DISCOVERING THE END OF TIME

Discovering the End of Time

Irish Evangelicals in the Age of Daniel O'Connell

Donald Harman Akenson

McGill-Queen's University Press
Montreal & Kingston • London • Chicago

ISBN 978-0-7735-4679-0 (cloth)
ISBN 978-0-7735-9849-2 (ePDF)
ISBN 978-0-7735-9850-8 (ePUB)

Legal deposit first quarter 2016
Bibliothèque nationale du Québec

Printed in Canada on acid-free paper that is 100% ancient forest free (100% post-consumer recycled), processed chlorine free

This book has been published with the help of a grant from the Canadian Federation for the Humanities and Social Sciences, through the Awards to Scholarly Publications Program, using funds provided by the Social Sciences and Humanities Research Council of Canada.

McGill-Queen's University Press acknowledges the support of the Canada Council for the Arts for our publishing program. We also acknowledge the financial support of the Government of Canada through the Canada Book Fund for our publishing activities.

LIBRARY AND ARCHIVES CANADA CATALOGUING IN PUBLICATION

Akenson, Donald Harman, 1941–, author
Discovering the end of time : Irish Evangelicals in the age of Daniel O'Connell / Donald Harman Akenson.

Includes bibliographical references and index.
Issued in print and electronic formats.
ISBN 978-0-7735-4679-0 (bound). – ISBN 978-0-7735-9849-2 (ePDF). – ISBN 978-0-7735-9850-8 (ePUB)

1. Darby, J. N. (John Nelson), 1800–1882 – Influence. 2. Evangelicalism – Ireland – History – 19th century. 3. Protestants – Ireland – History – 19th century. 4. Millennialism – Ireland – History – 19th century. 5. Elite (Social sciences) – Ireland – History – 19th century. 6. Ireland – Church history – 19th century. I. Title.

BX4839.A44 2016 280'.40941509034 C2015-907089-9
C2015-907090-2

Set in 11/14 Minion Pro
Book design & typesetting by Garet Markvoort, zijn digital

TO REV. EDWARD J.R. JACKMAN, O.P.

In gratitude for his counsel and encouragement over the years and for his generous support of the program of McGill-Queen's Studies in the History of Religion.

CONTENTS

MAPS AND ILLUSTRATIONS

MAPS

ILLUSTRATIONS

ACKNOWLEDGMENTS

I am grateful to several institutions and their staff, and most especially to two. The first of these is the Christian Brethren Archive of the University of Manchester Library. This collection is splendidly curated by Dr Graham Johnson. It is far and away the richest source of material on the Brethren who originated in County Wicklow and south County Dublin and also their cognates and associates in England, North America, and, indeed, around the world. Considering that during much of their development in the nineteenth century the Brethren were among the more hermetic of Christian groups, the material in the Christian Brethren Archive is of unique value.

Further, I am deeply indebted to the staff of Interlibrary Loans at Queen's University, Kingston, Ontario, for a level of assistance and patience that borders on the supererogatory. Because a significant proportion of the material related to the early Brethren and to their affiliates among Church of Ireland evangelicals has been reproduced in our own time in malleable electronic form by ideologically or theologically energized enthusiasts, I have attempted in every possible instance to see an original copy of the items that are employed here as evidence. The kindness of the Queen's University library staff has been well beyond exemplary.

Individual scholars who have helped me are acknowledged with gratitude in the relevant notes to the text.

The engraving of John Nelson Darby is by kind permission of the Christian Brethren Archive, the University of Manchester Library, and that of Powerscourt by generous permission of the National Library of Ireland. The remainder of the contemporary engravings are public domain items originally disseminated by the *Dublin Penny Journal*, which was published between 1832 and 1836, inclusive.

ABBREVIATIONS

BDEB	*Blackwell Dictionary of Evangelical Biography*, 1730–1860
CBA	Christian Brethren Archive, the University of Manchester Library
CDGBSL	*Clergy of Dublin and Glendalough: Biographical Succession Lists* (Belfast: Ulster Historical Foundation, 2001)
CDIB	*Cambridge Dictionary of Irish Biography* (Cambridge: Cambridge University Press, 2010)
CW	*The Collected Writings of J.N. Darby* (see Bibliographic Commentary concerning editorship and editions)
LJND	*Letters of J.N.D.* (see Bibliographic Commentary concerning editorship and editions)
ODNB	*Oxford Dictionary of National Biography* (Oxford: Oxford University Press, 2004)

DISCOVERING THE END OF TIME

INTRODUCTION

Present-day historians of Protestantism rarely get into barroom arguments with each other. On the other hand, historians of Ireland do. This book sits on the borderline between those two groups.

Here is a question for debate. If you were asked to name, in order, the four most influential (post-biblical) figures in the formation of present-day Protestantism, who would they be? The primary bone of contention probably would be for number 1: Martin Luther or John Calvin? Almost certainly number 3 would be John Wesley.

After that there would be a lot of names put forward, the equivalent of local candidates for sainthood. If one takes the perspective of twenty-first-century influence, both as an immediate matter and as a predictable product of present trends a generation from now, I think two figures stand out: the American Joseph Smith Jr, the prophet of the Church of Jesus Christ of Latter-day Saints, and his parallel in time, the Anglo-Irish voice of prophecy, John Nelson Darby. Paradoxically, neither one of these prophets claimed to have founded a Protestant denomination. Joseph Smith Jr was adamant about that; it is only in the last twenty years that the so-called Protestantization of the Mormon church has been a conscious public posture of the Latter-day Saints as they have moved into the mainstream of influence in Western Hemisphere social and political life. Similarly, John Nelson Darby refused to affirm that he and his followers were anything except universal Christians (he reluctantly accepted the need for "Brethren" and, late in life in North America, "Plymouth Brethren") and this despite his being so deeply anti-Catholic that he could have marched with the seventeenth-century Puritans.

John Nelson Darby is probably the most influential modern religious figure whose name, if heard, is almost always forgotten. This is not surprising, because Darby was as crabbit and judgmental as a religious leader could be, and at the same time he taught his followers to act as stealth insurgents among other faiths, leaving few traces. David Hempton, a very shrewd observer of transatlantic religious history, has noted that Darby was the "father-founder of the theological tradition of Dispensationalism, which has exercised such a profound influence on American evangelicals/fundamentalists and their perceptions of events in the Middle East."[1] Actually, there is more to Darby's influence than that, because the views that he pounded away at, decade after decade, on both sides of the Atlantic – the Rapture of believers, the Second Coming of Jesus, the apocalyptic bestiary of Revelation, the battle of Armageddon, and on and on – seeped into evangelical groups that do not recognize Darby as one of their own. In many ways, Darbyite beliefs became the fist within the evangelical glove, especially the wing of the evangelical movement of the twentieth and twenty-first centuries that has its hub in North America. Without conscious notice of Darby's influence, many of the things that he was one of the first to systematically and forcefully push – such as turning the hallucinogenic imagery of the book of Revelation into literalized scenarios for the end of time – are now part of everyday culture: just scroll through the movie channels any night of the week. Of course John Nelson Darby was not the only source or the only vector for transmitting these ideas (that is one of the points of this study), but the big story of modern Protestantism does not make any sense without including him as a major historical player.

The problem with talking about John Nelson Darby is that there is no biography that comes even close to decent scholarly standards. Most emphatically: this is not an attempt to fill the void. For reasons that are explained in the text and especially in the bibliographical commentary at the end of the book, I do not believe a satisfactory life of Darby can be done for at least another generation. This unfortunate situation stems from several characteristics of Darby and the Brethren of which he was a central figure (though not, certainly, the only person

1 David Hempton, *Evangelical Disenchantment: Nine Portraits* (New Haven 2008), 13.

of weight). As a cohort, the first generation of "Brethren" (or "Christian Brethren") in the 1820s and 1830s kept few records: partly because they had revived the ancient concept of the literal Second Advent of Jesus, which they believed was to occur very soon; and in part because they were clubby, socially and educationally selected, and, really, the right sort of people. They did not need to write down things that were automatically understood by those inside the social circle. Further, when in the 1830s, '40s, and thereafter, the Brethren starting pouring out an ever-expanding stream of tracts, pastoral booklets, and theological monographs, they did so without the niceties of dating or, in many cases, indications of authorship. They were very big on codes. As for John Nelson Darby himself, when, after mid-century, he did start to compose a fragmented history of his own life and beliefs, it was characterized by an almost complete cauterization of information about his own personal life before young adulthood. One is not being arch in noting that the New Testament gives more information about the family life of Jesus of Nazareth than Darby and his immediate circle ever intentionally provided to outsiders in regard to his family. Moreover, much of Darby's reconstruction of his own early spiritual path and behaviour as reported in the mid-1850s and thereafter is not merely wobbly but also demonstrably inaccurate; in places it is whoppingly counterfactual.

If we cannot engage a full biography of John Nelson Darby, we can nevertheless analyze a situation in which he became the final catalytic agent in a cascade of concepts, events, and beliefs that formed themselves into a recognizable, robust, and potent pattern. Thus, this book presents a series of chapters, each of which is a layer of relevant circumstance. Rather like engaging in the methods of traditional oil painting, one starts at the base layer and each subsequent level of definition is simultaneously dependent upon the previous one and a preparation for the subsequent overlay. Thus, we begin with "Dalyland," the social canvas that provided the basis for the distinctively Irish form of evangelicalism that arose after the Napoleonic wars. Dalyland is found on no map: yet it was a region of the Irish Anglican Church that was both geographically real – it included most of Wicklow and the posh parts of southern County Dublin – and a communal and devotional realm characterized by social exclusivity and by keen evangelism among many of the elite. The doyen of this socioreligious entity was the Rev. Robert Daly, rector of Powerscourt, which was probably the most desirable and influential single parish in all of Ireland. Once we have the geography and social physics of Dalyland clear, we can understand its central position in the great swell of evangelicalism that yielded the Second (or "New") Reformation movement of the 1820s. That is where the young priest John Nelson Darby enters the picture. Subsequently, as the chimerical attempt to convert the Irish Catholics to Protestantism turns thuddingly unsuccessful in the late 1820s, one sees Darby coming to the fore as a leader of the disappointed in formulating a break with the evangelicalism of the Church of Ireland and its replacement (for the truly devout few) by a new way of reading the holy scriptures and of defining the nature of the Christian Church and God's kingdom. Although Darby throughout his life exhibited his own originality, he picked up some of his ideas from the shop floor of religious discourse of the time. The way he arranged his own ideas and those of others into an (almost) workable religious machine accounts for much of his subsequent influence: that and his obdurate, driven, ice-coldly charismatic personality. By the mid-1830s, he had articulated enough of a new vision of Heaven, Earth, and time to qualify as a prophet. That is where we stop, with Darby in his thirties, a strong voice in a very large wilderness.

If the layering process involved in my exposition, unlike that in a traditional chronological essay, does not yield an exposition that is entirely linear, that it is both necessary and logical: the generative work of John Nelson Darby becomes the plinth on which later events are built, and Darby's construction of that plinth was itself a process of his own layering of social structures, political events, and devotional insights. This book stops in the mid-1830s when Darby, with help from some of his Brethren friends, had completed the first stage in the creation of a set of Christian scriptures that were brand new, quite brilliant, and quite different in narrative content from those that the framers of the Christian canon had settled on in the fourth century. The process of articulation continued throughout his own lifetime and was completed by others after his death, but according to his pattern. It is possible to trace in a very tight causal ladder the Darbyite mode of reading the Bible through the seminal figures of some of the major strands of nineteenth- through twenty-first-century evangelicalism: those represented by Dwight L. Moody, William Bell Riley, and Billy Graham, however quietly each of those figures recognized his debt. That process, showing the stealth-infusion of Darbyism into mainstream evangelicalism, is for a later book: here my brief is to get the foundation solidly laid and that means recognizing that John Nelson Darby's formative years must be chronicled where they happened, Ireland. Possibly, John Nelson Darby could have formed his distinctive views of the Bible and of the way God's hand was about to press out the dross from humankind if he had been something other than an evangelical Anglican curate someplace other than Ireland, but I doubt it. What is certain is that it was his experience of the social physics of a very small socially and economically elite region of southern Ireland that formed the way he looked at the celestial mechanics of God interacting with Man. Undeniably, his continual reading and rereading of the scriptures formed the way he looked at Ireland; equally, the Ireland that he experienced formed the way he reinterpreted the Bible.

Not a lot of people who read Irish history extensively also spend time studying the Bible or the various Protestant takes on the scriptures; and not many Bible students spend much time reading Irish history. Hence, if I sometimes seem to be explaining things that you already know, that is necessary. In this regard, two points of clarification. First, if my presentation of the texts that are employed in the Darbyite revolution in biblical interpretation is simultaneously secular and appreciative (the scriptures are wonderful objects, whether or not one has devotional faith in them), I would hope that various sets of Christians, and especially present-day evangelicals, can engage with my line of reasoning without feeling that doing so compromises their faith. Also, I hope that readers familiar with Irish history will permit me to deal with a socioeconomic set of families that usually is known for its secular influence on Irish events. We will see in some detail that families such as the Hutchinsons, Synges, Guinnesses, Parnells, Howards, and La Touches – all families famous in Ireland to the present day – had, in the first third of the nineteenth century, members who were in the forefront of several evangelizing agencies. They were not fakes or cynics any more than the devout of any religion are. To a remarkable degree, many of the elite of secular society spent much of their life in an alternative, and very deeply spiritual, universe. One of the main points of this study is that in a brief and singular period historical events in Ireland and the personalities of keen biblical students met in a fashion that should be recognized as one of the formative causal intersections in the evolution of modern Christianity as a world religion. The Irish situation, in a very tight social sphere and in a limited period, seems to suggest an interesting time when (*pace* Jesus of Nazareth's suggestion in Matthew 19:24), it seemed not too difficult for a rich man to enter the kingdom of Heaven.

PART I

God's Petrie Dish

CHAPTER ONE

Dalyland: The Shape of a Hidden Kingdom

"Dalyland" was the early home of many of the habits and ideas that make up the mental kit of modern evangelical beliefs worldwide. This land's character was so different from those we usually associate with evangelicalism that it has been virtually ignored in historical writing concerning the evolution of one of modern Christianity's main wings. The architecture of present-day evangelicalism is remarkably complex and deeply convoluted; the palisades of modern mega-churches should not entirely obscure the lineaments of earlier formative structures: after all, there are catacombs beneath the Coliseum and vaults beneath the Vatican.

Dalyland was a state a mind, a religious mentality, and it was also a network of real-world geographic coordinates, a web of complex social relationships, regulated mostly by the gentry and above; and all this rested on the peculiar economic and governmental structure of post-Union Ireland. Although it was no Garden of Eden, from roughly 1800 to the mid 1830s, Dalyland was the potting soil from which came forth not only some of the early fruits of evangelicalism but also – from the viewpoint of orthodox Christianity of the nineteenth century – the worm that was hidden in the surrounding foliage. Like so many things in the natural world, these two spiritual phenomena were an instance of elaborate co-evolution.

Because the definition of words has been so important in the development of Christianity – entire communities have been wiped out for getting the words of a creed wrong – it is well to be clear how the words "evangelical" and "evangelicalism" are here used. My intention is eirenic and to be as inclusive as possible without lapsing into boundary-free fuzziness. With a slight amendment, it seems to me that the most useful definition still is that of David Bebbington, whose work deals primarily with England. He has put forward a template that several historians have used for studying evangelical evolution over time.[1] Bebbington himself begins with the 1730s. In his reading: (1) evangelicalism was (and still is) a form of Protestantism;[2]

1 David Bebbington, *Evangelicalism in Modern Britain* (London 1989).

2 I am listing Protestantism as a specific aspect of Bebbington's work, although he does not make Protestantism a separate criterion but simply takes it for granted. "Evangelical religion is a popular Protestant movement that has existed in Britain since the 1730s" is the opening sentence of his book (1). David Hempton has argued that severe anti-Catholicism became a characteristic of English evangelicalism and has asked what happened to transform the "enlightened and thoughtful respectability of the Clapham Sect to the bigotry" of the leaders of English evangelicalism in the late 1820s and thereafter ("Evangelicalism and Eschatology," *Journal of Ecclesiastical History* [April 1980], 179–94, esp. 179–80). As for Irish evangelicalism, it had no era of "enlightened and thoughtful respectability" in the sense of being soft on Catholicism. To some extent, David Bebbington's taking for granted the strong Protestantism (and often extreme anti-Catholicism) of evangelicalism illustrates David W. Miller's observation that in North Atlantic history the "literature is written by scholars who are committed evangelicals themselves" and thus they run the danger of constructing as history their own deeply held religious views ("Varieties of Irish Evangelicalism," *Field Day Review* [2007], 215). The semi-biography of Bebbington by his wife indicates his lifelong commitment to evangelical beliefs. Further, there were several generations of Brethren in his family background and he had been taken to a Brethren assembly until he was eight years of age, before the family moved house and became Baptists. He nevertheless thereafter revered the Brethren practice of weekly Lord's supper and has been highly respectful of the Brethren (Eileen Bebbington, *A Patterned Life* [Eugene, OR, 2014], esp. 9–11, 23–4).

Does this personal investment by Bebbington imply that we should distrust his historical generalizations? I think not, for two reasons. One of these, admittedly secondary, is that he has shown an admirable ability to modify his own work as new data have become available. Thus, on the basis of late-career research into eighteenth- and early nineteenth-century sources, Bebbington came to recognize that conversion could be real without being sudden, dramatic, or dateable to a specific moment in an individual's life (David Bebbington, "Evangelical Conversion, c. 1740–1850," *Scottish Bulletin of Evangelical*

(2) it is marked by "conversionism," meaning a personal embrace of repentance and of a faith-commitment; (3) its functional pivot is "crucicentrism," meaning the doctrine of atonement by Jesus Christ for both the primordial Original Sin of all humanity and also for individuals' sins; (4) it looks to the Bible as the supreme authority in all matters of faith and practice; and (5) it is activist in its moral radicalism and public witnessing, especially in its energetic attempts to convert others to share in the evangelical experience. This final criterion is here being eliminated, in part because it is excessively loose in its meaning and also because it excludes a significant tranche of individuals who have been committed to points 1 to 4 but have lived quiet lives, practising their faith with the simplicity of modern-day Anchorites.[3] With that amendment, Bebbington's definition is an admirable and a necessary

---

Theology [2000], 102–27, esp. 108–9). Crawford Gribben, in *Evangelical Millennialism in the Trans-Atlantic World* (Basingstoke 2011), provides a discussion (4–10) of the possible limits of Bebbington's classic definition as it intersects with more recent historical studies. The qualifications are thoughtful, but none of the more recent studies has the same robustness of usefulness and of cross-cultural ductility that characterizes Bebbington's work.

One should emphasize that in employing David Bebbington's definition as an historical implement I am not being ungrateful for an entire range of historiography on early years of western European evangelicalism and particularly for the works of W.R. Ward and David Hempton. Among Ward's wide range of work on society and religion, *The Protestant Evangelical Awakening* (Cambridge 1991) is a prodigiously researched discussion of the European aspects of the eighteenth-century revival, with shrewd observations on interactions of Europe, North America, and the British Isles within early evangelicalism; also pivotal is *Early Evangelicalism: A Global Intellectual History, 1670–1789* (Cambridge 2006). Several of the writings of David Hempton will be cited in later pages as they often are relevant to specific Irish matters. Here, the central items are his *Methodism: Empire of the Spirit* (New Haven 2006) and (co-written with Myrtle Hill) *Evangelical Protestantism in Ulster Society* (London: 1992). The latter volume has a broad swatch of background observations that relate not just to Ulster but to Anglo-American evangelicalism in the broadest sense.

3 Bebbington's own criteria – conversionism, crucicentrism, biblicism, and activism – are employed in one of the most useful, but underappreciated, of reference books: *The Blackwell Dictionary of Evangelical Biography* (Oxford 1995, 2 vols), edited by Donald M. Lewis (hereafter BDEB).

inflection point for approaching evangelicalism as a cross-cultural historical phenomenon. This is not to ignore the fact that there have been big gaps as between various cultures on matters of taste, sensibility, mode, and method of evangelical worship. But commonalty of core experience must be recognized or we will lurch from nationalism to provincialism to parochialism and finally, as historians, become the equivalent of the pastors of those hillside chapels whose congregants deny commonality with other believers and rain down anathemas upon their perceived rivals.

Another reason Bebbington's approach is valuable is that it allows the historian to note that the concepts of evangelicals and of evangelicalism are applicable to both organizations and individuals. Thus, one can find individual evangelicals within denominations or congregations that do not fit the criteria of evangelicalism.

This analytic distinction between individuals and their institutional affiliation is valuable in a broad variety of contexts. It is more than merely useful, however – it is crucial – for us to catch the character of the ultimate religious product of Dalyland, namely the "Wicklow Brethren" (to use an accurate neologism). As they emerged from Ireland into Great Britain and then into the various New Worlds, the Wicklow-descended Brethren managed the difficult paradox of being intensely inward-looking as a group, yet willing to work as stealth agents within existing denominations and in various ad hoc evangelical alliances. They were very good at hiding their footprints, or at minimum, in refusing to advertise their affiliation. That, in part, is why they have been a palimpsest, rather than a feature page, in the history of evangelicalism.

By the time the Rev. Robert Daly (1783–1872) became the bishop of the united sees of Cashel, Emly, Waterford, and Lismore in 1843, his most important work was already done. For three decades before that elevation, he had been a parish clergyman and the most energetic and widely effective power broker for evangelicalism in the Church of Ireland. He was not the most beloved of clerics, for outside of his own circle he was snobbish, ambitious, and bumptious. He was highly energetic, a strong orator, a viciously effective debater, a very skilled organizer, and a great hater of Roman Catholics (always under the guise of loving them to death); he had a sincere humility before his God, but before few others who held less than 10,000 acres. His biographer, a former parishioner, Mrs Hamilton Madden, approvingly relates the following anecdote from the 1820s:

> In later years Mr Daly was much pleased with an answer made to him by a poor man. He was about to leave home for a time and said to his gardener, "Well, John, I have found a good man to look after my poor people while I am away."
>
> "Oh!" replied John, "but who will look after the *poor rich* people, sir?"[4]

That encapsulates why Robert Daly and the world that he dominated have been downplayed in the history of Irish Anglicanism.[5] The Church by the late nineteenth century was lean, mildly evangelical, and quite respectful of its everyday parishioners whatever their social class. By the late nineteenth century, outside of Ulster, the Church of Ireland was fairly careful about not publicly stepping on the toes of the members of the advancing Catholic majority, even while glaring contemptuously at them from behind drawn curtains.[6]

4 Mrs Hamilton Madden, *Memoir of the Late Right Rev. Robert Daly* (London 1875), 90. She also wrote a more personal and less document-based memorial, published anonymously as *Personal Recollections of the Right Rev. Robert Daly* (Dublin 1872).

5 Although the term "Anglican" was rarely used in the early nineteenth century, it has become an accepted term. On the other hand, "Episcopalian," which is freely employed in the United States, in the early nineteenth century in Ireland either referred to the Scottish cognate of the Church of England or was used by Irish Presbyterians as a slightly derogatory reference to the Church of Ireland.

6 The classic history of the Church of Ireland, especially volume 3, is still worth attention: Walter A. Phillips (ed.), *History of the Church of Ireland* (London 1933), 3 vols. The somewhat mysterious, often caricatured history of Irish Protestants from the later seventeenth through the eighteenth centuries is dealt with by three fine works: Alan Ford, *The Protestant Reformation in Ireland, 1540–1641* (Frankfurt am Main 1985); Toby Barnard, *A New History of*

In the early nineteenth century things were very different – and that is precisely why Dalyland matters. This eponymous entity is a heuristic construct, a way of breaking out of the usual categories that split religious, social, and economic history into separate dominions.

As a first glimpse into the early nineteenth-century world, we observe in its bare-bones detail the background and career of Robert Daly himself. He was born in 1783, the second son of the marriage of Denis Daly, longtime MP for County Galway and of Lady Henrietta Maxwell, who after her marriage and subsequent widowhood was generally referred to as "Lady Harriet Daly." She was the only heir of the first (and last) earl of Farnham (of the first creation), which meant that when her husband died in 1791 she nevertheless had a large personal fortune, more than adequate to take care of herself, her own sisters, and her two sons and six daughters. She moved from County Cavan to one of her own family houses, Bromley, near Delgany, County Wicklow. In

---

Ireland (New Haven 2003); and S.J. Connolly, *Religion, Law and Power* (1992). Organizational details and financial matters are treated (perhaps excessively) in my *The Church of Ireland* (New Haven 1971). The best recent history is Alan Acheson, *A History of the Church of Ireland* (Dublin 2002). This volume is especially good on specific personalities, and the material is usefully read in tandem with Acheson's contributions to *BDEB*. For an indispensable conspectus of the range of historical studies available as of 1992, see the collective article by James Murray, Alan Ford, J.I. McGuire, S.J. Connolly, Fergus O'Ferrall, and Kenneth Milne, "The Church of Ireland: A Critical Bibliography, 1536–1992." *Irish Historical Studies* (1993).The Presbyterian Church in Ireland did not directly interact significantly with the southern Irish Anglicans with whom we are here dealing, but it did so in the north later in the century. For the present period, an excellent recent discussion is Andrew R. Holmes, *The Shaping of Ulster Presbyterian Belief and Practice* (Oxford 2006). The Methodists interacted more directly with southern Anglican evangelicals, although not so much in what I am calling Dalyland. The Methodist literature is rich. On the one hand, it broadly involves Great Britain and on the other hand is very site-specific in Ireland. Thus, as framing, see David Hempton, *Methodism and Politics in British Society, 1750–1850* (Stanford 1984), and compare it to Robert Haire, *Wesley's One-and-Twenty Visits to Ireland* (London 1947). For an attempt, not entirely successful, at drawing everything together, see Desmond Bowen, *History and the Shaping of Irish Protestantism* (New York 1995).

retrospect, this was a fortuitous pivot in Irish religious history, for it put young Robert Daly in a genteel locale – substantial house, wooded demesne, splendid views – exactly the world where he was to spend most of his later religious life. Bromley was close to the parish of Powerscourt, which became his longtime charge. In the general area were estates of Lords Powerscourt, Meath, and Wicklow and the families of Synge and La Touche, among others. Lady Harriet was well connected. Besides her own family associations (her stepmother, Lady Farnham, had held possession of Bromley), her late husband had been a confident of Henry Grattan, who was voted a Wicklow estate, a former inn, renovated as Tinnehinch, as a portion of the gratitude-payment by the Irish parliament for his patriotic service to the nation. Young Robert was tutored at home by a succession of Englishmen recommended by Dr Euseby Cleaver, at that time bishop of Ferns, who usefully was married to a close cousin of Lady Harriet: Lady Harriet counted the bishop as her own cousin, meaning a family relative who was socially valuable. Robert took a very good degree at age twenty in 1803 at Trinity College, Dublin, where he was also a gold medalist in the classical competition. In practical terms, he was faced with three classic younger-son choices: study the law, buy a military commission, or enter the church. St George Daly, Robert's uncle and apparently the most significant male figure in Robert's life, seems to have hoped that he would read law: this Daly had been prime serjeant at law for Ireland just before and after the Union and had been rewarded handsomely for supporting the Union by being named a baron of exchequer in 1801. The uncle, a lifelong bachelor, spent summers at a cottage near Delgany and became an advisor to his nephew. He convinced Robert, still in his early twenties, to spend two years at Oxford and perhaps follow the Daly family tradition of politics and legal practice. Instead, Robert came down from Oxford in 1805, keen on the shooting and country sports, and became an enthusiastic member of the Kilcool Yeomanry, a parish band of Protestant volunteers who had assisted the government in putting down Emmett's rebellion of 1803 and who still were enjoying amateur soldiering. Robert was down to two alternatives: become a real soldier or enter the Church. The classic Irish meditation on that common young gentleman's choice is that of Sir Jonah Barrington, who in the 1798 Rising had briefly taken a commission and then resigned it only to find that a friend who had taken his place had his brains blown out in the very first engagement:

> Having thus rejected the military, I turned my thought to that very opposite profession – the clerical. But though preaching was certainly a much safer and more agreeable employment than bush-fighting, yet a curacy and a wooden leg [were] pretty much on a parallel in point of remuneration.[7]

Robert Daly did not need to worry about the remuneration – his mother would keep him in ready funds and his bachelor uncle promised an eventual inheritance, so he could safely take holy orders. Why he did so is unclear, for he had never shown any religious sensibility. Still, Lady Harriet arranged things well. Robert did not undergo any serious formal theological training but was ordained deacon by letters dismissory (Lady Harriet's "cousin," the Rev. Dr Euseby Cleaver, was still bishop of Ferns). She arranged for her son's appointment in 1807 to the curacy of the united parish of Malrancan and Kilturk in County Wexford where the rector, the Rev. Thomas Gore, was another one of her cousins of one degree or another.

The interesting thing about his two years in this curacy is that the Rev. Mr Daly (he was priested in 1808) began to catch religion. He was a compelling preacher and began to think of himself as an evangelist. The long excerpts from his journal that Mrs Madden reproduces in her biography of Daly show a sense of personal surprise that he does indeed love the faith, and this grows into a set of self-critical devotions and contemplations and especially to a concentration on biblical study. Mind you, the young cleric was not about to cast his everyday life upon divine providence: in autumn 1809 his mother's cousin, Dr Cleaver, was translated from the see of Ferns to the archbishopric of Dublin and thus in 1810 Daly was offered a desirable curacy in Newcastle, in north Wicklow. Among other things it carried the signal advantage that Newcastle was close enough to his family home so that he could live at Bromley with his mother and six sisters. There Daly resided until 1814, when he gained one of the plum parishes in all of Ireland: the parish

7 Hugh B. Staples (ed.), *The Ireland of Sir Jonah Barrington* (Seattle 1967), 128.

of Powerscourt. With it came a prebendal stall in St Patrick's Cathedral and also a sinecure prebend in St Fin Barre's Cathedral, Cork. The entire income was merely genteelly comfortable – at most £500 a year plus a glebe house – but Daly had independent means and a promise of significant future wealth. Crucially, the parish of Powerscourt gave him entry to some of the most influential aristocrats of the south of Ireland: most importantly, the Wingfield family of Powerscourt;[8] the Howards of Bushy Park (the family held the Wicklow earldom), who were his first real converts; and the Jocelyns (successive earls of Roden), one of whom was the brother of the first wife of Richard Wingfield, Fifth Viscount Powersourt.

Daly, by now a self-converted evangelical, was in equal parts energetic and unctuous and he converted Lady Anne Jocelyn, the Fifth Viscount Powerscourt, and, notably, Theodosia Howard who eventually became the widow of Lord Powerscourt and was herself a major figure in Irish evangelical circles. That was just a tithe of his work among the privileged, but Daly also carried on a larger ministry among the poor, much of it aimed at converting Catholics. Daly was fortunate in having his local pastoral duties lightened by having one of his cousins, the Rev. Arthur Wynne, serve for a time as his curate. Daly was an early supporter of the Hibernian Church Missionary Society (founded in 1814); a deep enthusiast for the work of the Irish Society for the Education of the Native Irish through the Medium of their Own Language (f. 1818, and usually known as the Irish Society – Daly himself was an Irish speaker); and strong supporter of the Hibernian Bible Society (known generally as "the Bible Society"), which was the Irish branch of the British and Foreign Bible Society, and it purchased thousands of copies of used Bibles in England each year and distributed them in Ireland. Daly did this despite the Bible Society's being disapproved of by many of the Church of Ireland bishops for being open to all evangelical Protestants. It says something both about Daly's pugnacious ecumenism and his physiognomy that he had a print of Martin Luther on his study's wall

8 The prebend had been attached to the parish of Powerscourt since 1303. This is worth noting as into the 1830s the parish is sometimes found in church and government records under the name Stagonil, the appellation of the prebend.

and that this was frequently taken to be a portrait of himself. With the perspective of a century having passed, Canon James B. Leslie, the Church of Ireland's assiduous annalist, laconically, and a trifle unfairly, summarized Daly's character as "rough in exterior, but well known for his charity."[9] There was more, much more, in his constant action and evangelical witness, and Daly continued at Powerscourt until 1843, when he became bishop of Cashel, Emly, Waterford, and Lismore. He never married. His mother, still in vigorous good health, attended his ceremonial elevation to the bishopric.[10]

The preceding telegraphic summary of the career of the Rev. Robert Daly instantiates several characteristics of the religious satrapy we are calling Dalyland in the years 1800 to roughly the mid-1830s. First, the existence of family networks was pervasive. Most of these connections are invisible to present-day historians, but they were well known to the contemporary players in the Church of Ireland. Certain families had clerical connections that were the keys to good careers. Secondly, social caste – gentry, aristocracy, substantial farmer – interwove with religious adherence. Of course the complex web of relationships among Anglo-Irish families has an existence based on land, inheritance, marriage, but in the period 1800–30 a remarkable number of families in Dalyland took to having relationships based upon their being seriously religious. If most of the adherents of the Church of Ireland were small farmers, labourers, and minor merchants, the bulk of the upper class was overwhelmingly Anglican and increasingly warm in their religious devotion, so long as this did not seriously reduce their style of life. Thirdly, women were notably important in this period of Irish religious history. This was more than the usual predominance at religious services of females. In this particular era emphasis was placed on obtaining the approval by women for the newly emerging evangelicalism.

9 James B. Leslie, *Ferns Clergy and Parishes* (Dublin 1936), 217.

10 Lady Harriet, born c. 1759–61, lived into 1852. In addition to Mrs Madden's memoir of Daly, see the entries on him in the *Oxford Dictionary of National Biography* (hereafter ODNB); in the *Cambridge Dictionary of Irish Biography* (hereafter CDIB); and in BDEB. See also *Fourth Report of His Majesty's Commissioners of Ecclesiastical Revenue and Patronage in Ireland,* "Diocese of Dublin," 90–1, H.C. 1837 (500), xxi, and A.R. Hart, *A History of the King's Serjeants at Law in Ireland* (Dublin 2000), 103–5, 153.

One finds considerable female leadership in charities and educational efforts – the soft aspect of Irish evangelicalism, as compared to the harsher, male-dominated confrontation with Catholicism. Fourthly, there is a very unusual temporary phenomenon in place as regards recruitment to evangelicalism among the clergy. That is – as Robert Daly's life indicates – it was not unlikely that a young man would first became a professionally religious person and then, sometime after taking holy orders, be converted to evangelicalism or something close to it. This is so different from the present-day evangelical situation, wherein a person is first converted and then feels a call to serve, that it must be underscored. Within the Church of Ireland, a collective process of evangelical self-persuasion was in train. Sometimes, like Robert Daly, individual men studied and prayed themselves into new views; other times, meetings of clerical study groups brought a man around; and occasionally contact with evangelicals outside the Anglican faith produced a conversion, but not necessarily any inclination to leave serving in the Church of Ireland. Thus, the Church of Ireland was not itself evangelical, but it increasingly held evangelicals within its ranks. Inevitably, the church's belief structure became increasingly complex: for even keen evangelicals, who emphasized the individual's responsibility in accessing spiritual grace, accepted that there also was validity in the institutional delivery of the sacraments.[11] Sometimes the ambiguities in this situation were more than a sensitive clergyman could bear. Yet, throughout most of this era all but a few of them managed. As we shall see, that began to change in the later 1820s.[12]

11 For a sensitive and sensible statement of these tensions, see the chapter "Evangelicals and the Established Church" in Grayson Carter, *Anglican Evangelicals* (Oxford 2001), 7–30.

12 The reader will notice that although I am providing probative material for the manner and mechanism by which evangelicalism grew within the Church of Ireland in the years c. 1800–30, I am not trying to explain its ultimate origin or attraction. Over the years, I have read hundreds of explanations of evangelicalism's rise and power all over the world; despite the excellent qualities of many of these studies, they end up analytically reductive or simply descriptive, or pieces of piety. This is not to be ungrateful, for I have learned from some wonderful scholars, but the categories and methods of explanation that we at present have in the academy seem largely inadequate to deal with the

Even though Dalyland was not a "real" place in the reductive sense of that concept, it was where an increasing number of leading southern Irish Anglicans lived, especially the social, economic, and religious elite. It was a site of the mind. Yes, it had geographic coordinates, social class and caste denominators, institutional associations, economic determiners, and creedal limitations, but what I am strenuously trying to prevent in our collective reading of the story is our analyzing the individual pieces so sharply that we miss the way the thought-machine worked as a whole, particularly on the religious level. If one wishes, Dalyland can be understood as being very close to an historical Ideal Type in Max Weber's sense of that concept: it shows how southern Irish Protestantism acted in an environment that was close to being a pure laboratory – and the sort of place where its clerical and social leaders felt completely at home. It operated by rules that Anglicans outside of its borders both envied and tried to emulate.

In physical-world terms, Dalyland was a portion of the archdiocese of Dublin and Glendalough, roughly half of it. Dalyland's boundaries were blurred. Dalyland included County Wicklow, a small slice of County Wexford, and parts of the diocese of Dublin that ran south of the River Liffey: not everything south, certainly not the Liberties or other impacted slums, but the fashionable eastward developments that included St Stephen's Green, Merrion Square, Ely Place, and Fitzwilliam Square, locations where the urban residences of the country gentry and aristocracy would be appropriate. Dalyland included the distinguished St Ann's Church[13] in Dawson Street, but at the top of

phenomenon. In order to stay away from concepts that too often provide chimerical understanding, I am using only very rarely the words Enlightenment or Romantic Movement. They are useful in other contexts, but one encounters too many discussions that swirl together these two constructs in a big Martini glass, add a dash of faith, and somehow come out with the British Isles version of evangelicalism.

13 St Ann's had the most fashionable of clergy. From 1774 to 1833 the vicar was the Hon. John Pomeroy. The curate from 1817 to 1836 was the evangelical

the street the walls of Trinity College (TCD) marked its border. Not that TCD was anything except deeply Protestant, but it was a world of its own and defended itself very skilfully against incorporation into anything that moved too quickly or with too much energy. As for the portions of Dublin north of the river, Sackville Mall/Street (now O'Connell Street) was no longer a satisfactory residential address for the upper class; in any case, the grandees who had lived there in the days of the old Irish parliament had not much overlapped with the families who dominated Dalyland.[14]

The legendary Irish historian R.B. McDowell, who loved the eighteenth century and disliked most of the nineteenth century, held firmly to the view that "the passing of the Act of Union is more than a constitutional landmark; it is the watershed about which modern Irish history inevitable divides."[15] He certainly was right that Ireland's political history changed radically when, in 1801, Ireland became a subordinate portion of the United Kingdom, but his secondary concern about the decline of Irish aristocratic society after Dublin was no longer a capital city was overwrought. "The decline spread quickly from Dublin throughout the country, and soon after 1800 the Irish landlord was transformed with remarkable suddenness from a cultured, if somewhat provincial gentleman to a philistine whose only interests were

---

John James Digges La Touche, from Ireland's most successful banking family, whose members owned multiple rural estates and fashionable Dublin residences. He was a nephew of Peter La Touche of Bellevue, County Wicklow, who is discussed in chapter 2. David Dickson, in *Dublin: The Making of a Capital City* (Cambridge 2014), 129, indicates that from its creation in the early eighteenth century St Ann's was a metric for fashionability in Dublin churches.

14 Eamon Walsh, "Sackville Mall: The First One Hundred Years," in David Dickson (ed.), *The Gorgeous Mask* (Dublin 1987). See esp. 41, list of residences in Sackville Street, 1795–99, table 1. An admirable collective history of Dublin City is F.H.A. Aalen and Kevin Whelan (eds), *Dublin City and County: From Prehistory to Present* (Dublin 1992); see esp. Louis M. Cullen, "The Growth of Dublin 1600–1900: Character and Heritage," 251–78.

15 R.B. McDowell and D.A. Webb, *Trinity College Dublin, 1592–1951* (Cambridge 1982), 74 (McDowell's co-author in this volume was the emeritus professor of Systematic Botany).

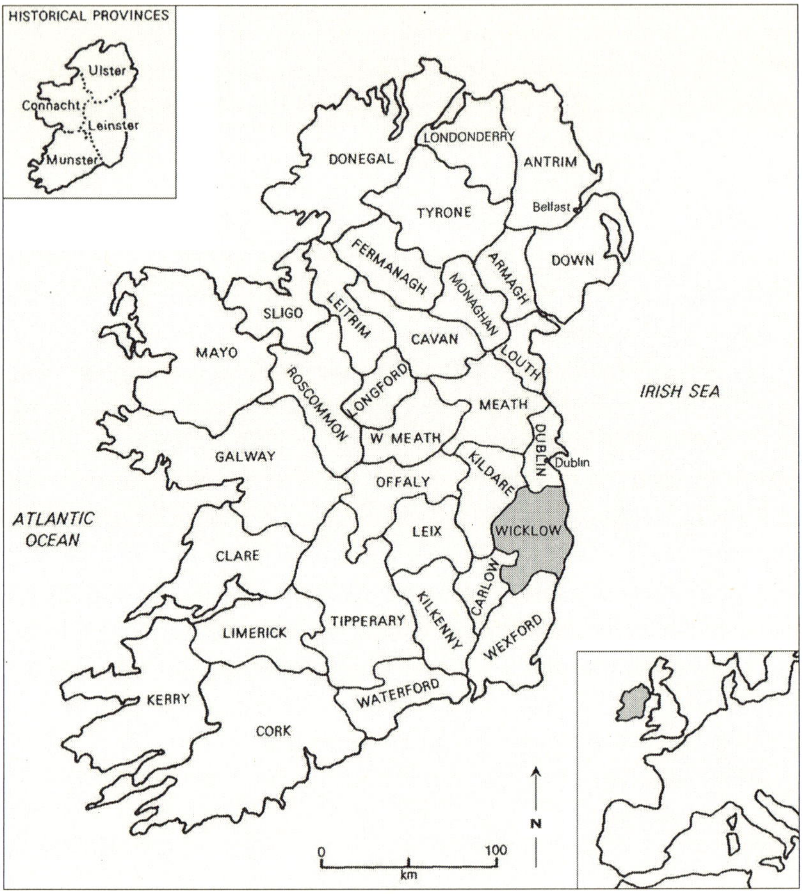

MAP 1.1 IRISH COUNTIES.

Note: before 1922, Offaly = King's County and Leix (var.: Laois) = Queen's County.

soldiering and sport."[16] Undeniably the Union made Dublin less central as a hub of political power and the byproducts of being a governmental centre – theatres, gentlemen's clubs, etc. – may have declined somewhat, although that is not entirely clear. Yet, the physics of the whole process yielded a result that McDowell either ignored or deplored: the areas around Dublin that were accessible in a single day's

16 Ibid., 85.

travel became more important and the ones that emerged as dominant were south, primarily in County Wicklow: this because coastal access to eastern Wicklow was relatively easy and because after 1804 a well-maintained military road was completed through the central Wicklow mountains, giving the entire county access to Dublin.[17] Thus, in many ways, the suppression of Dublin as a capital was actually a displacement of social authority from a small strip of land that ran along Dame Street, to a social caste of well-off and multi-residence owners, whose minds now obsessively took in demesne vistas and who planned ways to engineer their rural environments according to their own concepts of order and beauty. McDowell missed the displacement effect and one grants that the post-Union gentry could be both gross and frivolous (examples to follow later). They were, however, much less likely to pierce, shoot, or otherwise puncture each other than when duelling was endemic in pre-Union upper-class male culture.

Evangelically based religion, as understood at the time, became the everyday "household religion"[18] in an influential set of landed families. Paradoxically – and strongly counter-intuitively – the Union of Ireland and Great Britain coincided with an increase in the independence and religious professionalism of the Irish Church. This occurred despite the theoretical merging in 1801 of the Church of Ireland and the Church of England. The two established churches were to be "united into one Protestant Episcopal Church, to be called the United Church of England and Ireland."[19] Since there were no provisions for actually merging the administration of the two churches, this was all puff, and it lasted only until disestablishment of the Irish state Church in 1871. Almost no one used the term United Church, or its alternative "Established Church of England and Ireland" and it was scarcely heard

17 The T.S. Roberts painting of the Wicklow military road under construction is reproduced in F.H.A. Aalen, Kevin Whelan, and Matthew Stout, *Atlas of Irish Rural Landscape* (Toronto 1997), 209. This is an extraordinarily successful volume, both intellectually and in its production values.

18 This useful concept is Fergus O'Farrell's, articulated in his section on the historiography for 1800–70, in Murray, Ford, McGuire, O'Ferrall, and Milne, "The Church of Ireland: A Critical Biography, 1536–1992," 372.

19 Irish Statutes, 40 Geo. III, cap. 38, article 5.

without wincing. More importantly, the fourth article of the Act of Union provided that only four of the twenty-two Irish archbishops and bishops should sit in the newly minted parliament of the United Kingdom of Great Britain and Ireland, and then only by a scheme of strict sessional rotation. This was a huge change, as in the days of the independent Irish parliament, all the bishops sat in the House of Lords and were expected to do their political duty. After the Union, the Irish bishops were much less useful to the government (just four votes in the newly defined House of Lords), so they were left with a good deal more time to reside and to do pastoral work outside of the old capital city. The proportion of resident bishops improved directly. That said, it is true that immediately after the Union the government paid off a number of bishops under so-called "Union engagements" for voting the right way (or for their relatives in the Irish parliament doing so) when the bill for the Union was in the legislature: this payoff came through the clerical promotion of relatives of parliamentary gamesmen to bishoprics or by the translation of right-voting bishops to more remunerative sees. Granting this point, after roughly the end of the Napoleonic Wars, one nevertheless sees a four-fold trend: more Irishmen were appointed to plum bishoprics that in the pre-Union period had gone to Englishmen; in terms of intellectual background, a better quality of person was appointed; the bishops became much more serious about doing their job; and, below the episcopal level, more of the desirable benefices went to Irishmen, especially those educated at Trinity College, Dublin. So, the professional leadership of the Church of Ireland in the first three decades of the nineteenth century actually became more Irish and more seriously religious.[20]

To return to the specific details of Dalyland, we need to be practical and a little bit philistine and adopt some secular categories. Although we should keep in mind that Dalyland ran into parts of south County Dublin and into delimited areas of south Dublin City, the way that successive governmental and ecclesiastical authorities collected information means that in practice the unit we have to deal with is County Wicklow. That is a secular designation, necessary because the county

20 Akenson, *Church of Ireland,* 73–9, 328–9, on the Union specifically, and 71–145 on what I have termed "the era of graceful reform, 1800–1830."

was the chief unit of social and economic accounting for successive Irish administrations. In the 1820s and mid-1830s, the Church of Ireland and the UK government, working rather reluctantly together, produced a set of down-to-the-ground investigations of churches, charities, and clerical endeavours. These, when tied to independent observations about the relevant social, economic, and religious structure, help us to understand why County Wicklow was the trustworthy heart of Dalyland and the place where the household religion of the rich often comfortably took the form of evangelicalism, or something close to it.

Although County Wicklow had made little sense as a social-governmental unit in the early days of the modern conquest of Ireland – its having been the last area to be shired, 1605–06, speaks directly to that fact – by the early nineteenth century the county's topography had taken on a sharp set of social meanings. The county is of sensible size – roughly half-a million statute acres (about 782 square miles, or 202,000 hectares)[21] – but it is surmounted by a large granite massif. Before 1804 this separated the attractive and profitable portions of the county – the eastern coastal strip and the western and southwestern pockets of arable ground, as well as areas of good pasturage – from each other. Archaeological evidence suggests that until the conquest of the seventeenth century, the natural settlement concentration was on the west and the south of the central highlands, and it was these areas that were tied to Dublin.[22] Certainly nothing changed the existence of the dozen or so "mountains" of central Wicklow (the highest, Lugnaquilla, is just over 3,000 feet) nor the huge, barely habitable sections of central blanket bog, nor the plethora of short rivers that run in every which direction by virtue of the straggly structure of the Wicklow watershed, yet by the end of the Napoleonic Wars the meaning, and in effect the social location, of all these features had been radically altered.

21 Unless specifically mentioned, all measures of distance (e.g., miles) and of surface (acres) are in statute, not Irish, measure.

22 Seamus O'Maitiu, "Lacken, County Wicklow," in *Irish Townlands, Studies in Local History*, edited by Paul Connell, Denis A. Cronin, and Brian O'Dalaigh, (Dublin 1998), 203–19, esp. 204–7.

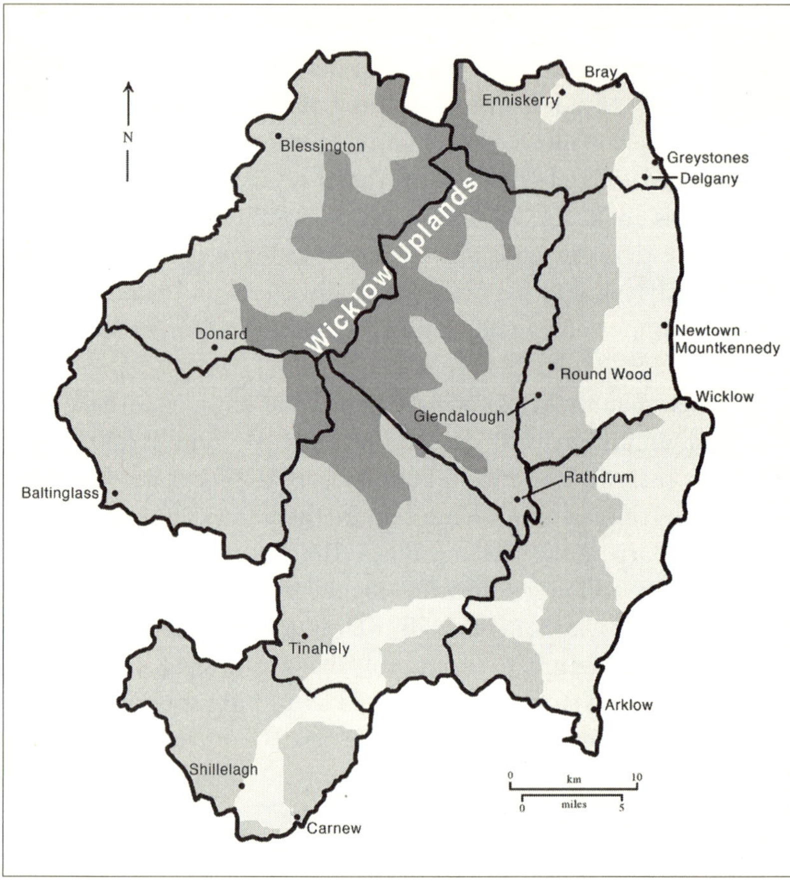

MAP 1.2 WICKLOW TOPOGRAPHY.

Slightly earlier, in 1801, the surveyor for the Dublin Society ("Royal Dublin Society," 1820) noted that "this circumstance of these rugged central mountains, with the fertile borders to the east, west, and south, has made the County of Wicklow be compared to a frize coat with a laced border."[23] Actually, by 1815, the county was being treated more like a big, rough semi-precious gemstone that was being chipped at and polished, to be shown off in a massive brooch. The military road

23 Robert Fraser, *General View ... County Wicklow* (Dublin 1801), 3. His figure of speech probably was a paraphrase of Jonathan Swift.

MAP 1.3 WICKLOW BARONIES AND PARISH BOUNDARIES.

of 1804 had opened the central wilderness and drovers' roads for livestock reticulated into a filigree of gaps and passes that would bear mounted riders; in 1811, the mail coaches that ran on both sides of the central massif were extended and by 1814 one could travel from Dublin to Waterford by coach. Bianconi cars began in 1816.[24] The major Wicklow landlords took to viewing their properties as big chunks of malleable environment, which could be drained, shaped, and planted so that the wild aspect of the county remained – they were great collectors

24 Arthur Flynn, *A History of County Wicklow* (Dublin 2003), 90–1.

of the Sublime and the Beautiful – while their own personal standard of amenities equalled those of comparable English estates. Thus, their collective project was like mounting a big piece of fossil-bearing amber (the wild vistas of Wicklow) in a thoroughly modern and artistically crafted setting.

Crucially, the religious-demographic structure of County Wicklow made it the best site in Ireland for a new religious movement. To sharpen focus, simply ask the following question: where in Ireland in the pre-Famine era would have been the best place to plan for an evangelical putsch? Recalling that adherence to Protestantism was an implicit item in Bebbington's primary criteria of evangelicalism, the intuitive response would be to suggest that the obvious place would be the province of Ulster, which is mostly Protestant, is it not? Actually, no. However one slices it: in the historic nine provinces of Ulster, or the slightly larger ecclesiastical province of Armagh, Roman Catholics were by far the largest single denomination and were in fact an overall majority.[25] But were not all Protestant denominations equally open to evangelicalism and thus in large areas of Ulster a potentially pan-denominational evangelical counterweight? Decidedly not: not until after the Great Famine was the Presbyterian faith fully open to the conversionist experience that is part of the evangelical syndrome.[26] Equally importantly, the level of ill-will between Anglican and Presbyterian, which had a rancorous pedigree running back to the early seventeenth century, did not subside into even an uneasy Protestant ecumenism until after the Church of Ireland was disestablished as the

25 For the exact numbers, based on the 1834 recalibration of the 1831 census as done by the Commissioners of Public Instruction in Ireland, see Akenson, *Church of Ireland*, 165, table 34.

26 David Miller has pointed out that a specifically Presbyterian "conversionist emphasis" had permeated synod meetings in the 1820s. However, the full shift to "conversionalist evangelicalism" came only with the late-nineteenth-century dominance of an industrially modernized economy in Ulster and the spreading of its mindset, if not its actual industrial methods, to the countryside (David Miller, "Presbyterianism and 'Modernization' in Ulster," *Past and Present*, 1978).

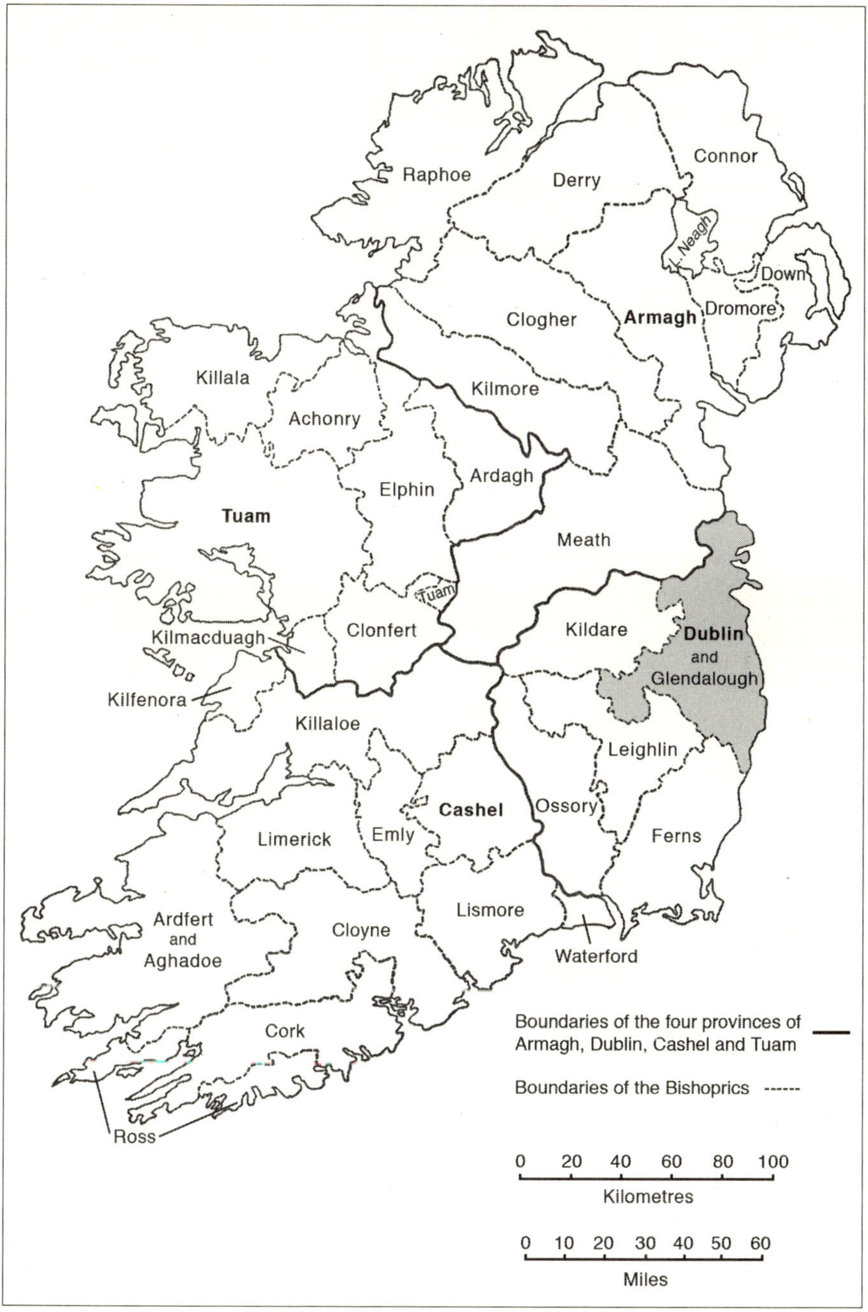

MAP 1.4 DIOCESES AND PROVINCES OF THE CHURCH OF IRELAND IN THE EARLY NINETEENTH CENTURY.

Irish state church in 1871.[27] Hence, our question is reduced, rather like an exercise in elementary algebra, to this form: in the early nineteenth century, where was the largest concentration of Anglicans, the group most open to evangelicalism? There are four possible answers which come from the 1831 census, and they are here put in terms of Church of Ireland dioceses:[28]

- Clogher, which was 26 percent Anglican, the highest proportion in Ireland. It was, however, located on the combat zone that ran across the lake-and-drumlin district of midsouthern Ulster. Two-thirds of the populace was Catholic, and Protestants were under day-to-day pressures that resulted in a low-level but consistent emigration.
- Dromore (22 percent Church of Ireland), just south of Belfast, was a more likely theatre of operations, except that 37 percent of the population was Presbyterian and they were clearly in social control except at the level of the largest landlords.
- the archdiocese of Armagh was a third potentially useful site but the Presbyterian split was distracting (21 percent vs

27 As is well known, the Presbyterians were subject in theory to the same early-eighteenth-century penal laws as were the Roman Catholics, although the government quickly backed off most of these enactments by way of annual indemnity acts or, from the 1780s, full toleration acts. However, it is easily forgotten how long the raspy collar of the penal days chafed the Presbyterians. Thus, not until 1844 was it made clear in United Kingdom statute law that a "mixed" marriage between an Anglican and a Presbyterian was legal in the case of its being celebrated by a Presbyterian clergyman; in contrast to one celebrated by a Church of Ireland rector, which always had carried legal legitimacy (James C. Beckett, *Protestant Dissent in Ireland* [London 1948], 122; Andrew R. Holmes, *The Shaping of Ulster Presbyterian Belief* [Oxford 2006], 216).

28 Akenson, *Church of Ireland*, 165, table 34. The original data are found in considerable detail in *First Report of the Commissioners of Public Instruction, Ireland*, 9–45 [45] H.C. 1835, xxxiii. The 1831 census had not inquired into religion, but with admirable ingenuity, this educational commission sent the parish-level reports back to the original enumerators and then on to the local Roman Catholic and Church of Ireland clerics for checking.

17 percent) and, like Clogher, much of the diocese lay atop a fault line in the settlement of Ulster, and a low-temperature war with the majority population (62 percent Catholic) was forever in train.

- the archdiocese of Dublin and Glendalough was 21 percent Anglican and 78 percent Roman Catholic. This yielded a degree of simplicity among Protestants that would be complicated only later, when some Anglican evangelicals decided to join ecumenically with smaller dissenting groups, especially those with ties to British Dissent.

Turning specifically to County Wicklow, according to Ken Hannigan the total Protestant population was nearly 22 percent (of a total population of about 121,500) and almost all of this was Anglican: there was one Presbyterian group of immigrant Scots who centred on the cotton factory at Stratford-on-Slaney, a Methodist congregation in Wicklow town, and Methodist groups in the mining settlements on the Fitzwilliam estate.[29] The Methodists in this situation were conservative and respectful of the landlord class and also sensitive to the desirability of not offending the lay leaders of the Established Church. If anything, the proportion of Protestants in the County Wicklow population may have been higher than the conventional recalibrations of the 1831 census suggest. Dr Garret Fitzgerald came to the conclusion

29 Ken Hannigan, "Wicklow before and after the Famine," in Hannigan and Nolan, *Wicklow History and Society* (Dublin 1994), 794–5. The entire volume is a major and indispensable achievement. Three notes about vocabulary are necessary. First, "Protestant" in the present discussion is used in its modern sense. In governmental documents in the era of the state church, it meant Church of Ireland (Anglican), and other groups were aggregated as "Dissenters" or occasionally as "Non-Conformists," or specified by their own corporate name. Secondly, the vocabulary of Methodism in Ireland in some ways is 180 degrees the opposite of that in Great Britain. Thus, "Primitive Methodists" in Ireland were those who wished to stay within the Church of Ireland; the primitives in England were a much more radical separationist set. Thirdly, in Ireland in this period, "chapel" was used for Catholic churches. Methodist places of worship were most often termed "meeting houses" or sometimes "preaching houses."

that "the proportion of Protestants in Wicklow was exceptionally high, at almost 24 percent rising to 28–31 percent in the baronies of Rathdown in the north of the county and in Shillelagh in the south."[30] Here the large Protestant landlords of Wicklow – there was only one big Catholic landlord in the county, Byrne of Croneybyrne, with 4,000 acres[31] – managed their properties' human resources with the same engineering mentality with which they chopped and changed their visual environment. Of course, the majority of tenants-on-the-ground on most estates were Catholics, but they were not thought to be very desirable, in part for security reasons, real or imagined. The more prudential landlords packed the areas around their own demesnes with Protestants. An unusually clear case of such arrangements was that of the Fourth Viscount Powerscourt. This is the situation as described by Robert Fraser, the observer for the Dublin Society, in 1801:

> What, independent of its grandeur and beauty, renders this district peculiarly interesting, arises from this estate of Powerscourt containing for its extent a greater number of respectable yeoman tenantry, than perhaps any of equal extent in the county. Of these there were no less than ninety-four, who with four officers kept guard at Powerscourt House, from the 6th of May 1798, for 18 months, and preserved the whole country safe from the depredations of the rebels and banditti, who infested the adjacent mountains; Lord Powerscourt himself constantly doing duty along with them, the greatest part of the time a subaltern in the corps. All his tenants have leases for 3 lives or 31 years, which ever last longest. Their farms are from 150 to 200, and some 300 acres.[32]

30 Communication to author. At the time of his death, Dr Fitzgerald was engaged in a statistical study of schools in the 1820s. He was being assisted by Cormac Ó'Gráda, Gillian O'Brien, and myself.

31 William Nolan, "Land and Landscape in County Wicklow," in Hannigan and Nolan, 663.

32 Fraser, 50–1.

The Powerscourt arrangements were exceptional in their clarity. However, the pattern was general in the sense that landlords and their agents used loyal Protestant small and middling farmers as a social buffer on the more desirable swatches of land. "There is a well-documented bias towards Protestant leaseholders at the scale of townland farms," notes William Nolan, "and this was significant in determining the shape and content of the countryside, particularly in the precincts of estate towns and villages, which were invariably sited in Wicklow's best endowed lands."[33]

By no stretch of the imagination can Wicklow's population generally be thought of as being anything very far above the subsistence line. In 1841, when the first inventory of Irish vernacular housing was taken, 28 percent of County Wicklow families were living in one-room mud cabins,[34] and the proportion probably was slightly higher in the 1820s. Recognition of this slight improvement over time (which runs against the grain of the general Irish experience of the era) is based on the clever work of the economic historian Joel Mokyr. He looked at the testimony of the 1,590 witnesses who appeared before the 1836 Irish Poor Law Commission about conditions in their respective parishes and counties. Of these, 1,362 were individuals who had been around at the end of the Napoleonic Wars and therefore they had two decades of observational experience. Mokyr's key conclusion was that only for

33 Nolan, in Hannigan and Nolan, 688. The data sources for the period do not permit a nominative tally that compares the size and nature of landholdings as between Protestants and Catholics. However, a fairly robust rule of thumb is that if one wants to know how the two groups were sorted out in any given area of contested landholding, simply use feet-above-sea-level as the independent variable. In pre-Famine Ireland, the Catholics usually were pushed into the higher elevations, where the holdings were less productive. This certainly was the case in County Wicklow, in which one finds the highest Protestant proportion of the population in the northeastern quadrant, the coastal-east strip, and southern lowlands (see ibid., 796, figure 20.1). Here, to my rule of thumb should be added a Wicklow-caveat: Catholics will be found on the higher elevations, *except* in places where singular vistas make the locales desirable for house-proud landowners.

34 Ibid., 795, citing the 1841 census.

the counties of Wexford and Wicklow in all of Ireland did experienced local witnesses report that things had improved since 1815.[35]

If Dalyland was blessed economically, at least in the sense that it was one of the few places in the south of Ireland that was not juddering downward, the reasons were prosaic. One of these was the benefit stemming from what one can call "domestic emigration." Wicklow, more than any other county in Ireland, had a notable portion of its locally born population living in Ireland but outside the home county. Wicklow-born persons of the farm-labourer class were migrating to Dublin to find employment. Mostly these were women, most often domestic servants and most commonly they were in the range of twenty-six to thirty-five years of age.[36] This is not some odd statistical irrelevance. It is, I think, a very similar situation to that which later prevailed throughout most of the twentieth century, when the most common place of Irish emigration was Great Britain, especially England: locations from which the migrants could come home at reasonable intervals and from which, in any case, it was easy to send the odd bit of money to family at home.[37] Thus, in County Wicklow, the economic impact of population pressure was relieved in two ways: first, some people left and when they did they were in a position to earn money and, if they wished, send or bring some of it back.

The second reason County Wicklow did reasonably well economically was that, as Roy Foster observes, there were many "secondary residences" in Wicklow that "were owned by people who drew their major income from larger estates elsewhere in Ireland but preferred to live in Wicklow."[38] In basic terms, this meant that the farming and

35 Joel Mokyr, *Why Ireland Starved* (London 1983), 12.

36 Hannigan, in Hannigan and Nolan, 793.

37 I am being somewhat tentative here because there are no systematic data on what one could call "domestic remittances" from in-country migrants. However, I am confident of the proclivity of Irish migrants, as evidenced over long periods of time, to send or to bring remittances home, and this was a perduring cultural characteristic. Indeed, as late as the early 1950s, remittances from Great Britain were 2.5 percent of the Republic of Ireland's national income and in the early 1960s were 3.2 percent (Enda Delaney, *The Irish in Post-War Britain* [Oxford 2007], 42).

38 Roy Foster, "Parnell and His Neighbours," in Hannigan and Nolan, 898.

Parishes of County Wicklow

Arklow

Arklow	A-1
Ballintemple	A-2
Castlemacadam	A-3
Drumkay	A-4
Dunganstown	A-5
Ennereilly	A-6
Glenealy	A-7
Inch	A-8
Kilahurler	A-9
Kilbride	A-10
Kilpoole	A-11
Redcross	A-12

Ballinacor North

Derrylossary	BN-1
Knockrath	BN-2
Rathdrum	BN-3

Ballinacor South

Ballinacor	BS-1
Ballykine	BS-2
Hacketstown	BS-3
Kilcommon	BS-4
Kilpipe	BS-5
Moyne	BS-6
Preban	BS-7

Lower Talbotsown

Blessington	LT-1
Boystown	LT-2
Burgage	LT-3
Crehelp	LT-4
Donard	LT-5
Dunlavin	LT-6
Hollywood	LT-7
Kilbride	LT-8
Tober	LT-9

Newcastle

Derrylossary	N-1
Kilcommon	N-2
Kilcoole	N-3
Killiskey	N-4
Newcastle Lower	N-5
Newcastel Upper	N-6
Rathnew	N-7

Rathdown

Bray	R-1
Calary	R-2
Delgany	R-3
Kilmacanoge	R-4
Powerscourt	R-5

Shillelagh

Aghowle	S-1
Ardoyne	S-2
Carnew	S-3
Crecrin	S-4
Crosspatrick	S-5
Liscolman	S-6
Moyacomb	S-7
Mullinacuff	S-8

Upper Talbotstown

Ballynure	UT-1
Baltinglass	UT-2
Donaghmore	UT-3
Dunlavin	UT-4
Freynestown	UT-5
Kilranelagh	UT-6
Kiltegan	UT-7
Rathbran	UT-8
Rathtoole	UT-9
Rathsallagh	UT-10

N.B. Some parishes cross the boundaries of one or more baronies.

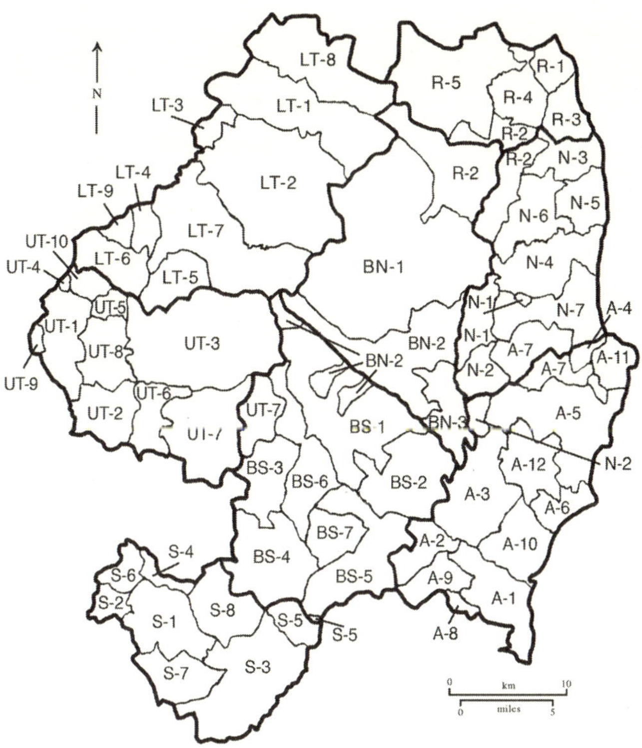

MAP 1.5 WICKLOW PARISHES BY NAME AND LOCATION.

farm-labourer classes of the county did not have to bear the full weight of their landlords. If County Wicklow had been a country, it would have been one with a national trade surplus; landlords were importing money from elsewhere in Ireland.

Whether the upper gentry and aristocracy were spending their money on primary or on secondary residences, they engaged in a good deal of conspicuous consumption and in its comfortable auxiliary, conspicuous leisure – in the classic sense that Thorstein Veblen established those terms. But this consumption and leisure were of a surprisingly disciplined sort. Although piles of Big Houses dotted the countryside, architecturally remarkable in the full ambiguity of that term,[39] the collective genius of the rich was to recognize, in William Nolan's sharp words, Wicklow's "inherent suitability for landscape engineering on a grand scale."[40] The archetypal engineered landscape consisted of a spectacular view – a glen with a glimpse of the sea beyond, or a mountain vista showing in the distance beyond a glaucous bog, or a sightline that opened on to running waters – so landowners wanted both lowlands and highlands, the high ground for visual purposes more than for actual farming. Entire villages were engineered into the pictures thus framed (note, thus, the Powerscourts' construction of Enniskerry). The moulding of the landscape required planning, obviously, and implied the imposition of a high degree of social discipline upon those lower down the social scale. The arrangement of the tenantry – especially the Protestant "yeomanry" – on big estates, was complicated in terms of leasing and restrictions on land usage and had to be well thought out. Also, religious facilities and schools were part of the necessary equipment of social control. On many large estates the landlords were engaged in cultural engineering almost as much as they were in contriving new physical landscape.

39 The indispensable reference work on the subject of Irish Big Houses is Mark Bence-Jones, *Burke's Guide to Country Houses, Vol. 1, Ireland* (London 1978).

40 Nolan, in Hannigan and Nolan, 687. It is worth emphasizing that the early nineteenth-century Wicklow landlords had excellent taste in topography. At the present time, roughly half of County Wicklow has been designated an "area of Outstanding Natural Beauty" by the government of the Republic of Ireland (see 256, plate, in Aalen, Whelan, and Stout).

For those on the upper levels of the pyramid, life could be quite satisfactory. Thus, in the mid-1830s, John Henry Parnell (father of Charles Stewart Parnell) did a grand tour of North America with his neighbour and cousin, the Sixth Viscount Powerscourt. Near Baltimore, Maryland, they visited a country estate and Parnell mentioned to the owner, "what a pleasant life it is to have a country house and farm if a man has sufficient income to support it."[41]

Dalyland, therefore, was a three-fold entity. It was a *reality*, consisting of real pieces of earth, awkward lumps of humanity (notably inconvenient Catholics and poor Protestants), and it held some real treasures of nature, as well as notable, indeed noble, human beings. In its engineered aspect, Dalyland was also a synthetic *illusion* in the same way that any well-realized portrait, any splendid piece of oratory, any great cathedral is. And it always sat on the knife edge of *delusion.* Dalyland's inherent and self-created danger was that the inhabitants of its thought-world would lose the distinction between reality and illusion – and that way lay not just delusion but also its obtrusive acolyte, madness.

41 Roy Foster, *Charles Stewart Parnell: The Man and His Family* (London 1976), 38, quoting from Parnell's unpublished journal of the tour.

CHAPTER TWO

The Fauna of Dalyland

Just for a moment, observe the most influential figure ever to live in Dalyland: not influential immediately, but ultimately he was a mind-maker, virtually worldwide. At the moment, though, the late autumn of 1826, he is a mess. He is working very hard at being an ascetic medieval holy man while occupying a curacy in a Church of Ireland parish in the mountainy bogs of County Wicklow. He was later to admit that in this phase of his life he had a horror of Protestantism and disowned the name: "I looked for the Church … I fasted in Lent so as to be weak in body at the end of it; ate no meat on week days; nothing till evening on Wednesdays, Fridays and Saturdays, then a little bread or nothing; observed strictly the weekly fasts too." He had been, he said, only saved from becoming "a Romanist" by the ninth and tenth chapters of the book of Hebrews which deal with the nature of covenant, of Jesus as the only true High Priest. This is John Nelson Darby.[1]

He is in what looks like a dumper post, an ad hoc arrangement of the sort that bishops cobble together for clerics who are either a moral embarrassment to the church and therefore need to be put where they

1 J.N.D. [John Nelson Darby], *Analysis of Dr Newman's Apologia Pro Vita Sua; with a Glance at the History of Popes, Councils, and the Church* (London 1866), quotations from 3, 19–20. Darby's medieval asceticism may have been operant before he was ordained, but there is no doubt that it continued well into his first (and, actually, only) formal religious posting. This is confirmed by the observations of Francis Newman, cited below.

could do least harm, or for those who are so potentially explosive that they had best be hived off into the wilderness. Darby's jurisdiction – later, after he has left, it formally becomes the parish of Calary – was over 13,000 acres of wildness, mostly boggy tableland, screened entirely from the sea, containing between 2,500 and 2,800 souls, of whom slightly more than 600 were Protestants.[2] There was no church and no glebe house for the clergyman to live in. A school founded and governed by the Association for Discountenancing Vice was the only really operational civic institution in the parish. It had roughly fifty pupils, of whom twelve to twenty were Catholics (depending on which faith was doing the counting); a Protestant schoolmaster; and a policy of reading the scriptures in both the Authorized Version (the King James Bible) and the Douai-Reims Version. The school was not John Nelson Darby's responsibility.[3]

Darby had been ordained deacon on 7 August 1825 and priested 19 February 1826.[4] He certainly was proficient in Latin, biblical Hebrew and biblical Greek, classical Greek, and probably in modern French. He was knowledgeable in the writings of the Church Fathers. He had, however, no experience as a servant of the Church, and in his era the Trinity College, Dublin, divinity course taught nothing so vulgar as practical pastoral techniques. Darby probably did not even bother attending, as young men with good connections frequently bypassed it. Francis Newman, the brilliant younger brother of the saintly (and eventual Cardinal) John Henry Newman, came to know John Nelson Darby in the autumn of 1827 and has left a famous, if slightly overegged, description of Darby's pastoral methods and martyrdoms:

2 *First Report of the Commissioners of Public Instruction in Ireland*, 128–30, [45], H.C., 1835, xxxiii; *Fourth Report of His Majesty's Commissioners on Ecclesiastical Revenue and Patronage in Ireland*, 20–1, H.C. 1837 (500), xxi. In governmental documents of the period, Calary is sometimes spelled Callary and, in at least one report, as Cabary.

3 *Second Report of the Commissioners of Irish Education Inquiry*, 850–1, H.C., 1826–27 (12), xii.

4 *CDIB*, Darby entry. Darby's diaconal ordination license is found in the Christian Brethren Archive [hereafter, CBA], the University of Manchester, J.N.D./1/1/34.

> Every evening he sallied forth to teach in the cabins, and roving far and wide over mountain and amid bogs, was seldom home before midnight. By such exertions his strength was undermined, and he so suffered in his limbs that not lameness only, but yet more serious results were feared. He did not fast on purpose, but his long walks through wild country and indigent people inflicted on him much severe deprivation: moreover, as he ate what food offered itself – food unpalateable and often indigestible to him, his whole frame might have vied in emaciation with a Monk of La Trappe.[5]

Add to this "a fallen cheek, a bloodshot eye, crippled limbs resting on crutches, a seldom shaven beard, a shabby suit of clothes and a generally neglected person," and one can understand how "the poor Romanists" might look on him "as a genuine 'saint' of the ancient breed."[6] Or a wandering madman. In either case, hospitality was the safest way to deal with him.

The singular religious-secular matrix of Dalyland was the one place in the world where John Nelson Darby could have been led to formulate and subsequently to amplify his unique personal mission. That assertion, of course, is open to dispute particularly from faith-based premises, but my argument has the virtue of applying to what did indeed happen in Dalyland, rather than an untestable counterfactual assertion of what the Almighty might have been pleased to let happen elsewhere. Hence, in practical terms, we need to understand more about the orbit of gentry and aristocratic evangelical Christians that was defined by the activities of the whirlwind religious and social entrepreneur, the Rev. Robert Daly. Crucially, the rise of Irish evangelical Anglicanism,

5 Francis William Newman, *Phases of Faith* (London 1850), 27–8. This book went through several editions. (It was in its ninth edition, London: Trubner, 1874.) The later editions included a good deal of new material and engaged in ongoing controversies, but the material related to Darby stayed the same.

6 Ibid., 28.

and especially its power in its homeland of County Wicklow and south Dublin, makes sense only if one goes to the most basic resource of Irish society: land and the power it provided to those who possessed it. Here we will isolate County Wicklow, since it was a civic unit for which contemporaries collected information in a fairly accurate form.[7]

Usually, when someone talks about nineteenth-century Irish landlordism, it is a quick jump to schoolbook discussions about a nationwide plague upon the Irish people. Well, plagues vary. Undeniably, several of the greatest estates of County Wicklow had absentee landlords and one might move to the stereotyped conclusion that here we have the indifferent Irish landlord, the dissolute landlord's agent, the rack-renting middleman, and that none of this has anything to do with religion. But in County Wicklow the absentees were of an unusual sort: because of the attractive nature of Wicklow estates, the absentees often were in residence part of the year.[8] Or secondary members of the family (unmarried sisters, for example) resided most of the year.

The least typical non-resident landlord (if living primarily in Dublin indeed was non-residence) was the second largest landholder in the county: the archbishop of Dublin held 26,500 acres in his corporate

7 Here again, one must recognize the economical and elegant manner in which William Nolan and Ken Hannigan collected and presented the fundamental data on County Wicklow in this period. See William Nolan, "Land and Landscape in County Wicklow," 649–92, and Ken Hannigan, "Wicklow before and after the Famine," 789–822, in Hannigan and Nolan, *Wicklow History and Society* (Dublin 1994). Nolan and Hannigan had to work with the awkward presentation by the early Ordnance Survey and subsequent land valuations, a great snarl of data. For the later Victorian data, which have a comparative usefulness and some historical value, see *A Summary of the Returns of Owners of Land in Ireland*, H.C. 1876 (422), lxxx. The original material for Ireland (and for Great Britain) tended toward underestimation of the extent of landowning oligopoly and the best contemporary reworking was by John Bateman; see his *The Great Landowners of Great Britain and Ireland*, 4th ed. (New York 1970; first published London: Augustus M. Kelley Publishers, 1883).

8 This is the observation of Roy Foster, citing the instances of the Fitzwilliams (the Wentworths), Powerscourts (the Wingfields), and the Carysforts (the Proby family) in *Charles Stewart Parnell: The Man and His Family* (London 1976), xiv.

capacity. The lands the archepiscopal see held in Wicklow were almost entirely mountainy or boglands with relatively few inhabitants. In any case, these church lands were not managed like a normal estate. Successive archbishops had been very lax in choosing their large tenants and agents and the result was that the estate had become fragmented and the leaseholds had degenerated (from a landlord's viewpoint) into holdings in perpetuity.[9]

The largest private landholding, just short of 80,000 acres in 1838, was the Fitzwilliam estate, most of which was profitable land in the southwest of Wicklow.[10] The relevant individuals were William Wentworth Fitzwilliam, Second Earl Fitzwilliam (well known in Irish history for having been cashiered from his post as Viceroy of Ireland in 1795 for supporting Catholic emancipation), and his son, the Third Earl Fitzwilliam, who succeeded on his father's death in 1833 and who up to that time had spent most of his civic duty as an MP for Yorkshire and an advocate of parliamentary reform. The estate was run from Coolattin in the barony of Shillelagh and here an important point emerges, applicable to Wicklow absentees in general. This is that the agents of the major absentees were chosen from a class above that of the normal land factors. They were men who acted not just as rent-receivers but as surrogate landowners or as gentleman farmers-cum-agents. The best example is the Fitzwilliam estates' Robert Chaloner, who was deputy lieutenant for the county and who married his daughters into Wicklow elite families.[11] Thus, it is revealing to note the local charities which

9 Nolan, in Hannigan and Nolan, 657–8. The basic conditions of the entire range of holdings of the Dublin archbishopric as of the early 1830s is found in *First Report of His Majesty's Commissioners on Ecclesiastical Revenue and Patronage, Ireland,* 62–71, H.C. 1833 (762), xxi. The overall picture is clear: from a management viewpoint, the situation was out of control. The three biggest tracts of land in County Wicklow, comprising several score townlands, brought in under £300 per year and were reckoned as having no "profitable" acres, and the "unprofitable" acres (bogland or scalped mountain) were not even calculated (ibid., 70–1).

10 Nolan, in Hannigan and Nolan, 656–8.

11 Foster (1976), xiv. Nolan has a valuable table (669, table 16.4) concerning the agents of the leading estates and their place of residence in the mid-1830s. Eleven of the twenty-six most important agents lived on or near the estates they managed. For a list of the magistrates of County Wicklow in the early

were supported by absentee landowners. The pattern suggests that their agents, in consultation with the landowners, effected a pattern of local involvement that was the same as if the owner were fully resident. Thus, in the 1820s, Earl Fitzwilliam was credited with providing aid to four schools for the poorer agricultural class: land to the value of £10 per year for the Protestant schoolmaster of a mixed school that was in connection with the Kildare Place Society in Cross Patrick, Shillelagh Barony; the schoolhouse for a free school (Protestant master, mixed pupils) and for the master's salary in Carnew, Shillelagh; and educational aid in the parish of Rathdrum in the northeast of the county, where the Fitzwilliams had long run a flannel factorship. The flannel hall was fitted out with desks and equipment for two pay schools, one Protestant, the other Catholic. That pattern, of the heads of families being influential locally without actually residing very often, is nicely documented for the Fitzwilliams in the field of education by virtue of a governmental commission of the 1820, and I strongly suspect that their local involvement held for other small local charities that have left no systematic records.[12]

Moreover, as far as education is concerned, the pattern certainly held for the other larger non- or occasional residents: the Brabazons of Kilruddery (earls of Meath, with nearly 24,000 acres), the Beresfords (marquises of Waterford with above 23,000 acres and a strong line in the most profitable Church of Ireland bishoprics), and the Probys (earls of Carysfort in the Irish peerage and barons in that of the United Kingdom, with 16,000 acres).[13] The Hill family (marquises of Downshire, with somewhat under 16,000 acres around Blessington in northeast

---

1840s – a mixture of landowners and their agents – and an identification of their estates, see George O'Malley Irwin, *The Illustrated Handbook to the County of Wicklow* (London 1844).

12 *Second Report of the Commissioners of Irish Education Inquiry*, 844–5, 852–3, 854–5, H.C. 1825 (12), xii. According to Lewis, the flannel hall, which the Fitzwilliams had built in 1793, was made nearly useless for its original purpose by the reduction of protective duties after the Union. In the mid-1830s, it not only held the two schools mentioned above but was also used as the local courthouse and as a Roman Catholic chapel. Samuel Lewis, *A Topographical Dictionary of Ireland* (London 1837), vol. 2, 495.

13 Nolan, 658, table 16.2, in Hannigan and Nolan; and see *Second Report of the Commissioners of Irish Education Inquiry*, passim.

FIGURE 2.1 KILRUDDERY HOUSE.

Built in the early 1820s as the seat of the earls of Meath, it shows the Wicklow ascendancy at its most self-confident.

Wicklow) were massive landowners in the north of Ireland. Admirably accurate estate accounts show that they supported several charities and poor pensioners and that in addition roughly 0.5 percent of the gross income of their estates was spent on building schools, paying schoolmasters, and providing books. As well, on the Blessington estate in Wicklow, they paid to clothe the schoolchildren.[14]

Rather more telling (because they left deeper traces) were the activities of aristocrats and gentry whom one may call "semi-resident." These were families who had one foot in Dublin and one in Wicklow and among them the La Touches and the Guinnesses stand out. Both were commercial families, but far from being in-trade: each family could have acquired titles in this period, but they did not bother, a form of righteous snobbery that is hard to beat. Take first the La Touches. Solely by landholding standards they were not a big deal: they held just

14 W.A. Maguire, *The Downshire Estates in Ireland* (Oxford 1972), 82. This volume is the standard by which all subsequent Irish estate studies are judged.

over 1,700 Wicklow acres.[15] But they were very big players indeed in the mental world that was Dalyland. Put simply, "the La Touches were perhaps the wealthiest, certainly the most enduring financial dynasty of Anglo-Ireland."[16] As Huguenots who had come to Dublin in the 1690s after the victory of William III of Orange, they had taken up being financial intermediaries for Huguenot nobles, pensioners, and remittance men. Essentially they were the Rothschilds of eighteenth-century Ireland: by mid-century they owned most of Ireland's biggest bank and a whole lot more. In the last decade of the eighteenth century they had five Dublin houses, residences that in themselves staked out the boundaries of fashionable urban territory: one in Ely Place, one on Merrion Square, and three on St Stephen's Green. In addition they held four significant rural estates around Dublin. The relevant one here is Bellevue in County Wicklow, owned by Peter La Touche II, where he turned the outbuildings into a glass-and-plant wonderland. He also bought a separate piece of Wicklow land surrounding Lough Tay (sometimes called Luggala Lake) near Roundwood, where he constructed in the early 1790s a Gothic fantasy retreat.

As an extended (but tightly knit) family, the La Touches had several signal characteristics in addition to their wealth: they were stoutly anti-Catholic (as Huguenots one could scarcely expect them to be otherwise); they were high-ranking Freemasons; they gave prodigiously to a wide range of charities; and they provided the standard number of younger sons to the Anglican ministry. As far as Dalyland was concerned, the notable clerics were: David La Touche (son of David La Touche II, who built Bellevue), appointed curate of Delgany in 1771, and John James Digges La Touche (a nephew of Peter La Touche), curate of the fashionable St Ann's church in Dublin from 1817–36.[17]

15 Nolan, 658, table 16.2, in Hannigan and Nolan.

16 David Dickson and Richard English, "The La Touche Dynasty," in David Dickson (ed.), 1987, 17. The entire essay (17–29) is valuable. See also the entries in *CDIB* on David Digues La Touche, David La Touche II (who built Bellevue in the 1750s), William George Digges La Touche, David La Touche III, and Peter La Touche.

17 Anyone who has worked on the history of the Church of Ireland will be aware that one of the unsung heroes who laid the foundation for later scholarship

The family was strongly predisposed to favour the evangelical movement. Indeed, one mainline son became a Methodist without disrupting familial relations.

The La Touches were the perfect part-time residents of Dalyland. Bellevue, in the parish of Delgany, Wicklow, was immensely self-indulgent in its architecture and especially its gardens. Paradoxically, it was also the site of continuing and sometimes sincerely selfless charity. Peter La Touche II, who had inherited Bellevue from his uncle in 1785, is credited with building entirely at his own expense the Delgany parish church in 1791.[18] That was very landlordly, the sort of thing many rich men might have done. However, in matters of more engaged charity, the operative figure (as in so much of the Irish evangelical movement) was female: in this instance Peter La Touche's second wife, Elizabeth. In 1792 she founded the Female Orphan House in Dublin. Mrs La Touche essentially was the committee of management, and she was very effective. The school in the Orphan House was one of the few boarding institutions for the poor that received the approval of the commissioners who investigated Irish education in the 1820s: "while we admire the singular benevolence and perseverance which

---

was the Rev. Canon James B. Leslie. He compiled numerous fasti of Anglican clergyman, parish by parish. All this was done by constant avocational application in roughly the first fifty years of the twentieth century. Nearly half of the clerical succession lists have been published, but for the most part they have necessarily been consulted in the archives of the Representative Church Body, Dublin. The archdiocese of Dublin and Glendalough has been splendidly served by the publication of Leslie's work, as expanded and corrected by W.J.R. Wallace, *Clergy of Dublin and Glendalough: Biographical Succession Lists* (Belfast 2001) [hereafter, CDGBSL]. Nobody is perfect and the entry on James Digges La Touche is in error in citing Peter La Touche as his father. Peter La Touche's two marriages were childless. He died in 1828 and left his estate to another nephew, who also was called Peter La Touche. See CDIB, entry for Peter La Touche.

18 *Saunder's Newsletter,* 19 February 1791, cited by Ruan O'Donnell (ed.), *Insurgent Wicklow, 1798* (Bray 1998), 11n6. That date, 1791, probably is for completion and consecration. *Fourth Report ... Ecclesiastical Revenue and Patronage* gives 1789 as the building date, which one can take as the start date. In any case, Peter La Touche saw building a parish church as one of his first duties as landlord.

distinguish the management of the asylum last mentioned [the Female Orphan House] we have to express our conviction, that it would be vain to reckon generally and constantly upon exertions of a similar nature in the direction of such institutions."[19] Not only was Elizabeth La Touche remarkably steadfast and competent, but she was also ambitious in her benevolence. As early as 1801, it was reported that "Mrs La Touche, to her school for female orphans, has lately added a day-school in the village of Delgany, where she has proper mistresses to teach any of the children and young women of the parish, who choose to attend, all manner of plain work and spinning, in addition to reading."[20] This day school, still under Mrs La Touche's supervision, was functioning very well indeed in the mid-1820s. The government's education commissioners found a school on the family estate, "built at the expense of Mrs La Touche, of the best materials." It was a free school, its expenses paid by the founder, and it educated twelve girls, all Protestants.[21] One suspects that these were the children of the Protestant tenantry with whom the La Touches filled the Bellevue estate: there were roughly 100 tenant houses on the estate, containing about 400 inhabitants, and as one later scholar noted "Gaelic patronymics" among the tenantry "were rare among the camellias of Delgany."[22]

That was not a frivolous comment, blending as it does notice of Peter La Touche's abhorrence of bog-born Romanism and his love of exotic plants; it points to the parish of Delgany as an exclusive little canton, equalling in tone that of its near neighbour, Powerscourt parish, and holding itself up as a shining light to the right sort of people. Thus, one finds in Delgany in the 1820s two extraordinary schools, places that boarded Protestant children from all over Ireland. One of these, run by a Miss Good, took fifteen girls to board in "a very convenient house," for the charge of 30 guineas a year.[23] This yielded an annual income above that of the average Church of Ireland rector. More impressive,

19 *Third Report of the Commissioners of Irish Education Inquiry*, 12, H.C. 1826–27 (13), xiii.

20 Robert Fraser, *General View ... County Wicklow* (Dublin 1801), 257.

21 *Second Report of the Commissioners of Irish Education Inquiry*, 848–9.

22 Nolan, in Hannigan and Nolan, 686, quoting Thomas Jones Hughes.

23 *Second Report of the Commissioners of Irish Education Inquiry*, 848–9.

FIGURE 2.2 THE OLD COURT, NEAR BRAY.
The vista was an excellent example of engineered landscape, antiquities, and crumbling monuments.

startling really, was the Delgany establishment of a Mr Anderson, who took Protestant boys into his "excellent house" for £30 per annum. In the mid-1820s, he had fifty-six students, meaning that his gross income was nearly £1,700 a year; were this sum a parish rector's gross income, it would have put Mr Anderson in the top 3 percent of the income distribution.[24] One desperately wishes to know more about these schools, not least because the only Old Boy I came across spent a portion of his life being worshipped in India as a god, preparation for which prob-

24 Ibid. For the comparative range of contemporary gross income for beneficed clergymen, see Akenson, *The Church of Ireland* (New Haven 1971), 87, table 22. Expensive as these private schools were, they pale in comparison to the amazing 80 guineas annual fee for a school in the nearby parish of Powerscourt. That school, kept by a Mrs Orsmby, employed a clergyman as its classics master and enrolled only twelve pupils, all boys (*Second Report of the Commissioners of Irish Education Inquiry*, 850–1).

ably was not included in the curriculum.[25] In any case, no one sent their children to these Delgany institutions without a sense that the parish was a very proper address, both socially and religiously.[26]

The second notable semi-resident family, the Guinnesses, was not so strong a social influence as were the La Touches in County Wicklow; but in the bigger picture they were even more influential in underwriting the sort of Irish evangelicalism that eventually produced, among many other religious variants, the Wicklow Brethren (to employ a term more accurate than the "Plymouth Brethren," which was forced upon later Brethren by outside observers), and contributed directly to the literalist-biblicist-apocalyptic tradition that became a major strand in world evangelicalism. The male members of successive generations of the Guinness family had a predilection for taking

25 I am referring to John Nicholson, who was at school in Delgany in the early 1830s. Nicholson is found, often inaccurately presented, in several collections of imperial stories. He badly needs a modern biographer, although the standard Victorian life is based solidly on documentary evidence: Lionel J. Trotter, *The Life of John Nicholson, Soldier and Administrator* (London 1897). The ODNB is too full of errors to be useful but the CDIB is serviceable. Surprisingly, the best modern approach is that done by two US professional military men, R.H. Haigh and P.W. Turner, *"Nickalsain": The Life and Times of John Nicholson* (Manhattan 1980). The name of Nicholson's school is never given, but there was only one male boarding institution in the parish, run in his day by the Rev. Dr Louis Delemere, and there he stayed for less than two years. He was the only Old Boy of the school to achieve the status of a god. In India, he gained the reputation among his foes during the Second Sikh War, 1848–49, of being bulletproof. Subsequently a Sikh-derived sect began to worship him as an avatar, wearing salmon-coloured clothes and black felt hats (EIC officer colours) and so enraging Nicholson that he frequently beat them, thus evidencing to them that he was a real divinity. This circle of belief and punishment continued until Nicholson at Delhi in 1857 proved not to be bulletproof. After his death two of the leaders of the sect committed suicide, and the rest disbanded.

26 Brian Gurrin's retabulation of the 1831 census data for Delgany parish suggests that it was the most Protestant parish in Wicklow, slightly more so than Powerscourt. His estimate is that in 1831 Delgany was roughly 45 percent Protestant (8/9ths of which was Church of Ireland) and had been so since the mid-eighteenth century (Brian Gurrin, *A Century of Struggle in Delgany and Kilcoole* [Dublin 2000], 21, table 8 and associated text).

Anglican holy orders. This made succession planning in the brewing business very difficult, since the lads of character left the business and the black sheep and the dim were the bulk of the remaining ruck. Thus, the first Arthur Guinness (1725–1803) found that his eldest and very able son Hosea was determined on spiritual service. In the next generation, the second Arthur Guinness (1768–1855) found that his eldest son, William Smythe Lee Grattan Guinness, was determined to enter the church. And several others in the extended family became clergymen. Patrick Lynch and John Vaizey's classic history of the great brewery captures the second Arthur Guinness's vexation at being the de facto bank of last resort for a disconcertingly saintly family: "Arthur Guinness once complained, with justice, of the burdens of 'many, so many relations,' most of whom appear to have been fecund and many, especially the clergy, feckless."[27] Here the economic historians are only half right: the clergy among the extended family undeniably were fecund (the Rev. Hosea Guinness had thirteen children and the Rev. William Smythe Guinness had seven), and there were indeed a lot of clerics in the Guinness families (in William Smythe's generation, among the various cousins, three young men took holy orders and three daughters married Church of Ireland clerics) but they were not feckless, merely impecunious.[28]

But what the economic historians may have considered to be religious recidivism actually was at the heart of the matter: indeed, the first three heads of the brewing business were concerned as much with salvation as with hops and yeast. The first Arthur Guinness had been very impressed with hearing John Wesley during one of his preaching tours of Ireland; although he remained a financial mainstay of the Church of Ireland, Arthur Guinness was notably ecumenical within the Protestant faith. He was one of the chief financial supporters of the Bethesda Chapel created in 1784 by William Smyth (var.: Smythe). This was an

27 Patrick Lynch and John Vaizey, *Guinness's Brewery in the Irish Economy* (Cambridge 1960).

28 The complex financial-religious and genealogical relationships of the Guinnesses (like many of their class, they frequently married cousins) are dealt with deftly in Michele Guinness, *The Guinness Spirit* (London 1999); on the matters mentioned above, see 1–79.

institution that did not fit into the template of Irish religious life. It was a halfway house between the Church of Ireland and Dissent, and its importance over its first four decades was that it became a virtual academy for evangelicals, especially among a minority of those Trinity College students who believed their religious training was desiccated and juvenile. It did not hurt that one of the assistant ministers at Bethesda was Edward Smythe, a cousin of Olivia, wife of the first Arthur Guinness. In the next generation, the second Arthur Guinness supported St Catherine's church. There in 1786 he co-founded with the Quaker Samuel Bewley, a Sunday school that became the non-denominational Dublin Free School in 1798. The second Arthur Guinness mostly worshipped at Bethesda. When there was a particularly nasty fight concerning Bethesda and the Anglican authorities in 1805 (more of that later), he paid the bills and kept the chapel going. He was surprisingly liberal in politics, supporting Catholic Emancipation. The head of the third generation, Benjamin Lee Guinness (1798–1868) formally took over leadership from his father in 1839–40, but had become influential within the family well before that date. He was deeply religious – he led family prayers each morning and evening – and his biggest charitable act, among many, was to prevent St Patrick's Cathedral, Dublin, from crumbling to ruins. His uncle Hosea had been chancellor of St Patrick's from 1810 to 1841. Benjamin Lee Guinness married his cousin Elizabeth (Bessie), who was extremely evangelical, and an adherent of Bethesda Chapel.[29]

29 Guinness, 24, 56 79; Alan Acheson, *A History of the Church of Ireland* (Dublin 2002), 98–9; Lynch and Vaizey, 114–15; *CDIB*, entry for Arthur Guinness (no. 2); *ODNB*, entry for Benjamin Lee Guinness. Two sidebars: (1) watch for the name Bewley – this mostly Quaker family drifts in and out of the margins of Irish evangelicalism-cum-Brethrenism and at one point is one of the early encouragers of the American evangelist Dwight L. Moody's crusade in the British Isles; (2) more immediately relevant to demonstrating the preferred clerical career lines of Dalyland is the career of the Rev. Hosea Guinness, who in his mid-twenties became the curate of Bray, then chaplain of the Magdalen Asylum in Dublin, 1803–06, then back to Wicklow as curate of Delgany, 1806–09, and from there to the chancellorship of St Patrick's Cathedral and the rectorship of St Werburgh's church, which was tied to the chancellorship, 1810–41 (*CDGBSL*, 690).

Now, play that into Dalyland. Later, we will look at the diffuse and subtle influence of Bethesda, but here we can focus on one name, that of the eldest son of the second Arthur Guinness: properly William Smythe Lee Grattan Guinness, who was appointed as vicar of Rathdrum in December 1824. The "Smythe" is a reference to his paternal grandmother's Bethesda-serving relatives mentioned above; the "Lee" is from his wife's family; and the "Grattan" was assumed in adulthood as a tribute to another of his grandmother's cousins, Henry Grattan, who not only was a famous Irish patriot but had been a strong supporter of brewers' interests in the pre-Union Irish parliament. Next, look at his education: the Rev. William Guinness was prepared for Trinity College, Dublin, through private tuition by the Rev. Benjamin W. Mathias, a church-licensed schoolmaster and, more importantly, the minister in charge of the Bethesda Chapel from 1805 to 1835 – at which point he semi-retired and served as a curate to his former pupil, the Rev. Mr Guinness, in Rathdrum until his death in 1841.[30] Then consider the unique nature of William Smythe Guinness's clerical appointment. Rathdrum was one of three benefices (of a total of 102) in the archdiocese of Dublin and Glendalough) that was in 1815 in the gift of the corporation of the city of Dublin. (The other two were Drumcondra in north Dublin where the church was in ruins and there was no glebe house and a perpetual curate received £70 annually from the corporation, and the other was Taghadoe in County Kildare, with a total population of 467 souls in 1831, a non-resident incumbent and a curate on £70 a year.)[31] Rathdrum was worth £610 a year, well above average, and had a first-rate glebe house, so it would be natural to think that the Dublin Corporation had simply made some prudent calculations and appointed to the benefice the eldest son of one of the city's major businessmen, the second Arthur Guinness, who in 1820 had become the governor of the Bank of Ireland and was well worth keeping sweet. Actually, no: the transaction was more direct than that, albeit a touch mysterious. In 1816, the Dublin Corporation had sold the advowson to Denis George, Esq., for the sum of £2,861. Then George died and

30 *CDGBSL*, ibid.

31 *First Report ... Ecclesiastical Revenue and Patronage in Ireland*, 212; *Fourth Report ... Ecclesiastical Revenue and Patronage in Ireland*, 12–99.

left the patronage of Rathdrum to Arthur Guinness, who appointed his own eldest son to the benefice.[32] The next observation: the parish carried with it a nice bit of inside patronage, or at least of extended influence: the attached parish of Ballinaclash (it is usually mapped under Rathdrum) from 1832 onward held a perpetual curacy, worth only £50 annually in formal stipend, but topped up by another £50 from the Rev. William Smythe Guinness, who had the right of patronage. Notably, this subpost included within its boundaries yet another ecclesiastical jurisdiction, the Royal Chapelry of Carysfort, a by then totally impoverished benefice that ran back to the time of Charles I. By licence of 1827 the Royal Chaplaincy was a separate post, its holder receiving roughly £80 a year from pew rents and offerings. And that appointment was vested in three trustees who, surprisingly, did not include the Rev. William Smythe Guinness, but rather, his father, Arthur Guinness, the Rev. B.W. Matthias of Bethesda Chapel, and the Rev. Dr William Thorpe, an assistant to Matthias at Bethesda and in the 1830s the minister and titular owner of a proprietary evangelical chapel in London.[33] Manifestly, in Rathdrum, sub-infeudation by evangelicals was taking place, but in a very quiet way. The parish's nearly 40,000 acres were located in the middle section of the eastern side of the chain of Wicklow hills. Rathdrum was described by the ecclesiastical commissioners of the 1830s as having one-fourth arable land, one-fourth pasture,

32 *CDGBSL*, 319. I have not been able to ascertain the relationship between Denis George and the second Arthur Guinness. However, the Rathdrum incumbency was something that seems to have involved long-term Guinness interests: namely that the man whom William Smythe Guinness replaced was the deceased longtime incumbent of Rathdrum (the Rev. Richard Powell, in Rathdrum 1796–1824), and he had been a curate (1775–96) at the Church of Ireland parish in Dublin, St Catharine's, which the second Arthur Guinness preferred when not at Bethesda Chapel; and Powell had been one of the co-founders of the Sunday School movement in Ireland, a cause the second Arthur Guinness strongly supported. See *CDGBSL*, entry for Richard Powell.

33 *Fourth Report … Ecclesiastical Revenue and Patronage in Ireland*, 14–15, 20–1, and also subnotes, 101. *CDGBSL*, entry for Ballinaclash. The Carysfort Chaplaincy was not a sinecure. In the early 1830s, duties included, in addition to holding church services and doing pastoral work, giving improving lectures every Thursday and Saturday.

and the rest mountainy ground.[34] That was the recipe the Wicklow landscape-shapers loved. Great vistas, deep valleys, the joining of the Avonmore and Avonbeg, where Thomas Moore sat and wrote the "The Meeting of the Waters," and visible but decently distant fine houses such as Avondale and Castle Howard. Small wonder that as he grew older Arthur Guinness used the Rathdrum glebe house as a rural retreat where he could talk to his son and worry about the approximately forty nephews and nieces who were on his list of begging relatives.[35]

The parish of Rathdrum was a microcosm of the sort of thing that was happening in several places in County Wicklow. It is one for which the documentation is particularly good and certainly it indicates that the semi-resident families, such as the Guinnesses and the La Touches, were influential in sculpting the socioreligious contours of Dalyland. Their interventions were strongly on the side of evangelicals in the Church of Ireland and were illustrative of the Dalyland belief that power spoke truth: Christian truth.

Earlier, we noted that in Wicklow the agents of the great, mostly absentee, landlords usually resided on the estates and performed the role of locum gentry. Roy Foster has observed that, in addition to the great landowners and their resident agents:

> there was also a large representation of what can be called "middling gentry": families like the Humes, Actons, Tottenhams, Synges, Tighes, Westbys, Grattans, Truells, and Parnells, who constituted the J.P. class of the county. They held more than one county office, owned estates of several thousand acres, and often maintained a Dublin or London house as well as a Wicklow seat. It is a class not usually considered characteristic of nineteenth-century Ireland; but the high incidence of this

34 *Fourth Report … Ecclesiastical Revenue and Patronage*, 62.

35 He died in 1855, leaving £400 in trust for each nephew and niece for their coming of age. This from an estate probated at £150,000 (Guinness, 80).

element in Wicklow is indicated even today by the large number of Victorian country houses in the county.[36]

The Parnells are a case in point. As owners of Avondale, they were under the goodly and godly spirit of the Guinnesses for a very long time. Not only was William Smythe Guinness rector of Rathdrum from 1824 to 1855,[37] but his predecessor was Richard Powell, who held the charge from 1796 to 1824 and was one of the founders of the Sunday School movement in Ireland – a cause dear to the heart of the second Arthur Guinness. Note that the Rev. Mr Powell had been appointed in the days when the patronage to the benefice was in the hands of the Dublin Corporation, one of the places where the Guinness influence was strong.[38] Although it is clear that the Parnells were not engaged in local good works, schools, or in direct efforts to convert Catholics in quite the way some of the other Wicklow gentry and aristocracy were[39] – they could have been called "soft on Romanism" as leading members of the family favoured easing up on the Catholics – but the Parnells could not escape being influenced by marriage and through local geography by the aggressive first generation of Dalyland evangelicals.

Among the resident gentry, the Parnells were latecomers. Their base was estates in Queen's County – roughly 3,700 acres in 1789 and smaller parcels in other counties. Their entry into Wicklow was effected in one

36 Foster (1976), xiv.

37 It is not of great moment, but CDGBSL has Rathdown as a vicarage, which it may have been before 1824. However, in the Guinness era, the tithes definitely went to the incumbent and the post was a rectory (see *Fourth Report … Ecclesiastical Revenue and Patronage in Ireland*, 62–3).

38 CDGBSL, entries on Rathdrum and on Richard Powell. In the person of the Rev. Robert Wyndham Guinness (incumbent 1874–1919) the Guinness evangelicals continued to preside ecclesiastically over Rathdrum both in Charles Stewart Parnell's lifetime and also that of the next inheritor of Avondale, his older brother, who had to sell the estate in 1899, as it was heavily burdened with mortgages.

39 Foster (1976), 39, makes this observation concerning John Henry Parnell (1811–59), and it is confirmed for earlier generations by the absence of the Parnell name in the censuses of supporters of schools, churches etc., that have been cited already concerning many of the other gentry and aristocracy.

FIGURE 2.3 THE VALE OF AVOCA.

The fame of the "Meeting of the Waters" was ratified by Thomas Moore's song.

big jump when in 1795 Sir John Parnell inherited the property that became Avondale from his cousin, Samuel Hayes. The family added to this base property over the years, so that in the late 1830s the Parnells of County Wicklow held nearly 3,800 acres.[40] This Wicklow branch of the Parnell family was distinctly separated from those in the midlands when, at the death of Sir John, his third son, William (1777–1821), was willed the formerly Hayes Rathdrum property.[41] (Because the towering figure of Charles Stewart Parnell, 1846–1891, looms over so much later Irish history, I will use him as a genealogical locus point; but the patterns and practices we are here observing were almost entirely antecedent to his birth and he really is not part of the story. William Parnell was the grandfather of C.S.P.) Whatever his worldly interests – writing novels and miscellaneous solutions to Ireland's

40 Foster (1976), 11; Nolan, in Hannigan and Nolan, 658, table 16.2.

41 He changed his name formally to William Parnell-Hayes in honour of the family's benefactor, but in practice he was known as William Parnell. See *CDIB*, entry on William Parnell, which suggests that his dates were not as usually thought (1780–1821) but actually 1777–1821.

problems – William's marriage in 1810 to Frances Howard meant that he now lived surrounded by the new piety. The three daughters of the Hon. Hugh Howard (the younger branch of the Wicklow earldom, the family holding collectively over 23,000 acres in the county) were famously evangelical and the daughters married splendidly: Frances, the eldest, to William Parnell in 1810; Isabella to the future third earl of Carysfort (over 16,000 acres) in 1818; and Theodosia, the youngest, to the Fifth Viscount Powerscourt in 1822.[42] Taken together, the sisters indicate once again how important the female component was in the configuration of Dalyland.

Certainly marriage made William Parnell start to pay attention to faith. His devotion to his wife was deep; he took in her piety with tolerance and then, after her tragic death in the late summer 1814, with something approaching affirmation.[43] A revealing correspondence took place after Frances's death between William Parnell and the Rev. Robert Daly, who offered himself as a personal and spiritual counsellor. Revealingly: because it shows both Daly's technique in working himself into the confidence of the local elite and also because it indicates Parnell's modest but marked spiritual turn. Robert Daly managed the relationship very skilfully. In consequence, Daly excuses Parnell for sending long letters, but goes on to complain about finding a place to live while the new Powerscourt glebe house is being built and about how a mutual problem – the grief Mrs Howard carried after the death of her daughter, William's wife – was to be assuaged. And then he gives spiritual counsel: "For you, who have suffered the greatest loss, I do hope you are resigned; and that when you join the spirits of the just, you will 'rejoice in your tribulation,' and say 'It was good for me to be afflicted; in very mercy has God visited me.'" Daly here is not taking

42 Turtle Bunbury, *The Landed Gentry and Aristocracy of County Wicklow* (Dublin 2005), 5–6; Nolan, in Hannigan and Nolan, 658, table 16.2.

43 Both ODNB and CDIB in their entries on William Parnell have Frances's death occurring in 1813. Foster (1976), 32, has it as 1814, and he is the more apt to be correct. GEC [Cokayne's *The Complete Peerage*] and several independent genealogical sites give her death as 14 August 1814. This fits much more closely with the chronology of William Parnell's relationship with his spiritual counsellor Robert Daly than do ODNB and CDIB.

liberties, for it is clear that he already has been taken on by Parnell as a spiritual advisor, "You speak of your vacillation and my steadiness," Daly notes, and then concludes "I wish I could live more up to my principles, for which I must watch and pray. This I recommend to you."[44]

Later, in April 1815, Daly is close enough to Parnell to postpone accepting an invitation for a repeat visit to Avondale and to reflect on what a good place that is: "I found there everything I could wish," especially the chance to sit relaxed in "the usual social hours" and "indulge the bent of my mind and say without constraint whatever was the real sentiment of my heart." Good manly stuff: "that is what I call society; not that unnatural state where form and stiff civility freeze and chill what should be warm and lively … For large and promiscuous company I have neither taste nor talents."[45]

By now Daly is part of the Parnell circle. He will see "Tom" in Dublin[46] – Thomas Parnell, the permanently unmarried younger brother of William, who was generally known as "Tract Parnell" for his manic engagement in papering the country with evangelical pamphlets. Thomas had become well known as an eccentric evangelical as early as the Napoleonic Wars. Thus, in his diary for May 1813, Sir Vere Hunt refered to him as a "swaddler," a term of abuse usually reserved for Methodists but sometimes applied to very keen Anglican evangelicals.[47] Thomas Parnell must have been a social lump. He was a big man, pockets filled with tracts that he was forever stuffing under doors; when he arrived as a guest, "the household knew that they were in for a discourse, at least an hour long, after evening prayers."[48]

But it was the older brother, the landowning William, who was worth cultivating. The Rev. Robert Daly and William Parnell became

44 Robert Daly to William Parnell, of n.d., but certainly after Daly's institution at Powerscourt, 17 March 1814. Indirectly, this confirms Frances Parnell's death as being in 1814, reproduced in Mrs Hamilton Madden, *Memoir of the Late Right Rev. Robert Daly* (London 1875), 54–6.

45 Robert Daly to William Parnell, 11 April 1815 in Maddden (1875), 56–7.

46 Ibid., 58.

47 Typescript of diary of Sir Vere Hunt, entry for 10 May 1813 (Limerick Regional Archives).

48 Timothy C.F. Stunt, *From Awakening to Secession: Radical Evangelicals in Switzerland and Britain, 1815–35* (Edinburgh 2000), 162, quoting J.B. Atkins, *Life of Sir William Howard Russell* (1911), vol. 1, 7.

close enough that William Parnell was telling Daly that he really ought to get married. "For your comfort I will tell you," the bachelor clergyman replied, "I am not in the least against it, if Providence (in whom I believe) should put it in my way."[49]

Whether or not William Parnell ever had the full conversion experience (however gradual) that is a mark of evangelicalism as it is usually defined is unclear, but under Robert Daly's care, he came to some kind of acceptance of God's will in ordering his life. "As to yourself," Daly wrote, "it is with the most gratified feelings that I have remarked you so humbly bending under the afflicting hand of our common God. Yours has been an afflicting of no common kind."[50] The affliction to which Parnell bent to the Divine will was the loss of his wife.

Although William Parnell never was counted among the stalwart evangelicals (he continued to publish material that was decidedly pro-Catholic in pointing to historical reasons for Catholic disaffection from church and state), an intriguing turn occurred in his civic interests. In 1817 he was elected an MP for County Wicklow and he spent a good deal of his energy trying to negotiate and promulgate an agreed set of the Christian Gospels for use of both Catholic and Protestant schoolchildren. This harkens, I think, to a period in his mourning for his dead wife when, with Robert Daly's encouragement and one infers guidance, he took to reading the Bible seriously. "I am very happy in thinking that you are reading the New Testament, and with interest," Daly wrote, "for I cannot conceive any one to read it without prejudice and not be made a real Christian by it."[51]

That sentence could serve as the mandate for Parnell's campaign to promulgate a set of ecumenical holy scriptures. He was quite taken with a set of extracts from the four gospels prepared by Sarah Kirby Trimmer (universally referred to by contemporaries as "Mrs Trimmer").[52] Parnell gave these to the Rev. Mr Doyle, the Catholic priest of

49 Robert Daly to William Parnell, 19 April 1815, in Madden (1875), 62.

50 Robert Daly to William Parnell, 11 April 1815, ibid., 58.

51 Robert Daly to William Parnell, [n.d., but 1814], ibid., 55.

52 That of course was standard contemporary usage, but Sarah Trimmer (1741–1810) has long been treated patronizingly by historians as being slightly ditsy by virtue of her writing religious works for children. Actually, she came from a very sophisticated home (her father, an artist, was drawing teacher to the

Bray, a town and locale where the relationship between the Catholic clergy and the Protestant gentry was particularly good, with the request that Parnell himself might be introduced to the Most Rev. Dr John Thomas Troy, Roman Catholic archbishop of Dublin. That was done, and after William Parnell's meeting with the Catholic prelate, Father Doyle was given by his superior the job of vetting the text Parnell was so keen on: he wanted to republish Mrs Trimmer's set of lessons from the four gospels and use them in schools for "the lower class of society." After Father Doyle suggested a few changes, all of which were accepted, Archbishop Troy signed his approval and Parnell ordered at his own expense 1,000 copies to be printed by the firm of Blenkinsop, the printer to Maynooth Seminary. Here it is worth emphasizing that Parnell was not a member of any Protestant proselytizing society, nor of the allegedly neutral Kildare Place Society, which had hundreds of purportedly non-denominational schools in its network and was later in the 1820s condemned by Catholic leaders.[53] William Parnell never-

future George III and among those passing through the family house were Reynolds, Hogarth, and Gainsborough), and she designed a quite effective ladder of evangelical education for children, including the innovative use of visual material. One emphasizes her pedagogic shrewdness as something to which one should be sensitive as a general matter in historical context. Although largely unnoticed well into the early twentieth century, some evangelical educators (for example, the Moody Bible Institute in the USA) produced lesson plans for both children and adults that in method and achievement of objectives were way ahead of what was being done in secular education. The text that so impressed William Parnell was Sarah Trimmer's *An Abridgement of the New Testament: Consisting of Lessons Composed from the Writings of the Four Evangelists. For the Use of Schools and Families* (London 1797). There were several iterations of the original edition and one does not know which one Parnell used. On Sarah Trimmer, see *ODNB* and the booklet by D.M. Yarde, *The Life and Works of Sarah Trimmer* (Hounslow 1972). Mrs Trimmer was irreproachably English. Mostly, she worked with the poor, but in her guide for teachers in schools for young ladies of the middle and upper-middle class, she advised as follows: "*French*, a sufficient knowledge was to be acquired to enable persons of condition to converse with foreigners. The French language has been the occasion for incalculable mischief by opening a passage for that torrent of infidelity and immorality" (Yarde, 44–5).

53 Documentation of the narrative here compressed is found in *First Report of the Commissioners of Education in Ireland*, 45–7, H.C. 1825 (400), xii. The

theless attended some of the Kildare Place Society's board meetings and pressed them to publish the now-revised version of Mrs Trimmer's work: rather optimistically, as he had 900 unsold copies still on his hands. They agreed after being certain that Archbishop Troy really had signed off on the work: 25,000 copies were ordered from Maynooth's printer. Then, in late July 1818, Dr Troy changed his mind: sort of. That was his way, havering, and it is how he had managed the choppy waters of his archiepiscopate (1786–1823) during the Catholic church's difficult passage from the late penal era to the early years of Daniel O'Connell's leadership of the Catholic cause.[54] Troy wrote to the society saying, yes, he had sanctioned the original scripture extracts, but that he now had some minor reservations over disputed passages, yet nevertheless he would assume that these would be corrected in later editions and that, therefore, he was not now withdrawing his approval. Troy was indeed good at being on all sides of an issue, but his coda was nothing less than a depth charge. "Allow me to observe," he said with apparent courtesy:

> that the Catholic church in all Ages has prohibited the indiscriminate Use of the Scriptures in vulgar Tongues without Note or Comment, also the Interpretation of them by every One's private Judgement. This Interpretation has been the fatal and prolific Hive from which Swarms of Sectaries daily issue, each One finding his Religion in the Bible, which has disfigured and distracted the Christian Church since the Days of Luther;

---

report states explicitly (45) that Parnell was not a member of the Kildare Place Society. Parnell died in 1821, but there also exists circumstantial confirmation of his non-membership. When the commissioners of Irish education inquiry visited Rathdrum in March 1823, there were only four children in a school reported to be in connection with the Kildare Place organization, hardly a sign of any commitment ever having been made to work with the society by any locals (including both Parnell and the rector). See *Appendix to Second Report from the Commissioners of Irish Education Inquiry*, 154, 1826–27 (12), xiii.

54 I am grateful to Vincent McNally for helping me to understand the difficulties of Troy's position. See McNally's *Reform, Revolution and Reaction: Archbishop John Thomas Troy and the Catholic Church in Ireland, 1787–1817* (Lanham, MD, 1995).

> wherefore the Catholic Church condemns the indiscriminate Use of Scriptures in vulgar Tongues without Note or Comment, and permits it only to the learned or the lettered of the laity.[55]

William Parnell died in 1821 and Archbishop Troy in 1823, without their having to experience the cultural war they had framed on the issue of Mrs Trimmer's New Testament selections. The matter of the Bible without note or commentary became one of the issues Daniel O'Connell pursued in the 1820s, and it was part of the fight the Catholic bishops had with the heads of the state school system that was set up in 1831 on the seemingly idealistic mandate of creating non-sectarian education.[56] Indeed, the matter, only suppressed in the nineteenth century, was re-fought in the 1920s in Northern Ireland.[57] The legacy was an unbreakable paradox: the classic evangelical Protestant position was that the Bible alone was enough for salvation; the classic Catholic position that the Bible without guided commentary yielded only

55 John T. Troy to C. Le P[oer] Trench, 23 July 1818, reproduced in *First Report of the Commissioners of Education in Ireland,* 46–7.

56 See the following items published by sanction of the Commissioners of National Education in Ireland: *Scripture Lessons, Adapted for the Use of Schools: No.1, Old Testament* (Dublin: 1832); *Scripture Lessons: New Testament No. 1, for the Use of Irish National Schools* (Dublin: 1835); *Scripture Lessons: New Testament No. 2, for the Use of Irish National Schools* (Dublin: 1835); *Scripture Lessons, for the Use of Schools: Old Testament, No. 2* (Dublin: 1846). In the 1830s the whole business had several more vectors than my overall summary above indicates. The Irish national education commissioners compiled their own biblical extracts with the help of the Catholic archbishop of Dublin (Daniel Murray), the Protestant archbishop of Dublin (Richard Whately), and one of the leading Presbyterian clerics, the Rev. James Carlile. On the other hand, some leaders from each of the three major faiths were against not only the extracts, but against the system of popular education itself. For details, see my *The Irish Education Experiment* (London and Toronto 1970; republished, London and New York 2012).

57 In Northern Ireland the Bible-cum-cultural war was fought under the label of "the religious instruction question," and in practice came down to modes of disadvantaging the Catholic minority in educational funding. See my *Education and Enmity* (Newton Abbot 1973; republished London and New York 2012), esp. 39–118.

dozens of varieties of heterodoxy. So, for evangelicals, the claim was that the Catholic hierarchy suppressed the Bible; and for Catholics that the Protestant's unvarnished approach to the Bible inevitably yielded heresy. And on and on.

When William Parnell died in 1821 at Castle Howard (one of the homes of his in-laws), his son John Henry (1811–1859; eventual father of C.S.P.) was too young to be a figure in the life of Dalyland. Indeed, throughout his life, he was almost excessively private, save for doing his county duties, playing cricket, and shooting things. The legacy John Henry Parnell's father had left him was this: a glorious piece of countryside and a social network where many of the main entities were Dalyland evangelicals – most especially his two Howard aunts, who, like John Henry's late mother, were nothing if not keen. As mentioned earlier, Isabella was married to the eventual third earl of Carysfort (he inherited in 1828)[58] and the elder, Theodosia, became the second wife of the Fifth Viscount Powerscourt in 1822. These were visible and energetic figures in Dalyland and not to be ignored. They were frequently around Avondale and neighbouring estates.[59] From the same

58 The second earl of Carysfort had been non-resident, being active in Westminster politics and living in England. Isabella in the 1820s supported with her own donation of £20 annually a school the absentee second earl had built. (*Second Report of the Commissioners of Irish Education Inquiry*, 837). The third earl and Isabella moved to Glenart Castle, near Arklow, in 1818. Thereafter they spent a good deal of their time in Dublin and London and are probably best thought of as semi-resident. Isabella was active in various local religious concerns.

59 John Howard Parnell, brother of C.S.P., wrote a charming, if not entirely reliable volume: *C.S. Parnell: A Memoir* (New York 1914). He remembers (3) that in the 1840s the local gentry and nobility came round to a tea cottage at Avondale and that Lord and Lady Wicklow would arrive to reminisce over old times with the Hayes and the Parnells. This is too late in the day if one were doing a biography of John Henry Parnell, but it suggests that the social fabric of the 1820s and 30s was kept continuously intact during his lifetime. In any case, the Hon. Hugh Howard, John Henry Parnell's maternal grandfather, was one of his de facto guardians, along with the future Lord Carysfort, who had married John Henry's aunt, as was his uncle, Thomas Parnell. One says "de facto" as technically John Henry was a ward of Chancery and these were "next friends" who represented him legally; Foster (1976), 35.

FIGURE 2.4 THE DARGLE.

The Dargle carved a glen that was prized for joining the mountainy uplands with picturesque views toward the coast.

generation, John Henry Parnell had at least to take some notice of his eccentric bachelor uncle, Thomas "Tract" Parnell. Thomas was the animating figure in the Religious Tract and Book Society (founded 1817), which was shepherded by himself and by James Digges La Touche (Dublin banker, son of William Digges La Touche), by the Dublin silk magnate Samuel Bewley, who was closely allied with both the Guinnesses and the La Touches, and by the bibliophile, evangelical, and Irish-language enthusiast, Henry Joseph J. Monck Mason. The last-named had been born on the Powerscourt demesne and was fated to spend his later days in "Dargle Cottage"[60] – the same place where the Rev. Robert Daly lived in the mid-1810s when his new glebe house was being constructed. The Dalyland evangelical sphere was a very small world, indeed.[61] The Religious Tract and Book Society had depositories all over the country and in its first ten years boasted it had sold – sold, they claimed that they gave away very few items – 217,000 books

60 *CDIB*, entry of H.J.M. Mason.

61 Smaller even than that implies. At this period "The Repository" (for texts, Bibles, and improving literature for sale or distribution) was one of the main buildings in the Powerscourt church complex (A.E. Stokes, *The Parish of*

and 2.5 million tracts.[62] Thus, Thomas Parnell was on the pointed edge of Dalyland evangelicalism and he later became one of the Brethren, as did his third cousin John Vesey Parnell. Catherine, the sister of John Henry Parnell (C.S.P.'s aunt) was deeply evangelical and became in 1835 the second wife of George Vicesimus Wigram, who was a strict religious disciplinarian and was to Brethrenism what sergeant majors are to firing squads.[63]

Was that merely ambiance? There is no evidence that John Henry Parnell ever had a conversion experience or anything close to it. He was conventionally Anglican: deeply anti-Catholic, which was hardly unusual, and affirmative of the need for regular, albeit formalistic, religious discipline. Even as a young man travelling in America with his cousin, the Sixth Viscount Powerscourt, he was taken aback by the laxity in religious practice of East Coast Americans. He was himself a regular church attendee even when on a grand tour. While in Mexico he wrote in his journal that he "did not think it altogether proper to spend Sunday shooting."[64]

What one is seeing here, I think, is the behaviour and attitudes of the Dalyland mentality being in part assimilated without specific doctrinal beliefs being embraced. Mental habits often pass on to children even if ideology does not. Thus, the comment of Roy Foster concerning Charles Stewart Parnell: "Parnell was a Protestant, a member of the Synod of the Church of Ireland; and dutifully took some part in local parish organisations like the Select Vestry when he was living at Rathdrum. His private religious feelings appear to have been agnostic; with an inclination (like others in his family) towards the Plymouth Brethren."[65]

Powerscourt [Bray 1986], 13). And even smaller yet: "Tract" Parnell was a road designer, at least in an avocational way, and he was the designer of the roads on the Powerscourt demesne (Foster, 1976), 12.

62 Acheson, 122. If true, and if spread evenly, this number of tracts would have provided at least one item for every family in Ireland.

63 The family ties of Catherine Parnell Wigram ("Tattie" was her nickname) are found in CBA, J.N.D./1/1/29.

64 Foster (1976), 40.

65 Roy F. Foster, "Parnell and His Neighbours" (1994), in Hannigan and Nolan (eds), 900.

Dalyland ruled, if only in muscle memory. If the mixture of evangelicalism and social elitism had such a long half-life even among those who were not evangelical, then it must have had a similar influence, but more robust, in its own time, even among those who saw it all as rather a silly waste of time. Evangelicalism was fashionable.

The Synge family was similar to the Parnells: Wicklow middle gentry with tendrils throughout Dalyland. As with the Parnells, we have to try to keep the developments of the first decades of the nineteenth century in our minds as independent occurrences, all the while accepting that there is a future reference point that sits in everyone's peripheral vision, in this case the master dramatist [Edmund] John Millington Synge (1871–1909).

Like the Parnells, the Synges were relative latecomers to Wicklow; as with the Parnells, they previously had significant lands elsewhere in Ireland; like the Parnells, their entry into Wicklow was facilitated by a fortuitous inheritance of significant size. The Synges, unlike the Parnells, found their place in Irish history through being professional clerics. One cannot skim the *fasti* of the Church of Ireland compiled by Canon James Leslie without finding them scattered among his list: in rectorships, archdeaconries, and bishoprics from the mid-seventeenth through the early twentieth centuries. They never quite made it to the top of the ladder of preferment – before 1801 the system was heavily loaded against Irishmen getting the big plums, the archbishoprics of Dublin and of Armagh, unless they were from noble families[66] – but the Synges did well in the far west and far south and made a habit of marrying well. For our purposes the relevant line begins with Nicholas Synge (1659–1771), who became bishop of Killaloe in 1745.[67] One of his sons, Edward Synge (1726–1792), was archdeacon of Killaloe from 1760

66 Akenson, *The Church of Ireland*, 10–28.

67 *CDIB*, entry for Edward Synge (brother of Nicholas, appointed archbishop of Tuam 1716). In the following discussion, I am relying on the admirable, and often entertaining, work of W.J. McCormack in his unravelling of the complicated Synge family relationships.

to 1785 and was squire of Syngefield, near Birr, King's County (now County Offaly). He married a Hutchinson (watch that name), and they had five sons. The eldest, Edward (1753–1818), took his father's place as archdeacon of Killaloe, but mostly spent his time at Syngefield, engaging in country pursuits.[68] Of the other brothers, the two that count for our purposes are Samuel (1756–1846), who became the Church of Ireland archdeacon of Killala, and Francis, the youngest (1761–1831), who became a minor politician and a rentier.

Here, before going on with some necessary family details, we should accept the fact that family history can be quite challenging if the family involved has the habit of recycling only a few first names. But here is why the Synges' own wee Book of Kells of interlocked ancestry counts: (1) because the Synges show – even in the simplified form that I will present – how convoluted, familial, and acquisitive the social network of Dalyland was, both for secular and clerical families; and (2) because the Synges as a family have been downplayed in histories of Irish evangelicalism in general, and most especially in the story of the creation of the Wicklow Brethren, we need to pay them heed. They are among the formative figures of present-day evangelicalism, worldwide. In the actual course of events, three male Synges (two brothers and a first cousin) were among the founding influences of the Brethren. Yet, only a very few of the modern historians of early Brethrenism have knowledge of the facts concerning a family triad whose members were well known among the Irish founders of the movement. This is not entirely the fault of modern writers, because, for reasons that are hard to identify, when memoirs and in-house histories of the earliest Brethren began to be compiled in the second half of the nineteenth century, the Synges were shoved to the margins of the story.

In 1787, the Rev. Samuel Synge married a niece of Sir Francis Hutchinson, who arranged that by special-remainder his baronetcy should pass to Samuel Synge, as his own sons were ageing and childless. Sir Francis died in 1807, and by 1813 the legal technicalities were sorted out and Samuel Synge received the baronetcy and at the same time by

68 *CDGBSI*, entry for Edward Synge (not to be confused with others of that name) and W.J. McCormack, *The Silence of Barbara Synge* (Manchester 2003), 102–3, 109.

royal warrant he changed his name to Synge Hutchinson.[69] His first wife never had the pleasure of seeing him become the Rev. Sir Samuel Synge Hutchinson, as she had died in 1788.[70] In any case, the promised baronetcy gave him scope for a useful second marriage to the right sort of heiress.

Previously, in 1786, his youngest brother Francis had married Elizabeth Hatch, daughter of John Hatch, a Dublin attorney and land agent who had a parliamentary seat for Swords in the old Irish parliament and several properties in eastern County Wicklow. These included Roundwood, where the young couple moved and a second residence, Glenmouth, which the Synges later rebuilt into the gothic extravaganza Glanmore Castle. The transfer of the central Roundwood property in the barony of Ballinacor North took place before the elder John Hatch died. How John Hatch had made his money is fuzzy, but his father seems to have been some kind of a factotum to the Temple family. That John Hatch was also closely tied by business transactions to the main branch of the Hutchinson family comes as no surprise: a very small circle here.[71] In any case, the elder Hatch died in 1797 leaving no heirable son, but two co-heiress daughters. One of these was Elizabeth (1766–1810), the first wife of Francis Synge.

The other heiress daughter was Dorothy. In March 1801, she married the widower the Rev. Samuel Synge Hutchinson. Thus, what W.J. McCormack resignedly terms "the confusion of two sisters marry-

69 McCormack (2003), 112; Charles Mosley (ed.), *Burke's Peerage, Baronetage and Knightage*, 107th ed. (Wilmington 2003), vol. 1, 1163, gets it all backward and has the family name becoming Hutchinson-Synge. (This is forgivable as in the west of Ireland there were members of the extended tribe who carried the name Hutchinson Synge and used the same small set of first names as did the people we are here dealing with.) Actually, the real problem is that the name Synge Hutchinson was not hyphenated in the first two generations (it was later), although in the second generation Francis Synge Hutchinson insisted on both names being on the title page of the evangelical monographs that he published.

70 McCormack (2003), 32, 122, 124.

71 W.J. McCormack, *Fool of the Family: A Life of J.M. Synge* (London 2000), 125–6.

ing two brothers"[72] was merely one of the complex, and mostly unrecorded, arabesques on the social roadmap of Dalyland. It is worth particular notice because it plays into the rise of evangelicalism among previously very lukewarm clerical families and later directly into the Wicklow Brethren.

The immediate practical result was that early in the nineteenth century two middle-aged men from a longstanding clerical family acquired the property of two wealthy co-heiresses. The split of the sisters' wealth was well arranged, but nevertheless was complex and involved Dublin houses and pieces of land in County Meath and elsewhere, plus the major pieces in Wicklow.[73] The inherited lands had straddled the mountains like a very uncomfortable, slightly broken saddle. The less splashy of the two sets of land were the parcels that lay on the less congenial west side of the Wicklow mountains, and these went to Samuel Synge Hutchinson. They were mostly in the baronies of Upper and Lower Talbotstown (with fragments elsewhere) and ran down from the Glen of Imail. By acquisition and subsequent minor inheritances, the Hutchinson estate had grown to slightly over 5,700 acres in 1838.[74] The parishes of Dunlavin, Donard, and Donaghmore were the ones that counted. The Rev. Samuel Synge Hutchinson had a residence, Castle Sallagh, in Upper Talbotstown, but it is not clear if he spent much time there – he was appointed archdeacon of Killala in the far west of Ireland and thus acquired the glorious compound title of the Venerable Sir Samuel Synge Hutchinson.

(Parenthetically, but pointedly: the person who actually did most of the religious work in the Hutchinson sphere of influence in west Wicklow was the Rev. Thomas Francis Greene, the long-serving – 1818–52 –

72 W.J. McCormack, "The 'Plymouth' Brethren?" *Religion and Literature* (summer–autumn 1996), quotation from 86.

73 McCormack, (2003), 104–5.

74 Nolan, in Hannigan and Nolan, 658, table 16.2, 658. I think this overstates the property actually held by the Rev. Samuel Synge Hutchinson, as the tally seems to have lumped together lands that really could not be called one estate, as they were held by various Hutchinsons. Still, given his Dublin houses and lands in Meath, he was not poor.

very effective evangelical curate of Donoughmore. The rector of Donoughmore parish was usually non-resident – in most of the period the incumbents were pluralists – and there were two curates who did the heavy lifting. One of them lived in the glebe house and the other – the Rev. Mr Greene – had to shift for himself. Yet poor Rev. Mr Greene was not a poverty-dodging curate from an English novel but, typically of the lower clergy of Dalyland, was well-born and not impecunious. He was a curate by choice. His father had been high sheriff of Wicklow in 1804 and during his long curacy he lived comfortably in his father's house, Kilranelagh, on the edge of the parish. In 1840, at age fifty, he married Elizabeth Heighington of Donard House, whose father had been high sheriff of Wicklow in 1803. Finally, in 1852, Greene gave up the hard labour of being a country curate and moved to nearby Donard Parish as the vicar and, one assumes, the semi-squire.[75] That's the way things worked in Dalyland.)

On three east Wicklow portions of the Hatch inheritance, mostly in Ballinacor North and Newcastle baronies, Francis Synge spent a good deal of the money he had inherited from his father-in-law in the form of rents and building land in Dublin (and by his own investment in local small mining operations).[76] He put turrets and crenellations onto an existing structure, one whose detractors referred to as a former artillery barracks. The result, at least if one were inside of the resulting Glanmore Castle, was amazing in that the view stretched from the famous Devil's Glen, edged with carefully planted parkland, and revealed in the distance the Irish Sea. Francis Synge did well financially;

75 CDGBSL, entry for Thomas Francis Greene. *Fourth Report ... Ecclesiastical Revenue and Patronage in Ireland*, 34–5. Other information on Greene is found in W.J. McCormack (ed.), *Memories of West Wicklow, 1813–1939* (Dublin 2005), 1–9.

76 Amid the recognition of scenic manipulation by major landholders, it is well to remember that landed proprietors – Powerscourt, Parnell, Synge, Fitzwilliam and their contemporaries – invested in mining ventures that were kept beneath the viewlines of the well-wrought estates. Copper, lead, sulphur, and silver were the chief yields, although marginal gold veins were worked off and on. Fraser, in 1801, reporting to the Dublin Society, believed that extensive gold finds were possible (ii, 13–18) (see Timothy Alborn, "An Irish Eldorado," *Journal of British Studies*, 2011).

by the time of his death in 1831 he had put together roughly 8,500 acres, mostly in the picturesque parts of Wicklow.[77] Although he lived in the middle of the evangelical belt, he was not notably spiritual himself. He did pay the schoolmaster of two small schools: five and twenty-four students, mostly Protestants, in Roundwood townland.[78] He provided in the mid-1820s £25 a year to the master and mistress of a school in Killiskey parish (part of the larger parish union of Newcastle) that was housed in a notably well-made structure of lime, stone and slate, costing £200.[79] This was a mostly Protestant operation, and was run by his son John Synge at Nun's Cross on the radical but sensible educational principals of Johann Pestalozzi.[80]

What transformed the branch of the notably clerical Synge family, who found such good fortune in Wicklow from holding a low-temperature adhesion to the Church of Ireland as a useful avenue of personal advancement, into persons who poked at the religious establishment with evangelical keenness? The answer, as in so many things, is that chiefly it was a generational change. The young caught the Dalyland fashion. They became fully converted Anglican evangelicals.

To compress matters (the individuals will appear again later), three men were involved, rooting around Dalyland like spiritual truffle

77 Nolan, in Hannigan and Nolan, 658, table 16.2. The tally was for 1838. See also Nicholas Grene, "Synge and County Wicklow" (1994), in Hannigan and Nolan, eds, esp. 693–4.

78 *Second Report of the Commissioners of Irish Education Inquiry*, 842–3.

79 Ibid., 846–7.

80 Acheson (131) has Francis Synge of Glanmore Castle building a church at Nun's Cross, Killiskey, and appointing a minister in 1817. The parish is not reported by the ecclesiastical commissioners of the 1830s, but the church undoubtedly existed at Nun's Cross from 1817 onward, as is indicated by engravings on the base of the steeple clearly visible at present. In the later 1830s it was noted that the church included a memorial to the now-late Francis Synge (Lewis, vol. 2, 144). I think one sees here the influence of Francis's evangelically inclined sons. The church probably was evangelical – all except eight pews (for the quality) were free. The intriguing point is that if (as Acheson suggests), the Synges had the right to appoint the minister to what was effectively a proprietary chapel, they were apparently engaging in the evangelical sub-infeudation of Wicklow, in a manner similar to the way the Guinesses operated elsewhere in the county.

hounds. The first was Francis Synge Hutchinson who lived an unfortunately short life (1802–1833), son of the Rev. Sir Samuel Synge Hutchinson, and cousin of John "Pestalozzi" Synge and his brother the Rev. Edward Millington Synge, of Glanmore Castle lineage. Francis Synge Hutchinson has left few secular traces, but several religious impressions. He was born in south Dublin, attended Eton, received a TCD first degree in 1823 and spent his entire life at one of the family's south Dublin estates. He had full access to the fixers and rentiers of post-Union Ireland. He married Louisa Frances Hely-Hutchinson, daughter of the Hon. Francis Hely-Hutchinson and the sister of the eventual (1832) third earl of Donoughmore. They had three children, one of whom became Sir Edward Synge-Hutchinson, Bart.[81] Francis Synge Hutchinson clearly moved in advanced evangelical circles in the 1820s, as did a cadre of recent TCD graduates. His house at no. 8 Fitzwilliam Square was the place where the first regular Sunday assembly that is generally accepted as being "early" or proto-Brethrenism took place.[82] He produced at least two religious works. One was a short monograph on Second Peter 1:19–21, a passage that validates biblical prophecy as a divine product and contains the famous verse 21, "For the prophecy

81 Latter-day Saints search site, "Francis Synge-Hutchinson." Dated 19 August 2011. Source: National Library of Ireland, Collection List no. 50 *Tighe Papers (Mss, 29,634–83),* xii. Because many scholars are somewhat afraid of using the LDS collections, I should emphasize that, with certain limitations, they are useful. Herein I cite only LDS items that are precisely sourced. For an extended discussion both of the value and the limitations of the LDS material to non-Mormon historians, see my *Some Family* (Montreal and Kingston 2007). On Francis Synge Hutchinson's education, see George Dames Burtchaell and Thomas Ulick Sadleir, *Alumni Dublinensis* (London 1924), 423.

82 Francis Synge Hutchinson's house is one of the few sites that modern Brethren recognize as something close to being a shrine. W.J. McCormack is right to insist energetically that it was at no. 8, Fitzwilliam Square, not no. 9, as is almost universally found in Brethren histories. No. 9 was occupied in the relevant period by a Robert Blakeney Jr: McCormack (1996), 86, 95n7, and McCormack (2000), 432. One should not confuse either residence with no. 8, Ely Place, a mansion built in 1814 by the uncle of Francis Synge Hutchinson (McCormack, 2003, 125).

came not in old time by the will of man: but holy men of God spake as they were moved by the Holy Ghost."[83] The other was a longer work that argued directly against "the opposition manifested by many in these days to the study of the prophetical parts of the word of God."[84]

The second relevant figure is even more shadowy: the Rev. Edward Millington Synge (1798–1859), the younger son of Francis Synge of Glanmore Castle.[85] Born in Cheshire, where his family held land, he was educated at Eton, received his BA from TCD in 1820[86] and then followed the path that the clerical members of his family had laid out generations earlier: a prestige curacy and next a desirable parish or two, and the hope of grace and the means for higher glory. The first post was the curacy of Tuam, a step toward a good career, and it was given to him at the request of his father, who apparently still carried weight in the archdiocese where his family had done so well over the years.[87] The archbishop of Tuam at the time was the Hon. Power Le Poer Trench; he favoured evangelicals, and young Edward certainly was that. In due time, 1829, he was given a parish of his own, Kilkerin (var.: Kilkeeran) Union, an amalgamation of three charges that covered 12,000 acres and yielded £485 a year. The local area consisted of much better land than was common in the far west, and much of it was tillage ground. The glebe house had been newly built in 1817, but there was only a dilapidated church and the Rev. Edward Synge held services in a schoolhouse and was reported to be doing so even in the mid-1830s.[88] Realistically, there was little hope of building new Anglican

83 Francis Synge Hutchinson, *Remarks on Second Peter, Chap. 1, Ver. 19–21* (Dublin 1830).

84 Francis Synge Hutchinson, *Letter to the "Christian Examiner"* (Dublin 1830).

85 Since the Rev. Edward Synge spent most of his clerical career in the west of Ireland he is sometimes confused with the extreme proselytizing estate manager, Edward Synge of Dysert, Co. Clare and neighbouring counties. That Edward Synge was a nephew of Francis Synge of Glanmore Castle and a friend of John Nelson Darby.

86 Burtchaell and Sadleir, 798.

87 Acheson, 158.

88 *Third Report of His Majesty's Commissioners of Commissioners on Ecclesiastical Revenue and Patronage in Ireland*, 522–3, H.C. 1836 (246), xxv.

churches in the west in the 1830s.[89] Despite being resident in a west-of-Ireland parish, Edward M. Synge clearly mixed with leading evangelicals, and he probably attended at least one of the epochal Powerscourt meetings in the early 1830s.[90] The family circle of the Wicklow branch of the family guaranteed his interaction with the front-edge Dalyland evangelicals, and it is another warrant of the social-religious-economic bonds of this matrix that when the Rev. Edward Millington Synge married in 1834 it was to a daughter of Sir Richard Steele. Her sister had become the second wife in 1832 of Edward's elder brother John,[91] who is discussed below. (This is the same marital pattern that had occurred a generation earlier among their father and uncle: two brothers marrying sisters, one of whom was a second wife, the other a first.) The ineluctable inference is that if one were a member of the generation of the Wicklow Synges who came of age in the 1820s, then one was in the swirl that led to Wicklow Brethrenism. Both the two brothers, Edward and John, and their first cousin Francis,[92] undoubtedly knew full well what it meant to swim in that evangelical Hellespont.

89 McCormack (2003), 125, has Edward Millington Synge become rector of Matlock in England later in his career. This suggestion has no date attached and no source is given. McCormack may be correct, but the information seems to clash with *Crockford,* which has the rectorship of Matlock being held from 1839 until at least 1868 by William R. Melville (*Crockford's Clerical Directory for 1868*, 453). It may be that Synge simply retired to the family property in Cheshire. It is clear that he resigned his rectorship in the west of Ireland in 1837 because his wife was made ill by the cold and damp (John D'Arcy Sirr, *A Memoir of the Honorable and Most Reverend Power Le Poer Trench* [Dublin 1845], 198–200).

90 McCormack (1996), 87.

91 A brave piece of early revisionist Brethren historical writing is T.C.F. Stunt, "John Synge and the Early Brethren," *Christian Brethren Research Fellowship Journal* (1976). The marriage reference is on p. 45. See also "Synge 1" (www.stirnet.comHTML/genie/british/ss4z/synge, accessed 31 August 2012).

92 McCormack (2003) concludes (I think convincingly, albeit instancing only one letter) that Francis Synge Hutchinson was addressed as "Francis Synge" by one of the early men of the Brethren, the Hebraist and sometime tutor of John Synge's children, Henry Craik. He cites W. Elfe Tayler's edited collection, *Passages from the Diary and Letters of Henry Craik* (London 1866), 119. This underscores again how curious the change of Synge Hutchinson to "Hutch-

Finally, the most well known of the three Synge young men, John "Pestalozzi" Synge (1788–1845): so-called because after entering TCD in 1805 and then transferring to Magdalen College, Oxford,[93] he went on a European tour during the Napoleonic Wars, and this experience led to the second conversion experience of his life. The first conversion had been to evangelical Christianity during his undergraduate years; the second was to the educational ideas of Johann Heinrich Pestalozzi, one of the pioneers of what later was called "child-centred education." John Synge saw the two revelations as fitting together as sources of spiritual and secular freedom. As an Oxford undergraduate, Synge was in correspondence with his young contemporary, James Digges La Touche – who was at TCD while John Synge was at Magdalen – and the bonding of religious feeling and shared social class assumptions that characterize Dalyland is very clear in a letter of La Touche to Synge in the autumn of 1808: "let the world think as it may, there is no stronger bond which cements friendships than joining to their other coincident affections that of fellow warriors in Christ."[94] John Synge's conversion to the Swiss educational prophet Pestalozzi came after Synge had studied with the master for a few months in 1814. Pestalozzi was not an obscure figure in the evolution of the educational profession: generations of training college and Higher Dip. Ed. students have had to listen to his being memorialized as part of the genealogy of child-centred education; nor was he as naively Rousseauian as he is often caricatured, for he did not think of human beings as inherently perfectable. Undeniably, however, he stood against the rote learning and brute force that was the modus operandi of most schools for the labouring classes – and, for that matter, the schools of the upper classes. Thus, his methods were a hard sell in Ireland, especially to a theologically acute community (such as the Dalyland evangelicals) who believed in Original Sin as

---

inson" is in early Brethren histories and how this has led to the misleading downplaying of the Wicklow Synges' familial influence when depicted by later historians.

93 Burtchaell and Sadlier, 798; McCormack (2003), 134.

94 James Digges La Touche to John Synge, 19 November 1808, quoted in Irene Whelan, *The Bible War in Ireland: The "Second Reformation" and the Polarization of Protestant-Catholic Relations, 1800–1840* (Madison 2005), 61.

the primordial state of all humans, not excluding children. John Synge opened his own school at Nun's Cross (also called Kilfee, in the ancient parish of Killiskey in the bigger parish of Newcastle) in 1815 and spent a bit of his father's money on it: £200 in building costs and £25 per year charged to his father for teachers. As an apostle of Pestalozzi, Synge wrote two publicity books[95] and opened his own print shop. This was at Roundwood, the roughly 700-acre estate he took over from his father on his marriage in 1818. (Synge apparently took marriage seriously: he had seven children, and after his first wife died remarried in 1832 and had another seven.) His print shop turned out small text books and hymn books, as well as his arguments for the Pestalozzian style of teaching.[96]

Does not some of this emphasis on education sound familiar? Recall that in the same post-Napoleonic period, William Parnell had come to the conclusion that education was one of the keys to reforming Ireland. As I will discuss in the next chapter, this, in various permutations, was a deeply held view in Dalyland and in its satellites. The educational issue was not only a very volatile matter between the two major Irish faiths from the early 1820s onward, but it has left an historical question whose answer remains lost in an impenetrable fog of animus.

95 [John Synge] *A Biographical Sketch of the Struggles of Pestalozzi to Establish His System of Education, by an Irish Traveller* (Dublin 1815). More interesting was John Synge's home-printed *The Relations and Descriptions of Forms According to the Principles of Pestalozzi* (Roundwood 1817). This was typeset in four parts and included sample classroom discussions, lesson plans, and four copper-plate engravings. The lessons had very precise goals in terms of information acquisition. Although the emphasis was on teachers' imparting information in a non-mechanical fashion, each set of lessons began with convincing pupils of their own ignorance. Thus, the system could be fit into the Christian doctrine of imperfection being the basic human state.

96 McCormack (2003), 134–56. John Synge had an additional four books of Petalozzian methods printed in his home print shop. An engraving of the Nunn's Cross schoolroom is found in McCormack (2003), 13. *Second Report of the Commissioners of Irish Education Inquiry*, 846–7. The Synge family, presumably with Francis Synge acting as paterfamilias, also supported a small set of poor schools at Roundwood (*Second Report of the Commissioners of Irish Education Inquiry*, 842–7).

That question: was it possible in Ireland in the pre-Famine era for the support of widespread schooling ever to be anything but proselytism? Perhaps yes, but the conspicuous involvement of the Dalyland evangelicals in the several school-promotion societies makes one alert: would they have supported schools if the long-term goal was not indeed to turn the children?[97] Turn: in nineteenth-century Ireland, a truly cruel, terribly explosive word, one that cannot be avoided.

97 The other matter that the Synges had in common with the Parnells is that a heavy cultural mortmain was passed from the first one-third of the nineteenth century on to the shoulders of the two icons of the late nineteenth and early twentieth centuries, Charles Stewart Parnell and John Millington Synge. We have already dealt with C.S.P., so here we note that J.M.S. had an Aunt Editha, née Editha Truell, who married the first Synge of Glanmore Castle and then as a widow married a man named Gardiner, one of the Exclusive Brethren. This second marriage of an aunt effectively banned J.M.S. from his family's prized gentry residence (McCormack, 2000, 70), at least after J.M.S. became a contrarian young thinker. J.M.S.'s own mother was deeply influenced by the Brethren, although she was not an Exclusive. "Come you out and be separate" was her favourite admonition (Terence Brown, *Ireland's Literature* [Mullingar 1988], 64n10). And J.M.S. had his deep love for a Brethren girl rejected on religious grounds. The Dublin-reared Synge managed to spend a good deal of time in the countryside. He clearly was well-acquainted with his start-of-the-century family heritage on both sides of the Wicklow mountains. In the early twentieth century he wrote a handful of essays on life in County Wicklow. W.J. McCormack adjudges that "these eight sombre prose articles" amount to "a psychopathology of County Wicklow" (McCormack, 2000, 219). That seems a little harsh, but certainly Synge only partially suppressed his anger at the more unbendingly pious aspects of life that were the dejecta membrana of now-disappeared Dalyland. At one point, he puts into the mouth of a tramp he met along the Dargle a mock-psalm that touches some Brethren shibboleths and indirectly mocks John "Pestallozi" Synge's having swanned about Europe during the Peninsular War (J.M.S., "The Vagrants of Wicklow," in *The Complete Works of John M. Synge* [New York 1935], 493.) For an intriguing suggestion that for William Butler Yeats and his followers both Parnell and Synge became the archetype of the figure of a great gentleman – meaning of a true Irish-Protestant gentleman – see Roy F. Foster, "Good Behaviour: Yeats, Synge and Anglo-Irish Etiquette," in Nicholas Grene (ed.), *Interpreting Synge* (Dublin 2000), 41–55, 201–3.

What we have seen thus far in Dalyland is a compact world that did not exist primarily as a physical concept, although its geographic homeland was County Wicklow, mostly, and the posh parts of south Dublin. Dalyland was a state of mind, one that interwove evangelical Anglicanism with landlordism and involved a web of complex social relationships based on assumptions and behaviours that we can see quite clearly in outline but not fully in their myriad details. At its most successful, the Dalyland mindset left few traces, because many people unreflectively acted as if what they were doing was just the way the world worked.

In the previous chapter, we saw that the leaders of Dalyland exhibited at a macrolevel a contradictory set of attitudes and related behaviours. One half of this mixed set was a deep and unfeigned appreciation of natural beauty, especially of the countryside in which the gentry evangelicals were privileged to live. And, in apparent contradiction, a propensity for engineering in the mechanical sense: for rearranging topography and flora and moving around quite ruthlessly the people who inhabited the landscape. So, a paradox: humility before nature and simultaneously an arrogant and a self-confident inclination to improve upon it. What held for landscape, held in parallel for human relationships. The evangelicals and those whom they influenced were truly committed to a belief in the value of each individual human soul and, at the same time, to rearranging the idea-content of the souls of their fellow human beings through schools, tracts, hectoring, and, on occasion, evictions.

We have moved from the macro to the granular and have talked about some of the Anglican elite of Dalyland. Here, let me be clear that concerning Dalyland I have *not* proved anything, in the sense that one can prove a theorem or a scientific hypothesis. What I am suggesting is a way of thinking about a complicated social system that is worth our time because it had long-term consequences for literally millions of people: it helped to determine the configuration of later nineteenth, twentieth, and twenty-first century evangelicalism. What I have presented (and will continue to develop) is a web of instantiation (not scientific demonstration; rather, litmus instances) that indicates the *probable* way (probable: but not irrefutably provable) that this relatively small but highly influential evangelically distinguished world operated.

Here, conceive of doing the equivalent of a geologist's transection of a portion of the Earth. In the heuristic that is Dalyland, we see the following instantiated. (1) That the elite leadership of the Anglican evangelicals intermeshed but was not identical with the social elite of County Wicklow and south Dublin. (2) That there was a good deal of intermarriage among members of the social elite in any case[98] and, mutatis mutandis, this meant (as we have seen in several cases) that the most religiously committed families often intermarried and, further, that as "serious religion" became more prevalent as the early nineteenth century progressed certain families became evangelical congeries; this selection by belief (belief in part; money and status were also required) was accelerated by the frequency of the cousin-marriages among the gentry and upper classes in general.[99] Further (and not surprisingly

98 This is a truism for the place and period and it is not something I am here spending time demonstrating. However, several monographs by A.P.W. Malcomson are germane, most especially *The Pursuit of the Heiress* (Belfast 2006).

99 Here, though, we have to recognize the limits of what we can know. Granted, from the family relationships that we can chart on a surface level one could make a small cartographic jungle – and that just by using the items in the basic reference sources such as *Burke's Peerage, Burke's Landed Gentry, Debrett's Peerage*, and G.E. C[ockayne']s *The Complete Peerage.* The trouble is that most of what was understood by the knowledgeable at the time (which cousin was "real family" and which one was not; and why was the sister of His Lordship's first wife erased from the genealogy?) went unrecorded or was spoken about only elliptically. Further, we are handicapped in any discussion of genetically based families by the inherent limits of the linguistic tools we have to describe even those relationships that we can chart accurately. The sad fact is that the English language has very low-resolution descriptive power (see "The Poverty of Terminology," in my *Some Family*, 217–26.) Some really important things are not well defined in our language. The difference between a blood cousin and a cousin-by-marriage is substantial, but often lost without a chart. And English, unlike many cultures, does not distinguish in blood cousins between parallel-cousins and cross-cousins, a matter of some genetic import. Aunts, uncles, nephews, and nieces can

given the rigours of childbirth) a striking number of early male evangelicals had two or more successive families, in a sequence of serial monogamy punctuated by bereavement.[100] (3) That there existed a chain of social being that ran from the resident aristocrats to the large gentry to the middling gentry to resident land agents and on to substantial farm tenants and then locked into the lower rungs, where it influenced the way land on many estates was allocated as between Protestants and Catholics among the small tenantry. (4) That the Church of Ireland as an organization had its own great chain of being. This was a hierarchy of preferment, and certain families did well out of the clerical system generation after generation; for some it was the family business.[101] (5) That, as we have seen in several instances in the diocese of Dublin and Glendalough, the evangelical social elite interposed their powers upon the Church of Ireland's ladder of preferment, putting their own people (sometimes their sons) into key positions and promoting their advancement; the evangelicals were not soft: they had their elbows out. (6) That, given Dalyland's social physics, the evangelicals within the Church of Ireland, especially those of good birth (such as the Rev. Robert Daly) used their leverage on the secular social ladder as a mechanism for promoting their own deeply held religious beliefs within the Anglican communion.

---

either be genetically related or not. None of this is fatal, merely limiting, and that should be acknowledged. Still, for example, when dealing with the Synges and their involuted marriage patterns, I do wonder what one calls someone who is simultaneously another person's brother and his brother-in-law, twice over?

100 The phrase is McCormack's (2005), 15.

101 The classic discussion of the way the ladder of preferment worked is that of Norman Sykes for the English church in the eighteenth century, *Church and State in England in the XVIIIth Century* (Cambridge 1934). It is a good model for early nineteenth-century Ireland, provided one bleaches it of some of the cynicism that Sykes documents for the English church. After the dust of the Act of Union had settled, the Irish Anglican Church was considerably more engaged in actual issues of belief and of pastoral care than the eighteenth-century English Church had been.

The preceding six observations have a high degree of probative force, but one final observation is necessary to keep us from being blinkered by our concern with religious history. Despite the fashionableness of "serious religion," we are not observing Holy Joe land. Certainly there is a great deal of evidence of household piety, but this existed in the same social network with gross acts of corruption, dissolute behaviour, and downright silliness. Compossibility – the ability to exist in two contradictory worlds at once – was one of the qualities that made citizenship in Dalyland possible. Here, one example will suffice.

This involves, albeit at a safe distance, the core evangelical aristocrats, the Wingfields (the Powerscourt peerage), the Howards (the Wicklow earldom), and their Counties Down and Louth satellites, the Jocelyns (earls of Roden). Richard Wingfield, Fifth Viscount Powerscourt, had married in 1813 Frances Jocelyn, eldest daughter of the second earl of Roden and niece of the third; one of his younger brothers, the Hon. Rev. Edward Wingfield, a rector in the diocese of Leighlin, had married in 1819 Louisa Jocelyn, a daughter of the Hon. George Jocelyn. After the death of his first wife in 1820, Viscount Powerscourt married Theodosia Howard, a niece of the third earl of Wicklow; one of her sisters was the wife of the earl of Carysfort, and another sister (d. 1814) had been the wife of William Hayes Parnell.

The Powerscourt-Howard wedding took place in August 1822, and springtime of that year was a flutter of anticipation. The date is worth noting, as is the fact that the Hon. William Wingfield, already a keen evangelical, came down from Oxford in the spring of 1822 and began to ready himself for ordination.[102] The late spring of 1822, then, should have been a propitious time for those in this close network of evangelical Anglican aristocrats.

Hence the stunning and deeply humiliating nature of the news that filled London's scandal press. Percy Jocelyn was being laughed at in public drinking places and tittered at behind fans and handkerchiefs in fashionable houses: Percy Jocelyn, son of the first earl of Roden, uncle of the third, and uncle of the wife of the Rev. Edward Wingfield, and also uncle of the late wife of Viscount Powerscourt. He had been caught in the backroom of a London tavern having sex with a

102 Bunbury, 62–70; *CDGBSL*, entries for Wingfield.

guardsman. This would have been bad enough if Percy Jocelyn had been an everyday son of an Irish aristocrat. However, he was also the bishop of Clogher. He was a throwback to the older generation of morally relaxed Anglicans; he had entered the Church without any apparent religious convictions. Through social and political allies, he had become, first, bishop of Ferns and Leighlin in 1809[103] and then was translated to the see of Clogher in 1820, which was both more lucrative and more convenient to the family estates. Hence, big splash when he was apprehended: the more so because his nephew, the third Irish earl, had just been created a British peer in 1821.

The aristocratic Dalyland evangelicals had to keep their dignity while obscene and satirical publications poured forth. To be fair, the charges were slightly indistinct. The London tavern regulars who had peeked through an outside window at the bishop and guardsmen at play apparently had not seen this sort of sexual circus previously, and they were not sure who was doing what to whom. Eventually Bishop Jocelyn, through political pressure, got off with a misdemeanour conviction – lenient, considering that the penalty for sodomy included execution as a possible sentence. Once he made bail, Bishop Jocelyn scuttled to the Continent and later quietly slipped into Scotland, where, for a time, he served under an assumed name as a butler to one of his elderly sisters. He died anonymously in Edinburgh in 1843.[104]

The scandal for the Rodens specifically, and the band of Dalyland evangelicals in general, was excruciating. Even worse, during the press's investigation of Percy Jocelyn it was learned that previously, when he was bishop of Ferns and Leighlin, he had been charged with sodomy by his coachman: not only had he beaten the charge but he had his accuser publicly whipped through the streets of Dublin and imprisoned for more than two years.[105] That was the good old Church of Ireland, and although they were new-style evangelicals the affected

103 A.P.W. Malcomson argues convincingly that this first bishopric came not from direct family influence by the Joceylns, but indirect: the pressure came from the Duke of Portland who was related to the Jocelyns and lobbied Pitt for the appointment (*Archbishop Charles Agar* [Dublin 2002], 606).

104 Matthew Parris, *The Great Unfrocked* (London 1998), 144–57.

105 Ibid., 152–4.

aristocrats closed ranks and the really nasty evidence sent to the archbishop of Armagh (Lord John George Beresford, whose family's massive estates in the south of Ireland included absentee control of over 23,000 acres in Wicklow)[106] was suppressed and the files were not opened until 1998.[107]

The evangelical aristocrats of Dalyland survived in desperately dignified silence. The marriage of Theodosia Howard to the widower Viscount Powerscourt took place in the shadow of the great scandal. She was destined to become a grand dame of Irish evangelicalism and the godmother of Brethrenism. The third earl of Roden (1788–1870) remained a keen evangelical but was caught up in the sectarian conflict in the north that increasingly ratcheted upward from the 1830s on. He served as the grand master of the Orange Order in Ireland.[108]

The Hon. William Wingfield was ordained deacon in 1823 and was appointed to the parish of Arklow in 1826, where the Parnells were in his charge. He became a famous hellfire preacher and died, aged eighty-one, in 1880.

His brother, the Rev. Edward Wingfield, continued to serve the church until his sudden death at age thirty-two: while at Powerscourt he died of "a surfeit of fruit." His widow, née Louisa Jocelyn, moved to England and married a wealthy brewer with ties to County Wicklow.[109]

So, then, John Nelson Darby, the ill-fed, bone-sore, unshaven priest in charge of Calary Bog was totally different from the privileged of Dalyland, a kommun run equally on the belief in the early Anglican form of evangelical Christianity and in the divine right of landlords and the preservation of social distinctions. How could a man like the young Darby fit into such a world?

106 Nolan, in Hannigan and Nolan, 658, table 16.2.

107 Parris, 144, 146.

108 Readers may be acquainted with the Orange song "Dolly's Brae." It concerns riots near Roden's estate on 12 July 1849 that killed thirty Catholics.

109 Bunbury, 64, 71; *CDGBSL*, entries for Wingfield.

CHAPTER THREE

John Nelson Darby Approaches Dalyland

Actually, John Nelson Darby would eventually fit very well into the warp and weft of Dalyland. He was a child of privilege, had close ties to the Wicklow ascendancy, was eccentric without being profane; and he was a very promising addition to the ranks of the seriously religious clergy. Of course he needed a lot of buffing, but the church capos of his time were willing to wait. They knew that he was not a round peg to be pushed into a round hole. Instead, they sculpted a topological space for him that fit his very angular, disjunctive personality. That is why he was ministering among the hovels of Calary Bog, one of the dreariest places in all Ireland. The path to Calary Bog was well laid out for Darby, but even in historical perspective it is mysterious in the sense that there are great big blanks in the chart. Some of these can be sketched in, but one has to maintain a full awareness that an awful lot of empty white space has to be left on the map.[1]

1 There never has been a biography of John Nelson Darby that comes close to meeting even minimal scholarly standards – and I certainly am not interested in presenting one in this book, as my subject is not his life, but the foundation of the transatlantic branch of evangelical Dispensationalism of which Darby was the major vector. There are three studies that come closest to being real biographies. One of these is W.G. Turner's *John Nelson Darby*, 2nd edition (London 1944). Turner was one of the Brethren and had access to some of the elderly veterans of the second generation of Darby followers. The book has little accurate to say about the first twenty-five to thirty years of Darby's life. The volume is devoid of documentation but was less *parti pris* than were most discussions of Darby done before that time: those either had Darby as

Take, for example, this simple question: how Irish was he? The answer is that by the time John Nelson Darby took up his priestly duties in Calary he was just as Irish as were the other Anglo-Irish evangelicals of his social caste – but that raises a volatile matter in Irish life and the inevitable assertion that these people were not Irish at all, a matter over which sectarian-national battles have been fought. The Anglo-Irish were a reality on the Irish scene – few places more strongly than in Dalyland – so drop the original question and inquire instead: how did John Nelson Darby became part of the Anglican evangelical establishment? Granted, to begin with he was born in England, but that is hardly a disqualification: many of the families we have been dealing with in defining the dominant social fabric of evangelicals in the Church of Ireland had a house in London or a rural estate in England, sometimes both. So the birth of a son to John Darby (1751–1834) and his wife Anne (var.: Ann) Vaughan Darby (1757–1847) on 18 November 1800 at their London house, 9 Great George Street, tells us mostly that they were well off.[2]

---

a saint or as a slightly demonic figure. The second biographical volume is Max S. Weremchuk's *John Nelson Darby* (Neptune, NJ, 1992; orig. German ed. 1988). This is a major step forward as Weremchuk was industrious in collecting verifiable facts and, in some cases, oral evidence. He documents the majority of his evidentiary assertions; although his faith-based inferences are beyond replication, they are not necessarily inaccurate. The biography deals in detail with only a ten-to-fifteen year period in Darby's early ministry. Third, Marion Field has written a popular-form biography, *John Nelson Darby* (Goldalming 2008). This contains some new information, tailored for an audience of Brethren adherents or sympathizers. Although he has not written a biography of Darby, over a period of more than forty years Timothy C.F. Stunt has published material on Darby and on the Brethren at a level of academic rigour that is impressive. His material will be cited frequently in the chapters that follow. For his own reflection on his historical work, see Timothy C.F. Stunt, "A Personal Odyssey," *Brethren Archivists' and Historians' Network Review* (2006).

2 By the time the UK censuses of 1871 and 1881 were taken, John Nelson Darby remembered his birth as being in 1801 (see censuses of England and Wales for Islington). That should not be taken as an indication of any mental slippage on his part but of the fact that, except for matters that held legal importance (such as coming of age), birthdays were not as widely celebrated as they are today and most particularly not among the Brethren.

The newborn son was the eighth of nine children and the youngest of six brothers.[3] What is more revealing is that he was christened, 3 March 1801,[4] "John Nelson"; this places the family in a specific strand of eighteenth-century Anglo-Irish tradition of families, part of whose identity was tied to the Royal Navy. (For example, one branch of the Beresfords of Waterford was notable in this direction.) Although among Brethren memorialists it has long been asserted that the patriotic hero Horatio Viscount Nelson was the godfather of the spiritual hero John Nelson Darby, this is highly unlikely: Nelson was on board ship off Spithead at the time of the christening.[5] Granted, a stand-in was possible, but Marigold Freeman-Attwood, a direct descendant of William Henry Darby and the author of an admirably sensible family history, indicates a more diffuse, less dramatic, more convincing situation. George Darby (1720?–1790), who was perhaps a great-uncle of the newborn John Nelson, had been an admiral and in 1781 became commander of the western squadron after the American war and had been in charge of the successful relief of Gibraltar.[6] Of more direct relevance to the naming of the new Darby infant was the career of his paternal uncle, Henry d'Esterre Darby (1749–1823), who, in charge of the *Bellerophon,* was one of Admirable Nelson's five captains at the battle of the Nile in August 1798. Lord Nelson spread the glory round his captains and Henry Darby became an admiral and was knighted

3 A useful simplified family tree is found as appendix A in Weremchuk, 199.

4 A copy (not an original) certifying the baptism as having taken place at St Margaret's, Westminster, 3 March 1801, is found in CBA J.N.D./1/1/21 and was issued 19 June 1821. I suspect this had to do with Darby's requiring documentation for his proposed career as an Irish barrister.

5 Weremchuk, to his credit, notes this fact (25) but then takes the possibility of a surrogate having represented Lord Nelson as being a probability. Failing sight of the original baptismal register, I think the exposition by the family history that I am following is more likely, if less dramatic.

6 *ODNB*, entry for George Darby. The best supposition is that he was a son of Jonathan Darby of Leap Castle, King's County, the Irish seat of the Darby family. While still a serving admiral, Darby became MP for Plymouth in 1780 and kept the post until 1784. Considering the later development of the misnamed "Plymouth" Brethren, this geographic coincidence is intriguing but probably leads nowhere.

in 1799. There is no doubt of Henry Darby's having been close with the great man, and after Nelson's death in 1805 several of his possessions, personal mementos, were testamentary gifts to Henry Darby and some still are in the family's possession. The direct result of the Darby-Nelson friendship was that the male born to John Darby and Anne Vaughan in late 1798 was christened "Horatio d'Esterre." Given that Admiral Henry Darby was a lifelong bachelor, it had fallen to his next-in-line, his brother John, to satisfy the family honour and thus occurred the naming of the wee nephew of Admiral Darby as "Horatio" – which became a Darby family name that pops up in virtually every subsequent generation. And, no surprise here, the next male in the family line of John and Anne Darby was christened "John Nelson." There was no godfather routine necessary here; a personal relationship between two heroic sea warriors was transmuted into a family memorial through the process of Christian baptism.[7] None of this hurt John Nelson Darby's later reception among the Anglo-Irish.

Nor was his having been a boarder at Westminster School in London from February 1812 to early 1815 any handicap among the Irish upper classes. At the time, the Anglo-Irish aristocratic and upper-gentry classes usually had their children tutored at home or educated at an English public school. Young Darby was formally enrolled in Trinity College, Dublin in July 1815, while still aged fourteen and he began studying in the autumn term, just before he turned fifteen.[8] That was not unusual: TCD, like the two older English universities, frequently took pupils who, by the standards of the later nineteenth century, would still have been in secondary school. Thus, by 1815, John Nelson Darby was well on his way to having a prototypically upper-class Irish education.

What is slightly bothersome, however, is the fulsome confidence of the Brethren biographer W.G. Turner, who laid down a compound fact that "in 1815 the family went to reside in the ancestral castle in Ireland, and for young Darby it was his first visit to that country."[9] The first part

7 Marigold Freeman-Attwood, *Leap Castle* (Norwich 2001), 75–9, 182.

8 George Dames Burtchaell and Thomas Ulick Sadleir, *Alumni Dublinenses* (London 1924), 210.

9 Turner, 13.

of this compound statement is so patently wrong that it is embarrassing: the immediate family of John Nelson Darby continued to live in England, and in fact both of his parents lived there until their deaths. Members of the immediate family did not move to the family's Irish estate until 1823, and one brother, George (1796–1878), continued to hold the family's English country estate, in Sussex.[10] The first half of Turner's compound fact being demonstrably inaccurate does not necessarily mean that the second half was untrue, but it leaves one deeply skeptical. Although it is not a matter of great moment (for his home up to age fourteen undeniably was England), it is improbable that John Nelson had not spent time in Ireland before the entry formalities for TCD were conducted at age fourteen. The reason for the guess (given the holes in the evidence, it can only be that) is twofold. First, his sister Susannah (often called Susan) married in 1816 Edward Pennefather, of a family that was very strong in three overlapping circles of power in Ireland: political (they were the owners of Cashel borough until the Great Reform Act of 1832), clerical (various members of the extended family held plum benefices in the province of Cashel), and legal (Edward Pennefather was well on his way to being a KC and eventually chief justice of the Queen's bench).[11] That sort of stylish Irish marriage does not usually come about if the bride's family had her locked up in a London tower like a princess in a fairy tale. The young Pennefathers soon had an estate in Delgany and a Dublin residence, and we know from their actions in the 1820s that Susannah and her youngest brother

10 For convenience of reference, the siblings of John Nelson were: Susannah (colloq.: Susan, 1795–1862, m. Edward Pennefather); Jonathan (1787–1809, died before inheriting); William Henry (1790–1880, chief heir of Irish property); Christopher Lovett (1792–1874, Irish clergyman); Sarah (1794–1877, English spinster); George (1796–1878, barrister and chief heir of English estate); Horatio d'Esterre (1798–1885, bachelor, resident at Leap Castle); Letitia (1802–?; died before majority). Compiled from Hugh Montgomery-Massingberd (ed.), *Burke's Irish Family Records* (London 1976), 322–3, with corrections from Freeman-Attwood, 182 and related text; from Weremchuk, 199; and from Darby family monuments, Aghancon Church, County Offaly.

11 A.R. Hart, *A History of the King's Serjeants at Law in Ireland* (Dublin 2000), 116–17, 154, 179. A.P.W. Malcomson, *Archbishop Charles Agar* (Dublin 2002), 286–93; *ODNB*, entry for Edward Pennefather.

were close, and clearly they had spent time together when John Nelson was young. Secondly, the Darbys as an extended family were deeply embedded in Ireland from the seventeenth century onward and, despite John Darby (senior) being a London counting-house obsessive, there were uncles and cousins all around the family's estate in King's County. This piece of property requires notice, for it is part of the background tinting of John Nelson Darby's character that is usually bleached from the devotional memoirs of his life.

Leap Castle (pronounced "Lepp") was typical of one genre of Anglo-Irish estate in that it was stolen from its Gaelic and Catholic owners in the seventeenth century, then fought over by the deposed and the new Protestants for generations, and finally in the high period of the anti-Catholic penal code became securely Protestant and stayed so until the rise of the Catholic nation left it in cinders in the early twentieth century. Specifically, the land involved in King's County (County Offaly) was that of the Ely O'Carrolls, to use the anglicized form of their name. In the sixteenth century, the O'Carroll chieftains were very much like the innumerable grand-dukes, margraves, electors, and princelings of the tessellating Holy Roman Empire: surrounded by foreigners, threatened by warlike kin, and caught in a 360-degree free-fire zone. Mind you, they were not inconsequential: the Ely O'Carrolls had five castles in the area that eventually was shired as King's County and the most formidable of these was Leap, which sat just beneath a 635-foot ridge and had twelve-foot thick walls as the foundation for its keep.[12] Although in the 1870s a myth was propagated that a John Darby had married in the 1550s a Finola O'Carroll – and thus the edge was taken off the deep Catholic-Protestant hatred that surrounded the castle – the reality was much uglier. As early as 1578, when squeezed hard by the government, the O'Carrolls had agreed to the "surrender and regrant" procedure, whereby they gave up their lands to Elizabeth

12 In addition to Freeman-Attwood's book, this discussion is based on two valuable articles by Andrew Tierney: "The Gothic and the Gaelic: Exploring the Place of Castles in Ireland's Celtic Revival," *International Journal of Historical Archaeology* (September 2004); "From Gothic to Gothic Revival: An Archaeology of Leap Castle, Co. Offaly," in Michael McCarthy and Karina O'Neill (eds), *Studies in the Gothic Revival* (Dublin 2008).

I and the Crown then granted them guaranteed title (or so it was promised) and gave most of the land back to them, plus some new tax burdens. Next, the O'Carrolls were trashed by the Great O'Neill during his rebellion and in 1599 the last strong O'Carroll chief was killed at the behest of his brother and the remaining claim to be the chief of the Ely O'Carrolls fell to a child who was made a ward of the court. The whole area was shired in 1605, but the remaining O'Carroll property, Leap Castle, was left in the hands of the young puppet chief, a reward for his family's agreeing to let the government plant the region with new settlers.

Where the Darbys appear is during the Cromwellian invasion and "Jonathan Darby of Leap" (mark I) appears on the tax rolls in 1659.[13] Even then, the whole business was messy. The restoration of the monarchy in 1660 meant that loyal Catholics, such as the O'Carrolls, had to receive most of their lands back, but that the Cromwellians could not easily be dislodged. An obvious problem: nationally, there were more entitlements than there was land; and locally, the O'Carrolls and the Darbys both coveted the same castle and its surrounding lands. For a time in the 1660s, the Darbys were turfed out, but then by the end of that decade Jonathan Darby of Leap (mark II) regained the land. What would have happened had the O'Carrolls not bet their lives on supporting James II against William of Orange is a fascinating speculation, but the result was that from 1691 onward, the significant Ely Carrolls (their name changed again) were spread around the Continent and North America. The latest Darby avatar – Jonathan Darby of Leap (mark III) – was the winner.

Surprisingly, some of the Ely Carrolls did rather better than did the Darbys. Charles Carroll of Litterluna ("Carroll the Settler," 1661–1720) saw the way things were going and emigrated to Maryland just ahead of the Catholic debacle. He had been well-educated in institutions run by the Jesuits, had studied law at the Inner Temple, and Lord Baltimore appointed him attorney general of Maryland in 1688 while it was still a private jurisdiction. He died very rich in 1720, true to the old faith, despite the Crown's taking away the right of Catholics to public worship. His son expanded the estate and became one of the richest men in the Thirteen Colonies and his grandson – Charles Carroll of Carrollton

13 Freeman-Attwood, 42.

(1737–1832) – was massively wealthy and the only Roman Catholic to sign the Declaration of Independence.[14]

That irony aside, the flight of the O'Carrolls, when combined with the anti-Catholic penal code of the late seventeenth and early eighteenth centuries, gave Jonathan Darby of Leap (mark IV) the holder, 1708–42, an opportunity to acquire large amounts of land. Probably he had amassed over 4,000 acres by the time his eldest son Jonathan Darby of Leap (mark V), the holder from 1742 to 1776, assumed his inheritance.[15] This generation, that of the eighteenth-century triumphalists, was the one that puts John Nelson Darby in touch with the bellicose history of his family, for the refurbished and enlarged castle was the one that he knew. This period's Jonathan Darby of Leap Castle and his wife Susannah Lovett from Buckinghamshire blocked off some of the fabric that was associated with the O'Carrolls, including three spiral staircases that threaded through the thick interior walls, and they Gothicized the place by keeping the central tower as the focus and adding two new wings and all sorts of ornamentation. The new architecture clearly said to the Catholics on the lands below that we stole all this fair and square, so live with it. Jonathan Darby (mark VI), holder from 1776 to 1802, in cooperation with the bishop of Limerick, William Cecil Pery (Baron Glentworth, 1790) built a new Church of Ireland house of worship in the local parish of Aghancon.[16] Cannily, he followed a policy of reserving the lands around Leap Castle for Protestants. This served the Darbys well during the 1798 Rising, when the

14 The standard study is Ronald Hoffman (with collaboration of Sally D. Mason), *Princes of Ireland, Planters of Maryland. A Carroll Saga* (Chapel Hill 2000). The Carroll family founded the chair of Irish history in Oxford University, the inaugural appointment being made in 1991.

15 The family held on to these lands very effectively well into the late nineteenth century. In the early 1880s, Jonathan Charles Darby of Leap held 4,637 acres in King's County (John Bateman, *The Great Landowners of Great Britain and Ireland*, 4th ed. [New York 1970; first published London 1883], 118).

16 Samuel Lewis, *A Topographical Dictionary of Ireland* (London 1837), vol. 1, 17. In contrast to the Gothic deformities of Leap Castle, the Aghancon church is a clean and simple architectural gem. It can be seen in detail in *All Creatures Great and Small* (BBC, 1978–80, 1988–90). Andrew Hewson, "Limerick and Killaloe," in Claude Costecalde and Brian Walker (eds), *The Church of Ireland: An Illustrated History* (Dublin 2013), 398.

FIGURE 3.1 LEAP CASTLE.

Leap Castle in the early nineteenth century (courtesy Sean Ryan)

tenants and the landlord mutually defended themselves against the rebels.[17] The ring-fort pattern (employing Protestant tenants as palisades) was continued down the generations. Thus the genial Rev. Richard Sinclair Brooke, upon visiting the castle in 1828, found "that a *very* large body of respectable Protestant yeomanry, numbering some hundreds" were among the Darby tenantry.[18] Comforting as this scene may have been to a Church of Ireland cleric, such as the Rev. Mr Brooke, the castle was located uncomfortably near to chronically disturbed portions of County Tipperary. It is hard to find much warmth in the social, or even the architectural, picture. Arthur Atkinson, who visited the place as part of his research for an early Irish tourist guidebook that he published in 1815, managed the following concerning the castle: "It is built upon a rock, and appears to look down upon the spectater [*sic*] in the valley with an air of ancient grandeur, and yet so tempered by modern improvement as not to look frightful."[19] Considering that one

17 Tierney (2008), 32–3.

18 Richard Sinclair Brooke, *Recollections of the Irish Church* (London 1877), 45.

19 Arthur Atkinson, *The Irish Tourist* (Dublin 1815), 160.

of the subscribers to the volume was Admiral Henry Darby, not looking frightful was faint praise indeed. If nineteenth-century engravings are anything to go by, Leap Castle, glowering down upon a hinterland of sullen Catholics and an infield of loyal but understandably nervous Protestant tenants, was closer to Transylvania than it was to Heaven.

The Darby family ties to Leap Castle and all that it represented – a perfect visual embodiment of the position of Anglican Protestants in the Irish midlands – continued well into John Nelson Darby's generation and beyond. Jonathan Darby of Leap (mark VI) died in 1802 without male issue and from there the estate passed sideways, rather than down a generation. It went first to the next eldest brother, the famous Admiral Sir Henry d'Esterre Darby, who was the holder from 1802 to 1823; then, because the admiral was unmarried, it went to the next brother, John Darby, the father of John Nelson Darby, who was in ownership from 1823 to 1834. All three holders in that single generation – Jonathan Darby of Leap (mark VI), Sir Henry, and John Darby had been born in Leap Castle and reared there until they went their very different ways as young men. (They were, respectively, two uncles and the father of John Nelson Darby.)

Whether or not the senior John Darby would have moved to Leap Castle had it passed to him earlier in life (he was seventy-two years of age when he inherited) is unknown. He had two uncles who were Dublin merchants, and he could have developed at least one of his activities – the sale of Irish linen – from his home country. He certainly was not alienated from his old home,[20] but in the years 1819–23 he was putting together an estate he called Marklye (var.: Markly) in Warbleton,

20 For instance, he visited his brother the admiral there (John Darby to George Lambert, 18 May 1819, East Sussex Record Office, Darby papers, AMS6146/112). Further, the family church at Aghancon, near Leap Castle, contains a carved memorial saying, "Near this place are deposited the Remains of Jonathan Darby, Eldest son of John Darby and Anne, his wife." It gives the dates for John of 1787–1809 and has a fifteen-line lament that focuses upon "Religion was his Ruling Principal." Manifestly, the King's County estate was not a piece of geography that had been erased from the senior Darby's mental map. Additionally, shortly before his own death, John Darby (father of John Nelson) had a plaque placed in the family's church in Aghancon in memory of his younger brother (b. 1757/58, the seventh son of the family), who had

Sussex. This he passed on to his third surviving son, George, and also a small farm nearby to his fifth surviving son, Horatio.[21] That Leap Castle was still the centre point of the Darby family identity is indicated by the Irish estate going to the eldest surviving son, William Henry, who held it from 1834 to his death in 1880.

Now, why beat so hard on the assertion that a large, unattractive, but profitable Irish midland estate counts? Chiefly because of the nature of the existing Brethren historiography, which, however unconsciously, wants to bleach John Nelson Darby of his Irish background and to see him as the result of a very long conversation with the Almighty, unmediated by social causation. Besides, Leap Castle is the sort of place that is very bad advertising for a purist religious movement. Its position as a citadel of Protestant landlordism in King's County was something to steer clear of; this was not County Wicklow, where the landlords were willing to lose money in pursuit of an engineered world that at last looked peaceful and idyllic. Moreover, as the nineteenth century progressed, the Darbys' castle became notorious for being haunted. Architectural realities, such as bricked-up passages, the Priest's House (a separate structure originally), the Murder Hole (an oubliette), and the Bloody Chapel (probably just a spare room) played alongside visions and sightings of ghosts and phantasms that were neither cute nor comforting. These were both known to the tenantry and, more directly, experienced by those living in the castle. Thus, the memory of Mary Charlotte Darby, a niece of John Nelson, recorded in her diary the opening of one of the interior walls in 1851 in response to a haunting reported by a guest.[22] Whatever the source

been a lieutenant general and late colonel of the 54th regiment of foot. This brother had died in January 1832 in his 74th year. It reads: "This monument was erected by his brother John Darby, Esq., as a testimony of affection."

21 I am relying on the excellent calendar of the Darby papers in the East Sussex Record Office. This is a trove of several thousand pages, mostly relating to the business affairs of John Darby as run from his London firm. These documents were discovered beneath a chicken coop at "Cralle Place," Warburton, a property that the Darbys neither rented nor owned. The basic Marklye estate was purchased by John Darby in 1819 and enlarged by purchase in the years 1819–23.

22 Tierney (2008), 40.

of the Leap Castle apparitions, they certainly gave licence for the dispossessed local Catholics and for the Anglo-Irish victors to share in a common projection of a very disagreeable communal history. The matter became nationally known after Jonathan Charles Darby, owner from 1880 to 1943, married in 1889 Mildred Dill, an Englishwoman who soon was wallowing in what a perceptive observer has termed "acute colonial guilt."[23]

Under the pen name "Andrew Merry," Mrs Darby took to writing short stories and novels, several of which were based on a disguised version of Leap Castle and upon the nastiness that had gone on there in the past.[24] In the castle itself, she opened up many of the old passages and storage rooms that the Gothicizing architects of the eighteenth century had concealed. She experienced several sightings of supernatural entities. The most sensational of these was of something she called The Elemental, a woman who turns into a ram. What probably had been demotic gossip around the countryside ever since the 1750s, when the architectural suffocation of the old Ely Carroll castle was begun, had by the twentieth century become a set of Irish national yarns. Oliver St John Gogarty in the 1950s called the house the most haunted house in Ireland.[25] In so doing, he already had been trumped by Sacheverell Sitwell, who, after visiting the remains of the castle, judged that "perhaps there is no house in the world that holds so many suggestions of the supernatural."[26]

23 Tierney (2004), 192.

24 I have not read any of the Andrew Merry novels. They were: *An April Fool* (1898), *The Naked Truth* (1900), *The Green Country* (1902), *Paddy Risky* (1903), *Anthropoid Apes* (1909), *The Hunger* (1910), cited by Freeman-Attwood, 106n4. Jonathan Charles Darby was a justice of the peace, a deputy-lieutenant of the county, and a stanch Orangeman; he was not pleased with his wife's covertly nationalist sympathies. In 1909, he forbade his wife to write anymore. In the next year she flipped her trotting carriage: she believed the ponies had seen an invisible spectre, she later reported. Thereafter she was a mental mess, and the marriage very uncomfortable (Freeman-Attwood, 106–7).

25 Oliver St John Gogarty, "The Most Haunted House of Them All," in *A Weekend in the Middle of the Week, and Other Essays on the Bias* (New York 1958).

26 *Dance of the Quick and the Dead* (London: Faber and Faber 1936), 9, cited in Freeman-Attwood, 111.

Beginning in August 1921, the Darbys began to be harassed by local Irish republicans: they were shot at several times, had crops burned, and could get no one to do the farm labour for them, so strong was the boycott and associated intimidation. They still farmed 500–850 acres of their own directly (accounts vary) and were attached to another 3,000-plus acres they had once held but that apparently were now under Land Acts in the process of being transferred to tenant ownership. On 30–31 July 1922, Leap Castle was torched by the Irish Republican Army: probably by the Irregulars, but in any case local vengeance was at the heart of the matter. The O'Carrolls had been driven out centuries before and now their conquerors were conquered. Righteousness, self-declared, inevitably was the form explanation assumed. The castle was a "cup of iniquity" one of the incendiaries, a former kitchen boy, declared in an interview decades later. It had been struck down, he said, "by the hand of God."[27]

27 Tierney (2008), 28. I am grateful to Leigh-Ann Coffey for providing me with a copy of the Darby family's claims for compensation to the Irish Grants Commission, which had been created to recompense in some degree the (mostly Protestant) civilian inhabitants of Ireland who had been victimized, intimidated, maimed, or most commonly burned-out or forced out of their homes and lands. The Darby file is large and complex, but a financial summary seems to be the following. Because the post-truce situation in King's County (Offally) did not return to economic normalcy, Jonathan Darby was unable to sell his land at a fair market price (bidders were threatened). He therefore sold most of the home farm (629 acres) to the Irish Land Commission for £5,477, the fair market value probably being £10,877. The Darbys then spent the rest of the 1920s pursuing a claim for damage to the castle, loss of livestock and crops, etc. They elected not to rebuild the castle but eventually converted the ballroom into the base of a residence and farmed on a reduced basis. Their total claim for loss was £37,297, and they were awarded £7,945. An interesting sidelight is that Mrs Mildrid Darby was awarded £1,250 in her own right, for loss of clothes and plate and for medical care and housing. Her claim showed that despite her husband's fiat she had kept writing, albeit not publishing. She claimed compensation for "40 or 50" typed short stories "her literary work over recent years never yet submitted," and for two complete long novels, never submitted, and for lost legal paperwork for the film rights to her novel, *Paddy Riskey*, which had recently been sold to Metro Goldwyn for $2,000.

Scant wonder that the historians of the Brethren wish to keep their distance. According to Max Weremchuk in his 1992 biography, "J.N. Darby's connexion with the family estate at Leap appears only to have been in the form of an occasional visit, if that much. There is no proof of his ever having been there."[28] Neither assertion is unreasonable, just wrong. Marion Field in her 2008 biography allows that "it is likely" that John Darby "visited the castle as he spent some time in Ireland during his ministry,"[29] which is slightly less misleading but still falsely distances Darby from his Irish roots. There is direct evidence of Darby's having been at Leap Castle and strong indirect evidence that he was religiously active in the area and used his own relatives at the castle as a mini-congregation. (As will be noted later, one of his brothers became an ardent follower of John Nelson and set up a Brethren assembly composed mostly of his own family at Leap.)

Here, the matter of ghosts and of evil supernatural manifestations is relevant. I mentioned earlier that in October 1851 a niece of John Nelson Darby had been present as a guest at the castle when an adult male guest perceived phantoms. Indeed, the guest was twice visited by them and the third time, according to the same girl's diary "Poor Mr B. came down looking more dead than alive having heard steps and a devilish sort of breathing close to his ears, which continued for a long time."[30] Now, to add a second layer, note that a very close neighbouring family to the Darbys was the Stoneys; John Butler Stoney was one of Darby's closest confidants and friends in the years of his mature ministry. In 1864, the not-yet-adult Anna Stoney spent a good portion of the winter at Leap at the invitation of William Henry Darby.[31] The significant point is that either at this time or close to it, Anna Stoney went over the hauntings with her spiritual counsellor, John Nelson Darby. According to Leap Castle's family historian, "She related in her

28 Weremchuk, 30.

29 Field, 24.

30 Tierney (2004), 195, quoting unpublished diary of Mary Charlotte Darby.

31 To his considerable credit, Max Weremchuk is working at expanding and correcting his earlier biography of Darby. This visit of Anna Stoney is cited in "Darby of the Leap," www.mybrethren.org/bios/by02jnd.htm (accessed 20 December 2011).

unpublished memoirs that she had discussed the ghosts with John Nelson Darby himself, who thought it quite possible that evil deeds might attract the devil to the scene of the crimes."[32] Not only did Darby visit, but he took the supernatural seriously; he was not just patting a young lady on the head to make her stop worrying. Darby was very much a literalist in his reading of the Hebrew and Christian scriptures; he believed in devils and angels and all sorts of intermediate spiritual entities, no doubt about it.

Further, although John Nelson Darby might not have been consciously aware of the fact, his Irish ancestral home carried a covert psychological meaning that was strong and pervasive. As Andrew Tierney has observed, the Gothic school of architecture "fetishized Catholicism as a part of an aesthetic ensemble of horror; what emerged was a distinctly Protestant gaze upon the vestiges of an older religion."[33] Indeed, literalism about the devil was necessary for literalistic Protestants. "The devil's overriding power was central to the new Protestant perception of the spirit world, which could no longer explain the supernatural as purgatorial souls returned from the dead."[34]

If Leap Castle at its darkest was a tiny window into John Nelson Darby's relationship with his Irish heritage, it also had more amiable aspects. The three brothers, William Henry (who inherited the castle in 1834), Horatio d'Esterre, and John Nelson, seem to have gotten along well together, at least some of the time. In 1828, even before Leap was formally inherited by William Henry, his father put him in charge of the place; Horatio lived here and seems to have taken over everyday matters.[35] Certainly this was the case later: in the 1860s, Horatio (a bachelor) was living in a secondary house on the estate and managing the enterprise, while William Henry and family lived in the main house.[36] Horatio, it will be recalled, had been given a small estate in

32 Freeman-Attwood, 111.

33 Andrew Tierney, "Return of the Repressed? 'Haunted Castles' in Seventeenth-Century Munster," *Eire-Ireland* (2010), 8.

34 Ibid., 20.

35 These arrangements are clearly implied in Brooke, 45.

36 Cf. Anna Stoney diary segments quoted in Tierney (2008), 35, and in Weremchuk "Darby of the Leap," www.mybrethren.org/bios/by02jnd2.htm

England by his father, so this arrangement was not one of economic necessity; apparently these two brothers got along well. John Nelson was certainly concerned that his brother Horatio be converted to his own religious beliefs. In a letter of 1835, written to Horatio at Leap Castle from Cork, where John Nelson was doing missionary work, John Nelson tells him of the respectable families in the neighbourhood of Birr, close by Leap, who have decided "to be separate from evil and serve the Lord with regular preaching." He encourages Horatio, who at that point was not buying the package: "May you find the comfort and joy of living thoroughly out for the Lord." The tone is not hectoring and is signed "Yr very affectionate brother, J.N.D."[37]

Those sort of relationships illustrates that, *pace* attempts to cleanse John Nelson Darby of unclean worldly and otherworldly associations – and Leap Castle was nothing if not a place of necromaniacal emanations – Darby was of the Anglo-Irish world. I suspect that John Nelson was the guiding force behind the small congregation of Brethren who worshipped near the castle. The family members who were Brethren (quite a number, as William Henry Darby had thirteen children by two wives) are buried just outside the Church of Ireland churchyard at Aghancon. They rest behind a set of iron railings on a hemisphere of land that touches the Darby's family churchyard but lies assertively outside of consecrated ground. This fences them forever from the general Protestant community and takes the precept of "come ye out and be separate" about as far as it can go.[38]

(accessed 20 October 2011). Horatio certainly was living at the castle during the Great Famine and was instrumental in arranging relief for the sufferers (Freeman-Attwood, 88).

37 John Nelson Darby to Horatio D'Esterre Darby, 5 October 1835, reproduced in full in Freeman-Attwood, 175–6. The letter is valuable as it is one of the relatively few that does not come from Darby's printed collected letters and their attendant censorship (see bibliography for extended comments).

38 Freeman-Attwood, 84. To fill in family relationships a bit more: Horatio, though in touch with John Nelson, never fully accepted John Nelson's views, and he remained Church of Ireland. Sarah died unmarried in England,

a follower of John Nelson's faith, and she left him some money. Susannah (Pennefather) will be discussed later, as will Christopher Lovett, who became an Anglican clergyman and a breakwater for John Nelson's own short career within the Established Church. William Henry Darby (1790–1880, and holder of Leap Castle, 1834–1880) is a special problem. As indicated earlier in the text, he and several of his offspring (and some of his grandchildren) are buried contiguously to the family churchyard but in such a manner as to make a strong statement that they were fervently and forever distanced from the Church of Ireland. In the late 1830s, he apparently was sufficiently in the good graces of the Brethren to be listed as one of the contributors for an edition of the New Testament with explanatory notes. Corinthians was apparently to be his patch. John Nelson Darby and B.W. Newton were to write the commentary on the Book of Revelation (CBA, J.N.D./1/1/16). In 1873, he had published a pamphlet that made it clear that he held strong Brethren beliefs (William H. Darby, *The Union of Believers*, printed for the author, 1873). The question is: what sort of Brethren was he? In the summer of 1848 William went to Dusseldorf as a colporteur of the faith; at that time he was in the good graces of John Nelson, who corresponded with the Germans with whom William was dealing. Clearly the two brothers were on the same page in religious terms. See August Jung, "Julius Anton von Poseck (1816–1898) and Brethren Origins in Germany," in Neil R. Dickson and Tim Grass, *The Growth of the Brethren Movement* (Carlisle 2006).

Yet, as an old man, John Nelson Darby's longtime ally, J.B. Stoney, recalled that in 1866 William Henry Darby had rejected his brother's then-new teachings about Christ's suffering and atonement and that for a time John Nelson was so affected by his own brother's rejection that he proposed to stop breaking bread ("A Review of Truth … J.B. Stoney, 1814–97," www.mybrethren.org/history/hy02revi.htm, accessed 17 February 2013). The recondite details of the theological split are found, mostly in the form of reproduced letters, in W.H.D. [William H. Dorman], *The Close of Twenty-Eight Years of Association with J.N.D.* (London 1866). Whether the two brothers ever made up is unclear.

A second, more corrosive matter is that it has become accepted among Brethren historians that William Henry Darby had for a time been a Roman Catholic. The source for this assertion is CBA, Fry MS 7061. This notebook by Frederick W. Wyatt states that "Darby had a brother, W.H. Darby, who joined the Church of Rome and afterwards came out again. He called J.N.D. 'potted ignorance'" (131). I am very skeptical of the accuracy of this report. Frederick W. Wyatt was the Boswell of Benjamin Wills Newton the mortal (some would say immortal) enemy of John Nelson Darby. His "fact" seems to be part of an oblique slag-job on John Nelson Darby. Finally, the simplest reason for skepticism about the report that William had been a Catholic for a time is also the most compelling: does anyone think that, if one of the better-known

Having established that John Nelson Darby was neither interdicted from communication or religious fellowship with his family, nor severed from his family's Irish roots, we can return to the more conventional matter of his parentage. Three main biographies – those by Turner, Weremchuk, and Field – are surpassing strange, at least in relation to secular standards of evidence. They paint a figure who very early in life was cut off from his mother's natural love and affection, a father who was inconsequential in worldly terms and distant emotionally, a relationship between the two parents that was cold to the point of estrangement, and brothers and sisters who did not have much to do with John Nelson.

The first of the biographies of John Nelson Darby, that of W.G. Turner, states that "his mother's death, when he was only five years old, made a deep and lasting impression upon young Darby."[39] Indeed, it probably would have, except that his mother's tombstone in St Mary's churchyard, Warbleton, Sussex, has her alive until 1847, dying at age ninety.[40] Max Weremchuk in his later biography granted Anne Vaughan Darby her long life, yet insisted that she and the young John Nelson Darby had been cut off from each other. He states that Darby did not see her "after his early childhood," and thus "for J. N Darby one can only feel sorry that his mother was so soon taken from him, causing a deep and lasting pain his own words only all too clearly testify to."[41] This is a "fact" derived from the biographer's narrative need – and from John Nelson Darby's curious refusal to acknowledge that he had much in the way of a family – not from any record. The two pieces of seeming

---

landowners in King's County had turned Catholic, it would not have been a matter of popular comment, not to say celebration?

39 Turner, 12.

40 For a photograph of the gravestone, see entry under Anne Vaughan Darby, www.findagrave.com. This photograph, however, is cropped so as to elide a culturally diagnostic fact concerning the Darby family's sense of identity: the plinth is surmounted by a large Celtic cross. Anne Vaughan's death date is confirmed by written sources, but the stone is the only direct confirmation of her age and thence of her birth, c. 1757. There is also a joint memorial in Aghancon church to Jonathan Darby (d. 1834) and to Anne, giving December 1847 as her death date.

41 Weremchuk, 232n11.

evidence that produce Weremchuk's conclusion are actually instances of spiritual parables that John Nelson Darby created and which are read by Brethen with excessive literalism.[42] One of these is two paragraphs in an undated letter, to an unspecified person, anonymously translated from the original French (does any of this inspire confidence?). The subject is about Darby's conviction that at communion the bread and wine remain just that, physically bread and wine, but that nevertheless some of the power of the Lord's Supper comes from the link in the believer's heart to the physical elements. As a comparison, he says:

> I have a charming portrait of my mother, which reminds me of her just as she was … The portrait has no value except as far as it is a good representation of her who is not there. I say, it is my mother. I could not throw it aside as a mere piece of canvas; I discern my mother in it. I cherish this portrait; I carry it with me; but if I stop at the perfection of the painting as a work of art, the link with my heart is lost.
>
> There is more than this in the Supper of our Lord … But it has pleased Him to give us a physical means by which we may be reminded of Him, so that I am authorized to speak of a portrait by way of comparison.[43]

Probably this letter was written some time after Darby's mother's death in 1847 ("a good representation of her who is not there"), but that is beside the point.

A similar midrash is at the heart of a long and wrenched reply (well over 200 pages) that John Nelson Darby published in 1853 to counter

42 Ibid., 26–7. for the two passages the biographer uses as evidence.

43 J.N.D. to ___, n.d., *Letters of J.N.D.* [hereafter LJND], vol 2, no. 9. Please see the bibliography for an explanation of the protocols necessary in the citation of Darby's collected letters. These are required in order to cover the various published editions (some of them undated) of Darby's letters that are found in libraries and in private collections held by Brethren. Because the pagination varies as between editions, giving a page number is false precision and is of no use in several of the editions. However, the item number remains constant, so that is the universal reference.

Francis Newman's *Phases of Faith*.[44] This book cut to the heart of Darby's *amour propre* and engaged him emotionally in his response in a manner unusual in his published writings: "I have long, I suppose, looked at the portrait of my mother, who watched over my tender years with that care, which a mother only knows how to bestow. I can just form some imperfect thought of her looks, for I was early bereft of her." After a brief panegyric of his mother, he returns to his parable: "That was my mother's picture. It recalled her, no longer sensibly present, to my heart." And here is the point: "Is Christ's picture in the Word less precious to me?"[45]

Now, without losing ourselves in a long argument about whether or not Darby's s story is entirely suppositional[46] ("I suppose" could be taken as a label of imaginative intent, although I don't read it that way), the interesting phrase is "for I was early bereft of her." Maybe something strange happened, maybe not. What we know is that Darby's mother lived a long life, but that Darby in middle age reported that he had in some ways been separated from her when he was young. It could be that Anne Darby spent some of John Nelson's youth with her own people back in the USA (more of her American background in a

44 Francis William Newman, *Phases of Faith* (London 1850).

45 The quotations are "The Irrationalism of Infidelity, Being a Reply to 'Phases of Faith,'" from vol. 6, p. 37 of Darby's *Collected Writings* [hereafter CW]. Because of the problematic nature of the *Collected Writings*, please see my discussion in the bibliography of the protocols needed in citing these items. Even more so than the *Letters*, the CW are subject to confusion through several editions. As for Darby's "The Irrationalism of Infidelity: Being a Reply to 'Phases of Faith,'" it has a publishing history that is not unusual in his work. It was first published in London by Groombridge and Son, 1853, without Darby's being identified as author on the title page, although a reader attuned to the Brethren would have recognized his authorship by the internal comment. Later it was reprinted in Darby's *Collected Writings*. The original item is found in the Taylor Library of the Iliff School of Theology, Denver.

46 Timothy C.F. Stunt was the first to note that Weremchuk had missed the parabolic nature of Darby's statement above, even though it did potentially refer to some undefined personal experience. See Stunt's review of the Weremchuk biography in *Brethren Archivists and Historical Network Review*, vol. 3 (autumn 1997), 47–50.

moment). Rather firmer is the fact that John Nelson was sent to Westminster School as a boarder at age eleven and, holidays aside, that was the end of the period when he was under his mother's kindly care.[47] Actually, that was not terribly young by the standards of the time, but young enough certainly to leave a mark, if that is what Darby is referencing here.[48]

The trouble with refusing to accept at face value that John Nelson Darby could have dearly missed the relationship he had as a child with his mother, but that she continued to exist as a viable human being within the family of John Darby Sr, is that a set of knock-on errors results: how do we get rid of mother from the story – if one accepts her continuing reality? Max Weremchuk did so by declaring the existence of a marital separation on the part of John Nelson Darby's parents, and he enriched this idea with a derogatory judgment on his father, the senior John Darby. Concerning the Darby marriage, it is confidently asserted that "the fact also remains that they separated and the only point that still is left unclear is why they did … In any case, the only person who could be cast in a bad light is John Darby and not his son John Nelson."[49] All this is quite amazing, as there is no evidence of a separation, even though there were reasonable legal facilities in England for separation from bed and board that did not involve anything so drastic as divorce.[50] Certainly one could grant that John Nelson

47 G.F. Russell Barker and Alan H. Stenning, *The Record of Old Westminsters* (London 1928), vol. 1, 245.

48 Chasing literalism here is a side path, but go down it for a moment. If we accept that being packed off to boarding school was in some way traumatic (the more so because the family was still living in houses in and near London, yet was unreachable by the young boarder), then the separation from mother was indeed hurtful. Was the portrait real or a figure of speech? I think the former. Of course Darby in the 1850s and '60s could only have an imperfect memory of his mother's appearance when he was a child (as he himself confirms). The portrait was most likely a miniature, as he carried it with him.

49 Weremchuck, 232n11.

50 The comparatively easily obtained *divorces a mensa et thoro* has a misleading ring to modern ears: it meant a legal separation, but the marriage and all its financial obligations were still intact. An absolute divorce with the right of remarriage had to pass through parliament and was almost always a male-

Darby's parents were not yet living in the era of what is frequently termed "companionate" marriage, but the couple was a product of the mid-eighteenth century and should be viewed as such.

Even if one loads the case toward a certain businesslike distance as between Darby's parents, the marriage seems to have been markedly successful. They did produce and rear nine children, of whom eight survived to adulthood. In the late 1820s, when a complex marriage agreement was being worked out for George, the heir of the Darby's English estate, with the daughter of the Homfrays, a well-connected Welsh mining, iron, and political family, both Anne Darby and John were involved. "Mr and Mrs Darby are most anxious that we should not inconvenience the Messrs Homfray and would willingly leave matters as they are."[51] Quite unusually for the time, the personal wishes of the female member of a married couple was being put forward as a significant factor in a familial-legal negotiation.[52] Despite what biographers Turner and Weremchuk have decreed, Anne Vaughan Darby certainly did not disappear from the family.

---

demanded procedure. Between 1700–1857 (when reforms were introduced) only four cases of women suing men for an absolute divorce were brought to parliament. O.R. McGregor, *Divorce in England* (Toronto 1957), 10–12.

51 George Chapple Norton, lawyer for the Darbys, to Charles Morgan, 5 February 1829, East Sussex Record Office, Darby Papers, AMS6146/243. There are a score of associated items in this transaction. The negotiation was around the Darbys putting £7,000 into a jointure and the bride bringing with her a dowry of £10,000. The Homfrays were apparently short of ready money and were stalling; the Darbys were willing to back off and take future payments as part of the dowry.

52 Although Weremchuk (28) considers the following action as evidence of the nastiness of John Darby and implication of family dysfunction, it is quite the opposite. That is, on the death of his wife's father, Samuel Vaughan, John Darby took the executors to chancery for the unpaid portion of his wife's marriage settlement. Considering that John Darby had waited the best part of fifty years for fulfillment of a £5,000 contract, one of the sort that customarily is paid promptly, usually before or just after the actual marriage, one might conclude that he had been remarkably restrained and very respectful of domestic feelings (East Sussex Record Office, Darby Papers, items 22 September 1830–10 January 1832, AMS6146/260).

More constructively, the third biographer of John Nelson Darby, Mario Field, notes that Anne Darby received £500 and lifetime residence at Marklye in her husband's will. She also points to some spongy, but not improbable, evidence that John Nelson Darby and his mother were in communication at least in the 1840s. She judiciously concludes that "mystery surrounds the relationship between Anne and her youngest son."[53]

John Darby, father of John Nelson, was not a negligible person, although he did not leave many traces except in the financial world. He may have been cold by nature, but he did not live in an age when fathers where expected to change nappies or teach young children much except to be politely fearful in their presence. By the time of John Nelson's birth in 1800 he was almost fifty years of age and he had become a significant transatlantic merchant, in part through family connections with his wife's family in the USA and in the West Indies. There is no charm in his business correspondence, bales of which are found in the East Sussex Record Office, but then business is business. He was a detail-driven manager and kept his attorneys jumping like puppets on a string. The years of the wars with the French were especially good for those in the provisioning trade. In his business dealings, John Darby brings to mind the men "one heard about in 1919: the hard-faced men who did well out of the war."[54] He had a brother who was an admiral, knighted for his heroism. According to at least one associate of John Nelson Darby, the senior Darby received victualing contracts from Lord Nelson with Admiral Horatio Darby acting as a presumed go-between.[55] John Darby also had a directly useful brother-in-law, William Vaughan (1752–1850), a sea-trading merchant and an alderman of

53 Field, 22. Although Field does not cite the item, the probated will of John Darby Sr is found in English National Archives (PRO), prob. 11/1841/135.

54 Evelyn Waugh, *Put Out More Flags* (New York 1961; orig. ed., Little Brown, 1942), 255, borrowing from Stanley Baldwin.

55 Timothy C.F. Stunt, "Influences in the Early Development of J.N. Darby," in Crawford Gribben and Timothy C.F. Stunt, *Prisoners of Hope?* (Carlisle 2004) 50n22. The source is Benjamin W. Newton, as found in a ms. book in the Rylands Library, Christian Brethren Archives. Newton was a sometime intimate and later a longtime bête noir of Darby.

the City of London. In the 1790s, Vaughan was one of the leading promoters of private dockage for the West Indian trade. In 1805 he became one of the founding directors of a different scheme, the London Dock Company, at Wapping.[56]

The senior John Darby respected legal expertise, commercial acumen, and estate management, but seems not to have had much enthusiasm for the professionally religious. The three of his five surviving sons who followed a secular path – William Henry, George, and Horatio – were given estates or sizable farms, while the two who went into religious life – Christopher Lovett and John Nelson – were shorted. In 1831, John Nelson and his then-friend Benjamin Wills Newton called in on the senior John Darby in Westminster; all they got out of him were two questions: "Well John, where have you come from?" "And where are you going to?"[57] Not very civil, but just maybe he should be given the benefit of the doubt: at that stage, the intellectually promising John Nelson Darby had already thrown away a law career, been priested, and now had abandoned his parish and was spending his time with religious radicals. For someone who prized the commercial world and rational calculation (the senior Darby tended toward rational religion, not enthusiasm) his youngest son must have been a terrible disappointment.

Actually, the best connections the Darby family possessed came through John Nelson Darby Sr's marriage to Anne (née Vaughan). Her immediate family, plus her mother's family, the Hallowells, were impressive indeed. Taking the Vaughans (var.: Vaughn, Vaughen) as a group, one concludes that they constituted not a social constellation, but rather an entire solar system. They deserve a collective biography, a very large one, for they were a fascinatingly powerful, and culturally and intellectually engaged congeries, one that was truly transatlantic in scope: through both friendships and business alliances in London,

56 www.museumoflondon.org.uk/Docklands (accessed 24 October 2012).

57 Weremchuk, 26, citing Fry MSS, now in the Rylands Library.

Jamaica, Ireland, New York, Philadelphia, they engaged with some of the truly big people of the early United States, such as Thomas Jefferson, Benjamin Franklin, George Washington, and the transnational scientist and philosopher Joseph Priestly. There are only two problems with the Vaughan connection as far as our present purpose is concerned: the first is that they were so talented, talkative, and interesting that they can upset the balance of our discussion, for we are trying here to understand the social physics that produced the Wicklow Brethren, not the pyrotechnics of an Anglo-American elite; the second is that the Vaughans were all over the map – ranging from being merchant and military pillagers of places that were vulnerable and profitable in Ireland, the West Indies, and mainland America, to being emissaries of real aesthetic grandeur and unaffectedly high cultural awareness in several transatlantic locales. That leads to a prosaically practical difficulty: it is hard to pin down the tiny highly particularized things we want to know about some of these individuals, the more so because they tended to have large families and to live long and apparently healthy lives.

So, start with what we do know. The signal point is that John Darby Sr and Anne Vaughan were married 21 July 1784 by the Anglican rector of Trinity Church, New York. Anne's family was mostly Unitarian or allegiant to a form of Presbyterianism that was virtually theistic.[58] The other matter we know is that the Vaughans were a family that historically had sprawling ambition and an edge to their actions honed by their origins in the Protestant-Catholic wars of the seventeenth century.[59] John Vaughan (1572–1634) had served in the earl of Essex's Irish campaign in 1599, had become an MP for the borough of Carmarthen

58 Again to his credit, Max Weremchuck has been improving his biography of John Nelson Darby and has dealt with Vaughan descendants to find new material, see www.mybrethren.org/bios/by02jnd.htm (accessed 12 October 2012) and www.mybrethren.org/bios/by02.htm (accessed 31 August 2012).

59 The standard print genealogy of the Vaughans is focused on Benjamin Vaughan (1751–1835), an uncle of John Nelson Darby, but has wider reference. John H. Sheppard, "Reminiscences and Genealogy of the Vaughan Family," *New England Historical and Genealogical Register* (1865). This was reprinted as a separate item as *Reminiscences of the Vaughan Family and Most Particularly of Benjamin Vaughan, LLl.D.* (Boston: David Clap and Son, 1865).

and controller of the household of Charles I when he was still Prince of Wales. He was rewarded with the earldom of Carbery in the Irish peerage and probably with Irish lands as well. It is certain that the family held considerable estates in Carmarthenshire, known as Golden Grove, a name that pops up later as the estate name of the principal holding of the Irish branch of the family.[60] The family was royalist during the Civil Wars and in the next generation was rewarded by the third earl of Carbery's being appointed governor of Jamaica in 1674 and apparently with further lands in Ireland.[61] (The great-grandfather of John Nelson Darby was born in Ballyboe townland, near Clonmel, County Tipperary in 1679.)[62] By the beginning of the eighteenth century, the Vaughans were prospecting for fortune not only in their native Wales but in Ireland, London, and the West Indies. The one place they had not really done any successful picking was mainland North America,

60 William Vaughan (1575–1641), brother of the first earl of Carbery, published a work in 1600 called *The Golden-Grove, Moralized in Three Books.* A critical edition was done by W.F. Marquardt as a PhD at Northwestern University (1949), which I have not seen. Although William Vaughan is usually known as a writer, he made two unsuccessful attempts after 1616 to found a colony in Newfoundland. In 1628 he was knighted. At that time he was in Ireland, for reasons that are unclear. See *Dictionary of American Biography,* vol. 1, 654–7.

61 The information on the early Vaughans was collected by Professor Sir James F. Rees for the *Dictionary of Welsh Biography* (online edition, wbo.llgc.org.us/en/s-VAUG-GEL-1500.html). John Vaughan (1640–1713), the third and last earl of Carbery, died without a legitimate male heir. He survived as governor of Jamaica only from 1674 until 1678, having been at war with Sir Henry Morgan. After that he became a landed gentleman, an MP, and a good amateur scientist (he was president of the Royal Society, 1686–89) and continued his lifetime avocation as a serious fornicator. Even before Vaughan was sent to the Gomorrah that was Jamaica, Samuel Pepys had described him as "one of the lewdest fellows of the age" (see *ODNB,* entry for John Vaughan).

62 The probable, but by no means certain, sequence of events seems to have been that a William Vaughan (1620–1698), denoted as "merchant adventurer for Irish lands of Ballyboe, near Clonmel in Tipperary, Ireland," was provided with Irish lands after the Restoration. His son, Benjamin Vaughan, should not be confused with the man of the same name two generation later (1751–1835). A solid genealogy of the Vaughans is found at www.lhughes.me.uk/familytree/family.php?famid=F333&ged=rummens_russell.ged (accessed 19 October 2012).

but that soon changed. The wedge into North America was Samuel Freer Vaughan (1720–1802; var.: Frier, Fuer), grandfather of John Nelson Darby.[63] As a young man he was entered into a London trading company and was eventually sent to look after the firm's affairs in Jamaica. He sailed via Boston and there met and married in 1747 the American-born Sarah Hallowell (1727–1809). She was not an heiress in the strict sense of the term in English law, but she came from a family that potentially was more than merely well-off, for they were among the chief inheritors of the "Kennebec Purchase," which covered 1.5 million acres of the land running along both sides of the Kennebec River, the best agricultural land in Maine. The tract was subject to long-running litigation, but by 1753 it was mostly cleared of legal impediments as the "Plymouth Company" and the town of Hallowell became something approaching a New England fiefdom. There members of both the Hallowell and the Vaughan families spent segments of their lives, broken by periods in Boston or London, pursuing commercial affairs.

For the moment, however, the important move was for Samuel Freer Vaughan, who, having married, continued on to Jamaica, where the Vaughan family still had considerable residual influence. He built up a trade-and-slave-labour business but moved about frequently between Jamaica (where the Vaughan's first son, Benjamin, was born in 1751) and London (1752) and back to Jamaica (1759), and so on. He was engaged in a nasty lawsuit in 1769, concerning his appointment to the lucrative post of chief clerk of the supreme court of Jamaica.[64] He also acquired land in County Waterford.[65] In any case, he put together three estates that were taken over and run badly by his fourth surviving son, Charles (b. 1759), and more efficiently by his fifth, Samuel

63 The recycling of names here is potentially confusing. Samuel Freer Vaughan should not be confused with his son, an uncle of John Nelson Darby, the gifted Samuel Vaughan (1762–1827). In fact, following a common custom of the time, the name "Samuel" was taken from a son of Samuel Freer Vaughan who had died in 1758 at age four.

64 See the "Grafton Estate catalogue, 1801–1820," Northamptonshire Record Office, items G1981–G1989.

65 One of the collective Darby family monuments in Achancon church refers to "John Darby, who married Anne, daughter of Samuel Vaughan of the County of Waterford by whom he hath a numerous issue."

(b. 1761). Both Samuel Freer Vaughan and Samuel Vaughan Jr were very good at talking about the freedom of mankind, but their heirs still had some residual rights to 1,367 acres of land, the third-largest plantation, Flamstead, in the jurisdiction of St James, Jamaica, at the time of slave emancipation in the British empire.[66] Between 1751 and 1768 Samuel Vaughan and Sarah Hallowell had five sons (four of whom survived to adulthood), and six daughters (five survived), among them the mother of John Nelson Darby, born in 1757, probably in London.

Samuel Freer Vaughan must have been some ilk of a charmer, perhaps a mesmeriser, for he played all three sides of the Atlantic triangle – London, New England, and the West Indies – with consummate skill. In September 1783 he returned to the now-independent USA, this time to Philadelphia, bringing with him his wife and three of his daughters, including Anne, the future mother of John Nelson Darby. Samuel Freer Vaughan already was friends with Benjamin Franklin and was acquainted with George Washington and Thomas Jefferson, with whom he shared a distrust of "irrational" religion and a keenness for the success of the new republic. He became a leading figure in the American Philosophical Society, and, rather amazingly, Vaughan was given responsibility for designing and planting the gardens of the State House Yard in Philadelphia, often called Independence Square. An almost-devout worshipper of George Washington, Vaughan twice visited the great man at Mount Vernon. He commissioned a Gilbert Stuart painting of Washington, which now is owned by the National Gallery, Washington, DC. He had a marble mantelpiece from his own London house sent to Mount Vernon, where it was placed in the banquet hall. Vaughan left Philadelphia to tend to his slave plantations in 1787, then came back to Philadelphia briefly in 1790 before going back to London, where he died in 1802.[67]

66 *1840 Jamaica Almanac*, jamaicanfamilysearch.com/Samples/AL40james.htm (accessed 24 October 2012). In addition to Flamstead, at least into the 1790s the family also owned the Crooked Spring Estate, and the Penn Estate.

67 A valuable if saccharine essay is Sarah P. Stetson, "The Philadelphia Sojourn of Samuel Vaughan," *Pennsylvania Magazine of History and Biography* (1949). Samuel Vaughan's architectural drawing of Mount Vernon and of the plan of its gardens is available at www.daacs.org/resources/sites/images/24/. George

Consider the perspective of the two persons who were eventually to become the parents of John Nelson Darby: Anne Vaughan and John Darby Sr. Anne, born in 1757, London, had been raised in a Unitarian household. She was christened in the Southwark Presbyterian Church, London,[68] which we can safely take as being rationalistic-dissenting in its theological leaning. Her two eldest brothers were educated at the famous dissenting academy at Warrington, but we know nothing of her education or, for that matter, that of her sisters. But even if one assumes that she had healthily demanding and independent tuition, she still had the problem any young woman of her station faced: she needed a suitable husband, and her father had to provide a dowry to make that happen. Samuel Freer Vaughan was willing. Fine: what about John Darby? Born in 1751, he was a third son and did not have a realistic hope of inheriting Leap Castle and its lands. (That this unlikely event actually occurred is not here in play.) He had two uncles who were Dublin merchants and, more importantly, an "uncle," George Darby, who was one of the Lords commissioners of the admiralty in 1780–82 and who was promoted from vice-admiral to rear admiral of the western fleet in November 1781.[69] This was a valuable asset to a young man in London maritime commerce, and, together with his undeniably gentry background, he was at least a presentable candidate for admission to the Vaughan circle. It is almost certain that some members of John Darby's family knew some members of the Vaughan family long before any marriage was suggested. By the mid-eighteenth century, one branch of the Vaughans held an estate, Golden Grove, in King's County, in the same barony as Darby's Leap Castle.[70] This is not

Washington's thank-you for the chimney piece was sent via son Benjamin Vaughan, 4 February 1785. "Calendar of Charles Vaughan Papers," Bowdoin College (the college has forty-one boxes of papers).

68 familysearch.org/search/records/index, citing christening record, 21 November 1757.

69 Robert Beatson, *A Political Index to the Histories of Great Britain and Ireland*, 2nd ed. (London 1787), vol. 1, 344. I put "uncle" in quotation marks because Freeman-Attwood suggests (78–9) that Admiral George Darby may have been a cousin of some sort rather than a brother of Jonathan Darby (mark v), as the family sometimes suggested to its advantage.

70 Mary Trench married William Vaughan of Golden Grove, King's County, sometime before mid-century. See Thomas R.C. Cooke-Trench, *A Memoir of*

to assert that Anne Vaughan and John Darby were acquainted with each other in Ireland, but their caste was a small one and, living off-and-on as they both did in London, they almost certainly had heard of each other and knew what the game was. Anne Vaughan, who was one of the three daughters whom Samuel Freer Vaughan brought with him from London back to Philadelphia, arrived 8 September 1783.[71] And barely three months later John Darby, who just happened to be in Philadelphia on business, asked her to marry him.

Anne refused. John Darby resolved to return immediately to London.[72] It all was a ritual dance that both parties performed. John persisted. Father Samuel Vaughan promised £5,000 as a dowry, Anne reconsidered. The couple married 21 July 1784, and by August they were packing to go to England. Anne's mother worried that she might never see her again.[73]

From the marriage alliance Anne acquired an increasingly successful husband, life in Westminster, children, and, later, life on a Sussex estate. John Darby's benefits were easier to calculate, and they consisted primarily of the contacts that Anne's very worldly, very gifted, very well-connected family yielded. We already have touched on the contacts, friends, and enthusiasms of Samuel Freer Vaughan and on the resources in Maine that came with his marriage alliance with the Hallowell family. Beyond that, the brothers of Anne Vaughan were pure bonus for John Darby for, though they varied from merely eccentric to truly pyrotechnic, they each had a battery of useful contacts in several places in the fast-developing Atlantic world. To take them quickly

---

the Trench Family (1897), 11 and 25–7. Thus, the Irish branch of the Vaughans became allied with the Clancarty branch of the Trench family, part of the ecclesiastical-landlord Trench dynasty that equalled that of the Synge family – and which, in the nineteenth century, like the Synges, favoured the evangelical wing of the Church of Ireland.

71 Stetson, 461.

72 John Darby to Charles Vaughan (in Jamaica), 10 December 1783, in the Charles Vaughan Papers, Bowdoin College. The phrase quoted makes two things clear: (1) that Darby knew Charles socially, and one suspects that he knew the other brothers as well; and (2) that he had been in Philadelphia primarily for the purpose of pursuing Anne.

73 Sarah Hallowell Vaughan to Charles Vaughan, 5 August 1784 (Charles Vaughan Papers, Bowdoin College). As a sidebar: Mrs Vaughan's worrying

in ascending order of achievement, Charles Vaughan (1759–1839) was a gentle screwup and even he had a wide network. Born in Jamaica, he was useless as a plantation manager in Jamaica and moved to New England in 1785. He invested heavily and ultimately unsuccessfully in developing a seaport in the Hallowell family's lands at the mouth of the Kennebec River, then became a London and later a Boston merchant-trader (the architect Charles Bulfinch and William Scollay were among his sometime partners), went bankrupt, and settled back in Maine, where he became something of a guru on Maine farming and stock-raising.[74] Samuel Vaughan the younger (1761–1827) ran the family plantations in Jamaica, which in 1802 had 300 slaves, and he traded widely within the Atlantic triangle.[75] As mentioned earlier, William Vaughan (1752–1850) was a very influential merchant trader and one of the chief promoters of the development of the London docks. Very well educated by Joseph Priestley at Warrington Academy, he was a fellow of the Royal Society and also a seriously practical philanthropist: he was involved in setting up the first retail savings bank in England, the first real protection the artisan class had for safely setting aside funds. William Vaughan was a director and subsequently governor of the Royal Exchange Assurance Corporation from 1783 to 1829. He hit rough financial times in the 1820s, but his value for anyone doing international trading was that he knew everyone who counted in West Indian-North Atlantic commerce.[76] John Vaughan (1756–1841),

that the family would be forever separated may indicate that at this point her husband Samuel was not intending to return to England, at least not *en famille*. As it turned out, she and the two daughters who were with the family in Philadelphia returned to England in 1786 and her husband did so in 1790. They retired to Buckinghamshire. He died in 1802, and she in 1809.

74 *Dictionary of American Biography*, entry for Charles Vaughan; and the Charles Vaughan Papers, Bowdoin College.

75 Vaughan Family Papers, 1768–1950. "Guide to the Collection" in the Massachusetts Historical Society (forty-two record cartons) cites a valuation of the Samuel Vaughan plantations, including categorized lists of his 300 slaves according to gender and age (carton 12).

76 ODNB, entry for William Vaughan. Late in life, when going blind, he collected and reprinted his early writing promoting the London docks. *Tracts on Docks and Commerce* (London 1839). His "Memoir" (4–22) is factually valuable, albeit not emotionally revealing.

a gentle Englishman in the wine trade, became in 1782 an even quieter, gentler Philadelphian in the wine trade. Mostly, his life was given over to the work of the American Philosophical Society, of which he was treasurer and librarian for decades. He was a close correspondent and friend of Benjamin Franklin and his grandson William Temple Franklin and served in the American Philosophical Society under Thomas Jefferson. Vaughan was a shy, generous, rich man who was willing to play second fiddle to some of the brightest minds in the new republic.[77]

The skyrocket of the family, however, was the eldest paternal uncle of John Nelson Darby, Benjamin Vaughan (1751–1835). He and his next brother, William, received a schooling that probably was the best available in England at the time: they lived with Joseph Priestley and studied, in large part under his tutelage, at the dissenting academy in Warrington. By all accounts, Priestley was an inspired teacher – and anyone who becomes the scientific discoverer of the element oxygen and who is burned out of home by a Birmingham mob for being a bit too keen on the French Revolution has claim to being a wide-gauged human being, and that does not even count his theological and philosophical writings; but it does make his exile to rural Pennsylvania from 1794 until his death in 1804 seem a cruel waste indeed. After Warrington, Benjamin Vaughan studied at Cambridge, where he could not take a degree: as a Unitarian he would not swear the Trinitarian oaths required for conferral. He read law for a time at the Inner Temple. During the American Revolution, of which he heartily approved, he used his family ties to become friends with Benjamin Franklin and, with Franklin's help, put together a book of Franklin's political and miscellaneous writings, which was published in 1779.[78] Thereafter, he studied medicine in Edinburgh for two years, although he did not actually practise until late in life. Vaughan made friends in Edinburgh

77 "John Vaughan Papers, 1768–c.1936," calendar of 850 items in the American Philosophical Society, Philadelphia. Among the correspondents listed are John Jay, George Washington, John Adams, Thomas Jefferson, Washington Irving, Henry Wadsworth Longfellow, Daniel Webster, and John Quincy Adams.

78 Benjamin Franklin, *Political, Miscellaneous, and Philosophical Pieces* (London 1779). This was expanded into a three-volume edition in 1796, which was also edited anonymously by Benjamin Vaughan.

with Adam Smith. In 1781 he married Sarah Manning, daughter of a very successful London merchant who had large West Indian slave plantations, and Benjamin became his business partner. In seeming contradiction to the West Indian slave business, he was frenetically keen on American freedom and later on the new French republic. For a time, Benjamin Vaughan served as an off-and-on private secretary to one of the eras most independent politicians, Sir William Petty, second earl of Shelburne (raised in 1784 be the first marquis of Lansdowne). Shelburne (as he was when Benjamin Vaughan worked for him) was home secretary and then prime minister from July 1782 to April 1783, when he conceded the independence of the United States in the Treaty of Paris. The interesting point is that during these negotiations Benjamin Vaughan was employed both as a confidential backstairs messenger between London and Paris by Lord Shelburne and was signed on by John Jay as a secret agent for the Americans.[79] The same ability to be on at least two sides or more of big issues was shown when Vaughan was sitting as an MP for the rotten borough of Calne, Wiltshire, in 1792–96. Although he was quite supportive of the new freedoms being invoked in France, he made only one speech in parliament. In February 1794, when William Wilberforce introduced his annual bill for the abolition of the slave trade, Vaughan warned of the need to prevent slave revolts in the British West Indies, which would follow from the French having abolished slavery in their colonies.[80] As a final starburst as an English enthusiast for freedom, Vaughan, while still a member of the Westminster parliament, accepted an invitation to attend the official opening of the first national assembly of republican France; this set in train a privy council investigation of his loyalty, not unreasonably

79 George S. Rowell, "Benjamin Vaughan" *The Magazine of History* (March 1916).

80 Ibid., 50; *Dictionary of American Biography*, entry for Benjamin Vaughan. He apparently had no problem with Africans as chattels. On 17 February 1798 he wrote to his brother Samuel, who was having trouble making money from the family plantations, and suggested in shudderingly modern management-speak that Samuel should sell part of the family properties and that he "concentrate negroes and mules" in a more profitable input balance on the remaining lands ("Calendar of Charles Vaughan Papers," Bowdoin College).

considering the state of English-French relations. Vaughan also was suspected by the French of perfidy and was arrested and only sprung through Robespierre's intervention. Reading the cards that were on the table in both England and France, Benjamin Vaughan decided to become an American and in 1796 settled in Hallowell, Maine, where he corresponded with the first six presidents of the USA and as a hobby practised medicine.[81] As one of his panegyrists said, "with an ample fortune he was placed beyond the torments of business, or corroding calculations to meet the wants of day-by-day."[82]

When John Nelson Darby began the Michaelmas term at Trinity College, Dublin, at the beginning of October 1815,[83] at age fifteen, he was not a cultural waif or a social cipher. This has to be emphasized because Brethren history has followed Darby's own later self-presentation and has strongly minimized his social background and has presented him almost entirely as a religious entity, one who did not quite spring full blown like Athena from the head of Zeus, but close. Actually, he was not reviled and despised by the world. First, he was vetted and then, being found highly promising, he was recruited, indeed courted, by the evangelicals who ran Dalyland. In the mid-range perspective, we can see that he was being channelled into a career funnel, one that started with a horizon of wide possibility and then narrowed into a

81 Rowell, 50–3.

82 Sheppard, 346.

83 Michaelmas Day fell on a Friday that year and term was put over to the beginning of October. The academic terms were Michaelmas, Hilary, Easter, and Trinity. These are not as irrelevantly antiquarian terms as they might appear, particularly not Michaelmas. The Christian year began, according to the Greek-derived calendar, about 1 September or on the Caesarean calendar on 24 September, and one major fourteenth-century English calendar had begun the ecclesiastical new year on Michaelmas Day, 29 September. To this day, the academic calendar in most of the western world begins with an autumn term, the start of an academic new year. See C.R. Cheney (ed.), *Handbook of Dates* (London 1961), 4–6 and, on the four terms as used in English law and English-derived legal education, 65–7.

FIGURE 3.2 TRINITY COLLEGE, DUBLIN: FRONT ELEVATION.
The front elevation as seen from the Bank of Ireland.

limited set of high-prestige alternatives, and finally into the Church of Ireland, where he would first take a curacy controlled by his evangelical recruiters, who lived in the posh parts of County Wicklow. The massive irony of the course of events as they unspooled is that the Anglican evangelicals thought to take over John Nelson Darby (ah, what a stout, crosier-banging evangelical bishop he would have made!), but he turned the tables on them: by the force of his singular personality, he became a much greater influence on evangelicals worldwide than ever they were.

Young Darby entered TCD with connections only slightly less valuable than those flashed about by the sons of the peerage or the eldest sons and heirs of substantial gentry. He was connected to the Leap Castle estate; had a father who made a fortune during the French wars and was assembling a Sussex estate; he had ties in London to several international trading firms (international trade, banking, and grand-scale brewing being the only socially acceptable forms of trade at the upper end of the Irish social scale); and he had uncles and cousins who were spread around the Atlantic world and knew world statesmen

FIGURE 3.3 TRINITY COLLEGE, DUBLIN: INTERIOR SQUARE.

and were on terms of friendship with some of the front-edge thinkers of the time. Naturally, the world of the Anglo-Irish ascendancy wanted Darby's allegiance and the Anglican evangelicals of Dalyland set about capturing him for their own cause. It took a while, but they were patient.

From his enrolment in Trinity onward, we begin to encounter John Nelson Darby in contexts that can be defined quite precisely and these encounters certainly are helpful historically. Yet he continually frustrates the curious and the concerned. Indeed, because he so ruthlessly cauterized large sectors of his own memory, there can be no interior narrative of Darby's emotions in everyday familial, social, and academic situations. His letters tell little of who he was or what he ever had been outside of his ultimate religious mission; and neither do his hundreds of published works. Granted, anything is possible, and perhaps someone will turn up the long-lost interior diary of Darby's feelings, but that would be nearly a miracle; even among his closest followers, he did not permit himself to recall things close to his heart. (As we shall see a bit later, he refused to remember even the year in which he was converted.) As one observes his life and mission as they evolve, it is hard to avoid the conclusion that John Nelson Darby did not like himself – no, indeed, that he abhorred himself in the same sense that the "Articles of Religion" printed in every Book of Common Prayer of his time described basic human nature: "Original sin … is the fault and corruption of the Nature of every man, that naturally is ingendered of the offspring of Adam; whereby man is very far gone from original righteousness, and is of his own nature inclined to evil" (Article IX). In his adult years, in his self-loathing he swithered about salvation and developed fevered and disjoined theories of higher spiritual gifts and of escape from future torments and always he was preternaturally busy, riding, walking, preaching throughout western Europe and the British Isles and later large patches of North America, writing thousands of letters on religious subjects, most of them admonitory, many of them bullying, and almost all of them syncopated, distrait, and ill-focused. Of course, to his followers that was (and still is) evidence of God's working within him. Whatever the case, the man could not sit still with himself. His unremitting drive was one of the things that made him a primary worldwide religious vector, the propounder and proponent of a set of revolutionary rewritings of nineteenth-century Irish Protestant Christianity and one of the founders of present-day American evangelicalism.

If we have no significant direct remembrance from Darby of his days at Trinity College, Dublin, we at least know how the university worked and can see that he exercised the one habit that was to serve as an emotional analgesic for the rest of his anxious life: he kept very busy. Not that he was forced to: TCD was remarkably flexible; one could obtain a degree with little real education being involved or could engage deeply with the system and very competitively with one's fellow students.[84] For someone such as John Nelson Darby, the entrance procedures were not so much a hurdle to jump as a low curb stone to step over. He completed the entrance procedures on 3 July 1815.[85] These consisted

84 In order not to confuse the text, I am referring in almost every instance to "Trinity College, Dublin." It was created by royal charter in 1591–92 and by Darby's time was sometimes referred to as the "University of Dublin," although it was not incorporated as such until later.

85 Burtchaell and Sadleir, 210.

of showing up with a financially responsible adult and dealing with whichever of the senior fellows was serving as bursar to guarantee that the fees would be paid; and then having a *viva voce* academic exam with another one of the senior fellows. No record is left of the character of Darby's exam, but an observant, slightly tart reminiscence of the procedure as it took place in 1795 turns out to be relevant, for the senior fellow who was bursar in that year, the Rev. Dr John ("Jacky") Barrett, was still one of the ranking senior fellows as late as the early 1820s, although by then he was librarian and more eccentric than ever. Barrett was famous for "his miserliness, his provincial expletives, his slovenly dress, his absorption in books and his ignorance of the world outside the college walls," according to a modern authority on Trinity eccentricity.[86] In a manuscript journal kept by William Blacker, son of the archdeacon of Dromore, the entrance process was as follows. He and his father called upon Dr Barrett in his college rooms. They encountered a man "in stature about five feet one inch, his figure stout and paunchy, his legs remarkably short and thick and appearing even more so from the long-skirted cut of his coat." Barrett's room had only two chairs, so the three met awkwardly in the middle of the room:

> "Ey-yere come to enter Trinity College?"
> "Yes sir."
> "So do, do ye see me now, you must go to Dr Hall, the sainor lecturer and be examined and then do ye see fetch me the money."

So saying, the Bursar spun about and disappeared into his inner sanctum. The exam itself was schoolboy stuff. "I spouted Horace and Virgil with due Carpendalian emphasis" and that was the end of things. His father paid the fees and Blacker was a Trinity student.[87] The process

86 R.B. McDowell and D.A. Webb, *Trinity College, Dublin, 1592–1951* (Cambridge 1982), 82. Unless otherwise noted, the information for my comments on TCD in what the authors call "Limbo: 1794–1830" comes from pp. 74–151.

87 Constantia Maxwell, *A History of Trinity College, Dublin* (Dublin 1946), quotations from 259–60. Maxwell has several pages of Blacker's journals on a range of topics.

had not changed by John Nelson Darby's time; for someone of his financial standing and coming from Westminster School, it was a stroll.

In Darby's time, the college staff – a provost, seven senior fellows, and eighteen junior fellows – was more selective and more academically competitive for staff membership than that of any of the Oxford or Cambridge colleges, save Oriel College, Oxford, the acknowledged leader in the English university reform movement. The TCD selection process for the appointment of faculty was rigorous to the point of brutality but fair in the sense that it severely limited patronage appointments. In Whitsun week of each year (assuming that one or more fellows had resigned or died, leaving a space for a new appointment among the junior fellows), the provost and senior fellows presided over a four-day public examination. Most candidates had read seriously for four to seven years beyond their BA, and, their heads about to explode with specialist details of every aspect of the college curriculum, they lined up together, a dozen feet apart, in the college hall. They stood and faced the examiners for four days of oral examinations with 500 or so spectators listening to each question and answer (and placing bets on who would be the first to crack and leave, and who the ultimate choices would be). All this for six hours a day. "Except perhaps that for admission to the Chinese civil service," the grilling "had a good claim to its reputation as the most gruelling public examination in the world."[88]

There were, then, some very good brains to rub against among the junior fellows, who did almost all of the teaching – all male, of course, as was the student body. With the exception of a staff in medicine and law, the fellows were required to be ordained as Anglican clergymen within three years of appointment. (This statute was abolished only in 1873.) The heavy predominance of clergy should not be read as meaning that the college was necessarily a hotbed of piety. Some of the clerics were genuinely gifted as theologians, but for the most part being priested was rather like picking up a licence to drive a motorcycle in the present day: rather less demanding, actually, as anyone selected as a junior fellow was ordained without any further religious training.

Nor should the requirement that the fellows be celibate – in the technical sense of being unmarried – be taken to be much more than a

88 McDowell and Webb, 105.

long-standing industrial requirement that was increasingly ignored. The practice of semi-clandestine marriage developed (an early precursor of the don't-ask-don't-tell policy of the US military). In 1811, for example, sixteen fellows actually were married, albeit without public admission of this fact. (The celibacy requirement was repealed in 1840.)[89]

One of the unusual but admirable aspects of Trinity in Darby's time was that students had a wide spectrum of choice as to how much adhesion they wished to have to the college during their four years. Seemingly paradoxical, the key to this variety was that TCD had (1) a single prescribed curriculum for everyone and (2) a set of quarterly examinations – sixteen over four years – conducted over an eight-day period each quarter. Almost the entire examination was oral. This focus on examination results as the sole mode of assessment for the bachelor's degree opened the following possibilities. First, it allowed men who could not afford to spend time being educated by the TCD staff to pay entrance fees and then show up for the examinations. This served a credentialing function for serious young men too financially strapped to engage in full-time education in Dublin. This was not just a path for the Irish; several Englishmen were usually on the books, taking a self-study degree in this way. (Not until 1858 did the University of London provide a similar facility.) Secondly, particularly within Ireland it was not unusual for a young man to be tutored at home on the material for the TCD examinations. Sometimes this was the case for clergymen's sons, who were tutored by their fathers; other times, the sons of the gentry and aristocracy were tutored at home by professional coaches. For example, both Robert Daly, the catalyst of most evangelical activities in the south-of-Dublin palatinate of the rich, and his older brother James (Lord Dunstable, 1845) were taught at home in Delgany by a full-time tutor who stayed with them for the entire degree course.[90] This does not mean that the genteel rich did not drop in on their TCD tutors now and again, especially during the social season, but it was convenient for the young men to spend the hunting months at home. Thirdly, most TCD students (roughly two-thirds) lived in

89 Ibid., 106–7.

90 Mrs Hamilton Madden, *Memoir of the Late Right Rev. Robert Daly* (London 1875), 7.

unsupervised lodgings in Dublin, usually near the college. They were expected to meet the daily demands of their tutors, but they were free from most harassments, such as daily early morning chapel. Fourthly, roughly 20 percent of the undergraduates lived in college and were more closely supervised: considering that most of the entrants were Darby's age – about fifteen – this does not seem a bad idea.

We do not know which of these environments John Nelson Darby lived in for each of his four years. Thus, in the autumn of 1818, he was not living in college, but where is unspecified.[91] Yet, even if he lived in college for some of his time, he was not trapped into a monklike existence. He got on well with his sister, Susannah, and her husband, Edward, an emerging legal luminary, and this gave him, at minimum, weekends in Delgany and access to their residence in Dublin.[92] Darby was enrolled as a "fellow commoner," which meant that in exchange for his father's paying double fees he was allowed to wear an academic gown with braiding and with substantial frogging on the front so that it could be looped closed like a great coat. More importantly, fellow commoners dined at the fellows' table, which guaranteed a reasonable quality of cuisine and decent wine.

From his own remarks, one would not know whether young Darby made any friends at Trinity or not. Later in life, in his few letters and published items that refer to life before his religious epiphany in the late 1820s, Darby sounds a tone of having been "sore let and hindered" in running the spiritual race that was set before him (to use a phrase in the Book of Common Prayer that he knew full well). At TCD he certainly must have been aware of his wealthy Anglo-Irish classmate John Gifford Bellett, who later became one of his enthusiastically loyal followers. Bellett, three years older than Darby, entered TCD in the spring of 1815 and took his degree in the same year, 1819, as did Darby.

91 CBA, HND 1/1/32, TCD account, September 1818. This is the only term account in the Darby papers and though at this time he was not resident, he could have lived in college at other times.

92 Weremchuk says that "Darby lived at school and not at their home" (31). Aside from the lack of any evidentiary citation, the statement that Darby did not live with his sister and brother-in-law does not necessarily mean he spent all his terms in college.

He was the classics prizeman, a demanding second-level award. Moreover, Bellett ate his terms at King's Inn in preparing for a career as a barrister, as did Darby.[93] But one would not know of any acquaintance from Darby's viewpoint: he later presented his own life before becoming a spiritual savant as a barren desert.

Only through indirect sources does one learn that John Nelson Darby had a blood-cousin, Jonathan Lovett Darby, who was a year behind him at Trinity. He entered in the autumn of 1816, at age sixteen, and took his degree in 1820 and certainly can have been no stranger to John Nelson. The name "Lovett" is important here, as in two successive generations a Jonathan Darby of Leap Castle (marks V and VI, as we have been counting them) married a daughter of a Lovett family, a kinship that had property in Buckinghamshire and in Tipperary. Thus, the Lovett name was more central to the Darby family identity than was the adventitious "Nelson" that was attached to John Nelson Darby. This particular cousin, Jonathan Lovett Darby (1800–1858), was from a branch of the Darby family that had moved north and settled in County Antrim. He was a very religiously inclined young man and, having taken his degree in 1820, became a curate in Collon, County Antrim, in 1821 and spent most of his clerical life as perpetual curate in charge of Acton, County Antrim.[94]

Amazingly, from the scorched earth of Darby's memory, one could not even extract the fact that during John Nelson's time at TCD, his own brother, Christopher Lovett Darby, became the curate of Delgany in 1817, after marrying into the extended kin network of the La Touche family. We will return to this slightly older brother later, but here the point is that in one of the most desirable rural locales close to Dublin, in the heart of the evangelical kingdom of Dalyland, John Nelson Darby had a brother, a sister (with two residences, one in Dublin, one in Wicklow), and a very influential brother-in-law from the Pennefather family. Yet none of this does he refer to in his spiritual musings.

93 *BDEB*, entry for J.G. Bellett, 81; Burtchaell and Sadlier, 57. Another of the three religiously inclined Bellet sons, George, entered TCD at age seventeen and graduated in 1820.

94 James B. Leslie, *Clergy of Connor* (Belfast 1993), 294; Burtchaell and Sadlier, 210; Darby memorials in Aghancon church.

John Nelson Darby's terms at Trinity may have been quite pleasant, with family and friends in comfortable proximity, but it is impossible to know if he ever permitted himself even a momentary pleasantry. He wipes out this period from his own record of his life the way a convicted felon would attempt to eclipse the record of his previous convictions.

The one point where we can see the future John Nelson Darby emerging has to do with his instinct for competition and for getting on with the job. In 1815, virtually coincident with his admission, the authorities of TCD announced a competitive system of academic honours that was separate from the grades awarded in the quarterly exams. They set up a separate category of distinguished students who were put into a more rigorous set of tutorials. Being on this list was an honour recognized upon graduation. Secondly a previously existing set of prizes – gold medals, which were sometimes multiply awarded – were redefined so that the best honour student in mathematics and philosophy ("science") was awarded one and the best in classics was awarded another.[95] Thus, the new structure fit Darby perfectly, and he set out to be the winner of the first of the newly upvalued gold medals in classics, which would be awarded at the end of the 1818–19 academic year.

Whom was he competing against? Mostly young men his own age, fifteen to twenty. Trinity at his time recruited roughly 300 entrants each year, so that was his competitive peer group.[96] Of these, only an elite, highly motivated few would really compete, but they would be very bright lads indeed. Considered as a contest, the gold medal race had the virtue of all the runners being on the same racetrack. Trinity had only a single undergraduate curriculum, and it was what a cultivated gentleman would need before going back to an estate or entering the law or the Church.[97] The basics were physics and mathematics (ele-

95 McDowell and Webb, 90.

96 Three hundred were admitted in 1817, with the number rising to more than four hundred in 1820 (McDowell and Webb, 86).

97 In his 1947 history of TCD, Kenneth Bailey, who at the time was serving as college registrar, looked enviously at the curriculum of the early nineteenth century: with a single curriculum, fewer staff could supervisor more students than when variations in courses of study became available (Kenneth C.

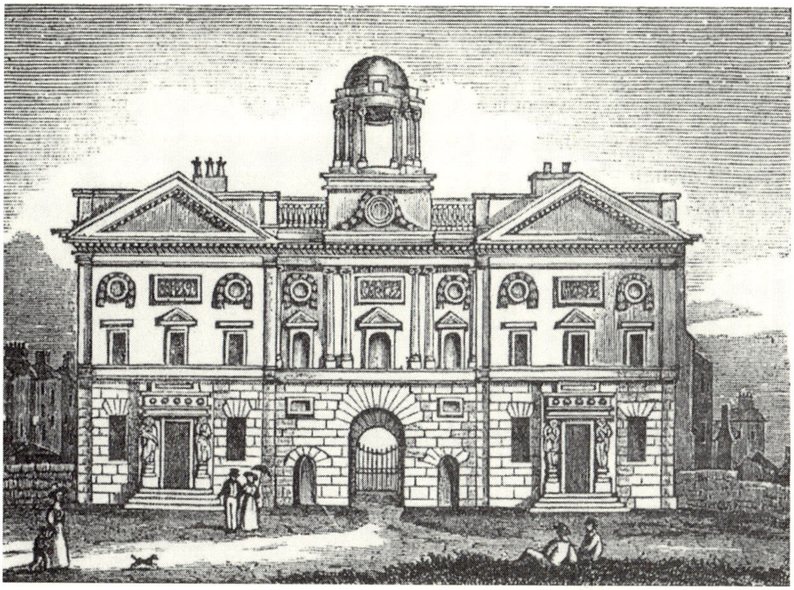

FIGURE 3.4 INNS OF COURT, DUBLIN.

mentary algebra being added in 1808 as the most difficult segment); philosophy, broken into logic and moral philosophy; and, most especially, classics: the latter at a quite high technical level in Greek and Latin, plus biblical Hebrew. Most of the teaching was done through tutorial lectures, which in practice meant that the tutor catechized his charges in a question-and-answer fashion. Memorization counted more than anything else on the classical side of the course of study and to excel in it either required almost rabbinic natural memory or a lot of dogged work. John Nelson Darby did not come first in his overall examination record.[98] However, he excelled everyone in the special examination for the gold medal in classics, which was mostly *viva voce*

Bailey, *A History of Trinity College Dublin* (Dublin 1947), 76. In Darby's time, approximately 1,200 undergraduates were the educational responsibility primarily of the eighteen junior fellows.

98 Darby's term-by-term results are found in appendix A of Floyd S. Elmore, "A Critical Examination of the Doctrine of the Two Peoples of God," 318 (ThD, Dallas Theological Seminary, 1990).

but, unusually for the time, included the requirement of an essay: in Latin, written on an assigned topic under a one-day time limit.[99]

Not only had John Nelson Darby scooped the highly desirable gold medal in classics in 1819, but he had been engaged elsewhere, setting himself in line for his chosen career, law. Even before having his name put down on the Trinity College entry books, Darby had been enrolled on the books of King's Inn, Dublin, a first step in becoming a barrister. This did not involve any hard work, but it shows decision. He ritually ate the requisite number of meals at King's Inn and was credited with nine terms by the time he left in November 1819 to complete his remaining terms at Lincoln's Inn, London.[100]

Notice what is not here: any indication of Darby's having a deeply religious experience while at Trinity College, Dublin. Not even a mild one: if TCD was a hotbed of the new spirituality, as is frequently asserted, then it somehow washed over the very young – not quite age nineteen upon graduation from Trinity – very goal-oriented, very competitive John Nelson Darby, and had no immediate influence whatsoever.

That fact is not small. It cues us to one of those trips and slips that we historians experience more frequently than we like to admit: it occurs when we provide explanations of things that really did not happen.

In 1970, Ernest R. Sandeen published a classic study, *The Roots of Fundamentalism: British and American Millenarianism, 1800–1930*.[101] It is disquietingly brilliant; it remains the best study of the interbraiding of strands from the British Isles and those indigenous to North

99 McDowell and Webb, 124.

100 Darby was admitted to King's Inn, Dublin during the Trinity term 1815, which was before his TCD admission. I am grateful to Professor Colum Kenny for providing me with a copy of Darby's final petition to the King's Inn for the Degree of Barrister, January 1822, which contains earlier details. The admission bond to Lincoln's Inn, London, including £100 as outfront fee, was signed by John Nelson Darby and co-signed by William Henry Darby, 10 November 1819 (CBA, J.N.D./1/1/48).

101 Chicago: University of Chicago Press.

America into the phenomenon known as American evangelicalism, especially its literalist, fundamentalist, and apocalyptic aspects. My own view is that Sandeen's work is undervalued in the present day, in considerable degree because of the unspoken, but bedrock, rejection of its foreignness. Historians of American evangelicalism (with a very few notable exceptions) have not been comfortable dealing with non-US cultures except as recipients of American missionary attention.

Here the irony is that one small group of American historians of religion, in counter-current to the dominant mindset, has paid too much attention to Sandeen – specifically, too much attention to a single clause in a question he raised about whether it was possible that the doctrines John Nelson Darby eventually espoused "were being taught simultaneously by several or even many prophetic students?" That is, was Darby alone in developing his very influential Irish theology? Sandeen speculated: "If more were known about early nineteenth-century Irish Protestantism and, particularly, the intellectual history of Trinity College, Dublin, a clearer light might be thrown upon these puzzling and difficult points."[102]

There are two suggestions implicit in Sandeen's reflections: (1) pay more attention to Irish Protestantism in its wider aspect and (2) focus especial attention on the curriculum and staff of TCD. In each case, the suggestion is for an open-ended query; there is no assumption that anything relevant actually will be found. Fine, have an open-minded look. In practice, however, historians who themselves have strong evangelical predilections have refused to pay much attention to what is implied in Sandeen's first suggestion, to use a wide-angle lens to assess the development of Irish Protestantism which includes the geographic, social, and economic context of Irish evangelicalism. But they have jumped on Sandeen's second idea – to look closely at the academic history of TCD – and have misinterpreted his question as being a statement of fact. In essence, he asked if the Trinity curriculum and faculty were directly and provably contributory to front-edge evangelicalism and to the sort that became Darybite dispensationalism. This is a sensible and legitimate query, but it has been mistranslated as being a

102 Sandeen, 90.

factual given – that TCD indeed had a robust evangelical, even apocalyptic component in its curriculum and on its staff and that this was directly causal in producing Brethrenism and, more particularly, the religious mind of John Nelson Darby.

This is a clear instance of what should be called the Professorial Fallacy,[103] the ill-founded assumption that most of the important beliefs, attitudes, and knowledge that students acquire at university come from the curriculum and the faculty. It is a vanity and when transposed into the past, it is a fallacy that produces bad history. Among evangelical historians there has indeed been a good deal of ferreting and sifting around the TCD confines, a search for the splinters of theology and fugitive discourses that resemble a half-missing Lego set and which can be re-formed into something approaching the full-blown evangelicalism of the mid-nineteenth century. Among Brethren historians, the fossicking around the TCD undergraduate curriculum for the basis of John Nelson Darby's mature beliefs has frequently been in equal parts imaginative and obsessive.[104] Actually, aside from one or two

103 I am here paying homage to one of the most academically courageous books of the twentieth century, David Hackett Fischer's *Historians' Fallacies* (London 1971).

104 See Floyd Elmore's thesis, cited above. And, as specific example, Gary L. Nebeker's "John Nelson Darby and Trinity College, Dublin" (2002). For comments on Nebeker's work, see Stunt in Gribben and Stunt (2004), 48. In the blog world of Brethren historians there is a mini-industry in finding potential spiritual godfathers for Darby at TCD. Mostly this search hinges on a continual confusion between the extramural writings of the members of the TCD staff (the text of which alumni usually encountered only years after their graduation) and the material that was taught in college for examination purposes. The chief casualty of the volitional misreading of the Trinity College educational structure has been Joseph Liechty's "Irish Evangelicalism, Trinity College, Dublin, and the Mission of the Church of Ireland at the End of the Eighteenth Century" (PhD thesis, St Patrick's College, Maynooth, 1987). This is a subtle and well-documented study that rather belies its title. It employs the term evangelical in a polysemous form, but most often to mean the "broad Protestant reform movement beginning in the eighteenth century which is usually known as evangelicalism" (36n1). Liechty analyses the defensive posture of the Church of Ireland at the end of the eighteenth century as a precondition to the aggressive evangelicalism (in its new form) in

odd birds who were turfed out early in the nineteenth century, the position of the TCD staff was, like the Church of Ireland itself, one of uneasy balance between mild evangelicalism and what T.C F. Stunt usefully terms "exact churchmanship."[105] Evangelicalism was growing, to be sure, but TCD kept its balance between the sacramental traditions stemming from its Catholic roots and the newer, more experiential evangelicalism. The curriculum of the institution was not much different in 1820 from that in 1750; the education was classical and philological, not theological or pastoral. Most pointedly, John Nelson Darby's own behaviour confirms that his four years at TCD did not move him from his pre-admission commitment to a career in law.

Actually, the suggestion of Ernest Sandeen that is ignored – basically, pay more attention to the non-academic, as well as the academic development of early nineteenth-century Irish Protestantism – points to where the paydirt is. Yes, in the early Irish evangelical movement there

---

the nineteenth century. His conclusion regarding the late eighteenth-century links of TCD to the new-style evangelicals of the nineteenth century deserves emphasis: "every attempt to find some individual or group directly responsible for transmitting evangelicalism proved unsatisfactory, and in fact *most of the evangelical Trinity graduates seem to have become evangelicals only after they left Trinity* (emphasis mine). Liechty proposes: "The question needed to be altered from 'why was Trinity producing evangelicals?' to "why were some Trinity graduates attracted to the evangelical option?" (470).

105 Timothy C.F. Stunt, *From Awakening to Secession: Radical Evangelicals in Switzerland and Britain, 1815–35* (Edinburgh 2000), 151–5. Concerning the situation in the Church of Ireland, the term "exact churchmanship," indicating a recognition of the sacramental conduits of divine grace, is preferable to "high churchmanship." In part this is because, outside of Ireland, as the nineteenth century wore on, the latter term implied a willingness to go much further in the direction of Anglo-Catholicism than was the case in the Irish Anglican communion. Paradoxically, the other reason is that, as Peter B. Nockles convincingly has shown, the post–1830 historiography of the Oxford Movement has tended to draw a set of historically unjustified distinctions between the old "high" church and the Tractarians and thus to miss the continuing interactions of evangelicals and the proto-Tractarians. All of which is to say that Anglican conversations in the first one-third of the nineteenth century were more fluid than later labels imply (Peter B. Nockles, *The Oxford Movement in Context* [Cambridge 1994], 1–43).

were many men who had been educated at Trinity College, Dublin, but it was not the formal TCD curriculum or any faculty indoctrination that made them evangelical. Their evangelicalism was something they usually embraced after leaving Trinity. Logarithmically more consequential than the direct effects of Trinity's rigid curriculum were the matters of ambiance and location. The young undergraduates (barely more than boys, most of them) and the recent graduates who remained in the Dublin region were situated in the one place in Ireland where evangelicalism was a social and economic reality of the first importance: County Wicklow, south County Dublin, and certain Dublin parishes – St Ann's, St Werburgh's, the Bethesda proprietary chapel and also the Magdalen Asylum and the Female Lockup, which had a fashion as evangelical missions with chapels attached – all these tied together high social contacts and evangelical sensibilities. These factors counted: unlike Trinity's curriculum.

The central case study here of course is John Nelson Darby himself. Over a decade or more the evangelicals of Dalyland funnelled him toward a career in the Church of Ireland and then toward their own brand of Anglicanism and simultaneously to the priesthood in their own part of the world. They acted independently of the formalities of TCD. Darby's early commitment to a legal career was no barrier to the senior evangelicals recruiting him: at minimum, if they failed, a really talented barrister on their side would be a plus.

To understand in some small degree the seemingly random way that John Nelson Darby developed between ages fifteen and thirty, we need to step back and observe his negotiating the formal hurdles of choosing and entering a desirable profession – while at the same time he mastered the social codes of the place he was likely to practise his not-yet-chosen profession, namely the upper class reaches of Wicklow and south Dublin – which in its guise as the home of serious Irish evangelicalism we call Dalyland.

The fact that Darby's name had been enrolled on the books of King's Inn, Dublin, even before he took Trinity College's entrance examination indicates that he (and whoever helped to arrange his life at that point) saw his legal future as being that of a barrister in Ireland. If

Darby had intended to practise in England, he would not have bothered with King's Inn, but would have waited until he left TCD and then enrolled in one of the English inns of court. However, in order to practise in Ireland it was strongly advisable (but not absolutely necessary) to eat the requisite number of dinners at King's Inn, Dublin, over nine terms with members of the Irish legal profession and with other law-aspirants; and then it was absolutely required by a seventeenth century Irish law that one enrol in one of the inns of court in London, eat one's way through eight more terms, and be certified as suitable – by English authorities – for the bar in Ireland. (This law of the Irish parliament of 1542 was only repealed by the United Kingdom parliament in 1885.) No real education, save that incidental to chatting with men of the law over large meals and claret was involved, and the teenage John Nelson Darby may even have enjoyed the process. Or not: he left no indication. At the end of the whole business, both in Dublin and in London, the King's Inn, Dublin, declared one the possessor of the "degree of barrister."[106] Another reason to take Darby's behaviour as implying he was headed for a career as an Irish barrister (rather than, for example, serving as a legal mouthpiece for his father's London businesses) is that he apparently had a close and easy friendship with his brother-in-law Edward Pennefather, who in 1816 was named a KC. He was considered remarkably brilliant in equity, and with his brother, Richard Pennefather, who also took silk in 1816, was a leading counsel

106 For the context of the projected path of Darby's legal career, see Colum Kenny, *King's Inns and the Kingdom of Ireland* (Dublin 1992). Because the English inns of court are the forms most readers are familiar with, the following differences as between the English template and the Irish form are relevant. First, unlike the contemporary English case, the King's Inn included on its rolls both the "lower forms" of law – attorneys and their betters, the solicitors – and barristers (and candidates for each level). Only in 1866 did attorneys and solicitors hive off as the Incorporated Law Society. Secondly, judges and other law officers stayed members even after being promoted out of adversarial practice. Thirdly, unlike the English inns, King's Inn had no actual chambers and did not provide any legal schooling. Fourthly, receiving the "degree of barrister" from King's Inn meant that one was admitted to practise, but, unlike the English situation, one still had to be called to the bar by a judge. This secondary step meant that there were quite a few credentialed barristers who were never called to the bar.

in chancery (and in 1821 was made chief baron of the Irish exchequer court).[107] Darby's family connections in Irish law were precisely what a young barrister would need to obtain briefs. And, further, albeit less importantly, the male line of Darby's own family had an intermittent history of qualifying as Irish barristers: Jonathan Darby (mark V) and Jonathan Darby (mark VI, died 1802) had qualified and so had a brother of Jonathan (mark VI) and later so too did a nephew of John Nelson Darby.[108]

Darby's potential career in law was comfortably intermeshed with social life and with just a hint of his religious future. The Pennefathers' Delgany estate was close to Powerscourt, and there is no doubt that the Rev. Robert Daly, rector of Powerscourt, was already bringing the very bright, very well-connected young Darby into his own social-religious circle. That John Nelson and Robert Daly were well acquainted as early as the spring of 1819 is indicated by a note written to young John Nelson by Edward Pennefather on the bottom of a printed inquiry that he had received from one of his favourite charities, the Dublin Foundling Hospital. The hasty, casual note said that Susan, Darby's sister (Pennefather's wife), "brought us last night a nice little girl, a very fine baby, both are quite well" (Darby would be the wee girl's uncle). Pennefather added a message to a mutual friend he and young John Nelson shared: "Tell Robert Daly that I missed seeing him."[109]

Still only eighteen years of age, John Nelson Darby was already mixing on terms of social equality with some of the power figures of Dalyland. The channelling of his future had begun.

The trajectory that turned John Nelson Darby from a probably lucrative law career into acting as one of the founders of modern evangelicalism depended upon two women: Lady Harriet Daly (born Lady

107 *CDIB* entries for Edward Pennefather and for Richard Pennefather; Edward Keane, P. Beryl Phair, and Thomas U. Sadleir, *King's Inns Admission Papers, 1607–1867* (Dublin 1982), 397.

108 Keane et al., 121.

109 CBA, J.N.D./1/1/36.

Henrietta Maxwell, but usually known by her married surname and shortened first name as Lady Harriet Daly) and Lady Theodosia (née Howard) Wingfield, one of the three then-living Dowagers Viscountess Powerscourt (more of that complexity later.)

Women are woefully underwritten and underestimated in the shaping of early evangelicalism in the British Isles, a historical vacuum that cannot be filled simply by assertion. Granted there are some exceptionally well documented female-led sectors – the Countess of Huntingdon's Connexion is a very early example – but in Ireland evangelical women (such as the La Touche ladies) were recorded almost entirely through their work in schools and charities. And, although the more-than-weekly meetings of evangelicals mostly had women in attendance, they invariably were led by men. The historical downwriting of women is almost inevitable because, first, most of the things women did were taken for granted and, secondly, evangelical ideology, even more than the habits of the time, affirmed the biblically derived subordination of women.

As an instance that indicates how a woman of rare power could be both massively influential and yet remain almost completely unknown to later historians in her exercise of power, Lady Harriet Daly is both illuminating and, like some of the Chinese empresses, a touch scary. (We will leave Theodosia Viscountess Powerscourt aside for the moment.) Lady Harriet quietly shaped Dalyland, the heartland of Irish evangelicalism, as much as did her famous and very public clerical son, Robert.

Lady Harriet's attributes included a long life (1759/61–1852) of fierce and intense commitment to furthering her second son's ecclesiastical career (the older of her two sons had a political career that was less in need of her management).[110] She had a remarkably shrewd under-

110 Her elder son James Daly (1782–1847) was MP for Galway and was created Baron Dunsandle in 1845. He rode efficiently on the Daly family's political coattails. The Dalys had controlled the Galway Corporation in the last decades of the independent Irish parliament. His father (Denis Daly, d. 1791) had represented Co. Galway and was an ally of Henry Grattan in promoting Catholic relief measures. His great-uncle, Denis Bowes Daly, was still active in the reform interest until his death in 1821. This great-uncle held various parliamentary seats until 1818, and among those was King's County (1790–

standing of Irish societal geometry – especially the ecclesiastical sector. For the main chance, she had the unblinking eye of a feral husky on the hunt. Above all, she had a first husband who died in the most desirable manner possible: unusually among upper-class women, she was left in full charge of wealth without male oversight. Her control of her own money was the plinth that made everything else possible.

This requires explanation. In wide perspective, in agrarian societies (and thus in most of the world until the twentieth century) the overwhelming majority of cultures have exhibited one of two sharply contrasting patterns involving the way family resources are re-arranged when a marriage occurs. One of these patterns involves cultures in which females are taken as being of positive value (speaking in economic terms). In such situations, it is commonplace for the male and his kin to pay what anthropologists call "bride-price" or "bride-wealth." Money or items of value are transferred from the male side of the new alliance to the parents or kin of the female. It could be called "womb price," for it allows the male to acquire the children of the union, in exchange for material goods.[111] The other, sharply contrasting, pattern occurs in groups (either entire cultures or smaller groups within a larger society) where females are not seen as being of positive economic value and therefore the parents of a woman must pay a dowry to induce a male to take her away.[112]

The Irish upper classes were an extreme case of the latter situation – one may think of it anachronistically, but accurately, as Jane Austen's world on steroids – and that, we shall see, is why Lady Harriet Daly was so unusual and therefore unusually powerful. If one were the daughter

---

1801), the home base of the Darby family (see *CDIB* entries for Denis Daly and Denis Bowes Daly).

111 The most extreme anthropological statement of this situation – one that was said, quite wrongly, to be universal – is found in the work of Claude Levi-Strauss; see his *The Elementary Structures of Kinship* (London 1969; orig. Fr. ed. 1949). The two volumes of his *Structural Anthropology* (London 1968 and 1973) make the same argument.

112 As a counterbalance to Levi-Strauss, based more closely on reality and less on theory, see Robin Fox, *Kinship and Marriage* (Cambridge 1983). The classic empirical tabulation of world family patterns (involving 863 societies) is George Peter Murdock, *Ethnographic Atlas* (Pittsburgh 1967).

of a family of substance, the goal was to find a husband who would improve your own family's social standing and, through carefully drawn legal contracts, would guarantee you a certain standard of living and an allowance big enough to keep you in moderate circumstances if your husband died. On the other side of the table, the potential groom and his parents (usually cash-poor, land-rich, and of good birth or, best of all, of title) wanted as much money as possible and as few restrictions on its usage as their negotiators could obtain. Not very romantic. The table was tilted very strongly toward the males' advantage. The legality that ran through all levels of Irish (and English) society was that of incorporation: not incorporation in the commercial sense that we now know it, but rather meaning that a woman as an economic entity was incorporated, first, into her father's domestic satrap and then into that of her husband. This spancelled the females of the gentry and aristocracy as tightly as if they had been indentured servants. A married woman did not own wealth on her own, nor could she conduct commercial activities without her husband's permission. He was limited by civil law and by the treaties negotiated upon marriage from alienating her freeholds and could only sell or pledge her personal property. (This did not change significantly until the passage of the United Kingdom's Married Women's Property Act of 1870.)

Almost all of the evangelical women we deal with here – the female side of the Guinnesses, the La Touches, the Synges, the Parnells, and the several families of title – were living in marriages (or living in widowhood) whose terms were fairly standard. (One must here call attention to one of the most perceptive pieces of Irish social history, Anthony Malcomson's *The Pursuit of the Heiress*). Their marriages were the product of individual treaties that required each of their fathers to pay a sum of money upon marriage, or in instalments after the marriage. Let us say £10,000 as an example. This was non-refundable. Her husband was required to treat her decently, whatever that meant. If the husband died, the widow received an annual sum from the late husband's estate – called a "jointure" – which had been agreed upon before the marriage ever took place. The going rate in the late eighteenth and early nineteenth centuries was an annual amount equal to about 10 percent of the original payment: in our example of a £10,000 dowry, the jointure payout would be £1,000 year. Crucially, in Ireland, unlike

England, it was not customary for there to be a dower house on an estate – a place where a widow could live rent-free. (There were only a few exceptions to this austere custom and these were considered to be eccentricities, not practices to be admired.) Therefore, when their husbands died, Irish dowagers were in the nasty position of being pushed out by the new male heir to the estate (and, realistically, his wife). Usually, the widow needed to rent a place. "Dowagers would usually want to make a beeline for a metropolis or watering-hole, and would not want to live close to, and thus be overshadowed by, their daughters-in-law in some isolated part of rural Ireland where few others of their class and kind were found."[113] Most jointure arrangements were set to stop payment if the widow remarried. Granted, their were variations and side deals – an unusually mushy groom might negotiate away many of his family's control rights over his bride's fortune – but in general, being an Irish wife in the gentry and aristocratic classes was a good deal more constricting and anxious than is implied by all those portraits of composed ladies gazing serenely into the middle distance.

The lottery win, meaning direct and virtually unfettered control of a significant amount of property and money, occurred in the cases of statistically unusual family structures that yielded only a female heir; or, for a married woman, a fortuitous skein of deaths in the family that left her in control of a large chunk of the estate.

Lady Harriet Daly was the penal-era product of a rapidly upwardly mobile Irish father and a mother from the English nobility. Robert Maxwell (1720?–1779) inherited both a substantial County Cavan estate and an Irish baronage from his father in 1759. He held both Irish and English parliamentary seats and in 1760 became Viscount Farnham and then in 1763 earl of Farnham (of the first creation). His first wife, whom he married in 1759, was Henrietta, Dowager Countess of Stafford. It can be taken as given that she brought with her sufficient protected wealth from her first marriage to make the new union worthwhile for the Maxwells. She died in 1771. The couple had two children, one of them a son who died in 1777 and the other, Lady Harriet. Robert Maxwell married a second time, but there was no issue from that union. Thus, when Lord Maxwell died in 1779, there was

113 A.P.W. Malcomson, *The Pursuit of the Heiress* (Belfast 2006), 17.

no direct male heir. The title earl of Farnham went extinct (temporarily) as did the viscountancy of the same name.[114] As for the family resources, what seems to have happened (no testamentary documents are available) is that the main landed property went back to Lord Maxwell's brother (as did the subsidiary title of Baron Farnham).[115] Lady Harriet had an annual charge owed to her by the Farnham estate (as a bypassed heiress, she probably received an amount equal to one-third of the estate), and she inherited houses, lands, and money composed of separate bits of property and also of the residual portions of her mother's dowry that had been protected in her own pre-marital negotiations. At minimum, Lady Harriet eventually had full control over Bromley, an estate in Delgany, County Wicklow, which her stepmother, Mary, the second Dowager Countess Farnham, occupied until she was bumped out by Lady Harriet.[116] Lady Harriet had ample funds to run the Bromley estate and to supply the needs of herself and her children.[117]

Clearly, prior to Lady Harriet's 1780 marriage to Denis Daly (1747–91), parliamentarian and member of a family that controlled the Galway Corporation, she had been able to negotiate a marriage treaty that through various legal trusts fully protected her own material rights. This was a suitable marriage, for the Daly family was wired into the Irish legislative class and had particular prestige because of Denis Daly's close friendship with the great Henry Grattan – who even-

114 Charles Mosley (ed.), *Burke's Peerage, Baronetage, and Knightage*, 107th ed. (Wilmington 2003), vol. 1, 1392.

115 At the risk of driving the reader cross-eyed with detail, the following is necessary knowledge. Barry Maxwell, brother of Robert Maxwell, whose earldom and viscountancy (of the first creation) went extinct in 1779, was automatically third Baron Farnham and became Viscount Farnham (of the second creation) in 1781 and earl of Farnham (of the second creation) in 1785. One way or another, various Lords Farnham were operative in County Cavan as the largest landlords in the county throughout the nineteenth century. They became very evangelical in the early 1820s and were part of Lady Harriet (née Maxwell) Daly's set of social and religious alliances.

116 Madden (1875), 3.

117 The Byzantine inheritance patterns around the Farnham estate, involving several generations of complexity, are noted in Malcomson (2006), 84–5.

tually became Lady Harriet's neighbour in County Wicklow. In any case, after Denis Daly died in 1791, Lady Harriet moved her two sons and five of her six daughters into her own estate in Delgany, County Wicklow. (The eldest daughter went to live with Lady Harriet's step-mother, Lady Farnham, in London; recall that dower houses were rarely provided in Ireland, and the dowager countess had joined the polite retreat to an acceptable address, in this case Cavendish Row, in the metropole.) Lady Harriet had a full-time tutor engaged for her two boys and a gamekeeper to accompany them whenever they wished to go shooting. The family was briefly discomfited by the 1798 rising. Lady Harriet took three of the five-at-home girls off to London, where her step-mother was ill, and sent the youngest two girls to the Daly grandmother in Dublin. The boys went into a private school at Donnybrook. After several months (during which Lady Farnham died), Lady Harriet reassembled the family at Bromley, set the girls to good works, mostly teaching among the locals, and had both her sons tutored at home for their Trinity College, Dublin, studies, which they completed in 1803.[118] It is a clear indication of how rare was the undiluted power Lady Harriet had over her own estate that when in 1827 G.N. Wright listed the names of the ninety-five major residences in County Wicklow and their owners, only Bromley was under female control.[119]

So, when Robert Daly took deacon's orders in 1807, one had an ambitious and able young man (he had taken a gold medal at Trinity) and an ambitious and independent and well-resourced mother. That would be interesting but not important in the history of world evangelicalism, except that there was more, a multiplying engine that turned Lady Harriet's considerable independent power into a true *force majeure* that shaped the entire landscape of Irish evangelicalism and, among other things, helped to channel John Nelson Darby into his religious vocation.

The machine was simple, resembling one of humanity's earliest mechanical devices. Think of Lady Harriet's unusual body of independent wealth, and consequent social power, as being a stable fulcrum.

118 Madden (1875), 3–7. Robert Daly took his BA in 1803 and a gold medal. James Daly did not complete his degree (Burtchaell and Sadleir, 207–8).

119 G.N. Wright, *A Guide to the County of Wicklow* (London 1827), 171–3.

Then visualize a very long lever that balanced on that fulcrum and was manipulated at one end by the full force of the ambition of Lady Harriet for her clerical son and the increasingly spiritual intensity of the young Rev. Robert Daly. Then ask: what could that device lift? The answer is: several of the pivotal appointments in the Church of Ireland as they came open in the Wicklow-South Dublin area, at least if they came open at the right time. Obviously, for this result to occur there needed to be a manipulable clenching-and-grabbing device at the far end. And there was.

In chapter 1, I mentioned that Lady Harriet had a "close cousin" who was married to a clergyman who held a succession of Irish bishoprics and then became archbishop of Dublin. For Lady Harriet's purposes, this cleric was a very useful man indeed, but, like so many industrial tools, he was bent, frequently undependable, and prone to become dirty and despoiled. The "close cousin," Catherine (c. 1767–1815, née Wynne) Cleaver was close in the contemporary sense of the term, meaning that she and Lady Harriet had a family relationship, however tenuous, and were reasonably near in age, of approximately equal social position, and willing to share enemies and exchange gossip, and to form an alliance for mutual advantage. Actually, the two women were first cousins, once-removed.[120] Catherine was the daughter of a long-established County Sligo family and her father, Owen Wynne, was MP for the county and was named to the Irish privy council in 1756. Catherine in 1788 made a good marriage to one of the last of the truly money-grubbing Englishman appointed to bishoprics in Ireland, the Rev. Euseby Cleaver (1745–1819). He owed his Irish career to his appointment as chaplain to George Nugent Temple Grenville, first marquis of Buckingham, who was the Lord Lieutenant of Ireland in 1782–83 and almost disastrously in 1787–89, during the Regency Crisis. Buckingham appointed Cleaver as his chaplain in 1787 because of pressure from Lord Egremont, Cleaver's patron, who had already appointed Cleaver to the rectorship of Petworth, site of his Sussex estate. (Not incidentally, Lord Egremont was also a large landowner in Clare and Limerick; and also not incidentally, the Rev. Euseby Cleaver's

120 Their common ancestor was a Maxwell, who was Lady Harriet's great-grandfather and Catherine's grandfather.

brother had been the tutor of the young George Grenville; not much was accidental in the upper reaches of the eighteenth-century Church of Ireland.) From the springboard of the vice-regal chaplaincy, Euseby Cleaver rose to the bishopric of Cork (March-June 1789) to Ferns (1789–1809) and finally to the archbishopric of Dublin (1809–19).[121]

Euseby Cleaver was famous for being complaining, grabbing, and generally unpleasant. Two acts were symptomatic of his character. First, while serving as bishop of Ferns, he also acted as land agent for Lord Egremont's Irish estates in the west of Ireland. Apparently he was very good at it – "finance happened to be the bishop's hobby."[122] He was not the only Irish bishop or lower clergyman of his era to serve as a landlord's agent,[123] but aside from the far-from-spiritual nature of wringing rents out of the Irish peasantry, the identification of the Protestant state church with landlordism was certainly detrimental to the long-term health of the Church. Secondly, during the 1798 Rising he lost any public dignity he had by scarpering to Wales: his extravagant newly completed episcopal palace was sacked and was only saved from burning by the actions of the local Catholic priest. The Right Rev. Dr Cleaver then made it his mission in life to prosecute exaggerated claims for governmental compensation.[124]

121 *CDIB* entry for Euseby Cleaver; A.P.W. Malcomson, *Archbishop Charles Agar* (Dublin 2002), 192–3.

122 Malcomson (2002), 193, quoting H.A. Wyndham.

123 Malcomson (2002), 192n32; As further example of clerical land agentry, the Rev. le Poer Trench (destined to be the last Church of Ireland archbishop of Tuam) was in his early career in the 1790s both a pluralist rector and land agent for his father, the earl of Clancarty. In fact, the practice of Anglican clerics holding land agencies only died in the 1860s, the last one being the dean of Ross, who managed to hold in addition to the deanship a benefice in Cork and a rectory in Lisburn and to be the agent for the marquis of Hertford, who held about 2,500 acres in Antrim and Down (George T. Stokes, "John Nelson Darby," *The Contemporary Review* [1885], 541–2).

124 *CDIB* entry for Euseby Cleaver; Malcomson (2002), 344–7. Cleaver's most egregious move, however, was to claim compensation for the abolition of the rotten borough of Old Leighlin by the Act of Union of Great Britain and Ireland. He claimed £15,000 compensation: "it had been usual and customary for the Lord Bishop of Leighlin and Ferns to nominate and appoint chiefly the beneficed clergy of the united dioceses of Leighlin and Ferns, as bur-

Unappealing as Bishop Cleaver was – serious scholarship ranks him among the most mercenary Irish Protestant bishops of the eighteenth century[125] – Lady Harriet Daly granted him the honorific of "cousin" and in the early nineteenth century used him like scoop in a granary. In chapter 1, I noted that the young Rev. Robert Daly had received his early education from English tutors that were recommended by Bishop Cleaver and that he was given his first post, a curacy in County Wexford, when the Rev. Dr Cleaver was bishop of Ferns. Next, soon after Cleaver became archbishop of Dublin, Robert Daly received a curacy in Newcastle, Co. Wicklow, and then in 1814 one of the plum parishes in the entire country, Powerscourt. That simple sequence disguises the real power of Lady Harriet – she could have been merely wheedling and flattering, but actually she had an iron fist inside her spidery black net gloves.

The opening for her to obtain real (albeit necessarily almost invisible) power in south Dublin and Wicklow occurred when Bishop Euseby Cleaver went totally mad. Surprisingly, considering the range of deep-dish eccentrics and bent personalities found on the Irish bench of bishops during the eighteenth century,[126] the Church had no rubric in place to deal with mental incapacity. So, when in 1810–11 it became clear that Cleaver was with Sweeney and the Nightingales, neither canon lawyers nor governmental officials knew quite what to do. Eventually a special act was passed, effective 29 August 1811, naming the Hon. Charles Brodrick, archbishop of Cashel, as coadjutor archbishop of Dublin. Problem solved? No, for legal counsel decided that

---

gesses of the said corporation" (John d'Alton, *The Memoirs of the Archbishops of Dublin* [Dublin 1838], 353).

125 Malcomson (2002), 490.

126 My own favourite, Frederick Augustus Hervey, fourth earl of Bristol and bishop of Derry (1768–1803) was wildly eccentric but not crazy. Immensely wealthy, he spent most of his time as a bishop on the Continent, where "Hotel Bristol" became the name of several fashionable hotels. He was particularly fond of Rome, where he went about in red plush breeches, a broad-brimmed white hat, and totally outclassed his Catholic rivals with the variety of chains, ornaments, and scapulars he wore around his neck. He did occasionally return to Ireland and expended a great deal of money in job-making projects for the peasantry.

the right of making new appointments to livings belonged to the Chancellor of Ireland (Lord Manners) in his post as custodian of the legal affairs of lunatics. And, as the Rev. Richard Wynne, brother of Archbishop Cleaver's wife, told Archbishop Brodrick, with evident satisfaction, the Lord Chancellor of Ireland had "kindly consented … to present such persons as Mrs Cleaver has reason to believe would have been objects of the [now-lunatic] Archbishop's patronage. She will from time to time submit to your Grace's [Coadjutor Bishop Brodrick] consideration those who may be proposed to her, or those whom she may wish to recommend to the Chancellor."[127] In other words, the wife of the lunatic archbishop effectively gained the exercise of the most important prerogative of an Irish bishop: to hand out jobs.

For Lady Harriet Daly, bright was the morning when her dear cousin Catherine became controller of clerical patronage in the archdiocese of Dublin and Glendalough. The litmus case that showed how much collateral power this situation gave to Lady Harriet was the appointment of her own son Robert to the parish of Powerscourt. This was not the easy slotting one would have expected, because Richard Wingfield, Fifth Viscount Powerscourt, had another candidate in mind. Even a healthy and fully functional archbishop would have hesitated to exercise his right of making an appointment in the face of opposition from the most powerful landowner in the parish; and he would have been even less apt to ride hard when the opponent was an aristocrat in his twenties who was just beginning to find his strength as a magnate. But the contest was not between a bishop and a seigneur, but between the imperious Lady Harriet Daly and a young man of limited experience. Lady Harriet stared down Lord Powerscourt and her son was lodged in the post that became the pivotal parish in the Irish evangelical revival.

It is an indication of the Rev. Robert Daly's skill in salving the feelings of the Wicklow rich (and, indeed, bringing them into the evangelical fold) that in 1820 Viscount Powerscourt, who was in Madeira at the time, wrote to Daly saying:

> I remember perfectly well my *anger* and *pride* at the time of your appointment to the living of Powerscourt, having applied

127 Richard Wynne to Charles Brodrick, 1 January 1812, quoted in Malcomson (2002), 503n131.

> for it for a good-humoured amiable person, whom I cannot be sufficiently thankful did not get it by my means, as all his accomplishments are utterly worldly; and the parish of Powerscourt would, in all probability, had I then been successful, not have possessed, or scarcely, one spiritual soul in it.[128]

Lady Harriet began a program of filling every available benefice and curacy in her locale with clergy of the sort approved by her son. This raises the question of whether either she or her cousin Catherine were given much to religion, much less to evangelicalism, and the answer in each case is unclear. Catherine Wynne Cleaver had a reputation for piety, although of what sort is uncertain: her being found in a position of prayer upon her death in May 1815 fit with her public reputation for godliness.[129] As we shall see, after Catherine Cleaver died, Lady Harriet's influence did not diminish: one suspects that the death of cousin Catherine simply left Lady Harriet to deal directly with the coadjutor bishop and with the Lord Chancellor. Although Bishop Cleaver died in December 1819, he was not replaced until April 1820 by Lord John George Beresford, who two years later was translated to the archbishopric of Armagh. Until William Magee became the archbishop of Dublin in June 1822, there was no strong pastoral hand on the tiller, and Lady Harriet and her son filled the void in northeast Wicklow. Mind you, that still leaves open the question of Lady Harriet's own brand of faith; with great tact the biographer of Robert Daly judges that "his mother, though an excellent woman, and most conscientious in the discharge of what she felt to be her duty, was not at that time under the influence of true religion."[130] That is a coded way of saying she was not an evangelical in these early years, but came around later to her son's beliefs. Her vocation from the mid-1810s to the mid-1820s was to promote the Rev. Robert Daly's career and to press for his being surrounded by like-minded evangelicals – in the same way she would have advanced his political allies if he were a politician.

128 Viscount Powerscourt to Robert Daly, 6 March 1820, reproduced in Madden (1875), 66–7. Emphasis in the original. The occasion of the letter was Daly's having been offered the deanery of Cashel, which he declined.

129 *CDIB* entry for Euseby Cleaver.

130 Madden (1875), 4–5.

Her particular religious faith at this point was irrelevant: Lady Harriet's works are what counted. In northeastern Wicklow one sees evangelicalism growing through lots of inside game-playing, the same sort of thing that we have earlier seen the Guinness family doing in mid-Wicklow and south Dublin. Survey for a moment the way the heart of Dalyland came together into an extraordinarily tight community of the evangelical and social elite. Lady Harriet did not create all this, but her fingerprints are clear. Here, we cannot rely on a set of documents but rather on pattern recognition. In her era, the way a woman, even an independently wealthy one such as Lady Harriet, pushed her causes was through the drawing room and country visits, not written petitions. But anyone who follows a premier league football team or who has owned a fantasy league baseball team will recognize the pattern: she was building a team and its headquarters were in the parish of Delgany (where Lady Harriet's estate was) and in the neighbouring parish of Powerscourt, where she had ensconced her son.

The wedge years for the evangelical hegemony in northeast Wicklow was the period between the death in 1815 of Lady Harriet's cousin, the wife of the officially lunatic archbishop of Dublin, and 1822, when a tough new archbishop came in. In that period, the character of Dalyland was firmly established and knock-on effects continued in Wicklow throughout the 1820s and into the mid-1830s. That example was followed elsewhere, notably in County Cavan (among the Maxwells, the Lords Farnham who were descended from Lady Harriet's uncle), Roscommon (the Lords Lorton), and County Down (the Jocelyns, or Lords Roden). Dalyland, with its dominance of south Dublin and Wicklow remained the evangelical centre, however.

As a related set of examples of how ecclesiastical appointments in Dalyland and its satellites worked, watch the following.[131] In 1816, the Trenches, one of the most powerful clerical families in Ireland, effectively turned evangelical. As Alan Acheson has rightly noted concerning the Irish evangelical movement in general, "the revival was,

131 Each of the appointments to benefices and non-episcopal dignities that I am here mentioning was under the direct patronage of the archbishop of Dublin, or his substitute; see *First Report of His Majesty's Commissioners of Ecclesiastical Revenue and Patronage, Ireland,* H.C., 1833 (762), xxi, 62–71.

FIGURE 3.5 GREAT SUGAR LOAF MOUNTAIN.

Wicklow landlords used the mountain as one of the primary anchor points in designing the sightlines of their estates' vistas.

above all, a family affair."[132] In this case the catalyst was the death of Lady Emily La Touche, sister of the earl of Clancarty, wife of Robert La Touche (nephew of Peter La Touche of Bellevue), and sister of the Honourable Power Le Poer Trench (bishop, successively, of Waterford, 1802–10, and Elphin, 1810–19, then archbishop of Tuam, 1819–39). As platoon leader of an extended clerical family, the noteworthy point about Bishop Trench is that in 1816 he was converted. He turned from being a hunting-and-shooting bishop to energetic evangelicalism. This radical change occurred because his sister, Lady Emily, died with a peace and a joy that laid open the emptiness of his own spiritual life. Subsequently, his own archdeacon, an evangelical, convinced him of the need to embrace justification by faith.[133] This conversion certainly

132 Acheson, 127.

133 Ibid.

was emotionally wrenching. Lady Emily had given birth and about six weeks after delivering a son had been taken with some form of sepsis. Her brother, then bishop of Elphin, was at her home, as were several other family members. The entire dreadful affair was marked by a fervent memorial sermon preached by the Rev. Robert Daly at the Female Orphan House on the Sunday after her death[134] and later by the conversion to evangelicalism through the counsel of Bishop Trench's archdeacon.

The reality of the Trench family's turn toward evangelicalism cannot be gainsaid. That granted, getting one of the Trenches into place in the parish of Delgany would be a great coup both for Lady Harriet Daly and for her son, Robert. But Delgany already had a rector, himself a sound evangelical, the Rev. James Dunne. Fortunately, he knew who his patrons were: Euseby Cleaver had appointed him to the curacy of New Ross in 1800 and to the rectorship of Delgany in 1810; he also knew that his real vocation was to become an evangelist of the Hibernian Bible Society, a position that was under the influence of the new wave of Anglican evangelicals. So, in 1817, he resigned Delgany and, in 1820, was given the chaplaincy of the Magdalen Asylum in Leeson Street (effectively, an evangelical satrap) and was named prebendary of Killybegs, in the archdiocese of Tuam that was by then under Trench influence.[135] The rectorship of Delgany now was open and the appointment was in the hands of the official guardian of lunatics in Ireland (for Archbishop Cleaver was not functional) and, no surprise, that official appointed an evangelical whom we can take for granted was acceptable to Lady Harriet Daly: Frederick Eyre Trench, a member of the clan of the clerical Trenches and a collateral relative of both the earls of Clancarty and the La Touches.[136]

The curate's post at Delgany came vacant at almost the same time, but that was less a matter of celestial mechanics than of old-fashioned log-rolling. The providential part was that the living of Kilgobbin in then-rural south Dublin, on the road to Bray, fell vacant in 1817 by

134 Alexander Knox to Hannah More, 22 and 23 April 1816, reproduced in [James J. Hornby, ed.] *Remains of Alexander Knox* (London 1837), vol. 4, 317–22.

135 *CDGBSL*, 598.

136 Ibid., 1121.

virtue of the death of the incumbent, and that parish was the perfect place to put a rising evangelical. The parish was socially and religiously dominated by the family of Alderman Frederick Darley (who had been Lord Mayor of Dublin in 1809). Darley was married to Elizabeth, daughter of the first Arthur Guinness. So, from Lady Harriet's parish of Delgany, the curate, Rev. Hugh Kearney, a warm, anti-Calvinist, moderately exact churchman, was moved to Kilgobbin, where he was a great success and, among other things, produced a new church edifice and inspired three of the Bellet brothers, who were in the forefront of the rethinking of Irish Anglicanism in the late 1820s and early 1830s.[137]

The sign of how tightly orchestrated these moves in County Wicklow and south County Dublin were is indicated by simple chronology. The Rev. Frederick Eyre Trench was formally installed as rector of Delgany on 7 October 1817, and on 18 October a new curate of Delgany was formally licensed: Christopher Lovett Darby.[138] He was one of the older brothers of John Nelson Darby; if one needs confirmation of my earlier argument that the Darbys were an Anglo-Irish family that was both coveted and recognized among the social elite in Ireland, this bears weight. Not a great deal is known (at present) about the Rev. Christopher Darby (1792–1874), although his career in the Church of Ireland was successful at a level of comfortable parishes and minor dignities, albeit no deanships or bishoprics. He had a Westminster schooling, followed by a seemingly unhappy Oxford career: he had matriculated at Christ Church but transferred to the decidedly downmarket St Mary's Hall and received his BA in 1815.[139] In 1817 he was at the canonical age for appointment in the Church of Ireland and needed a

137 [Dorothy Bellett], *Memoirs of the Rev. George Bellett* (London 1889), 24–5; Michelle Guinness, *The Guinness Spirit* (London 1999), genealogical frontispiece and 33. In regard to Bellet's memoir, T.C.F. Stunt makes the important correction of a running typographical error, wherein "Darley" is printed as "Darby," a fairly big problem if one is engaged in sorting out early evangelicalism in Ireland (Stunt, 2000, 153n16). The proper spelling, Darley, is set out in [Letty M. Bellett], *Recollections of the Late J.G. Bellett by His Daughter* (London 1895), 11ff. Alderman Darley was a fairly hard-edged Orangeman who did well out of municipal corporation construction jobs.

138 *CDGBSL*, 273–4.

139 Barker and Stenning, 245.

patron. Fortunately for his career, he married in 1817 Mary Boyle, who was a niece of Elizabeth La Touche of Bellevue.[140] It is clear that the appointment of Frederick Eyre Trench as rector of Delgany and Christopher Darby as curate was a package deal. Given the absence of both the insane archbishop of Dublin and the unfortunate death of his admirable wife, a good guess is that the real patron of Christopher Lovett Darby in his first religious post was Lady Harriet Daly in concert with the La Touches. Granted, the young Rev. Christopher Darby was a secondary acquisition, but he definitely had the sort of background that made him collectible in Dalyland, even if merely as a curate.

A rather tighter trade (I cannot use any other word) involving the parish of Delgany occurred in 1819. Frederick Eyre Trench was collated to Donoughmore, where he was permitted to be non-resident; a curate did the parish duties, and Trench lived on a second benefice in the diocese of Leighlin. As a throw-in, Trench received a more desirable prebend in St Patrick's Cathedral.[141] But why was the parish of Donoughmore empty? Because the clergyman in charge of Donoughmore, who had only been appointed 16 January 1819 resigned on 24 July and Trench was in office 30 July 1819. The cleric who vacated Donoughmore was William Cleaver (1789–1860), son of the insane archbishop of Dublin. But where was he to go? Of course, to the rectorship of Lady Harriet Daly's parish, Delgany, which, as part of the deal, the Rev. Mr Trench resigned.[142] William Cleaver was trading down in terms of financial rewards, but he was right to do so. His father, the lunatic archbishop, was near death's door and the moment he died

140 Montgomery-Massingberd, *Burke's Irish Family Records* (1976), 322; Weremchuk "Research Paper 13," www.mybrethren.org/bios/by02jndx.htm (accessed 31 August 2012).

141 *CDGBSL*, 279, 1121; *A List of the Parishes in Ireland with the Names of Their Respective Incumbents; and Distinguishing Those Parishes in Which the Incumbent Is Not Resident*, H.C. 1824 (436), xxi, 14.

142 *CDGBSL*, 273, 279. In common with Christopher Lovett Darby and John Nelson Darby, William Cleaver was a product of Westminster School. His son, the Rev. Euseby Digby Cleaver (born in Delgany in 1826, d. 1894) was a longtime pioneer in the Irish-language movement and was vice-president of the Gaelic League, 1893–94 (*CDIB* entry for Euseby Digby Cleaver).

Cleaver would be vulnerable, at least in the sense of having a reasonable chance of finding a benefice where he would be happy. The Rev. Mr Cleaver, still only thirty years of age, was one of those souls who is often mentioned in memoirs as saintly, as a gentle soul, and certainly he was evangelical in a caring and non-confrontational way.[143] So very unlike his father. In essence, what Lady Harriet was doing was paying off a moral promissory note to her late cousin Catherine: taking care of Catherine's son by placing him in a protected position (no one messed with her protégés) in a splendidly salubrious locale where he served until 1847. The younger Cleaver was very active in Delgany parish in a genteel way; fully resident and, unusually, helped by two curates. One of those who served for a time as curate was his brother Henry Owen Cleaver,[144] thus again illustrating Alan Acheson's observation that, among the social and clerical elite, evangelicalism was a family affair. Finally, what about the Rev. Christopher Lovett Darby, whose

143 For example, in his *Recollections* (1877, 18–19), the Rev. R.S. Brooke recalled that the Rev. William Cleaver, a Christ Church Oxonian, and the son of the late archbishop, held the parish of Delgany, "a gem of rural beauty … He was a scholar, and a refined gentleman in mind and bearing and united in himself things that were 'true, and just, and pure, and honest, and lovely' in a singular degree. His influence was as extensive as his kindness, and through both he drew within the circle of his beneficence, not only the neighbouring clergy but also the gentry, and a number of young men preparing for orders, who gladly listened to his eloquent Gospel pleading, and profited by the example of his pastoral activity." A tougher critic, James Anthony Froude, stayed in Cleaver's home for a time and found in his household "a beautiful principle of unobtrusive piety" (Waldo H. Dunne, *James Anthony Froude: A Biography* [Oxford 1961], vol. 1, 65–6, quoted in T.C.F. Stunt, "Evangelical Cross-Currents in the Church of Ireland, 1820–1833," in W. J. Sheils and Diana Wood (eds), *The Churches, Ireland and the Irish* [Oxford 1989], 217n14). In the early 1840s, Froude was resident with the Cleavers as tutor for one of their sons who was preparing for Oxford. See the excellent recent biography by Ciaran Brady, *James Anthony Froude* (Oxford 2013), 75–80. Brady, in assessing William Cleaver's influence on Froude, makes the salient observation that "Irish evangelicalism was both sociologically and ecclesiologically a phenomenon entirely different from the English version" (77).

144 *CDGBSL*, 485; *A List of the Parishes* (1824), 14.

curacy formally ended when William Cleaver was moved to Delgany? He simply disappears from the clerical scene in 1819 and then pops up in 1822 as rector of Killenaule in the diocese of Cashel. In the ordinary chronicling of Irish clergy, that lacuna would be a very unsatisfactory state of affairs. However, as I will indicate in the next chapter, something else was going on. This is the same period that his brother, the young John Nelson Darby, falls farthest from conventional historical tracking systems. Perhaps this is coincidental, but I doubt it.

The way that Lady Harriet Daly operated in aid of her evangelical son in northeast Wicklow, and the manner that the evangelical Guinnesses used their influence farther south in Wicklow and also in Dublin (discussed in chapter 2), provide detailed instantiation of the way that the early Dalyland evangelicals used their secular power to further their spiritual ends. The evangelicals within the Church of Ireland understood office and they understood power.

Four points need underscoring. The first is one of interpretation. If one is a person of faith, these Irish events (and their later American knock-ons) can be read under the rubric of providentialism: meaning that, however strange or grossly worldly some of the jobbing actions were, they can be interpreted as being guided by the divine plan as part of a pattern of cause and effect. This possibility requires emphasis because many evangelical scholars seem to fear that engaging the historical development of evangelicalism, especially in its social and economic aspects, is part of a project whose goal is to explain away evangelicalism: and thus they shun any history that is not a succession of shimmering ideas. If one is not a person of faith, the historical events discussed here have as much empirical validity and eventual cultural impact as any other comparable set: you may or may not like the emergent patterns, but chronicling event and impact is what historians do. Either way: take the even, take the odd.

Secondly, the richness of detail presented here is intended to overcome one of the fundamental problems of all historical narrative, that "everywhere in the past we encounter things which remain unexplained only because they were completely self-understood in their time, and like all daily matters were not thought necessary to write down": thus Jacob Burckhardt, the generative historian of renaissance art and culture.[145] In the early history of Irish evangelicalism, everyone knew who was related to whom and how prayer sessions and ecclesiastical patronage overlapped. They knew, but we can only occasionally reconstruct, the invisible everyday social web that bound people together, or, alternately, defined whom one should ignore. Things that everyone knew are actually the very matters that most often disappear historically, for the knowledge of them is so ubiquitous as to rarely require formal records. Hence, when one sees patterns as clearly as in the case of Dalyland, we should not let them slip into our collective blind spots concerning the past.

Thirdly, and related to general forgetting, is the specific matter of evangelical women. This is a problem in almost any era of evangelical history, for women are underdocumented in virtually every record set, save those of exclusively female groups, such as are found in most churches and denominations. The big things all seem to be run by men, with self-conscious recognition sometimes being accorded to darling wives and saintly mothers. Even taking into account the debilitating admonition of Saint Paul – "Let your women keep silence in the churches," 1 Cor. 14:34 – I think there have been a lot more powerful women behind the scenes than ever we shall know, but they are very hard to catch on film: they knew they were supposed to keep out of the frame of history's camera. That is one reason why persons such as Lady Harriet Daly (and, in the next chapter, Viscountess Powerscourt) are worth particular historical attention.

Fourthly, when one comes to the Brethren, they present us with an extreme case of willful amnesia. With the exception of Lady Powerscourt (of whom the Brethren were inordinately and inaccurately proud), and the occasional sere and suffering missionary wife, the first and second generation of Brethren memorialists simply removed women from the story. (In this regard, the standard compendium of

145 Quoted by Martin E. Marty, *A Nation of Behavers* (Chicago 1976), xi.

Brethren biography running from the 1820s to the early twentieth century tells everything in its title: *Chief Men among the Brethren* (*Acts 15:22*).[146] Later historians, even if they had been so inclined, would have had a terribly difficult time documenting notable women: after the first and second generations of Brethren were gone, there was little in the way of written material to fall back on. This problem haunts the present study.

146 Henry Pickering, *Chief Men among the Brethren* (London: 1st ed. 1918; 2nd ed. 1931).

PART II

The Real World

CHAPTER FOUR

The Missing Years (1): 1819–1822

John Prine, a splendidly original, albeit not very reverent, songwriter, did very well with a song entitled "Jesus, the Missing Years."[1] He referred to the big lacuna that should intrigue any serious student of Christianity – namely, what was Jesus doing and with whom was he studying between ages twelve and thirty? Or to put it in terms of another time, what was Yeshua of Nazareth doing between his Bar Mitzvah and his becoming a rabbi? We are not allowed to know, and the hints we have in the scriptures are not very satisfying.

There is a similar erasure in the life of John Nelson Darby. We know that he was a driven young man, but what was he doing between mid-1819, when he left Trinity College, Dublin, and August 1825, when he took deacon's orders in the Church of Ireland? Characteristically, Darby himself is not much more forthcoming about this than about how he spent his spare time when at TCD. This is striking, given the cultural richness of his family and the wealth of genteel Irish evangelical hosts and hostesses of pious disposition who were conveniently available to divert or to improve him. The missing years break into two segments, 1819–22, when becoming a barrister was a stated goal, and 1822–25, when Darby went through a period of spiritual development that led him into the priesthood of the Church of Ireland. The operational key in dealing with John Nelson Darby's life in the first and most mysterious period, 1819–22, is two-fold. First, the most likely boundaries of his experience at this time can be set out and this can be

1 Album title: *The Missing Years* (Oh Boy Records 1991).

done without wild speculation, but with clear caution. Secondly, the period is one of observational opportunity, for it was in these years that the formative context of the Irish socioreligious situation in the 1820s was articulated. Thus, one watches the development of crucial institutional entities that played directly into the creation of the radical wing of Irish evangelicalism and at the same time one recognizes that the collective expression of nascent evangelicalism formed a significant portion of the cultural landscape that John Nelson Darby experienced in these years.

On paper, John Nelson Darby's life-course between 1819 and 1822 is deceptively clear. He entered Lincoln's Inn, London, in Michaelmas term 1819, completed his obligations in Hilary term 1822, and thus was admitted to the "degree of Barrister" of the Society of King's Inn, Dublin.[2] Although there is one report that Darby actually was called to the Irish bar in 1825[3] (in Ireland, qualifying as a barrister did not automatically mean one was called to the bar), I doubt its accuracy: to the extent that Darby ever practised – "I was a lawyer," he stated in the 1850s[4] – he was done with the law by late 1824, when he purchased a

2 Edward Keane, P. Beryl Phair, and Thomas Sadleir, *The King's Inns Admission Papers, 1607–1867* (Dublin 1982), 120. Max Weremchuk, *John Nelson Darby* (Neptune, NJ, 1992; orig. German ed. 1988), 32, dates Darby's calling to the Irish bar as 21 January 1822. (This fits with his oath-taking; see below.) This dating would imply that Darby took his ritual three meals at Lincoln's Inn at the earliest possible dates in Hilary term, or had his meals taken by proxy, which was a not unusual practice.

3 G.F. Russell Barker and Alan H. Stenning, *The Record of Old Westminsters* (London 1928), vol. 1, 245.

4 John Nelson Darby, *Letter by J.N.D. to Prof Tholuck, "translated from the French," 185__* (Dublin: F.G. Burkitt, 2nd ed., n.d), found most conveniently in *LJND*, vol. 3, no. 226. Despite being presented in *LJND* as a private letter, it was in fact a message, via Tholuck, to Darby's Continental followers, and it was subsequently put into print, although when exactly it was printed is unclear (before or after Darby's death?). The item was originally in French and probably was translated by William Kelly. The frontispiece of the printed version (but not the *LJND* version) states that "This letter, found among the papers of J.N.D., had not been sent to his correspondent. There is reason to suppose that the reluctance as to having the appearance of speaking of himself and his work had given up thought of forwarding it" to Tholuck. The

clergyman's gown prefatory to entering the church.[5] The prudent view is to accept that he was registered as a law student at Lincoln's Inn from 1819 to 1822, "kept eight terms in the dining hall and paid all dues and duties to the Society," and left to be certified as a lawyer in Dublin.[6] And that is about all one can document.

Actually, even what that tells us is not very revealing, for in the period we are dealing with, there was little that anyone today would recognize as legal education. To be anachronistic, but accurate: we are not here dealing with the nineteenth-century equivalent of Yale Law School.

---

problems this raises as to both authenticity and accuracy are obvious. Almost all the letters in *LJND* had an implicit, if minimum, check for authenticity in that the three volumes of Darby's letters were compiled mostly from items that had been kept by Darby's correspondents and were lent to the editor of *LJND* (William Kelly) by the recipients. This Tholuck item, however, lacks that basic check; though I take this draft to be authentic, that is at least a small leap of faith –Professor Tholuck was dead before the publication occurred, so any possible denial by him that he was this close to Darby was silenced. There certainly was a good deal of room for creativity here. F.A.G. Tholuck (1799–1877) was professor of Divinity at the conservative Protestant University of Halle from 1826 onward and previously, 1824–26, had been professor of Oriental Languages at the University of Berlin. He tended toward devout Pietism, but from the mid-1820s onward he had entry into a broad range of United Kingdom religious leaders, ranging from Edward Pusey to John Nelson Darby (see entry for Tholuck in *BDEB*). One scholar has suggested that he "was one of a select few European theologians considered worthy of general trust by the English Protestant public" (Kenneth J. Stewart, *Restoring the Reformation: British Evangelicalism and the Francophone "Réveil," 1816–1849* [Milton Keynes 2006], 213). Individual testimony to the direct influence of Tholuck upon young seekers after spiritual knowledge is detailed in the autobiography of George Müller, the famous orphan-house leader and an adherent of Open Brethrenism (G. Fred Bergen, ed., *Autobiography of George Müller* [London 1905], 8–15).

5 Bill rendered 9 December 1824 for making of a clergyman's gown (CBA, J.N.D./1/1/31).

6 The quotation is from the certificate of completion of Darby's terms at Lincoln's Inn, drawn 26 November 1821. I am grateful to Dr Colum Kenny for generously providing me with a copy of this Lincoln's Inn document and also of Darby's petition to be admitted to the degree of barrister in Ireland, countersigned by Edward Pennefather, and Darby also signed a copy of the oath of allegiance (with its anti-Catholic abjurations), 21 January 1822.

Legal education in Darby's era was entirely a solo enterprise – learn as you will, being the rule – and the formal requirements were minimal, the predictable competences of the students (apprentices, really) even less. Darby was required to "keep" eight terms at an English inn of court and to be attested (but not given any examination in law) by English legal authorities before returning to Ireland and automatically being certified by King's Inn, Dublin, as an Irish barrister. Since eating three of the meat-and-claret meals in hall counted as keeping a term, Darby could have had as few as twelve dinners (four terms) at Lincoln's Inn for each of two years, and then, after paying the appropriate fees, become a barrister. At its worst, this system produced barristers with as much knowledge of horseshoeing as they had of law.[7]

An alternative possibility is that Darby could have been well served by taking advice from his eldest brother, William Henry Darby, who had been admitted to Lincoln's Inn at Michaelmas term 1811. He had been called to the English bar in November 1817, and had begun to know the winding sidepaths of being a barrister (he eventually became an Irish landowner and non-practising Irish barrister). Also, John Nelson would have done well to have listened attentively to another older brother, George Darby, who, while at Cambridge, had been admitted to Lincoln's Inn in June 1816 and was called to the English bar in November 1821.[8] Under the protocols of the time, John Darby Sr would have paid at least 100 guineas to find his youngest son a place in a fashionable law office where John Nelson could sit in a corner and observe and then be allowed to copy out documents and to read over old folders that showed the various practical requirements of a law case proceeding from complainant to solicitor to barrister to trial. John Nelson would have spent his spare time watching trials or attending one of the houses of parliament and watching bills as they proceeded to enact-

7 Joseph Napier, in the House of Commons speech cited above (*Hansard*, col.155), quotes the advice of one experienced barrister who had practised at both the Irish and the English bar and who counselled young Irish candidates in England that all they needed could be learned over wine at dinner and the only book they needed to crack for the Irish bar was Joe Miller's Joke Book. The suggestion was seriously made.

8 Barker and Stenning, 245.

ment. At the scanty mock trials the inns held, he would show up and be intent on the proceedings. He would have returned to Ireland, paid £45 to complete his registration, and practised law in a system that still had few Catholics (they had been allowed to become barristers only in 1792) and that until 1829 had only Protestant judges.[9]

Where John Nelson Darby fit between those two extremes is impossible to say with any firmness. One suspects that he did not spend most of his time from 1819 to 1822 studying law in England. Because he was so serious and hard-working it is easy to forget that between his leaving Trinity College, Dublin and receiving the degree of barrister he still was very young: just his nineteenth through twenty-first years of age, and any privileged young gentleman of that age was susceptible to a wide range of possibilities. For example, he could have been earnest about husbanding his time and have decided to make good use in his own way of the freedom of the Lincoln's Inn system: with a little planning, one could go five months at a stretch without even showing up in London, and that was without employing a proxy to eat some of his meals. Here, I can only note three relevant facts about Darby's family and suggest one fairly strong probability statement about his social situation.

In addition to his older brothers, who were part of the English legal system, Darby's other family members formed a frame for his expectations in the years 1819–22. First, as mentioned in an earlier chapter, his father had bought Marklye in Sussex in 1819 and enlarged it with adjoining lands in the years 1819–23. Secondly, one of John Nelson's older brothers George (b. 1796, the eventual heir of Marklye) was a bit more relaxed about education than was John Nelson. He had left Westminster at age sixteen, and he had not enrolled in St Catherine's Hall, Cambridge, until he was nearly twenty years of age. He took his BA in 1820.[10] He was great mates with a charismatic Anglo-Irish medieval enthusiast and European traveller, Kenelm Henry Digby – of

9 On the variable possibilities of legal education, see Keane, Phair, and Sadleir, vii–x; Kenny (1992), 162–9; Colum Kenny, *Tristram Kennedy and the Revival of Irish Legal Training, 1835–1885*, 146–217. See the vivid speech of the legal reformer Joseph Napier, *Hansard* (Commons, 1 March 1854), cols 147–69.

10 Barker and Stenning, vol. 1, 245.

whom a brief note later. Here the relevant point is that if John Nelson Darby spent any time in the English countryside it most likely was at Marklye in the company of his brother George and his faux-medieval world. And, thirdly, another older brother (b. 1792), the Rev. Christopher Darby, was at liberty in the years 1819–22. Recall that Christopher Darby had left the curacy of Delgany, being replaced 7 May 1819[11] as part of the complex set of trades engineered by Lady Harriet Daly to increase the power of evangelicals in Dalyland. Christopher Lovett Darby was not in any clerical disgrace: in 1822 he was appointed to the rectorship of Killenaule in the diocese of Cashel and thereafter had a conventionally successful career in the Church of Ireland and a brace of clerical sons who did even better.[12] Most likely, he took his leave by choice. The Darby family had money, and in any case Christopher

11 *CDGBSL*, 274.

12 After being appointed as rector of Killinaule in Cashel in 1822, Christopher Lovett Darby was appointed to the Kells Union in the diocese of Ossory in 1828. He was granted a faculty for pluralism, so he kept both benefices until his death in 1874. The Kells Union was worth £875 annually (gross) in the mid-1830s and afforded two curates. Darby was resident in Kells. The glebe house was built in 1830 but carried the splendid address of Kells Priory, which referred to an imposing ruin, a sometime Augustinian priory that had been built on the plan of a castellated secular fortress. Christopher Darby inherited in 1835 an estate of undefined size in County Tipperary and a docket of perpetual rents in Queen's County upon the probate of the will of John Darby Sr. Certainly, Christopher Darby can be said to have done well financially out of his time in the church. In the early 1870s he owned seventy-six acres in County Kilkenny and just before his death in 1874, he compounded under the Irish Church disestablishment arrangements for an award of £3,233. Christopher Lovett Darby used the Anglican Church as a job bank for his family. He appointed his youngest son John Lionel as the curate of Kells, 1868–71, and this was the stepping-off point for the son becoming diocesan inspector of the diocese of Chester, England, and then archdeacon and subsequently dean of Chester. An older son, Christopher Lovett Darby (who often is confused with his father in historical discussions), was his father's curate at Kells, 1854–63 and then rector of Killegney (diocese of Ferns), 1863–64, and then rector of Gowran in Ossory, 1864–84. At disestablishment of the Church of Ireland, he compounded Gowran for £6,122. Perhaps most intriguing, as it hints that the Darby family (other than John Nelson) kept extended ties alive over a considerable period of time, is that Christopher Lovett Darby's second

was married to a La Touche niece. For people of his class, a three-year sabbatical was not beyond their means.[13]

What is clear from John Nelson Darby's later behaviour is that, in the years 1819–22, he was simultaneously seduced by all the riches of Dalyland and intrigued by the serious spiritual mien of some of Dalyland's social elite. The ambiance of the fine houses and engineered landscapes; the correct manners of the upper classes and the forelock tugging of their inferiors; the serious and improving conversation of rich men and women; and the pleasure of being treated as a member of a club of serious minds, men of the world who avoided the sin of being merely worldly: potentially very intoxicating for a very young man, just reaching age twenty. Even if one assumes that for a time John Nelson Darby was serious about entering the practice of law, he would have had reason to spend a good deal of time in kindly Dalyland, talking Irish law to good purpose with the husband of his sister Susan, Edward Pennefather, who like his brother Richard, was a KC and headed for the top level of the Irish legal profession. (Richard became chief baron of the exchequer in 1821, and Edward, as chief justice of the Queen's bench, eventually presided at the state trial of Daniel O'Connell in

---

daughter, Mary, married the Rev. George E. Haviland of Warbleton, Sussex, where the Darby family's English estate was located.

Sources of the above: James B. Leslie, *Ossory Clergy and Parishes* (Enniskillen 1933), 79–81, 281, 283–4 (this corrects St John Seymour, *The Succession of Parochial Clergy in the United Diocese of Cashel and Emly* (Dublin 1908), 42); James B. Leslie, *Ferns Clergy and Parishes* (Dublin 1936), 182; George Dames Burtchaell and Thomas Ulick Sadleir, *Alumni Dublinenses* (London 1924), 210; *Fourth Report of His Majesty's Commissioners of Ecclesiastical Revenue and Patronage in Ireland*, 162–5, H.C. 1837 (500), xxi; *Irish Church Act (Commutation) Return*, 17, H.C. 1875 (52), lvii; C.A. Empey, "The Sacred and the Secular," *Irish Historical Studies* (1984), 131–51; N.U.I. Galway, Landed Estates Database, Family Lovett, landedestates.nuigalway.ie/LandedEstates/jsp/family-show.jsp?id=3374 (accessed 21 February 2013), will of John Darby, National Archives (PRO) prob. 11/1841/135, probated 16 January 1835.

13 The birth spacing in the family is relevant. Married in 1817, the Christopher Lovett Darbys eventually had seven children, born 1818 (Anne); 1820 (Jonathan); 1823 (Mary); 1825 (Christopher Lovett); 1826 (Elizabeth La Touche); 1828 (Catherine Frances); and 1831 (John Lionel). Hugh Montgomery-Massingberd (ed.), *Burke's Irish Family Records* (London 1976), 322.

1844.) The Pennefather family until 1832 controlled the borough corporation of Cashel, so there was plenty of chance to discuss the ways and byways of the Irish legal system, its legislative formation, and its political realities.[14] Darby's sister and brother-in-law had residences both in Delgany and on Fitzwilliam Square, Dublin.

Yet, clearly, serious religion and the people who adhered to it became more attractive to Darby than did a future arguing cases before irascible judges. This was a continuation of a process begun while he was a TCD undergraduate – the Rev. Robert Daly was friendly with him while John Nelson was still a student – and young Darby must have come to know Delgany quite well when his brother Christopher Lovett was the parish curate. The entire area of northeastern Wicklow was an extremely beguiling environment. Just a half-day from Dublin, it was socially rich, religiously serious, and incredibly beautiful physically. In addition to the strictly clerical arrangements that we have seen being set in place in this sector of Dalyland, there were major religious attractions embedded in fine landscapes and imposing Big Houses. Within a fifteen-mile radius of his sister Susan [Susannah] Pennefather's country house were several elegant citadels of serious religion: the Howards' Bushy Park, which was within walking distance of the Pennefathers; and Charleville of the evangelical Monck family also was close at hand. Of course in the nearby parish of Powerscourt, with its great house of the Wingfields (the Powerscourt peerage), there was the Rev. Robert Daly himself, who paid flattering attention to young John Nelson Darby.

At Bellevue the second Mrs La Touche had become the patron of a long-term resident (from 1803 to 1828, when her husband died), the luminous Alexander Knox (1757–1831). A remarkably unworldly man, Knox had been private secretary to Lord Castlereagh before the Union, and had been a brilliant writer of position papers, but was unable to master filing things or, indeed, how to ride a horse. He settled into a life of advocacy of semi-mystical churchmanship: he had an appreciation of John Wesley and, in a massively impractical prospectus, pro-

14 *CDIB* entries for Edward Pennefather and Richard Pennefather; Malcomson (2002), 291.

pounded the joining together of the Greek Catholic Church and the Church of Ireland. Although preternaturally shy, he was one of those rare people who inspire trust, imagination, and devoted friendship: six years after his death four very large volumes of his essays and letters were put into print, and they are rare in their clarity and readability.[15]

Crucially, just as the estates of the eastern side of County Wicklow were carefully massaged pieces of topography, so too were the spiritual landscapes of the great and the good. Consider just two of many available descriptions of these manicured evangelical palatinates:

> The beautiful county of Wicklow, abounding in resident gentry, and possessing a fine body of Protestant yeomanry, was studded with good ministers, between whom and the wealthy laity much cordiality of feeling and community of action existed. The Rev. William Cleaver, a Christ Church Oxonian, and the son of the late Archbishop, held the parish of Delgany, a gem of rural beauty, made up of landscape contributions from sea, and valley, and forest, and down, and mountain. He was a scholar, and a refined gentleman in mind and bearing, and united in himself things that were 'true, and just, and pure, and honest, and lovely' in a singular degree.
>
> … In the next parish – beautiful and romantic Powerscourt – resided Robert Daly … a man of strong sense, thorough inflexibility of principle, and singular honesty of purpose.

15 *CDIB* entry for Alexander Knox. The four-volume collection of Knox's letters and writings was anonymously edited by James J. Hornby, as *Remains of Alexander Knox, Esq.* (London 1834–37). It was in a third edition by 1844. As early as 1803 we find Knox living primarily in Bellevue, although he had rooms in Dawson Street, Dublin, as well. See Knox to Thomas Stedman, ___1803, in vol. 4, 134–7, in which he says "It was because Mrs. La Touche deemed me religious that she wished so much to have me here" (136). Sometime in the 1830s, Robert Daly told Archbishop Richard Whately that he had sat at the feet of this "Gamaliel," but that he had rejected the erroneous doctrines of Knox, which Daly believed were close to those later put forward by the Tractarians in England. (Mrs Hamilton Madden, *Memoir of the Late Right Rev. Robert Daly* [London 1875], 34).

FIGURE 4.1 POWERSCOURT WATERFALL.

> Powerscourt under its rector became a model parish, in which Dissent was scarcely to be found.[16]

That is the way things looked in memory to the Rev. Richard Sinclair Brooke, who had spent his early career in Ireland before taking an English parish. The following picture, focused more tightly on Powerscourt parish, has the same character, being the religious equivalent of a hand-tinted postcard of a sublime, albeit slightly touristy, view:

> Over Lord Powerscourt's tenantry, Mr Daly exercised a most salutory influence, and was greatly beloved by them. The Buckleys, Burtons, Evanses, etc., were most regular in their attendance at church; and as many of their farms were located

16 Richard Sinclair Brooke, *Recollections of the Irish Church* (London 1877), 19–20.

FIGURE 4.2 ENNISKERRY.

The designer-village established by the Viscounts Powerscourt and completed shortly before the death of the fifth viscount in 1823.

under the mountain, at the back of Powerscourt demesne, the situation of the old church was convenient to them. They had perfect liberty to walk and drive through the demesne, and to put up their horse in the stable-yard belonging to the house, which was quite near.[17] It was indeed a pleasing sight on the Sabbath day, morning and evening, to see all the avenues of this beautiful demesne traversed by persons of all classes going to the house of God, the elevating and softening influence of the beauties of nature helping to lead the mind to holy thoughts.[18]

17 Madden (1875), 51–2. This describes the situation in the time of the Fifth and Sixth Viscounts Powerscourt. Mrs Madden tactfully omits the fact that the seventh viscount became fed up with the sturdy yeomen tramping through his demesne and had the church torn down in 1859 and rebuilt nearby the village of Enniscorthy.

18 Ibid., 52.

Not much of this was reality: the mountains were full of Catholics, most of whom little more than two decades earlier would have been pleased to see the sturdy Protestant yeomanry and the gentry and aristocracy burned to a crisp. Most of Dalyland was illusion, well managed, nicely arranged, deftly presented, and nothing wrong with that. Yet for those who could not understand that illusion is an art form to be enjoyed, the ground of Dalyland was, like tundra, the source of a delusive sense of security. But seductive, entirely.

During these "missing years," John Nelson Darby got saved: most likely in 1820 or 1821, although that is not entirely certain. Of course his conversion could have happened any place, but it was more apt to occur in a community of believers, especially Dalyland, than among the clattering glasses of lawyers' dinners. Darby's conversion took a form characteristic of Irish Anglican evangelicals of his era. Granted, saying that he "got saved" is an anachronistic transatlantic howler, but putting it that way provides an opportunity to emphasize a point made earlier: that conversion among the early Anglican evangelicals in the British Isles usually was a deeply spiritual experience, but much slower than we are accustomed to associate with the lightening-bolt conversions that occurred in the great crowd-driven religious revivals of the past – or those of the present day. Those conversions are associated with altar-calls and come-to-Jesus-moments, not the sort of thing the Anglo-Irish upper classes would embrace. Recall that the Rev. Robert Daly had gradually been converted through his own reading and self-discipline, after becoming an Anglican priest: not before and not with any fanfare. Much of the muffled quality of early Irish evangelical conversion is ascribable to social class: the genteel classes and their imitators were not willing to flail about in public at moments of spiritual vulnerability – although when converted they were willing to argue stoutly, like true gentlemen, for the new principles they came to embrace. If one is willing to think in terms of geometry: whereas swift revivalist conversion can be represented by a line that suddenly is changed from running in one direction to another vector entirely, the conversions one finds in early Irish Anglicanism more often take the shape of a constant-radius arc that over a certain distance gently ceases to move in one direction and takes another path. In the former case, the date, indeed even the moment, of conversion is memorable and often is cited by the spiritually newborn. In the second instance, the change is equally real, but the person who has been converted cannot quite pinpoint when it occurred.

Add to this the fact that the early generation of Anglican evangelicals in Ireland had a socially derived inhibition against rabbiting on about their own sins that had preceded their individual conversions – the vivid self-description of their own pre-conversion sinfulness that became a stock in trade of many later evangelical preachers was beyond the bounds of good taste for the serious Protestant Christians of Dalyland. Hence, the thin memory that John Nelson Darby preserved of his own conversion is not quite as strange as it might first appear, but it is indeed maddeningly imprecise. Late in life, in the margins of a specially bound set of study Bibles, he wrote that he had "loved Christ, I have no doubt sincerely and growingly since June or July, 1820, or 21. I forget which."[19] Note the vague dating.[20] Probably this conversion marked the start of a period of wrestling with the existence of a religious vocation. "In my own case, I went through deep exercise of soul before there was a trace of peace, and it was not till after six or seven years that I was delivered."[21] That fits nicely with Darby's period of intense self-reflection that runs into 1827–28, which resulted in his withdrawing from his work as a parish priest and becoming a self-declared Pauline missionary. The 1820s were a period of religious turmoil for a young man who had a life to invest and who desperately cast about for direction; at certain moments, the process easily could have been recalled as one long blur. Darby's longtime colleague and editor of his

19 The entire long piece of marginalia is usefully reproduced in Weremchuk, 204–6, appendix C. The set of Darby's study New Testaments now are in CBA, J.N.D./3/2–5. See esp. J.N.D./3/5.

20 Also note that Darby does not credit any particular person with leading him to God's path. He does refer to the essays of the Rev. Thomas Scott as being helpful, but the reference is to his spiritual development after conversion, not before.

21 J.N.D. to ____, 1874, *LJND*, vol. 2, no. 196. The letter is translated from the original French by an unknown hand, probably William Kelly.

letters, the Rev. William Kelly, believed that Darby had been converted "when a barrister."[22] The certainty is that the early 1820s were a time of intense internal spiritual work on the part of John Nelson Darby. And, being John Nelson Darby, he did not wish to share details.[23]

Without being simplistic about Darby's silence (he was a very complicated man indeed, and rarely understandable by a single, simple explanation), we should mention that there were good reasons for his not wishing to remember too precisely what took place in the early 1820s: secular events associated with the comfortable and graceful figures of Dalyland's evangelical elite were of a disturbingly worldly nature that Darby, later grown into a grave and ascetic religious leader, would inevitably recall with discomfort. In chapter 2, we saw that the spring of 1822 had been a period of public humiliation for the Dalyland evangelicals, because of the buggery scandal involving Percy Jocelyn, bishop of Clogher. This raw humiliation melded with a procession of other secular events that under different circumstances would have

22 Weremchuk, 34 and 233n27, cites the *Kelly Letters*, 22 June 1899. His usage here is doubly misleading. (1) *Pace* Weremchuk's citation, there is no printed version of the Kelly letters that any other historian has yet found, including Kelly's biographer. There is, instead, a collection of letters of the Rev. William Kelly in the CBA. It mostly consists of photocopies of a typescript of some of Kelly's letters made by E.B. Dolamore in the 1940s. These had been held by Edwin Cross, the Brethren publisher of the firm Chapter Two. The location of the original letters is not at present known. (2) The letter by Kelly says that "Mr Darby was converted when a barrister," which would have meant after he took the degree of barrister in early 1822. Weremchuk ascribes an additional statement to Kelly, "a barrister (or studying to be one)," which would cover any period from 1815 to 1824 and, then, somehow he says that Kelly thus "confirmed the correctness of the 1820/21 date" (Weremchuk, 34).

23 The most sensible summation of the situation is that of Timothy C.F. Stunt: "In the absence of any more specific details of his conversion, we may perhaps reasonably conclude that it was an experience in which submission to God and a decision to follow the Saviour were the principle elements" (Stunt, "Influences in the Early Development of J.N. Darby," in Gribben and Stunt [2004], 49).

been triumphs, but instead were plastered with the smut and ashes of vain flummery of worldly excess – at least if one chose a career of saintliness, as did John Nelson Darby.

For example, we can take as genuine the conversion to evangelical Anglicanism in 1818–19 of Richard Wingfield, Fifth Viscount Powerscourt, under the influence of the Rev. Robert Daly; and we can accept the depth of Lord Powerscourt's grief when his first wife, Frances Theodosia Jocelyn, died of tuberculosis in 1820 at age twenty-five. Equally, the highly eligible young widower (he was born in 1790) can only have been chuffed to learn in the spring of 1821 that the newly crowned George IV would be making a state visit to Ireland and would like to see the Powerscourt estate. Also, Viscount Powerscourt was to be given a representative Irish peerage in the United Kingdom parliament and hence a seat in the House of Lords, and that certainly would enhance his political prestige and influence.

The new king was especially interested in seeing the estate's 400-foot waterfall. So the Viscount had his men build a viewing platform; to be sure that George IV would have something really spectacular to see, he planned to dam the Dargle above the waterfall. Then, when his majesty was in proper viewing position, estate workers would pull out the tranches of the dam, one after another, so that a truly massive cascade continued in train as long as royalty was taking in the view.

All that construction was being hastily completed while the highly successful and gloriously ridiculous twenty-two day Irish royal tour was taking place from 12 August to 3 September 1821. Although George IV had acceded to the throne in late January 1820, his coronation had been put off for a variety of reasons, not least his continuing adultery case against his estranged and very strange wife, Caroline of Brunswick-Wolfenbuttel. Only in January 1821 did she agree to accept £50,000 a year as hush money from parliament and to renounce her privileges and position as Queen consort: not exactly a divorce, but close enough. Even so, she tried to gatecrash the coronation at Westminster Abbey on 19 July. Turned away, she attempted to poison herself and then conveniently died on 7 August 1821.

Conveniently: because George IV was already scheduled to arrive at Howth on 12 August. He had left London on the sixth and was slowly progressing toward Ireland. The king had no intention of attending her

FIGURE 4.3 KINGSTOWN PIER.

Begun in 1817, the pier made possible the harbour's development as a regular cross-channel terminus and, later, as a railway connection point.

funeral.[24] The not-grieving royal widower arrived in Ireland and spent the first five days "in private" at the vice-regal lodge in the Phoenix Park. Actually, most of his time was spent with his latest infatuation, Elizabeth, marchioness of Conyngham who, like the king, was in her fifties and heavy enough to threaten the bedposts. The king emerged from his porcine fornicating on the seventeenth and there followed a fortnight-plus of public ceremonies. These included his appearing in public with so many shamrocks around his head that he resembled

24 The classic contextualization of the "Queen Caroline Affair" is that of Élie Halévy who had the dual advantage of being French and Jewish and of perceiving how bizarre the English could be. See vol. 2 of his six-volume *A History of the English People in the Nineteenth Century* (London 1961; orig. ed. 1923), 84–105.

FIGURE 4.4 KINGSTOWN HARBOUR AND OBELISK.

Dunleary was renamed Kingstown in honour of the Irish visit of George IV in 1821. The obelisk is intended to mark the spot where he stepped ashore.

a topiary; cringe-making protestations of loyalty from all quarters, most notably from Daniel O'Connell; and the renaming of Dunleary as "Kingstown," an appellation that lasted until the creation of the Irish Free State. During this time, the king managed to get four nights at Slane Castle with his portly mistress.

Meanwhile, Viscount Powerscourt, who still in good conscience could recite the prayers for the royal family in the Book of Common Prayer, was looking forward to his own royal moment. Powerscourt waterfall was to be the last stop before the king left Ireland from the newly named Kingstown. On Sunday 2 September 1821, George IV listened to a sermon at the Chapel Royal in Dublin Castle and then was scheduled to be taken smartly to Powerscourt. He dawdled, however, and there are few large mammals harder to hurry than a dissolute monarch. So he arrived late. Just as well. At the time he was scheduled

FIGURE 4.5 POWERSCOURT WATERFALL, NEAR ROYAL PLATFORM.

The bridge is close to the location of the royal viewing platform where George IV would have encountered the ill-planned flood resulting from the Fifth Viscount Powerscourt's meddling with natural hydraulics.

to be on the viewing platform, Lord Powerscourt's inexperience with hydraulics became clear. The men in charge released the pent-up Dargle, and it came with such a rush that the entire royal platform was violently washed away.[25] That was one of the last events on the royal *opera buffa* tour of southern Ireland.

Then the farce turned briefly to dignified felicity and then sadly and quickly into tragedy. Viscount Powerscourt became attentive to one of the most hyper-evangelical souls in all of Ireland, Theodosia Howard, niece of the earl of Wicklow. She was his neighbour and a cousin of his late first wife. A convert of the Rev. Robert Daly, she eventually became a necessary and influential link in the story of evangelicalism worldwide, most especially the branch that emphasized millennialism. In June 1822, they married.

On 9 August 1823, Viscount Powerscourt died from causes unrecorded. He had been in declining health since the spring of 1823,[26] and near the end it was reported that he had been deranged for a time.[27] He left a seven-year-old son and a twenty-two-year-old widow and one of the most prestigious estates in Ireland. His widow became widely known as "good Lady Powerscourt" and more formally she adopted the courtesy title of Viscountess Powerscourt or Theodosia Lady Powerscourt. (She was not in strict law the Dowager Viscountess Powerscourt, as there were two Powerscourt widows from earlier generations who took precedence.) Theodosia was deeply spiritual, unreserved

25 Constantia Maxwell's *A History of Trinity College, Dublin* (Dublin 1946) has a long summary (231–5) of an anonymous eyewitness pamphlet chronicling the royal visit and sizable extracts from the acerbic journal of a strongly loyalist TCD graduate (275–8). Turtle Bunbury's article, "George IV's Royal Visit to Ireland," is a well-documented recent summary: www.turtlebunbury.com/history_georgeiv.htm (accessed 28 November 2011).

26 Robert Daly to Viscountess Powerscourt, 25 March 1823, reproduced in Madden (1875), 77–81. The couple had left Ireland for health reasons, one guesses to a southern clime such as Madeira (where the viscount's first wife had been taken before her demise). Daly notes in his letter to Lady Powerscourt that he has arranged for substitutes to step in and take over the Sunday School classes that each of the couple usually taught.

27 John David to Anne La Touche, June 1823, quoted in Turtle Bunbury, *The Landed Gentry and Aristocracy of County Wicklow* (Dublin 2005), 70.

in expressing her religious opinions, and ever-willing to take in new ideas about the nature of the Church and of biblical prophecy. In her volatile way, in the later 1820s and 1830s she became as influential in Dalyland as Lady Harriet Daly earlier had been in her carefully calculated manner.

The narrative of the main events on the Powerscourt estate in the years 1821–23 is not a parable. The events were real. Yet, certain aspects do serve as a parallel to the fortunes of the evangelical cadre of the Church of Ireland in the years between the end of the Napoleonic Wars and the mid-1830s: the achievement of advantageous social arrangements; the hubris of trying to create and control a natural phenomenon; the disinclination to separate reality and illusion; and ultimately the necessity of dealing with disaster that, like death, comes swiftly, calling on silent feet.

Most readers of Irish history perceive the 1820s as the decade of the great drum roll for Catholic Ireland, and rightly so. This period is caught almost perfectly by Sean O'Faolain's *King of the Beggars: A Life of Daniel O'Connell*, which appeared in 1938. Decades after its publication the book still takes one's breath away in its mixture of hard-headed observation and perfectly apposite lyricism. There are scores of other more recent discussions that cover the political rise of Catholic Ireland and Catholic Emancipation, and several of these are excellent. What O'Faolain has that is unique is, on the one hand, a big-picture sensibility that gives his writing the same unfashionable sweep (in modern academic eyes) one finds in Edward Gibbon's histories; and, on the other hand, an ability to provide to the reader a portal into the mind not only of the Liberator but also of individual members of the peasantry and the fallen gentry who by a mixture of courage and low cunning had kept their complex Hiberno-Anglo culture alive during the long winter of the anti-Catholic penal laws. O'Faolain is right: it was Daniel O'Connell in the 1820s who brought the Irish Catholics off their knees and taught them to march as a nation.[28] This liberation

28 Sean O'Faolain, *King of the Beggars: A Life of Daniel O'Connell* (London 1938).

process was the background reality of the 1820s, and it, more than anything else, determined the path of the Church of Ireland for the rest of the nineteenth century.

Yet, a lot was going on in the 1820s besides Catholic Emancipation. One reality was the messy matter of a sectarian contest that was fought outside the political arena between evangelicals and the Catholic bishops and clergy. Among the prizes were souls: many, many souls. Irene Whelan's *The Bible War in Ireland* (2005) is a sharp and readable study of this conflict.[29] Curiously, when it appeared, it was reviewed relatively rarely and has not yet been built into Irish historiography: I think that such neglect should sensitize us to the danger of permitting the dominant political narrative to shove the religious conflict aside. Of course religious discourse and politics did not exist in completely separate compartments, but vital religious differences within Ireland had an integrity of difference that was not dependent upon politics – although politics certainly came into play in expressing those differences.

Considering for the moment only the Anglican side of the equation, the Church was a professionally religious institution with a wide variety of personnel and a set of lay adherents who ranged from indifferent to enthusiastic, so any set of generalizations excludes outliers. But, generalizations are necessary. I believe that in the years from 1815 to the mid-1830s we can legitimately infer from the words and behaviour of those who cared a bit about the Church (meaning clergy who actually lived in their parishes and laymen who turned up for service more than twice a year) that there were three overlapping mentalities in play: a realistic sense that accepted improvement in efficiency in delivering pastoral services to the Church of Ireland population as necessary and not very painful except to the most indolent of clergy; a second mindset, held mostly by evangelicals, who were pushing for greater spirituality, and were willing to live with the knowledge that any set of goals had to be slightly beyond reach and thus intentionally employed as motivating illusions; and a third mentality, one that was delusional,

29 Irene Whelan, *The Bible War in Ireland: The "Second Reformation" and the Polarization of Protestant-Catholic Relations, 1800–1840* (Dublin and Madison 2005).

which embraced with fervour the idea that the Irish religious world actually could become a New Jerusalem.

The New Jerusalem was to be a four-walled structure: (1) the Church of Ireland would become a true national church representing the Irish moral component of the new Union of Great Britain and Ireland; (2) a new relationship with the state would be forged wherein antiquated privileges would be surrendered by the Church in turn for its being given increased resources from the state for specific tasks that related to the moral welfare of the Irish people; (3) a great number of adult Catholics would convert to the Anglican form of Protestantism; and (4) the most important instrument of the new national spiritual reign of the Church of Ireland would be the control of the minds of the young. It is this New Jerusalem mindset that, under the torsion and acute disappointment of the 1820s and early 1830s, yielded the phenomenon that we can call the Wicklow Brethren and ultimately the Irish stem that begins the so-called Plymouth Brethren. That, however, is an aeon later in ontological time; many things had to happen before the Brethren emerged.

In the long sweep of post-Reformation Irish history the idea that the Anglican Church could become the true national Church of Ireland and that a large minority, maybe even a majority, of Roman Catholics would convert to Protestantism seems just plain crazy. But every big delusion has within it a kernel of reality and usually a touch of consciously artful illusion – and an individual does not have to be crazed to become convinced of a crazy set of ideas. There existed a bundle of social and pragmatic realities that when stacked a certain way – and then reinforced by institutional propaganda and by local enthusiasm, social pressure, and religious activism – allowed serious believers to swaddle themselves in the New Jerusalem ideas. These people were not individually loopy: just very wrong in their collective view of the realities of Irish life. It is not perverse to suggest that the most fervent and optimistic and (inevitably, highly sectarian)[30] of the Church of

30 In this study, "sectarian" is used in the modern Irish sense of the term, meaning unthinking anti-Catholicism or anti-Protestantism. The point is worth making because in the nineteenth century "sectarian" and its derivatives (such as "sectary") was sometimes used by Anglicans to refer to Dissenters,

Ireland's clergy and laity actually had some accurate information that could be arranged so as to channel their thinking to a set of communal beliefs that when twisted a certain way were indeed delusional: because the accurate ideas were presented bereft of realistic context and thus became untrue.

What were these accurate apperceptions, the ones which could be misread as meaning a bright sunrise for the Church of Ireland? First, it is undeniable that from the 1790s onward, the Church of Ireland was becoming better at serving the Anglican community.[31] For example, the number of churches increased from 1,001 in 1787 (a good base date, thanks to the contemporary investigations of Daniel Beaufort)[32] to 1,293 in 1832, an increase of close to 30 percent. In the same period, the number of benefices grew by almost 25 percent. Not only were there more benefices for clergy, but the proportion of charges without a church dropped: from 10.6 percent to 7.4 percent. Equally importantly, the practice of the minister residing within his benefice continually increased: from 46.4 percent in 1806 to 65.2 percent in 1819 to 74.8 percent in 1832. In part this was because the bishops, encouraged strongly by the secular authorities, became stricter in enforcing residence, and in part because a number of glebe houses for the clergy to live in grew from 354 in 1787 to 829 in 1832. And there was a remarkable increase in the number of ordained clergy serving the Church of Ireland: 1,253 in 1806 and 1,977 in 1826, an increase of 57.8 percent. These numbers lie very still and cold, but to church loyalists in the first decades of the nineteenth century, they were the adumbration of an exciting fact: as an institution their church was growing; it was on the march.

Secondly, serious evangelicals recognized, rightly, the presence of more and more clergy and laity like themselves within the Church, and many others that were ripe for turning. This is a prediction that

---

and it was often used by Brethren to refer to individuals who belonged to any of the extant denominations, by which the Brethren referred to anyone other than themselves. For a thoughtful consideration of the term, see Joseph Liechty, "The Problem of Sectarianism and the Church of Ireland," in Ford, McGuire, and Milne, eds. (1995), 204–22, 278–9.

31 Data for the statements that follow and the primary sources are found in my *The Church of Ireland* (New Haven 1971), 112–31.

32 Daniel Beaufort, *Memoir of a Map of Ireland* (London 1792).

says: "there will be more of us because there already are more of us." It is one way that movements, secular or religious, grow: through self-belief and self-promotion.

Thirdly, the United Kingdom government was putting bigger and bigger dollops of money directly into the Church of Ireland. The straight-ahead payments were primarily to the wonderfully named Board of First Fruits. The pre-Reformation origin of the term was that the first year's income from a bishopric, dignity, or benefice was paid – as "first fruits" – to Rome. In other words, a tax. By the late eighteenth century in Ireland its incidence had been turned around completely, and the Board of First Fruits became a conduit by which parliament gave money to the Church of Ireland to build churches and glebe houses. The amounts involved after the Union were substantial: between the Union and the end of the year 1822, more than £1,020,000 passed through the board's hands, a noteworthy sum of money that overwhelmingly went for capital investment in churches and clergy residences: this at a time when the annual total net income of all the bishops, dignitaries, and beneficed clergy was roughly £702,000.[33] The United Kingdom government's spending on Irish churches and clergy residences, items that put an increasing number of Anglican clergy in local parishes, had a variety of motivations, but undeniably among these was the belief that this was a cost of improving social order in Ireland.

Fourthly, a sympathetic contemporary observer of the Church of Ireland would have been pleased to see that the state was providing the Church with ever-larger amounts of money in what would today be termed "cross subsidies." That is, the United Kingdom government paid for some social services in a manner that the Church could easily cash in on. Mostly, this was in the form of school aid, a matter discussed below. Here, however, as an example of a less-than-obvious form of government expenditures that was trawled up by the Church, is the case of the Foundling Hospital in Dublin. Founded in 1704, from the era of Jonathan Swift onward, the hospital (meaning a refuge, not a medical hospital) had been a source of scandal, benevolence, and a depressing indicator of the helpless poverty at the bottom end of the

33 Akenson, *Church of Ireland*, 83–7, 113–19.

Irish social scale. In 1798 it had been reformed and was supervised by nine Protestant governors. The hospital had a variety of side activities (mostly educational), but its main purpose was, indeed, to deal with foundlings. These were not, as later was suggested, mostly the product of out-of-wedlock births, but for the most part were from families that could not afford to feed another child. In the first two decades of the nineteenth century, roughly one-third of the infants were "left in" by their mothers; one-eighth by their fathers, and the rest were foundlings in the most literal sense: "children that were exposed," meaning infants left out to die or dumped on the doorstep of a Catholic priest, Protestant minister, or gentry house. These infants were brought in by a variety of benevolent persons of both faiths. The largest number (roughly one-third) originated in Dublin City and Dublin County, but the rest were from all over Ireland with only the far west being sharply unrepresented. Two thousand or so children were left-in each year. That babies who had been left unfed by their parents were in danger of starvation was obvious, which makes the necessity of one of the reforms of 1798 so questionable: efforts at "artificial feeding" were replaced by the tried-and-true employment of wet nurses. These were women from Wicklow (the greatest number), Kildare, and Carlow. They were paid £3 a year to feed and foster a child, and if the baby survived its first year they received a £2 bonus. The women fostered the children in their own homes. After the first year they were to show up at the hospital at a specific date and if the child were alive they would be paid another £3 annually. This continued until ages five to eight, and at one of the annual inspections the child would be taken back and put into education at the hospital and then "apprenticed," which usually meant sent into service, not any artisanal work. (The exceptions were the smartest, most biddable, and luckiest children who were apprenticed to schoolmasters and sometimes came to head their own primary schools.) The whole system was out of control, and the hospital authorities could not even distinguish in their records between the large proportion of foundlings who had died from those whom the foster mother had refused to return and who had thus become part of her family (actually these were the children who were winners in this system) or from those who, when old enough, had simply absconded: the hospital managers could account for about one-fifth of those who passed through their hands between 1796 and 1825. This was a disaster, but a lucrative one. To take 1820 as an example, the Dublin Foundling Hospital's annual budget was £40,814, of which £32,500 came from a parliamentary grant. From the perspective of the present study, the point is that an opportunistic churchman could see that further reform of the hospital was necessary and simultaneously perceive it as an easy chance to continue to keep government money under a Protestant (overwhelmingly Anglican) governing board and to use it to gain souls: for example, by no longer allowing Catholic women to be foster mothers and to require that all the foundling children who survived to school age be educated as Protestants under the examining eye of the parish clergyman. The keener evangelicals were pressing for these changes in the early 1820s and had a realistic expectation of winning.[34]

The Foundling Hospital is merely a single example of cross-subsidization by the government of Protestant-controlled institutions, and there are many others. For example, the management, and at minimum the chaplaincies, of penitentiaries, reformatories, and homes for "profligate" women were funded by the state, yet largely controlled by the Church.

A massive arena of opportunity involved mass education. Emphatically, Irish schooling in this period of history was not necessarily sectarian; even less was it inevitable that it be a form of proselytizing. But in the perception of those who believed that the Church of Ireland could become a true national church and could assimilate the bulk of the Irish population to Protestantism – all the while acquiring large grants of government monies – the schools were a bright ray of hope. Since the Reformation there had been sporadic and inefficient and poorly funded attempts at putting "parish schools" in each benefice in the country. This was essentially a defensive measure designed to protect

34 38 Geo 3, cap 35 (Irish statutes); Fred Powell, "Dean Swift and the Dublin Foundling Hospital," *Studies: An Irish Quarterly Review* (summer/autumn 1981), 162–70; Joseph Robins, *The Lost Children: A Study of Charity Children in Ireland* (Dublin 1980), 15–44; *Papers Relating to the Foundling Hospital in Dublin,* H.C. 1824 (281), xxi, passim; *Third Report of the Commissioners of Irish Education Inquiry,* 1–156, H.C. 1826–27 (13), xii. One should note that neither Robert Daly nor James Digges La Touche, each of whom testified before the commission, approved of the foundling system.

the English language and customs against a native Irish revanche and against English settlers going native. As the security of the conquest increased, the focus changed to emphasizing the advancement of the Protestant religion. The parish schools were clearly identified as proselytizing agencies, and the better-off Catholics avoided them, although the education-hungry members of the lower classes did not. In 1823, there were 782 parish schools, containing 36,408 children, of whom 15,303 were Catholic. Typically, these schools ran on about £10 a year in the combined benevolence of the local Church of Ireland minister and the local landlords and were held in a cabin or in the better-off parishes in one or two-room schoolhouses. Parents paid pennies per month. The scale of the parish school system was small – Ireland had a population of more than six million in the early 1820s – but it indicated a hunger for education among the peasantry.[35]

The "Charter Schools," so called because they were the product of a private charity founded in 1717, received in 1733 a royal charter as the "Incorporated Society in Dublin for Promoting English Protestant Schools in Ireland." At first the society's efforts depended on private charity, and then parliamentary grants were obtained. The schools were of dubious quality and were run as boarding schools based on the "transplantation" principle. Children, mostly Catholics, were taken from their homes and sent away to learn basic literacy, Protestant religion, and hard manual labour. If the children did well when they left school they were "apprenticed" to a Protestant master and success was declared. The actual numbers were small – 2,150 children were enrolled in thirty-four of these boarding schools in 1824 – yet the parliamentary grant was very large: it reached its apogee at £38,000 in 1818.[36] It

35 Irish statutes: 28 Henry VIII, cap. 15; 7 Will. III, cap. 4; 8 Geo I, cap. 12; 5 Geo II, cap. 4; *Report from the Commissioners of the Board of Education in Ireland: Eleventh Report, Parish Schools,* passim, H.C. 1810–11 (107), vi. *First Report of the Commissioners of Irish Education Inquiry: Appendix,* 14–15, H.C. 1825 (400), xii. There are several good modern histories of seventeenth- and eighteenth-century Ireland that give the broad background on the parish schools and parallel efforts. A convincing and nuanced discussion of religious issues is Sean Connolly, *Divided Kingdom: Ireland 1630–1800* (Oxford 2008).

36 *Report from the Commissioners of the Board of Education in Ireland, Third Report: The Protestant Charter Schools,* passim, H.C. 1809 (142), vii; *A*

was this level of governmental largesse that made shrewd evangelicals believe that if they could crowd out the Charter Schools, the monies could be turned to forming a nationwide system of state education under Church of Ireland control. (Dominated as the Anglican evangelicals were by County Wicklow and County Dublin interests, they were always a bit vague about what they would do about the Presbyterians in the north of Ireland.)

There existed a vehicle that, if subverted, could work nicely: the "Society for Promoting the Education of the Poor in Ireland," which was known generally and in most official documents as the "Kildare Place Society." Founded in 1811, it was genuinely liberal in affirming that the education of the Irish poor was necessary and that it could only be accomplished if a network of schools were created "divested of all sectarian distinctions in Christianity." The Bible was read in the Kildare Place schools, but without interpretation; in the early nineteenth century that worked fairly well, as the school time was religiously neutral, but, by silent concordat, clergy of both major faiths were allowed to teach in the school building after hours: not ideal, but acceptable to both sides as long as no one became too aggressive. The Kildare Place Society wedded private support to state funding and by 1821 was receiving £10,000 a year from parliament, operating 513 schools with well over 51,000 pupils on the rolls, and growing quickly. In fact, trouble was already in train due to keen evangelicals using the schools to proselytize, but that was obscured by the belief (realistic, it turned out) that the number of schools could triple within five years and so too could the parliamentary grant. If manipulated properly (meaning away from its original religious neutrality), the Kildare Place system would be a key to catching the minds of the Catholic young.[37]

Statement of the Grants Voted by Parliament on Account of Miscellaneous Services for Ireland in 1818, 1, H.C. 1819 (515), xv. The full history is found in Kenneth Milne, *The Irish Charter Schools* (Dublin 1997).

37 The Kildare Place Society evolved after 1831 into being solely a training college. That is the primary focus of Susan M. Parkes, *Kildare Place: The History of the Church of Ireland Teaching College* (Dublin 1984). See also the discussion and references in the same author's *A Guide to Sources for the History of Irish Education* (Dublin 2010), esp. 30–4.

Finally, the New Jerusalem enthusiasts were emboldened by the kinetic energy generated by a tangle of ginger groups that, whatever the differences in their agendas, were dedicated to promoting some form of Protestantism (not necessarily Anglicanism) in Ireland. A skeletal list: the Association for Discountenancing Vice and Promoting the Knowledge and Practice of the Christian Religion (founded 1792, and later referred to as the APCK, the Association for Promoting Christian Knowledge); the British and Foreign Bible Society (founded 1804), with an auxiliary, the Hibernian Bible Society, often called simply "the Bible Society" (founded 1808); the London Hibernian Society (founded 1806 by Congregationalists); the Sunday School Society for Ireland (a union of local societies, founded 1809); the Baptist Society for Promoting the Gospel in Ireland (founded 1814); the Irish Society for Promoting the Education of the Native Irish through the Medium of their Own Language (founded 1818, usually called "the Irish Society"). And there were several other groups as well. From 1815 onward such bodies were growing in activity level and in financial resources, mostly private subscriptions. (The APCK received governmental grants for its schools.) Further, various English mission groups episodically ran branch operations in Ireland. These several groups overlapped and the relationships resembled a pile of electric eels, being hard to follow individually but yielding surges of energy collectively.

We have here an instance of practices and policies (six forms of which are discussed above) that in each case has a level of primary verifiability, for each existed and we can do a financial and behavioural audit of all of them. Nevertheless, when contemporary Irish Anglican adherents joined together apperceptions of these realities, the result was a massively unrealistic belief system. That is because a perception may be accurate in a narrow sense, but for it to be true a perception must be not only exact and true to itself but also accurately affixed to the context in which it is found. Those who deeply embraced the beliefs that the Church of Ireland could become the true national Church of Ireland and that large numbers of Catholics could be converted to Protestantism were effectively delusional. They forcefully occluded from their own viewpoint the relevant Irish context by which each of their apperceptions was surrounded, namely that the Roman Catholic Church was rising like a Leviathan from Ireland's eighteenth-century penal laws and was forming itself into an entity that could defend itself very effectively, indeed triumphantly. From Anglican blindness followed the intemperate ambition that needed no outside intervention to accomplish its own downfall.

The Bible War effectively was declared 24 October 1822 by William Magee, archbishop of Dublin. That is the opinion of Stewart J. Brown in his Chalmers Lectures, published in 2001, and it is convincing.[38] Magee, who had been translated from the see of Raphoe to the archbishopric of Dublin on 24 June 1822, gave his initial formal charge to his clergy in St Patrick's Cathedral, Dublin. He was nothing if not direct. He believed that his main task was to shape up his clergy, so he sounded like a drill sergeant in canonical garb. Archbishop Magee granted that the church reforms of the previous decades had left the Church of Ireland in the best shape it had ever been. However, his goal was that: "We should prove ourselves to be the genuine ministers of that APOSTOLICAL and CATHOLIC church which has descended to us freed from the abuses of antiquated error; and present ourselves to the world, as worthy depositaries of the sacred trust committed to our keeping."[39]

38 Stewart J. Brown, *The National Churches of England, Ireland, and Scotland* (Oxford 2001), pp. 93–4. An alternative dating is that of Alan Acheson: "Sharing the faith with Roman Catholics gave rise to developments known as the 'Second Reformation.' The phrase is generally attributed to William Magee, though what the archbishop had said, essentially, in 1825 was 'in truth, with respect to Ireland, the reformation may only now be said to have begun'" (*A True and Lively Faith*, 1992, 24; all subsequent references to Acheson's history of the Church are to his general history, 2nd ed., 2002. The Rev. Dr Acheson's PhD thesis, "The Evangelicals in the Church of Ireland, 1784–1859," Queen's University of Belfast 1967, is the essential background to his general history of the Church).

39 William Magee, *The Collected Works of the Most Reverend William Magee*, two vols, A.H. Kenney, ed. (London 1842); the quotation is from "A Charge Delivered at His Primary Visitation," vol. 2, 440–1, emphasis in the original.

As a very exact churchman, Archbishop Magee believed strongly in the supervisory power of a bishop over his clergy; he told them in unambiguous terms that henceforth they were to reside in their parishes and that they would be allowed to be non-resident or to have curates assist them in their duties only with his permission. He said he would no longer accept new clergy ordained for his archdiocese by anyone other than himself. The Anglican clergy were to act and dress like priests, not like country gentleman, and they were not to encourage the new fashion of the faithful going about and listening to sermons here and there. In part, Magee was trying to sort out the mess that had been created during the lunatic decade of Archbishop Euseby Cleaver, who had died in December 1819. He had been replaced for a two-year period by Lord John George Bereseford, who turned out to be a surprisingly good administrator (surprising because the several Beresfords who held benefices over the years were not distinguished by attention to duty), but he had been translated to Armagh before he could do much real improvement.

The trouble with Magee's parade-ground barking at his clergy was that as a theologian (he was a nimble one, actually)[40] he felt the need to wrap his pragmatic directions for clerical performance in his own theology, which yielded the conclusion that as a group the clergy were "fearful of incurring the charge of bigotry" if they contended "for the *apostolical origin and succession of the Christian ministry;* the only ground on which the just rights of the church can be maintained."[41] Then, in probably the most quoted portion of an Irish sermon of the

40 Magee was well-known in England and Ireland for a major two-volume work, *Discourses and Dissertations on the Atonement and Sacrifice*, based on lectures given in 1798 and 1799, and published in 1801. The fourth edition of 1816 is reproduced in Kenney's edition of *The Works of the Most Reverend William Magee*. An anonymous appreciation of Magee's career up to his promotion to the bench of bishops, and particularly the place of his work on the atonement in securing his reputation, is "Gallery of Illustrious Irishmen – no. XV. Wm. Magee, Archbishop of Dublin," *Dublin University Magazine*, vol. 26 (1845), 475–93.

41 Magee, "A Charge Delivered at His Primary Visitation," 444. Emphasis in the original.

nineteenth century, Magee stated: "We, my reverend brethren, are placed in a station in which we are hemmed in by two opposite descriptions of professing Christians: the one, possessing a church, without which *we* can properly call a religion; and the other, possessing religion, without which *we* can properly call a church."[42] These words were being spoken by a man who was easy to dislike on sight, if one were so inclined, and many were: in 1824 Magee wrote to a friend that he feared he would soon be obliged to be armed when he left his episcopal palace.[43] Also, Magee was easy to ridicule. He had a small body and seemingly a large head, and because of a circulatory problem he had to hold himself perfectly erect or he would pass out[44] – something of a handicap for an office that required a fair degree of kneeling, bowing, and reverencing.

In his inaugural charge as archbishop of Dublin Magee had made the distinctions between the Roman Catholic Church and Protestant Dissenters quoted above, and then had continued by saying that, on the one hand, "the one so blindly enslaved to a supposed infallible ecclesiastical authority, as not to seek in the word of God, a reason for the faith they possess; the other, so confident in the infallibility of their individual judgment as to the reasons of their faith, that they deem it their duty to resist all authority in matters of religion." Therefore, he continued: "We, my brethren, are to keep clear of both extremes; and holding the Scriptures as our great charter, whilst we maintain the liberty with which Christ has made us free, we are to submit ourselves to the authority to which he has made us subject."[45]

That last paragraph, citing the scriptures as ultimate authority, was enough to keep the Anglican evangelicals in line, but most of Ireland – 89 percent was non-Anglican – was outside the veil.[46] Arch-

42 Ibid. Emphasis in the original.

43 S. Brown, 96.

44 A.H. Kenney, "Memoir of the Late Most Reverend William Magee, Archbishop of Dublin," in a preface to his edition of William Magee, *Collected Works*, vol. 1 (1842), xxi and xxxi.

45 The quotations are from "A Charge Delivered at His Primary Visitation," 444.

46 See the tabulation of Irish religious distributions, 1834, in Akenson, *Church of Ireland*, 165, table 34; 8 percent were Presbyterian, less than 1 percent other-Dissenters, and 81 percent Roman Catholic.

bishop Magee genuinely believed that "the established Church in Ireland now had the potential to succeed where the sixteenth century Reformation had failed; there was a real opportunity to unite the Irish people within the true Protestant faith."[47] Still, even with the most generous of interpretations, it is mysterious that Magee could imagine that the conversion of Ireland would be successful if it began by insulting the largest group in the nation, the Catholics, and then wrote off the most useful extra-Church allies, the Presbyterians, Methodists, and other Dissenters.[48]

That the evangelicals of Dalyland did not reject Archbishop Magee as being excessively exact in his churchmanship (meaning very strong on episcopal authority and unbending in recognizing that the Church's sacraments were one of the conduits of divine grace) is due in part to their being as devoted to the supernal liturgies found in the Book of Common Prayer as he was – and, conversely, to Magee's being as fervently anti-Catholic as most of them were. He was more friendly

47 Brown, 95.

48 This writing-off of non-Anglican Protestants largely explains why the Bible War did not much involve the Presbyterian north and why it was not of much interest to Methodists as a denomination. The Presbyterians in any case did not become a significant evangelical force until the 1830s and 1840s. Although the Methodists were closer to the Established Church in Ireland than they were in England – the mainline Methodists only stopped taking communion in the Church of Ireland in 1816–17, and the Primitives not until 1878 – and although they had their own attempts at converting Irish Catholics, they were not as a denominational group part of the Bible War of the 1820s. That being noted, it is significant that under the leadership of London, the Methodist conference began in 1799 a campaign of subsidizing missionaries to convert Catholics through preaching in the Irish language. The effort made few converts but was a model upon which in 1818 Henry Monck Mason, Robert Daly, William Smythe Guinness, Archbishop Trench, and others founded the Irish Society for the Education of the Native Irish through the Medium of Their Own Language (Whelan, 86–93, 115). I must emphasize that there exists a rich historiographical tradition for both the Irish Methodists and the Irish Presbyterians, each of which is worth reading for its own merits. Starting completely from scratch, I would approach the Irish Methodist tradition through the modern works of David Hempton. Similarly, the recent works of Andrew Holmes are an efficient way to enter the large historical literature of Irish Presbyterianism.

in practice toward evangelical activities than his formal theological positions would imply. For example, he had been one of the earliest supporters of the APCK. As early as 1796, when the association was struggling and he was a young fellow of Trinity College, Dublin, Magee had lauded its members as "a sacred band," leagued together to fight "the giant strides of infidelity."[49] As a fellow and then senior fellow of TCD from 1788 to 1811 he had been popular among students. During the early years when he was heavily engaged in teaching, he had an unusually large number of tutees. When he left TCD he was given a spontaneous gift of silver, not at all a common tribute.[50] His TCD contacts served him well and took some of the harsh edge off his uncomfortable exact disciplinary style. He kept two houses in the south of County Dublin and was well taken socially while at Trinity.

Let us examine two quick examples of Magee's willingness to trim in practical matters as long as his theology remained intact. The first is that in October 1821 his predecessor, Lord John George Beresford, condemned the Hibernian Bible Society[51] (often referred to simply as the Bible Society): his grounds were that it was cooperating too much with Dissenters, primarily Baptists and Congregationalists based in England, and this undercut the state church in Ireland. In a quick row of dominoes, those bishops and archbishops of Ireland who were patrons of the society resigned, all save the evangelical Power le Poer Trench, archbishop of Tuam.[52] Game over? Not at all: the Bible Society was one of the educational-proselytizing darlings of Dalyland. Robert Daly, when advised by Archbishop Beresford to resign from the society, told

49 William Magee, *A Sermon … May 1796* (Dublin 1796), 2.

50 Magee left TCD to become a pluralist, taking two livings under the patronage of the college, one in County Tyrone and the other in County Down. He soon was dean of Cork and then bishop of Raphoe. While a Trinity fellow, Magee had ignored the college statutes and married. He had fifteen children, of whom four of the boys made a career in the Church and three of the girls married clergymen. *CDGBSL; CDIB; ODNB;* Burtchaell and Sadleir, 545; A.H. Kenney, "Memoir of the Late Most Reverend William Magee, Archbishop of Dublin," in William Magee, *Collected Works*, vol. 1 (1842), xxxii–li.

51 Whelan, 138.

52 Brown, 105–6.

the primate that "as a servant of God, I dare not desert it."[53] When the society met in the spring of 1822 Archbishop Trench (a Dalyland convert, it will be recalled) took the chair and the Rev. Edward Wingfield (of the Powerscourt dynasty) became hon. secretary and the members rejected criticism of their society.[54] Effectively, the social elite of the evangelical world said "no" to the Irish bishops and made it stick. Perhaps Lord John George Beresford, with his aristocratic wealth and mien, could have fought them, but he was soon gone to serve as archbishop of Armagh and Magee, as the new archbishop of Dublin knew better than to cross the great and the good evangelicals. Besides, William Magee, who had made his way up the ladder from beginnings as a pensioner at TCD to an archbishopric through ability and application, had little inclination to accept the judgment of those who had gained high Church office as a heritable birthright. "The production and maintenance of Beresfords is not the final cause of the Irish church" was his acid judgment.[55] So, as archbishop of Dublin, William Magee publicly denounced Dissent and yet permitted the growth of the Bible Society, and the half dozen other proselytizing groups that popped up at this time, fungi on a damp forest floor, to work away.[56]

Similarly, although Lord John George Beresford, during his short term as archbishop of Dublin, had possessed the brass neck to dismiss a petition that the Bethesda proprietary chapel be licensed as a fully approved site of divine worship – a petition that was signed

53 Undated letter in Madden (1875), Robert Daly to Lord John George Beresford, 99–100. See also the following letter by Daly, 100 1.

54 Alan Acheson, *A History of the Church of Ireland* (Dublin 2002), 137.

55 Ibid., 76.

56 Thus, in the case of the Bible Society, he told an investigatory committee of the House of Lords in April 1825 that "I am not myself a member of the Bible Society, and I have not been one. Not that I do not in the fullest manner approve of the object of that society; but as a churchman I felt it not so eligible to adopt the mode which it pursues, as another which presents itself." (His favoured choice was the APCK.) *Minutes of Evidence Taken before the Select Committee of the House of Lords appointed to inquire into the State of Ireland*, 391, H.C. 1825 (521), ix. Note: although this was a Lords committee, the bulk of its work was reprinted in the Commons papers.

by the La Touches, the Lords Wicklow and Roden, and several other major lay leaders – William Magee quietly let the matter cool down and then in 1828 gave this evangelical citadel a full licence.[57] This was a continuation of the strain of realism that coexisted alongside Magee's sometimes bombastic exact churchmanship. "The evangelicals, both Episcopal and Dissenting, had unquestionably laid the foundation of the new-Reformation movement, and at the time when it was given official expression in 1822 by Archbishop Magee, they held control of all the agencies through which its expansion was to be attempted."[58]

All of the excitement came at just the time that John Nelson Darby, not long converted, was moving from being a non-practising barrister to his lifetime religious vocation. These were heady times. A holy war against infidels was beginning, and the Church cried out for young officers. Exciting times, indeed, but in Dalyland, also sensual, perhaps sexual, in a mortuarial sort of a way. From the autumn of 1823 onward, a black-clad figure hovered over the moral landscape of Dalyland, that of the young, pale, intensely spiritual Theodosia Howard Wingfield (1800–1836), the grieving Viscountess Powerscourt.[59]

57 Acheson, 137; Whelan, 19.

58 Whelan, 139.

59 Aside from the usual details in *Burke's*, there is a useful handwritten note concerning her family background and relations in CBA J.N.D./1/1/29, written by an unnamed family member in probably the 1840s. Theodosia was the third daughter of the Hon. Hugh Howard, third son of the first earl of Wicklow. Her mother was the second daughter of the Very Rev. Robert Bligh, dean of Elphin, and was a niece of John, earl of Darnley (of the third and Irish creation). Theodosia was the youngest of five children of Catherine Bligh and the Hon. Hugh Howard. Her father outlived her, dying in 1840. One of Theodosia's sisters married William Parnell of Avondale, who was the brother of the first Lord Congleton (the second lord became a Brethren ornament) and grandfather of Charles Stewart Parnell. Theodosia was the aunt of Catherine (usually called "Tattie" within the family), who eventually married George V. Wigram, wealthy bankroller of early Brethren activities and a stout disciple of John Nelson Darby.

She had every right to wear black. She had become the second wife of Richard, Fifth Viscount Powerscourt, in June 1822, after one of her cousins, who had been his first wife, had died in 1820. Theodosia seemed to be surrounded by death. An unnamed infant child of her marriage to Viscount Powerscourt was interred in the family vault at Powerscourt.[60] Then her husband died 9 April 1823. Not long after the formal period of mourning was over, the Rev. Hon Edward Wingfield, brother of the late fifth viscount and a stalwart defender of evangelizing societies, died at Powerscourt on 6 September 1823. He expired from "a surfeit of fruit," which one takes to be an oblique way of saying that he choked to death after taking too big a bite of something; the alternative possibilities are not nice to visualize.[61]

Theodosia was one of the Rev. Robert Daly's prize trophies in his crusade to bring the privileged into the evangelical wing of the Church of Ireland. Her conversion, according to Daly, came in 1819,[62] and one takes it in part to be the response of a sensitive nineteen-year old to the tubercular sufferings and approaching death of her cousin, the first Lady Powerscourt. She was effusive in her expressions of gratitude to Daly for his part in her conversion:

> Strive hard for me in your prayers. I owe you more than I can say, humanly speaking, and I would not write you this way, did I not feel that you are the only person who feels for my soul as I feel for it myself, for we both have to give account of it … Oh! May I still be your joy and crown of rejoicing in the last day.[63]

60 Stunt (2000), 162n49.

61 Bunbury [and Kavanagh], 71; *CDGBSL*, 1193.

62 In her funeral sermon in 1836 Daly said, "She always stated to me that she was converted to God in the year 1819. The dangerous state of health of her near relative, the former Lady Powerscourt, appears to have prepared her heart for receiving the word of truth of the gospel; and during the season of the last illness of that dear child of God, she conceived she was born again," Madden (1875), 53n1.

63 Ibid., 83. The date of the letter is not specified by Mrs Madden, although she clearly had the originals of Daly's collected correspondence. It was written from London, 9 April 1823, during Lord Powerscourt's final illness, to Robert Daly. See Lady Powerscourt's *Letters and Papers* (discussed below), 3–6.

In another letter, from the mid-1830s, she tells him, "I shall yet be a very great joy to you, and I joy to believe it. In the day of His appearing, I may have many masters, but only one father."[64] As mentioned earlier, after her marriage, both she and Viscount Powerscourt taught Sunday school in Daly's parish. After her husband's death she continued to support (in his name) two local mixed-religion schools, both unusually well housed and with teachers paid far above the standard.[65] She was good at being "good Lady Powerscourt."

More importantly, however, Lady Powerscourt continually resonated, like a spiritual tuning fork, and sought both to bring solace and to receive enlightenment. For those with whom these harmonics found sympathy, she was a saint; for others she can only have been tiresome and enervating. The Rev. Robert Daly collected and published a large, but thoroughly unsatisfactory, collection of her letters after her untimely death at age thirty-six.[66] When Lady Powerscourt was

64 Madden (1875), 84, again undated. This letter has additional significance because it is sometimes lifted by Brethren and turned into a final Dear John letter from Lady Powerscourt to John Nelson Darby. This is done in a STEM electronic e-version and in Field, 112. There is no doubt that Mrs Madden had the original and that it was written to Robert Daly. As clearly indicated in the previous letter, Lady Powerscourt regarded Daly as her spiritual father. John Nelson Darby may have been close to her emotionally, but he certainly was not in a position to be regarded as her father.

65 *Second Report of the Commissioners of Irish Education Inquiry,* 850–1, H.C., 1826–27 (12), xii. The teachers were paid somewhat more than £35 a year, and one of the schools was a four-room structure built by Lord Powerscourt at a cost of £600.

66 Robert Daly (ed.), *Letters and Papers by the Late Theodosia Viscountess Powerscourt* (Dublin, 3rd edition 1839). Even given the conventions of Victorian collections of letters – the collection was compiled from originals sent to Daly, copied, and then returned – the collection is vexing: (1) he tries to scrub them ("I have studiously omitted everything in the least degree personal," v); (2) dates are often missing, and he so carefully redacts names and identifying references that some of the items are close to being incoherent; (3) the chronology of the letters is somewhat scrambled; (4) there is almost nothing on prophecy, one of Lady Powerscourt's major interests. Daly defends himself by noting that there was very little in the collection on this topic (viii–ix), which is no defense at all as she had broken with him on this and other issues

in an optimistic frame, her vibrant spirituality was of this sort: "Sweet thought! Our being now vessels of mercy (because of the great love wherewith He loved us) evidence that He has set us apart, to display in us the riches of His glory!"[67] But, equally often she was storm-tossed and given to Gothic fainting spells: "Now I feel *my tale is told*, and ties of friendship are drawing towards an hereafter, while we are only left in Satan's kingdom, for the Lord to finish his work in us and by us."[68]

Whatever one may think of the viscountess, she was a compelling figure. She was young (John Nelson Darby's age, born in 1800) and willing to engage in religious relationships that were intensely personal and ran across age and gender lines. Without being sub-Freudian about things, one can scarcely miss the near-lubricious quality of some of her letters, especially when she lingers on the Bride-of-Christ theme. Her sign-offs would have been taken as flirtatious if the body of the letters were not about the soul, mostly her own. As has been written concerning the Brethren mother of John Millington Synge, Lady Powerscourt "was not always able to conceal the interconnection of erotic and spiritual need."[69]

Above all, the oscillating harmonics of her religious life were amplified by the great fortune of which she was a partial caretaker. The approximately 49,000 acres that the Wingfields owned in various parts of

---

and one can scarcely suspect her allies to have sent to Daly her private letters on the subject; (5) not surprisingly, then, there is no direct reference to her having left the Church of Ireland and joined the embryonic Brethren; (6) as much as some avocational historians have wanted to find in the letters signs of a romance and then holy renunciation thereof between Darby and Viscountess Powerscourt, it is not there; (7) nor is there any letter that can be inferred as being sent to John Nelson Darby by Lady Powerscourt. Darby and Daly were at war in the mid-late 1830s and Darby, a most private man, could not be expected to have sent such items to Daly; (8) irritatingly, Daly includes letters from Lady Powerscourt to himself, but without identification. One can identify two or three, however, from comparison to items in Madden's biography of Daly, which was based on her having the original material.

67 Letter of 28 December 1828 in Daly (ed.), 54.

68 Letter of 12 May 1826, ibid., 30.

69 W.J. McCormack, *Fool of the Family: A Life of J.M. Synge* (London 2000), 31.

Ireland was the unseen support of the Powerscourt demesne, which in turn was one of the lynchpins of the conglomerate that was Dalyland's crown jewel:

> The unbroken demesne swathe which began at Kilruddery and extended west encompassing Wingfield, Bushy Park, Tinnehinch, Powerscourt and Charleville before ebbing at the eastern head of Glencree in Ballyorney. Here in almost 3,000 acres of countryside girdled by trees and bounded by crafted walls, lay the grandeur and statuary of imperial Wicklow.[70]

Powerscourt House itself was so large that it defied an accurate count of the number of its rooms. Included in the inventory of the house was a throne prepared for the royal visit of 1821. One could be a very spiritual person and nevertheless be aware of the opportunities such a worldly situation offered.

70 William Nolan, "Land and Landscape in County Wicklow," in Hannigan and Nolan, eds (1994), 686.

CHAPTER FIVE

The Missing Years (2): 1822–1825

Although he later viewed them as a false start, the years 1822–25 were pivotal for John Nelson Darby. Despite his extreme reticence in discussing his own spiritual development, Darby makes it clear that following his conversion – in "June or July, 1820 or 21, I forget which" – he was very uneasy in his soul. It took him six or seven years, he recalled, before he found true and full peace.[1] That is how he remembered things fifty years later and how he wanted his followers to build the narrative of his life. In fact, this skates over a period of his life that he had every reason to later downplay, namely the sincere and deep quest that led him to become a priest in the Church of Ireland.

Downplay? Naturally: Darby spent most of his life as a religious professional bashing both state churches and voluntary denominations and in creating his own branch of Christianity, so one hardly expects him to celebrate his youthful commitment to a form of Christianity he later came to despise. Yet, in his twenties he became not only an Irish Anglican cleric but one of the aristocratic species he later contemptuously dismissed, one of the Dalyland-elect. Nevertheless, between his conversion and his entering the priesthood in 1825, a lot happened in his heart and mind, as he uneasily admits.

His summation of events bears attention, for it pivots on one psychologically diagnostic word. Darby's excessively economical explanation is that he was "induced to be ordained."[2] *Induced*: that is John

1 J.N.D. to ___, 1874, *LJND*, vol. 2, no. 196.

2 *Letter by J.N.D. to Prof. Tholuck*; *LJND*, vol. 3, no. 226.

Nelson Darby *pure laine.* It makes Darby passive in the process and not fully responsible. That is a characteristic which runs through his writings and his letters and, indeed, his entire adult life. He refuses to take responsibility for his actions. He is always being led astray by someone, in the case of what he considers his mistakes, or is being led by some variant of God (the Holy Spirit, Jesus) into decisions that are sometimes heroic but that often cause other persons immense pain and divisiveness. Significantly, he does not often take direct credit for accomplishments of which most persons would boast. Putting this perpetual passivity in self-concept together with his very slim personal recollections will make for difficulties for any future biographer[3] – the more so because in his actual behaviour throughout most of his life he was fiercely self-willed and a virtual berserker in the protection of his own religious constructions. Here the word "induced" has just enough of the tone of someone being led maliciously astray that it allows Darby off the hook. He says in effect: I really should not be blamed for my period of devoted churchmanship.

Not surprisingly, Brethren historians have embraced the idea that John Nelson Darby was induced into this wrong turn and have suggested specific individuals as being responsible for leading him into the priesthood. This effort, I think, is misplaced. No one person was responsible, but several persons, plus the interaction of Darby's own hungry soul with the richness of Dalyland and the excitement of being in the war room of a spiritual crusade intended to win all Ireland for

3 Because of the slimness of Darby's personal recollections, including his very rare admissions that he even had parents and brothers and sisters and relatives, the Tholuck "letter" is useful as it gives another touch of information about his eldest brother, William Henry Darby, the inheritor of Leap Castle (see chapters 2 and 3 for earlier references to him). Here J.N.D. says, clearly referring to William: "My elder brother, who is a Christian, spent two years at Dusseldorf. He is engaged in the work of the Lord, wherever he may happen to be at the moment. He has been blessed to several souls in the neighbourhood of Dusseldorf." One might add that William's freedom to leave his home and lands for a period of two years was probably made possible by the family pattern we saw earlier: a younger bachelor brother, Horatio de'Esterre Darby, resided at Leap and acted as estate manager. To avoid any confusion of historical reference, note that William Henry Darby's tenth child, born in 1864, was named John Nelson Darby.

the Lord. This was admixed with his clearly prodigious reading in church history, which certainly influenced him throughout his life.

Still, there were important individuals who often are pointed to in turning Darby to the religious life; as long as no single one is put forward as the sole agent, they are worth noting, for each was part of the causal swirl. For example, though Darby would not be keen to admit Robert Daly's significant influence – they later were at loggerheads, not only about ecclesiastical matters but about personal primacy in the religious life of Lady Powerscourt – yet Daly was the animator of several evangelizing societies and invited the younger man's participation.[4] Also, Daly worked at influencing the diocese's clergy and the divinity candidates by having summer gatherings where they would have discussion and dinner and in the season's long evenings "saunter amidst the thick oaks of the Dargle glen, along whose hollow a mountain torrent thundered and foamed amidst rocks and boulders."[5] Timothy C.F. Stunt, surveying the clergy of County Wicklow, concluded that "there can be no doubt that Daly stood head and shoulders above his fellows, being a natural extrovert and possessed of boundless energy."[6] Concerning John Nelson Darby's becoming an Anglican cleric, one of Darby's biographers, Max Weremchuk, for a time believed that Daly "was the one who induced him"[7] – an excessive personalization, but a useful acceptance of Daly's being influential. Later, Weremchuk came to question his own emphasis on Robert Daly and began to consider that Darby's being "induced" "was not so much Rev. Robert Daly's influence as it was his brother's? … or [William] Cleaver'? or all in some way together?"[8] That last phrase – "all in some way together" – is

4 Thus, the formal invitation with a personal note from Daly to Darby, August 1823, to attend the tenth annual meeting of the Wicklow branch of the Bible Society (CBA, J.N.D./1/1/30).

5 Richard Sinclair Brooke, *Recollections of the Irish Church* (London 1877), 33, reporting his own experience in 1827.

6 Timothy C.F. Stunt, *From Awakening to Secession: Radical Evangelicals in Switzerland and Britain, 1815–35* (Edinburgh 2000), 165.

7 Max S. Weremchuk, *John Nelson Darby* (Neptune, NJ, 1992; orig. German ed. 1988), 37.

8 Max Weremchuk, "Research Paper No. 4," www.mybrethren.org/sitefram.htm (accessed 31 October 2012).

FIGURE 5.1 MOSS HOUSE, DARGLE GLEN.

A rusticated bench, protected from the weather, was set on an elevated rocky point, and the visitor was able to take in the wild landscape without much physical exertion.

the beginning of wisdom, at least if one adds to the mix Darby's theological reading, some unspoken family ties, and the background aura of Theodosia, Lady Powerscourt, to the entire evango-snobbish social matrix of Dalyland.

In 1822 John Nelson's brother, the Rev. Christopher Lovett Darby, was given his first sole charge as rector of Killinaule in the diocese of Cashel, and then in 1828 added the Kells union of parishes in Ossory to his portfolio.[9] The relevant point is that Christopher was a serious exact churchman, given both to the efficacy of the sacraments and to the need to convert Catholics. A senior colleague in his first appointment was Henry Woodward (1775–1863), another exact churchman, whose father, Richard Woodward, had been a strong defender of the Protestant Ascendancy in his years as bishop of Cloyne (1781–94). A rather obscure but germane fact is that the father of Christopher Lovett Darby and John Nelson Darby was a cousin of the late Bishop Woodward.[10] In any case, the sort of Anglicanism that John Nelson Darby assimilated was close to that of his brother, but even more exact. Thus, more than forty years later, Darby remembered that: "I fasted in Lent so as to be weak in body at the end of it; ate no meat on week days; nothing till evening on Wednesdays, Fridays, and Saturdays, then a little bread or nothing; observed strictly the weekly fasts, too. I went to my clergyman always if I wished to take the sacrament, that he might judge of the matter."[11]

We should grant a certain degree of retrospective exaggeration – Darby in 1866 was in a fire-red competitive frame of mind, jealously responding to the huge public reception given to John Henry Newman's *Apologia pro Vita Sua* (1864). Thus, Darby claimed, concerning the early devotional system of John Henry Newman, that "I knew it and walked in it years before Dr Newman, as I learn from his book."[12] But, allowing for rhetorical inflation, these self-statements indicate a sacerdotal exactness that was just at the far edge of what could exist

9 Charles Lovett Darby's clerical career is outlined in chapter 4, note 12.

10 Stunt (2000), 164, and 170; *CDID* entry for Richard Woodward.

11 "J.N.D.," *Analysis of Dr Newman's Apologia Pro Vita Sua: With a Glance at the History of Popes, Councils, and the Church* (London: W.H. Broom 1866), 19–20.

12 Ibid., 19. Thus, it seems that his competitive mettle makes Darby somewhat rewrite his own early beliefs. He certainly did not see the "union of Church and State to be Babylonish" (20) until he had been a clergyman for three or four years and had run into a fight with Archbishop Magee on the topic. There are other assertions that are likely counterfactual concerning his own beliefs on his way to the priesthood, but this response to Newman's book has the redeeming feature of being one of the few of the hundreds of published monographs and tracts written by Darby that can be read straight through with a fair certainty of what his prose actually means.

within the Church of Ireland. For example, writing in the mid-1860s, Darby had acquired a sufficient (and unusual, for him) awareness of the slightly lugubrious nature of his practices in the mid-1820s ("I was rather a bore to my clergyman by acting on the rubrics"),[13] so that one tends to accept as authentic that he recognized the apostolic character of the Anglican Church but disowned the name of Protestant: "I looked for the Church. Not having peace in my soul, nor yet knowing where peace is, I too, governed by a morbid imagination, thought much of Rome and its professed sanctity, and Catholicity and antiquity … I looked for something more like revered antiquity."[14] Note those terms: *morbid imagination*; *revered antiquity*; *professed sanctity.*

Uncharacteristically, John Nelson Darby was willing to own them as his own mistakes and do so quite candidly in the context of his 171-page denunciation of John Henry Newman. What Darby will not tell us here, or elsewhere, is where those beliefs came from, particularly his youthful love affair with a romantic version of medieval Catholic Christianity. Or, even if that affinity of the medieval world was self-generated, did anyone encourage him to develop it?

On this matter, one suspects that Darby was shrewdly avoiding any association with a topic that was, by the time of his writing in 1866, a matter of some derision. This was a once-attractive form of pseudo-medievalism based upon an extremely romantic view of medieval chivalry and a rosy view of the medieval church. Of course the novels of Sir Walter Scott were in play here, but the primary evangelist of ersatz-chivalry among people of Darby's social class was the Anglo-Irishman Kenelm Henry Digby. His family were King's County neighbours of the Darbys, and they had done very well out of Catholic lands and Anglican church appointments. Digby's father was rector of Geashill in King's County, as had been several of his ancestors, for the appointment was in the hands of successive Lords Digby, heads of the family. Although only a second son, Kenelm Henry Digby was left well off at his father's death in 1812. He was sent to school in England and at age eighteen entered Trinity College, Cambridge. He was an almost exact contemporary of John Nelson Darby's brother, George, and they

13 *Analysis of Dr Newman's Apologia pro Vita Sua*, 2.
14 Ibid.

were boon companions. Although he took his degree in 1819, Digby kept rooms in Trinity until 1829 and spent his summers inhaling the glories of the most picturesque ruins of Europe. When not travelling he spent his time trying to reinvent chivalry, increase reverence for the monarchy and remedievalize the Anglican Church. In these pursuits, George Darby was a valuable ally, "the model of a knight" in Digby's opinion. The year 1819 is significant as this was when the senior John Darby began turning his London fortune into an east Sussex estate. He purchased Marklye in 1819 and had completed its expansion with further purchases by 1823. It was at Marklye that Kenelm Henry Digby and George Darby held what Digby's biographer called "a solemn tournament in the approved fashion."[15] The number of participants in the tournament is not specified, but the "approved fashion" included using ponies as steeds and hop poles as lances. These medieval fantasies were not ironic games but an attempt to revive the values of the chivalric past in the devalued present.[16]

In 1822, Digby published anonymously *The Broad Stone of Honour, or, Rules for the Gentlemen of England*, which he rewrote twice by 1830.[17] This was not an obscure volume: it was influential among the right sort of athletic, imaginative young gentleman of the ancient universities. In 1825 Digby turned Catholic and spent the rest of his life as a mixture of apologist and knight errant. He rewrote the *Broad Stone of Honour* to include a picture of the Catholic priest as chivalric figure, an ascetic noble warrior expending himself in the propagation of the

15 Bernard Holland, *Memoir of Kenelm Henry Digby* (London 1919), 10. The close Digby-Darby links are tied down, ibid., 9–11. A valuable large frame discussion is Mark Girouard, *The Return to Camelot* (London 1981). Digby is discussed 56–66. I am grateful to Dr Andrew Tierney for introducing me to the quite considerable literature on faux-medievalism among one cohort of the gilded youth of the late Georgian era.

16 Other chivalric exercises of Digby and Darby were: the attempt to recreate an overnight ride from Marklye to Herstmonceux Castle. Also, Digby, the keener of the two, kept vigil one night by sneaking into the chapel of King's College, Cambridge, and he actually rescued a maiden in distress on one of his rides.

17 The first anonymous edition was London: C. and J. Rivington, 1822, and a second anonymous edition, expanded into two volumes, was published by the same firm in 1823.

faith[18] – uncomfortably close, one might note, to John Nelson Darby in his march on Calary Bog. That John Nelson Darby later excised everything to do with his brother George Darby and the Marklye circus from his already highly censored personal history is understandable.[19]

18 Expanded into four volumes, the book now was subtitled *The True Sense and Practice of Chivalry* (1826–29).

19 Two consequential details. First, two of the biographers of John Nelson Darby flatly assert plausibly (albeit without documentation) that when he took the Calary charge his father cut him out of his will but later reinstated him (Weremchuk, 38, and Marion Field, *John Nelson Darby* [Godalming 2008], 29). The asserted temporary disinheritance by his father has a ring of authenticity, for not only was John Nelson Darby giving up the practice of law, but he was contemplating going into the hills and bogs of Wicklow and doing so in medieval mode: the ecclesiastical version of the chivalry-mad behaviour that the commercially minded senior John Darby had been forced to permit at Marklye. I cannot find any testamentary document of John Darby Sr in which John Nelson was temporarily disinherited, but later in life John Nelson wrote to a co-religionist in Barbados referring to the mid-1820s: "I honestly began by giving up everything, though in point of fact my faith was never tried in that way, as an uncle left me something before I was run out, or very soon after" (J.N.D. to Sydney Smith, 9 March 1869, *LJND*, vol. 2, no. 2). This implies that his father also cut off any regular allowance John Nelson may have had. In the final event, John Nelson was included in his father's will, but as something of an afterthought and on terms markedly less favoured than any of his father's other male children (Will of John Darby, National Archives, PRO, prob. 11/1841/35, probated 16 January 1835). Secondly, as for John Nelson's need in the mid-1820s for everyday money, the letter to Sydney Smith, cited above, indicates that his family came through. Field asserts (33, again without documentation) that his uncle, Henry d'Esterre Darby, left him £2,000 in government stock, which is correct in general but not quite right in detail. William Kelly, who first met Darby in the 1840s, wrote in the 1890s that Sir Henry had left John Nelson "with enough to provide amply; as his cousins borrowed the capital and paid him good interest, avowedly to hinder his giving it away" (photocopy of typescript copy of letter of William Kelly to "P. of Rotherham," 22 June 1899, CBA Kelly papers, box 33). The will of Sir Henry d'Esterre Darby is a complicated document (National Archives, PRO, prob. 11/1691/401, probated 22 November 1824.) It was proved, as were substantial Irish wills of the time, in the Court of Prerogative Causes under the archbishop of Armagh, in this case Lord John George Beresford. My reading is that John Nelson received from his uncle (as did each of the seven living children of John Darby Sr) lifetime interest on £5,000 annually in a portfolio of

To be "induced," even if only to a limited degree, in his spiritual life by youthful faux-medievalism was cringingly embarrassing.[20]

While accepting that in his late middle age John Nelson Darby would want to erase such interpretations of his early religious career, we should nevertheless recall the thorough demonstration by Peter B. Nockles that in the Church of England's history it is important not to push the evangelical/Anglo-Catholic split into the period before the 1830s,[21] and this is even more true of the Church of Ireland. There were many people, both lay and clerical, who could be both exact churchmen ("high church" in some vocabularies) and evangelicals at the same time. Adherents of these two variants of Irish Anglicanism in the 1820s were united in their anti- Roman Catholicism and therefore in their backing of the new-Reformation movement, paradoxical as that may seem. Thus, for example, Archbishop William Magee could be both strong on exact churchmanship and quite willing to unleash almost every sort of proselytizing society.

One would like to know whom John Nelson Darby referred to as "my clergyman," the priest he consulted concerning his worthiness to receive the eucharist, but he gives no real clue. Crucially, his metropolitan, Archbishop Magee, both knew of his ascetic, almost medieval, devotions and did not disapprove. By late 1824, Darby was confident both of his own spiritual fit as a cleric and also that he would be welcomed into the priesthood of the Church of Ireland: he could order a canonical gown without fear of making a fool of himself.[22] He spent the better part of the next year preparing himself for his new role, probably by reading, discussing, and praying, as he had been doing.

East India Company bonds that yielded 3 percent each year. That would have given young Darby £150 annually. This was two to three times the amount of an Irish curate's salary in this period but markedly beneath the income of beneficed clergymen, their median annual net stipend being in the £300–400 range (Akenson, *The Church of Ireland,* New Haven 1971, 87, table 22).

20 The more embarrassing, indeed, because in 1833 Kenelm Henry Digby married into the Catholic tranche of the Dublin-Wicklow world. He wed Jane Mary Dillon, the wealthy co-heiress of Thomas Dillon of Mount Dillon, County Dublin (*ODNB,* entry for Kenelm Henry Digby).

21 Peter B. Nockles, *The Oxford Movement in Context* (Cambridge 1994).

22 Bill dated 9 December 1824 (CBA, J.N.D. 1/1/31).

It would have been *infra dig* for one of his social class and intellectual standing to be required to take the divinity course at Trinity, and indeed he probably had read as widely, if not quite so deeply, as had his potential professors.[23]

Instead of making John Nelson Darby jump through hoops, on his behalf Archbishop Magee did a bit of horse-trading that would have made even Lady Harriet Daly admire his dexterity: he created a virtual parish for Darby – Calary – if not out of pure air, at least from the nearly profitless tailings of four solid parishes. Essentially, Magee did a whip-round of Dalyland's senior clergy and convinced four of them that there was a really promising new applicant for their club and that they should help pay the first few years of his dues. He was the right sort of chap and, besides, he would work very very hard. Thus, from their own pockets each year the four benefice holders promised the following amounts: Robert Daly of Powerscourt, £7.13s.10d; Lambert W. Hempenstall of Derralossory, £15; William Archer of Newcastle, £7.13s.10d; William Cleaver of Delgany, £15, plus an optional annual payment of £30. That sum – a total of £75.7s. 8d – was within the usual range of stipends for curates.[24] To satisfy the supervision requirements of canon law, Calary was made a curacy of Delgany, but that was merely formal: nobody would be supervising Darby; indeed, rarely would anybody even visit him, so isolated was Calary Bog.

To send out an ornament of the finely educated Anglo-Irish genteel classes to a site with no church (a schoolhouse would have to

23 The TCD postgraduate divinity course was dispensable for persons like Darby, but it was indeed on the books as a requirement supposedly honoured by the Irish bishops in their recruitment of pastoral personnel. Until reforms were effected in 1833, the course was impressive on paper, but not in the actual delivery of training. See Thomas P. Power, "'Of No Small Importance': Curricular Change in the School of Divinity, Trinity College Dublin, 1790–1850," in Power (ed.), *Change and Transformation* (Eugene, OR, 2013).

24 *Fourth Report of His Majesty's Commissioners of Ecclesiastical Revenue and Patronage in Ireland,* 20–1, 30–3, 56–7, 90–1, H.C. 1837 (500), xxi. This report deals with the early 1830s, but in the case of Calary simply codified what had been the practice since Darby's appointment. Calary in 1831 became a perpetual curacy, which meant that it would be a parish of its own, albeit slightly second class. Part of the deal that Magee engineered with the four clergymen was that the right to appoint clerics for Calary would rotate between the holders of their respective parishes.

do), no place to live (the new cleric would have to find and pay for his lodgings, roughly £12 annually), and no gentry company within half a day's ride sounds strange and wasteful. But it suited John Nelson Darby down to the marrow: he could promote ascetic, apostolic, and evangelical Christianity and at the same time practise his personal mortifications and venerations. No more would Darby have to experience even the most fleeting contact with fly-blown three-bottle parsons; no tallow candles dripping away untended. He, like the ancient desert fathers, would convert the local people by his own example of self-renunciation. All this also suited both Archbishop Magee and the evangelicals who chipped in to underwrite Darby's mission. The very young John Nelson Darby could promote the new-Reformation by converting Roman Catholics and with little public risk if he went astray (he would be preaching in some spots not even marked on the maps drawn up by the military engineers), and the odds were that after a year or two or three he would take on the grave and stolid mien of a parson who had the makings of a conscientious bishop.

Once he had arranged things with the four local incumbents, Archbishop Magee was in a hurry to have Darby in the field. He used his son Thomas, who was the rector of Kilcar in the diocese of Raphoe (the archbishop's previous bishopric), as an arranger. He told him concerning John Nelson Darby that "upon ordination [to deacon] I propose to appoint him to Calary district which is important to have attended immediately."[25] Apparently it was up to Thomas to arrange the ordination by the bishop of Raphoe (the Rev. Dr William Bissett), and this was done on 7 August 1825 in St Eunan's Cathdral, Raphoe.[26] Darby went off to his spiritual charge. He was priested by Archbishop Magee in Christ Church Cathedral, Dublin, on 19 February 1826, and at age twenty-five was a full-time soldier in the army of the Lord.[27]

25 William Magee to Thomas Magee, 2 August 1825 (CBA, J.N.D./1/1/11; duplicate in J.N.D.5/1). The Rev. Thomas Percival Magee (1797–1854) had, at age twenty-five, published a book on the nature of the visible church. He moved about during his early career but settled down (1830–54) to being the archdeacon of Kilmacduagh and held the prebend for Wicklow in St Patrick's Cathedral, Dublin (*CDGBSI*, 866).

26 Embossed licence, 7 August 1825, CBA, J.N.D./1/1/34.

27 Field, 25; receipt for fees for Darby's letter of holy orders, 27 February 1826 (CBA, J.N.D./1/1/14).

John Nelson Darby later felt strongly that becoming a clergyman of the Church of Ireland was a great mistake and, indeed, was dancing with the devil. Rewriting his own life story was his prerogative and is something every human being does. Yet, in fact he and the Church of Ireland were a good marriage at that period in his life, his mid-twenties. He was given real responsibilities and a great deal of freedom to carry them out. Brutally bucolic as Calary Bog may have been, Darby was actually receiving very special treatment: virtually no just-deaconed young man was given a charge of his own. Darby was. He was put in this rare position by the primate of Ireland, Archbishop Magee, the second-highest ranking figure in the Irish Church.[28] Magee did this in cooperation with the spiritual leaders of Dalyland, the Church of Ireland's most solidly Anglican-dominated local social hierarchy. Of course John Nelson Darby outgrew his first posting. He was expected to; that was one of the points of the whole exercise. Appointing Darby as the pastor of Calary was not a wrong decision by the Church leaders, but a stage in his spiritual maturation, intentionally planned as such. Nor was his accepting the post a mistake: by his own admission he was a devotional work-in-progress. That in the mid-1820s the Church of Ireland was undergoing a vitriolic spasm of overt anti-Catholicism and unrealistic evangelicalism is irrelevant; so too is the fact that, by his own account, in his mid-twenties John Nelson Darby was something of a mess spiritually. Unless one is willing to dismiss the historical notion of cause and effect, then John Nelson Darby's Church of Ireland priesthood is an essential segment in the evolution (or, if one prefers, invention) of the beliefs that eventually became part of the ideological spine of most evangelical constituencies worldwide.

In the spring of 1825, not long before he negotiated the creation of the Calary charge for John Nelson Darby, Archbishop William Magee was called before a House of Lords select committee on the state of

28 The Lord Primate of All Ireland, the archbishop of Armagh, took precedence over the archbishop of Dublin, but it was not a command relationship. Each archbishop ran his own province.

Ireland. Several other notables, both Catholic and Protestant, were also called, but Magee received more time and attention in examination than anyone else, mostly because of his part in the new-Reformation. Magee's answers under hostile probing had the considerable intellectual virtue of being either short and direct or well-argued and rational; and these same characteristics made Magee's responses very awkward politically. Thus, if one wanted to know why the 1820s were known as the period of the Bible War, this interaction explains it very well:

> Question: Is your Grace of opinion that the lively attention to the subject of religion, which you state has not existed in Ireland to the same degree since the Reformation, can possibly exist without a strong disposition and determination towards Protestantism?
> Answer: So I feel. I conceive that it cannot exist without exciting attention to the Bible; and that I take to be (rejecting all minor considerations) the grand distinction between Protestants and Roman Catholics.[29]

This examination took place roughly halfway through the Bible War, and at that point Magee thought that the new-Reformation (or Second Reformation) was doing well in the archdiocese of Dublin and Glendalough. In Dublin itself, he said, more churches were being built in the fashionable areas (near Merrion Square, chiefly), and they were filling up; also, the poor Roman Catholics were pressing into the Church of Ireland places of worship. Equally, in the countryside, a noteworthy social chemistry was developing. Magee said that poor rural Protestants, who previously had been afraid to show their religious allegiance because of Catholic intimidation, were coming forward, and, significantly, their better-off Protestant co-religionists were stepping forward to protect them. In perhaps too clear and too accurate a sentence, Magee noted that "the state of affairs having changed lately in

29 *Minutes of Evidence Taken before the Select Committee of the House of Lords Appointed to Inquire into the State of Ireland*, 393, H.C. 1825 (521), ix. Magee was examined on 29 April and on 3 May 1825. This quotation is from the first day.

Ireland, so as to force upon the higher class of Protestants a recollection of the difference between Roman Catholic and Protestant, and to compel many of them, from regard to their personal safety, to make some distinction in favour of the latter."[30] The conversion of Catholics was going along well, Magee believed, and he instanced that several schoolmasters had changed religion. He also stated that he had had several Roman Catholic priests come to him to change faiths, but that he had "almost uniformly rejected them."[31] Although the nature of parliamentary reporting bleaches out the tension between the two or three peers on the select committee who were Magee's critics because of his anti-Catholicism, there are other unofficial reports that make this obvious and fill in some blanks spots in the official reporting. The hostile peers cross-examined Magee in roughly the same way that a prosecuting attorney would examine a witness, walking back and forth portentously while the short, erect, unbending Magee answered them in irritatingly full sentences. At one point Lord Holland hectoringly inquired "Does your Grace really think that there is any person capable of holding such a monstrous opinion as that the Roman Catholic religion is idolatrous?" Magee paused and then, after a silence, stared straight at the hovering peer and replied, "My Lord, *some have sworn to it.*"[32] That reminder of the abjuration clause in the House of Lords' oath drove Lord Holland back to his seat in silence, and it is a good example of Magee's propensity to win small battles and hurt his overall position in the big war: it reminded everyone of the way the political system was tilted. Moreover, when asked directly about civil rights, he elaborated:

30 Ibid., 384. A similar pragmatic observation probably also was correct and is exactly the sort of thing understood at the time and now forgotten. Magee noted that there needed to be a change in internal Anglican church architecture, for almost all of the space in churches was taken up by the large square pews of the "respectable families of the parish," so "that the lower classes are too commonly unprovided for … We have not in Ireland adopted the plan of single rows. We are doing it now" (386).

31 Ibid.

32 A.H. Kenney, "Memoir of the Late Most Reverend William Magee, Archbishop of Dublin," in William Magee, *Collected Works*, vol. 1 (1842), lxvi–lxvii.

> Question: Is your Grace of opinion that there would be any danger to the Established Church from the equalization of the civil rights between Roman Catholics and Protestants?
> Answer: My impression is that the equalization of civil rights will unavoidably lead to an endeavour to overturn the Protestant establishment in Ireland and tend of course to endanger its existence.[33]

Here Archbishop Magee was right in his long-term historical prediction – it took until 1871 for the Catholics to disestablish the Anglican Church, but win they did. Yet again, Magee was inanely insensitive in answering directly. Did the majority of the Irish population need to be reminded that the existence of the Church of Ireland as a state church was predicated upon the continuation of legal impediments to full political equality for Roman Catholics?

As it evolved from the mid-1820s onward, the Bible War (or, new-Reformation or Second Reformation movement) is a rich topic, well-covered in most of its aspects, and almost irresistibly fascinating in some of its macabre details: one watches it rather like one watches a horror movie, wanting to look away, but then peeking through one's fingers at an inevitably messy wreck in train.

A very compressed summary of the Bible War in full cry is provided below. Given our discussion in chapter 4 of the strategic goals of the new-Reformation, only the barest summary of its tactical methods in the mid to late-1820s is necessary: these matters are handled in detail in other studies.[34] The interpretive key is that in each tactical action of

33 *Minutes of Evidence Taken before the Select Committee of the House Lords appointed to inquire into the State of Ireland*, 398.

34 Especially in Irene Whelan's *The Bible War in Ireland: The "Second Reformation" and the Polarization of Protestant-Catholic Relations, 1800–1840* (Dublin and Madison 2005). Desmond Bowen's *The Protestant Crusade in Ireland, 1800–70* (Dublin and Montreal and Kingston 1978) is still useful; some of its excesses are corrected in Alan Acheson's *A History of the Church*

the Bible War lay the antithesis of the overall strategic intention of the new-Reformation, namely the creation of the New Jerusalem with the Anglican Church becoming a true national Church. Even if this goal had been obtainable (I have already expressed my doubts), it could only be approached by tactics that moved softly-softly. But the Bible War was noisy, and its officers were greedy.

Here we should distinguish between core matters and those that were pyrotechnical, drawing popular attention (such as public debates between Protestant and Catholic clergy), but not truly central and those tactical behaviours that really counted. The latter involved things that could be counted – meaning money, mostly, and bodies. If the Church of Ireland were to move toward becoming a real national Church it had to push ever-upward the curve of state spending on its operations: but quietly. At the end of the Napoleonic Wars, the United Kingdom parliament was unlikely to vote more publicly identifiable direct aid than it was already providing for the religious activities of the Church of Ireland. Hence, everything depended on the Church receiving either covert or semi-covert governmental monies.

As a small example, useful to sensitize us to cross-subsidies and their tactical management, we return briefly to the sadly memorable matter of the Dublin Foundling Hospital. "About the year 1820," according to a governmental commission of 1826, the way the hospital was run "produced so much embarrassment as to lead to one of the

---

of Ireland, 1691–2001 (2nd ed., 2002). The several school societies and the way their often-proselytizing activities led to their replacement by the Irish national system of education is covered in my *The Irish Education Experiment* (London and Toronto 1970; republished London and New York 2012). The post-Emancipation history of the various Protestant societies is aphasic, and then comes alive with a nineteenth-century historiography of controversy concerning activities during the Famine and its aftermath. In the quieter later twentieth-century literature, Desmond Bowen's *Souperism* (1970) deals with the issue head-on. Miriam Moffitt has chronicled the long-term history of matters that usually are dropped soon after the Famine period is discussed: *Soupers and Jumpers* (Dublin 2008) and *The Society for Irish Church Missions to the Roman Catholics* (Manchester 2010). A distinguished contribution to understanding the long half-life of the Protestant evangelizing societies is David Fitzpatrick, *"Solitary and Wild": Frederick MacNeice and the Salvation of Ireland* (Dublin 2012).

most remarkable changes of system that has occurred in the management of the Institution."[35] This certainly was not what would have been recognized as reform in the Benthamite tradition. Instead the number of admissions of deserted infants was cut from roughly 2,000 each year to a maximum of 500, with preference going to the City of Dublin. Each parish from which an infant originated was to be charged £5 per child.[36] In future, only Protestant wet nurses were to be employed, in contrast to the existing practice wherein most nurses were Roman Catholics. All children over the age of four who were in Catholic care were to be transferred to Protestants – this being done to the number of 2,150 children in 1824 and 1825.[37] And the clergy of the parish that received foundlings should require them to attend Protestant schools and learn the Anglican catechism when they were of suitable age. These religious arrangements were to be enforced by the Protestant archbishop of Dublin,[38] and his fingerprints are on the sectarian aspects of the reforms. Since almost all of the wet nurses were in Counties Wicklow, Kildare, and Carlow, Archbishop Magee's ecclesiastical province stood to acquire the most children. (It is worth noting that despite the parishes of Powerscourt, Delgany, and Rathdrum being among the biggest gainers through this forced Protestantization of young children, the Rev. Robert Daly disapproved of the whole Foundling Hospital system: although he dryly admitted that it did indeed meet the hospital authorities' desire that the children be brought up "as Protestants and not Roman Catholics.")[39] All this was happening while the Foundling Hospital was receiving an average of nearly £32,500 in

35 *Third Report of the Commissioners of Irish Education Inquiry*, 8, H.C. 1826–17 (13), xiii.

36 3 Geo. 4, cap. 35. Rather unconvincingly, the commissioners reflected "that an increase in infanticide might have been the consequence, but the inquiries which we have made upon that subject have not afforded any ground for supposing that such has been the result" (*Third Report of the Commissioners of Irish Education Inquiry*, 9).

37 See *Third Report of the Commissioners of Irish Education Inquiry* (141) for the transfers from Catholic to Protestant wet-nurses by parish.

38 "Circular Letter to the Clergy of the Diocese of Dublin" [1824] reproduced ibid., 142.

39 Robert Daly testimony, ibid., 128ff.

annual parliamentary grants. Obviously, the number of children here involved was small in relation to the total population, but that is why it is such a revealing case, almost a laboratory experiment. It shows clearly what was meant if the continuance of the Anglican establishment depended, as Archbishop Magee stated, upon the continued diminution of Catholic civil rights.[40]

The big-number case of cross-subsidization of the Church of Ireland was the matter of popular education. It was a very complicated business both in financial terms (wherein it approached the complexity of modern money-laundering) and even in the simple matter of how many children were in what sort of schools: neither matter has been fully resolved historically. However, a fair summary is that until the late 1810s the Established Church was quiet, if not restrained, in its siphoning of governmental funds. Thereafter the evangelicals became aggressive and the Catholics, who were becoming restive concerning their long-impaired civil rights, became confrontational. Here are only three examples of the myriad ways governmental money went to cross-subsidize Protestantism through educational enterprises. First, a relatively simple operation. The Association for Discountenacing Vice and Promoting the Knowledge and Practice of the Christian Religion (referred to now as the Association for Promoting Christian Knowledge) was a solely Anglican-controlled institution (Archbishop Magee's favourite), and since the year 1800 had received parliamentary grants, running to £9,084 in 1823, plus a larger amount from appeals to private citizens. The society both published books and tracts and helped fund local Church of Ireland schools. Up to roughly 1820 (when it was assisting schools with about 9,000 pupils, about half of whom were Catholic) it stayed clear of heavy proselytizing and of cooperation with overtly proselytizing societies. This policy changed sharply in the early 1820s, and, besides becoming more ginger itself, the society slid money sideways to the London Hibernian Society, which was very aggressive indeed. That is a simple case. Secondly, and much more complicated, is something called the Lord Lieutenant's School Fund. It had been initiated in 1819 in response to an appeal on behalf of Catholics put forward

40 The Foundling Hospital received so much hostile criticism that it was out of operation by 1835.

by William Hayes Parnell; its original purpose was to erect schools for poor Catholics. The three trustees were Protestants, including James Digges La Touche, a very serious evangelical and adept money-man. The amount of governmental money that the Lord Lieutenant's School Fund distributed began at £3,250 in 1819 and was up to £15,000 annually in the 1825–26 financial year. During that period it granted only 12 of its 481 new school subsidies to Catholic schools. Moreover the fund's trustees made direct grants to schools that were run by proselytizing societies, as well as sliding monies sideways to the governors of various societies. This sectarian tilt was so obviously noxious as to be publicly unsupportable, and the fund in its original form was extinguished in 1826. Thirdly, there were several overtly anti-Catholic organizations. An example in the educational field was the vigorously anti-Catholic London Hibernian Society. When one pries into its funding, one discovers it receiving money from the APCK (which was receiving parliamentary money) and also from the Lord Lieutenant's School Fund. These cases – the APCK, the Lord Lieutenant's School Fund and the London Hibernian Society – are only three examples of a deeper pattern of semi-covert subsidization of Protestant religion, a pattern of subvention that was much more generous than it appears if one simply scans the parliamentary financial votes and accounts.[41]

Despite the abrasive nature of the three activities just mentioned, there was a fourth effort that seemed to have reached an equilibrium between the desires of the two major religious groups: the Kildare Place Society (f. 1811), which for a brief time had a truly ecumenical board of control and a serious intention of educating the Irish poor in a non-sectarian manner. In its first decade it was impressive, devising a series of school books that were pedagogically way ahead of anything published elsewhere in the British Isles. The leaders of the

41 The rough details are in Akenson, *The Irish Education Experiment*, 1970 and 2012, chiefly 80–6. In order to aid historians in coming to terms with the nature of the Irish governmental structure in the 1820s, an historical accountant needs to examine not only the cross-subsidization of the church and various education societies but also other social welfare expenditures that covertly aided the Church. The challenge will be to document the filigree of sub-rosa interconnections that permitted funds voted for one purpose to slide unaudited to quite another.

Roman Catholic Church were willing to give the society a chance, because the Irish peasantry had an immense hunger for education and the Catholic Church, recovering as it was from the penal years of the eighteenth century, could not meet that demand. By 1824, the Kildare Place Society was operating 1,490 schools with about 100,000 pupils on the rolls and was receiving £22,000 annually from parliament, plus private donations. Nevertheless, the society was also on the edge of a losing battle; from roughly 1820 onward, it had let itself become less vigilant about proselytization of Catholics and had allowed itself to be used for the cross-funding of various sectarian societies. Thus, Daniel O'Connell resigned from the board after its 1820 annual meeting. From then onward, a major question was whether or not the various educational activities paid for by the United Kingdom government (both overtly and covertly) were to continue as charges on the public purse.[42]

The best estimate of the number of children in Ireland receiving some form of basic schooling in 1824 – ranging from mud-cabin hedge schools upward – was reported as being somewhat over 500,000 pupils in roughly 12,000 schools (although that probably is an underestimate, of roughly 9 to 14 percent).[43] About 36 percent of Irish children six to

42 On the Kildare Place Society, in addition to Parkes (1984), see the classic by H. Kingsmill Moore, *An Unwritten Chapter in the History of Education* (London 1904). An appreciation of the publishing work of the society and of its relationship to both the earlier hedge schools and the later national schools is J.R.R. Adams, "Hedge Schools and Popular Education in Ireland," in Donnelly and Miller, eds (Dublin 1998).

43 The *First Report of the Commissioners of Irish Education Inquiry*, H.C. 1825 (400), xii, is a very rewarding but frustrating document. Cannily, the commissioners had a set of duplicate returns, filled out by the Catholic and the Protestant clergy. The amount of detail collected was quite amazing, running all the way down to the type of building provided and the sources of the teachers' income. The material was not, however, systematically analyzed or cross-tabulated or related to the available census data on the number of children in the various catchment areas for the schools. The late Dr Garret FitzGerald had completed the first stage of a complete reconfiguration of the data and a full analysis of the student enrolment data and the characteristics of their schools and that is being completed by other authorities. His analysis, together with the financial audit that I suggested above, are the two prerequisites to future improvements in our understanding of the educational flux of the 1820s.

thirteen years of age were enrolled in school.[44] Immense room, then, for evangelizing.

Amid the snowstorm of information on schooling that came out in the 1820s was an intriguing outlier among the data on rural schools, and this singularity points to the most contested salient in the Bible War: County Cavan. In contrast to what can be thought of as the other border counties (Fermanagh, Monaghan, and, in Leinster, Louth), County Cavan had 48 percent of its boys and girls in education; the other border counties had not much more than half that. Moreover, 71.3 percent of the pupils on the County Cavan rolls were Roman Catholic.[45] These numbers were an indirect and accurate indication of the apparent success of the new-Reformation in an area that was overwhelmingly Catholic and, unlike Dalyland, not under an uncontested upper-class evangelical social order. The efforts here were directed, successively, by John Maxwell (1760–1823), Fourth Baron Farnham, and John Maxwell (1767–1838), the fifth. Using their Kingscourt estate as a centre point, they became the pivot of what was grandly called the Kingscourt District of the Irish Society for Promoting the Education of the Native Irish through the Medium of their Own Language. One says "grandly," because although the proselytizing district covered counties Cavan, Louth, Meath, Monaghan, and Tyrone, it was only in Cavan, where the Maxwells were supreme, that the Irish Society's schools truly flourished. In a sense, the Maxwells' effort more closely resembled a frontier colonial venture – one thinks of the latafundia of Spanish South America – than a venture in nineteenth-century evangelical conversionism. Their estate employed a full-time "moral agent" who had been brought up in the slave islands of the West Indies and whose previous managerial experience was in the Napoleonic Wars. The Maxwells in 1826 claimed that 300 Catholics had publicly recanted in Cavan town. That is hard to verify, but in the political arena the ultra-evangelical Maxwell family undeniably beat the Catholic Association in the election of 1826.[46]

A telling point about the Maxwells and their uniquely (if temporarily) successful evangelical dominion was that it was not nearly as

44 The tabulation is FitzGerald's.

45 Ibid.

46 Whelan, 172–82.

independent as it seemed: its closest ties were to the heart of Dalyland. It will be recalled that Lady Harriet Daly's father, Robert Maxwell, had been the first earl of Farnham. The earldom went extinct upon his death in 1779, but she was left an heiress. The subsidiary title of baron stayed intact, so that there were plenty of Lords Farnham still in the picture. Lady Harriet's uncle had inherited the Maxwell lands in Cavan, and it was her cousins (one and two generations farther down the family tree) who were in close touch with her son, their distant cousin the Rev. Robert Daly, about the Irish Society. Of all of Robert Daly's evangelical involvements, this was his favourite. He learned the Irish language and became quite an adept lexicographer, revising one of the standard Irish-English dictionaries of the time.[47] Daly's interest in the language was essentially instrumental as he did not wish to preserve it, but to use it to save souls.[48] However, the Maxwell family went the whole road, tying the security of land rentals to faith, publishing messages on the desirability of abandoning "Popery" and, at minimum, admonitions on the need to send children to the proper schools. There were other, less successful attempts at creating spiritual satrapies (those of the Rodens in Louth, the Lortons' several estates in Connaught, and the Synges of Dysert come to mind) but nothing like the demonstrable efficiency of the County Cavan exercise existed: outside, of course, of Dalyland, which was another world entirely, a kingdom of interlocking landlords and parsons and Sunday schools and surplus wealth and an evangelical example to be envied by those outfield Protestant landlords who were surrounded by an ocean of unregenerate Catholic tenants just barely within their social control.

On another flank, the Bible War tactic that set off the most smoke and had the least potential for actually converting anyone was a series of debates between Protestant and Catholic clergy that had all the dignity of an argument in a fish market. During his examination before the

47 *CDIB*, entry for Robert Daly; Madden (1875), 93–6.

48 As was the case with the other Dalyland power in the Irish Society, its co-founder and first secretary was Henry Joseph Monck Mason (1778–1858). He was born on a gentry tenancy on the Powerscourt desmense. He funded the chair of Irish at TCD. He spent his retirement at Dargle Cottage, Delgany (*CDIB*).

select committee of the House of Lords in late April 1825, Archbishop William Magee referred approvingly to a public meeting in Carlow, where the differences between the Roman Catholic and the Protestant (meaning Anglican) faiths was debated by leading clergymen of each side.[49] This debate was one of a whole series that had taken place in 1824, wherein the various proselytizing societies ("Bible societies" in the vocabulary of the time) as meat for their annual meetings invited Catholic priests and lay leaders to debate Protestants about big issues – the place of the Bible in determining faith being the most important, but also the topics of purgatory, transubstantiation, and the position of the priesthood. The Carlow meeting of 18–19 November 1824 was the annual meeting of the Carlow Auxiliary of the Bible Society. This was the occasion on which the Rev. Robert Daly became a national figure. His auxiliaries in a two-day debate were the Hon. Rev. Edward Wingfield, and the Rev. Richard Pope, a just-priested, very energetic Church of Ireland clergyman whose family was influential in Cork City. Four Catholic priests faced them and the two sides argued over the Bible. Eventually the discussion, if such it was, ended with the Protestants escaping just before an armed mob broke in threatening grievous bodily harm.[50] The Carlow affray was one of many such mixtures of debate-and-melee that continued well into 1827.[51]

When in the autumn of 1825 John Nelson Darby threaded his way through the mountain passes to his isolated charge, he was fully aware that a multi-front sectarian contest was taking place and that he was a young militant tapped to be a future leader: thence his singular degree of independent responsibility as a Church of Ireland deacon.[52] In the 1850s Darby recalled that "as soon as I was ordained, I went amongst

49 *Minutes of Evidence Taken before the Select Committee of the House of Lords Appointed to Inquire into the State of Ireland*, 391 H.C. 1825 (521), ix.

50 *BDEB*, entry for Pope; Bowen (1978), 99–101; Whelan, 208.

51 Bowen (1978), 106–9, 399–400.

52 To emphasize an earlier point: in this study, when "sectarian" is used it is in the modern sense of the term.

the poor Irish mountaineers, in a wild and uncultivated district, where I remained two years and three months, working as best I could."[53] This memory fits well with external sources. It is unusual in its degree of precision, for the statement is one of the few occasions in which Darby was both willing and able to use the secular calendar to define with any real accuracy what he had done in the past. Manifestly, this was one of the most memorable times of his life and coincided with the latter portion of the "six or seven years"[54] of spiritual unease that he had felt since his conversion, whose year, much less its specific date, he could not remember.

While granting that the Rev. Mr Darby, as he was then known, had real theological issues to grapple with, it is useful to frame some of them in somewhat less spiritualized terms than Darby later employed. Thus, it is fair to recognize that, roughly, from late 1824 to the beginning of 1827 one of his difficulties was how to reconcile his romantic embrace of faux-medievalism with the real world of Irish poverty. His brother George Darby at Marklye was still a running-mate of Kenelm Henry Digby, and the Darby family's Sussex estate was the home of medieval tournaments that were as solemn as they were ridiculous. To a skeptical eye (including, one infers, that of his own mature vision), John Nelson Darby's becoming a self-styled medieval monk was of a piece with this flummery.[55] Had he been play-acting as a knight at Marklye, one imagines that he would have tied Lady Powerscourt's handkerchief to his lance. But in his Calary charge he was not play-acting, and he later asserted that he sought "assiduously to fulfill the duties of the ministry confided to me, working day and night amongst the people, who were almost as wild as the mountains they inhabited."[56]

Related to the tension engendered between his own romantic medievalism and everyday economic deprivation of Darby's parishioners was the more fundamental matter of just what Catholicity and Prot-

53 *A Letters by J.N.D. to Prof. Tholuck*, LJND, vol. 3, no. 26.

54 Ibid.

55 In a late-life letter wherein Darby refers to himself as a "poor worm," he refers to "honest monks' labour, which I have tried." Darby to ___Mahoney, 28 May 1880. *LJND*, vol. 3, no. 77.

56 *A Letter by J.N.D. to Prof. Tholuck*; LJND, vol. 3, no 226.

estantism meant in his own ministry. As far as the institutional Roman Catholic Church as it existed in Ireland was concerned, Darby was a lifelong anti-Catholic, at as deep a bile-dripping level as the most ardent Orangeman. However, his knowledge of the early Church fathers and of their medieval spiritual descendants permitted him at this stage of his life to develop an idea of a form of true Catholicism that was unbesmirched by the fingerprints of the actual Church. Somehow, he had to align his being anti-Catholic in Ireland (he was knowingly a soldier in the Bible War) with a refusal to be a Protestant in the sense of rejecting the true Catholic Church. He had the same "horror of Protestantism" that John Henry Newman had, and Darby "disowned … that name. I looked for the Church."[57] The capitalization of "Church" is Darby's, and it indicates something that he never was able to define: an affirmation of an ancient perfection equally satisfying to the mind and emotions. In his mid-fifties, the middle-aged Darby explained well, albeit now with clear revulsion, what the young Darby had found attractive about "the root of Romanism": "it is a sensuous religion, fills the imagination with gorgeous ceremonies, noble buildings, fine music, stately processions. It feeds it [the imagination] with legends and the poetry of antiquity." Then with remarkable economy he explained why this did not work for him: "But it gives no holy peace to the conscience, ease it may, but not peace."[58] That is the conclusion toward which John Nelson Darby was working when, in 1825, he took march to Calary Bog.

57 [J.N.D.] *Analysis of Dr Newman's Apologia pro Vita Sua*, 2.
58 Ibid., 13.

CHAPTER SIX

Everything Implodes, 1825–1829

Among the things that everyone once knew, but now is largely forgotten, is that a braided line – think of a ship's hawser – is stronger than one that is simply made up of two or three strands twisted together. And both are much stronger than a single filament. Even today, in the age of malleable steel and of extruded polymer lines, the really tough sheets are braided and fused from multiple strands. Whether done by hand or through chemical glues, braided lines are made of interlocking knots so that, as in the case of a hawser, if the line is cut at any point, it does not unravel but holds form and strength right up to the point that it is interrupted.

In setting in place the Irish background of a significant component of world evangelicalism, I have tried to interbraid four lines. These are, first, the unique socioeconomic character of the south Dublin region that I have called "Dalyland." This was a singular area in terms of its being relatively rich, an area whose big landowners drained money from their distant estates in order to engineer a landscape and a style of life that were both artful and artificial. After the 1798 Rising was definitively settled, Dalyland became as secure an Anglican bastion as existed anyplace in Ireland. Secondly, the religious affiliation of Dalyland was not merely Church of Ireland, but, from the end of the Napoleonic Wars onward, increasingly evangelical, and by the mid-1820s dominantly so. A series of complex family relations and of close social ties knotted together the economic power structure with the ladder of power and preference within the southern part of the Diocese of Dublin and Glendalough. This we have seen in detail with families such as the Guinnesses, Parnells, Synges, Wingfields, Howards, La Touches, and others. Thirdly, the Church of Ireland as a nationwide institution faced problems that seemingly had been solved in Dalyland, most notably the question of how to tie together Anglican economic, governmental, and religious hegemony with the necessity of gaining mass acquiescence to that order. Thus, it was not surprising that the clerical and lay leaders of Dalyland were in the forefront of several evangelizing agencies. Fourthly, we have seen that John Nelson Darby came from a family background that was culturally rich, financially privileged, and, even though cosmopolitan in its network of useful contacts, ultimately Anglo-Irish. Because Darby himself worked hard at bleaching his backstory out of existence and because the Brethren historians who have followed him have kept the page almost as empty as he left it, I have braided together what we can know about Darby as a young man, together with the social structure of Dalyland and its leading families, with the Church of Ireland's power games, and with the ongoing Bible War – and I have done this at several points.

More than two decades ago, *Irish Historical Studies* commissioned a multi-author bibliographic study of the history of the Church of Ireland. Fergus O'Farrall was assigned the period 1800–70, and he was a shrewd reader indeed. Among his observations:

> Darby's career as the most seminal thinker in formulating the theological system known as Dispensationalism is important; this system came to dominate late nineteenth-century American millenarianism and is a most significant element in the history of fundamentalism. The apparently God-forsaken state of the Established Church, which so dismayed Darby, had enormous consequences for Protestantism, particularly in the United States of America. There is an obvious need for a detailed local study of the north Wicklow/south Dublin area in the 1820s and 1830s.[1]

1 Fergus O'Ferrall, in the collective article: James Murray et al., "The Church of Ireland: A Critical Bibliography, 1536–1992," *Irish Historical Studies* (1993), 374.

Concerning John Nelson Darby, the single most salient conclusion is this: Darby as an historical figure makes sense only if one recognizes that he was the product not just of revelation but of situation.

Although John Nelson Darby never would have used anything as vulgar as the language of a tradesman, he seems to have come to understand that, despite being assiduous in his efforts, he was not very good at this job as a priest of the Church of Ireland – or, alternately, that priesthood in the Church of Ireland was not a fruitful occupation no matter how good at it he was. "Working as best I could, I felt, however, that the style of work was not in agreement with what I read in the Bible concerning the church and Christianity; nor did it correspond with the effects of the action of the Spirit of God."[2] That self-judgment runs against the grain of Brethren folk history, which wishes to see John Nelson Darby preaching fluently in Irish and converting Catholics in numbers.[3]

One grants, however, that Darby's self-presentation while serving as a Church of Ireland clergyman was arresting – virtually performance art – and it was natural for the drawing-room class to assume that it was effective. His performance as an ascetic medieval monk can be considered as an ecclesiastical parallel to the landscape engineering of the Dalyland aristocracy, a successful attempt at creating an illusion, a vision that levitated above crude reality. The famous description of "the Irish clergyman" by Francis W. Newman is worth attention, particularly because Newman wrote at least fifteen years after he broke with Darby, and yet he unintentionally still acts as a publicity agent for him. Thus, one can see how Darby's reputation came to considerably exceed his actual performance. Newman in his memoir of his own spiritual

2 *A Letter by J.N.D. to Prof. Tholuck; LJND*, vol. 3, no. 226.

3 These beliefs are widespread. The most recent example is Marion Field's biography of Darby: "He preached to the villagers in Gaelic, their native language; this pleased them as the Irish Roman Catholic Priests suppressed Gaelic and insisted that English should be spoken. Folklore said that the devil could tell no lies in Gaelic and because of this the superstitious peasants accepted the truth of what Darby told them and many came to accept the Lord Jesus Christ as their Saviour and Lord" (*John Nelson Darby* [Godalming 2008], 32).

development provided a compelling picture of the indefatigable Darby roving out each night amid mountains and bogs; seldom home before midnight; sallow and lamed by his work, and his frame becoming more and more skeletal as he ate the food the locals offered, unpalatable and often indigestible. Newman asserted that Darby's saintliness "intensely excited the poor Romanists … The stamp of heaven seemed to them clear in a frame so wasted by austerity, so superior to worldly pomp, and so partaking in all their indigence." Newman than postulated "that a dozen such men would have done more to convert all Ireland to Protestantism, than the whole apparatus of the Church Establishment." So the unstated conclusion was that John Nelson Darby must have been a wonder at converting Catholics.[4]

Actually, there is no direct evidence that he either spoke Irish or converted any Catholics from within Calary; indeed what we know suggests the opposite.[5] Nevertheless, Francis Newman's unintentional advertising for Darby is a useful pattern as it indicates in writing what must have been going on verbally throughout the drawing rooms and salons of Dalyand: Darby was becoming a country-house legend, his public performances being taken as guarantors of his ecclesiastical production. Note in the case of Newman's observations that there is no indication that Newman ever visited Darby's charge, much less observed him in ministerial work with the peasantry. Newman in

4 The quotations are from Francis William Newman, *Phases of Faith* (London 1874), 27–8.

5 Although there is no evidence that I have found to suggest that Darby converted any number of Roman Catholics to Protestantism, that could merely be a reflection of the loss of parochial records. A more reasonable inference is that in Calary he brought forth out of their silence some of the at most 300 adult Protestants in the parish, of a total population of 2,500 to 2,800 persons of all ages. These would be the sort of individuals whom Archbishop Magee had described as being too frightened to show themselves for fear of their Catholic neighbours. Yet, even on this front Darby was only marginally successful. In 1829, after he abandoned his parish to become a roving preacher, his former parishioners presented him with a memorial of "our love and grateful thanks." It was signed by only thirteen persons, representing just seven families, not a large turn-out. And all the names were Anglo-Irish, not "native Irish" as the term is sometimes used. The memorial of 28 March 1829 is found in CBA, J.N.D./1/1/23 (duplicate in J.N.D./5/1).

September 1827 had become a tutor for the sons of Susan and Edward Pennefather, chiefly at Temple Carrig, their Delgany country estate. The Pennefathers also had a Dublin residence, 20 Fitzwilliam Square. From encounters at those two addresses – not Calary Bog – Francis Newman became convinced of John Nelson Darby's great missionary powers and was one of Darby's first disciples and himself participated in an epic missionary journey with other Brethren to Baghdad.[6] Here the point is that the world of fashionable evangelicalism was accepting of Darby's reports on his social visits as despatches from the front and as indications of battles fought and won.

Privately, John Nelson Darby was feeling ripped up about his own spiritual state and the fruits of his mission. Late in the year 1827, Darby, somewhat dispirited and confused, had some good luck (call it providential intervention, if you prefer), although at the time it appeared to be just the opposite. He had what his devotees later called a "riding accident," though it was nothing quite so toney as that. "An accident happened which laid me aside for a time; my horse was frightened and had thrown me against a door-post."[7] One does not have to have spent much time with horses to realize that a tired and hungry horse will go for anything resembling a stable door and letting that happen is not something one can view with pride. Hence, in the Brethren telling, it becomes a riding accident. But in truth it was a blessing, for Darby had to take to his bed and then to crutches and at best to limited activity, at minimum for the period of December 1827 through February 1828.[8] In his enforced inactivity, he had time to think, pray, and pay critical attention to what was happening in the Church of Ireland as it carried on its Bible War.

Concerning the efforts of the new-Reformation movement, a basic evaluative question both for Darby at the time and for present-day

6 *ODNB*, entry for Francis William Newman.

7 *A Letter by J.N.D. to Prof. Tholuck*; *LJND*, vol. 3, no. 226.

8 Timothy C.F. Stunt, *From Awakening to Secession: Radical Evangelicals in Switzerland and Britain, 1815–35* (Edinburgh 2000), 171.

historians is: were significant numbers of Roman Catholics really being converted? David Miller, one of the most skilled historians of nineteenth-century Irish religion, came to the conclusion that, despite the furore surrounding the County Cavan efforts of successive Lords Farnham, "very little, if any, evidence has come to light that Catholics were induced to have the sort of experience understood to be conversion by evangelicals of the English, methodistical type."[9] That conclusion is technically right but, as Miller quickly clarifies, historically irrelevant. "English, methodistical" conversions – here Miller means fall-down responses to hellfire sermons – were not what the Irish new-Reformation conversions were all about. As I have emphasized repeatedly in previous chapters, Anglican evangelicalism in the period from the Union to the mid-1830s in Ireland was a somewhat different phenomenon from contemporary English and American models. Irish evangelicalism was much lower in emotional temperature, much less oriented toward single-moment individual conversion experiences, much more willing to grant the validity of collective worship through liturgy and sacrament, and in the 1820s was tied very closely to producing conformity with a specific state church. Yet, undeniably the movement was evangelical, not just in its self-labelling as such but especially in its deep commitment to biblicism: hence the immense effort to teach the Irish nation to read and thus to encounter the scriptures directly. Irish evangelicalism fit the famous criteria of David Bebbington concerning evangelicalism (see chapter 1), but with a different weighting of its various elements, a different mix than we are accustomed to observe in most of the English-speaking world.[10] Paradoxically, it was the singular configuration of Irish evangelicalism that yielded the creation of the Brethren and, secondarily, was a necessary precondition to the adoption of the Brethren's intellectual stepchild, pre-millennial Dispensationalism.

9 David Miller, "Varieties of Irish Evangelicalism," *Field Day Review* (2007), 216.

10 Lewis W. Rambo, *Understanding Religious Conversion* (New Haven 1993), provides a useful antidote to narrow definitions of the conversion experience. Such definitions usually are culturally constricted. He particularly emphasizes that conversion is a process that usually takes place over a considerable period of time and whose shape is sharply chiselled by specific cultural context.

Whatever form conversion by Catholics to Protestantism assumed, some did indeed take place. One must remember, however, that this had always been the case. For example, between 1703 and 1800, a period largely characterized by intense anti-Catholic penal legislation, some 6,000 Roman Catholics were officially recorded as having converted to the Church of Ireland.[11] Overwhelmingly, these were Catholics from the landed class who converted in order to preserve their property or to access gainful occupations, particularly the practice of law.[12] The new-Reformation conversions of Catholics seem to have been quite different, being mostly poor-to-modest farmers and a set of interesting, but not statistically significant outliers, Catholic priests. The County Cavan crusade of the Maxwell family on the Farnham estates, combined with the focused efforts of the Irish Society, into which the Rev. Robert Daly invested so much energy, ramped into full gear in the autumn of 1826; local newspapers reported 252 converts between September and December. This number was claimed to have risen to 450 persons by the end of January 1827.[13] As the Cavan efforts developed, a separate crusade was begun in County Carlow in January 1827. This mostly involved cadres of evangelical preachers sermonizing on Sundays and acrimonious debates staged during weekdays.[14]

When the April annual meetings of the various evangelical societies came around in 1827, it was claimed that, in Ireland, 1,340 converts had been brought into the fold (presumably during the previous year).[15] An even higher estimate, provided by an English magazine, the *British Critic,* stated that between September 1826 and September 1827 almost 2,400 Roman Catholics had conformed to the Church of Ireland – in this case, conforming being the synonym of conversion.[16] So buoyed

11 Emmet Larkin, *The Pastoral Role of the Roman Catholic Church in Pre-famine Ireland* (Dublin 2006), 215.

12 An excellent set of essays on eighteenth-century conversions is Michael Brown, Charles Ivar McGrath, and Thomas P. Power (eds), *Converts and Conversion in Ireland* (Dublin 2005).

13 Thomas McGrath, *Politics, Interdenominational Relations and Education in the Public Ministry of Bishop James Doyle* (Dublin 1999), 133–4.

14 Ibid., 135–9.

15 Stewart J. Brown, *The National Churches of England, Ireland, and Scotland* (Oxford 2001), 126.

16 Ibid., 130.

were the Anglican leaders by reports like these, that in December 1827 a Dublin Metropolitan Reformation Society was formed, with Archbishop William Magee in the chair. Subsequently, county Reformation societies were formed in Carlow, Kilkenny, and several other places in the countryside to support local Bible instructors and home visitors and to be conduits for the distribution of Bibles and tracts.[17] Thus 1828 was to be a prophetic year, a year of miracles.

At that point, late 1827 to early 1828, on the verge of a promised miraculous moment, individuals with education and leisure could well have used the opportunity to do their sums: if so, they could only have concluded that what was going on, as far as advancement of the Church of Ireland was concerned, was exactly nothing, at best. Even if one does not question the score-keeping of the evangelical societies – let us assume 2,800 converts per year in the mid 1820s – that is only two conversions each year per ecclesiastical benefice. Really, that is not a national religious reformation or even a potential one. Indeed, the actual situation was even less flattering: the claims of the various new-Reformation societies always dealt in *gross* numbers, while an accurate picture requires *net* numbers. To put it another way, the real scorecard should have answered the question: did more people convert from Roman Catholicism to Anglicanism in this period, or was it the other way round? Dr James W. Doyle, the remarkably able and realistic Catholic Bishop of Kildare and Leighlin, did a tally of his own dioceses, asking each of his priests about how many specific cases they had of conversions from Protestantism *to* Catholicism. Doyle's episcopal responsibilities covered a geographic crescent that enclosed the Church of Ireland's archdiocese of Dublin and Glendalough: running from County Kildare to King's County and then south to Queen's County and into small parts of counties Kilkenny, Carlow, and Wexford and a bit of the far south of County Wicklow.[18] This jurisdiction included most of the hot spots of the new-Reformation, save County Cavan. In 1825, Bishop Doyle had computed that the average number of conversions *to* Catholicism per parish under his control (he had

17 Ibid., 129–30.

18 For maps of the Roman Catholic diocese of Kildare and Leighlin, see Thomas McGrath, *Religious Renewal and Reform in the Pastoral Ministry of Bishop James Doyle* (Dublin 1999), viii–ix.

forty-seven parishes, the number varying somewhat over time) was 200 annually. This number actually increased during the heightened Protestant crusade of 1826 and 1827, although the number never exceeded twenty in any single parish. Usually it was three to ten a year and mostly these were done quietly. Sometimes they were deathbed conversions, thus perhaps illustrating the folk belief that the best way to be happy in both this world and the next was to live as a Protestant and to die as a Catholic.[19]

Since Bishop Doyle did not compute his diocese's losses to the Established Church, the picture is incomplete, but paradoxically it is conclusive: namely, that whatever gains were claimed by conversions to Protestantism by new-Reformation activists had to be discounted by losses through counter-conversions. The dispiriting effect of this fact was multiplied if anyone quietly reflected upon the fact that there were many more Catholics in the population than Protestants; in the late 1820s roughly 75,000 Catholics were being born each year and only 15,000 Protestants, and not all of those Church of Ireland.[20] During the course of the new-Reformation movement the Anglican Church had to have fallen several hundred thousand souls farther behind the Catholic church.

The 1987 edition of *The Oxford Companion to the Mind* has a rare and wonderful essay on human intelligence. This virtuoso piece by H.B. Barlow avoids everything that makes one wince when psychologists start talking about intelligence – there is no discussion of the psychometrics of intelligence testing, no borrowed neuroscience, no half-formed epistemology of knowledge. Instead, Barlow discusses in-

19 McGrath, *Politics*, 139–41, 290n217. The case of one parish that claimed 139 converts to Catholicism is taken as being of doubtful accuracy.

20 This was the calculation of Thomas Wyse in *The Political Catechism Explanatory of the Constitutional Rights and Civil Disabilities of the Catholics of Ireland* (London 1829), 101–2, cited in McGrath, *Politics*, 143. Wyse was a Catholic, educated at Trinity College, Dublin, and in 1830 was MP for Tipperary. He was an enthusiast for the creation of a non-sectarian national system of education. For details see Akenson, *The Irish Education Experiment* (London and Toronto 1970; republished London and New York 2012), 108–15.

telligence as "the art of good guess-work." Good guess-work is the ability to detect new, non-chance associations, and to get it right. Really intelligent people can do two things. One of these is to look at a minimal pattern and somehow know what the completed pattern will be. The standard puzzles kids still play with show a few dots against a solid background and slowly more dots are added. Smart individuals guess the pattern more quickly and more accurately than do others. Secondly, intelligent people can look at a mass of information and guess quickly which of the pieces really count. Swift and accurate pattern recognition leads to more sensible and more timely plans of action than does blinking uncomprehendingly at a world of swirl.[21]

As the sectarian moil and malice of the 1820s moved toward its conclusion, two leading individuals in the Anglican communion showed considerable intelligence by good guessing – that is, by salient pattern recognition – and one missed the memo entirely. These were: most impressively, the Rev. Dr Richard Lawrence, the archbishop of Cashel, who is worth brief acquaintance as an indication that the mind of the Church of Ireland was not entirely intoxicated by Dalyland; the second is the Dowager Viscountess Powerscourt, who could recognize a dark cloud when others could see only an empty horizon. In contrast, surprisingly, John Nelson Darby never did understand the fundamentally flawed strategy of the new-Reformation, much less its self-defeating tactics.

Richard Laurence (1760–1838) was appointed by the Crown (effectively meaning by Lord Liverpool, the prime minister of the United Kingdom) as archbishop of Cashel in July 1822. This appointment ran against the grain of the Church of Ireland's administrative culture as it had developed after the Union of Great Britain and Ireland for, despite an in-name-only union with the Church of England, the Irish church was becoming more and more Irish in its personnel, and the best posts now were going to Irishmen. Laurence was one of two English archbishops thrust upon the Irish Church in the 1820s and 1830s (the other was Richard Whately, appointed archbishop of Dublin in 1831, of whom more later) and each was resented as a blow-in. This was

21 H.B. Barlow, "Intelligence: The Art of Good Guess-Work," in Richard L. Gregory (ed.), *The Oxford Companion to the Mind* (1987), 381–3.

unjust in each case, as neither had wanted the appointment and each was a religious thinker and humanities scholar of distinction markedly above that of the average Irish bishop. In Laurence's case, he left the post of regius professor of Hebrew at Oxford as well as a canonry at Christ Church, Oxford. He was, in 1822, a widower in his sixties who had spent his life in the study of Ethiopic and had done a pioneering edition of a major item among the Judaeo-Christian pseudepigraphical writings. Archbishop Laurence was essentially a gentle, unworldly old man who had little direct knowledge of Ireland.[22]

But he was very intelligent and the several dimensions of confusion that blew across the Irish religious scene in the 1820s did not blur his vision. He recognized the pattern of social physics that encompassed the new-Reformation. Every Irish bishop was expected to make a formal visitation of his diocese every three years, and in the case of archbishops it was expected that the occasion be marked by a major address to the assembled clergy of his province and the publication of the address soon thereafter. As our earlier discussion of the 1825 address of Archbishop Magee indicated, this was an opportunity to make a statement to which the Anglican laity would pay notice. Archbishop Laurence's head-snappingly direct point was contained in a simple question he addressed to his clergy about the new-Reformation attempts at converting Catholics: "Can you flatter yourselves that you could gain a single proselyte?"[23] Here the Rev. Dr Laurence was putting forward the gross-vs-net issue, without using those words. To his clergy he suggested that they could carry on with their missionary work (he hoped it would be temperate in tone) but that they should

22 *ODNB*, entry for Richard Laurence. It appears that his only significant contact with Ireland came through his elder brother (regius professor of Civil Law, Oxford), who had been a good friend of Edmund Burke and was his literary executor. That put the future archbishop on two sides of the fence as far as the Church of Ireland was concerned: (1) Burke as a founding conservative, anti-French, pro-monarchist fit well with Irish Anglicanism, but (2) anyone close to him knew of his Catholic family history and of the encoded way that he inclined toward the abolition of Catholic civil disabilities. See Conor Cruise O'Brien, *The Great Melody: A Thematic Biography and Commented Anthology of Edmund Burke* (Chicago 1992).

23 Richard Laurence, *A Charge Delivered … 1826* (Dublin 1826), 12.

realize that the Catholic priests would be doing the same thing. In his view it all led to no gain for the Church of Ireland or, indeed, to loss. Thus: a null transaction, or less, for this competition for souls would hurt Irish Christianity considered as a whole.

This realistic exercise in pattern recognition earned Archbishop Laurence several public rebukes from promoters of the new-Reformation. One of the more widely published was in *Blackwood's Edinburgh Magazine*, where, as part of a larger discussion of "the Catholic Question," it was noted that: "The archbishop of Cashel lately put forth the unaccountable doctrine that the efforts in favour of the Reformation, whatever they may do in other respects, are pretty sure to injure Christianity in Ireland."[24]

That viewpoint had to be counteracted in Great Britain, as much of the money for the more aggressive proselytizing societies came from frequent Irish fundraising tours of England and Scotland:

> We will not deal harshly with the archbishop of Cashel; but we must be permitted to advise him to read the oath taken by the clergy – to examine certain laws which bear upon the duties of the clergy – to peruse the New Testament – to make himself thoroughly acquainted with the example, precepts, and commands of the Divine Founder of Christianity in all matters touching the Reformation of Ireland.

In case there were any doubts that Archbishop Laurence had perceived with nerve-pinching accuracy the Irish situation, this desperate insult followed:

> If our Saviour had resembled the Archbishop – if the instructions of the one had been the same as the instructions of the other – what would have been the case at present with Christianity? If the example of the Archbishop had always been followed, what would have been the present condition of Christianity? We dare not express all that we feel touching his conduct, but we are

24 [anon.], "The Catholic Question," *Blackwood's Edinburgh Magazine*, vol. 21 (May 1827), 580.

> very sure that this conduct will be thought of as it ought to be by our countrymen.[25]

A second person who had early pattern recognition about the new-Reformation – though not as acutely as Archbishop Laurence – was Lady Powerscourt. This may sound surprising, as she was used by the Dalyland evangelicals as a high-tone resonator for their message (what a wonderful amplifier a really Big House was), and she certainly was a committed evangelical herself. Yet, behind the fluttery prose and the expression of spiritual joy that one finds in her collected letters from the middle 1820s, there was also a critical, sometimes morose, sensibility. At times, she was dispiritedly condemnatory of her own failings, or of those of some preacher, and at some moments she had a particularly harsh view of the prospects of the Church, as well as of her own life. In the spring of 1826 she was writing that "now I feel *my tale is told,* and ties of friendship are drawing towards an hereafter, while we are only left in Satan's kingdom, for the Lord to finish his work in us and by us."[26]

Lady Powerscourt had a right to feel that the religious world was not turning properly – "Satan's kingdom," indeed – but this was in part because her own position on Earth was less enviable than her Big House and social position might make one expect. For one thing, she had a serious eye problem that for a time made her almost blind.[27] More

25 Ibid. The idea that differing Christian faiths should live together as being under the same salvation was particularly incendiary to hyper-evangelicals. It implied that salvation through the Roman Catholic Church was possible and was part of a larger plan of divine salvation and thus had legitimacy. In any case, this is the appropriate place to correct the misapprehension, found in some modern studies, which suggest that Robert Daly was the author of the anonymous piece quoted above (for which the author is not definitively known but is not Daly) and that writing as "Senex," Daly wrote several inflammatory anti-Catholic articles in *Blackwood's* in this period. "Senex" actually was Horatio Townshend, a Church of Ireland clergyman in the diocese of Cork, in his mid-seventies and thoroughly disinhibited verbally.

26 Lady Powerscourt to ___, 12 May 1826, in Robert Daly (ed.), *Letters and Papers by the Late Theodosia Viscountess Powerscourt*, 3rd ed. (Dublin 1839), 30, emphasis in the original.

27 Lady Powerscourt to ____, October 1827, ibid., 35.

debilitating, however, was another matter: she was conscious of living with a temporal calendar that each day brought her closer to what, in the terms of her social class, was disaster. Several times in her letters she quotes the biblical phrase "let thy widows trust in me" (Jer. 49:11). This usage was not only immediately after her husband's death, but it referred to a continuing aspect of her life, a recognition of her own vulnerability.[28] Without in any way impugning Lady Powerscourt's spirituality, she had a this-world problem of the sort that we mentioned in the previous chapter: even women of the aristocracy were liable to experience severe social and economic decline if their husbands died. This was true throughout the British Isles but was especially severe in Ireland, where (with rare exceptions) there was no custom of the dower-house.[29] The day that the Fifth Viscount Powerscourt died, the calendar pages began to turn for Theodosia, the youngest of three Dowager Viscountesses Powerscourt. The minority of her stepson, the sixth viscount, would end in January 1836 and that was the date Lady Powerscourt would be shipped off to a good address in Dublin, just as inevitably as a brindle beast would be sent to the knackers. It was a very cruel world, and anyone raised in its confines understood the rules. Lady Powerscourt could of course remarry, but her religious devotion limited the pool of potential second husbands. In any case, she was no longer a very attractive economic proposition: jointures usually ended at remarriage. In a strange way, Lady Powerscourt as a widowed aristocrat had the same basic problem that even the yeoman tenantry of her estate had: traditionally such persons lived under the "hanging gale," meaning a half-year's rent that they were allowed to run in arrears, the result being that upon eviction, or even voluntary change of location, they were in danger of being impoverished.

Crucially, Lady Powerscourt responded to the pains and travails of her present life and the dark clouds on the horizon of the years ahead of her by a wonderful piece of cognition: she found a future world and brought it home to Powerscourt. This occurred by her being fascinated by the teaching of the Scottish magus Edward Irving, for a time

28 Thus: Lady Powerscourt to ____, 18 February 1824, ibid., 20; Lady Powerscourt to ____, 26 November 1833, ibid., 192.

29 A.P.W. Malcomson, *The Pursuit of the Heiress* (Belfast 2006), 17.

London's most popular preacher and by the "prophecy conferences" that were held at Albury Park, the Surrey estate of Irving's patron, Henry Drummond. The first was in December 1826, and they continued annually through 1829. Lady Powerscourt probably was an observer at the first conference. In any case, as an inveterate sermon-taster, she approvingly heard Irving preach at his church in London. In 1827, she seems for a time to have organized every second Tuesday evenings at Powerscourt for informal discussions of prophecy, with Robert Daly in the chair.[30] These were not the famous Powerscourt Conferences of the early 1830s, but they were the start.[31] Whatever the mixture of personal and spiritual interest was that drove Lady Powerscourt, she had divined that the present church was not working and that an alternate future was required.

John Nelson Darby, in contrast to Archbishop Laurence, never did understand why the new-Reformation was a failure, but by a complicated, almost random path he concluded that a different future was necessary. In his convalescence in winter 1827–28, during what he later called "my solitude,"[32] he had the entire spiritual world on his mind and a fair amount of the institutional Church to consider as well. Mind you, the divans at the Pennefathers' two residences were not exactly the appointments of an Anchorite cell. Whether in their Dublin or their Wicklow residence (he seems to have spent time at both), he not only had family for company, but old friends, such as John Gifford Bellett,

30 *ODNB*, entry for Theodosia Wingfield; see also Mrs Hamilton Madden, *Memoir of the Right Rev. Robert Daly* (London 1875), 149–50. The chronology here is wobbly both because the Albury meetings were not well recorded and were officially male gatherings and because Mrs Madden (150–1) is uncharacteristically unclear. Lady Powerscourt wrote to the Rev. Mr Daly, "I am going to the prophets' meeting at Mr Drummond's" (Madden, 150; the date is most likely 1827, not 1826). It appears that Mrs Madden is wrong in dating the start of Lady Powerscourt's full-blown prophecy conferences (as distinct from bursts of fortnightly discussions) to autumn 1827. On this misdating, see Grayson Carter, *Anglican Evangelicals* (London 2001), 203.

31 Lady Powerscourt was not the only Irish person at the Albury meetings. The most significant official attendee was the Rev. Hugh NcNeile, the rector of Albury, which was under the patronage of Henry Drummond. McNeile, who organized the event, was the son-in-law of Archbishop Magee of Dublin.

32 *Letter by J.N.D. to Prof. Tholuck*; *LJND*, vol. 3, no. 226.

a contemporary from TCD and now a young barrister, who lionized him.[33] And, Francis William Newman, fresh from a double first at Oxford and a fellowship at Balliol, had been engaged in September 1827 as tutor for the sons of Edward Pennefather and was a fine mind for Darby to rub against. Add to that the probable condolence visits of the Dalyland elite (the Revs Cleaver and Daly, Lady Powerscourt, and others) and John Nelson Darby's convalescence probably was not as ascetic as he remembered it decades later.

Still, he was peering into a world where to him the pattern made less and less sense. His response, I think, was twofold: he immersed himself in the Bible and tried to harmonize his place in the Irish Church with the scriptures – and found it impossible. That he would bathe his mind in the scriptures is a blindingly obvious suggestion, but if we are not careful it leads to a hiccup in our own thinking. Because John Nelson Darby almost never granted anyone credit for any idea he borrowed, it is tempting to read a marginal note Darby left in his special Bible study notebook, as referring both directly and causally to this time of incapacity: "I had once had my soul brought I knew not where – so deep as no tongue, I suppose could tell … I think Scott's essays gave a strong determination to my thought at one time, while my mind was working upon it."[34] The reference is to Thomas Scott (1747–1821), a Church of England cleric, an early evangelical, and a prolific writer. It is impossible to know which of Scott's dozens of books Darby read, but there are two reasons to think that the reference to Scott is probably retrospected memory and an indication of Scott's writings being helpful later in Darby's life, not in the 1820s. The first reason is that Darby's muted praise of Scott was found in the pages of the ongoing commentary on scripture that he was putting together, most likely in the 1850s and '60s. And as the *Dictionary of National Biography* notes, Scott's "major work, however, for which he is now alone remembered

33 See [Letty M. Bellett], *Recollections of the Late J.G. Bellett* (London 1895), 27, on a planned visit to the convalescing Darby. The ambiguous dating of the letter mentioning this visit (John Gifford Bellett to George Bellett, 31 January 1828) is straightened out in Timothy C.F. Stunt, (2000), 171n86.

34 Max S. Weremchuk, *John Nelson Darby* (Neptune, NJ, 1992; orig. German ed. 1988), 204, appendix C, reproducing marginal notes to 2nd Timothy, chapter 3. This fascicle of the study New Testament is found in CBA J.N.D./3/5.

was his commentary on the Bible (4 vols, 1788–1792)."[35] This commentary was an impressive piece of scholarship, especially in its remarks on the Old Testament, as Scott was an accomplished Hebraist. Essentially, it is a Bible with footnotes added, and a good model for Darby to have in mind as he did his own work. Moreover, the Rev. Mr Scott commenced his large commentary with a long preface that argued in detail for a literalness in interpretation of biblical stories and for accepting both testaments fully, for he believed "beyond dispute the whole Bible to be a divine revelation."[36] This was exactly Darby's view in the personal Bible commentary he was himself constructing. Secondly, one suspects that Thomas Scott was on Darby's mind in the mid-1860s because John Henry Newman, the iconic convert to Catholicism of the Victorian era, had published his *Apologia* in 1864, a volume that enraged Darby and brought forth a long reply from him. In his *Apologia,* Newman discusses his early evangelical views and says that "the writer who made a deeper impression on my mind than any other, and to whom (humanly speaking) I almost owe my soul – Thomas Scott of Aston Sandford … I had been possessed of his essays from a boy; his commentary I bought when I was an undergraduate."[37] So, thirty or forty years after his series of spiritual crises of the 1820s, John Nelson Darby most likely had Thomas Scott on his mind for reasons other than accurate historical memory.

Instead of searching for spiritual godfathers for John Nelson Darby's second conversion, it is better to simply recognize that from late 1827 into early 1828 he was in both physical and mental pain. Bodily, he hurt: smashing up a leg is not a comfortable experience. And, despite the visits of obliging friends, Darby was left to his own devices to define his personal and professional position within the Church of Ireland and whether or not it fit with the scriptures. "He had practically given up all reading except that of the Bible" was the memory of Francis W. Newman, "and no small part of his movement towards

35 *ODNB* entry for Thomas Scott. For convenient memoirs of Scott, see the works by his son, John Scott, *The Life of the Rev. Thomas Scott* (London 1822) and *Letters and Papers of the Late Rev. Thomas Scott* (London 1826).

36 Thomas Scott, *The Holy Bible, Containing the Old and New Testaments with Original Notes …*, 2nd. ed. (London 1792), xiii.

37 John Henry Newman, *Apologia Pro Vita Sua* (orig. ed. 1864; London 1912), 32.

me soon took the form of dissuasion from all other voluntary study."[38] Clearly, he was holding the Irish Church up to the unbending metrics of the scriptures, as he interpreted them.

In practical terms, his relationship to the Church of Ireland now came down to his view of his patron, William Magee, archbishop of Dublin. Whatever gratitude he had once felt toward Magee for creating the Calary charge for him disappeared. In part, this was a matter of generational conflict – it evolved into a snarling match of a young cub vs an old and injured lion; in part, it was related to a jagged edge of Darby's personality, made clear here, but consistent through his life: namely, he could not abide other alpha-males.

Darby's issue with Archbishop Magee was projected onto the theological question of the nature of authority in the Church of Ireland. The authority of Magee was legitimated by a pattern of apostolic succession that ran back to Saint Patrick and thence to Jesus-the-Christ. (By virtue of being ordained by bishops the clergy shared in this apostolical succession, but as subordinates.)[39] Once Darby started to question Magee's behaviour and pastoral directives it was a psychologically natural step to question the ecclesiastical theory in which the archbishop's authority was embedded. In the period of reflection granted to him by his accident, John Nelson Darby was thinking very big thoughts indeed (nothing less than the nature of divine authority in the Christian Church), and at the same time was dealing with practical authority as expressed by Archbishop Magee. In the best of circumstances, it would have been hard to keep these two matters apart, and these were actually very hard circumstances: choppy and frightening times for the Church and all sorts of issues were jumbled together as clergy and the devout members of the laity tried to find a course forward.

38 Francis W. Newman (1850), 28.

39 "High churchmen stressed the primitive and catholic aspects of their church's heritage, and generally taught what they called 'church principles' or 'sound churchmanship' … Magee, for his part, urged his Dublin clergy to contend for 'the apostolical origin and succession of the Christian ministry." Alan Acheson, *A History of the Church of Ireland* (Dublin 2002), 154.

Two vague chronologies are possible through this confusion, but no satisfactory logic exists – which is a signal point, really, for Darby's volatility before his enforced retreat in the winter of 1827–28 was a precondition for the insights that he later presented as a series of revelations. The two chronologies that can be held up to probative tests are: (1) the narrative John Nelson Darby dictated in his sixties, when as a full-scale prophet he was becoming a world figure through his quiet, insistent, almost covert selling of his form of evangelical millennialism to Protestant free-church leaders around the English-speaking world; and (2) our own estimate of what was the most probable story that Darby affirmed when he was much younger, in his late twenties. The former narrative has either been accepted by Brethren and other evangelical historians as being essentially correct, usually without any examination of the evidence, or those who have had doubts have tiptoed carefully away as if leaving a minefield. Even partially sorting out the course of events (and in the present state of evidence a partial job is all one can do) is wearying. It is necessary, however, because, at minimum, John Nelson Darby was one of the initiators of a major declension within evangelicalism in the English-speaking world; and, at most, these events of 1826–28, in Darby's own estimate, initiated the true Church of God.

Fortunately, a few things are clear. On 10 October 1826, Archbishop Magee delivered a triennial charge to all the clergy of the province of Dublin. Whether or not Darby was present at St Patrick's Cathedral for the very long sermon-cum-lecture is uncertain, but in any case the charge eventually was published in mid-1827. Although Darby later used that sermon as the text, or pretext, for a denunciation of Magee's alleged Erastianism, the archbishop's charge of 1826 was not what set Darby off.

The sharp, attention-demanding event that triggered Darby's attack on Magee stemmed from the bales of petitions for and against Catholic Emancipation that flooded the parliament of the United Kingdom, especially from 1825 onward. For the most part, the petitions from Protestants were generalized rejections of the wisdom of allowing Catholics to sit in parliament, but as the Catholic Association became increasingly efficient, a more frightened tone began to be heard among Protestant leaders. The following is an example from the lodging of an anti-Emancipation petition with the House of Lords on 23 February 1827 by Viscount Lorton on behalf of the inhabitants of the County of Sligo:

> He wished to see an emancipation in Ireland. He was an advocate for emancipation of the Protestants, not the emancipation of those who urged their claims in a manner hostile to the constitution of the country. He could assure their lordships that the Protestants were persecuted and proscribed in Ireland and would be forced out of the country or annihilated, if they were not protected.[40]

That speech was given in an emotional register very different from the triumphalism of the new-Reformation movement. Note the overlay with a petition that Archbishop Magee endorsed and that most of his senior clergy in Dublin and Glendalough signed on 1 February 1827, before it was presented to the House of Commons. The Church of Ireland clergy were appealing to the government: "for protection against the hostility and calumny, with which they and their religion have been, for a length of time, systematically assailed, under the pretence of seeking civil and religious liberty, but with the real design of obtaining powers subversive of both." And the Church of Ireland clergy: "were desirous, though exposed to daily vexations, and insults, and injuries, to submit in silence, and to endeavour by the quiet discharge of their proper duties, to soften the violence of their enemies."[41]

One has to be aware that Archbishop Magee was a less combative, much more flaccid personality in 1827 than he had been earlier in his episcopate, and that is analogous to what was happening to his Church as the Catholic Emancipation movement surged. Certainly he was not the same man who in September 1823 had brashly courted the wrath of the Catholics of Wicklow by refusing to allow the time-honoured right of Roman Catholics to be buried by a Catholic priest in one of the

40 2 *Hansard (Lords)*, vol. 16, cols. 647–8, 23 February 1827. Robert King, First Viscount Lorton in the Irish peerage, was a representative Irish peer in the UK parliament.

41 The entire petition is found in Field, 35–6, and in Weremchuk, 212–13.

country's most venerated sites, St Kevin's churchyard, Glendalough.[42] Now Magee was weak and indeed injured: his wife of thirty-two years (and mother of their sixteen children) had died in late 1825, and he never recovered emotionally. He was deeply depressed. His physical health, never good, worsened and the frequent fainting he had always experienced now increased. He was doing the best that he could when he took yet another petition to London, this time from the bench of Irish bishops, and made the case for protection for Irish Protestants directly to George IV.[43]

The old and now-frightened archbishop's asking for protection for the Church of Ireland enraged the twenty-six-year-old John Nelson Darby and catalyzed him into action.[44] He most particularly objected to the February 1827 petition to the house of commons signed by most of the clergy of the dioceses of Dublin and Glendalough. Additionally, Darby had a delayed reaction to what he believed Magee had said in

42 John D'Alton, *The Memoirs of the Archbishops of Dublin* (Dublin 1838), 359, with dating from the *Chronology* of the *New History of Ireland*, vol. 8, 305.

43 A.H. Kenney, "Memoir of the Late Most Reverend William Magee, Archbishop of Dublin," in William Magee, *Collected Works*, vol. 1 (1842), lxvii–lxxiv.

44 This was the opinion of John Gifford Bellett, one of Darby's earliest Irish followers (*Interesting Reminiscences* [London 1884], 2). This was the printed version of the final iteration of a circular manuscript that began with an 1858 letter of Bellett to James McAllister and grew through additions by members of Darby's phalanx of the faithful (called Exclusive Brethren for most of the relevant period) and was published by Brethren in 1884. I have not seen any of the original manuscript copies, and, as T.C.F. Stunt notes, "there are several variant versions of this document which circulated in MS before it was printed" (2000, 173n94). The 1884 printed version was reprinted as an historical exhibit by George M. Ware in an untitled item in his *A Review of Certain Contentions for the Faith* (London 1937), 14–32. Ware's version does not preserve the pagination of the first printed edition. A German Brethren PDF shows the original 1884 pagination (which I use). This version indicates the pagination on the 1884 first printed edition (www.bruederbewegung.de/pdf/reminiscences.pdf (accessed 20 December 2012). The pagination of the 1884 first printed edition is indicated in the German reprint and is here employed in references. The versions reproduced by George Ware and the German Brethren vary slightly on titles (Dr vs Mr, etc.) and on small emendations. Herein only items on which the two versions agree are either cited or quoted.

the charge that the archbishop had addressed to his clergy in October 1826. (More of the content of that document in a moment.)

Here things become very strange. According to Darby's memory in late middle age (probably the mid-1850s to early 1860s) in the autumn of 1827, before his accident, he was upset by what he saw as Anglican truckling to the Catholic Church and, further, by indications that the Church of Christ was asking the civil state to protect its existence: corruptions, in his view. By his own account (left as marginalia in a New Testament study attached to 2 Timothy, chapter 3) he spent three months in medical confinement in 1827–28 and during that time he underwent what he called "a great trial of judgment": "Would I rest the faith of my soul as a living man on the Word of God?" He found that "Grace determined me to do so."[45] That was the big decision. Yet, what simultaneously ate at him was his own relationship to authority within the Church of Ireland. His response was to write a pamphlet and to have it printed. This is the first entry in the Darby canon and it is typically fraught. Darby had his essay privately printed as *Considerations Addressed to the Archbishop of Dublin and the Clergy Who Signed the Petition to the House of Commons for Protection.* Then he withheld it for a time – although he had the piece marked "not published," which was a very narrow point indeed. If having multiple copies printed for his colleagues and ecclesiastical superiors was not commercial publication, it certainly was intended to be a promulgation – a publishing – of his views. Darby's name was not printed on the title page, in perhaps the hope that he could keep his identity secret, an idea that in the closely knitted social-religious web of Dalyland had no practicality whatsoever. Finally, just as he was ready to distribute his printed opinions, according to Darby's later-life memory, a major "humiliation" directed by God produced another "whole trial." There was a cock-up at the printers sometime in the spring of 1828, and the pamphlet lay at the print shop, nothing being done for a time. Then, after the essay was in print, "another passage of the trial" occurred: "some persons related to me – who I believe were under grace," disagreed

45 Darby marginalia on 2 Timothy, ch. 3 (CBA, J.N.D./3/5), reproduced in Weremchuk, 205.

with him and he cut them off – the first of many excommunications he effected during his long religious career.[46]

The swirl in Darby's mind that courses around this, his first effort in print – the massive issue of the nature of divine authority, the smaller one of the relationship of the Irish Church to the state, and the familial one of not being backed by his own people[47] – carries over to his pamphlet. For one thing, Darby shows here a tick that later develops into an identifying characteristic: he says he is not doing something and then does it. Here he declares that "I am not going to discuss the merits of the Archbishop's Charge at all," and he immediately spends several pages on it. Secondly, Darby writes paragraphs of three to five hundred words, or more, compounds non-sequiturs, and makes one fight hard to get at what he means. That is unfortunate, because he actually has a strong case to make against the Irish state church and, indeed, against state churches in general. Thirdly, he demonizes his opponents, a trait that comes out most clearly later when he has battles within his own Brethren group. In this essay he demonizes Archbishop Magee indirectly, by contagion. He refers several times to the work of Satan, and then uses phrases such as his reference to "the office which the Charge proposes to the clergy. But with this in view, it is manifest they must let Satan alone." The derogatory slur of meaning is not accidental and later in Darby's life becomes an habitual mode of argument. Finally, there is great emotional energy behind whatever he says; this continued throughout his career: I doubt if John Nelson Darby ever wrote a casual or recreational word in his life.[48]

46 Ibid., 205–6.

47 The family members with whom he was closest at this time were his brother the Rev. Christopher Darby, his sister Susannah, and her husband, Edward Pennefather. It is most likely that it is the Pennefathers whom he cut off for not agreeing with his views. Because (1) he was living on their couch during much of his recovery from leg injury and seeing them frequently and (2) in his marginalia, Darby uses the plural – "persons" – suggesting a married couple. A cautionary point: this breach with family members did not necessarily follow printing of the pamphlet; it could equally have been caused by disagreements during unrecorded verbal discussions of Darby's views before the pamphlet appeared.

48 See note 50, below, for the quotations employed above.

A conflicted, somewhat confused document, disproportionate by a quantum-level to the words and actions of Archbishop Magee, and yet it has an even stranger place in the historiography of the schism stemming from Anglican-derived evangelicalism: for John Nelson Darby's inaugural diatribe metastasized – through laziness, solecism, honest error, and occasional fabrication, to become a lurid node in the received history of Brethrenism and of evangelical Dispensationalism. Those are hard comments, but eventually to get at what I believe to be Darby's genius, we need to clear out, as much as we can, the artificial and the meretricious parts of the story, and also to recognize the powers of invention possessed by the mature John Nelson Darby. First, and of least importance, among the many historians and followers of Darby who have discussed this, his first known publication, I can discover none who actually has seen the original printed version. That is unusual, but understandable in that it is not in the comprehensive collection of the Christian Brethren Archive, the British Library, nor the archives of the Representative Church Body of Ireland. In fact, it is bound in a fugitive place in the National Library of Ireland's collection of a volume of Archbishop Magee's pamphlets, not the place one would immediately look for a denunciation of the archbishop by one of his clergy.[49] The matter turns out to be more diagnostic than substantively injurious as the Darby item is found in all of the editions of Darby's *Collected Writings*,[50] as edited by the Rev. William Kelly with Darby's cooperation, and one can retroactively take the necessary foundational step and ask: was the version as republished in the first volume of Darby's assembled writings that appeared in 1866 the same as the original

49 National Library of Ireland Pamphlets 540 (7). I am grateful to Professor Brian Walker for calling this item to my attention. I suspect that originals may also be found in the private collections of Darby material that are maintained by devout collectors of Brethren material, and, further, that in some rare devotional publication the original edition is noted, although I have been unable to find such an item.

50 "Considerations Addressed to the Archbishop of Dublin," *CW*, 01001, 1–19; the quotations in the previous paragraph are from 4 and 8. Because the anonymous printed version is virtually unobtainable, citations here and hereafter are to *CW*.

of 1828? Answer: both the body of the text and the postscript that was printed with the text are the same as in Darby's *Collected Writings.*[51]

Thus, despite a little laziness here, no harm done. Yet, secondly, another niggle, this one slightly more significant. The date in the *Collected Writings* for Darby's first publication, one that is taken as being authoritative in Brethren and Irish-evangelical histories, is 1827. Yet we know from the detailed, if slightly confused, chronology of publication that we discussed earlier – the marginal note by Darby's Greek New Testament near 2 Timothy, ch. 3 – that Darby's first pamphlet actually was printed in 1828, after he had recovered from the worst aspects of his leg injury. Hence, what is the source of the 1827 misdating? It is John Nelson Darby himself in a preparatory note written in 1865 to the first volume (published in 1866) of his reprinted writings. This dating forces the false inference that Darby's denunciation of Magee was printed and uttered in 1827, not 1828, and naturally Brethren writers have taken that year as the start of the entire Darby corpus.[52] Apparently Darby had forgotten that earlier he had left a conflicting and much more circumstantial chronology in his private study New Testament. By pre-dating the pamphlet, Darby presents himself as having been an immediate and unflinching opponent of the ideas that he believes Magee presented in his October 1826 charge to his clergy, as well as being a response to his colleagues in Dublin and Glendalough having signed the 1827 petition to parliament for protection.[53]

Again, not the end of the world: but the canary has started to cough. Thirdly, Darby in his new prologue to his first pamphlet makes in the mid-1860s the following factual statements that are a response to things Magee allegedly had effected following his 1826 charge and preceding Darby's privately printed pamphlet that he misdates to 1827, namely: (a) that Magee "imposed, within the limits of his jurisdiction, the oaths of allegiance and supremacy" on converts; (b) that, before

51 The total anonymous printed pamphlet is 33 pages. The postscript is pp. 32–3. The NLI copy is missing p. 33, which is *CW*, 01001, 19. Since all the other pages are the same as between NLI and *CW*, it is safe to believe that p. 19 of *CW* also accurately recapitulates p. 33 of NLI. That page (really a half-page) does not refer to oaths.

52 Ibid., 1.

53 Ibid., 1–2.

this ecclesiastical fiat by Magee, 600 to 800 Roman Catholics were turning Protestant each week; and (c) that thereupon this great success (effectively the new-Reformation of Ireland) "instantly ceased."[54] Did Darby actually believe these assertions to be true? Almost certainly: in the early spring of 1865, while in Toronto, he wrote to an Irish follower, W. Kelley, that "I ought to have somewhere a copy of my [printed] letter to the Archbishop. I forget it. But his course was ruinous – really stopped the deliverance from popery of masses, perhaps all of Ireland; they were leaving from seven to eight hundred a week. He [Archbishop Magee] required the oath of supremacy and abjuration; it stopped as a shot."[55] In 1869 he published commentary on the approaching disestablishment of the Church of Ireland as a state church: "At the time I refer to [1827], Roman Catholics were passing over to Protestantism many hundreds in a week. The Archbishop of Dublin insisted that the Protestant Establishment suited the State, made them take the oaths of abjuration and supremacy, and the work stopped."[56] In a moment, it will become clear that each of Darby's facts was a fabrication, but not, I would argue, cynical ones. Rather, they were part of a full-on delusion, a creating of history of the very sort that one needs be able to effect if one is to be a prophet in the Jewish-Christian tradition. Therefore, understanding the amazing degree John Nelson Darby was able to treat everyday, documentable historical reality as a plastic substance, an entity to be massaged, manipulated, and shaped into higher truths, is a window into his mind – and, to a lesser degree, into the consciousness of his followers. Historians of evangelicalism, however, should be wary of reading Darby's non-theological assertions as necessarily being of weight.

Hence, fourthly, briefly cast an eye on Archbishop Magee's 1826 charge to the clergy of the province of Dublin.[57] Magee presented a

54 Ibid., 1.

55 J.N.D. to W. Kelley, ____, 1865, *LJND*, vol. 1, no. 242.

56 "Disendowment – Disestablishment: A Word to the Protestants of Ireland in a Letter to the Ven. Archdeacon Stopford," dated 20 February 1869 in *CW*, 20021, 288.

57 William Magee, *A Charge Delivered at his Triennial and Metropolitan Visitation in St Patrick's Cathedral, Dublin in Oct. 1826* (London 1827). It is in the National Library of Ireland, Pamphlets 315(1) and in a Google ebook accessed

rather elegant, rather academic defense of the Church of Ireland's relationship with the state, theologically considered, one that emphasized toleration as one of its defining characteristics. Formally, Magee's argument was framed as an intra-Anglican debate correcting the views of William Warburton (1698–1779), bishop of Gloucester, who in 1736 had written a defense of the anti-Catholic and anti-Dissenter test acts. That being the formal structure, Archbishop Magee was talking over the heads of the clergy, pitching his words toward the governing class in the United Kingdom parliament. His encoded message, at a time when Catholic Emancipation loomed large, was that the union of Church and state was necessary for civil stability and that the Anglican communion was tolerant in that the "church would act with great inconsistency indeed, if she refused toleration to those who cannot conscientiously conform to her discipline and worship."[58] This was scarcely a form of zealotry. At *no* point did Magee suggest the possibility of introducing oaths or other tests for new converts to the Church of Ireland; much less propose oaths as desirable, for the whole point of his long essay is that the Established Church is not a sectarian body. The closest Magee came to endorsing religious tests was a too-clever paragraph in which he tried to justify the existence of the residual test acts in England as being consistent with religious toleration.[59] That is the kind of paradox academics love to defend in a display of their own dexterity, but it was gauche and self-indulgent: especially because at the time Magee wrote, the English test acts were clearly on their way to being abolished, as indeed they were in May 1828.[60] That said, Magee's small exercise in

---

2 August 2014). It is reprinted in Magee, vol. 2, 463–98, as "The Principle of the Union between Church and State in Christian Communities Explained; and its validity defended against the fictions of Warburton, and the usurpations of Popery; in a Charge Delivered to His Clergy in St Patrick's Cathedral, Dublin in the Year 1827." Note that in the reprinting Kenney, the editor, has provided a new title and has the year wrong. The substantive content is the same as the original, save for one editorial footnote. A further cautionary note: there are several versions of the Google ebook and in at least one version Magee's 1822 charge is mislabelled as 1826.

58 Magee, vol. 2, 487.

59 Magee, vol. 2, 407.

60 9 Geo. 4, cap. 17.

pettifogging was a far distance from being an endorsement of the imposition of new oaths and tests for converts to the Church of Ireland. It is impossible to reconcile Magee's actual charge to his clergy with John Nelson Darby's 1865 preface to his original pamphlet of 1828, for there is no foundation in Magee's text for what Darby claimed Magee had proposed. It is hard to understand why historians of Brethrenism and of Irish evangelicalism have taken as gospel Darby's cartoon of Magee's argument instead of reading what the archbishop said.[61]

There is no joy in any of this, but it is necessary because of the fundamental character of John Nelson Darby's first public essay and the gloss that he later put on it. As he stated in the 1860s, this was "the first germing of truth which has since developed itself into the Church of God."[62] It is difficult to think of a higher imperative for examination than that.

Therefore, as a fifth mode of examining John Nelson Darby's creativity and the critical generosity (or, perhaps, credulity) of those who have accepted his statements of historical reality as being the true milk of the word, we can for the moment prescind all that we know concerning Archbishop Magee's writings and of Darby's spiritual inclinations and act momentarily as purely secular historians observing political and social events. Even from a position of complete secularity, Darby's assertions concerning the origins of his first, epiphanous writing – *"the first germing of truth which has since developed itself into the Church of God"* – slew eccentrically out of Earth's orbit. To be specific: John Nelson Darby's estimate of the rate of Catholics being converted to the Church of Ireland is roughly fifteen times that of even the most boastful of proselytizers – and that is setting aside entirely his singular assertion (made in the mid 1860s) that in the late 1820s all of Ireland might have been on the way to conversion, a simply hallucinogenic

61 I can find only one historian of Brethrenism and its related forms of evangelicalism (surely there must be more) who shows evidence of having actually looked at both the original charge of 1826 by Magee and at the preface Darby wrote in 1865 to his 1828 privately printed pamphlet concerning Magee's charge. This is Grayson Carter (212–13) and, curiously, he does not note that Magee indeed did not suggest the imposition of tests.

62 "Considerations," [later-added preface] *CW*, 01001, 1.

belief. Given his belief that the Irish nation was converting to Protestantism is counter-factual, his assertion that the process was blocked by Archbishop Magee is merely a logical fallacy: one does not explain something that was never happening by saying that someone caused it to cease in mid-track. Equally diagnostic is Darby's explaining the failure of the new-Reformation by pinpointing Archbishop Magee as the single individual who allegedly killed it. Personalization of cause and effect (and thus of blame) is a characteristic that runs in and out of Darby's writings: he rarely thinks in abstract logical terms but adopts instead the vocabulary of personal animus. From personalization there follows demonization, a rhetorical undertow that moves from being fairly oblique in Darby's first pamphlet to later being a standard method of dealing with persons with whom Darby disagrees.

To lock down the point that, despite Darby's energetic assertions in 1865, Magee certainly had not recommended the imposition of oaths, much less imposed them, at the time Darby had composed the body of his anonymous essay, we should consider the most severe of outside witnesses: the Rev. Dr James Doyle, the Irish Catholic hierarchy's vigilant guardian against the new-Reformation and a compelling proponent of Catholic Emancipation. In late 1827, he published an examination and refutation of Archbishop Magee's 1826 charge. Doyle provided a comprehensive review of Magee's argument and concluded that the Church of Ireland was not indeed a beacon of toleration. Yet, even in that confrontational context, Doyle does not mention Magee's imposing, or proposing, any new oaths.[63]

The reason for our inevitably wearing examination of John Nelson Darby's later-life version of the events of 1826–27 is in part because his summary in his *Collected Writings* has become a standard narrative and inevitably will mislead historians in the future. That is salient but not all-important: Darby's historical waywardness can be turned inside-out and used as affirmative evidence about certain aspects of Darby's theology and personal character. It is clear that in his late maturity Darby had settled on an interpretation of his own life that used

63 [James Doyle], *A Reply by J.K.L.* (Dublin 1827) (Professor Brian Walker kindly provided me with this item.) National Library of Ireland, Pamphlets 315(2). The monograph is now available as a Google ebook.

apocalyptic thinking as its template. In his sixties and seventies, he rewrote the hesitations and anxieties and bothersome medievalisms of a young cleric who had tried to fight against his archbishop by printing an anonymous pamphlet, and he turned those haverings into a near-apocalyptic story. Archbishop William Magee became a powerful demon whose actions lost for all eternity thousands and thousands of souls, and John Nelson Darby heroically stood against evil; though he lost the immediate battle, he had begun the "Church of God" and that Church was bound for eventual eternal victory. In the long view, Darby's ability to create facts, ignore reality, and to establish a coherent narrative that transcends mere accuracy was a prerequisite for his performance in his maturity in the role of a full-fledged religious genius, a prophet who broke free of the present world and established an alternative universe.

John Nelson Darby's ability to reject reality was abundantly clear in the mid-1860s, when he put forward the standard narrative of his actions in the late 1820s. The probative material is heavy indeed. The danger here is that, believing we have freed ourselves from the narrative hand of Darby as he wrote in the mid-1860s, we still may be in his grasp: because it is easy to clean out the nettles from Irish Church history in the late 1820s by assuming that the young Darby had the same ability to transcend reality that he clearly possessed when he was much older. Perhaps he did, perhaps he did not, but it would be an unusual person who had the same personality structure and the same belief system in his later twenties as he was to have in his mid-sixties. Essentially, one wants to know, when did John Nelson Darby turn into a prophet? Was Darby, the rattled curate of the 1820s, a prophet in chrysalis?

The functional answer to the question again turns on old-fashioned empirical evidence. If one examines Darby's privately printed pamphlet of 1828 and when one scrubs it of the misleading preface that Darby added in the mid-1860s, it is an entirely different product. Nevertheless, it still is somewhat mystifying, because it hangs in two portions – the body of the essay and a postscript that Darby added after the main argument was complete. The body of the pamphlet is a frazzled, albeit self-contained, jeremiad directed against Archbishop Magee's 1826 charge and opposing the clerical petition wherein the Anglican clergy asked for governmental protection. It has no mention whatsoever of any intention by Magee to introduce compulsory oaths for new converts. It does, however, contain a very cloudy sentence, one that might be stretched to indicate that in his late twenties he actually believed in the success of the new-Reformation: "the manifestation of the power of the Divine Spirit which has begun a work in this country, which I fully hope will not end in it, and is of no country, but of the power of that kingdom which shall fill the whole earth."[64] That nearly opaque expression is as close as young Darby comes to saying that the new-Reformation was gaining traction, and actually it is not much of a claim of success. Thus, the body of the privately printed pamphlet that Darby wrote for distribution to his fellow clergy in the diocese of Dublin and Glendalough was not of a piece with the preface that he added in the mid-1860s. There was, then, in 1827, when the body of the essay was composed, a fair distance between John Nelson Darby the time-bending prophet of the high Victorian era and the inexperienced priest of the later 1820s.

Except there is just a hint of his later delusion about Magee's killing the new-Reformation by oaths. In a postscript to the main pamphlet that was written in 1827, Darby, probably writing in early 1828, says:

> The oath of supremacy is proposed by the Archbishop to the converts, which, instead of opening the door of Christ to the soul in bondage, makes the admission into the Establishment a necessary condition: and I would suggest, that such a measure is exceedingly analogous to the conduct which created such difficulty at Antioch, on the admission of the Gentiles, and puts a stumbling-block in the way of a weak believer.[65]

Three alternatives: first, perhaps the young Darby in early 1828 had discovered an intention to impose oaths, which Magee has cleverly encoded in his 1826 charge. Not likely: based not only on a modern

64 "Considerations addressed to the Archbishop of Dublin," CW, 01001, 2.
65 "Considerations addressed to the Archbishop of Dublin," CW. 01001, 18.

historical reading of Magee's writings but also upon his great Catholic rival Bishop Doyle's failing to discern any such secret intent. Secondly, young Darby may have been projecting his own dark fantasies into the clucking clerical gossip of his own time. Or, thirdly, it has been suggested by Peter Embley, a serious scholar, that in late 1827 Archbishop Magee issued another pastoral letter and that this contained the requirement that converts from Roman Catholicism with the diocese of Dublin and Glendalough should take the oaths of supremacy and allegiance to the Crown. The existence of such a late 1827 pastoral is possible – although Embley's making its alleged oaths normative ("should") flies in the face of Darby's own words, that Magee had been speculative: "proposed" (see the quotation above). Perhaps such a new pastoral was indeed published, but if so I can find no one who has ever seen it.[66] It is not pleasant to report that among those who have not seen it is the historian Peter Embley, despite his noising abroad its alleged contents and providing a citation. This is yet another case of an historian being hypnotized by the backsplash of Darby's technique, in full bloom in 1865, of truth by assertion.[67]

If Archbishop Magee, in failing health and weighed down by the march of Catholics toward civil equality, muttered something, some

66 Dr Raymond Refaussé, chief librarian and archivist of the Representative Church Body of Ireland, finds no material in the Church's collections on Magee's alleged conversion-oaths fiat, nor of a late 1827 pastoral by Magee (communication to author, 27 May 2013). That said, it still is possible that a rare late 1827 pastoral by Magee may indeed not be a phantasm and may turn up, but it would scarcely have scuttled the new-Reformation.

67 Peter Embley, "The Origins and Early Development of the Plymouth Brethren," (PhD thesis, St Paul's College, Cheltenham, 1967), 64, pointed to the existence of a late 1827 pastoral letter by Magee that was completely separate from the 1826 charge. His cited evidence (238n97) for that item as being found in the National Library of Ireland, Pamphlets 315(1). Actually, the document there is the 1826 charge by Magee. Apparently, Embley never saw any late 1827 pastoral letter by Magee and certainly not one that contained a requirement for oaths. Had he seen such a pastoral letter he would have been able to quote from it; he did not do so. It is also clear that Embley did not read the 1826 charge, in which there are no indications of the future imposition of oaths, but instead simply accepted as facts the untenable assertions made by Darby in 1865.

place, about wanting Catholic converts to take some oaths, one would not be surprised: old men often cough out panaceas to fix the world they think is going to hell, and these are of no more consequence than flecks of pipe tobacco speckling an autumnal waistcoat. Recall that 1827–29 saw the epochal simplifying of the civil code of the United Kingdom through the removal of most of the remaining oaths and tests that impaired Catholic civil rights. Of all the times in Irish history to impose anti-Catholic oaths, even within the Established Church, this was not it. To be obvious, note the continued silence of Daniel O'Connell and of the Rev. Dr James Doyle, sentinels against any such move by Magee in 1828–29. Moreover, James Thomas Law's definitive collection of ecclesiastical statutes, including historical items, contains no such imposition during Archbishop's Magee's archiepiscopate.[68]

If John Nelson Darby in the spring of 1828 was working himself into a paroxysm of anxiety about the unlikely possibility that his archbishop would introduce a new oath for Catholics converting to the Church of Ireland (the numbers of which were hardly overwhelming), then he was using the fear of a phantom to keep himself from dealing with the real problem: Bible-based evangelical Anglicanism had no chance of becoming the dominant religion of the Irish people, and, as Darby had made clear in the body of his privately printed anti-Magee philippic, he was himself not at all comfortable with the existence of an Established Church that was a partner with the civil state. Darby was immensely confused about everything. He did not, as one might expect him to have done, resign his priesthood in the Church of Ireland. Indeed, he never did. Instead, he went AWOL from his parish,

68 James Thomas Law, *The Ecclesiastical Statutes at Large* (London 1847). Because of the long history of anti-Catholic penal legislation in Ireland, the whole matter of conversion to the state church had been more closely controlled and more clearly articulated in statutes that required parliamentary approval than was the case elsewhere in the British Isles. There is some doubt of whether or not Magee would have had the legal power to introduce such oaths in 1828ff, even if he had wished to do so. Additionally, given the "parsons freehold" – the fact that Anglican rectors had what we would today call tenure and that their income was received independently of central control – it is hard to see how Magee could have forced his clergy to do anything against their inclination.

became a wandering, almost mendicant preacher for a time, and then in the early 1830s grew into a full-bore, time-bending, word-swirling, God-loving, man-judging prophet – a mixture of the caterwauling Old Testament brimstone annunciators and, his own favourite, the forever ambulatory presence, the ultimate inconvenience on every believer's doorstep, the Apostle Paul.

In terms of everyday realty, as a young curate John Nelson Darby did not immediately see the pattern and was not yet able fully to create his own alternative. That would come soon. In his short-term impercipience about the day-in, day-out position of the Church of Ireland within Irish society, he was typical of both the clergy and the evangelical laity of the faith.

That few Anglican evangelicals in Ireland showed intelligence of the sort that H.B. Barlow talked about in *The Oxford Companion to the Mind* – that art of good-guessing or, if you prefer, swift pattern-recognition – is surprising: as a group they were very highly educated, were well connected to political insiders, and had plenty of leisure to employ in figuring out the swirls and filigree of the social and economic world around them. Their failure is doubly surprising because the pattern was so obvious and so loudly announced.

The relationship of the Anglican and the Roman Catholic Churches from, say, the 1820s onward can be visualized in the shape of a cursive X – the Protestants wavering and then declining sharply, the Catholics moving gradually upward and then accelerating into a victorious flourish. As I have argued earlier, the new-Reformation was self-contradictory both in its strategy and tactics. It was poking a stick into a wasps' nest. Evangelical revival within the Church of Ireland population was religiously valid and organizationally useful; attempting to become a true national Church and to take over the educational guardianship of the entire population was a declaration of sectarian war: not productive of violent conflict but directly resulting in heightened religio-ideological strife.

As a course of campaign, the new-Reformation had the bad fortune to encounter the Rev. Dr James Doyle, who was arguably the most able

Catholic churchman of the nineteenth century,[69] and Daniel O'Connell, who was an imperfect politician but unparalleled as a nationalist leader.[70] At the leadership level, the Church of Ireland was heavily outmanned.

Earlier, in order to make it clear that during the 1820s and thereafter both a political and a religious strand ran through the Irish Catholic revival, each with its own integrity, we kept the two strands separate as much as possible. However, in contemporary history they intertwined. Although each of the two chief Catholic leaders pressed primarily for his own brief, Doyle also fought for Catholic civil rights, and O'Connell for protection of the Catholic Church. Up to 1820, when O'Connell resigned from the board of patrons of the Kildare Place Society because it was tipping against Catholics, both Doyle and O'Connell had been willing to give Catholic-Protestant cooperation in schooling a chance.[71] Doyle, though sharp at protecting his flock, was more aware than was O'Connell of the financial weakness of the Catholic Church and was willing to negotiate a neutral system of Ireland-wide primary schools, and this is the reason for his making the single most famous statement of educational principles in Irish history (and, sadly, the most ignored in practice):

69 Paul Cullen, archbishop of Armagh (1850–52) and then of Dublin (1852–78), undoubtedly had more power: by the late 1860s he was probably the most powerful Catholic in the world, save for the pope. But in his theology and political work he was much less nimble than was Doyle and the organizational matters he dealt with were mostly exercises in exerting power, much less complex than were Doyle's challenges at the dog-end of the penal era. Historians are fortunate in Doyle's biographers of both the nineteenth and the twentieth centuries. The two thorough and well-argued volumes by Thomas McGrath (1999) have already been cited. A fine nineteenth-century work is William J. Fitzpatrick, *The Life, Times and Correspondence of the Right Rev. Dr Doyle* (Dublin 1861).

70 The only rival would be Charles Stewart Parnell. The literature on O'Connell is very large, and there are a score of biographies. The easiest way to encounter O'Connell directly is through Maurice R. O'Connell's exemplary eight-volume edition of *The Correspondence of Daniel O'Connell*, 8 vols (Dublin 1972–1980).

71 John Coolahan, "Primary Education as a Political Issue in O'Connell's Time," in O'Connell, ed. (1991), 87–100, 107–9.

> I do not see how any man, wishing well to the public peace, and who looks to Ireland as his country, can think that that peace can ever be permanently established, or the prosperity of the country ever well secured, if children are separated at the commencement of life on account of their religious opinions. I do not know any measure which would prepare the way for a better feeling in Ireland than uniting children at an early age, and bringing them up in the same school, leading them to commune with one another, and to form those little intimacies and friendships, which often subsist through life. Children thus united know and love each other, as children brought up together always will; and to separate them is, I think, to destroy some of the finest feeling in the breast of men.[72]

This testimony before the 1830 select committee on the Irish poor was simultaneously idealistic and a coded attack on Anglican-run education. Doyle's view soon was governmental policy, at least for a time.[73]

In highlighting Daniel O'Connell and James Doyle as representative of the two strands of Catholic resurgence in the 1820s and early 30s, one does not mean to focus on leaders only, but economy of space is necessary. Simply put, at ground level a byproduct of the clash between the Catholic push for civil rights and the new-Reformation's pressure for the Church of Ireland to become a true national Church was a heightened awareness of their own sectarian identity by both everyday Protestants and Catholics.[74] If we adopt the perspective of Church of

72 *Second Report of Evidence from the Select Committee on the State of the Poor in Ireland. Minutes of Evidence 18 May–5 June*, 427, H.C. 1830 (654), vol. vii.

73 It took roughly twenty years for the neutral system created in 1831 to become mostly sectarian and eventually effectively segregated. For a summary of the physics behind this development, see Donald H. Akenson, "Pre-university Education, 1782–1870," in Vaughan (ed.), vol. 6, part 2, 523–37.

74 One should not assume that this automatically meant violence. Among the Catholic population, increased religious awareness cut both ways, with the Catholic priests being active in damping down the less respectable aspects of popular sectarian aggressiveness. For landmark studies of this complicated matter, see: Sean Connolly, *Priests and People in Pre-famine Ireland, 1780–1845* (Dublin 1982), esp. 236–63; James S. Donnelly Jr, *Captain Rock: The Irish*

Ireland adherents, especially those who backed the new-Reformation from the mid-1820s to the mid-1830s, their optimism about the turning of Ireland ran into the following cascade of realities (notice that almost all of these are specific to Ireland and not to Great Britain):

- 1823. Formation of the new Catholic Association; publication by "J.K.L." (Bishop James Doyle of Kildare and Leighlin) of his landmark *Vindication* of the religious and civil rights of Irish Catholics.
- 1824. The nationwide "Catholic rent," collected monthly by Daniel O'Connell's organization instituted: apparently based on the small-group bonding principles used so successfully by Methodists.
- 1825. First report of critical investigation of Irish schools by commissioners of Irish education, marking the beginning of the end for Protestant control of governmental funding for primary schooling.
- 1826. Lord George Beresford loses County Waterford seat to pro-Catholic Emancipation candidate.
- 1828. Parliamentary select committee recommends that the government take control of state-funded primary education; Daniel O'Connell elected MP for Clare, although he cannot yet take his seat because of the required oath.
- 1829. Catholic Emancipation passes parliament and receives royal assent.
- 1830–33. Tithe War in Irish midlands and south against payment of tithes to support the clergy of the Church of Ireland.
- 1831. Richard Whately, liberal Oxford logician, appointed Protestant archbishop of Dublin; he and the Catholic archbishop of Dublin and Presbyterian lay leaders cooperate with the government in establishing the Irish national system of education.

Agrarian Rebellion of 1821–1824 (Madison 2009); Patrick O'Farrell, "Millennialism, Messianism and Utopianism in Irish History," in *Anglo-Irish Studies*, vol. 2 (1976).

- 1832. The government provides grants for Irish clergy in financial distress due to the Tithe War; UK government appoints a royal commission to investigate Church revenues and patronage; four detailed reports follow.
- 1833. United Kingdom parliament forces the reorganization of the Church of Ireland; parliament abolishes ten Church of Ireland bishoprics, reduces two archbishoprics to bishoprics, lowers bishops' incomes; ecclesiastical commissioners to suspend or rearrange parochial livings.
- 1834. Another governmental commission appointed to inquire into public education and religion.
- 1835. First detailed census of Irish religion published: shows 11 percent of the nation was affiliated with the Church of Ireland.

No single one of these events yielded an irreparable injury to the Church of Ireland, but each was a defeat for the new-Reformation's advocates and the effect was cumulative. The pattern from the viewpoint of, say, 1835 is clear. Any attempt to exert force as a national Church or to convert large numbers of Roman Catholics was chimerical – and always had been.

Although many of the spiritual experiences of Irish evangelicals were shared with evangelicals elsewhere in the British Isles, the total force of the pressures listed above was specific to Ireland. The Irish new-Reformation movement was unique: its ambitions were logarithmically greater than those of any similar evangelical effort in England and Wales, or Scotland. Each of those other countries was overwhelmingly Protestant and had a state church that already claimed, with varying degrees of accuracy, to minister to the bulk of their respective populations. The dreams of the Church of Ireland evangelicals, to create a New Jerusalem in Ireland's green and Gentile land, were destroyed by events of which they had only a very imperfect understanding.[75]

75 To very briefly complete the story: although weakened by the UK government's reform activities, especially those of the early 1830s, the Church of Ireland held together remarkably well. The inevitable occurred in 1871, when it

was disestablished as a state church (Ireland was a Catholic country and had a large Presbyterian minority, so an Anglican establishment was untenable in an increasingly democratic age). After disestablishment, the Church's constitution was remodelled and the position of the laity was made much stronger, close indeed to being dominant. After 1871, as a religious institution cleared of its responsibilities to the state, the Church was considerably improved in its devotional life, albeit reduced in funds and in professional personnel. In reading memoirs of clergy of the disestablishment era, one frequently comes across a forced, slightly ironic, optimism. It reminds one of Greta Garbo's fine performance in the 1939 American film *Ninotchka*. Asked about the news from the USSR, she replies, "The last mass trials were a great success. There are going to be fewer but better Russians." Similarly: fewer but better Irish Anglicans. Irish developments are well covered in: Raymond Gillespie and W.G. Neely (eds), *The Laity and the Church of Ireland* (Dublin 2002); Michael Hurley (ed.), *Irish Anglicanism, 1869–1969* (Dublin 1970); R.B. McDowell, *The Church of Ireland, 1869–1969* (London 1975). For a generalized discussion of present-day evangelicalism that touches upon the Church of Ireland, see Robert Dunlop (ed.), *Evangelicals in Ireland* (Dublin 2004).

PART III

Into Deep Eternity

CHAPTER SEVEN

Ecclesiology: Rebuilding the Fallen Jerusalem

The New Jerusalem that enthusiasts for the new-Reformation in Ireland so devoutly desired had been a virtual reality, a vision etched in the heavens. It possessed all the vain hopefulness of a silhouette projected onto a gauze sheet in an early magic lantern show. It was never going to be real. To a remnant of the serious Irish evangelical faithful, their virtual New Jerusalem had indeed been ruined. They searched for some way to rebuild it, this time with sturdier materials. By the end of the 1820s, the overwhelming majority of Irish evangelical Anglicans realized that the New Jerusalem had been a big miss, but only a small tranche embraced the idea of radical reform of the Church.

Once Catholic Emancipation became a reality in 1829, the "era of cooperation" between exact churchmen and evangelicals within the Church of Ireland diminished swiftly "and within two years many high churchmen seem to have washed their hands altogether of the evangelicals, claiming that in their desire to convert Roman Catholics they were ready to sacrifice the Establishment."[1] Overwhelmingly the Irish evangelicals stayed within the Church, and in fact their influence grew so that well before the Irish Famine they clearly were the most influential sector among both laity and clergy.[2] They were changed,

1 T.C.F. Stunt, "Evangelical Cross-Currents in the Church of Ireland, 1820–1833," in Shiels and Wood (1989), 219.

2 One cannot precisely date the arrival of evangelical ascendancy, but Alan Acheson is not being excessive when he states that "the period of evangelical ascendancy in the church (c. 1845–95) lasted some 25 years each side of

however, by the trauma of the slow-motion implosion of their Church: now they concentrated on bringing into active fellowship with the Church of Ireland the big band of nominal Anglicans who either were intimidated by social-class barriers to church participation or who had kept their heads down because they lived in Catholic-dominated communities and were very much afraid of sectarian trouble. The overall result of the continued growth of evangelical influence was that, as Ireland's greatest historian, W.E.H. Lecky, noted "the Irish Establishment became by far the most evangelical section of the Anglican Church."[3] He was referring to the entire British Empire, and the observation is valid as long as one remembers that Irish Anglicanism had a very cool temperature in terms of public display: in the first half of the nineteenth century private baptism was the norm and public baptism was an innovation (the Rev. William Cleaver of Delgany was the first to administer baptism as part of formal public worship),[4] and hymn singing, even during the 1830s, "was still dismissed as un-Anglican"[5] – metrical psalms sufficed for congregational singing. Among Anglican evangelicals, daily family worship, or at least prayers, became a common feature, and fervent prayer sessions among clergy and the more devoted of the laity were common. But these were bounded by the deep and habitual sense of personal privacy that was virtually instinctive among Irish Anglicans.[6] A small but very energetic band of Church of Ireland

---

disestablishment [of 1871]" (*A History of the Church of Ireland* [Dublin 2002], 182).

3 William E.H. Lecky, *A History of England in the Eighteenth Century* (London 1879), vol. 2, 611.

4 Acheson, 183.

5 Ibid., 159.

6 References to the historiography of relatively small (but highly controversial) post-new-Reformation conversion efforts are found in chapter 5, note 34. The period of the Famine is the most controversial, and the phenomenon is easy to exaggerate. Still, one must note that some Famine souperism involved the now-aging veterans of Dalyland. Thus the *Freeman's Journal* of 24 October 1851 carried a story that was compiled from reports from the *Hull Examiner* and the *Limerick Examiner*: "The 'reformation' game of 1825 is now playing over again in Ireland," the English paper reported. Specifically the papers noted that the lord bishop of Cashel had recently confirmed at the Dromkeen, Co. Tipperary, a number of poor Catholics in the Anglican faith. That

evangelicals (of whom John Nelson Darby was only one) came to question both the efficiency and the legitimacy of the organizational structure of the Church of Ireland. Their reasons for doing so were widely various, but that is irrelevant. Whatever their individual reasons were, the keenest of them not only asked if the Anglican Church was truly Christian but also whether any of the formal churches of Christendom were legitimate.

As these evangelical radicals moved toward creating a new and authentic Christianity (all the while insisting that they were merely discovering the old and true forms of the faith) they worked on three fronts. First, they rethought and attempted to reshape Church forms. This is often called *ecclesiology* and although tied to some complex theologies, matters of Church organization inevitably involved everyday, this-world practicalities. Secondly, they defined the future. The form this took most often was apocalyptic and is often discussed as *eschatology*. Thirdly, they dealt with text: they examined the holy scriptures with microscopic attention to details, while simultaneously reshaping the texts through meta-level interpretative patterns. The stated

---

bishop was Robert Daly, who in 1842 had been raised to the episcopate (at the same time the see was reduced from being an archbishopric to being an ordinary diocese, as part of the continuing church reforms dictated by the UK parliament). According to the report, before the confirmation, the "Rev. Dr [*sic*] Darby," the incumbent, had promised clothes to those who went through the ritual. This was the Rev. Mr [not Dr] Christopher Lovett Darby, brother of John Nelson Darby, whose pluralism covered the rectory of Killinaule in the diocese of Cashel and Kells Union in the diocese of Ossory. (For his career and that of his two clerical sons, see chapter 4, note 13.) After the service of confirmation he "distributed among them plenty of warm clothing for the winter, not omitting some rather gay dresses for the female brands snatched from the burning." The only difficulty, the *Hull Advertiser* reported, was that the next Sunday most of the converts went to their respective Roman Catholic chapels and recanted and were granted readmission to the Catholic Church. Here the *Limerick Examiner* took up the story, reporting that the Rev. Mr Darby was threatening to take legal action to recover the clothes unless they returned to the Church of Ireland. The peasantry resisted, on the grounds that they had honoured the letter of their agreement with Darby. This story is set in context in the Thomas Davis lecture by Irene Whelan, "The Stigma of Souperism," in Cathal Poirteir (ed.), *The Great Irish Famine* (Cork 1995).

goal of the radical reading of the scriptures was to discern the original intention of the texts, which, they believed, was nothing less than the direct product of personal revelation from God.

In a statement that was only narrowly accurate, but certainly untrue in its implied importance, John Nelson Darby in his mid-fifties asserted that in 1828 he and "four persons who were pretty much in the same state of soul as myself, came together to my lodgings." He was living in Dublin at the time, having walked away from his parish. "We spoke together about these things, and I proposed to them to break bread the following Sunday, which we did. Others then joined us."[7] This can be taken as a direct self-declaration by John Nelson Darby of his being the founder of the Brethren movement: others joined his group. Almost certainly, it is what he believed when he was in his mid-fifties and was looking back on the course of his life. It is a characteristic attempt to create his own life as an autochtonous entity in which he, in discussion with the Almighty, was the primary righteous actor. Given that Darby becomes the dominant figure in the Brethren movement and the most compelling international colporteur of a singular and effective mode of biblical invention, one very much wants him to be more directly revealing – and if not revealing, at least truthful – rather than merely accurate. In point, Darby, still in his late twenties, was only one of the several young Irish evangelicals who were struck by the painful realization that a New Jerusalem was not in view any place on the Irish horizon, and they required an analgesic – a new mode of Christian fellowship.[8]

7 *Letter by J.N.D. to Prof. Tholuck; LJND*, vol. 3, no. 226.

8 The historiography of the early Brethren movement is difficult, and the bulk of the historical writing done before roughly the 1960s is cloudy indeed. The challenges in dealing with John Nelson Darby's own work are discussed in detail in the bibliography to the present study. However, though Darby was the figure who most influenced Brethrenism in general and American evangelicalism in particular, he had a large and vibrant sounding board composed of acolytes, enemies, and a few strongly independent minds. The indispens-

Exactly when the Brethren came into being is a question that has invited assertion over the years, but has never produced a satisfactory answer, in part because the early Brethren refused to admit that they were a this-world organization. As a group of evangelicals with similar spiritual reflexes they were well established several places in the British Isles by June 1838, when a set of meetings lasting almost three weeks was held at the Gloucester Hotel, Clifton, near Bristol. The event was attended by adherents from all over the British archipelago, and it marked the shift of their religious metropole from Ireland to England.[9] Up to 1838, various events and conferences in Ireland had dominated, but thereafter Irish events became secondary. From 1838 onward, it is

---

able discussion of the printed sources is Arnold D. Ehlert's *Brethren Writers: A Checklist* (Grand Rapids 1969). This is an update of an extended essay Ehlert wrote for the American Theological Library Association, originally published in 1957. On a specifically bibliographic level, the Brethren publications are very difficult to corral and contextualize because of: the Brethren predilection for anonymity or for initials-only indications of authorship (the insiders of course knew who the authors were); the habit of not dating most publications; the general refusal until the twentieth century to recognize the state and thus to lodge legal-deposit copies (hence, the usual repositories, particularly the British Library and the Library of Congress, are very thin and often miscatalogued); until very recently – when the heroic work of the curators of the Christian Brethren Archive, the University of Manchester, began to make headway in collecting and identifying large numbers of items – this was the situation: "the best of the older works never come into the open market, but are passed along privately … The classics of the first generation of Brethren writers can be seen almost nowhere except in the private collections of connoisseurs" (Ehlert, 18, whose work is particularly valuable in providing identification of initials-only authors and in indicating code words that help one identify otherwise stealth Brethren publications, particularly the tracts that were distributed freely, sometimes in editions of more than one million copies). Beginning in the 1960s, academically trained scholars began touching on the Brethren and their influence on evangelical Protestantism. Those works are referred to in this study and employed with gratitude.

9 Timothy C.F. Stunt, "An Early Account of the Brethren in 1838, with Some Explanation of Its Origin and Context," *Brethren Historical Review* (2012), 5–9. The move of the increasingly large assemblies of Brethren from Ireland to England was confirmed in the printed *Collectanea* of the 1839 conference held at Leamington (Edinburgh: J. Roberston, 1840. CBA 1173).

reasonable to accept the label given the Brethren by outsiders – the "Plymouth Brethren" – even though many of them refused any name other than "Christian." Before that, there is no strict genealogy of the creation of the Brethren because it was a firefly phenomenon. That is, in scores of places all over the British Isles, but especially in Ireland, little assemblies of believers came into existence, flourished for a bit, and then some went extinct, others coalesced and formed a longer-lasting coalition of belief. The flickering, evanescent nature of early assemblies being granted, and their widely spaced distribution noted, the first home of Brethrenism in a form that has a recognizable and causally robust continuity with the later Victorian movement was southern Ireland in the mid-1820s. What does one call these people? Some later Brethren referred to them as "earlies," and that is not a disrespectful term; sometimes "proto-Brethren" is used, and that has the advantage of pointing toward the later, brighter, more vigorous iterations of this new form of faith; and, if one wishes both historical and geographic accuracy, they can be termed the "Wicklow Brethren," for that was their home county within the physical and mental space we earlier surveyed as Dalyland. (And how much misdirected modern religious history could have been avoided if something indicative of their Irish origins and concerns had been applied to the Brethren, rather than the misleading "Plymouth," with its connotations of seventeenth-century English Puritanism.)

The surviving word-pictures of early Brethrenism, from, say, 1825 through 1829, are so far out of focus that one can just make out the main players but not their actual relation to each other. The backdrop is easy enough to recognize: the better parts of Dublin City south of the River Liffey, semi-rural southern County Dublin, and County Wicklow – in other words, Dalyland, in this case with a bit more of the urban drawing room than of sweeping demenses. Even if one did not have to rely on memoirs written decades after the fact, the waters are muddied by this question: among this particular group, what counts as a litmus act that was the warrant of a few serious evangelicals becoming "earlies," or proto-Brethren? The accepted answer has become: when a small group of nineteenth-century evangelicals came together to "break bread." That is, to remember the death of Jesus in a manner they believed was practised by the earliest primitive Christians. This is a useful criterion as it potentially distinguishes the comings-together of the earliest Brethren from the "drawing-room meetings" that Grayson Carter has pointed out were popular during the 1820s among the serious evangelicals of Dublin and environs.[10] Bible readings, sermons, and extemporaneous prayers were one thing: going over the line to celebrate communion – a function reserved for priests in the Catholic-derived faiths and for ordained clergymen in the Dissenting denominations – was a distinctive and radical act.

Most likely, the first group to coalesce and then cross the line to performing house-communion was the least typical of the sort of persons from whom the Brethren were formed.[11] This occurred in 1825 or 1826,

10 Grayson Carter, *Anglican Evangelicals* (Oxford 2001), 197. Carter usefully provides the anecdote of a Quaker gentleman who was invited to dine at a fashionable Dublin house and was taken aback when, after dinner, a sermon was preached and thereafter everybody dropped to their knees and prayed.

11 The high degree of indeterminacy between 1825 and mid-1829 must be emphasized. Also, there is the tendency in the literature for downward-dating creep, that is, an unconscious tendency to wish for (and thus to find) signal events occurring earlier than their actual occurrence. As a countervail, if I mention two possible dates, the later one is chronologically the more likely, although the first is possible. In the discussion of the proto-Brethren groups, I am guided by the material in the following secondary studies and by their citation of primary sources: Grayson Carter (as listed in note 10, above); especially the work of the pre-eminent historian of the period, Timothy C.F. Stunt, in several of his essays, but most particularly in his *From Awakening to Secession: Radical Evangelicals in Switzerland and Britain, 1815–35* (Edinburgh 2000), 172–81; Tim Grass, *Gathering in His Name: The Story of the Open Brethren in Britain and Ireland* (Milton Keynes 2006), has material on early formation and is valuable because his work serves as something like a loyal opposition to the overemphasis on Darby. In particular he has an appreciation of Anthony Norris Groves. See also the historiographical material in Neil T.R. Dickson and Tim Grass (eds), *The Growth of the Brethren Movement* (Carlisle 2006).

Harold H. Rowdon's *The Origin of the Brethren, 1825–1850* (London 1967) was the first of the Brethren histories to use footnotes and bibliographic techniques in the fashion that makes factual assertions verifiable. The book is based on a University of London doctorate. On the early meetings, see 37–57. Rowdon's work appeared at almost the same time as Peter L. Embley completed his PhD thesis at St Paul's College, Cheltenham, "The Origins and Early

when a former Roman Catholic medical student, Edward Cronin, converted to evangelical Protestantism but could find no Dissenting churches to accept him; and he was averse to conforming to the Church of Ireland. His steadfastness of purpose attracted the support of the Nonconformist assistant secretary of the Bible Society. These two men, along with two Misses Drury (cousins of Cronin), and Richard Tims, a Grafton Street bookseller and a skilled printer and who for a time became the publisher for most Irish Brethren books and pamphlets, met frequently in Cronin's Dublin home, 13 Lower Pembroke Street. They celebrated house-communion. A second group, tilted slightly less toward Dissenting denominations, was apparently formed in Dublin at about the same time. That cohort of four or five men included William Stokes, who later became a mainstay of the Dublin Brethren, and a Dissenting scripture reader (that is, a colporteur) named Patterson. Most importantly, the Church of Ireland was represented by John Vesey Parnell, who eventually became a prized ornament among the Brethren group. He was one of the Parnells of Queen's County (for which his father was a longtime Liberal-Whig MP) but was under the influence of his Wicklow bachelor uncle, Thomas "Tract" Parnell, the large and voluble proponent of evangelicalism by means of the printed word. Wealthy to a significant degree, John Vesey Parnell became the second Baron Congleton in 1842 when his older brother committed suicide. A third group, entirely Anglican at this point, seems to have coalesced in 1827 when Anthony Norris Groves led a small group to meet in Dublin at widely spaced intervals. Groves was a West Country Englishman, a dentist who came to Trinity College, Dublin, to sit examinations for a bachelor's degree. (Trinity, it will be recalled, was the first British Isles

Development of the Plymouth Brethren" (1967). See also Peter L. Embley, "The Early Development of the Plymouth Brethren," in Bryan R. Wilson (ed.), *Patterns of Sectarianism* (London 1967). F. Roy Coad, *A History of the Brethren Movement*, 2nd ed. (Exeter 1968), is semi-documented (the foundation material is 15–35) and somewhat given to moralizing. Prior to those works, almost all Brethren history and memoirs were by allegiant writers and were collections of anecdotes, snippets from unpublished manuscripts, and restatements of printed material – none of it necessarily wrong, but hard to judge for quality. The standard reference sources used elsewhere in this study – *BDEB, CDGBSL, CDIB, ODNB* – continue to be helpful.

university to permit non-resident students to study its curriculum and take degrees.) Groves planned to be ordained as an Anglican minister and to become a Church Missionary Society worker, but his conscience intervened when he discovered that he would have to affirm belief in just war, something he could not do as a pacifist. At Easter season, 1827, Groves was accompanied by a Miss "Bessy" Paget (the Groves family lived with the two Paget sisters, Charlotte and Elizabeth, in Exeter) and – with no ordained cleric present – they apparently celebrated holy communion with Francis Synge Hutchinson and John Gifford Bellett, both of whom we previously have encountered as young evangelical stalwarts of Dalyland. (Bellett later separated from the Church of Ireland; Synge Hutchinson did not.)

Distant and meteorlike as these tiny house-communion groups are to modern viewers, they certainly were known to each other. Dublin was a very small, very gossipy city and the cohort of young, educated men and women who had the deep need to become distinct in some way from all existing religious denominations was not very large. One suspects that the chief reason the recollections of the earliest era in Brethren-formation so often conflict with each other is that the personnel sometimes fellowshipped with each other and whoever saw them at such a time froze that particular moment in memory. Undeniably, something was going on, but to overdefine the issue of personal priority misses the point.

Where was John Nelson Darby? Although in mid and late life he believed he had founded the whole breaking-bread movement, in fact he was late to the feast. When he was in his seventies, Darby told a follower that "I was myself the beginning of what the world calls Plymouth brethren, though we began in Dublin."[12] In September 1864 he wrote to John Gifford Bellett that "it was no small thing to me that you, with dear C [Edward Cronin] and H [Francis Synge Hutchinson], were one of the first four who, with me, through god's grace the fourth, began to break bread in Dublin, what I believe was God's own work."[13] This identifies the four persons referred to earlier in Darby's mid-1850s

12 J.N.D. to unknown, writing from Boston probably in 1873. *LJND*, vol. 2, no. 128.

13 J.N.D. to J.G. Bellett, September 1864. *LJND*, vol. 1, no. 232.

letter to Professor F.A.G. Tholuck. Thus: there were four alleged founders, counting Darby as one of the four. The curious matter is that in another letter of the 1860s (the date is unclear), Darby wrote to John Gifford Bellett with a somewhat different story of what he believed to be the central moment in early Brethrenism:

> I was laid up in Fitzwilliam Street with a hurt. [His leg injury, so the date was early 1828.] We had reading meetings, and these things came up among others.
>
> Five of us met at Fitzwilliam Square – [James G.] Bellett, Edward Cronin, [Francis Synge] Hutchinson, the present Master [William] Brooke (who was frightened away by Hutchinson) and myself. As H. was willing I proposed meeting next Sunday.
>
> We did at H.'s house. Brooke did not come. I have read since that Cronin had already met with Wilson and some others, but they had broken up. Of that I know nothing.[14]

Notice the troika of young comrades whom Darby credits as being his assistants in his self-claimed founding of Brethrenism: Cronin, Synge Hutchinson, and Bellett (Brooke was excised).[15] Each had been part of earlier house-communion groups, an indication of the fluidity and inter-connectedness of what was really a very small group of kindred souls.

14 J.N.D. to J.G. Bellett, [n.d.] reproduced in [John Gifford Bellett], *Interesting Reminiscences* (London 1884), 14.

15 William Brooke (1796–1881) was of the same generation as the other young Anglican evangelical radicals; his deletion both from Brethren history of the 1820s and from general Irish evangelical history of that period erases a consequential figure from the picture. He was an example of a strong evangelical, close to the Brethren in many regards, who stayed with the Church of Ireland and influenced it significantly toward "low church" forms and toward the greater influence of the laity. He became master of the court of Chancery, a lucrative and prestigious post. He was a main figure (perhaps *the* main figure) in the revision of the Prayer Book when the church was disestablished, removing a number of non-Reformed (that is, historically Catholic) elements in the catechism, liturgy, and rubrics and redefining the meaning of "priest" (see Akenson, *The Church of Ireland* [New Haven 1971], 303–9).

Some of the historical ambiguity about the movement dissipated when Francis Synge Hutchinson made his home at 8 Fitzwilliam Square into a house-church for those who needed a place of solace to study the Bible, pray, and break bread. This was in November 1829, and the arrangement lasted until May 1830, when, the group's numbers having grown, a room in an auction house-cum-cabinetmaker's establishment at 11 Aungier St, Dublin – about halfway between Stephen's Green and St Patrick's Cathedral – was rented on a continuing basis. The rental was paid for by John Vesey Parnell, and it probably opened the doors to middle-class and clerical-class worshippers who had not felt quite at ease on Fitzwilliam Square. This should not obscure the major social trend in the other direction: most of the interest in the subjects raised by the Brethren came from the elite of Dalyland. As we shall discuss in the succeeding chapters, the massive Powerscourt estate became the central location for the discussions of the wrenching issues that deeply concerned Irish evangelicals.

No one would criticize the successive generations of Brethren memorialists for their continuing interest in the folklore of their movement's foundation by tiny groups of Irish believers. This micro-focus, however, sometimes blocks the recognition of bigger social patterns. Basic to the social matrix of the proto-Brethren was the catalyzing fact that the Brethren movement arose in Ireland because it was an analgesic reaction to the rapid slide by the Church of Ireland in its power and influence in the late 1820s and early 1830s. For an especially vulnerable group – the young men who had invested so heavily in the new-Reformation and who had actually believed that a New Jerusalem would be formed from Ireland's civil polity – the nondenominational house fellowships of the late 1820s and (as we shall see in the next chapter, the elaborate Powerscourt conferences of the early 1830s) were a poultice for some and a source of hope that there was another way to bring about God's kingdom.

Although only a small minority of the disappointed Irish evangelicals eventually went all the way from the Established Church to the small assemblies of the new faith, the pool of individuals who were hospitable to many of the proto-Brethren ideas was quite large and that larger group is the social medium from which the core of Irish Brethrenism emerged. We must remember that the new-Reformation had been chiefly an Anglican movement. After its failure, the pool of persons who were searching for a more effective form of Christian community was also overwhelmingly Anglican. Yet, while unhappy with the way things had turned out, "what is striking … about the discontented members of the Established Church in the late 1820s is that, although they might attend the preaching of some dissenting ministers, they rarely became members of the existing nonconformist institutions."[16] Thus, if a new faith-community was to be recruited from the disaffected Anglicans, it would not succeed if it resembled any of the existing Dissenting organizations.

The relative youth of the pool of available recruits to new ways of worship was striking. Most of the core cohort of potential proto-Brethren were in their late twenties and early thirties. However, the prevalence of relatively young persons somewhat obscures the pivotal importance of older individuals: established Anglican clerics and senior landowners – Robert Daly,[17] William Cleaver, and several of the Synges and Parnells, for example. Still, the driving energy came from the younger Anglican evangelicals. The great unknown is: to what degree did the earliest forms of Brethrenism appeal to women? Aside from Lady Powerscourt, the influence of women is a matter of mystery. Either they were silent (or were silenced) or the records have left them largely unrecorded. They are heard to speak in the diaries and memoirs

16 Stunt (2000), 172.

17 Robert Daly's continuing influence and his long-term commitment to aggressive evangelicalism are worth emphasizing. As Desmond Bowen notes, even after he became bishop of Cashel, Waterford, Lismore, and Emly in early 1843 (nom. 1842) "his evangelical militancy in no way lessened, and until his death in 1872 he represented the uncompromising anti-Catholic party in the Established Church which considered itself at war with a religious and cultural world of superstition and ignorance, protected and nurtured by the Antichrist in Rome" (*The Protestant Crusade in Ireland* [Dublin and Montreal and Kingston 1978], 76).

of the Anglo-Irish praying caste[18] but not in the newspaper reports of the Irish conferences on Bible interpretation or on prophetic exegesis.

As for social-class matters, by the early 1830s, the group of men who were fervently petitioning the Almighty, sermon-tasting, and studying together were thoroughly gentrified and more than a touch aristocratic, even more so than had been the case in the mid-1820s. Reflecting on this, in the 1840s Darby admitted to a Swiss brother that the Brethren movement at home had passed for an aristocratic movement and, implicitly, that this had favoured its rise.[19] The dentists and medical doctors were still admitted, but the sons of landowners and bishops and barristers and politicians and well-beneficed clergy were more and more preponderant among the seekers. This was a band of privileged young men: very well-educated in the classics, accustomed to being fed without earning their keep, and unaccustomed to being baulked. For the most part they were remarkably cosmopolitan, although not worldly in the negative religious sense of that term. They met each other not only in the prayer rooms of Dublin and the drawing rooms of Wicklow but in fashionable churches in London and occasionally in Parisian restaurants. There was something resembling a Masonic set of

18 Thus, in 1839, Mrs Francis Howard, a frequent visitor to County Wicklow, wrote of "the great stride religion has taken into the fashionable world." She meant Anglican evangelicalism of the sort that shared prayers and Bible study with the emergent Brethren. R.F. Foster, *Charles Stewart Parnell: The Man and His Family* (London 1976), xviii.

19 Neatby, 42. Darby, with characteristic emphasis upon self-control, wrote a foreign colleague that he was in Dublin and would be travelling about: "I am in a different position here, as I have to be on my guard. I meet many I have known of old, some relatives, more of the upper classes of society interested in divine things. The revival brings people of all sorts, gentlefolk of the Establishment (besides, everybody knows everybody in Ireland) – persons really interesting, and I have to watch as to being as absolutely and solely a Christian as I am wont in England and abroad" (J.N.D. to G. Gausby, 16 May 1854. *LJND*, vol. 2, no. 124). Neatby notes (1902, p. 42) that "in this respect things have changed inevitably, but even yet fashionable people often find it easier to pass from the Church of England to Brethrenism than to any of the older forms of Dissent."

codes among these young gentleman that facilitated their recognizing each other as being the proper mixture of piety and property.

Strikingly, in counter-current to their privileged social status, several of the young men assumed the mantle of ostentatious poverty. Both in the larger pool of concerned Anglican evangelicals and in the smaller group who eventually became Brethren, one encounters a contradictory admixture of humility and arrogance. They abased themselves before the Saviour found in the gospels and at the same time many of the "earlies" (most effectively John Nelson Darby) claimed both the right and the wisdom to reformulate, indeed replace, almost all existing Christian denominations with their own reformulation of earliest Christian organization. As a group, the most serious evangelicals, both those who remained Church of Ireland and those who separated, were notably selfless and also simultaneously selfish. Frequently they gave of themselves and of their worldly goods, but mostly to those who might possibly become allies or converts.

To the framers of the Brethren mindset, human beings, whether as individuals or as members of social cohorts, were merely the mud and straw that was provided by the Almighty as building material for the foundation of their new Church order. The theory of Church construction is often referred to as "ecclesiology"; although it is not a household term, it is a useful second-level descriptor. Ecclesiology has two main meanings: the science and art of the physical architecture of religious buildings and, more abstractly, the way the organizational architecture of a religious denomination is arranged. The first usage is quite common in Ireland because of the work of Augustus W.N. Pugin (1812–52), the incandescent proponent of the revival of the splendour of the Gothic era in Christian architecture. As a convert to Roman Catholicism, he was considered trustworthy by the Catholic Church in Ireland and his having designed the Gothic interior of the Palace of Westminster after the 1834 fire certainly did not hurt his reputation. Thus, in the south of Ireland, most especially County Wexford, one finds the best collection of post-Reformation architectural work put up by the Irish Catholic

Church, a short-lived Gothic revival that was mostly displaced by the glowering grey churches of the post-Famine era. This sort of ecclesiology, consisting of stones and stained glass made to soar upward in God's praise, is definitely not what one means when one talks about the emerging ecclesiology of the Brethren. To them, such physical forms were mere vainglory; their own taste in physical architecture ran from the banal to the banausic, with no stops in between for the decorative praise of the Almighty.

Instead, Brethren ecclesiology goes right to the intangible heart of everything they came to hold sacred. The early Brethren were as much concerned about what the proper organization of their faith should be as they were about anything else, save their supreme shared belief in salvation through Jesus Christ and their spiritual animation through the Holy Spirit. The present necessity of examining their almost prosaic ecclesiology may disappoint readers who wish to deal immediately with the fascinating way that the Brethren built a massive, idiosyncratic, neon-lit superstructure of belief that includes rococo descriptions of the final Apocalypse and Tribulation, the revival and divine redemption of Israel, the snipping of all history including the future into parcels (called "dispensations"), and, most intriguing of all, the doctrine of the secret Rapture into Heaven of true believers before all Hell breaks loose on Earth. But the organizational blueprints are crucial.

The closest analogy in physical architecture to our task here is this: if we are to respect and to at least partially understand the early Brethren's building of a faith, we are like architectural engineers trying to comprehend the wild wonders of the Basilica and Expiatory Church of the Holy Family (Sagrada Familia) designed by the genius Antoni Gaudí. Before becoming mesmerized by the turrets, hidden stairways, majestic spires, and lurid interior decorations, a student of church architecture must survey the foundations, the part that few visitors pay much attention to, but without which distinct portions of the whole magnificent edifice would list in different directions and crash ignominiously to earth. Similarly, with the Brethren, we have to look at foundations first. And here the analogy works nicely, for Gaudí was the master of sequentially built foundations. He would do one segment of foundation and put up something amazing, say a paraboloid vault, and then he would have an incremental vision and would build more foundations and then join a forest of columns that resembled the branching of trees in a forest, to the original structure. And on and on. Never quite completed, the Sagrada Familia is a work still in progress long after the death of its chief architect.

The Brethren worked the same way, and this holds despite one school of the faithful's preferring to believe that the whole faith – ecclesiology, doctrines of salvation and spirit, and prophecies of the future – came as a single unified vision, chiefly one vouchsafed to John Nelson Darby, as if he had been on the summit of a mountain conversing with higher powers. Actually, the foundations were partially built, then some of the superstructure was put in place, then the next bit of organizational foundation was added and then more cosmic ornamentation. The elaboration continues into the present day. The first stage of the process ran from roughly 1827 to 1837. John Gifford Bellett wrote to a close friend on the eve of Catholic Emancipation that:

> Many persons are confidently anticipating sorrowful times for our land. The condition of the public mind here they think to be very alarming. I would that I felt myself more in an Abraham state, looking for a city that hath "foundations." You know none of the present Kingdoms of earth have foundations, they are all either shaken, or to be shaken. (Hebrews xii: 27, 28)[20]

John Nelson Darby too felt the need for proper foundations. Mark Sweetnam and Crawford Gribben have noted that "one of the most interesting things about the way in which Darby's interpretations of prophetic scripture emerged is that his development of Dispensationalism was a result of his disaffection with the ecclesiastical status quo … Eschatology followed on from church doctrine. It was ecclesiological concern that led to Darby's rethinking of prophecy." Much of this followed from his gloom over the condition of the Irish church, which he generalized: "Darby became deeply pessimistic about the future of the

20 John Gifford Bellett to __ Reynolds [1828–29], reproduced, with elisions in [Letty M. Bellett], *Recollections of the Late J. G. Bellet* (London 1895), 28.

world and disillusioned about the prospects of global evangelicalization and the growing success of the gospel."[21]

The defining and constructing of a new and trustworthy foundation was a conflicted process, not least within the personality of John Nelson Darby himself. Along the way, most "church brethren" – Anglicans who in the early years often met with the keener brothers and sisters – decided to stay within the Church of Ireland, rather than separate. Others left the Anglican communion or, less often, some Dissenting fellowship, formed a small assembly, and then had deep disagreements with each other. The passage toward an agreed ecclesiology among the proto-Brethren was an untidy historical progress, not a nice clean evolution. In the discussion that follows, I am being intentionally untrue to the deep messiness of emergent Brethren ecclesiology and instead am suggesting three historical pivots that serve as legitimate ordering points that make the process understandable; but, emphatically, the discussion is not comprehensive. That made clear, I believe the inflection points were as follows: (1) the reading of the New Testament as an historical document that contained a set of plans for the "true" Christian Church; (2) a radical approach to the Old Testament, particularly the awkward question that had so long bothered most schools of Christians, namely whether or not the Hebrew scriptures provided patterns of organizational behaviour for the Christian Church to emulate; (3) a remembered constellation of previous attempts in Ireland at setting up "primitive" Christian congregations; these were more part of the atmosphere than directly causal, but they were not forgotten.

INFLECTION POINT NO. 1

The New Testament can be read by a believer as a document that is both divine and also has secular historical truths within it. If one believes that the Church of the present day has failed, it is the natural place to look for blueprints for reconstructing Christianity. In doing

21 Mark S. Sweetnam and Crawford Gribben, "J.N. Darby and the Irish Origins of Dispensationalism," *Journal of the Evangelical Theological Society* (2009), 573.

just that, the educated young men who felt that Irish Anglicanism, even in its most evangelical form, had failed them, were engaged in a way of thinking that was far from being heretical: just the opposite. In their development, whatever their interpretative arguments among themselves, the Brethren always insisted on the "literal" interpretation of the biblical texts. In the actual course of events, their proud literalism came to be a multi-level system that most outsiders would conclude involved allegories, typologies, tropes, and redactions of the texts that, in sum, were anything but literal in the common meaning of the term. In the early days – the late 1820s and early 1830s in Ireland – a simple form of agreed literalism was to read the New Testament and to ask: how did the early Christians arrange themselves once Jesus of Nazareth was no longer with them? This pattern of ancient organization was then to be taken as normative, the one to adopt as the blueprint for rebuilding the faith. The term "primitive church" is often used for the object of their search, and "primitivism" can be employed as long as it is scrubbed of any negative overtones. Another aspect of this style of literalism is that the sacred texts were read for their "original intent," a term that one borrows from American constitutional law. The characteristics of this mode of innocent, "common sense" literalism are worth filing for future reference, because when they become secularized they are a powerful pattern in determining how one reads foundational documents of any sort – trust deeds, legal statutes, and constitutions.

The early Irish seekers after the New Testament's ecclesiological blueprint were anything but simple-minded, even when they were being their most literal. Almost all of the male participants in discussions were competent in classical Greek and could read the much less difficult Greek of the New Testament in the original. They understood that no translation of the ancient text was completely accurate, or even universally acceptable, so they harried ancient words for their root meanings. (John Nelson Darby in his mature years did impressive amounts of direct translation of the Bible, including portions into French, German, and Italian.) The philological sophistication of the Irish proto-Brethren granted, the phalanx that eventually left the Established Church made a crucial commitment to the belief that each portion of the New Testament in its canonical post-Reformation form was of full authority. (The Apocrypha, which was standard in many

Protestant texts, was soon dropped out of proto-Brethren discussions as being of lesser, if any, authority; in any case, its direct historical references were pre-Christian.) This commitment to the divine authority of the full twenty-seven books of the New Testament, as found in the Authorized Version, delivered the students of scripture from the awkward nature of the New Testament when it is used as a blueprint for later Christianity: in their central content, these scriptures are mostly about Jesus and not much about the primitive Church. The four gospels are Jesus-centred and do not tell very much directly about Church organization, as distinct from information on the way Jesus dealt with his disciples. The Acts of the Apostles contains a good deal of material on what might be called Church practices, but it is very late in the first century in its composition. To the extent that there is any direct information in the New Testament about the primitive Church that was written before the traumatic destruction of Jerusalem and its temple in 70 CE, it is found in the letters of Paul. The immediate problem this raises is that six of the thirteen (and sometimes fourteen) letters eventually ascribed to Paul, as well as the "catholic epistles" of various writers and also the book of the Revelation of St John, were all questioned by the early Church fathers before being reluctantly accepted as canonical. In a very effective sidestep, the Brethren declared all parts of the New Testament to be equally of divine origin. This avoided their having to do a stratigraphy of authenticity: the standard Protestant canon was accepted as being divine in its entirety. Thus the entire New Testament was open to a hunt-and-peck search for anything that might be relevant concerning proper Church organization, each piece being equal to every other, provided that it was read properly in its immediate literary context.

Therefore, the following questions could be addressed directly by close and literal reading: where did authority over a local congregation reside? were there bishops in the primitive Church? were there priests? could divine grace be transmitted via sacraments, or did grace descend entirely without an intermediary to the individual believer? was holy communion more than a symbolic act of collective affirmation? could a truly Christian Church ever make an alliance with the state? And more. Virtually universally the evangelicals who eventually became Brethren dealt with one awkward question by playing it into the long grass. That is, they did not deal directly with the foundational question: do the blueprints for the primitive Church begin when Jesus was alive or after his crucifixion? Without open reflection, they opted for the latter. The reason is that if they saw their central collective act, the breaking of bread, as being normatively set down by Jesus of Nazareth, then they needed an authority figure to stand over holy communion – and that road leads very quickly to the position they abhorred, that of the Established Church or, worse yet, of the Roman Catholics. So, instead, they followed the Acts of the Apostles and the communion service that is embedded as a performance metaphor in the writings of Paul (1 Cor. 11:23–26). The liturgical decision to adopt the practices of the apostolic era over that of Jesus's own ministry inevitably flattened the ecclesiastical structure. Priests were not really necessary, separating Brethren decided.

INFLECTION POINT NO. 2

Among those early Brethren who eventually left their parent church, the response to the question, what can we learn about church organization from the Old Testament? was contradictory. On the one hand, they were fully willing to assimilate one of the primary metaphors of the Hebrew scriptures, namely the Jerusalem Temple. The Old Testament contained, etched in sharp and loving detail, the lines of Solomon's Temple. When Zerubbabel began the rebuilding of the Jerusalem Temple after the Babylonian Exile, the Israelites' ambition was to reconstruct Solomon's edifice just as it was found in the texts that were possessed at the time of the re-building by the leaders of the covenanted nation. The Brethren studied both the original temple and its rebuilding. Similarly, after the destruction of Herod's massive temple (the "Second Temple"), the Mishnah recorded the temple's lineaments with obsessive, and one assumes accurate, precision. This provided the blueprint not only for those Jews who believe that a Third Temple will be the final step in the restoration of Israel but also for many messianic Christians. (Usually, Christians have quietly borrowed from the Jewish dévotes the drawings and architectural projections derived from the Mishnah without acknowledging where they come from.) So, although in the late 1820s and early 1830s the disappointed, angered, or simply the bewildered among the religiously sensitized Irish Anglican community were directly threatening orthodox institutions, they were not doing so as rejectors of ancient tradition, but, in their view, as its protectors. They would rebuild the temple.

On the other hand, with an almost-regal sweep of hand, the early Brethren cleanly rejected the long-standing idea that the Christian Church evolved from the same covenant that had produced ancient Judaism. Both the Reform and the Catholic traditions have viewed the Church as in some way fulfilling the mission that Yahweh had trusted to the Jewish people and which, it was believed, the Jewish people had failed to fulfill. This basic concept has led to entire libraries of theology that detail, and argue about the details, concerning which principles of ancient Hebrew ecclesiastical organization and behaviour should be carried over into Christianity and which should not. In an early pamphlet, John Nelson Darby erased the entire complex problem from the blackboard when he declared that the death of St Stephen marked the close of the Jewish possibility of being part of the continuous sequence of God's dispensations.[22] One of Darby's and his followers' notions was that the Anglican Church had been corrupted by its conforming to Jewish conceptions of Church order.[23] Statements revolving around this Brethren principle of Church order could be multiplied by the score – and in each repetition one would run the danger of inferring, wrongly, that Darby and the Brethren were anti-Semitic. They were not and indeed were part of a philo-Semitic phalanx within the evangelical movement of the British Isles that was fascinated with Judaism and was deeply knowledgeable about certain narrow strands of both ancient Hebrew literature and aspects of post-70 Rabbinic Jewish traditions. Actually, a key point with the Darbyites (as they eventually became) was that they were the most energetic of groups that predicted – indeed longed for – the reestablishment of Israel in the old homeland. That desire, however, had nothing to do

22 "The Character of Office in the Present Dispensation," in *CW*, 01007, 97. The pamphlet was not dated in *CW* but probably was written in 1833 or 1834.

23 Floyd D. Elmore, "A Critical Examination of the Doctrine of the Two Peoples of God" (ThD, Dallas Theological Seminary, 1990), 25.

with their rejection of there being any continuous tie between their purified form of Christianity and ancient Israel.[24]

INFLECTION POINT NO. 3

Neither the early Brethrens' definition of issues to be settled, nor their method of employing the entire New Testament as a unified divinely provided historical source, was totally new. From the second half of the eighteenth century onward these questions were raised and similar attacks upon the issues were common in western Europe: the more so in the first half of the nineteenth century. All across the Protestant states of northern Europe and into parts of France and Switzerland, "conventicles" were popping up, house churches or at least Bible study and prayer groups that operated outside the ambit of the state churches and usually were treated as a threat by the clergy of the various state-established denominations. The activities of these small faith-groups were frequently reported in evangelical papers in the British Isles.

Within Ireland, there were three groups that could be labelled "pre-Brethren" – that is, their beliefs and practices, though not directly leading to the Brethren, anticipated in various ways later Brethren practices. At the same time, these small assemblies were consequential for their contribution to the climate of evangelical excitement that was so strong in the 1820s. These three were the Kellyites, the Walkerites, and a cohort that has no name but can be usefully labelled the Camowen Green emigrators. The first two are well-known in Irish history, the third is almost invisible in Irish religious documents but was a highway for primitive-Church enthusiasts and their ideas to move back and forth between Ireland, Great Britain, the USA and the Canadas. It was a theological conduit well known to serious Irish evangelicals of the 1820s and '30s.[25]

24 The case for Darby as a philo-Semite is made with considerable enthusiasm by Paul Richard Wilkinson, *For Zion's Sake: Christian Zionism and the Role of John Nelson Darby* (Milton Keynes 2007).

25 The most tightly focused discussion of the Kellyites and Walkerites that I have encountered is Grayson Carter, chapter 3, "Thomas Kelly and John Walker, and the Revival of 'Apostolic' Practices within Irish Evangelicalism" (58–104).

The Rev. Thomas Kelly (1769–1855) was in many ways close to being the Ideal Type of the Irish early evangelical Anglican clergyman. He was from a wealthy family (his father was a judge of Irish common pleas), he studied at Trinity College, Dublin, and married in 1795 the future-heiress, Elizabeth Tighe, of a family of substantial landowners in County Wicklow, several of whom became keen evangelicals. Thus, the Rev. Mr Kelly was wired into the Wicklow spiritual world even before it became Dalyland. Later, in 1830, his daughter married the Rev. Hon. William Wingfield, the evangelical younger son of the fourth Viscount Powerscourt, and thus Kelly was tied directly to the Powerscourt circle. At first Kelly studied law, but then, over the objections of his family, became an Anglican priest. (The parallel in both family wealth and in his rejecting law as a career, obviously similar to the path later taken by John Nelson Darby, is apparent.) As a clergyman, Kelly was open to the idea of free grace descending from the Almighty without its involving the Church, was hospitable to pan-denominational evangelicalism, willing to practise the breaking of bread outside of the bounds of canonical buildings, and sought after a vague sort of primitive churchism. He came to believe that the early Church had possessed only two spiritual orders – elders and deacons. A brilliant preacher, Kelly was perceived as a serious threat to Church order and in 1803 he seceded from the Church of Ireland, a prudential move as he was on the verge of being silenced. An able band of young followers – formally called the Church of Christ but almost always known as the Kellyites – tended congregations several places in Ireland, including Blackrock, County Dublin, on the Proby estate, indicating Kelly's continuing ties to the Anglican evangelical social elite even after he had seceded and become an opponent of all national Churches. Kelly was wealthy enough to build at least four churches with his own money. He seems to have been a genuinely sweet man and was gifted as a hymn writer: several of his 765 published hymns found their way into the hymnals of the Anglican communion worldwide, into those of the Brethren,

---

Useful commentary on a wide range of secessionists, mostly English, is found in Harold H. Rowdon, "Secession from the Established Church in the Early Nineteenth Century," *Vox Evangelica* (1964).

and into those of several Dissenting denominations. If by 1830 Thomas Kelly's separate organization had ceased to grow, it still had a long half-life ahead. Kelly himself lived into the mid-1850s. There is no question that the devoted and distraught young persons who were grappling with the what-next? problem in their own religious lives were aware of the Rev. Thomas Kelly and of the partial precedent his ecclesiology might offer.[26]

For a time in the late eighteenth and early nineteenth centuries the Rev. Thomas Kelly was yoked with the Rev. John Walker (1769–1833) at the extreme edge of the nascent evangelical movement within the Anglican communion. At various times, each of them supported Bethesda Chapel, Dorset Street, Dublin. Walker was a joint-chaplain there, 1793–1805, and over several decades both Walker and Kelly intersected with the Rev. Benjamin Mathias, who took over the chaplaincy of Bethesda in 1805 and became Dublin's most popular Anglican evangelical preacher.[27] Walker's relationship with Mathias was

26 In addition to Carter, see entries on Thomas Kelly in *BDEB*, *ODNB*, and *CDIB* and the entry on William Wingfield in *CDGBSL*. See also Patrick Comerford, "An Innovative People," in Gillespie and Neely, eds (Dublin 2002), 192–3. The comment of the hymnodist E.E. Cornwall is germane: "Hymns by Thomas Kelly are to be found in all the principle hymn-books of Great Britain and America and have been freely used in Church of England hymnals that are evangelical, but probably none have drawn more upon them than those known as 'Brethren,' many of whom were themselves Irish and well acquainted with his hymns, so widely known in the early part of the nineteenth century. Their own hymns were as yet mostly unwritten, and those of Kelly contained in large measure the truth which to them had become so real" ("Thomas Kelly, 1769–1855," an excerpt from his "Songs of Pilgrimage and Glory," found at www.stempublishing.com/humns/biographies/kellyt.html, accessed 5 July 2013).

27 In chapter 2 of the present study, I indicated that the Rev. Benjamin Mathias (1772–1841) was supported in his career by the Guinness family and was grafted into the Dalyland network through the Guinnesses' control of benefices in Wicklow and County Dublin. According to Alan R. Acheson, during Mathias's Bethesda pastorate (1805–35) "his congregation was one of the most influential ever assembled in Ireland" (*BDEB*, entry on B.W. Mathias). This was in spite of the chapel not being fully licensed as a Church of Ireland sanctuary until 1825. Two minor notes from [anon.], *Brief Memorials of the Rev.*

cold, Kelly's cooperative, and that reflects their very different personal temperaments. Walker was abrasive and often bitter, Kelly soft and sweet-tempered. Still, Walker and Kelly left the Church of Ireland at almost the same time: Kelly in 1803, Walker in 1804–05. In Walker's case, while still an Anglican priest, he began a group called the Church of God,[28] which was rigidly separatist: its members were not to worship with anyone with less than perfectly correct beliefs, meaning almost nobody in Ireland or the rest of the known world. (Walker had made a six-week tour of Scotland and found not a single person who was up to standard.) The Walkerites viewed a state church as being non-biblical. This was not quite the thing for a fellow of Trinity College, Dublin, to preach; when, with admirable integrity, he told the provost of TCD that he was resigning his position, he was terminated the next day. The Walkerites practised the breaking of bread each week. Walker himself was a Calvinist in the strict sense of that term – thus he deeply loathed Methodists – and saw the maintenance of discipline as a prime commandment. At their peak, the Walkerites had perhaps a dozen congregations in Ireland, and large ones in Birmingham and London. As is frequently the case with extreme congregationalist groups, the Walkerites had their schisms, the most notable being the division in the home-church in Dublin in 1815–19: the perhaps-biblical practice of greeting one's fellow believers with "an holy kiss" on entry to service and upon leaving led to an oscular schism in the Church and to Walker's leaving Dublin for quieter locales. (The story, perhaps inaccurate, is that the schism started with a blacksmith kissing the gentry ladies

---

B.W. Mathias (Dublin 1842): one is that both Thomas Kelly and Robert Daly were among the subscribers to this memorial of Mathias; secondly, Mathias, although only three years younger than John Walker, had been his student at TCD and the memorial volume reproduces (10–12) a letter of advice (19 August 1795) from Walker to his tutee.

28 "Church of God" was the descriptive name that John Nelson Darby gave retrospectively in the 1860s to his own efforts that began in the late 1820s. He referred to his first effort "which has since developed itself in the Church of God" (J.N.D., "Considerations Addressed to the Archbishop of Dublin, CW, 01001, 1). Although Darby's term was merely descriptive (it never was the formal name of the Brethren), its usage may indicate a latent, if minor, influence of Walker upon Darby.

with much too much enthusiasm.) Walker, unlike Thomas Kelly, was not born rich and did not marry an heiress, so after being turned out of his fellowship at TCD he was forced to rely on coaching undergraduates and writing books of classical scholarship. From 1819 onward he lived in Scotland and then in London and was reliant on wealthy patrons. Grayson Carter is certainly right that Walker had put forward "a radical 'primitivism' which in some respects foreshadowed the views advanced by a number of other evangelical seceders, including John Nelson Darby, Edward Irving, Theodosia Powerscourt and members of the [English] Western Schism."[29] Walker also had a more general cultural currency despite his extreme views: in 1833 Trinity College, Dublin, in public amendment for its treatment of him early in the century, voted him a life pension of £600 a year. Walker returned to Dublin, but he died before he could collect any of his reward, unintentionally separatist to the very end.[30]

29 Carter, 83.

30 For a broad-spectrum analysis of Walker, see Joseph Liechty, "The Popular Reformation Comes to Ireland: The Case of John Walker," in R.V. Comerford, Mary Cullen, Jacqueline R. Hill, and Colm Lennon, *Religion, Conflict and Coexistence* (Dublin 1990). Although one should not slight the Rev. Mr Walker's substantial classical scholarship, he comes down to us as a religious figure. In that regard, he was fortunate in the quality of the opposition he elicited; the opposition, as much as his own devotional stance, made him well-known in the 1810s and 20s. In particular, the Rev. Peter Roe (1778–1842) of St Mary's, Kilkenny, in the diocese of Ossory, was his opponent. Roe was the only major Irish evangelical cleric who had a centre of influence outside of Dalyland or urban Dublin. In 1815, he edited and wrote the introduction and an essay in *The Evil of Separation from the Church of England, Considered in a Series of Letters Addressed Chiefly to the Rev. Peter Roe* (London: 1st ed. 1815, 2nd ed. 1817). The letters written to Roe were actually essays by heavy hitters within the Irish and English Established Churches. Peter Roe is the subject of one of the best Irish clerical biographies published during the Victorian era: Samuel Madden, *Memoir of the Life of the Late Rev. Peter Roe* (Dublin 1842). This has not only Roe's clerical correspondence but private letters with family and friends as well. Madden, unlike so many early Victorian biographers, is not coy about identifying the correspondents. A noteworthy point about Roe is that his anti-Catholicism was limited to religious matters and did not spread to economics or politics. During the Catholic Emancipation flap, he preached a notable sermon to the Dublin clergy advising them to "preach the Word"

The group that I call the Camowen Green emigrators was unusual because of its contribution to the atmospherics of the debate among (chiefly) young Anglican evangelicals about how to rebuild the Church. This occurred through most of the founding members emigrating to North America. Their leader, James Buchanan (1772–1851), became one of the most influential persons in facilitating and directing the pre-Famine migration flow from Ireland to the USA and to the Canadas. James Buchanan was born to a gentry linen family in Strathroy, County Tyrone. As a young man, Buchanan had acted as an agent for the Irish under-secretary of state concerning the 1798 Rising in County Tyrone, a service that was translated later into both a political plum for Buchanan and, indirectly, special treatment for certain types of Protestant migrants. He was one of the few Irish Presbyterians in the emerging constellation of primitive-Church believers. In 1805 he held Lisanally, a substantial farm and linen operation near Camowen Green, close to Omagh. He and his wife had become upset in 1799 with the problem of finding a proper Presbyterian minister for the Omagh kirk, and they despaired of the quality of young candidates. Eventually, in 1805, Buchanan offered to pay for anyone suitable who would celebrate service at his own house each Sunday. He built thereafter a meeting house and though several trained pastors rotated through the post, Buchanan was the director of the assembly, which constituted itself as a church outside the Presbyterian (and of course the Established) Church system. This body became "a Church of the Living God," with five original members. The assembly modelled itself on what it believed was the pattern in the book of Acts, breaking bread every Sunday, with no ordained cleric being required, and practising adult, rather than infant, baptism.[31] This essentially Ulster Presbyterian movement did

and, implicitly, to stay out of politics ("Address of the Rev. Peter Roe," *The Christian Examiner and Church of Ireland Magazine*, vol. 7, June 1829, 393–7).

31 James Buchanan printed in May 1834 a letter to his children and grandchildren concerning his religious beliefs. It was reprinted by one of his grandchildren, George Whitlaw, as *The Religious Belief of James Buchanan* (London 1896), and reprinted again in the mid-twentieth century under the same title (Omagh 1956). Grayson Carter makes two rare mistakes (94) in stating (1) that James Buchanan was a protégé of the famous early Scottish

not grow dramatically or noisily. By the end of the Napoleonic Wars, it had at most five congregations and at most one hundred members.[32]

Why pay attention to these small assemblies? After all, John Nelson Darby noted in April 1833 that "I hear the north is dotted with little bodies … though I do not know the places."[33] And probably few of the south of Ireland evangelicals could have named the congregations. Nevertheless, they were consequential because of James Buchanan. He emigrated in 1816, leaving his brother John in charge of the Camowen Green group. James Buchanan was not the usual emigrant. He was a man of money and was owed by the government for his work in 1798: in a word, he was connected. Thus, in 1816 he was appointed British consul in New York. That was not just a ceremonial post. At the time it served as one of the two most important control points for Irish migrants to the northern parts of the United States and to Lower and Upper Canada. (The other control point was the city of Quebec.) James Buchanan held his post until 1843. In 1824, his daughter married a distant cousin, Alexander Buchanan (1798–1851), who became a major law officer of Lower Canada. An unmarried brother of James Buchanan, Alexander Carlisle Buchanan (??–1840) was chief British agent for emigration to Lower Canada from 1828 to 1838. The son of James Buchanan (also named Alexander Carlisle Buchanan, 1808–1868, and easily confused with his uncle), acted as the assistant and locum for his uncle in the emigration business in the mid-1830s and in 1838 himself became the superintendent of emigration for Upper and Lower Canada.[34] That the Buchanan family had a near-lock on one of the

---

evangelicals, the Haldane Brothers, and (2) suggesting that the Buchanans' Camowen Green meeting house was probably a Walkerite group. The former statement is based on an overreading of Coad (81), who says that the Haldanes "influenced" Buchanan, which they certainly did. The second is refuted by Buchanan himself (*Religious Beliefs*, 7–13), who makes it clear that he accepted ideas from clergy of the Established Church, the Haldanes, and John Walker but did not affiliate with any of them.

32 Peter Embley is informative on this matter; see "The Origins and Early Development of the Plymouth Brethren," (PhD, St Paul's College, Cheltenham, 1966), 30–1.

33 J.N.D. to "Beloved Brother and Brethren," __April, 1833. *LJND*, vol. 1, no. 6.

34 *Dictionary of Canadian Biography*, entries on the Buchanans in vols 8 and 9. For genealogical details, see Arthur W.P. Buchanan, *The Buchanan Book*

more powerful sets of governmental positions in the empire is obvious. Alexander Carlisle Buchanan in 1828 claimed to have brought 6,000 migrants from Ireland and his brother James in New York had by that time sent thousands to Upper Canada.[35]

James Buchanan had an especially fine opportunity to both do well and to do good. He kept his primitive-Church faith, and he also did very well for himself: he acquired land in what is now Ontario, and in 1836 one of his sons (John Stewart Buchanan) became the owner of the heart of the mill town of Strathroy. Crucially, James Buchanan was involved in the proto-Brethren congregation in New York City, which in the years 1818–20 collected and printed a correspondence with similar congregations in the Canadas, the USA, and the British Isles.[36] This is one of the earliest exhibits in the history of the nineteenth-century's transatlantic evangelical network. Although the publication is today a rare item, it was well-known among evangelicals on both sides of the Atlantic, was circulated hand-to-hand, and its contents were summarized in vol. 1 (1835) of *The Millennial Harbinger; and Voluntary Church Advocate.*[37] The consequential matter is that it was no secret in Ireland that the British consul in New York City could open the way to opportunities both in the US and in British North America. For serious Irish

(Montreal 1911). In case the family relationships of the Buchanans still seem simple: James Buchanan articled as a lawyer with a family friend, an Omagh solicitor named Alexander Carlisle, whose practice he took over. The ship that James Buchanan and his family took to New York in 1816 was the 221-ton "Alexander Buchanan." It is worth noting that the records of the offices charged with effecting emigration to Upper and Lower Canada in the era of the Buchanans are somewhat less clear than they would have been if the major players had not shared the same name.

35 J.I. Little, "A.C. Buchanan and the Megantic Experiment: Promoting British Colonization in Lower Canada," *Histoire Social/ Social History* (November 2013). The brothers had a cousin, William Buchanan, who ran charter ships out of Londonderry to Quebec.

36 [anon.], *Letters Concerning Their Principles and Order from Assemblies of Believers in 1818–20* (1st ed. privately printed; reprint ed., London 1889). I have not been able to find the first edition.

37 [William Jones], "Prefatory Matter," *The Millennial Harbinger; and Voluntary Church Advocate*, vol. 1 (1835), 10–15. The primary London distributor was G. Wightman of Paternoster Row; the Dublin distributor was R.M. Tims, who was the unofficial printer and bookseller for the early Brethren.

evangelicals, it was clear that the Buchanan family machine was particularly useful to the right sort of believer. The Buchanans' form of pre-Brethrenism was well known in the Irish homeland in the 1820s and 1830s, because the family had left the country and magnified themselves abroad.

None of the pre-Brethren separatist groups mentioned here – or any of the several others scattered around the British Isles at the time – should be considered as being directly causal to the creation of the Irish Brethren; nor should they be viewed as completely irrelevant. Evidence concerning the chain of provenance of any given idea simply is not there. As a sympathetic mid-twentieth century historian noted, "the Brethren are still shadowy figures to many even of their fellow-Christians. This fact arises partly from their quixotic (though well-intentioned) practice of anonymity."[38] This shadowiness was deepened by the later Brethrens' following John Nelson Darby's consistent refusal to cite the source of his ideas, save the Bible. Thus, the leading present-day scholar on the matter has noted in controlled frustration: "Looking in Darby's publications for the sources of his ideas is on the whole, a fruitless task. In the vast bulk of his writing, Darby tended only to quote from the works of other writers when he was disagreeing with them in controversy or when he was giving a source of information rather than an opinion."[39] A well-informed but very unsympathetic nineteenth-century Londonderry Presbyterian clergyman, the Rev. Thomas Croskerry, stated that "Plymouthism" (a nasty term at the time he used it) "is indeed, theologically the least original of systems."[40] Perhaps the Rev. Mr Croskerry was correct, but except in the vaguest terms it is hard to substantiate where basic Brethren ideas came from. Asserting that they borrowed from this group or that is easy enough, but actual probative material concerning transmission and assimilation of specific idea-forms is hard to come by: the Brethren throughout the nineteenth century were not inclined to leave

38 Coad (1968), 7.

39 Timothy C.F. Stunt, "Influences in the Early Development of J.N. Darby," in Crawford Gribben and Timothy C.F. Stunt (eds), *Prisoners of Hope?* (Carlisle 2004), 56.

40 Thomas Croskerry, *Plymouth-Brethrenism* (London and Belfast 1879), vii.

much evidence of their borrowing from earlier forms – in this case the earliest Irish separatist assemblies. One must admit that an idea can be invented several times over, each creator seeing himself as the recipient of an original revelation.[41]

Planning and then creating a new form of religious organization required some heavy lifting. The Brethren liberated and expended a remarkable amount of emotional energy in their early days. A good deal of that energy took the form of an incandescent negativism. Anyone who has seen a pure-alcohol flame burn has a visual image of what was occurring among the front edge of the Wicklow Brethren: an immense amount of energy was being released in a form that gave off a startling amount of heat, but much less light. Several of the leading figures of proto-Brethrenism shared a strong negative valence toward the Church of Ireland on grounds that were personal rather than purely theological, and the chief of these was John Nelson Darby.

In his ("not published") 1828 pamphlet blasting Archbishop Magee and the Anglican clergy who had asked for governmental protection for Protestants (discussed in the preceding chapter), it is clear

41 Again at this point one should mention the fact that the Irish Methodist movement had essentially no influence on the narrative that is evolving here, save an immeasurably small increase in the general temperature of Protestant religious devotion: "No connections whatsoever have come to light between Irish Methodism and the origins of the Plymouth Brethren in that country. 'Powerscourt' Castle, which figures so prominently in the annals of those sections of Irish evangelicalism from which the Brethren movement sprang, is not even mentioned in histories of Irish Methodism" (Embley [1967], 12). This is unfortunate, because the Methodists kept quite good records (in sharp contrast to the Brethren) and had a clear leadership structure from earliest days. And the quality of their present-day historiography is high. Special attention should be paid to David Hempton, "Methodism in Irish Society, 1770–1830," *Transactions of the Royal Historical Society* (1986). He points to the relatively urban and market-town concentration of Irish Methodists (very different from Dalyland) and, after 1815, the Methodist membership becoming predominantly located north of the line from Sligo to Dundalk, as a result of growth in the Loch Erne region and in the Ulster linen triangle.

that Darby had a heated contempt for several individuals within the Church of Ireland. At the same time, he was afraid of them: he tried to keep his first pamphlet from being recognized as having been published, in the technical sense of the term. A similar duality existed as far as the form of Church organization was concerned: he had strong reservations, for example, concerning the powers of bishops, but at the same time (the late 1820s and early 1830s) he was not willing to condemn the entire structure.

Very ambivalent: hence, we should start with the simplest questions, ones of obvious and observable behaviour, or so one might hope. When did John Nelson Darby formally leave the Church of Ireland? When did he demit his office as priest? When did he turn in his papers for Calary? The compressed answer in each case is either "nobody knows" or "he never did." Or "he did it all informally and to his own satisfaction."

In late middle-age, Darby created his own narrative of seceding from Anglicanism, piecemeal in its published form but clear enough in the fragments we have. The theme was exceedingly simple: like the apostle Paul, with whom he identified as a human figure much more closely than with Jesus of Nazareth, Darby presented his life as pivoting on a single massive moment of revelation. This Damascene moment occurred in 1827–28 and almost everything from then on was clear, a working out in the sordid world of his all-encompassing moment of truth. In late 1828, he rewrote and expanded his original jeremiad of early 1828 aimed at Archbishop Magee in the form of a more temperate argument entitled "Considerations on the Nature and Unity of the Church of Christ."[42] Although Darby at the time clearly was twitchy about the Established Church, he says that "I am supposing here, of course, that the great truths of the Gospel are the professed faith of the churches, as they are in all the genuine Protestant churches."[43] The closest he comes to rejecting the Church of Ireland is the following:

42 "Considerations on the Nature and Unity of the Church of Christ," in CW, 01002, 20–35. Originally pub. Dublin, 1828, no publisher given. Grayson Carter (215) shrewdly suggests that this is a rewrite of Darby's anti-Magee piece.

43 Ibid., 20.

> Where two or three are gathered together in His name, His name is recorded there for blessing; because they are met in the fullness of the power of the unchangeable interests of that everlasting kingdom in which it has pleased the glorious Jehovah to glorify Himself, and to make his name and saving health known in the Person of the Son, by the power of the Spirit.[44]

Not terribly radical and certainly not a declaration of separation from the Irish Established Church.

John Nelson Darby's next significant essay on ecclesiology (as distinct from minor pieces in religious periodicals) was much more stinging – and exceedingly curious. Its title was "The Notion of a Clergyman, Dispensationally the Sin against the Holy Ghost," and it was published in Darby's *Collected Writings* in the 1860s with a long, new preface that was part of his late-life creation of his own, factually ropey narrative of his development on Church matters. The item as reprinted has no date or publisher ascribed to it and that is because, according to late-life Darby, the original work had a publisher behind it and was set in type, but then it was spread abroad in pre-publication form and "I was surrounded and entreated not to publish it."[45] He gave in and suppressed the essay. The piece, as reprinted (clearly Darby in his sixties had access to one of the original printer's copies), was fairly yeasty. Given that in Darby's view the Holy Ghost's talking directly to the Church was a new divine dispensation, he declared that "I believe the notion of a Clergyman to be the sin against the Holy Ghost in this dispensation … that the notion of a Clergyman puts *the dispensation* specifically in the position of the sin against the Holy Ghost, *and that every Clergyman is contributing to this* … that not half a dozen, or possibly none of the Bishops are of God's appointing; and this is the case with the highest churchman, in consequence of their being appointed simply by the King's Letters Patent."[46] That would be a fair platform for leaving the Established Church, but once again (as with his first pamphlet) Darby

44 Ibid., 25.

45 Later preface added by J.N.D. to "The Notion of a Clergyman, Dispensationally the Sin against the Holy Ghost," *CW*, 01003, 36.

46 Ibid., 39, 40. Emphasis in original.

backed away from having a Martin Luther moment: he refused to have his views exhibited in public. In his sixties he justified himself by the following argument, which is typical both in its rationalization of his youthful behaviour and his lifetime rhetorical habits:

> We can all understand (at least, any who have had deep convictions on points which affect the whole standing of the church of God) how (however deep internal convictions of any such truths may be) a serious and conscientious mind may hesitate as to putting forth what may shock the feelings of many godly persons, and violates established order; and in such matters all ought to be not only conscientious but serious, have the fear of God and not merely an opinion on that which may work deeply in the minds of any, and affect so sacred a thing, the only sacred thing in the world, as the church of God. It never therefore appeared.[47]

That was his story, and he stuck to it, leaving an initial impression that denouncing the Established clergy and bishops was part of his divine mission and that, in contrary motion, temporarily suppressing truth was also part of his mission. Darby foresaw his readers catching this contradiction and covered himself with a deft diversion, rather like that a professional magician employs. He indirectly asserted that he already had left the Church of Ireland before "The Notion of a Clergyman" was printed and suppressed. He said, "when I left it, I published the 1828 tract '[Considerations on] the Nature and Unity of the Church of Christ.'"[48]

That is, Darby as an older man, implied, first, that he had on high principle left the Anglican communion in Ireland in 1828 (as we shall see, he still was undecided as late as 1834) and, secondly, that the content of his 1828 tract on the nature and unity of the Church had been a declaration of independence from the Established Church (which, as we have seen, it certainly was not).

47 Ibid. (new preface), 36.
48 Ibid.

Like the fabrication that Darby wove around his first pamphlet (the attack on Archbishop Magee, which we discussed in the previous chapter), here the slightly soiled nature of Darby's creation of his own fictional past is actually a useful window into his mind and personality. First and clearly, he was very conflicted as a young curate: he twice had written substantial essays, conveyed them to the printer with the intention of their being distributed in some form and twice had suppressed them. As an older man these perhaps-craven acts still gnawed on him, and he felt the need to explain in his *Collected Writings* the printings-and-suppressions and to frame non-factual explanations. Secondly, related to the matter of ecclesiology, in his twenties and early thirties he clearly had fundamental problems with authority. That is an issue that stretches from his tense relationship with his father into his problems and volatile behaviour in relations with Archbishop William Magee and, later, with Archbishop Richard Whately, and from those personal relationships into the deep theological questions of authority within the Christian faith. Thirdly, as I suggested in chapter 6 when viewing the embroidery that Darby wove around his first pamphlet (the one printed but marked "not published"), his ability to create, fully and unselfconsciously, an alternative to everyday prosaic reality was the platform on which his later standing as a prophet was based.[49]

49 Concerning "The Notion of a Clergyman, Dispensationally the Sin against the Holy Spirit," in CW, 01003, 36–50, I have not seen the original printed pamphlet that was suppressed; nor has anyone in any Brethren history or memoir I have encountered claimed to have seen it. Everyone has relied on the item reprinted in CW. I suspect that an original copy or two may exist in private collections, which is to say that one or more of the copies that the publisher showed about to Anglican clergymen were preserved. The reason to infer this is that Darby felt the necessity of having the item, which greatly embarrassed him, reprinted in his collected writings. A reasonable explanation (although certainly not the only one) would be that Darby in the 1860s knew that some copies were afloat and that it would be harmful to his assertion of integrity if he deleted the item from his CW and it subsequently appeared elsewhere. The other point to note is that there is no indication in CW of when "The Notion of a Clergyman" was written and printed, and there are insufficient internal clues to its dating in the actual text (as distinct from Darby's new preface of the 1860s). Thus, it has become something of a Rorschach test. Of course later

Actually, Darby did not separate from the Church of Ireland in 1828, either by formal resignation or by preaching publicly against the Church's fundamental doctrines. Instead, he abandoned his Calary parish and went walkabout. Characteristically, in writing to an Italian co-religionist in his later years, he turned this abandonment of his post and of his people into a holy act: "At first, when I left the Episcopal church, there was no one with whom I could walk; I was led on and guided simply by the word of God."[50] Quite like Saint Paul. "After his time of convalescence he does not appear to have returned to Calary, but for a year or two worked in a variety of parishes as a freelance missioner."[51] This was within Ireland, and he acquired something of a medieval-monkish reputation by going about in old clothes little different from those of an ordinary beggar.[52] Did he ever resign the post that Archbishop Magee had specially cobbled together for him in

---

devotees of Darby put it as early as possible, usually meaning 1828. Grayson Carter (412) suggests c. 1834 as a publication date. Elmore (25) has it "near 1830"; John Percy Ward places it in a sequence of events that begins in 1832 (see "The Eschatology of John Nelson Darby," (PhD, University of London, 1976), 22–3. Ward suggests, but provides no evidence for the assertion, that this pamphlet was part of a fight Darby was having with the evangelical Archbishop of Tuam, the Hon. Power Le Poer Trench. I think Ward is confusing this with a disagreement Darby had about this time with the Rev. Frederick FitzWilliam Trench. The contretemps with Archbishop Trench came later (see Stunt, in Gribben and Stunt [2004], 60–1, and Stunt [2000], 277).

50 J.N.D. to ___ Spignio, 5 March 1877 in *LJND*, vol. 2, no. 252. Translated from the Italian, translator unspecified. Significantly, in this letter of his sunset years Darby was dating his leaving the Church of Ireland to a time prior to his meeting to break bread with John Gifford Bellett, Francis Synge Hutchinson and Edward Cronin, the moment when (as discussed previously) the aged Darby fabulously believed that he was himself the beginning of the Brethren movement.

51 Stunt, in Gribben and Stunt (2004), 59.

52 Most of the Brethren folktales on this theme descend from and are elaborations on the basic picture in Francis William Newman, *Phases of Faith* (London 1874), 27ff. The story of Darby's being taken for a beggar in Limerick is found here (27) and, as Newman notes, "if not true, the story was yet well invented." A version of it has a gentleman in Limerick tossing a penny to Darby, having taken him for a beggar (George T. Stokes, "John Nelson Darby," *Contemporary Review* [1885], 544).

Calary? The Church of Ireland's compiler of clerical succession lists, Canon J.B. Leslie, has the charge being empty after 1828.[53] It was not filled until mid-1831, when the mishmash of a jurisdiction that had been put together for Darby was formally constituted as a perpetual curacy and a church was built in 1834.[54] Since Darby was technically a curate under his friend in Delgany, the Rev. William Cleaver, he may simply have given his resignation verbally to Cleaver: there is no formal record.

Leaving the Calary curacy aside, did John Nelson Darby ever resign his Anglican priesthood? I think never, although this did not preclude his separation as a self-generated act – one that did not imply any recognition of Church of Ireland authority even in his exit. He was never formally dismissed from any charge, much less defrocked, and from the viewpoint of the Church of Ireland's canon law he was a priest until the day he died: not that the mature Darby cared a fig for the kirtled surplices of the Church. From mid-1829 to late 1831 he mixed his Irish missionary work with visits to Paris, London, Oxford, Cambridge, and Plymouth. From 1832 to 1837 Darby was primarily doing freelance missionary work in Ireland and in the west of England before beginning a six-year sojourn, mostly on the Continent. Sometime in the period 1830–34 Darby was offered the post of assistant chaplain at the Magdalen Asylum in Dublin.[55] The position was one that required a clergyman of the Established Church; though Darby did not take the position, he would not have been offered it if he had already broken decisively with the Church of Ireland. Darby was still able in 1833 to inform some of his Brethren friends that "I am no enemy to episcopacy abstractedly, if it be real and done from the Lord."[56] John Gifford Bellett, one of Darby's earliest and most loyal supporters, noted that as late as 1834 Darby was "all but detached from the Church of England,"

53 *CDGBSL*, entries for Calary (265) and for J.N.D. (536).

54 Ibid., 265; *Fourth Report of His Majesty's Commissioners on Ecclesiastical Revenue and Patronage in Ireland*, 20–1, H.C. 1837 (500), xxi.

55 Stunt, in Gribben and Stunt (2004), 60. Stunt (60n59) suggests 1832 as the most likely date for the offer and its refusal. [Bellett], *Interesting Reminiscences*, 8, gives 1834.

56 J.N.D. to "Beloved Brother and Brethren," ___April 1833. *LJND*, vol. 1, no. 6.

apparently meaning not yet fully detached, but almost.[57] This fits with Darby's having confided to James Butler Stoney in June 1834 that he was not himself quite confident that he was right in believing he should separate from the Established Church.[58]

Something – or, more likely, things – were holding John Nelson Darby back. To identify one of these tendrils, Darby's life in this period must be braided once again into the social matrix of Dalyland. One clear reason that Darby hesitated to definitively and permanently sever his relations with the Anglican communion was that most of the people whom he respected in the evangelical wing of the Church of Ireland were sympathetic to his questioning but unconvinced by his answers. The totemic case is the Synge family, especially the Dalyland wing, several of whose members were intertwined with the Brethren, but few of whom left the Anglican Church. Indeed, none of the Dalyland Synges who are counted as contributing to the early history of Brethrenism actually abandoned the Church of Ireland.[59] Francis Synge Hutchinson had given his Fitzwilliam Square house over to the first Brethren fellowship and had written two short books on prophecy before his death at age thirty-one in 1833. He remained Anglican all his life and was an early example of what in Ireland was called "church brethren." His first cousin, the Rev. Edward Millington Synge, served as a Church of Ireland rector in the west of Ireland and was sympathetic to the Powerscourt prophecy conferences of the early 1830s. He served as a

57 [J.G. Bellett], *Interesting Reminiscence,* 8. See also [Letty M. Bellett], *Recollections,* 76. According to his brother, the Rev. George Bellett, John Gifford Bellett and his wife Mary had seceded from the Anglican communion and had joined the Brethren, probably in 1831. In any case, it was before John Nelson Darby was reckoned to have seceded. [Dorothy Bellett], *Memoir of the Rev. George Bellett* (London 1889), 73.

58 Note by James Stoney Butler, written 12 July 1871 in [Bellett], *Interesting Reminiscences,* 20.

59 The complicated family relationships of the Wicklow Synges is discussed in chapter 2 of the present study.

parish priest all his life. Edward's elder brother (and also first cousin of Francis Synge Hutchinson) was the almost-famous John "Pestalozzi" Synge. At the time of John Nelson Darby's 1827–28 convalescence he held Roundwood, a 700-acre estate equipped with a print shop that turned out religious items as well as educational documents. The Synge family's senior residence, Glanmore Castle, was favoured as a discussion site in the late 1820s for summer gatherings of Church of Ireland clergy from Wicklow and Dublin and for promising divinity students.[60] From mid-1827 to mid-1832 John "Pestalozzi" Synge resided chiefly at Buckridge House near Teignmouth in Devon, although he was back and forth across the Irish Sea fairly often. This coastal residence was chosen to provide sea air for his ailing wife (she died in 1830). It may also have been to be near Anthony Norris Groves, who, after being converted while visiting Dublin to take examinations at Trinity College, was becoming an early lodestone in the Brethren movement in England. In the actual event, Groves left on a missionary trip to Baghdad within months of Synge's arrival. Synge hired a remarkable Scot, Henry Craik (1805–1866), who for two years had been tutor to Groves's children as tutor for his own sons. In fact, Craik came with cultural gems in his baggage.[61] A formidable classical scholar who knew biblical Hebrew well, Craik became something of an adult-tutor and colleague to his employer: John Synge was wonderfully willing to learn new things, almost to the point of distraction. Working with Synge, Craik wrote at least two books of instruction in basic Hebrew for students. Craik left tutoring in April 1831 to become a Baptist minister,

60 Richard Sinclair Brooke, *Recollections of the Irish Church* (London 1877), 32–4. Brooke began attending these meetings in 1827. John Synge did not actually become owner of Glanmore Castle until his father Francis's death in 1831.

61 Craik left a highly readable diary and collection of papers (W. Elfe Tayler, ed., *Passages from the Diary and Letters of Henry Craik, of Bristol* (London 1866), see esp. 99–124). A fair indication of the perils of Brethren history is that Craik's almost three years with John Synge are erased from standard sources as part of the industrious airbrushing of the Synges from the Brethren story. Thus, see the article on Craik in Henry Pickering, *Chief Men among the Brethren* (1st ed. 1918; 2nd ed., London 1931), 32–5; and Harold H. Rowdon's entry on Craik in *BDEB*.

but he and Synge remained close and Synge introduced him into the Powerscourt circle of prophecy exegetes – and in turn Craik put Synge in touch with George Müller, who, along with Anthony Norris Groves, represented a gentler, less strident form of Brethren ecclesiology than that John Nelson Darby was creating. Synge's own father died in 1831, and soon John Synge was permanently back in Ireland. There, at Glanmore Castle, he was an eccentric, generous grandee, with his own printing press and a qualified printer and was attended by a "moral agent": a former naval doctor, William G. Rhind (1794–1863), who was allocated a cottage at the mouth of the Devil's Glen and whose task was to mix charity with the religious improvement of the tenantry. John "Pestalozzi" Synge was one of the hinge points of the Dalyland evangelicals, along with Robert Daly and Lady Powerscourt. (The second son of Synge's second marriage was named Robert Daly Synge.) Synge, though a layman, chaired several daily sessions of the Dalyland conferences on prophecy.[62]

Thus, John Synge was the sort of upper-gentry layman one did not ignore, at least if, like John Nelson Darby, one was calibrating whether or not to jump forever away from the Church of Ireland. Synge disagreed with post-1829 evangelical assessments that the Church was heading for ruin, and he argued his case very effectively in print. In 1831 Captain Percy Hall,[63] an early Brethren teacher at Plymouth, had sent Synge a copy of a secessionist pamphlet. This was *A Call to the Converted,* by William George Lambert, an evangelical of Corpus Christi College, Oxford. Lambert's *Call* was for a pure Church, one

62 The most useful discussion of John Synge in his social matrix in this period is found in W.J. McCormack, *The Silence of Barbara Synge* (Manchester 2003), 168–83. An informative appendix on the knock-on effects of early Brethrenism in the Synge family is found in W.J. McCormack, *Fool of the Family: A Life of J.M. Synge* (London 2000), 431–6. The supplest reading of the religious aspects of Synge's activities is Timothy C.F. Stunt, "John Synge and the Early Brethren," *Christian Brethren Research Fellowship Journal* (1976).

63 "Captain Percy Hall, RN" in Pickering, 19–21. Hall (1804–1884) had resigned his commission and his half-pay as being incompatible with true Christian principles. Percy F. Hall, *Discipleship* (London [1848]). Hall was not the rough seaborne character his naval rank might imply: his late father had been dean of Christ Church, Oxford, and the regius professor of Divinity (Carter, 240).

that would be filled with the Holy Spirit and would push aside as unnecessary formal ecclesiastical arrangements. It was idealistic, spirit-besotted, and emotionally adolescent in its lack of practicality.[64] John Synge responded with a thoughtful sixteen-page essay that was notably practical and tactically shrewd. He argued against any secession from the Established Church on scriptural grounds: the members of the earliest, purest apostolic form of Christianity had continued to worship at the Jerusalem Temple. Since the Christian Church stood higher spiritually than the Jewish faith, it followed in Synge's argument that continuing to respect the forms of the Established Church was an even higher ecclesiological custom in the present day than respecting Temple forms had been in the days of Jesus's original apostles. As for practicality, Synge pointed out that the Church was a conduit for the Word of God and that refusing to have anything to do with it simply because it was not perfect was not merely a counsel of perfection but of moral callousness: Brethren should make room for Anglicans to participate in Bible and prayer sessions and should not try to pull them out of their church homes. In a figure of speech that worked perfectly in a rural world, he said that the Established Church was a "*store-fold*, rather than a *fattening-fold*." That is, the Anglican churches were not to be looked at as mere encampments to be plundered by proselytizing, but were best respected as safe houses for God's people. Most practical of all, Synge did not wish Brethren meetings to conflict with the hours of holding normal Sunday services.[65] John Nelson Darby took this in, and in April 1833 he observed that the Brethren "church" (an interesting term for a local assembly, later to be eschewed by Brethren) at Limerick "have so multiplied, that they must seek some place of meeting, and one has offered, and the hour they talk of changing to twelve

64 I have not seen the first edition of Lambert's pamphlet, but the quotations and summary given in Stunt (1976), 44–5, 50–3, agree with the abridged edition (Hereford: County Press Office, 1837).

65 John Synge, *Observations on "A Call to the Converted"* (Teignmouth 1831). The quotation is from p. 8. The introduction is dated 1 November 1831. This is a scarce item, found in CBA, ref. 12,010 in photocopy. It was retailed in London by L.B. Seeley and by J. Nisbet, and, more tellingly, in Dublin by R.M. Tims.

… this is a cause of anxiety to me"[66] To Darby, the Church of Ireland still counted.

In worrying about the impact on the Church of Ireland of Brethrenism's potentially becoming fully separatist, John Nelson Darby was evincing something that can only be called class interest, however unconscious Darby may have been of that valence. John Synge of Glanmore Castle,[67] the Howards, the Parnells, the Pennefathers, and the La Touches were his people, the fabric of Dalyland. Some of them, like the Synges, became church brethren, worshiping in both environments, but most simply stayed Church of Ireland evangelicals and only a very few (notably Lady Powerscourt) became fully separated as Brethren. That was the laity. Obviously the clergy of the Church of Ireland also constituted a class interest, a sector to which Darby belonged despite all his protestations. In contemplating full separatism from the Established Church he must have felt a deep shiver of loneliness.[68] No heavyweights from among the Church of Ireland evangelicals were willing to contemplate separatism. Granted, the idea attracted a small cadre of minor lights: the Bible Society evangelist Thomas Tweedy; the Rev. Charles Hargrove, rector of the embattled parish of Westport, Co. Mayo; John M. Code, the curate of Westport; and, most congenially

66 J.N.D. to "Beloved Brother and Brethren," ___April 1833. *LJND*, vol. 1, no. 6. Note the comment of Stunt (1976), 57.

67 John Synge stayed with the Church of Ireland and also fellowshipped with Brethren. He violated the code of anti-worldliness that developed among the more severe Brethren in that he took public office, albeit locally only. He and John Parnell of Avondale served on the original Rathdrum Poor Law Union, established in 1839, and Synge subsequently served as chairman. He maintained this social welfare involvement until his death in 1845 (McCormack, 2003, 202–3). Synge was never one to stint his enthusiasms and charities: on his death his estates were found to be bankrupt (Nicholas Grene, "Synge and County Wicklow," in Ken Hannigan and William Nolan, eds, *Wicklow History and Society* [Dublin 1994], 693–4).

68 Thus, although Darby early-dated in his own narrative the time when he left the Church, the line in his letter to his Italian colleague quoted earlier, concerning his walking alone when he left the Anglican communion, has an emotional authenticity that is rare in his writings. One accepts that for a serious clergyman leaving his original church home indeed was a terribly lonely business (J.N.D. to ___Spignio, 5 March 1877, in *LJND*, vol. 2, no. 252).

for Darby, the young James Butler Stoney (born 1 May 1814, he entered Trinity College, Dublin, autumn 1829), whose County Tipperary gentry family was similar to his own. Darby was willing to make expedient alliances with other stripes of separatism (such as that of the Rev. Edward Hardman), but they really were not his sort of people. Peter Embley has usefully gone through the reference book *Chief Men among the Brethren,* and of men in Darby's age cohort (those born before 1820) only twelve in the entire British Isles were Anglican clerics or young men in training who became Brethren separatists.[69] Grayson Carter's list of secessions from the Established Churches of Ireland and of England shows that before 1840 there were at most fifteen seceders to Brethrenism from among the ordained clergy of the United Church of England and Ireland.[70]

✠

Eventually John Nelson Darby overcame his hesitations, stopped his haverings, abandoned his class interests, and left the Church of Ireland. Every serious historian who has dealt with this issue over the past half-century has hedged the discussion with "probably," or "most likely," or "one assumes that," or similar phrases meaning that they do not actually know when the event took place and that they are speculating or, indeed, guessing. The proximate reason that we do not know when that occurred is that the Brethren were People of the Booklet.[71] That is, they put out tons of little booklets, usually undated: and in the

69 Embley (1967), 215.

70 Carter, appendix, 399–403. Both Embley's and Carter's data fit well with the informed but undocumented assertion of Harold H. Rowdon that "at least ten or a dozen clergy and several who were about to take Orders seceded from the Established Church in England or Ireland" (Rowdon, 1964, 76n2).

71 To adapt a phrase of W.J. McCormack's from a discussion of John Synge (McCormack [2003], 150). McCormack in *The Silence of Barbara Synge* is entertainingly frustrated with the evidentiary problems he encountered, especially in dealing with the Darbyites in the British Isles: "Without an identifiably clerical body, and without training colleges or libraries, Brethrenism is an elusive set of beliefs to authenticate or interrogate. Over a period of a century-and-a-half, shifts of emphasis have taken place; schisms and expulsions have occurred, indicating acute disagreement among members" (433).

high Victorian era they were putting out as many as a million copies of various items annually. The larger monographs written by Darby can be confidently dated, but most of the things he published in the 1830s, when he was framing the outlines of several of his basic beliefs are of indeterminate timing, despite the confidence with which a year is stamped on them by Brethren enthusiasts. My own speculation – it is here explicitly labelled as merely being an informed guess – is that Darby probably became a full-blown secessionist in late 1834 or in 1835, and almost certainly by 1838, absolutely certainly by 1840.[72]

Here we should back away a bit and reckon with certain salient aspects of John Nelson Darby's personal behaviour. First, he had a real problem with his father. One would not even know he had one if all we had was Darby's writings. His father had been opposed to his abandoning his training as a barrister and becoming a clergyman, and Darby in late life stated that his father for a time had cut him off. Secondly, Darby had immense difficulty with his religious superiors, especially those on the bench of bishops. Thirdly, and crucially, when Darby had a fight with someone on a religious issue, he personalized matters. Thus, he had placed personal blame on Archbishop Magee for the failure of the new-Reformation. There was very little room for disinterested theological discussion in the way John Nelson Darby thought. He personalized things and fought hard and dirty.

This bring us to a time when we can observe Darby working himself into an extreme emotional pitch and publishing a set of pamphlets that were more free-swinging and vituperative than any he was to write until the seismic Brethren schism of the mid-1840s. In this

72 "On the Formation of Churches," according to Darby or Kelly's editorial note, "published originally in French, in Switzerland, about 1840. In English it has been entitled 'Reflections on the Ruined Condition of the Church; and on the Efforts Making [*sic*] by Churchmen and Dissenters to Restore It to Its Primitive Order'" (*CW*, 01011, 138–55). The first relevant ecclesiological item with an actual publication date (though not the name of the publisher) was dated "Geneva, 1841." It probably was originally published in French but was entitled in English "Some Further Development of the Principles Set Forth in the Pamphlet, Entitled 'On the Formation of Churches' and Reply to Some Objections Made to Those Principles" (*CW*, 01012, 156–205).

case, the specific opponent was the successor to Archbishop Magee, Richard Whately (1787–1863), appointed archbishop of Dublin in 1831. Aside from being on the side of the unrighteous in Darby's view, Archbishop Whately drove the young cleric into a frenzy by insulting Darby's vanity: Whately simply ignored him. (Whately's own life is well enough documented to permit it to act as a calendar to date some of Darby's publications.)

In his attacks on Archbishop Whatley in 1832–34, John Nelson Darby was chanting in harmony with most of the clergy of the Church of Ireland, especially the evangelicals, and Darby stood out only in the intensity and gross bad form of his attack. The problem with Whately, as far as Irish clergymen were concerned, began with his not being Irish. To his own surprise and mild dismay he had been appointed to Dublin, one of the two plum posts in the Church of Ireland (the other was Armagh, which paid more but was not in the old capital), by a Whig government. Whately never knew exactly why he was put in place, nor do later historians. Not only was he unsuitably non-Irish at a time when the Church of Ireland clergy were feeling put upon by the state, but he had favoured Catholic Emancipation. Worst of all, he did not think much of the brains and education of the Irish clergy or most of their bishops, and he did not hide his opinions. He was unfair to the Irish bishops, several of whom had been through the academic winnowing of winning the competition to become fellows of Trinity College, Dublin; but he was correct in pointing out that there really was very little in the way of rigorous training for the Irish clergy at TCD, whence most of his new subordinates came. (Whately tried to found a real divinity school in Dublin but was blocked by interests loyal to TCD.) Whately's contempt for Irish levels of professional competence was partially veiled by a laboured sense of humour – mostly because of his horrible puns, he had the misfortune to be labelled a Dublin wit – but what he could not veil was his sure knowledge that he was a Champions League regular in a scrappy provincial conference: he had published a treatise on logic (1826) that was the standard in English for the first half of the nineteenth century, a pioneering work on rhetoric (1828) that was still being used in American universities in the mid-twentieth century, had been head of a minor Oxford hall and the second professor of economics in Oxford University.[73] Still, in the eyes of the Church of Ireland bishops, clergy, and concerned laity, Whately's worst sin was that he did not hate Catholics nearly enough. Although he looked at Roman Catholicism as superstition, he was against proselytizing, Orangeism, and keen evangelicalism. Together with Daniel Murray, the Roman Catholic archbishop of Dublin, and the Rev. James Carlile, a leading Presbyterian minister with a congregation in Dublin, he formed a clerical breakwater for the founding of the "national system of education in Ireland." The intention of the government and of these men was that a non-sectarian, but Christian, system of mass elementary education was to be made available throughout the country. All three of the major Irish denominations – Anglican, Catholic, and Presbyterian – had a large number of lay persons who were skeptical of the new system, but the clergy of the Church of Ireland were the most upset of any group of Protestants. This new governmental system promised to erase any hope they still had of operating a national network of Anglican schools. Seven commissioners of national education, all major citizens, were appointed, including among Church of Ireland figures not only Archbishop Whately but also the Duke of Leinster and the Rev. Dr Franc Sadleir, professor of mathematics (and later provost) at Trinity College, Dublin. Government money flowed to the new system.[74]

John Nelson Darby in 1832–34 published three pamphlets, each of which would be libellous in our own time, and each of which moved back and forth between the education question and his own problem with authority as represented by the government and, more directly, by Archbishop Whately and his fellow national education commission-

73 William J. Fitzpatrick wrote an entertaining and informed and not-at-all Victorian biography: *Memoirs of Richard Whately, Archbishop of Dublin*, 2 vols. (London 1864). In contrast, Whately's daughter's production is censored and misleading: Elizabeth Jane Whately [with Herman Merrivale], *Life and Correspondence of Richard Whately*, 2 vols. (London 1866). (This is an appropriate point to warn the reader against paying any serious attention to her philippic *Plymouth Brethrenism* [London 1877]). My own biography of Whately is *A Protestant in Purgatory* (Hamden, CT, 1981).

74 The details of the entire business are found in my *The Irish Education Experiment* (London and Toronto 1970; republished, London and New York 2012).

ers.[75] The first of these was a series of observations on a set of ecumenical scripture lessons that the commissioners of national education had put together for the new school system. These lessons were part of a series of textbooks that became the most widely used in the British Isles and in several of the overseas dominions, as they were sequential, pedagogically easy to work with, and cheap.[76] That was irrelevant to the religious issue. Animated by the Rev. James Carlile and aided by Dr Arnold of Rugby, the three main commissioners – the Reverends Whately, Murray, and Carlile – had put together a set of four volumes of scripture extracts that were drawn from both the Authorised Version and the Duoay Version of the scriptures. The extracts were structured rather like Diatessaron of Tatian (c. 150 AD), a harmony of the four gospels, except in this case they joined together the entire narrative spine of the Old and New Testaments. The scripture extracts usage was not compulsory, but most schools adopted them. Darby went mad. In a letter that was addressed to some periodical, but which apparently was rejected (he had it published as a booklet by R.M. Tims, the Brethren's unofficial publisher), he focused first on the Presbyterian James Carlile and noted sarcastically, "Mr Carlile, I suppose, knows Hebrew … I trust, sir, you will give due publicity to this important fact, for the benefit of others as well as the poor Irish children, that the translator knows Hebrew." Darby cited errors in Hebrew implied in the new scripture extracts and then returned to the Rev. Mr Carlile. "And the translator knows Hebrew – knows Hebrew! Knows enough of that, and everything else too, to set at rest all the difficult questions which have hindered Irish education time out of mind, and give just the quantum of scripture which will satisfy Papists and Protestants, Presbyterians,

75 The three items are found in volume 32 of CW, somewhat obscurely labelled. All three are found in the table of contents under the title of the first item "Some Observations on the Scripture Lessons of the Board of Education," which is CW, 32014, 281–305, The second item, "A Letter on a Serious Question Connected with the Irish Education Measures of 1832," is CW, 32015, 306–14, and the third is "Speech Delivered at a Meeting Held for the Purpose of Supporting Scriptural Education," CW, 32016, 315–22.

76 On the textbooks generally, and also on the long-running scripture extracts crisis, see Akenson, *The Irish Education Experiment*, 225–74.

Arians and Socinians and above all himself (God, sir, we must remember is put out of the question), with just the right sense and nobody to dispute it. Oh happy ages, that we should have one such man!"[77] As for the government of the United Kingdom: "The existing government, of which these commissioners are the instruments, have acquiesced in this. The principles of the Roman Catholic religion are in this to be acquiesced in."[78] As for Archbishop Whately, he gets off relatively easily in this, the first of John Nelson Darby's letters on education: "Dr Whately – I cannot bring myself to call him Archbishop of Dublin … If Dr Whatley must be recognised after this book and its preface have gone forth, in the place of authority in what God heretofore set as the Protestant church, the judgement of God must be recognised also by the church to which he belongs as impending on it."[79]

Darby truly found his rhythm in an undated pamphlet (either 1832 or 1833) set in the form of an epistle to an unnamed clergyman who was on his side as far as disapproving of the scripture extracts. "The scriptures are the witness, not only of the holiness of god, but of His love, of His prerogative love in Christ. The Archbishop has set himself forward as the main effectuator, as under the circumstances he certainly is, of a scheme which is professedly to meet the [Roman Catholic] priests, in accordance with their principles, in excluding from schools this witness of God's love in Christ."[80] In case there was any doubt about Whately's turpitude, Darby declares, "the Archbishop of Dublin is a Sabellian,"[81] an insult that had more impact in the nineteenth century than at present – Sabellius was a third-century heretic who did not keep God the Father and God the Son sufficiently distinct for the taste of later Christian theologians. Thereafter, Darby engages in a heresy-hunt through the appendix of the fourth edition of Whately's *Logic*, an exercise so pilpulistic that it would have impressed

77 "Some Observations on the Scripture Lessons," quotations from CW, 32024, 281.

78 Ibid., 284.

79 Ibid., 290, 297.

80 "A Letter on a Serious Question Connected with the Irish Education Measures of 1832," CW, 32015, 306.

81 Ibid., 307.

a tenth-century rabbi. His conclusion was a charge of heresy: "Let it be known only that, though God may be in a distinct position, there is, according to Dr Whately, no distinction in the person of the Father and the Son. What may be the duty of the clergy in such a case I leave to themselves: of that of a Christian I can have no doubts."[82] In case one still had any question of Darby's views on the national system of education, in a speech in Banbridge in 1834, Darby concluded: "I believe this Board [of education] to be simply the work and instrument of Satan, though God shall overrule it to His own purpose. For to Him all power belongs; and though Satan may be permitted for wise ends to manifest himself for a time, yet the Lion of the tribe of Judah will ultimately overcome him, for He is King of Kings and Lord of Lords."[83] That is how John Nelson Darby spoke and wrote when under a full head of steam, orotund, but unmistakably clear as to who his enemy was.

With no psychobabble, we can note that John Nelson Darby's behaviour tells us that between 1827 and 1834 he was in an acute bind. He was immensely uncomfortable in the Church of Ireland, although he had not yet finally decided to get out – whatever form secession might take, formal or informal, it meant escaping. In his two animated and personalized ventings – against Archbishop Magee and against Archbishop Whately – he attacked them and their authority and implicitly the concept of hierarchical human authority within the Christian Church. Yet, despite his discomfort with the Church and his disdain for those in its highest levels of authority, he hesitated and hesitated some more. It is fair to surmise that he was in a bind that was more a function of his own emotional configuration than an issue of spirituality or of theology. On the personal level, he required an outside event to free him.

In the late autumn of 1834, Darby's father died. He was eighty-three years old and testamentary records show that for some time he had been carefully planning for his demise. His decline and death cannot

82 Ibid., 314.

83 "Speech Delivered at a Meeting Held for the Purpose of Promoting Scriptural Education," [editor's note in STEM edition: Banbridge, 1834], *CW*, 32016, 322. The dating fits with the chronology of Whately's work in favour of the system of national education.

have come as a surprise to any member of his family. The legal preparation had been meticulous, so the will was probated unusually quickly, 16 January 1835. John Nelson Darby's father had never approved of his youngest son's choice of a career but did not cut him off. However, unlike the other male children, he was not given an estate, even a small one.[84] He was left the life interest on £7,000, as were each of the other immediate children. There is some significance in the chronology of John Darby Sr's arranging his final estate. The basic will was carefully written and executed 25 September 1832. Assuming it was not a secret document (among the upper classes, death arrangements, like those for marriage, were carefully defined and usually were not secret), this means his heirs knew the score from late autumn 1832 onward. They all knew exactly what angering the old man would cost them. John Darby Sr executed codicils in January 1833, August 1833, and September 1834, none of which affected John Nelson Darby, but his father, clearly, was keeping his eye on things right to the end.[85]

On the purely financial level, from early 1835 onward, John Nelson Darby could count on the annual income for life from £12,000 of stock (£7,000 from his father and a previous £5,000 from his uncle). This yielded between £300 and £400 a year, the median net income of a Church of Ireland rector, without the disagreeable features of being tied to one place. Nor, if he chose to become an ecclesiastical independent, would John Nelson have to depend on the charity of his flock, like one of the Dissenting clergy he so looked down upon. He was not rich, certainly, but he became a man of sufficient independent means. In 1840 he wrote to a French colleague that, "as to your temporal circumstances, dear brother, it will always be to me a great pleas-

84 William Blair Neatby, who knew well several of the second generation of Brethren, explained the situation as follows: "Darby enjoyed under his father's will a very comfortable annuity; but I have heard that he lost a handsome property through his father's want of sympathy with his ecclesiastical course" (*A History of the Plymouth Brethren*, 2nd ed. [London 1902], 78n1).

85 Will of John Darby, National Archives (PRO), prob. 11/1841/135, probated 16 January 1835. The date of John Darby Sr's death is between his signing a final codicil 14 September 1834 and his attorney's presenting the will for probate 26 November 1834.

ure to help you. I am not very rich, but what I have, I hope, through the grace of our God, will be always devoted to His work."[86] In the world in which he chose to operate, this made John Nelson Darby forever a rich young ruler.

John Nelson Darby did not attend his father's funeral.[87] Just as he was provided with financial freedom by his father's death and subsequent legacy, so on the emotional level he was freed of the need to truckle to the original alpha-male in his life, his father. I would suggest that after his father's death – but not until then – he quickly freed himself of the other alpha-males whom he so resented and did so by leaving behind the Church of Ireland, its bishops and archbishops, its willingness to bow to the civil state, and, above all, the dead weight of the long chain of Christian history, the impediment that Darby came to believe kept the faith from following the holy pattern of the primitive Church.

86 J.N.D. to __Maylon, 2 January 1840 (tr. from French, translator not stated), *LJND*, vol. 1, no. 13.

87 In his early eighties, John Nelson Darby told a co-religionist that he had not attended his father's funeral. This was noted in a characteristic conjoining of two disparate phrases. "As to funerals, I would not go to any where the clerical system is kept up, I did not to my father's" (J.N.D. to______1881, *LJND*, vol. 3, no. 353). The first phrase is prescriptive for his co-religionist's future behaviour; the second is historical, related to his own. The reader is expected to infer that the principle of the former produced the action of the latter, which is not the best historical logic as it depends upon the future being the cause of the past. Actually, the most one can logically accept is that in his eighties John Nelson Darby recalled having not attended his father's funeral and now, in late life, Darby would like that earlier behaviour to be ascribed to high principle, not filial disrespect or resentment.

CHAPTER EIGHT

Eschatology: Lady Powerscourt Points to the Heavens

From the late autumn of 1830 onward, Lady Powerscourt felt the spiritual need to plan a momentous event. It would be one of the most exclusive house parties in Ireland, and it would take place early in October 1831. Of course it would be held on the Powerscourt estate. This was to be the first of the concerted collective efforts of the mostly spirit-filled, righteous, and well-born of Dalyland to stencil the ongoing ruination of Ireland onto their own map of the invisible cosmos. They were willing to accept help from gifted outsiders, but this was to be very much an Irish venture, designed to deal with a specifically Irish problem, which, in their view, was a micro-version of the problem with the whole universe.

In essence, Irish evangelicals, Wicklow Brethren, and a few genuine early separatists were together building experimentally on new foundations – their ecclesiology. But they were building before the footings had fully settled, so some of their sketches for heavenward arches and Jerusalem Temple-style walls were inevitably skewed and later were modified or abandoned. This is a crucial historical observation; yet again, it involves our breaking the tyranny of one of the most powerful of all religious narratives: namely, the Road to Damascus model provided by the conversion of St Paul. That momentous conversion was given demotic form in the later nineteenth century in the singlemost ubiquitous phrase of evangelicalism: "Are you saved?" The question is a query that is designed to lead to an oracular moment of personal transformation. When translated to the historical narrative of the large tranche of the world evangelical movement that owes much of

FIGURE 8.1 POWERSCOURT HOUSE.

The house as situated in the time of "Good Lady Powerscourt." In 1842 a major project began the present system of terraces and formal gardens.

its ideology to Irish roots, and especially to John Nelson Darby, the temptation is to adopt a similar verbal tactic and to hang the story on The Big Moment.

That is a mistake. We have already seen in earlier chapters how John Nelson Darby personalized and fictionalized Big Moments: for example, the effect of the putative fiat of Archbishop Magee that allegedly caused the failure of the new-Reformation movement; and how in midlife Darby claimed the originator's role among the early Brethren, despite his being a later runner-in. That is natural and understandable. So too is the desire among many historians of the Brethren to find the designers' template for later Brethren beliefs fully sketched out in early meetings. My argument in this book has been that the beliefs and orthopraxy of the Brethren were the products of a longer evolution, one that in part flowed from the social configuration and mentality of a specific caste who dominated Anglo-Irish society in County Wicklow and the south of County Dublin. The evolution from within this caste was simultaneously intellectual, devotional, and social in character and was also the product of the personal idiosyncrasies of various proto-Brethren leaders, not least John Nelson Darby. Further, any such process necessarily has a good deal of cumulative randomness about it. Unforeseeable as it was in the 1820s and 30s, the main features of John Nelson Darby's method of parsing the scriptures and of prophesying about the end-times turned out to be directly useful to the generative figures in modern North American evangelicalism, such as Dwight L. Moody. Darby's way of reading holy texts fit the needs of the cadre of clergy and lay leaders who attended the formative evangelical/fundamentalist Niagara Conferences at the end of the nineteenth century. Eventually, Darby's views on the unfolding of history were written into the Scofield Bible, the standard-issue piece of weaponry in the arsenal of twentieth-century evangelical preachers. All this took stretches of time, not merely a singular moment.

Given the case for Dalyland's being the specific, long-term, and unique micro-environment for the creation and articulation of an innovative set of beliefs, it must be emphasized that the biblical prophecy movement of the nineteenth century was widespread throughout Europe and North America. Among historians, that larger movement is only a small tranche of the field of scholarly study of a variety of mostly religious (but occasionally political or revolutionary) phenomena frequently called "apocalypticism."[1] The term "apocalypse" itself

1 The bibliography one could compile on apocalypticism is huge. The following are suggestions for a strategy of approach for the interested reader. A useful place to start is the three volumes of *The Encyclopedia of Apocalypticism* (New York 1998), edited by John J. Collins (vol. 1), Bernard McGinn (vol. 2), and Stephen J. Stein (vol. 3). Despite its title, this is a connected series of non-technical essays that provides something close to the present-day view of the subject in the academy. The now-classic study of the medieval view is Norman Cohn, *The Pursuit of the Millennium* (London 1957; rev. ed., New York 1970) (it was the 1970 revised edition that proved highly influential). Despite its generative force, the work has been underappreciated by the evangelically based historians who dominate Christian apocalyptic studies, because Cohn treats millenarians as persons inspired by a fantasy of salvation to be gained through a transformation of the Earth by supernatural agencies: not phrases that are comfortable, even to believers with tenure. Although it unsettled American scholars with its transatlantic perspective, the pioneering work of Ernest R. Sandeen still impresses with the crispness of its insights and the prodigious originality of its research; See *The Roots of Fundamentalism: British and American Millenarianism, 1800–1930* (Chicago 1970). Another scholarly touchstone has been J.F.C. Harrison, *The Second Coming* (New Brunswick, NJ, 1979). For a social scientific reading of the phenomena, a very useful study is Charles B. Strozier, *Apocalypse: On the Psychology of Fundamentalism in America* (Boston 1994). Crawford Gribben in "Evangelicalism, Historiography and the Possibility of Millennial Theory" (in Searle and Newport, eds, 2012) surveys the recent literature, particularly in the social

is not complicated – it comes from a Greek word for unveiling or uncovering – but it has become a linguistic weed that is used in everyday speech to speak of a genre of catastrophe films, to discuss big-time trades in sports, and as an ironic term for some major music releases; in the theological world, it is employed as an umbrella for dazzling, but often puzzling, taxonomies of how the final truth will reach humanity in the end-times; and, among semiotically fixated cultural chroniclers, it has become an exercise in restating in postmodern terms the apocalyptic details that believers hold close to their hearts. Academic historians have often dealt with apocalypticism by creating narrow definitions that allow us to focus only on the wee group or on a tiny set of ideational components that we find fascinating.

Fair warning: that last behaviour is what I am engaged in here, although one hopes in a way that is intellectually generous. Instead of trying to find a suitable global definition of apocalypticism I am dealing only with the Judaeo-Christian tradition and mostly with the Christian portion. That said, the entire historical discussion of apocalypticism inevitably occurs within the ground rules set by the Hebrew scriptures. As Robert Alter notes, "it is peculiar, and culturally significant, that among ancient peoples only Israel should have chosen to cast its sacred national traditions in prose."[2] This is in contrast to the verse epic in which other ancient national texts are preserved; it means that

---

sciences, and explains his skepticism concerning the possibility of a general theory and his resistance to attempts to conflate Christian apocalypticism with that of other religions. Within the several faith traditions there is a massive body of interpretive writing. One volume that has been ignored by most students of Christian apocalypticism, nearly to the point of *todschweigen,* is that of the Adventist Le Roy Edwin Froom, who in 1946 published a massive four-volume work, *The Prophetic Faith of Our Fathers* (Washington 1946), which includes an extraordinary range of material that most historians of Christian apocalypticism are not well acquainted with; if used as a reference set, these volumes have great value. Froom's being a Seventh-day Adventist made his work objectionable to most evangelicals, and, it must be added, he leaves out the most direct rivals to his own denomination. Still, his study of the equivalent of a library of scarce small-run materials from eighteenth- and nineteenth-century Europe (many now permanently lost through war) is valuable for documenting trends that prevailed before it became general archival practice to preserve religious ephemera.

2 Robert Alter, *The Art of Biblical Narrative* (New York 1981), 25.

apocalypticism within the Judaeo-Christian template was talked about in prose narrative, a form that is accessible to every sentient human being. In turn, that permits the future to be discussed using the same narrative tools with which people talk about the past. Undeniably there are amazing segments of soaring rhetoric and luminous figures of speech in the Judaeo-Christian tradition, but inalterably the apocalyptical is tethered to both the past and the present by the everyday medium of storytelling. Judaeo-Christian apocalyptic talk is always the presentation – in narrative prose – of the history of the future.

Apocalypticism in the Christian portion of the Judaeo-Christian tradition has two words associated with it, the one simple enough, the second another linguistic weed. The first of these is a term that, from its use in the previous chapter, we are already familiar: eschatology, the study of the endtimes. Admittedly, the term can be somewhat pretentious, but it is not ambiguous.

The second term and its variants – "millennium," "millennialism," and "millenarianism" – are slightly more wobbly because they have developed a conventional attachment to Christian apocalypticism and have come to imply automatically a thousand-year period in the history-of-the-future that lies very close to the final judgment and to the end of earthly time (interpretations vary as to just how close). Although "millennial" and its variants have a narrow range of meanings in Christian thought, at present it is often used in everyday speech to mean apocalyptic in the wider sense of any world-ending big bang, nice or nasty.

Given that millennialism has become a customary synonym for the dominant school of evangelical Christian apocalypticism, it is surprising that the concept of "the millennium" only appears directly once in the scriptures: in Revelation 20:1–7. This passage refers to a period of one thousand years in which Satan is bound and cast into a bottomless pit, after which he is let out (v. 7) and after a final battle is thrown into a lake of fire and brimstone and a new Heaven and Earth and a New Jerusalem appear (20:8–15, 21:1–2).

One accepts the judgment of Crawford Gribben that the terms "millennialism" and "millenarianism" are not distinguishable.[3] Essentially,

3 Crawford Gribben, *Evangelical Millennialism in the Trans-Atlantic World* (Basingstoke 2011), xiii, based on the work of Ernest Sandeen.

they are synonyms in the time period we are focused on. Contemporaries used them interchangeably.[4]

The Irish evangelicals who eventually convened at Powerscourt in October 1831 had the entire history of the world on their minds and especially the future. Not only were they trying to work out the proper biblically based form of Church fellowship – should they stay connected with the Established Church? should they be ecumenical, worshiping with those from whom they were denominationally separate? were all true believers priests? – but what did the Bible mean in its very puzzling projections of the future? The questions were massive; some of the egos were almost equally as large. The material they were working with was the entire Christian canon, from Genesis through Revelation, but certain portions were strongly privileged in their discussions. Everything in their thinking hinged on the identification of the millennium and thus on texts that might illuminate that God-driven disjuncture in future time. The following scriptures (listed in their order in the King James Version, rather than in their probable sequence of composition) were the focal points for the Powerscourt discussions of the future: Daniel 7–12; Matthew 24; Mark 13; Luke 21; John 14:2–4 and 18:35–6; 1 Corinthians 15:20–54; 2 Corinthians 5:1–5; Philippians 1:21–3; 1 Thessalonians 4:13–18, 5:1–2; Hebrews 12:22–4; and the book of Revelation, especially chapter 20.[5] Accepting the risk that mere summation entails as necessary, it is not a digression to characterize briefly the apocalyptic texts that the Wicklow prophets had in the forefront

4 For an example – almost a definitive experiment – that indicates the futility and ahistorical nature of imposing a split between millennialism and millenarianism on mid-nineteenth century material, note Ernest Lee Tuveson, *Redeemer Nation: The Idea of America's Millennial Role* (Chicago 1968), passim, but esp. 34.

5 My listing of the New Testament material follows the general example of Stanley E. Porter, "Was Early Christianity a Millenarian Movement?" in Stanley E. Porter, Michael A. Hayes, and David Tombs (eds), *Faith in the Millennium* (Sheffield 2001). Although I depart from some of his interpretations, Porter's essay is a piece of adept and economical scholarship that raises basic questions about the nature of the early Church.

of their minds. Nothing they said or did makes any historical sense unless we share with them an awareness of how certain biblical texts could be read as unlocking the path to eternity.

First, the book of Daniel joins with the book of Revelation in being one of the two distinct entities in the Christian version of the scriptures that are unambiguously apocalyptic. These two documents book-end most prophetic readings of the scriptures. There are of course several other prophetic documents before Daniel in the Hebrew scriptures, but these are so tightly focused on various specific situations in ancient Israel that they require the equivalent of an hermeneutic jackhammer to break them out of that situational context. In contrast, the book of Daniel, while engaging with a specific historical problem, is rhetorically loose and highly vivid in its use of encrypted language. Thus it becomes something like the initial problem set given by a university math professor to a lecture class: by the end of the term, that is, by the time the book of Revelation is read, the smart students should be able to solve the problem set themselves.[6]

The book of Daniel was the last document in the Old Testament to be admitted to the Jewish canon (save possibly the book of Esther, which does not mention the Almighty and may be a vernacular folk tale). It is the only text in the Hebrew scriptures for which the date of composition of the final version is firm: between 167 and 164 BC. This is because the work centres around the hideous desecration of the Jerusalem Temple by Antiochus Epiphanes and the Maccabean revolt. It shows a direct familiarity with several historical events attested in other sources – while getting quite wrong some of its predictions about the immediate future. Thus, indirectly, it provides the reader with a sound channel for dating its composition. Both in its period of writing and in the nature of the political problems that the author had to deal with, the book of Daniel is closer to the Christian scriptures that were written after the Temple was destroyed in 70 AD than it is to the

6 Nothing that I am suggesting in this brief conspectus of the relevant Judaeo-Christian texts is original, although inevitably anything that anybody says about the scriptures is controversial. The full argumentation and documentation for this conspectus is found in the text and notes of my *Surpassing Wonder* (New York 1998).

ancient prophets of Israel. Daniel is one of the three major apocalyptic visions of roughly the same era that were known to Jewish scholars at the time of Jesus (the other two were the book of Enoch and the War Scroll), and it is not a great stretch to suggest that all three influenced the book of Revelation, directly or indirectly.

What gives the book of Daniel life beyond the immediate exigencies of the situation in Jerusalem (mostly described symbolically, but occasionally with a direct and plaintive wail, as in 8:11–13) is that the author issues a menu of images and time-usages that later Christians were to view as profound riddles to be solved. The most famous of these is the "seventy weeks of Daniel" (9:2ff), often glossed as being weeks of years. This period of prophesied time has sub-segments, several wild and largely undefined beasts, and under the direction of the Archangel Michael (12:1–13) a resurrection of the dead, a sealed book, and a mysterious saviour figure clothed in white linen. It is impossible to know what the overlapping visions of the book of Daniel were intended to mean to the people of its time, save for the obvious statement that Yahweh would be victorious over the Seleucids. For some later Christians, Daniel became the foundation puzzle, the point at which decoding of the future must begin.

The "Little Apocaplyse" of the synoptic gospels – Matthew 24, Mark 13, and Luke 21: most biblical scholars suggest that these three passages are taken either from Mark or from a fragment the author of Mark was using. They all are distinguished by having Jesus "predict" that the Temple will be destroyed. This (similar to the third-party verifiable portions of Daniel) is highly valuable; it provides one of the few trustworthy markers concerning when the synoptic gospels, in the form we have them, came together: after 70 AD, when the Temple was destroyed. Mark and Matthew have Jesus referring to a time when the faithful shall see the "abomination of desolation" (spoken of by Daniel the prophet) standing in the holy place. This is an adoption of Daniel's screed against Antiochus Epiphanes (cf. Matthew 24:15; Mark 13:14; Daniel 9:27, 11:31, 12:11), and it is also an adaptation: for in the hands of the gospel writers, the specific reference in the Hebrew scriptures to the Seleucid regent and to his defilement of the Temple by offering sacrifices in it to Zeus – an action well past – becomes a prophecy of a future defilement. Moreover, in the Little Apocalypse, the term "tribulation" is introduced (Matthew 24:21; Mark 13:24). This may not be the "Great Tribulation" one later finds in Revelation – it lacks a specific article, but that is not the kind of thing to bother later fossicking readers. We have here a splendid bridge, one that needs only a little shoring up to form a textual joining of the encrypted prophecies of Daniel and of Revelation. Each of the synoptic gospels speaks of hideous troubles and then of the appearance of the Son of Man coming down from the clouds in power and glory. Never mind that it is not at all clear that the authors of this material meant that Jesus should be understood as saying that he was himself the Son of Man – scholarly opinion is fairly evenly divided on this. But undeniably each of the passages resonates strongly with two of the most powerful works of Jewish-formed apocalyptic writing, Daniel and Revelation, and reaffirms the need for a new Heaven, a new Earth, a New Jerusalem.

John 14:2–4 and 18:35–36: in the former, Jesus is reported as saying that he will come again and take his followers to his father's house; in the latter, he tells Pilate that his own kingdom is not of this world. Neither of these passages indicates anything to do with the physical world but rather with the initiation of an otherworldly kingdom, a spiritual reign.

1 Corinthians 15:20–54: This authentic Pauline letter is crucial because it is one of the few references to a possibly apocalyptic scheme in the New Testament that undoubtedly predates in its writing the destruction of the Temple in 70 AD. As a prelude to his apocalyptic views, Paul provides (15:4) what is probably the earliest written account of the resurrection from the dead of Jesus of Nazareth. He then (15:20–8) states that the risen Jesus shall overcome death not just for himself but for all those who follow him, will reign over his enemies. and finally will put both himself and all things he has conquered under God, "that God may be all in all" (15:28). Paul, one might note, is no believer in the Trinity, for Jesus is subordinate to God, but that fact is only a theological inconvenience. The real awkwardness occurs if one keeps reading the chapter and encounters verses 40–54, where Paul takes a deep dive into Hellenistic mind-body dualism and explains that not all similarly named entities are the same. Thus, there are celestial bodies and terrestrial bodies. Equally, there are corrupt bodies (the natural body of human beings) and incorrupt bodies (the spiritual body) of

which the Lord in Heaven is the archetype. Paul concludes: "Now this I say, brethren, that flesh and blood cannot inherit the kingdom of God; neither doth corruption inherit incorruption" (15:50). A later reader has a choice: read only verses 20–8 and infer that Paul propounded a faith in a physical apocalypse, replete with Jesus's return, a triumphant bashing of his enemies, and a resurrection (maybe one, maybe two), and all that easily could be literal and physical; or, continue to read his exposition and discover that he is talking about a non-physical apocalypse – since present-world corporeality is incompatible with the sublime heavenly state, it would follow that all resurrections are cosmic, not corporeal events.

2 Corinthians 5:1–5: the first verse is the powerful one, pointing out that each believer has an earthly "house" and, were it to be dissolved, believers also "have a building of God, an house not made with hands, eternal in the heavens." This is a direct restatement of the physical/spiritual distinction made in 1 Corinthians, chapter 15.

Philippians 1:21–3: again, the post-death experience wherein Jesus and his followers are united is unambiguously stated as being non-physical. From this passage, it is very hard to infer that Paul believes in a literal apocalypse.

1 Thessalonians 4:13–18 and 5:1–2: in contrast to the previous item, here Paul apparently is both directly apocalyptic and physical about it – albeit in a gentle manner that seems to be free of bloodshed. He says that Jesus shall come in the air with a massive degree of noise and that there shall be two resultant reorganizations of the biosphere. In the first stage, those who died in the faith ("asleep") shall be raised from the dead and, secondly, those who are alive and believe in Jesus shall be taken up into the clouds to meet the Lord and spend eternity with him. In a perfect phrase, Paul warns his fellow believers that they cannot predict when the "day of the Lord" will occur: it will arrive "as a thief in the night" (5:2). This is one of those biblical passages that is argued about endlessly. At minimum one has to take it that when Paul is talking about a massive world-rendering thunderclap and about believers being elevated into the clouds, he is not writing allegory. Some physical apocalypse, however vague in its details, is implied here. This passage (running from 4:13 through 5:2) is the only place in the Christian scriptures that portrays clearly the cloud-descent of Jesus and the

Rapture of believers to meet him in the air. (The word "rapture" is not used, but nevertheless this is the key rapture text for many modern Christian apocalypticists.) Where all this becomes potentially problematic is that Paul's physical-world references in First Thessalonians are at odds with his virtually Platonic interpretation of the incorporeal nature of the Second Coming of Jesus in First Corinthians. However, this is only a difficulty if one denies Paul the basic right we grant to all individuals: the right to develop spiritually and intellectually over time. The writings of Paul do not have to be consistent with themselves, for he grew in faith as time passed. If the almost universal scholarly view is correct, that First Thessalonians was the first of the authentic Pauline letters to be written, then we have a case of Paul's having a literal view of the return of Jesus and its accompanying events in his earlier years. However, as the years passed and no thief-in-the-night appeared, he allegorized and spiritualized the apocalypse. He did not stop believing but refined what he believed.

Hebrews 12:22–4: the "Epistle" to the Hebrews (if it was indeed a letter) contains the New Testament's most elegant argument for Christianity aimed at a Jewish audience, apparently one already Christianized but under pressure. Scholars suggest that it is written in the best Greek of the New Testament, which is rather a problem: certainly it is not by Paul and aside from the writer's making it clear that he had never heard Jesus in person (2:3), there is no useful hint of who the author was and when he wrote. In crafting his argument, the author rewrites the major images and narratives of the Hebrew scriptures, of the book of Jubilees (which, from the Qumran caves, we now know was ubiquitous among Jewish dévotes at the time of Jesus), and portions of the early Christian scriptures, or at least of early oral knowledge by Jesus followers. The fascinating point theologically (although vexing historically) is that when he is speaking of the Jewish past, the author assiduously focuses on the pre-First Temple era, the time when the portable Tabernacle was Yahweh's house. This was the period of the primordial covenant, and it is employed as a metaphorical parallel to the primitive Church whose purity the Christian Church has forever been seeking to recover. Only in the beginning of his peroration (12:22–4) does the author of the book of Hebrews invoke a future that includes the holy site, Mount Sion, and the heavenly Jerusalem, "the city of the living God" (2:22). Even then, the Temple is implied, not defined. Clearly, though, the vision is apocalyptic, for in the heavenly Jerusalem there will be an assembly, consisting of an innumerable company of angels, and including those faithful who died before Jesus returned, and also of living believers. A judgment by God (not by Jesus) will occur, and Jesus will be the new high priest, sprinkling the altar with blood and thus being the mediator of a new covenant with Yahweh; or, to be faithful to the ancient Hebrew concepts the author knows his audience is familiar with: Jesus will be the broker in cutting a new contract with Yahweh. The lack of specifics in this small apocalypse makes it very plastic indeed and thus useful for quotation by anyone who takes a notion to explain what the Old and New Testaments mean when they seem to predict the future.

The book of Revelation is referred to in various Christian traditions as the Apocalypse of John and as the Revelation of St John the Divine, or that of John of Patmos. It is thoroughly and completely and intentionally the terror at the end of the Bible.

The power of this text can scarcely be overestimated. Never mind that no convincing case has been made as to who wrote it (certainly it was not by the same author as the Gospel of John). Never mind either that it consists of a syncopated pastiche of visions that are possibly divine in origin, but if uttered today would be adjudged diagnostically schizophrenic in character. (Remember, however, that God gets to reveal his wonders in strange ways.) And forget for the moment that the leaders of the early Christian Church as they emerged into the harsh light of later imperial Rome were strongly divided about whether or not Revelation should be included in the canon of authoritative Christian texts. Only in the later 300s did it gain majority (but not unqualified) acceptance in the Rome-based Church. In the eastern branch of Christianity it was not accepted until late in the seventh century. (Mind you, as stout a defender of scriptures as Martin Luther was tempted to exclude the entire book from his translation of the Bible.) However, once the western Church had decided to accept Revelation, the canon makers put it at the back of the Christian scriptures, probably for no more complex a reason than that it was the last manuscript to be added. But for whatever reason, the placement of the book of Revelation at the end of the canon completely changes the meaning of the Christian message by turning the entire text of the New Testament into an apocalypse, one that starts with the birth of Jesus and ends with Christ's kingdom in eternity. In fact, because the Christian texts are a rewriting of the Hebrew scriptures (the Christian texts are called quite accurately the New Covenant), the theatrical placement of Revelation at the farthest distance from the book of Genesis makes the entire history of Creation and of God's relationship with humanity a narrative that leads to the insane maelstrom that is the end-times. Consider how differently the New Testament, or the entire sets of Hebrew and Christian scriptures, would be read if the Church fathers had decided to place at the conclusion the rhetorically polished Epistle to the Hebrews (like Revelation, a disputed book), whose apocalyptic sections are gentle and whose idiom is not attack but persuasion.

That Revelation is an always vengeful, thoroughly violent, often salacious attack on the Roman Empire is not a point that anyone would argue against, although exactly which Roman emperor and his administration is being vilipended is open to discussion. Crucially, it is also a great deal more than simply anti-Roman Empire: in part it is a hate-filled attack by the author on Christian groups other than his own. Yet, the encryption of the author's venom is so complex and luridly splattered that one cannot tell exactly whom he is denouncing.[7] Even granting that Revelation is both an attack on imperial Rome and a pamphlet in a fight as between various early forms of Christianity (a term, incidentally, that the author of Revelation does not use), there remains the seemingly independent power of the text itself. The evangelical interpreters of the early nineteenth century with whom we are ultimately concerned, cared only peripherally for the circumstances of the book's creation and focused intensely on its mysteries.

7 In *Revelations: Visions, Prophecy, and Politics in the Book of Revelation* (New York 2012), Elaine Pagels makes a provocative case (43–72) for Revelation, written c. 90 AD, being an all-out attack on Pauline Christianity, which is to say it is a warning against the inclusion of Gentiles except those fully ritually converted to Judaism.

And it is harder to find a text more mysterious.[8] Both everyday readers and lifelong scholars disagree over the most basic issue: is the story that washes through the text a linear narrative or is it a series of repetitions forming a set of concentric circles that revolve around a single hub of truth? The text of Revelation begins simply enough: a man who calls himself John and is an itinerant missionary in the Mediterranean basin, claims in the very first verse that Jesus's own angel has passed along to him a revelation that Jesus himself has been given by God. There is a very clear hierarchy here: Jesus is not God, but a conduit for God's message. Thereafter we are given sets of messages that become more and more hallucinogenic at each revolution. The literary figure that almost holds them together is the magic number seven (with sidebars for the number twelve and its multiples and for the number two). The first vision (1:10–3:22) was given to John at an auditory level as loud as a trumpet. It is a dictation of a set of letters to each of seven churches in Asia Minor. This involves various sevens: the church of Ephesus is saluted by an angel who holds seven stars in his right hand and walks among seven golden candlesticks; the memorandum to Sardis opens with the seven spirits of God and with seven stars. And the church at Philadelphia, if it remains faithful, is promised incorporation in a new Temple in a New Jerusalem. The second vision (4:1–4:11) has John opening a door in Heaven, again hearing a mighty voice, and he then encounters twenty-four elders around a jewelled throne, and sitting there, lighted by seven lamps, "are the seven spirits of God." And in front of the throne are four beasts, each with six wings praising the being who sits on the throne, presumably the Almighty. The third vision (5:1–7:17) is a continuation, with a seven-sealed book, which previously could not be opened, being unwrapped by a "Lamb as it had been slain" (5:6) and having seven horns and seven eyes, "which

8 Here I should call attention to a remarkable work of what is sometimes called "popular scholarship," but which actually is masterful in breadth and wit: Jonathan Kirsch, *A History of the End of the World* (New York 2006). Other, less accessible works are cited in my *Surpassing Wonder.* The article in *The Anchor Bible Dictionary* (New York 1992), on Revelation (vol. 5, 694–708) is an admirable summation of the issues.

are the seven Spirits of God sent forth into all the earth." And so follows an opening of the first six seals with details of starvation, warfare, murder, and martyrdom. As a parenthesis, chapter 7 seems to suggest that 144,000 Jews and an unspecified number of Gentile martyrs will be granted a time-out from this particular reign of terror. Continuing to his fourth vision (8:1–11:19), John gets to the seventh seal, and, when it is opened, he drops into an internal spiral, for he hears seven trumpets, each of which announces its own blood-drenched or fire-consumed or sea-destroying woe ("the third part of the sea became blood," 8:8) to those who are on the wrong side of the Almighty, or at least of John of Patmos. The visionary escapes from that internal spiral and in his fifth vision (12:1–14:20) opens the seventh seal and introduces seven figures ranging from Satan to Jesus to the archangel Michael to the Son of Man to sea-beasts and earth-beasts never before seen; John sees a figure "like unto the Son of Man" with a great sickle in his hand and he sits on a cloud and reaps the tainted figures of humanity with such vigour that blood runs as deep as the bridles of war horses. The sixth vision (15:1–16:21) consists of seven agents emptying seven vials, each a plague, some involving putrescence, all involving blood by the shipload and pain beyond measure. A particularly deft touch is that during the fifth vial the citizens of the kingdom of the beast gnawed their tongues to assuage pain (16:10). In the seventh vision (17:1–20:15) seven dooms are announced against the world power Babylon (Rome), and John encounters the scarlet-dressed woman who has seven heads (and, confusingly, ten horns) and is the mother of all harlots; one also has what may be taken as the Second Coming of Jesus, out of whose mouth issues a sharp sword (19:15) and one has the Bible's only mention of a thousand-year reign of peace (20:3) followed by Satan's making a brief escape and then being punished forever in the lake of fire. Thereafter, John of Patmos produces a vision of a New Jerusalem, one that descends out of the heavens. and he gives his audience its dimensions and details – the most significant of which is that there is no temple in the New Jerusalem, "for the Lord God Almighty and the Lamb are the temple of it" (21:22). Here the writer seems to have forgotten that earlier – 3:12 – the Philadelphians were promised a New Jerusalem with a temple. That, though, is only a distraction. The virtuous have won and their enemies are tortured intact or are strewn about in small pieces, all to the greater glory of God.

There is no way to see Revelation as a compassionate piece of work, and it is hard to take it as morally edifying. Still, it became an indispensable item in the biblical toolkit with which the depressed and resentful evangelical elite of south Dublin and County Wicklow – Dalyland – tried to recapture control of their world.

Despite the considerable rhetorical force of some of the apocalyptic sections of the Jewish and Christian scriptures, it may seem puzzling that anyone save cultural historians of the ancient Middle East pays much attention to them. After all, the prophecies that predicted a physical apocalypse involving the Second Coming of Jesus of Nazareth all had one seemingly fatal flaw: *they were demonstrably wrong*. Take the items we surveyed above. Jesus is reported as telling his disciples that "this generation shall not pass" without his prediction being fulfilled of the Son of Man appearing in the clouds (Matthew 24:34; Mark 13:30; Luke 21:32). Paul writes to the Thessalonians that "we which are alive" will be caught up into the clouds when the Lord descends from Heaven (1 Thessalonians 4:17). Most tellingly, the book of Revelation begins by promising that it is about "things which must shortly come to pass" (1:1). Jesus, through the medium of his angel and of John of Patmos, encourages the church at Philadelphia by saying "behold I come quickly: hold that fast which thou hast, that no man take thy crown" (3:11). And the penultimate verse of this master apocalypse says this: "Surely I come quickly; Amen. Even so, come, Lord Jesus" (22:20).

Despite the apparent inability of the main figures in early Christianity – Jesus and Paul – to get the immediate future right, in the early 1800s, almost nineteen centuries after the death of Jesus, many believers throughout Europe and North America were parsing Christian apocalyptic prophecy more closely than ever. How did that come to be? The question has exercised Church historians for generations, and I cannot see that we are very close to an explanation and certainly I am not propounding one here. Instead of dealing with the question directly, let us go at it from the side and ask: what did the apocalyptic notions in the scriptures do for – or to – the Church? In other words, of what benefit were these notions and at what potential cost?

At the most fundamental level, the apocalyptic rhetoric seemed to solve the huge problem that arose when Jerusalem and its temple were destroyed in 70 AD. Apocalyptic thinking, and especially the book of Revelation, is the device for replacing the Jerusalem temple and, in one way or another, the temple of Herod the Great with a structure that is not tainted by the present corrupt world. A New Jerusalem descends from Heaven "prepared as a bride adorned for her husband" (Rev. 21:2). This new city is described in careful, albeit fevered, detail. In a melange of metaphors, Jesus, the Lamb of God, becomes, together with Yahweh, the ruler of the New Jerusalem (22:1ff); further, the two reconstitute the temple itself (21:22), and this presentation of the Lamb, the primary sacrificial animal of Israel, permits the ingrafting of all of the lamb-and-blood images that are found elsewhere in the scriptures, of which the pivot is "Behold the Lamb of God which taketh away the sins of the world" (John 1:29). In practical terms, the joinery accomplished by the wildness of apocalyptic thought permits both the Catholic liturgy of the Eucharist as an actual blood sacrifice and also licenses the nineteenth-century evangelical interrogatory, "Are you saved? Are you washed in the blood of the Lamb?" For the believer, each of these very different approaches provides a personal experience that is outside of time. And if the experience is outside of earthly time, then the niggling details of inaccurate prophecy are immaterial.

Apocalypticism has provided demonstrable benefits for the Christian Church, but it has always been worrisome. The classic and deeply brilliant attempt to build a containment shield around apocalyptic thinking and especially around the book of Revelation was the work of Augustine, bishop of Hippo, in north Africa. The fall of Rome to the Vandals in 410 led to his serial composition of *The City of God against the Pagans*, which deals with a situation akin to the fall of Jerusalem.[9]

9 The version employed here is William Chase Greene's bilingual edition, *The City of God against the Pagans* (London: William Heinemann, and Cambridge: Harvard University Press, 1960), vol. 6. The citations follow standard protocol of citing chapter and section number.

For our purposes, the signal chapter is number 20, which deals with the final judgment and with various forms of prophecy and what they mean. Augustine's exposition is so quietly confident, so reasonable, so tactful in asking for the reader's assent that one seems at first to be encountering someone who does not have much hope of dealing with the adrenaline-fuelled enthusiasts of apocalyptic prophecy. Their disputations make a sound like a migrating colony of wild bees. What can he have in common with them? Surprisingly, quite a lot. Augustine's discussion of apocalyptic matters is thoroughly and consistently based on reference to the scriptures. He believes strongly in the last judgment as declared by "the Saviour himself" (20:5). He unreservedly believes in the Second Coming of Christ. He believes that Jesus will be the final judge in eternity and that this is indicated even in the Old Testament although the person of Christ is not actually mentioned therein (20:30ff). He links together both Old and New Testament texts that deal with the end-times and the final judgment. He believes that before the final judgment takes places the Jews will be converted to "the true Christ, that is, our Christ" (20:29). He believes in two resurrections, the first when Jesus returns and the second at the ultimate end of time (20:6).

Was St Augustine a fellow traveller with John of Patmos? Up to a point, yes: he takes Revelation wholly seriously. Augustine understood the crucial point about Christian apocalypticism as it was most likely to be assimilated by agitated minds – namely that the operational centre of the entire edifice is those seven verses in Revelation (20:1–7), the Bible's only mention of the elusive idea of the millennium. Thus the centrepiece of Augustine's discussion (20:7) has the long section title "About the Two Resurrections, and the Thousand Years, Dealt with by John in His Apocalypse, and What Opinion We May Rationally Hold about Them." Somewhat unfairly, Augustine ridicules those who have a "carnal" understanding – meaning a literal view – of the millennium: he says that such people think that when Jesus comes back those who rise from the dead will have a thousand years of food and drink and one long banquet. That is a straw man and unworthy of him. Augustine's real arguments are, first, that the number "one thousand" is an expressive number, one of particular mathematical perfection and is intended to be indicative of spiritual perfection. Secondly, the kingdom of Heaven is not some future concept: "the Church, even now is the kingdom of Christ and the kingdom of heaven" (20:9). And, thirdly, therefore the millennium is the history of the Church. The wild things found in the Revelation of John are not empirical predictions of soon-to-occur current events but are metaphorical expressions of the dangers and difficulties Christ's Church must and shall overcome.

The containment vessel developed by Augustine worked well for several centuries, almost up to the Protestant Reformation. Indeed, slightly reformulated, it serves well today in most forms of Catholic dogmatics and in the "mainline" Protestant denominations.

Because, manifestly, Augustine's containment device did not fully control the more enthusiastic forms of Christian apocalypticism, it is easy to underestimate his genius on this particular topic; unlike the actual writers of the several pieces of apocalypse, he saw the future accurately, at least in regard to its reception by generations of future believers. He understood that, despite its belated appearance near the very end of the book of Revelation, the concept of the millennium was the functional heart of the Christian apocalyptic system. This is the reason he makes it the centrepoint of his own interpretation of Judaeo-Christian prophecy. That recognition by Augustine was only partly theological or philosophic, despite his emphasis on rational methods of analysis. Augustine's intuitive understanding of human nature (for want of a better term) tells him that the millennium is the one point where everyday people and workaday priests will grab "carnally" onto prophecy. They will do this by seeing the millennium as a real temporal-physical entity that occurs in a future that could be close to hand: one that offers them immeasurable future benefits and also the promise that their enemies will feel the terrible sword of divine vengeance. Augustine summarizes: "Those who are spiritually minded call those who believe these things, in Greek, 'chiliasts,' and we may in Latin translate the term literally as 'millenarians'" (20:7).

In chapter 6, I mentioned the idea that real intelligence is the art of good guessing – that is, of seeing accurately complex patterns for which one has only a few datum points. That is Augustine's genius. He foresees the strong possibility that the millennium will become the mouse that eats the lion, the small paragraph at the end of the holy codex that turns all the other pages upside down.

As a rhetorical convenience, we can accept the conventional modern shorthand that makes "millennialism" and "apocalypticism" synonyms in discussions of Christian theology, at least within evangelicalism. "Millennialism" is convenient and not misleading as long as one accepts that it is an abbreviation for "apocalyptic millennialism." Remember that the dominant theology throughout most of the life of the Christian Church has been *non*-apocalyptic millennialism: meaning that the prepotent interpretation of all that biblical prophecy was *not* that a physical apocalypse of great gore and violence was to be the necessary harbinger of the final and eternal reign of God (in concert with his son Jesus) over the universe.[10]

10 My intention in introducing the term *non*-apocalyptic millennialism is to save the reader from having to wade through a swamp of terminology that various dévotes use to distinguish their own form of belief from that of their rivals who decode the scriptures in some manner other than their own. An entire arcane taxonomy and hermeneutic vocabulary has developed that has the effect of turning the genuinely curious reader of good will away from trying to understand evangelical apocalyptic viewpoints as something other than pathology; an unfortunate result, given the influence of evangelical apocalypticism upon present-day demotic thought, not least in the geopolitical realm.Simply put, the historically dominant position of *non*-apocalyptic millennialism consists of members of the Christian tradition who reject entirely the idea that there is any useful prophetic material in the scriptures; for them, their present experience of the divine, however experienced, is sufficient, and if there is indeed any millennium, it is within each believer; those who, like St Augustine and the overwhelming majority of Catholic theologians. see the apocalyptic prophecies as metaphors that deal with the spiritual life of the Christian Church; those who conclude that the events in the prophetic books – particularly Daniel and Revelation – are mostly encoded descriptions of far-past and specific historical moments and that these predictions of future events are well past their sell-by dates. This is the dominant view of scholars in the secular academy, but not in most instances of those employed by various denominational universities, colleges, and Bible schools. There was, and is, a gentle school of belief that there will be a "millennium," but that it will be a time of gradual improvement in the present world and that, when the world has become thus pacified, Jesus will return and he will reign for eternity; no sanguinary hydraulics in most forms of

That granted, apocalyptic speculation has always been at least a tiny slice of Christian thought. Mostly, it was kept under tight control until the Protestant Reformation, when the scriptures in various vernaculars became more widely available to the minority who could read among the several populations of Christendom. The scriptures in local languages were intoxicating texts indeed, and their reading by lay persons resulted in the creation of scores of little sects and hundreds of conventicles. These groups, despite their small size, were unsettling not only to the Roman Catholic Church but to the Protestant denominations (such as European Lutherans) that had become state-established institutions after the Reformation.

Still, the grand flowering of millennial thought did not occur in Europe until the age of the French Revolution. That observation is hardly controversial; it holds whether or not one believes that the French Revolution was the product of a whole new way of thinking, or if the revolution itself created new thought patterns, or both. Certainly Irish society, at virtually all levels, was affected by the world-changing character of the French Revolution, its prelude, and its aftermath: the hopes and the counter-alarums of the period, from Grattan's parliament through the 1798 Rising and on to the Act of Union of Great Britain and Ireland, were all tinctured by French vocabulary, by the vast if temporary expansion of the French revolutionary empire and by the excesses of the revolution. To many Bible students in the British Isles and in northern Europe, events at the end of the eighteenth century were a broad hint of the apocalyptic millennium to come.

The point that requires emphasis is that as Ireland entered the nineteenth century Irish society also had its own unique awareness of

---

this view. This view – that the world has to get better, not worse, before Jesus comes back – is non-apocalyptic; though it uses the concept of millennium for a time of human-brought peace, it is not "millennialist" in the sense of requiring a round of apocalyptic cleansing as a prior condition. Of the various forms of *non*-apocalyptic millennialism, it is the only one that is discussed more than peripherally in the present study. Confusingly, this form of belief is usually labelled by historical theologians as "post-millennialism," a term we will avoid. For a sensible and comprehensible approach to the arcane taxonomy of evangelical apocalyptics, the Brethren historian F. Roy Coad has a conspectus in *Prophetic Developments* (Pinner, Middlesex, 1966), esp. 8–10.

millennial thought. One here cites two sets of evidence from widely differing strata of Irish society: the bestseller status of the writings of Francis "Millennium" Dobbs at the end of the eighteenth century and the start of the nineteenth and, secondly, the widespread popular acquaintance in Ireland in the 1820s with anti-Protestant interpretations of various prophecies. Neither of these exhibits is very sophisticated, but taken together they provide something quite rare in observations of theological history: direct evidence of widespread acquaintance with developing theological ideas on the part of a large portion of a national population.

First, Francis Dobbs (1750–1811): son of the Church of Ireland rector of Lisburn; member of the Irish parliament; leading Irish Volunteer in the 1780s; barrister; supporter of all sorts of reforms, including the payment of clergy of every faith; successful negotiator with the Wicklow rebels of 1798; author of more than one multi-volume history of the world[11] and of several efforts at biblical prophetic application[12] – and, above all, ardent opponent of the Union of Ireland with Great Britain. God was against the proposed Act of Union of Great Britain and Ireland, he explained in one of the most famous speeches of the old Irish parliament, as could be proved in detail by reading the books of Daniel and of Revelation and of some scriptural bits elsewhere. Dobbs gave three speeches in the Irish House of Commons that he thought were worth reprinting – 5 March 1799,[13] 5 February 1800, and 7 June 1800[14] – and the third of these certainly caught the public's attention. He was in apprehension, he told his fellow members of parliament, on hearing the words "That this bill do pass" come from the chair, meaning that Ireland would almost certainly be swallowed up in a new United Kingdom. As was the case with almost all millennialists throughout history, Dobbs confided that he did not consider himself to be living in ordinary times – "feeling as I do that a new and better

11 Francis Dobbs, *First Volume of Universal History*; *Second Volume of Universal History*; *Third Volume of Universal History*; and *Fourth Volume of Universal History* (London 1787–1788).

12 Francis Dobbs, *Millennium, a Poem in Four Books* (London 1787). The poems was variously revised and repackaged, notably in 1800.

13 Francis Dobbs, *Mr Dobbs's Speech ... of March, 1799* (Dublin 1799).

14 Francis Dobbs, *Memoirs of Francis Dobbs, Esq.* (Dublin 1800).

order of things is about to arise and that Ireland, in that new order of things is to be highly distinguished indeed."[15] A new order of things?

> I shall for the present confine myself to such passages [of scripture] as will support three positions: – the first is the certainty of the second advent of the Messiah; the next, the signs of the times of his coming, and the manner of it; And the last, that Ireland is to have the glorious pre-eminence of being the first kingdom that will receive him.[16]

Undeniably, Francis Dobbs was a disconcertingly original interpreter of millennial prophecy – not many other scholars have seen Jesus's Second Coming to Earth as occurring first in Ireland, or have perceived Armagh as being the Celtic variant of the word "Armageddon" and thus the prospective site of the greatest of end-of-time battles[17] – but, as far as his reading of the biblical references to biblical chronology as found in Daniel and Revelation prophecy was concerned, he had good bloodlines. As he noted several times in his speech, Dobbs relied strongly on the authority of Sir Isaac Newton, who also had views on as-yet-unfulfilled biblical prophecy, albeit more architectonic than Dobbs's and certainly non-Hibernian in detail.[18] It is fair to add that

15 Ibid., 35.

16 Ibid., 36.

17 This latter point is stated ibid., 44.

18 For example, ibid., 36, 39, 40. This was not mere window-dressing. Much of Dobbs's chronology comes from Newton. Compare Dobbs's longer work (279 pages) of 1800 with Newton's earlier work. Francis Dobbs, *A Concise View from History and Prophecy of the Great Predictions* (Dublin 1800). Newton's work that was available to Dobbs was his posthumously published *Observations upon the Prophecies of Daniel and the Apocalypse of St John* (London 1733). In this version of Newton's work one has a close reading of the texts and interpolating of historical information, without his asserting any specific future predictions. He does, however, affirm belief in a physical resurrection and a thousand years of life in the rebuilt and enlarged Jerusalem (171). However, in other private writings, it appears that Newton came to the conclusion that human civilization arose just before 1000 BC and that it would end with the return of Jesus in 2060 AD (see Jed Buchwald and Mordechai Feinigold, *Newton and the Origin of Civilisation* [Princeton 2012]).

Francis Dobbs also followed his own father, the Rev. Richard Dobbs (1694–1775), who in 1759 had produced a remarkable study of fulfilled scriptural prophecy, arguing that the seven seals in the Apocalypse of St John yielded a timeline, cut into twenty-year segments, that fit nicely the development of "the present happy British constitution," from 1620 to 1760.[19] Reading prophecy as a political guide was a family matter within the Dobbs clan.

The idea that when the 144,000 Jews apparently specified in Revelation were assembled it would be in Ireland has never been widely popular in millennialist thought. However, Francis Dobbs explained to the Irish parliament that the book of Revelation refers to the Jews "harping with their harps," and that they were to be "clothed in fine linen, white and clean," and this most probably meant that their assembly would be in Ireland, where else?[20] Since Satan is spoken of as a serpent, "what I rely on more than all is our miraculous exemption from all of the serpent and venomous tribe of reptiles."[21] And what has all this to do with Dobbs's opposition to the Act of Union of Great Britain and Ireland?

> I do not hesitate, even in this moment again to proclaim it to this House, and to the British and the Irish Nations, that the Independence of Ireland is written in the immutable records of Heaven.[22]

That Dobbs's speech invited waves of laughter from his fellow MPs and the gallery of fascinated observers is not surprising. One would not have guessed that Dobbs would quickly repackage his parliamentary words together with some of his other messianic predictions and extracts from his poem "Millennium" and very quickly sell 30,000 copies.[23] Even accepting that many of the copies may have been purchased with a sense of levity, the point is that virtually every middle- and

19 Richard Dobbs, A *Remarkable Accomplishment* (London 1762).
20 Dobbs, *Memoirs* (1800), 44.
21 Ibid., 45.
22 Ibid., 46.
23 Entry on Francis Dobbs, *CDIB* and *ODNB*.

upper-class family in Ireland must have had access to a copy and that millennialism in a form clearly recognizable as such was widely afloat in Ireland well before the development of the Dalyland evangelical complex or the proto-Brethren of County Wicklow and south Dublin.

The second case, more demotic and more diffuse, indicates that among the Catholic peasantry and middling farmers in the southwest of Ireland a form of Christian millenarianism was abroad, and it was distinctly threatening to Protestants. The theological source of this movement was the writings of the Rev. Charles Walmsley (1722–1797), longtime Roman Catholic vicar apostolic of the southwest of England. A talented astronomer and mathematician, he was a fellow of the Royal Society and a Church historian with an interest in the Revelation of John of Patmos. (The overlap with the interests of Sir Isaac Newton is obvious.) In 1771 Walmsley had published pseudonymously – as "Signor Pastorini" – a history of the Christian Church, which was republished several times in England and also in Dublin in 1790. The local interpretation of the book of Revelation – usually known as "Pastorini's prophecies" – was that beginning in the early 1770s there would be a fifty-year punishment of Protestant heretics. This was taken to culminate in 1825. Significantly, the cleansing was not to be achieved by the Second Coming of Jesus Christ but was to be a prelude to it. From 1817 onward, the prophecy spread throughout Munster and parts of Connaught and was related to a significant degree of violence against Protestants. Ironically, the Protestant Bible societies helped the spread of the Pastorini prophecies by making the scriptures more widely available as part of their attempts at converting the Catholic peasantry. Although the Catholic middle and gentry classes found the millennial beliefs to be an embarrassment, the evidentiary point is that millennial concepts and expectations based upon Bible prophecies percolated deeply into the social class and sectarian fissures of Irish society.[24]

24 Charles Walmsley, *The General History of the Christian Church: From Her Birth to Her Final Triumphant State in Heaven* (Dublin 1790). The standard historian's discussion is James S. Donnelly Jr, "Pastorini and Captain Rock" in Clark and Donnelly, eds (1983). This essay includes a bibliographic summary of the Irish publication of the "Pastorini" editions. The piece is a response to Patrick O'Farrell, "Millennialism, Messianism and Utopianism in Irish

None of this should surprise us. Ireland from the 1770s onward had undergone political and social stresses unequalled elsewhere in the British Isles: a Protestant parliamentary revolution in the 1780s, a real threat from French radicalism, a bloody attempted revolution in 1798, a further revolutionary spasm in 1803, deep financial depression after the end of the Napoleonic Wars, a typhus epidemic in 1817, and near-famine in 1821–22. Ireland, an outside observer would have concluded, was rich soil for the variant seeds of millennialism. Shrewdly, Gary L. Nebeker has concluded that "at least one part of the theological discord between Irish Catholics and Protestants of the early nineteenth century can be attributed to a battle of competing politico-prophetic convictions."[25]

The first native-grown interpreter of Christian apocalypticism whose work can be directly shown to have demanded the awareness of the evangelicals of Dalyland, and especially of the early Powerscourt set, was William Burgh (1801–1866). His anonymous work of 1821, a polished, compressed, and rhetorically compelling discussion of Christian apocalypticism, begins with a discussion of a usually ignored set of three verses in Second Peter (3:11–13) and develops into a prophetic tour de force. But it is even more than that: William Burgh and his strong apocalyptic views, his background, and his ecclesiastical career form a constellation one encounters only rarely in history – a natural experiment. His career suggests an alternative narrative line that easily could have developed within the circumstances and cultural values of the sector of society that he and John Nelson Darby shared. Indeed, William Burgh had so much in common with Darby that he can be used as a virtual counterfactual suggesting that Darby's own self-agency was among the reasons that Darby became such a strange and strong voice, crying loudly in the wilderness.

William Burgh was born within a few months of Darby and came from a family even more deeply seated in Ireland than was Darby's: old

History," in *Anglo-Irish Studies,* vol. 2 (1976), which minimized indigenous demotic millennialism in Ireland. For useful commentary, see Irene Whelan, *The Bible War in Ireland: The "Second Reformation" and the Polarization of Protestant-Catholic Relations, 1800–1840* (Dublin and Madison 2005), 141–7.

25 Gary L. Nebeker, "John Nelson Darby and Trinity College, Dublin" (2002), 92.

Norman, and indeed in 1848, the Burgh family reclaimed their former name of "de Burgh." His father was for a time MP for Athy. Burgh entered Trinity College, Dublin, at age sixteen (two years after Darby), and took his first degree in 1821, also two years after Darby. The two men were very much part of the same generation, the young cohort that claimed the right in the 1820s to reframe the Church of Ireland.[26]

At TCD John Nelson Darby was a gold medalist, but William Burgh was much more of a golden boy. He was a genuine spiritual leader and that quite independently of the Trinity curriculum. Burgh became an adept at reading and teaching the scriptures, and he conducted a regular morning seminar in his college rooms for the interpretation of the New Testament in Greek.[27] He impressed his friends with an extended essay whose main point was the reality of the Second Advent of Jesus as being an actual physical personal reign (a view that he found almost unpublished at the time in the British Isles). His friends pushed his publication of *The Coming Day of the Lord*, which appeared in 1821.[28] This was technically anonymous, but within the emerging young evangelical elite it was an identified item; its publication was a much bigger distinction than a gold medal: a book coming out almost in synchrony with the time of degree conferral. The publisher was Richard Moore Tims, who was one of the earliest proto-Brethren who formed the

26 George Dames Burtchaell and Thomas Ulick Sadlier, *Alumni Dublinenses* (London 1924), 113, with dating correction by Timothy C.F. Stunt, "Trinity College, John Darby and the Powerscourt *Milieu*," in Searle and Newport (eds), 61n51.

27 R.W. Harden, *St John's Monkstown* (Dublin 1911), cited by Stunt (2012), 61n52.

28 [William Burgh], *The Coming of the Day of God* (Dublin 1821). The first edition of 1821 sold well enough to warrant a second slightly revised edition by Tims in 1826. My reading below is from the first edition. That the anonymous work was indeed Burgh's is confirmed by William Burgh, *Lectures on the Second Advent* (Dublin 1832; 2nd ed. Dublin 1835), iv. It is worth noting Burgh's assertion of the importance of the 1821 work: "I may mention, that it is upwards of twelve years since my attention was turned to the subject of the Lord's Second Advent, and my mind convinced of one doctrine which holds prominent place in these Lectures – the personal reign of Christ. At that time this expectation was but beginning to revive in the Church, so much so that with the exception of 'The Letters of Basilicus' (first published in the Jewish Expositor) there was no publication on the subject in these countries."

movement in the mid-1820s, and who into the 1830s was de facto the official publisher of Brethren-friendly material.

William Burgh's anonymous 1821 essay (slightly revised and republished by Tims in 1826) is a splendidly economical (forty-two pages, plus a short appendix), very well-written conspectus of most of the questions that Irish evangelicals focused on in their discovery of biblical prophecy; and in its answers to the questions posed it is an accurate predictor of what most early Brethren (and sympathetic evangelicals) came to espouse. This is not to say that Burgh framed the eventual Brethren view of the apocalyptic future – everything may have been fortuitous duplication – but he got it right as far as most items were concerned. What did the twenty-one-year-old TCD prodigy suggest? A coarse summary is as follows and is somewhat unfair to Burgh in that it obscures his fine, direct sense of style, owing more to Addison and Steele than to the involuted periphrastics of his era's divinity texts. The prophetic portions of the Bible were not the property of the learned but were written to be interpreted according to good-sense meaning. When dealing with scripture in its good-sense meaning, the default position was that it was literal – some poetry, yes, some word-pictures, but literalism was the central interpretive mode to be employed; most importantly, this meant that all references to the Second Coming of Jesus were to a real physical event that would occur at some time in the future. All parts of the scripture were of equal authenticity; given that this indeed was divinely designed authenticity, then pieces from one text could be taken and made into a spiritual mosaic with textual tiles from any other portion the conscientious reader found relevant. Burgh's essay was a virtuoso exercise in the mode of thought that the Right Rev. John Jebb (bishop of Limerick, 1823–33) called "gymno-biblism."[29] Indeed, the young William Burgh rearranges the Bible with a dexterity that is as swift and sure as any of the thousands

29 Charles Foster (ed.), *Thirty Years Correspondence between John Jebb, Bishop of Limerick and Alexander Knox, Esq.* (London: 1836), vol. 2, 245, quoted in Timothy C.F. Stunt, "Evangelical Cross-Currents in the Church of Ireland," 218. Bishop Jebb is one of the fascinating figures whom I do not have space to discuss adequately. Fortunately, Alan R. Acheson has recently produced a valuable biography, *Bishop John Jebb* (Toronto 2013).

of *explications de texte* that I have encountered over the years. Without appearing to strain or to engage in the distractive tricks that often are employed, Burgh threaded a small, fine tapestry that began with his main text concerning the "Coming Day of God," in 2 Peter, and was interwoven with gobbets from all the gospels, from Isaiah and the other major prophets, and from almost all the letters ascribed to St Paul; he also managed to include verses from the Psalms and some fragments from Joel, Amos, Micah, and more.

Does this not all sound familiar? Up to this point we are in the same playbook that we described in chapter 7 – by which the early Brethren and their sympathetic fellow evangelicals approached the scriptures in their attempt at finding the right form of "primitive" Church organization: literalism, common-sense reading, with the Bible being its own interpreter, and the weaving together of disparate texts to give the plan for the right future ecclesiastical architecture. As we noted previously, the proto-Brethren worked on their ecclesiology as a basis for their apocalyptical thought, but with the cement not being completely set for the organizational foundations before they began their construction of the sweeping heavenward arches that defined future time.

To continue with Burgh: not only will the return of Jesus be literal, but it will be the Day of God or, the Day of the Lord and that will be Judgment Day; at this point there is to be no millennium or other pause in the proceedings – the present Heaven and Earth are destroyed and then a new set appears and immediately has Jesus as judge and king; Burgh posits two resurrections, the one of the dead in the Lord, the rest of everyone else deceased; the Jews will have their own new Canaan. Burgh notes references to a millennium in scripture, which he accepts as a literal concept but presents as almost a divine afterthought, a period after the big events of the destruction of the old Earth and Heaven and the creation of the new. Indeed, Burgh's argument pays much less attention to Revelation and more attention to other New Testament texts than is usual in later evangelical eschatologies: it is almost as if he were bent on proving that one could do Christian apocalypticism without leaning heavily on John of Patmos. With wisdom well beyond his years, Burgh does not engage in any predictions of the actual date of future events or even of how to discern that the end may be quickly approaching.

In using 2 Peter rather than the book of Revelation as his primary entry into future shopping, William Burgh reports that he had "valuable ministers of the gospel of Christ, and all of them persons of sound judgement and piety," in full agreement with him, and "they now see a harmony and clearness in the divine book, that they never did before."[30] Forgiving him his youthful hubris, Burgh was the first Irish evangelical to raise the central points of interpretation for the new, literalist approach to biblical prophecy. He was taken seriously by both the older generation of clerics within the Church of Ireland and by the new wave of evangelicals, including proto-Brethren. As a promising young cleric (ordained deacon 1824, priested 1825), he was given the prize curacy of Wicklow town and a year later the simultaneous appointment as chaplain to the Female Penitentiary, which was something of an evangelical fief.[31] He was as solidly a citizen of Dalyland as one could be. He married and his two successive wives (the first died in 1851) produced eighteen surviving children. He was part of Lady Powerscourt's prophecy circle, was friends with the early proto-Brethren, notably George Wigram, and attended the Powerscourt conferences.[32] In the mid-1830s, being a person of means, he built his own (ecclesiastically approved) church in Kingstown. A massive and distinguished writer on theology, particularly prophecy (forty books), he was Donnellan lecturer at TCD in 1854.[33]

The Rev. William Burgh had a truly fine mind, but he was scrubbed from Brethren history and thus from the history of evangelicalism in the English-speaking world. Why? At an operational level, because the first and second generation of Brethren refused to permit him to be remembered and that has provided a difficulty for twentieth-century and more recent historians. More efficiently than the Synge family, which was only partly erased from Brethren history, he was expunged from memory as being one of those who remained in the Church of Ireland: there was something of a Stalinist tinge to early Brethren memory

30 Burgh (1821), 4.

31 *CDGBSL*, entry for William Burgh.

32 Stunt, "Trinity College," 62–3.

33 *CDGBSL*, entry for William Burgh.

(people became unpersons), and there is no profit in avoiding the difficulties and misdirection that raises.

More directly contributory to Burgh becoming an unperson in standard Brethren histories is that in 1832 he ran afoul of John Nelson Darby's inability to tolerate other alpha-males. The specific instance was Burgh's delivering a set of a dozen lectures in Dublin in 1830–31, which were published as a book on the Second Advent of Jesus in 1832 by Richard Moore Tims.[34] Burgh's work was substantial (252 pages) and was part of a small library on prophecy he published over the subsequent twenty-five years, eventually making him the doyen of Church of Ireland commentators in the field. Already in 1832 he had another major book in press, this one on Revelation.[35] If one were a rival, he really had to be stopped. This was not easy to accomplish from an evangelical perspective, as Burgh continued to expound his belief in the literal Second Coming of Jesus Christ and of his rule throughout eternity. Most of his theological development since his precocious triumph of 1821 was in the same direction that the proto-Brethren, including John Nelson Darby, were taking. Burgh in the early 1830s now spent more time on, and gave more credit to, the concept of the millennial reign of Jesus than he had previously; at times he now wrote, somewhat hazily, of periods of history as "dispensations"; and he seems to have found room for a concept that John Nelson Darby was to develop more fully, namely a blank period in which prophetic events seem to take a break – "the thread dropped so long" is Burgh's way of saying this.[36]

William Burgh's biggest new idea since 1821 was that the prophesied Antichrist was not the institution of the Roman Catholic papacy (as most Protestants of the time believed) but rather was to be a "personal Anti-Christ." Burgh did not engage in any predictions of who this might be, but he argued strongly that several of the events prophesized before the Second Coming require a real individual of remarkable nastiness. Thus, when John Nelson Darby felt the need to clear Burgh from the playing field, he could gnaw away at the edges of this conclusion. He

34 William Burgh, *Lectures on the Second Advent.*

35 William Burgh, *An Exposition of the Book of Revelation*, 5th rev. ed. (Dublin 1857). The first edition appeared in 1832. I have not seen a copy.

36 Burgh, *Lectures on the Second Advent*, 127.

did so very effectively in a long article in the *Christian Herald*, a short-lived (1830–35) Irish evangelical serial that focused on prophecy and was open to early Brethren opinions.[37] Darby reviewed Burgh's *Lectures on the Second Advent* and skipped over another of Burgh's item he was to review, *The Apocalypse Unfulfilled*.[38] Darby's scattergun prose, as always, is somewhat difficult to interpret as to the meaning of any individual paragraph, but it characteristically includes sentences that, when taken out of their rhetorical context, are memorable. In this case, Darby says some nice things about Burgh's work (especially on the Jews) and discusses his own view of the seven seals in Revelation, murmurings that are incomprehensible. Darby accepted the idea that the Antichrist was to be a real individual, but he did not like the way that Burgh had come to that conclusion: it was too rational in deduction, too systematic in presentation. The Rev. Mr Burgh, Darby suggested, had locked himself into systematic thinking: "I do not think he has interpreted the book of Revelation rightly or successfully, and by making a system of it, he has made all his errors hang together."[39] Darby had preceded this judgment with a seemingly modest sentence of self-reference: "I confess I find it more profitable to learn from Scripture than to frame a system."[40] A more efficient effort at poisoning a rival's well – divine scripture over mere systematic thinking – is hard to imagine.

The Rev. William Burgh did not jump into the ditch and fight with the Rev. John Nelson Darby. He simply went his own way within the Church of Ireland as an evangelical (and later high church) interpreter of prophecy and also as a notable student of the Hebrew Bible. His life and works suggest two conclusions. One of these is a fact often overlooked – that an Irish tradition of apocalyptic millennialism existed

37 Thomas Kelly, "'Come, Lord Jesus, quickly come!' The Writing and Thought of Edward Nangle, 1828–1862," in Crawford Gribben and Andrew R. Holmes (eds), *Protestant Millennialism* (Basingstoke 2006), 104. The prophetical journal was edited by the Rev. Edward N. Hoare, rector of St Lawrence, Limerick. It is relevant that the city of Limerick was one of John Nelson Darby's focal points when he went on missionary rambles in the 1830s.

38 William Burgh, *The Apocalypse Unfulfilled* (Dublin 1832; 2nd. ed., 1833).

39 Reprinted as "Review of 'Lectures on the Second Advent,' and 'The Apocalypse Unfulfilled,'" CW, 33001, 11.

40 Ibid., 9.

within the educated strands of the Church of Ireland well before the era of the Powerscourt conferences. The other is that one could develop an elaborate millennial apocalyptic (one that had roughly a 95 percent overlap with that of the later Darbyist eschatology) and could do so without basing it on hatred of the Church of Ireland or of any other denomination. In other words, the highly negative tincture that was a central feature of the ecclesiological foundation of Brethren apocalyptic was not really necessary. Burgh's form of millennialism indicates clearly that an Irish mode of apocalypticism could develop without a declaration that all existing Churches were in ruins.

"Foreign" interpretations of Christian apocalyptic (meaning contemporary influences from outside the country) came into Irish evangelicalism by a process of cultural osmosis that was as subtle as it was pervasive: ideas often wander about on invisible legs.[41] Unusually, however, a specific conduit of transmission can be documented in the development of Dalyland's prophetic consciousness, namely the Prophetic House Party (which later in the century became the less exclusive

41 For reasons of space I am not dealing here with the back-and-forth influence of early evangelicals and a small number of Continental European theologues. This whole matter is discussed in depth in Timothy C.F. Stunt, *From Awakening to Secession: Radical Evangelicals in Switzerland and Britain, 1815–35* (Edinburgh 2000). See also Kenneth J. Stewart, *Restoring the Reformation: British Evangelicalism and the Francophone "Réveil," 1816–1849* (Milton Keynes 2006), which is particularly strong on the Haldane brothers. The following work may have influenced John Nelson Darby: [Père] Bernard Lambert, *Exposition des prédictions et des promesses faites à l'Église pour les derniers temps de la gentilité*, of undetermined date. [Joshua William Brookes,] *A Dictionary of Writers on the Prophecies* (London 1835), li, has a new edition being published in Paris in two volumes, publisher unspecified. Froom (vol. 3, 324) has an 1806 first publication date. Froom (ibid., 324–5) notes that the volume was of limited circulation, but that Fr Lambert put forward the idea of the Second Coming being the prelude to a time of violence and then the millennium. In "The Tribulation of Controversy: A Review Article," 97–8, Stunt restates a useful point that he had made decades previously, namely that S.P. Tregelles cited the Lambert book as having been studied by Darby in the mid-1830s.

"residential conference" conducted in hotels or, in North America, at camp grounds. The house-party concept came from Albury Park, Surrey, and was adopted wholesale by the Irish evangelical radicals, most spectacularly by Theodosia, Viscountess Powerscourt.

The style-setting venue, Albury Park, was the residence of Henry Drummond (1786–1860), one of the heirs to Drummonds, a London private bank. Henry Drummond was one part dandy, one part philanthropist, and one part an English nineteenth-century explorer – in his case not of distant lands but of far spiritual universes. He was well connected with the world of English influence. His grandfather, the first Viscount Melville, took over his care when Drummond was in his teens. Drummond was at Harrow with Lord Byron and Robert Peel. He took a seat for Plympton Erle, Devon, 1810–12, and then resigned to travel with his wife to the ancient Holy Land and then on to the new holy city, Geneva.[42] There in 1817 he encountered Robert Haldane, one of two amazingly energetic Scottish brothers who became influential religious independents, and Drummond agreed with Haldane on the need to bring the city of Calvin back to stricter Calvinism.[43] The effort did not last all that long as Haldane soon returned to Britain, and Drummond landed in trouble with the Swiss authorities, who were not keen on the unsettling civic implications of calls for righteousness from an English banker. Drummond and his wife left for France and

42 *ODNB*, entry on Henry Drummond. The Royal Bank of Scotland has a strong archival site, the basic summary of which is on heritagearchives.rbs.com/wiki/Henry_Drummond_of-Albury (accessed 6 March 2013).

43 The Haldane brothers, Robert (1764–1842) and James Alexander (1768–1851), are yet another of the robust pioneering evangelicals who seem one-and-a-half times life-sized. An admirable Victorian joint biography is Alexander Haldane, *The Lives of Robert Haldane of Airthrey, and of His Brother James Alexander Haldane* (London, 1st ed. 1852, 3rd ed. 1853). The European work of the Haldanes is well covered in Kenneth J. Stewart (2006). As mentioned in the present study, chapter 7, note 31, the Haldanes had been active in the north of Ireland in the early nineteenth century and had some influence upon the group of proto-Brethren that was formed by James Buchanan of Camowen Green. In the early 1820s, when in Ireland, Robert Haldane moved in the circles that included not only the Powerscourt set but also the Jocelyns (earls of Roden), and he kept ties with the Rev. Thomas Kelly (ibid., 499–500).

then went back home. Tired of the fripperies of the world, Drummond had sold The Grange, his residential and sporting estate in Hampshire, in 1817 and had bought the Surrey property, Albury Park, in 1819. He had Augustus Pugin turn the mansion and a portion of the local Anglican church into a Gothic monument.[44] The estate was an ideal place to hold a far-from-this-world religious retreat.

Without at all burlesquing the proceedings, which ran annually from 1826 to 1830, inclusive, one can fairly note that the leading figures in the Albury Park prophetic discussions seem to come from the pages of a well-drawn, fully colour-inked graphic novel. They were big men, about forty in number each year, oversized in ideas, reputation and ego, and they do not settle into a single frame, but jump right out of the usual boundaries. They had their brief and flaming moment as a prophecy college and then by mid-1830 were on their separate paths.

Given the egos involved and the habitual impracticality of Henry Drummond, credit for assembling (at Drummond's direction) the group of prophetic savants goes to the "moderator" (and sometimes chairman) of the proceedings, the Rev. Hugh McNeile (1795–1879). A TCD graduate, originally from Ballycastle, County Antrim, McNeile was handsome, a gifted orator, and the heir of his wealthy uncle. He would have been a natural parliamentarian (he took his law dinners at King's Inns, Dublin, and Lincoln's Inn, London), but an evangelical conversion led him to take holy orders. He was ordained in 1820 and given a County Donegal curacy by the then-bishop of Raphoe, William Magee. McNeile had the good sense to wed properly: in May 1822 he married Margaret Ann Magee, daughter of his bishop. The wedding took place less than six weeks before William Magee was nominated for translation to the archbishopric of Dublin.[45]

All this fit well with McNeile's coming to the attention of Henry Drummond, who owned the patronage rights to the rectory of Albury and who appointed him to the benefice in the same year.[46] Despite his

44 A. Haldane (1853), 452–7. See also RBS history, cited above, note 42.

45 *CDGBSL*, entry for William Magee; F. Maurice Powicke and E.B. Fryde, *Handbook of British Chronology* (London 1961), 370.

46 The old print edition of the *ODNB* (1903ff) has McNeile being appointed by Drummond after the patron heard him preach a sermon at Percy Chapel,

relative youth (age thirty-one in 1826), McNeile carried himself with personal authority. He brought from Ireland a heightened sense that the world was on a downhill slide, an unswerving personal loyalty to the Established Church, an openness to apocalyptic millennialism, and a visceral anti-Catholicism that was an active bonding agent across the spectrum of Protestant apocalypticism. (Later, in 1834, when he broke decisively with Henry Drummond, McNeile became the perpetual curate of St Judes's, Liverpool, and a leading sectarian agitator in Liverpool, the chief entrepôt into England for Catholics from Ireland, and the cockpit of English anti-Catholicism.)[47]

The Albury meetings were conducted under what might be anachronistically termed the Chatham House Rule: they were not to be recorded; speakers and their affiliations were not to be identified. The conference had the air of big secrets being discussed in hushed tones. No direct record remains of even who attended – and that is one of the reasons the importance of the Albury Park meetings has been underestimated – although the pieces were later partially put together by attendees and by historians.[48]

London. The present *ODNB* deletes this statement. However, there is no doubt that McNeile was a spell-binding preacher.

47 In many ways, McNeile spent his life fighting the same battles he would have fought in Ireland, save he did it in England. In the mid-1830s, he was the leading opponent of the attempt by the Liberal-controlled Liverpool corporation to introduce the Irish national system of education into Liverpool. He won by backing and organizing a system of Anglican schools (see James Murphy, *The Religious Problem in English Education* (Liverpool 1959). Besides continual anti-Catholic writing, McNeile fought strongly against the Maynooth College Act of 1845 (8 and 9 Vict. cap. 25) and favoured strongly the delimiting of the territorial titles of Catholic dignitaries (14 and 15 Vict. cap. 60). The broader, mostly English, aspects of the anti-Catholicism characteristic of evangelical Protestantism is well covered in John Wolffe, *The Protestant Crusade in Great Britain, 1829–1860* (Oxford 1991).

48 The most dependable summary of the unfortunately spare evidence is that of Columba Graham Flegg, *"Gathered under Apostles"* (Oxford 1992), esp. 34–41. One should add that Flegg's history of what became the Catholic Apostolic Church is a very useful insight into one of the most secretive of the new sects and denominations that arose during the evangelical upsurge of the first half of the nineteenth century.

The first conference of November 1826 was of course animated by Drummond and McNeile but also by notables such as Lord Mandeville (later Duke of Manchester) and Spencer Perceval, whose father had been assassinated while prime minister. Two-thirds of the forty or more guests (depending on the year) were Anglican, but with others from several Protestant denominations in attendance, and an unreported number of silent wives. A striking aspect of the focus of the Albury Park discussions was that they were predictive of the later concerns of many apocalyptic millennialists: in particular, Drummond's guest list included a number of influential persons with interests in Jewish matters. They held not just the traditional Christian concern with the Hebrew scriptures but also with modern Jewry. Henry Drummond as early as his twenties had fixed considerable attention on the Jewish issue and had long been a strong supporter of the London Society for Promoting Christianity amongst the Jews, founded in 1809 (commonly called the Jews Society at the time). The conversional interests of this society played into the interest in prophecy that flourished in the 1820s by virtue of the imprecise, but strong, suggestion in the scriptures that the Jews would return to their ancient homeland as part of the final times of the present world.[49] At the first Albury conference, an electric figure in promoting this view (though certainly not the only enthusiast) was Joseph Wolff (1795–1862), who had just returned from five years of missionary work with the Jews of the Middle East, which had been paid for by Henry Drummond. Wolff was the son of an Ashkenazi rabbi from the Germanies who had been educated at Tübingen (Protestant), had been a Redemptorist (Catholic), and in 1818 had joined the Church of Ireland and then had studied for a time at Cambridge by gift of the London Society for Promoting Christianity amongst the Jews. After his 1821–26 missionary journey he was a returned hero at Albury. Before he left for yet another series of adventures (including making it all the way to present-day Afghanistan and Ethiopia), he took the opportunity to marry a younger daughter of Horatio Walpole, earl of Orford. Wolff, like several of the figures of the

49 An excellent study is Donald M. Lewis, *The Origins of Christian Zionism* (Cambridge 2010). Particularly relevant here are pp. 25–103, indicating the linkeage of the Rev. Hugh McNeile and philosemitism.

early evangelical movement, arguably was a larger, more fearless figure than were most of the exploring and military figures who feature so strongly in Victorian mythology.[50]

Yet, at the Albury Park conferences the largest figure of them all was a Scot, the Rev. Edward Irving (1792–1834), a man so complex, so innocent, so handsome, so eloquent, so ill-fated that his being for a time an ecclesiastical actor for whom it seemed as if London was a mere stage set is not a condemnation but just another fact of a very strange and ultimately sad life.[51] Irving was a lad of parts, the son of a substantial Dumfrieshire tanner; as a licensed cleric of the Church of Scotland he was called to what was a second-line Scottish pulpit, the Caledonian Chapel in London in 1822. Within a year it became a fashionable church for the praying portion of the English preying class. The chapel was so crowded that it had to be replaced by a massive Regent Square neo-Gothic building, completed in 1827. At one time in 1824 it was said

50 ODNB has an unusually sharp sketch of Wolff. He strongly deserves a full new biography. His own volumes of memoirs are somewhat self-serving. The present standard life is by Hurly Pring Palmer, *Joseph Wolff* (London 1935). In a fitting arabesque, Wolff, who had joined the Church of Ireland as a layman when in his twenties, in his forties (1838) was ordained a Church of Ireland priest by the formidable Richard Mant, bishop of Dromore. Wolff settled down for a few years as a clergyman in Yorkshire and then was off again on his adventures in central Asia.

51 The standard biography of Irving is by "Mrs Oliphant" (Margaret Oliphant Wilson Oliphant), *The Life of Edward Irving*, 2 vols (London 1862). Quotations used herein are from the one-volume second edition (New York 1862). Subsequent English editions were in the one-volume format. This biography has not been adequately replaced. Oliphant received sharp criticism from Anglican churchmen for being too worshipful of Irving; and those who joined the Catholic Apostolic Church saw her as being too hard on those within that new-minted denomination. In fact, given Mrs Oliphant's generous quotation of primary sources, this is as straightforward a Victorian biography as one could find for someone as controversial as Irving. Less successful than Mrs Oliphant in presenting Irving as a full-fledged human figure are Andrew L. Drummond, *Edward Irving and His Circle* (London 1937), and Arnold A. Dallimore, *The Life of Edward Irving* (Chicago 1983). A very well-balanced modern biography is Tim Grass, *Edward Irving: The Lord's Watchman* (Milton Keynes 2011).

that a queue of carriages four miles long was waiting to pick up the quality after Irving's Sunday sermon: doubtlessly an exaggeration, but Irving was a major celebrity long before the term was employed. He was feted at fashionable houses and was a close companion of Samuel Taylor Coleridge, entwined as savants of the spiritually exotic. Irving was arrogant and instinctively manipulative, but he was no conman: "On the contrary, there was a kind of sublime humility in his egotism, like that of a Dominick or a St Frances; and while he believed in himself, in his powers, his mission, his convictions, and scrupled not to speak of them, and to deal with them as divine infallibilities, he was yet quite willing to become as nothing, if only the world would just believe with him." Those were the words of the astringently critical *North British Review*, nearly three decades after his death, and they fairly illustrate that most of those who saw him as being wrong also perceived his unusual innocence.[52]

The inaugural conference of 1826 began on Advent Sunday (3 December, that year) and involved eight days of residence. Breakfast through evening discussions were carried on each day, save Sundays. The Rev. Edward Irving published a description of the topics covered,[53] but it is misleadingly self-effacing in that Irving arrived with his head full of a strange and wondrous piece of Spanish language millennial writing and the ideas in that exotic piece were the pivot around which discussion revolved.[54] This was a not yet fully translated item that must have seemed to have come from outer space; an almost-secret treasure whose translation Irving still was labouring to complete (it was completed in January 1827 and was the tangible centrepiece of the 1827 Albury conference); an item that sounds so preposterous that it must have been a hoax.

52 [anon.], "Edward Irving," *North British Review* (1862), 96.

53 Irving in his introduction to the prophetic work of "Ben Ezra" (see note 56 below for citation), published in 1827, gives a description of topics covered in 1826 (vol. 1, clxxxviii–cxiv).

54 See Oliphant, 272–3, who makes it clear that whatever the formal agenda of the 1826 conference may have been, it was the Spanish work that was the catalyst of Irving's thought.

Providentially, at least in his own eyes, Irving had begun to study Spanish in the winter of 1825–26, and this study was said to have begun shortly before an amazing book was placed in his hands.[55] With the help of Spanish colleagues, Irving translated the book as *The Coming of Messiah in Glory and Majesty by Juan Josafat Ben-Ezra, a Converted Jew.*[56] Irving preceded the published translation with a 194 page "Preliminary Discourse," which could scarcely have been less convincing in its presentation of the provenance of the document. Irving began by rehearsing his own views of the Second Coming and of the millennium and the restoration of the Jewish nation and pointed out that the present book was by happy coincidence in agreement with him. He talked of the writer as being Jewish – "my worthy master Ben-Ezra" – but noted that he had discovered that the author really was a Catholic priest, a Chilean Jesuit, and that his surname was Lacunza and that the book had various editions in Spanish and that "there is no Protestant writer whom I know of to be at all compared to him. His book is the finest demonstration of the orthodoxy of the ancient system of the millenarians which can be imagined; indeed I may say perfect and irrefragable."[57] Irving disagreed with his sublime author on details and these matters took scores of pages, and put Irving as well as Lacunza in the centre of the frame.

The whole business positively calls out "fraud." Irving's introduction has the texture of the "discovery" of the papers of the Victorian arch-bully Harry Flashman.[58] Yet, despite Edward Irving's self-referential and distracting preface, the volume was real. It was the product of Manuel de Lacunza y Diaz (1731–1801), a Chilean Jesuit who spent a life in peripatetic exile as the result of the papal banning of the Jesuits.

55 Ibid., 266–7. Lewis (84) indicates that Henry Drummond called the book to Irving's attention.

56 Two vols (London: L.B. Seeley and Son, 1827). For reasons that are explained in the text, the item is usually listed in English language bibliographies under the authorship of Manuel Lacunza, *Coming of Messiah.*

57 Irving, "Preliminary Discourse" to Lacunza, vol. 1, xxvi.

58 George MacDonald Fraser, *Flashman* (London 1969) and subsequent volumes.

His world slipping badly into chaos, he turned to the scriptures as his source of diagnostics and of future hope. The publication history of his writing on the coming of the messiah has been well documented and Irving's translation confirmed as authentic.[59] One suspects that in part because of its exotic origin (by evangelical Protestant standards) it received both a good deal of attention in prophetic circles in the 1820s and early '30s, and for the same reason its articulation of several of the central ideas of apocalyptic millennialism was infrequently cited thereafter: Protestant enthusiasts for biblical prophecies of the end-times were not apt long to advertise that their views either stemmed from a Chilean Jesuit or even to acknowledge that their own views, if independently arrived at, nevertheless had been foreseen clearly by a Romanist priest.[60] The Rev. Edward Irving's translation of Lacunza's pseudonymous work certainly was the primary driver of discussion at the 1826 and 1827 Albury conferences. Significantly, John Nelson Darby cited the treatise in what was probably his own first published work on prophecy.[61] The Lacunza work was a sotto voce part of the Powerscourt conferences of the early 1830s, and an abridgment was published in Dublin in 1834.[62] Cult publication though for a time it was

59 David Pio Gullen, "Two Hundred Years from Lacunza," *Journal of the Adventist Theological Society* (1998). In addition to his own work, Gullen cites Spanish- and French-language studies that also provide a bibliographic history of Lacunza (73n6).

60 Stunt (2004, 57) cites the opinion of the French scholar of Lacunza, Alfred-Félix Vaucher, that if the "Plymouth Brethren" had been in the habit of citing their sources Lacunza's name would have frequently occurred in their writings.

61 J.N.D., "Reflections upon the Prophetic Inquiry and the views advanced in it," in CW (02001); pp. 5–9 deal with Irving's "Preliminary Discourse" astringently but with some approval amid his negative criticisms. Interestingly, Darby refers to the original author as Ben-Ezra rather than Lacunza. That this was Darby's first prophetic writing is taken on the basis of CW assigning it to "Dublin, 1829." Whether it was 1828 or 1829 is not material; it certainly is a response to Irving's 1827 publication and probably comes out of the period of intense reflection that was initiated by Darby's incapacitation in late 1827. The pamphlet is found in the National Library of Ireland, pamphlet 535(8). There is no indication of the publisher, and the work was published anonymously.

62 Brookes (1835), l.

(and to some small extent still is), the 1827 English-language version of Fr Manuel Lacunza's 1791 publication is a significant marker: not for his propositions as things in themselves, but rather because their translation became a centrepiece of discussion and therefore tells us indirectly what the prophetic adepts who assembled at Albury were thinking about.

The necessary modesty of that suggestion – that the material presented in Lazunza's work is best read as the real, but unreported, agenda of the Albury conferences – is disappointing because the five annual Albury Park conferences had the tantalizing promise of a visit to an uncharted rainforest, a venue full of flashy creatures never before assembled together, and beliefs, previously only presented as dry calculations, that now glowed as they were assembled together. Alas, the events at Albury Park lack a record that can be taken seriously in any detail. In line with his habitual self-indulgence, Henry Drummond, besides funding the conferences, kept control of the public version of the discussions. He insisted on controlling publication of any record of his Albury Park house parties. What a weird hash he made of it: he wrote a set of three volumes that contain well over 1,000 pages of pseudo-Ciceronian dialogue, purporting to give the true import of the discussions at Albury with fictitious names for participants, but real names for modern authors to whom the fictive speakers refer in arch and convoluted passages. Drummond had no intention of recording what actually had been said.[63] Here is a fair example, reasonably clear, from the opening of a conversation of "Philalethes" and "Anastasius" on the second coming of Jesus:

> *Philalethes.* You told me in our first conversation upon the times of the Gentiles, that you would on a future day point out to me the Scriptures which relate to the throne of David; will

63 [Henry Drummond], *Dialogues on Prophecy*, 3 vols. (London 1828–29). As Drummond averred, "the published Dialogues have borne little or no resemblance to these real conversations: much that was spoken was not printed; and much that was printed was never spoken. Fictitious names were assumed, and sentiments put into the mouths of the supposed collocutors, without any reference to the real opinions of any one who was actually present," vol. 1, iii.

> you now be so kind as to inform me, whether you consider that this throne is to be set up at the beginning, or at the end of the millennium?[64]

And on the conversation goes, taking in some big prophetic topics in a remarkably dull fashion. Interestingly, as Drummond winds his imitations of classic dialogues over hill and dale, he presents an argument that is intended to confirm prophetic interpretation as a property of an educated elite:

> *Philalethes.* I have observed, with great regret, that the works published by some of the ablest clergymen, who attained in their younger days to high academical honors, and who have displayed their power subsequently on other subjects, have hid their talents in matters of more important concern: their printed sermons contain little more of mind or power than could be found in the exhortations of unlettered piety from an old woman in a country cottage; and they seem to justify their indolence by saying, that their works are "chiefly designed for the poorer classes"; "or for a country congregation"; or "for domestic worship," etc.[65]

One should not bin Henry Drummond's school-boy faux-classic exercise as being entirely useless, but to consider the three volumes as a fundamentally accurate indication of proceedings would be to miss the point that Drummond's *Dialogues on Prophecy* was as much a work of suppression as an attempt to get things right. That this is the case is indicated by the primary fact that his agenda deletes discussion of the intellectual centrepiece of at least the first two conferences, Edward Irving's electrifying discovery of the Jesuit prophetic adept, Manuel Lacunza. One accepts the counsel of Ernest Sandeen that Drummond summarized "*to some extent* the substance of those meetings."[66] Drum-

64 *Dialogues on Prophecy,* vol 1, 159.

65 Ibid., 364.

66 Sandeen, 20–1n34.

mond probably did not meddle with the formal agenda of topics that the prophetic interpreters marched through, day by day.[67] However, one has to dilute sharply Drummond's one effort at straight factual reporting, namely his 1829 listing of six items on which there was a "perfect unanimity" among all the participants at his gatherings.[68] If there was such perfection among the big personalities who were guests at his house parties, it was miraculous. Still, if one takes his list as being a general, but far from universal, indication of what many front-edge prophetic exigetes were propounding in England in the late 1820s, the following summary is sensible:

1. The present age would not move smoothly into the millennium, but would be terminated by severe judgments upon the Christian Church;
2. while the judgments were falling upon the Christians, the Jews would be restored to their ancient homeland;
3. the most powerful portions of the Church would be held most responsible and would be most strongly punished;
4. the collective judgments would be followed by the millennium;
5. the Second Coming of Jesus would take place at the beginning of the millennium;
6. the French Revolution marked the beginning of the end-times and Jesus would soon return.[69]

67 Sandeen notes (Ibid., 21n34, emphasis mine) that the list of topics covered at the 1826 meeting as reported by Irving in his preface to Lacunza (vol. 1, clxxxviii–cxiv) was the same as the headings for the topics that Drummond had his fictional conversants discuss in volume 1 of his *Dialogues on Prophecy*. This does not necessarily mean that either Drummond or Irving was accurate in reporting the agenda of the first two years' debates or that Drummond accurately listed the agenda items of the subsequent years, but it tilts the probability table in that direction.

68 *Dialogues on Prophecy*, vol. 3, iv. Even here Drummond leaves it cloudy as to whether the "unanimity" was a prerequisite for participation (he had sent around a trial set of questions to see if a meeting would be productive) or if unanimous agreement was the product of the meetings as he saw them.

69 Ibid., vol. 3, iv.

These matters doubtlessly were discussed at a recondite level (the decoding of the seventy weeks of Daniel alone would have produced an encyclopaedia of arcane interpretation). The salient point is that the main matters –the actual physical Second Coming of Jesus before a literal millennium of 1,000 years, the literal return of the Jews to the land held by the ancient Israelites, and the inevitablility of there being a period of suffering before the millennium – were assertions that the overwhelming majority of Christian theologians in the 1820s would not have accepted, and this held in particular for the Protestant Churches in the British Isles. (The sixth point, about the French Revolution being the divinely determined start of the countdown to the end-times was a crotchet, and even the Church of England prophetic exigetes who dominated the Albury Park guest list would not have unanimously endorsed it.) Given the novel, or at least radical, nature of the six propositions that Henry Drummond said were unanimously agreed by himself and his savant guests, he should hardly have been surprised that his conference proceedings, despite being reported with all the vividness of a damp blanket made of fulled cloth, excited some vigorous criticism. In 1829, in his third volume of the *Dialogues on Prophecy,* he expressed wonder that anyone could not agree with his prophetic formulations. To his surprise, he had discovered after his first volume of *Dialogues* was published that:

> Several other works upon the subject of unfulfilled prophecy made their appearance, or were called into notice about the same period; and then it was for the first time perceived with amazement and grief that the doctrines advanced in them, and in the Dialogues, were charged with being "novel," and of "modern invention."[70]

"Amazement?" Only if one had paid attention solely to the religious beliefs of those inside one's own self-selected prophecy circle:

> This charge was not made in one, or only in some, of those publications, which assume to be the sole legitimate teachers and

70 Ibid., v–vii.

> judges of theology, called "Religious Matters" and contradicted in others; but they all, of every party, creed, and denomination, united in one concurrent testimony that these opinions were novel and heretical.[71]

Of course Henry Drummond overstated things, but he was encountering the disapproval that was experienced by so many of the prophetic enthusiasts of the first half of the nineteenth century. The "prophets" frequently were genuinely puzzled that they met disapproval when they put forward new ideas that they believed were actually old ideas being based, they believed, upon the original intent of the Almighty as expressed in the scriptures. Being anything but a man who accepted criticism, Drummond continued:

> Not being in the habit of reading Magazines, from considering them, even in their best form, as calculated to furnish spurious and superficial information, and to be therefore rather prejudicial than otherwise to sound doctrine and practical godliness, we were much surprised at what was advanced; and still more so at finding that however their respective opinions varied upon every other branch of religion, doctrinal and ceremonial, they were unanimous in spurning the belief of the personal coming of our Lord before the millennium, and in rejecting the idea of His kingdom on earth ever being more remarkably displayed than in a wider extension of the present state of Christendom.[72]

Unlike so many meetings, documents, and collective events in Church history, the Prophetic House Parties of 1826–30 held at Albury Park have been underplayed in the chronicles of nineteenth-century developments. This is not the fault of historians, for they have not been left much to work with. Henry Drummond was just the opposite of a good publicity agent: he suppressed accurate information and handed out a version of the Albury meeting that was almost perfectly designed to kill historical interest. Further, the cohesiveness of his study group

71 Ibid., vi.
72 Ibid., v–vi.

dissolved at the 1830 meeting, held unusually in the summer months. This assembly dealt with, and in large degree endorsed, speaking-in-tongues as being inspired by the Holy Spirit. This then-rare practice was being engaged by some Scottish women and was catching on in England, particularly in the Rev. Edward Irving's London church.[73] The phenomenon made Irving uneasy (although he eventually accepted speaking-in-tongues as spiritually valid) and made Drummond excited. On top of this, at this time Drummond and some of the senior elders of Irving's congregation were beginning to talk of founding a new denomination – again, Edward Irving was hesitant; but he finally accepted a subordinate role in what eventually became the Catholic Apostolic Church, a wondrous amalgam of proto-Pentecostalism (speaking-in-tongues was practised) with a synthetic high-church ritual and secret formularies that made even the highest of the Tractarians seem liturgically pallid.[74] Most members of Drummond's college of prophetic exigetes scuttled away, and very few of the individual members of the Albury Park coterie later recorded their memories of the sessions. As for the larger circle of individuals who were indirectly influenced by Albury Park, they seldom admitted any significant debt; the Albury consortium of the 1820s came to be (unfairly and anachronistically) associated with what was called in derision in the 1830s "Irvingism": a combination of alleged heresies that, by endorsing the disorder and indiscipline of speaking-in-tongues, and by creating an entire new liturgy and a new form of apostolic order, repulsed almost all the Protestant prophetic enthusiasts.[75]

73 Grass (2011), 173.

74 See Father Flegg's sympathetic history (1992), based on his unusual access to the tightly restricted archives of this secretive and virtually extinct group.

75 The retrospective distancing of Anglican (and former Anglican) students of biblical prophesy from "Irvingism" was a two-way street. Not only did the former group both minimize and directly deny being influenced by Albury, Drummond, Irving, and/or the Catholic Apostolic Church, but the latter group and its heirs denied having been directly influenced by other denominations. Flegg argues (435–9) that the eschatology of Brethrenism in general and of John Nelson Darby in particular had nothing to do with the Catholic Apostolic Church. He suggests that his group only came to influence Angli-

One picks up only a few indirect indications of Albury Park's influence on the Irish strand of English-language evangelicalism, but not many. As mentioned earlier, John Nelson Darby's first extended writing on biblical prophecy (most likely written in 1828 or 1829) was primarily a response to Edward Irving's translation and publication of Manuel Lacunza's 1791 treatise. Darby was critical, but Irving's name was not demonized, which for Darby was unusually tolerant.[76] Indeed, if one goes a bit earlier, to the beginning of 1828, when Darby was on his convalescent bed, he seems to have become conversant with the front-edge prophetic notions that circulated around Irving, Drummond, and their associates. Thus, an extract from the late-life memory of John Gifford Bellett, one of Darby's earliest and most faithful followers, is revealing:

> In the beginning of 1828 I had occasion to go to London, and there I met in private and heard in public those who were warm and alive on prophetic truth, having had their minds freshly illuminated by it.
>
> In my letters to J.N.D. at this time, I told him I had been hearing things that he and I had never yet talked of, and I further told him on my return to Dublin what they were. Full of this subject as I then was, I found him quite prepared for it also, and his mind and soul had travelled rapidly in the direction which had thus been given to it.[77]

Bellett was writing at a time (c. 1870) when to indicate with specificity that he had himself learned great things from the members of the Albury circle, much less from the Rev. Edward Irving himself, would have been nearly impossible. Bellett was willing to state that John

---

can views of the prophetic scriptures in the first half of the twentieth century when, as the denomination dwindled rapidly, most of its surviving members began to worship in Anglican churches (438–9).

76 "Reflections upon the Prophetic Inquiry," CW, 02001, passim.

77 This is in a printed extract from a letter by Bellett to James McAllister, c. 1870 in [John Gifford Bellett], *Interesting Reminiscences* (London 1884), 3.

Nelson Darby was informed of what was going on in advanced prophetic circles in England and that he was at least moderately sympathetic with the notions of the colloquia of "prophets" – but to mention the words "Irving," "Drummond," or "Albury Park" in connection with Darby would have been close to committing the mysterious sin against the Holy Spirit.

That reminiscence by Bellett concerned early 1828. To go back slightly farther among the Dalyland evangelical Anglican elite – to a time when Irving and Albury were not words that could not be spoken – Lady Powerscourt in 1826 knew about the impending inaugural Albury Park meetings. She was confident of her right to attend and modestly optimistic that it would be illuminating. She wrote to the Rev. Robert Daly that "I am going to the prophets' meeting at Mr Drummond's"[78] and returned to start her own fortnightly meetings at Powerscourt and eventually to host a series of seminal conferences. She was a deeply spiritual person and, in addition, very well understood Protestant Irish religious chic. As a reviewer in the *Christian Examiner and Church of Ireland Magazine* noted in 1829, "the notion of the personal advent of Christ to reign with his saints upon earth for a thousand years, is becoming, if we might so express ourselves, absolutely fashionable." The comment was in a review of a book on the last-days by the Rev. Edward Irving. "And among its many advocates, the Rev. writer in question towers aloft, a very Ajax above his fellows."[79]

78 Quoted in Mrs Hamilton Madden, *Memoir of the Late Right Rev. Robert Daly* (London 1875), 150. The letter is from 1826 but otherwise undated, although certainly written before the early December start of the prophetic meetings. The Albury lists that have been reconstructed include no women, but that is not an indication that no women were there. On Lady Powerscourt's own prophetic soirées, see ibid., 119, and [Mrs Hamilton Madden], *Personal Recollections of the Right Rev. Robert Daly* (Dublin 1872), 18. These events are not to be confused with the large house parties Lady Powerscourt hosted later.

79 Anon. review in *Christian Examiner and Church of Ireland Magazine*, vol. 8 (April 1829), 288–92, quotations from 288–9.

The first Prophetic House Party in Ireland took place in the west of Ireland in 1829. The Rev. Edward Synge (1798–1859),[80] curate to the archdeacon of Tuam from 1823 onward, was appointed rector of Kilerin Union in the province of Tuam in March 1829. One of his first actions was to convene a week-long residential party in his new glebe to encourage the clergy of the province to study prophecy. Following the Albury Park pattern, "the whole period of their abode under his hospitable roof, from early morn till their separation at night, was devoted to the word of God and prayer."[81] This differed from the later Powerscourt conferences in its being limited to west of Ireland Church of Ireland clergymen. However, it was very much Dalyland in character: the Rev. Edward Synge was the younger son of Francis Synge of Glanmore Castle, the brother of John "Pestalozzi" Synge, the Anglican lay leader who worked most closely with the early Brethren, and a cousin of Francis Synge Hutchinson, who had provided his Dublin residence for the first Brethren meeting house. The Rev. Edward Synge was active in evangelical and prophetic circles until the ill health of his wife drove him into early retirement in England in 1837.

The Rev. Edward Synge's house party in the far west may have encouraged the Viscountess Powerscourt to hold her own residential meetings; but probably more influential was the visit to Ireland in mid-September 1830 of the Rev. Edward Irving and his wife, along with their five-year-old daughter Maggie. In person, away from his pulpit personality, Irving was a figure of mixed sadness and exaltation, domestic devotion, and spiritual self-confidence. He was perfectly constructed to appeal to an emotively spiritual person such as Lady

80 Not to be confused with two other Revs Edward Synge who were also part of the Darby families' social ambit: the Ven. Edward Synge who was archdeacon of Killaloe and resided on his estate, Syngefield, King's County; and his son the Rev. Edward Synge (1753–1818), a sporting clergyman of the same address who was rector of Birr. (There are other Revs Edward Synge in Church of Ireland chronology, but these are the most likely to be confused with the man discussed in the text.) *CDGBSL*, entries for Edward Synge.

81 Joseph d'Arcy Sirr, *A Memoir of the Honorable and most Reverend Power Le Poer Trench* (Dublin 1845), 198; pp. 195–200 are based mostly on a memorandum-memoir by Edward Synge.

Powerscourt, who oscillated between her depressed observation of the declining state of the world (her world, that is, that of the Anglo-Irish Ascendancy) and her fervent affirmation of a great-day-coming. It is easy to understand his appeal. Irving was 6'4" and darkly handsome; yet he carried a load of domestic pain with dignity and without denial. He and his wife had lost their infant son in July, and the melancholy this cast was unmistakable.[82] Further, the once-unassailable giant was at the beginning of religious difficulties that, by the time of his premature death from tuberculosis in 1834, were to see him crumpled and diminished, allotted a minor role in the new organization formed by those who took over his London ministry and turned it into the Catholic Apostolic Church.[83] At the time of his visit to Dublin, Irving was weathering the first wave of a virulent attack on his allegedly heretical Christology led by James Haldane. Irving accepted the orthodox doctrine that Jesus took on human nature and then, as thorough-going a Romantic as one could find, had empathetically extended it to mean that Jesus shared all human suffering and pain; and so Irving was open to the debater's charge that he believed Jesus was capable of sin.[84] On top of that there was the problem, already mentioned, of some of his female associates in Scotland having begun to speak in tongues.

Irving's longtime friend, Thomas Carlyle, remembered seeing Irving in mid-1830 or 1831 (the date is fuzzy): "He was by this time deep in prophecy and other aberrations, surrounded by weak people, mostly echoes of himself and his inaudible notions."[85] That may have been the case in London, but in Ireland, Irving was a palpable force. Essentially, he was sponsored by Lady Powerscourt – he and his wife and young daughter stayed mostly at Powerscourt and were conveyed to and from

82 Oliphant, 387–91.

83 In addition to Flegg's generous history of the Catholic Apostolic Church (1992), see the more astringent Edward Miller, *The History and Doctrine of Irvingism*, 2 vols (London 1878).

84 Oliphant, 354; A. Haldane, 566–7.

85 Thomas Carlyle, in James Anthony Froude (ed.), *Reminiscences* (London 1881), 309. The Victorian historian and polemicist Thomas Carlyle (1795–1881) is not to be confused with Thomas Carlyle (1803–1855), a lawyer who became a major figure in the Catholic Apostolic Church and a colporteur in Germany.

meetings by one of her carriages. Irving preached thirteen times in eight days, probably 15–23 September. These included seminars for clergy and laymen (and women) in south Dublin, Bray, studies for the Wicklow Bible Society, a large meeting at the Rotunda in Dublin, and a night in Delgany (probably with the Rev. William Cleaver) that included an evening meeting and sermon.[86] Undoubtedly, Irving's still-formidable physical presentation was impressive and went down well among the evangelicals in the Anglo-Irish Ascendancy. In this period, Carlyle remembered that Irving, "from the broad hat, brown skin, and flowing black hair," was mistaken for "the one-string fiddler Paganini – a tall, lean, taciturn abstruse-looking figure – who was then, after his sort, astonishing the idle of mankind."[87] Yet, when with his family in the company of Lady Powerscourt, Irving was the model of enviable domesticity. She took Irving and his family in her carriage from Powerscourt to the boat at Kingstown. There they found that the vessel was late. Lady Powerscourt sat with the family at an inn, five-year-old Maggie on her knee, and the wee child unselfconsciously sang a song of her own creation.[88] A family scene that a still-young widow could long to emulate – and a prophet ripe with truth. The next year, 1831, Lady Powerscourt introduced into Dalyland the practice of the Prophetic House Party, and she did so without stint.[89]

86 Oliphant, 392–3, quoting large excerpts from a letter of Mrs Irving to her sister (September 1830), and *Saunder's News-Letter*, 18 September 1830. The dates 15–23 September are the most probable given indirect calendral evidence, and excluding two travel days. The Rotunda meeting is reported by Carter (221); also, Carter (221n122) suggests that John Nelson Darby was not in Ireland at the time of Irving's tour.

87 Carlyle, 311.

88 Oliphant, 393–4, quoting extensively a letter from Irving to his sister, 13 October 1830.

89 During the early 1990s it became "known" to the cognoscenti that a rare old tract established that the first Powerscourt meeting was held in 1830, not 1831. This came from the discovery and circulation of a small pamphlet apparently owned by William Trotter (1818–1865). He was a one-time English Methodist preacher, turned Brethren, who used the pamphlet for his *Plain Papers on Prophecy* (n.d.); see Pickering (2nd ed., 1931, 31–2). The tract that Trotter once owned and that was circulated in the 1990s was a resetting and extension of

an original: [anon.], *Questions for Eight Weeks' Consideration: Addressed to the Church of God* (London 1838). At my request the original 1838 item has kindly been put up in a permanent form by the Duke University library on archive.org, 16 September 2013. The original item listed the dates and topics for the first seven Irish prophetic meetings. The extended version that Trotter owned carried on through three additional meetings, all of them in England. The extended reprint was substantially accurate in its reprinting, although it added a spurious, albeit inconsequential, introduction that actually was not in the original 1838 text. The extended version of the tract owned by Trotter was reprinted in 1998 by Chapter Two, a London faith-based house.

Both the original tract and reprint have Irish conferences occurring annually in the years 1830–36 inclusive and English conferences in 1838, '39, and '41. All these years include a precise indication of dates of meeting and fairly full agendas – except for 1830. The alleged Powerscourt meeting of 1830 is said to have taken place on an unspecified Monday, Tuesday, and Wednesday in September 1830. The actual dates were not known by whoever wrote the original pamphlet in 1838 and the default position should be that, lacking other evidence, the dates were unknown because there was no such conference. Further, not only was the putative conference uncharacteristically brief (only three days), but the agenda of topics is not a good fit with the way the agenda of the 1831–1836 conferences focused discussion. A charitable explanation would be that someone of good intention, but no source of accurate information, confused the various meetings in south Dublin and Wicklow that were held during Edward Irving's whirlwind visitation with the actual Powerscourt conferences that began in 1831. There is no doubt that Lady Powerscourt facilitated Irving's holding several seminars with Dalyland clergy and leading lay people.

CHAPTER NINE

The Drawing Room Prophets, 1831–1832

"It often seems to be God's way to begin with the upper classes to raise up a testimony before kings and rulers."[1] That was the candid view of Miss Anna M. Stoney (1839–1936), as she reflected on her family's long and deep attachment to the Brethren and especially their loyalty to John Nelson Darby. Her father, James Butler Stoney (1814–1897), came of a Tipperary gentry family and he was a longtime Darby loyalist.[2] Her grandmother had been so keen on the prophetic meetings of the 1830s that she shut up her country house and moved to a cottage on the Powerscourt demesne.[3] If one glosses Miss Stoney's observation to mean that the Brethren and their brand of radical evangelicalism had its seed bed in the Irish upper classes, she certainly was right. What she does not say is that, however much this suited the purposes of the Almighty, the arrangement also served the emotional and social needs of a well-defined tranche of the Irish upper and gentry classes – especially the caste we have found in the spiritual satrap of Dalyland, the upper-class reaches of Co. Wicklow and south Co. Dublin.

Yet, while we can scarcely ignore the "worldly" background of the evangelical crisis in County Wicklow in the early 1830s, one must equally accept that the beliefs that developed had an integrity of their own that can be recognized and analyzed independently, on their own

1 Anna M. Stoney, *An Account of Early Days of the So-Called Brethren Movement* (London 1995; orig. pub. date unknown), 1.

2 Henry Pickering (ed.), *Chief Men among the Brethren* (1st ed. 1918; 2nd ed. London 1931), 88–9.

terms as ideational constructs. As Professor Sean Connolly has recently written, "there is now a greater willingness to focus on reconstructing, on their own terms, the beliefs and experiences of particular times and places." He added an important codicil: "If today's historians of religion operate in a more encouraging intellectual climate, however, they also face a new problem: the declining familiarity across society as a whole of the cultural forms that are their central concern."[4] That is why it is necessary at points to explain things to the general reader that are known chiefly to dévotes and to historical scholars – and I hope to do so by ironing away some of the creases and crinkles in terminology that really serve no purpose except as labels among insiders who are fighting each other over microdots of theological difference. In my view, one has to be aware that the texts the evangelicals were working with – the Hebrew and the Christian scriptures – are among the strongest texts ever written and that each set has a power independent of its immediate receptive context: they make us think in certain ways; we do not own them. Thus, the well-beyond-hubris work of the radical evangelicals was truly amazing, for they melded the two texts, Hebrew and Christian, together in totally new ways. By their brashly innovative new hermeneutic techniques they rewrote the story. Whether that was for better or worse is not here for discussion, but it was an intellectual feat of great magnitude, and one does not need to affirm the new beliefs in order to recognize their power.[5]

3 A.M. Stoney, 2. As mentioned in chapter 3 of the present study, Anna Stoney had spent time at Leap Castle during her childhood as a guest of the Darbys and as a friend of their children.

4 Sean J. Connolly, Foreword to J.N. Ian Dickson, *Beyond Religious Discourse* (Milton Keynes 2007), xv. Dickson's study, dealing as it does almost entirely with Ulster sermon literature in the second half of the nineteenth century, is not directly relevant to the present study, but it deserves mention as a model of the methods that can be applied to sermons in a much wider variety of locales.

5 A generation ago, Mark A. Noll, David W. Bebbington, and George A. Rawlyk wrote that "for more than thirty years, a cadre of professional historians (many of them evangelicals themselves, or at least sympathetic to evangelicalism) have been rescuing evangelical movements of the eighteenth and later centuries from historical neglect." That was a percipient statement at the time. The point at present is that an everyday historian – meaning an academic

Timothy C.F. Stunt, the doyen of historians of the Brethren movement and of related evangelical phenomena, has suggested to those on the other side of the intellectual equation – chroniclers of religion, mostly from within the denominational subset being studied – that they can survey social contexts and build them into their discussions without undercutting the faith. Thus: "we are stepping away from the attempt to define millennial hopes solely in doctrinal or exegetical terms. Instead, we are explaining the roots of millennial thinking as much in terms of the millennialists' social, intellectual and psychological presuppositions as in their doctrinal or ecclesiastical interpretation of the scriptures."[6]

This admixture of awareness of the external social contexts of various religious beliefs with an awareness of the within-the-faith logic of those beliefs should not, I must emphasize, be "balanced." The variety of methods are not arguments that are put on some sort of intellectual seesaw and made to go up and down in synchrony by virtue of their being artificially balanced. The complexity of the situation we are dealing with requires two complementary resolutions: to use the variety of historical tools at hand and to realize that nobody is going to be entirely happy with what you do. That is simply the nature of the business.

Jaroslav Pelikan, one of the truly great historians of early Christianity, wrote that "the core of the Christian faith is pessimism about life and optimism about God."[7] This formulation certainly fits the young Irish Anglican evangelicals who came of age during the 1820s. Born

---

historian who has no particular inclination toward evangelicalism – nevertheless has to recognize it as a major cultural constellation and should try to understand on a wide perspective basis how it came to be such. Noll, Bebbington, and Rawlyk, "Afterword: The Generations of Scholarship," in Noll, Bebbington, and Rawlyk (eds), *Evangelicalism: Comparative Studies of Popular Protestantism in North America, the British Isles and Beyond, 1700–1990* (New York 1994), 411.

6 Timothy C.F. Stunt, "Trinity College, John Darby, and the Powerscourt *Milieu*," in Searle and Newport, eds (2012), 73.

7 Jaroslav Pelikan, *The Shape of Death* (New York 1961), 5.

just before or after the turn of the century – Lady Powerscourt and John Nelson Darby shared 1800 as their birth year – in their chrysalis and imago years the Anglican evangelical cohort underwent the emotionally and cognitively disruptive experience of being members of a highly privileged elite whose purchase on power began to slip sharply. This slippage was hard on Protestants of privilege in a general sense, but religiously it was more than a mere declination. Those young persons who were most allegiant to the Church of Ireland felt the sharpest pain. They watched, or tried to fight back, as the Catholics gained Emancipation, as the United Kingdom government reduced and then abolished the Anglican dominance over state-financed primary education, and then began to carry out the systematic reduction of the Irish Church's revenues. That is why a cadre of the most spiritually devoted became so pessimistic and (as I suggested in chapter 7) began to consider alternative forms of organizational architecture for the faithful in Ireland. Their ecclesiological blueprints were blurred, and when they began building the new foundations they frequently made false starts and went off at crazy angles. Nevertheless, their ecclesiological concerns served as a foundation for their new and strangely optimistic eschatology, a mixture of projected violence and a happy future.

Lady Powerscourt illustrates this well. In spring 1831 she observed to a friend that "the church and the world are like tumbled drawers." As an apocalyptic hope, she quickly added: "May the great Head of the church, the King of the universe, quickly come and put all in order!"[8]

It is fair to examine in more detail one probable source of deep pessimism that characterized Lady Powerscourt; and we will deal with her apocalyptic hopes later. Even her sanitized published letters frequently cry out in spiritual distress. She shared the pain of devoted Anglicans of her generation as her Church lost purchase in the Irish polity, but there was more going on than that. Even as she planned the first grand Powerscourt conference for the autumn of 1831, she was situated in a highly uncomfortable social ambiguity, one that most likely could be resolved only painfully.

8 Lady Powerscourt to ____, 14 May 1831, reproduced in Robert Daly (ed.), *Letters and Papers by the Late Theodosia A. Viscountess Powerscourt*, 3rd ed. (Dublin 1839), 151.

Despite her occupation of the magnificent Powerscourt estate, it all was on loan. Her stepson (Richard Wingfield, sixth viscount) would come of age 18 January 1836, and thereafter the estate would be his. That was a dark cloud, growing blacker with each passing year, and Theodosia, Viscountess Powerscourt (her usual formal title; less formally she was known simply as Lady Powerscourt), knew full well that only rarely (and not in her case) were dower houses provided for widows of Irish aristocrats. Yet there was more: Theodosia's future descent into renting rooms in Dublin – or living in a distant wing of the big house, barely tolerated by whomever her stepson married – would for her be a social eviction even more galling than that experienced by most Irish upper-class widows: in strict protocol, she was in fact not even the Dowager Viscountess Powerscourt.

The painfully bizarre situation was that Richard Wingfield (c. 1730–1788),[9] Third Viscount Powerscourt, had married in 1760 Lady Amelia Stratford (??–1831), daughter of the first earl of Aldborough. Lord Powerscourt was a great builder: he completed the massive County Wicklow house, designed by Richard Cassels, which had been begun at about the time of his own birth, and himself commissioned Powerscourt House, on William Street, Dublin, designed by Robert Mack.[10] This was his own townhouse and definitely not a dower house. When the third viscount died in 1788 the main estate was inherited by the fourth viscount and the Dublin house was put in trust for the three sons and three daughters of the fourth viscount. Lady Amelia (née Stratford) Wingfield was left an annuity of £600 per annum, which was in addition to considerable resources she had brought with her at marriage and which were protected by jointure.[11] Lady Amelia, now Dowager Viscountess Powerscourt, was not poor, but she owned no

9 The basic genealogical details on the third and subsequent Viscounts Powerscourt and their wives are taken from Charles Mosley (ed.), *Burke's Peerage, Baronetage and Knightage*, 107th ed. (Wilmington 2003).

10 The facade and elevation of Powerscourt House, William Street, are found in Niall McCullough, *Dublin: An Urban History* (Dublin 1989), 107.

11 National Library of Ireland, *Collection List No. 124: Powerscourt Papers*; "Report Number 510" refers to material "now lost," which included the details mentioned above.

estates or dower-protected residence and in 1831, near the end of a remarkably long widowhood, was living on North Great Georges Street with Martha, her unmarried daughter.[12]

Lady Amelia may indeed have been a pleasant person and the fact that Theodosia, Lady Powerscourt, was not the ranking Powerscourt widow was in itself not a functional issue – Irish widows of aristocrats were not too fussy about the title of dowager as it very rarely carried real money with it – and instead tended to call themselves (for example) Lady Powerscourt, as if their husband still were alive. Yet, no matter how deeply spiritual Theodosia may have been, within the tight social world of Dalyland, every time someone made a reference to a Lady Powerscourt, it required a moment of hesitation: which one was being referred to? This was an embedded reference, a citation of the fact that no one of breeding really needed to mention: that even Theodosia, "Good Lady Powerscourt," was just another relict passing through the system.

There was more: if one were being strict, there was a second-in-line to the title of Dowager Viscountess Powerscourt, namely the second wife of the late Richard Wingfield, Fourth Viscount Powerscourt (1762–1809). This was the termagant Isabella (née Brownlow) Wingfield), who had married the fourth viscount in 1796 and bore him three children: two daughters married Anglican clergymen and her son became the famous Church of Ireland preacher the Rev. Hon. William Wingfield. Isabella lived a notably long widowhood: until 1848. The Fourth Viscount Powerscourt was a man of considerable energy and passion. He had vigorously commanded the local yeomanry corps in protecting his part of Wicklow in the 1798 Rising; and a little later he kicked out of his house the messenger whom William Pitt had sent to offer him a marquisate if he would vote for the Union of Great Britain and Ireland.[13] He was one of the last of the old lot, the fiercely patriotic Irish Protestant aristocrats whose style of romantic allegiance to country was so very different from the Catholic nationalism that would be

12 Turtle Bunbury, *The Landed Gentry and Aristocracy of County Wicklow* (Dublin 2005), 62.

13 [Mervyn Edward Wingfield], Seventh Viscount Powerscourt, *A Description and History of Powerscourt* (London 1903), 14.

led triumphantly by Daniel O'Connell. His passions also ran to quality urban buildings and to an attachment to his second wife that went beyond the usual formal requirements of Irish upper class domesticity. Early in the new century, he built a house at no. 6 Ely Place, a quiet road just one street off St Stephen's Green. The family's former Dublin mansion was sold in 1807 to the Irish administration, which used it as an office building. Soon after moving into the new residence on Ely Place, the Fourth Viscount Powerscourt wrote a last will and testament that, while providing most of his estate to his senior male heir and to the other children of his first marriage, left his second wife, Isabella, with something rare in Ireland: an honest-to-goodness dower house. Lord Powerscourt's last will gives no indication that he was unusually aware of impending mortality and seems to have been occasioned instead by the completion of the new house and by his passion for his second wife. He died in July 1809, and Isabella was left with a lifetime right of occupation of a splendid Dublin house and all its furnishings. Therefore, she had an unusually secure position for an Irish widow, particularly a second wife.[14] (The only women in a stronger position were those few individuals who, like Lady Harriet Daly, mother of the Rev. Robert Daly, held title to lands and residences in their own name.)

The generosity to his second wife defined in the testamentary records of the fourth viscount stands in marked contrast in tone and substance to the last will of Richard Wingfield, Fifth Viscount Powerscourt (1790–1823). Written, as was legally necessary, as follow-up to the jointure agreement that preceded his marriage to Theodosia Anne Howard, the will, although far from being generous, was an unusual and touching document. Dated October 1822, it contained a hope that we now know went unfulfilled, the conditional provision of £10,000 to any children of this, his second marriage, when they reached the age of majority; the second marriage was childless. The children of the first marriage were of course provided for and the bulk of the estate was reserved for Richard Wingfield, sixth viscount, who would

14 PRO, (NA), cat. Ref: prob. 11/1511, last will and testament of Richard, Fourth Viscount Powerscourt, probated 11 May 1810 (accessed 12 November 2013). Lady Powerscourt also had jointure rights, but they were not great: 5 percent annual interest on £1,000.

become legally an adult 18 January 1836. The will made thoughtful provision for Lord Powerscourt's primary servants. But what is unusual is that almost every bequest, whether to family or friends or staff, was wrapped in phrases such as "the glad tidings of salvation," "debt of gratitude to our Lord," and "I trust in better hands than merely earthly ones." Considering that Viscount Powerscourt executed the document when he was in the bloom of health and could reasonably expect three or four decades of prosperity and influence, it is clear that the Rev. Robert Daly indeed had led him to a deep sense of evangelical commitment: this was no death-bed document but a statement of abiding religious faith. Thus, £500 was left to the Reverend Thomas Mackie, curate of the parish.[15] A set of three trustees, including the English evangelical leader, the Rev. Charles Simeon of Trinity College, Cambridge, were provided with £3,000 to spend on converting the Irish poor, on bringing the Christian gospel to India, and for the aid of the "poor blacks" in Sierra Leone. Still, the bequest to Theodosia, though kind, did not follow the romantic precedent of the fourth viscount. There was no dower house, though as one of the legal guardians of the children of Lord Powerscourt's first marriage, Theodosia had the right to occupy the Powerscourt estate until young Richard came of age. In a noteworthy gesture, Theodosia was to be given £1,000 in addition to whatever she was due under her marriage contract. In perspective, however, one notes that the governess who raised the children of the first marriage was also to be given £1,000, plus £200 annually for life. The total amount was roughly what Theodosia, with the aid of her jointure income, likely would receive.[16] When the will was drawn up, however, all that was expected to be in the far future.

Then, suddenly, in early August 1823, Theodosia, not long into her twenties, was thrown into a bear pit. Her husband died, and she was expected to be a chatelaine, manage a massive household, and keep

15 Mackie, who had been appointed in 1814, served under Robert Daly until 1835 (*CDGBSL*, 318).

16 PRO (NA), cat ref: prob. 11/1682, last will and testament of Richard, Fifth Viscount Powerscourt, probated 21 February 1824. As was the practice with major Irish estates that involved property and investment in both Ireland and England, this will was probated in both London and Dublin.

the children of the first marriage on the right path spiritually. It is surprising that she did so well, and one has to feel considerable sympathy for her: she was caught in a domestic oubliette; although to outsiders it may have looked as if she had a soft life, she had to find her situation increasingly painful. Consider: she was by far the youngest and least worldly of the three living women who had been widowed by successive Viscounts Powerscourt (specifically, the third, fourth, and fifth). Those who had preceded Theodosia were of families at least as influential as her own. Lady Amelia Stratford, a daughter of the earl of Aldborough in the Irish peerage, and secondly Isabella Brownlow, who is sometimes mentioned as being the daughter of an Ulster linen merchant, as if he were in trade. Far from it. Her father, William Brownlow (1726–1794) was one of the largest landowners in Co. Armagh and was an MP for the county for more than forty years. He was one of the Wide Streets Commissioners of Dublin, a charter subscriber for the creation of the Bank of Ireland, and the owner of a large residence on Merrion Square. The half-brother of Isabella (she was the product of a second marriage), was also named William Brownlow (1755–1815); he not only inherited the massive Armagh estates and almost automatically a county seat in parliament for Armagh (held both before and after the Union) but was rich enough to found his own bank.[17] From 1809 onward, Isabella, widow of the fourth viscount, had full control of the house and furnishings of 6 Ely Place, Dublin.

There is no doubt that Isabella was an absolute terror, and the young widow Theodosia, Lady Powerscourt, could not defend herself against her predecessor's aggressiveness. The evidence for this is the candid observation by the Seventh Viscount Powerscourt that all the family pictures he displayed at Powerscourt had in the past been looted by Isabella "sometime in my father's minority and before his marriage," meaning between mid-1823 and early 1836, the period in which Theodosia was in charge of the big house. The old dragon had not only removed the family portraits, but had taken the family miniatures, and these she kept at the Ely Place dower house, save for some she gave to a niece who lived in Gorey. That the young widow Theodosia could

17 *CDIB*, entries on the two William Brownlows.

not protect Powerscourt from a campaign of pillage by the virago is clear; the humiliation implied is obvious. Indeed, Isabella was sufficiently formidable that when the sixth viscount came of age in 1836, he determined to get the pictures and miniatures back – but he did not dare confront the gargoyle directly and instead directed a van to Ely Place when she was away and only then had the pictures carried back home. Even so, some of the miniatures still were missing and had to be purchased from Isabella's niece by the seventh viscount.[18]

The reason that the painful and inevitably humiliating social tectonics that pressed upon Theodosia are important is that they provide one of the few windows we have into the private social pain, torsion, and constriction to which the members of the cohort of young Anglican evangelicals could be subject, quite apart from their shared perception of the decline of Irish society as they knew it. One feels sympathy for the young Lady Powerscourt, but without being in any way patronizing: she had courage and her own intellectual and religious resources. Of course she is not typical, but she is representative – in the sense that she reminds us that the young men and women who were so wrenched by what they understood as the increasing perversity of the political and the social order and the rapid decline of their Church's position also were individuals with their own personal problems. The self-control and costive personal dignity that was common among the young Anglo-Irish evangelicals means that they rarely complained about such things, and certainly their Victorian biographies, even when they are spiritually revealing, rarely peek behind the social curtain. Those individuals who eventually became Brethren were distinguished at life's end by obituaries that are chiefly about God and reveal very little about mortal life. When we make the empathetic leap and recognize that there were self-specific as well as general social-class considerations that made Theodosia, Lady Powerscourt, feel at times that her life was a hell to be escaped, we can legitimately do the same for her co-religionists, socially privileged though they too may have been.

None of this explains away the new religious beliefs, or the embryonic system of theology, through which the young Anglican evangelic-

18 [Wingfield], *Powerscourt*, 16.

als tried to cope. Their nascent theological revolution had an ideational integrity that was not dependent upon its pained origins. Still, the beginnings are worth remembering: Christianity has always taught that origins count.

The Powerscourt conferences break into two sets: those held in the massive rural estate in 1831 and '32, under the chairmanship of the Rev. Robert Daly, and those of 1833, '34, '35, and '36. The former were intended to operate within the spiritual guidelines of the Church of Ireland and were kept just barely within those bounds. After 1832 Daly resigned his association, and the 1833 conference at Powerscourt was chaired by John Synge of Glanmore Castle, a stay-in-the-church lay sympathizer with Brethren concerns. The next two conferences were held in Dublin in 1834 and '35 at the no. 6, Ely Place dower house, which suggests that Theodosia, Lady Powerscourt, was able to make some sort of temporary truce with her predecessor. Then the 1836 meeting had a suburban Dublin hotel as its venue, a decided comedown from the previous events and an indication that grand prophetic house parties in Dalyland were no longer in fashion.

The Powerscourt house parties were a basic skeletal structural component of the semi-opaque history of early transatlantic evangelical development: they, and certainly not the allegedly "Irvingite" Albury Park residential meetings of the 1820s, were the acceptable acknowledged template for the Islington, London, meetings of the Mildmay Park Second-Advent Conferences of 1876ff (convened by the Anglican clergyman, the Rev. William Pennefather, a collateral relative of John Nelson Darby)[19] and thereby of the Niagara Conferences of 1883ff that were instrumental in forming twentieth-century American

19 The Rev. William Pennefather (1816–1873) was educated at TCD and priested in 1842. He began his career in Ballymacagh in the diocese of Kilmore. His father, Edward Pennefather, was the brother-in-law of Susannah Darby Pennefather, the sister of John Nelson Darby. See the Pennefather entries in *BDEB* and the various references to John Nelson Darby's family ties in the present study.

evangelicalism in its more fundamentalist guise. Nevertheless, historians have frequently written more confidently about the Powerscourt parties than is justified.[20] In fact, we know what the guests talked about, but do not even have a list of who attended or an accurate idea of who said what: the only direct transcript of anyone's opinion is the regretful, almost heartbroken peroration of Robert Daly as he left the group in 1832. There are a few anecdotal memoirs written years later that mention events, and there is a Brethren-printed tract of 1838 that gives the schedule of annual topics, but even this is derivative from very spare newspaper accounts and has significant inaccuracies.[21] Mostly one must proceed inferentially, and here I think the best strategy is not to fossick for agreed-conclusions from the meetings but rather to look at

20 My direct point is that Brethren beliefs (and thus the Dispensationalism that runs through one form of evangelicalism) developed less clearly than is often taken to be the case by chroniclers from within the tradition. That granted, ideology around early Dispensationalism did evolve quickly in the early 1830s. I will signpost clearly the inferences of probable developments, but with the awareness that these are only probability statements and certainly not beyond all reasonable doubt.

21 [anon.], *Questions for Eight Weeks' Consideration. Addressed to the Church of God* (London 1838). See my discussion of the character of this item in chapter 8, note 89. The topic list appears not to have been compiled by anyone who was present. The alleged 1830 meeting was a non-event. The usually cited sources for 1831 and 1832 are program listings in the *Christian Herald*, vol. 2 (December 1831), 287, and vol. 3 (December 1832), 290 (cited in Grayson Carter, *Anglican Evangelicals* (Oxford 2001), 203n34). In fact, the report of the discussion menu for 1832 originated in the *Christian Examiner and Church of Ireland Magazine,* new ser., vol. 1 (October 1832), 790–2. A discursive but guarded discussion of the 1832 conference was written anonymously by John Nelson Darby for the *Christian Herald* (December 1832), republished in LJND, vol. 1, no. 2, attached to a letter he wrote to Plymouth friends 15 October 1832, just after the second Powerscourt conference closed. The discussion program in LJND is an addition by the editor of the *Christian Herald* to the report Darby made of the conference of 1832 and is a lift from the *Christian Examiner.* A letter by "Dionysius" in the *Christian Examiner and Church of Ireland Magazine,* new ser., vol. 4 (September 1835), 639, 641–2, gives the 1835 program. Besides Darby's report, the only direct contemporary published testimony of the actual program is for 1833 and comes from the diary of Henry Craik and was first published in 1866: W. Elfe Tayler, *Passages from the Diary and letters of Henry Craik, of Bristol*, 2nd ed. (London 1866), 166–9.

the ground rules of the discussions and then to infer what the participants were most apt to argue about and where the boundaries of their disagreements were located and also where they were most likely to be in harmony.

The key to understanding this first Powerscourt conference, particularly its being a success at least in terms of semi-amiable discourse, is that it was conducted within the canons of *noblesse oblige*. Some thirty-five clergyman, fifteen laymen, and about a score of ladies were in attendance. (The acknowledged presence of women was unusual in theological circles of the time; not so unusual is that they were not to speak during the formal sessions.)[22] Most participants probably were local; some, though, came from England and distant parts of Ireland. The guests from outside the Wicklow and south Dublin area easily could be accommodated as houseguests of Lady Powerscourt, and this was not an irrelevant detail: the inhibitions and good manners of a civilized house party were in effect. As far as debate was concerned, the house rules were those of the Church of Ireland as regnant in Dalyland. The chairman of proceedings was the Rev. Robert Daly, whose evangelicalism was increasingly energized by a faith in the Second Coming of Jesus and an interest in the biblical prophecy related to it: all within the Church. The Synge family was important at this meeting, and one detects the gentle, almost revered voice of Francis Synge Hutchinson who had given over his house in Dublin to the first Brethren meeting, as well as the louder tones of his cousin, John Synge of Roundwood, the heir-designate of Glanmore Castle. A Dalyland gentleman (married to the daughter of the Hon. Frances Hely-Hutchinson), Francis Synge Hutchinson's abbreviated adult years (d. 1832) were given over to spiritual contemplation and encouragement of churchmen to study prophecy.[23] Among the clergy were John Nelson Darby and Edwin Hoare, a Limerick rector who reported very briefly on the conference

22 Carter, 204, based on *Christian Herald*, vol. 2 (December 1831), 287.

23 Frances Synge Hutchinson, *Remarks on Second Peter, Chap. 1, Ver. 19–21* (Dublin 1830), and *Letter to the "Christian Examiner"* (Dublin 1830). Synge Hutchinson was remembered by John Gifford Bellett as a churchman who was a model of decency and gentle open-mindedness. Bellett says that he was introduced to him by John Nelson Darby ([John Gifford Bellett], *Interesting Reminiscences* [London 1884], 3–4).

for his prophetically focused journal, the *Christian Herald*, and the Venerable William Digby (1799–1866), archdeacon of Elphin, who (like Robert Daly) had strong prophetic interests but was determined to keep the Church of Ireland intact.[24] Given the very strong social conventions that restricted this meeting (see below), in the absence of any guest list it seems most likely that this first conference was very much a Dalyland set piece, with perhaps the odd Dissenter present under the veil of vague ecumenism.

The genteel conventions that kept this first Powerscourt conference a polite house party were two-fold. One of these was that the participants in formal meetings were restricted to reading prepared statements on the several questions that were on the agenda. And there was no public debate or argument.[25] With these conventions accepted, and with the Rev. Robert Daly in the chair, the whole week of meetings, conducted in the grand ballroom of Powerscourt, seems to have been carried out with great politesse. This is not to say that deep religious fervour was missing, or that there were not sessions of intense private prayer and deep conversations on long walks, but genteel decorum was maintained.

Secondly, the house-party conventions were respected because Lady Powerscourt combined her religious enthusiasm with her aristocratic responsibilities to the local gentry and to her more substantial yeoman tenants. She made the meetings a public event. Mrs Hamilton Madden, a young girl at the time, recalled that "all the neighbourhood were invited to hear them twice a day." She meant, of course, respectable Protestants, not the entire populace. "At the evening meeting they had tea first, and the ladies went dressed for the evening; on which occasions, I think a little more vanity than usual crept in, as I well remember one of my aunts being very particular about her 'discussion cap.'"[26]

24 Jonathan D. Burnham, *A Story of Conflict* (Carlisle 2004), 116.

25 *Christian Herald*, vol. 2 (December 1831), 287, cited by Burnham, 117.

26 [Mrs Hamilton Madden], *Personal Recollections of the Right Rev. Robert Daly* (Dublin 1872), 18–19. Mrs Madden was capable of muddling theological subtleties but was very sharp on social details, and she possessed a large cache of Daly letters and related material.

The dear old Aunt had every right to be vain, for the venue was definitely where the Quality met. In the later vocabulary of Victorian evangelicalism, the term for colloquia of several days duration was a "residential conference," and that is accurate as far as it goes. But, in this case, what a residence: more a palace, actually, and certainly one designed to affect the mind of any of its residents, temporary or permanent. It was the mid-eighteenth century design of Richard Cassels, whose Palladian monuments include Carton House and Leinster House, the latter being the present home of the Irish parliament. Sixty-eight or more rooms comprised Lady Powerscourt's residence (no one was exactly certain how many there really were), and the house was nothing if not an exercise in style over function. For example, the ground floor contained a massive entrance hall (40' × 60'), minor reception rooms, and a dining room in one wing of the house and the kitchen and cellars in the opposite wing, so that for any major meal servants ferrying dishes and wines were flying through the main entrance hall in an effort to get things to the table before everything reached a tepid temperature. Guests arriving late for dinner faced the danger of being run over in the entrance hall by the evening's menu. Curiously, the important social rooms were on the next floor. The dominant location was the salon, or ballroom, which today would be large enough to hold the finals of the Olympic beach volleyball competition. Just add sand: the room was sixty feet long, forty wide, and had a forty-foot high ceiling. The ultimate umpire's chair was the throne carved for George IV's visit in August 1821. Around this room were marble statues and busts of the great thinkers in classical history, plus those of some modern statesmen and a few Irish-themed paintings. Over all this hung two massive chandeliers. It must have been a joy to conduct a parliament of the spiritual future in such a space and, when necessary, adjourn to one of the panelled side rooms to have an intimate conversation; or to walk on the terraced lawns. These were not the famously strict gardens laid out later in the century: these informal lawns, with their terraces falling away gently into the mist, must have been restful on the soul.[27]

The formal agenda for the week of 3–7 October 1831 was as polite as a handwritten dinner card, albeit more confusing. The meetings were convened on a Monday at six in the afternoon and concluded Friday

27 Terence Dooley, *The Decline of the Big House in Ireland* (Dublin 2001), 18–24.

in the late afternoon: that fit the schedule of the clergy who were attending, and for the rest of the guests it was assumed that they took the usual Friday-through-Monday for recreation. This was not a working-class audience. The program of discussion, somewhat confusing in places, was as follows:[28]

MONDAY.	*Evening,* October 3. The gifts of the Spirit to be considered.
TUESDAY.	The intention of the end being first in the ordering of the Lord's decrees declared to be the end of creation and redemption? How does each dispensation further the means and answer the end? In this view, are Christ's people now in their right position? (including, Is it present duty to resist and endure corrupt institutions?)
WEDNESDAY.	Proof if 1260 days means days or years, connected with which, the sketch of Daniel and Revelation, whether it be literal or symbolical?
THURSDAY.	Last great and terrible conflict at the coming of Christ. Who the power that heads it? Against whom? Signs by which this power to be known? Proof whether saints to suffer in it?
FRIDAY.	What to be the state of the world and state of the Church at coming of Christ? What cause to think from Scripture that these are or are not the last days? This to include whether Ezekiel's temple is to be before or after the Millennium.

No matter how hard one tries to get into the mind of the organizers, the program makes little sense either logically or emotionally or indeed, in places, syntactically. Yet, certainly, the attendees were very bright and very well-educated persons, and they had things in mind that they believed might well fit together, albeit not like a neat two-dimensional jigsaw puzzle. They were working in several dimensions at

28 [anon.], *Questions for Eight Weeks' Consideration*, 6.

once. These dimensions included not just geographical space but time and additionally dimensions that they halfway perceived and tried to investigate: most especially, the mind of the Almighty. All that was entwined with a set of emotional experiences some of them shared with other participants, various epiphanies, the sense of personal imperfection and of their failings eventually being washed away by divine grace. Above all, they shared a belief in God's definitive intervention in the real world sometime in the future: quite soon, many of them believed. Rather than parse the 1831 program in detail (who knows what was said and by whom?), the issues that arose in 1831–32 and thereafter can be put into a semi-logical framework of questions and possible answers.

This is useful, but only if one accepts that one is dealing with fuzzy logic, in the technical sense of the term, for much of the material is related to other items not by deductive thinking but by association and by the imbrication of related concepts and of scriptural references. These things intersect uneasily with each other like the swerving rows of shingles put up by a crew of drunken roofers on a Friday afternoon. Obviously, the issues that the participants debated related to the arguments about proper Church structure (ecclesiology) discussed in chapter 7, but here we are dealing only with the bare bones of their prophetical concerns. Below, within the confines of the participants' shared logic, is the first half of a large program of end-times matters that one infers were the basics of the Powerscourt conference of 1831 (the second half will be taken when we get to the 1832 meeting):

(1) By virtue of the selectivity of the guest list, it is probable that almost all of the participants believed that Jesus-the-Christ would return to Earth again: the Second Advent, or Second Coming, and that this would occur soon. Most (but probably not quite all) accepted, or were at least amenable to, the idea that Jesus would appear in literal physical form: nail prints in his hand, the product of his crucifixion being the proof of his physicality. This physical literalism was certainly not the dominant form of Christian belief at the time and had been rarely voiced in post-patristic mainstream theology before, roughly, the beginning of the nineteenth century. Not that Jesus's Second Coming had been rejected, but it had usually been interpreted either as an allegory for God's final judgment, or as occurring through an undefined, larger-than-the-universe cosmic figure subsuming the temporal order

of Earth. In fact, some of the latter character was attached even to the physical Jesus in the literalistic interpretation, for he was expected to come down from the heavens with power and majesty and to direct great events (details varied enormously).

(2) The selective nature of Lady Powerscourt's guest list meant that most of the invited participants were pre-sold on the idea of the Second Advent of Jesus being an apocalyptic event. It was not going to arrive as a culmination of a long period of increasing righteousness, but with a crash, an interruption of ever-more-evil earthly life.

(3) Given the apocalyptic nature of the Second Coming, the next question was: would it be a single, explosive event that immediately ended human time and led swiftly to the final judgment of all humanity, or would it be a massive event that would introduce a new temporal order that would itself last until the later execution of the final judgment? Both theories involved an apocalyptic end to everyday human history. Most probably the majority of participants at the Powerscourt conference came around to the idea that there would be some sort of time gap[29] – the "millennium" being the most frequent and literalistic label for that period – before yet another appearance of Jesus and the clearing up of Satan and evil once and for eternity. That this approach involved something its proponents almost never labelled accurately – it would be a Third Coming of Jesus – is significant and probably sensible: given that the bulk of the Christian community still was resistant to the idea of a physical Second Coming, propounding a Third rather loudly would have been counterproductive.

(4) Was there to be one resurrection of the dead or two? The theory that involved a millennium usually tied the Second Advent to the lit-

29 See chapter 8's discussion of the Rev. William Burgh, who, in his early twenties was a leading articulator of the single big-ending interpretation. He came around to accepting the idea that some indeterminate time gap would follow the Second Advent and the ultimate end of time. One should emphasize that several leading Irish evangelicals agreed with Burgh's original position and rejected both the idea of a millennium (or its equivalent) and of the necessity for two resurrections of the dead. For example, the highly esteemed Rev. Peter Roe, who attended the 1832 conference but apparently not the 1831 conference, was of this view (Samuel Madden, *Memoir of the Life of the Late Rev. Peter Roe* [Dublin 1842], 441).

eral bodily resurrection of the faithful dead and their assumption into Heaven. (Again, details varied and provided wide space for debate.) A second resurrection at the end of time would sort out everybody else as part of the last judgment.

(5) The matter that probably pinched most deeply on the emotions of those present was the question of whether or not the literal and apocalyptic Second Advent (in whichever of the forms one embraced it) could be predicted. The predisposition of Lady Powerscourt's guest list almost certainly was that it would be occur soon, but how soon? If one were a serious evangelical student of scripture, there were three possibilities. (a) The interpretative position that holds the prophetic parts of the scriptures were already fulfilled in the past history of the Christian Church. This concept was unpalatable to most evangelicals, as it implied that the Second Advent might not be literal after all. That idea not being taken on board, the Powerscourt people seem to have been split between (b) those who believed that one could use the biblical prophecies to make some sort of reasonable prediction about when the great event would occur and (c) those who believed that prediction was impossible.[30] It is hard to know who believed what, as beliefs were in flux.[31] Views on whether or not one could actually

30 Here, I should indicate that as later doctrinal and hermeneutic disputes have taken place, a somewhat misleading, pseudotechnical vocabulary has emerged. The first group mentioned above are sometimes called "preterists," the second "historicists," and the third "futurists." This is very confusing. The first term is unnecessary jargon, and the second and third are confusing in normal speech. The so-called "historicists" were trying to predict the future. Everyone who expected the Second Advent believed, by definition of their expecting it, that it would be in the future. To outsiders, a curious point is that those of the predictability school and those of the unpredictability school of apocalyptic evangelicals both expected the Second Advent to occur soon. For other comments on avoiding pseudotechnical terms in dealing with nineteenth-century apocalyptic evangelicals, see chapter 8, note 10.

31 Burnham, 116–17, suggests that William Digby and John Nelson Darby at this point held the predictability position and that the unpredictability position was held by Robert Daly and by William Burgh. Re: Burgh, see also Le Roy Froom, *The Prophetic Faith of Our Fathers* (Washington 1946), vol. 3, 658–9. I think Burnham may be wrong about Darby, but, given Darby's volatility in this period of his life, one does not wish to be dogmatic. In a remarkably

calibrate the future arrival of Jesus's Second Advent did not correlate with views about whether or not there would be a millennium or its equivalent. These concepts cross-hatched, so four positions were possible when these two basic issues were put in play together.

(6) One item on the program of the 1831 house party demands particular attention at this point. This is the matter of the 1,260 days, and it requires notice because it provides a clear indication of the nature and detail of the scriptural epigraphy that the bright young evangelicals were engaged in. In addition to their drive for spiritual knowledge, one has to recognize that these minds were attracted by the intellectual challenge of code-breaking. Hundreds of these puzzles, having all the addictive power of a good double-acrostic, were engaged by the exegetes. The 1,260 days is one of the best known, and it shows clearly some of the ways the minds of the decoders could work. The way that the item was phrased for the 1831 Powerscourt house party – "proof if 1260 days means days or years, connected with which, the sketch of Daniel and Revelation, whether it be literal or symbolic?" – is a schmier. Yet, it is revealing of one of the emotional-cum-theological needs that the houseguests shared, namely to affirm that in holy scripture there was some sort of a demonstrable line of continuity between the main apocalyptic text of the Hebrew scriptures and its counterpart among the Christian texts: aside, that is, from the authors of Daniel and of Revelation sharing a genius for the description of loathsome imaginary beasts and, manifestly, of John of Patmos's having been familiar with the filigree of the book of Daniel and having adopted several of its tropes and images.

To avoid grounding the new evangelical apocalyptic in something other than the base texts' historical circumstances (Daniel being

ill-tempered set of letters published in the *Christian Herald* (December 1830 and February 1831), he attacked the views of the Irvingite *Morning Watch* (perhaps accurately) and those of the major scholar, the Rev. Samuel R. Maitland (thoroughly inaccurately, as Maitland had never published a word in the *Morning Watch*, though Darby's first letter carelessly made that assertion). Amid several pages of argument about the gender of Hebrew nouns, Darby concluded: "The mystery of Babylon and the papacy have no place in the prophets, or the 1260 days mean years." The letters are collected as "On 'Days' Signifying 'Years' in Prophetic Language," in CW, 02002, quotation from 39.

about the Seleucids, and Revelation about the Romans; therefore, if one took that tack, both were stale-dated and of no use as guides to the ultimate end-times), the common notion among prophetic noetics was to tie together two sets of magic numbers, namely 1,260 from Daniel (9:2ff) and 1,000 from Revelation (20:4). The number 1,260 is in itself a second-level concept, and its usage at Powerscourt indicates that the guests were expected to be quite advanced in their studies. The primary mental habit here on display comes from the famous "seventy weeks of Daniel," wherein modern Christian interpreters learned the use of calendral time as an analogic concept. The seventy weeks are understood by the author of Daniel to be the period from the time when "the word of the Lord came to Jeremiah the prophet, that he would accomplish seventy years in the desolations of Jerusalem" (9:2).[32] In Daniel's usage, this verse could be taken several ways. Depending when one dates the existence of the prophet Jeremiah, it

32 The implied reference is to Jeremiah 25:11, where the prophet predicts that certain nations will serve the king of Babylon for seventy years. It is not a metaphorical usage of time, but a straight prediction in normal reckoning. That is here irrelevant because it is Daniel's rewrite that counts. Using Daniel's allegorical rewrite of Jeremiah's literal prophecy as a base, the remarkable Joseph Mede (1586–1638; see *ODNB)* had constructed a path of decoding that asserted the seventy weeks meant 490 actual years. Mede's posthumous works were influential among late eighteenth- and early nineteenth-century enthusiasts who encountered his ideas in the English translation of his Latin works. I am following his path of exposition, in which he first established the year-day concept by reference to Daniel chapter 9, and only after that construct was secure did he move to the quite different and less compelling reading of chapter 7. Mede's base-date for the 490 years was an equation of Jeremiah's prophetic uttering with the first year of the reign of Darius the Mede (Dan 9:1), who, incidentally, did not exist; Darius I was a Persian. Mede then states that the Destruction of Jerusalem by the Romans happened 490 years later and therefore the seventy weeks of Daniel are weeks of days. That the actual chronology does not work did not bother later adopters of the system. But note that the central magic number of Second Temple apocalyptics was here involved (7, and its variants 49 and 490). This is hardly accidental and similar usage of 7 is also fundamental to the (not known to Mede) Book of Enoch and the Book of Jubilees, as well as to the Revelation of John of Patmos (Joseph Mede, *Daniel's Weekes: An Interpretation of Part of the Prophecy of Daniel* [London 1642], 1–5).

could have been predicting the destruction of the first Temple in literal years, the debasement of the Second Temple by the Seleucids, or of the later destruction of the Second Temple in analogic years, or perhaps literally. The operational point is that prophetically inclined Christians took the seventy weeks of Daniel as a directive to read Daniel's use of the calendar as *non*-literal. Clear enough: what was rarely commented on was that this approach to end-times prophecy was expected to merge seamlessly with the reading of the only text that mentions the thousand-year reign of Christ (Rev. 20:4), and that blessed period was always taken to be a literal one thousand years. For a few, this was unsettling. "To be consistent," one concerned Anglican wrote to his church paper, "should not all be interpreted alike?" He went on to point out that, using the seventy-weeks method and assuming a 360-day year, the millennium after Jesus's return would last 360,000 years. Almost plaintively he asked, "by what right, or with what fairness, can we interpret days to signify years in the former parts of the book, and reject that meaning here?"[33]

That was only the ground-level complication. The seventy weeks taught one use of analogic time but led to a derivative and the guests at the first Powerscourt conference were expected to be able to cope with this complication: Daniel chapter 7 spotlights a mysterious concept for measuring duration: "a time, and times and the dividing of time" (7:25 and 12:7). These units are taken as measures of a sequence of empires that begins with the reign of Belshazzar, an alleged king of Babylon (7:1), and this was to run until four successive evil empires came to an end at God's hand and this would all take "until a time and times and the dividing of time." By a very recondite set of arguments, this becomes 1,260 "days," a period mentioned in Revelation (11:3; 12:6).[34] And, so, a "time" (value=1) and "times" (value=2) and a divided time (value=1/2) is taken to say that 3½ "time" = 360 something. That sum is 360 "days." But previously the prophetic exegetes of this school had

33 "Politelos," letter to the editor, "On the Calculation of Prophetic Time," *Christian Examiner and Church of Ireland Magazine*, vol. 8 (June 1829), 413.

34 Revelation also mentions 42 months (13:5), which could be taken as 1,260 days if months have 30 days. Revelation also uses "time, and times, and half a time" (12:14).

shown that a day in the book of Daniel is equal to a year. Therefore, 1,260 years from some mysterious starting point, something big would happen – or, indeed may already have happened.[35]

Hence, once the houseguests at Powerscourt began their discussion, they were being asked to think in five different time worlds at once; the everyday passage of time; the seventy weeks equals 490 years of Daniel; the year-day principle in reading certain other prophetic texts; the "times" metric when reading others; and simultaneously they were required to decode who or what the various beasts, dragons, and humanoid figures that were sequenced through these multiple time principles were – and to decide what parts of this massive puzzle referred to the infinite time of eternity. This was a prescription for cognitive dissonance on a grand scale, the more so because one aggressively articulate phalanx of the evangelical exigetes held that the biblical prophecies were to be read as being literal – as if deciphering magic

35 I have read Mede (ibid.) fully and cannot understand his reasoning or, alas, that of any of his later followers whom I have read. His approach to chapter 9 of Daniel (seventy weeks) at least has a metric against which to measure the days or years. In contrast, there is no metric for the "time, times, and the dividing of time" in Daniel that makes the figure come out to 1,260 day-years. The number apparently is imported from Revelation. There are in Daniel totalizing numbers of 1,290 (12:11) and 1,335 (12:12), but Mede ignores these and they cannot easily be squeezed to mean 1,260. That said, the entire Mede-derived exercise has some curious problems, not least is the use a calendar year of 360 days duration. Most of the Hebrew writers of Daniel's time were using a 354-day lunar year with an interpolation of an extra month every third year; and others were using a 364-day solar calendar. In whatever case, the calendar year of 360 days enforced by the 1,260 year-day theory loses five days each solar year and over a 1,260-year period, which represents a good deal of slippage, a demerit in a scheme that prophecies the future. How Mede interpreted the linkage of 1,260-year-days to the millennium of Revelation is unclear as he certainly believed in the 1,000-year period. However, as his translator Richard More pointed out, he suppressed some of his writings out of political fear. Thus, one finds Mede summarizing his interpretation of Revelation by showing how Daniel chapter 7 and Revelation 20:4 fit together and foretell Christ's literal 1,000-year reign on Earth with his saints. Mede abruptly concludes by saying, "I leave the whole matter to the Church to be determined by the Word of God" (*The Key of the Revelation* [London 1650], 127).

numbers and unveiling the identity of such things as "a woman clothed with the sun, and the moon under her feet and upon her head a crown of twelve stars" (Rev. 12:1) was not a meta-reading of a cryptogram; it certainly was not literalism, whatever anyone said.

These, and other matters even more confusing and emotionally charged, were on the program card of the first Powerscourt conference. In a later section of this chapter I will discuss the second conference, that of 1832, and will continue the identification of the train of fuzzy logic (again: in the formal sense) that informed the thoughts and prayers of Lady Powerscourt's houseguests.

The great wonder of the 1831 Powerscourt meeting was that the centre held. With Robert Daly, rector of Powerscourt, in the chair, decorum and manners were maintained.

On 11 October 1831, just days after the close of the house party, Amelia, the senior Dowager Viscountess Powerscourt, died. This slightly simplified the life of Theodosia, Lady Powerscourt. The demise and the celebration of Lady Amelia's life was most revealing in that her family drafted an epitaph to be cut into her stone memorial, one that fulsomely praised her virtues. However, the Rev. Robert Daly ruled that no such monument would be allowed unless a scripture text were added: "For all have sinned and come short of the glory of God."[36] Daly still was very much in charge, but that would not continue forever.

"The students of prophecy saw themselves as prophets" William H. Oliver observed concerning Edward Irving, Henry Drummond, and their associates in England.[37] This aspect of the interpreters of proph-

36 [Wingfield], *Powerscourt*, 72.

37 William H. Oliver, *Prophets and Millennialists* (Auckland and London 1978), 124. Oliver is best known as a poet and as a cultural historian of New Zealand and that may explain in part why his perceptive and beautifully written set of observations is frequently ignored in the literature on the history of apocalyptic millennialism. Because his book effectively walls off England from the Celtic countries, he has space to provide for several English exigetes, such as James Hatley Frere of the Society for the Investigation of Prophecy, a student who can best be described as an English millennialist-nationalist, given his view that England was uniquely placed to receive divine mercy.

ecy, at once vatic and aggressive, holds even more for several of the young Church of Ireland evangelicals who came to understand the Second Coming of Jesus as the only cure for the way that the rise of the Roman Catholics and the governmental diminution of the Anglican establishment were leading to a ruination of the world: not just their own world, but the entire world. More than English students of prophecy in the early 1830s, the Irish had a lot to worry about in their immediate vicinity. Granted, the rioting and disequilibrium associated with the electoral reform bills of 1831–32 were unsettling in England, but they were nothing close to the sequence the Irish upper classes experienced from the late 1820s right through the 1830s: Catholics in parliament; loss of Church of Ireland control over most social welfare institutions; the creation of the national schools; the reduction of Church of Ireland revenues ("temporalities") and suppression of several bishoprics (mooted in 1831 and passed into law in 1833); all this amid a "tithe war" by Roman Catholics (and some Presbyterians) against payments to local Anglican clergy. Scant wonder, therefore, that some of the privileged young "prophets" turned against the existing order; equally, it was natural that they used Lady Powerscourt's prophetic house party of September 1832 as a forum for their disquiet.

Besides the belief of the more engaged of the Irish evangelicals that their world was sliding ever-faster toward a precipice, I would infer (or, to be even more circumspect, merely speculate) that one big change occurred between October 1831 and September 1832 and that this radically affected Lady Powerscourt`s meeting: the behaviour and focus of John Nelson Darby. Within the limited evidence we have, a pattern is discernable – not the only possible pattern, but the one that seems to be likely. Darby from the time he walked away from his Calary charge was mightily busy in his own spiritual life, undeniably. That granted, like all human beings, he was living within a specific social world and trying to find his rightful place within it. He asserted himself with increasing effect. It is not an outré metaphor to see the Rev. John Nelson Darby in the later months of 1831 and throughout 1832 as something akin to a once-juvenile buck that emerges from his time of wandering in the wild and judges that he just may be ready to challenge the big stags; and the autumn of 1832 was to be the start of his time of serious combat.

As we have seen in earlier chapters, Darby had trouble with other alpha-males: his distance from his father was barely within telescope range; he poured scorn upon his early benefactor, Archbishop Magee; he quietly put a stiletto into the work of the rising star of Church of Ireland eschatological thought, the Rev. William Burgh; and in 1832 Darby began a vituperative set of pamphlets directed against Archbishop Whately. These cases instance how his personality was constructed. In 1832, John Nelson Darby endeavoured to push aside two big stags, Edward Irving and Robert Daly, both leading evangelical divines. The last thing Darby wanted was to take over the Rev. Mr Daly's parish or the London flock of the Rev. Mr Irving. He desired, however, his views to overcome theirs, at least to the extent that their ideas of evangelical Christianity were in the forefront of those embraced by Lady Powerscourt. Robert Daly had converted the young Theodosia Howard to evangelical Anglicanism and she recognized him as her continuing spiritual mentor; and Edward Irving's apocalyptics had first attracted Lady Powerscourt to prophecy, and his reluctant acceptance of the idea of special higher spiritual "gifts" were on her mind. (The "gifts" – meaning speaking-in-tongues, faith healing, and perhaps divination – were a very explosive issue and had been the topic for the first evening of the 1831 house party, but apparently they had been pushed quietly aside in the bustle of guests' arrival.)

Whether or not there was what St Augustine would have called a "carnal" attraction between Lady Powerscourt and John Nelson Darby is not documentable. What counts here is that Darby managed to dislodge, if not entirely defeat, his two rivals for the spiritual attention of Lady Powerscourt, and the 1832 house party was the scene of his muted triumph.

As mentioned in chapter 7, Darby had travelled a good deal from mid-1829 to late 1831, spending time in Paris, with excursions to London, Cambridge, Plymouth, and Oxford, among other places. These English trips led to encounters that Brethren memoirs later showcase. However, for understanding his character and especially his toughness, I would suggest that Darby's beginning hard-scrabble missionary work in Ireland – intermittent, small pay-off, small-group work – tells us more than his discussion with Oxford dons and Continental theologues.[38]

38 I should warn the reader against taking as genuine an item that is sometimes used as the starting point for a definition of Darby's missionary career. It first

The first stage in John Nelson Darby's hardening was that he tried to convert Roman Catholics. He probably had attempted this in the days of his Calary curateship,[39] but, as we have discussed earlier, with no known results. Yet, he believed it was within his powers, so one finds him linking up with Edward Synge of Dysert (var.: Dysart) in County Clare. This Synge is not to be confused with the other Edward Synges we have already encountered: he was a layman, a second son of George Synge of Rathmore, King's County, which was near to Birr and to the Darby estate. In general, the extended Synge family had done well from Church of Ireland benefices and from acquiring formerly Catholic lands. In this case, Nicholas Synge, bishop of Killaloe from 1745 to 1771, had left his two grandsons roughly 2,000 acres of land in Clare, as well as about 1,100 acres in King's County. Edward Synge of Dysert became estate manager of the Clare land in 1823 for his father and uncle. He had been converted to keen Anglican evangelicalism shortly before his arrival in the west and soon set up three schools for the education of the local Catholics. At first this went well, but Edward Synge of Dysert was a keen proselytizer and soon was using his powers as landlord's agent to try to force school attendance and to encourage Catholics to turn religion. From 1826 onward, a small-scale local war was in train, with shots fired, a school house partially burned, and one

appeared, as far as I can tell, as an unsourced tract printed in 1930, entitled *How the Lost Sheep Was Found: An Incident in the Life of the Late J.N. Darby.* It allegedly is Darby's telling of how he walked up and down over steep hills of Kerry and found an old woman in a cottage and a suffering lad of seventeen or eighteen, in the last stages of consumption. The lad had taken ill after looking for one of his father's lost sheep. With Darby's help, the lad realizes that he himself is the lost sheep. Having accepted Christ as his saviour, and comforted by Luke 15 (where Jesus tells the parable of the lost sheep), he dies. This item has several times been reprinted. T.C.F. Stunt calls this a "romanticised account," and that is gentle comment (Timothy C.F. Stunt, *From Awakening to Secession: Radical Evangelicals in Switzerland and Britain, 1815–35* [Edinburgh 2000], 170n82). The item is bogus. It is written entirely according to twentieth-century literary protocols. Beyond that, it is entirely different in style, register, and (diagnostically) clarity from anything John Nelson Darby ever wrote.

39 A muddy, perhaps accurate, memory held by Darby was of "going from cabin to cabin to speak of Christ," which might be taken as referring to his Calary period. J.N.D. to ___ "Dear Brother," April 1877, in *LJND,* vol. 3, no. 334.

of the local men who attacked Synge's house being sentenced to death (subsequently commuted). John Nelson Darby's ties to this situation were two-fold: social ties in that Edward Synge of Dysert was from the Anglo-Irish ascendancy of the Birr region, as were the Darbys, and he was a nephew of Francis Synge, who owned Glanmore Castle, and a cousin of John "Pestalozzi" Synge, the heir to the estate, and thus an occasional member of the social circle of Wicklow evangelicals; secondly, the three schools were connected to the proselytizing agencies, the London Hibernian Society and, later the Irish Society for the Education of the Native Irish through the Medium of Their Own Language – which was a great favourite of Robert Daly, with whom Darby had not yet broken. In the severe winter of 1828–29, when violence flared, Darby went out to Dysert to support Edward Synge in converting Catholics, keeping the schools open, and encouraging the Protestant tenants and labourers of the Synge estates to be brave and not give in to threats by Catholics against their persons and property. There, in harsh County Clare, John Nelson Darby seems to have had an epiphany. It came in the form of a sheet of paper containing a message from "Captain Rock," one of the names used to issue warning to their opponents by gangs of Catholics who were aggrieved on economic or religious issues.

> I hope you will take notice for your own sake Not to be Disturbing the people of Corofin [where one of the schools was located] by your spreading business. coming like a Thief at night, seducing the people of Corofin by your Bible business and if you don't mind what I say you will meet with your fate at last in Corofin. So, darby return to your own native place. We have heard who you are and What your screaming way of living is [illeg] you rascal. We have listened a long time to your [illeg] which has brought you to the county and if you attempt to come anymore it is your life will end …
>
> Written by Captain Rock[40]

40 CBA, J.N.D./5/2. The Rockite movement is analyzed in James S. Donnelly Jr, *Captain Rock: The Irish Agrarian Rebellion of 1821–1824* (Madison 2009).

Edward Synge stayed on for at least two more years before being driven out temporarily,[41] and Darby, wisely one judges, decided that his talents did not run to converting these people to evangelical Protestantism. He was not quite like the famous Spanish officer at the battle of Kinsale in 1601 who concluded after the disastrous attempt to rescue the native Irish forces from those of the Crown that "surely, Christ didn't die to save these people."[42] But John Nelson Darby, though he was willing to make the occasional attempt,[43] decided not to concentrate his powers on bringing them to the new faith.

Instead, he spent a good deal of the next two years in Paris (where, in the spring of 1830, his stay overlapped with those of both Lady

41 Edward Synge in 1831 had to have police protection. Even so, one of his servants was fatally shot and Synge was saved from mortal injury by a Bible that caught a bullet that would have hit his heart. This was on 16 February 1831, Ash Wednesday. He left Dysert, probably for at least two years, but eventually returned and lived long enough to have acquired estates (most likely long leaseholds) of roughly 5,000 acres by 1851. An admirable discussion of the Dysert events, based on ms. sources, is Flan Enright, "Edward Synge: The Dysert Proselytiser," in *The Other Clare* (1982). Synge family landholdings in Dysert are found in the land data base of the National University of Ireland, Galway, "Estate: Synge (Dysert)," landedestates.nuigalway.ie/landedEstates/jsp/estate-show.isn?id=1840 (accessed 25 December 2013). The three-volume history of the Catholic diocese of Killaloe is relevant. See Ignatius Murphy, *The Diocese of Killaloe in the Eighteenth Century* (Dublin 1991), esp. 162–5 and end maps of the diocese; *The Diocese of Killaloe, 1800–1850* (Dublin 1992), esp. 37–49; *The Diocese of Killaloe, 1850–1904* (Dublin 1995). The bare administrative details of the relevant Anglican parish, Kilnaboy Union, are found in *Fourth Report of His Majesty's Commissioners on Ecclesiastical Revenue and Patronage in Ireland,* 634–5, H.C. 1837 (500), xxi.

42 Thomas J. Mullen Jr., "Sayings by and about Irishmen at War," 3.

43 Thus, in late autumn 1832 he reported to his now-close associate, George Wigram, that "we have had too, readings among the Roman Catholics, with very comfortable success." Darby was referring either to activities in Limerick City or in Westport, Co., Mayo; the letter is unclear, but I think Limerick more likely (J.N.D. to George V. Wigram, undated, *LJND,* vol. 1, no. 5). In this instance, the date "1833" put on the letter by the later editors probably is wrong and should be late 1832, as the letter forms part of a related set dealing primarily with Limerick that runs from *LJND* vol. 1 nos 4–7.

Powerscourt and of the Rev. Robert Daly)[44] and also made visits to Oxford and Cambridge universities and to Plymouth and perhaps Bristol. His expeditions to Cambridge (where he was ill-received by the evangelical pioneer, the Rev. Charles Simeon) and to Oxford (where he made a strong impression among some young evangelicals and picked up some followers, notably George Wigram) have been solidly documented.[45] Undoubtedly, being lionized, if only by a small and youthful Oxford coterie, increased his certainly that he was on the right spiritual path. Certainly he gained confidence. Writing in the late 1850s to the evangelical Prussian theologian, Prof. F.A.G. Tholuck, Darby recalled that in 1830:

> I went to Cambridge and Oxford. In the latter place, some persons who are still engaged in the work, shared my convictions, and felt that the relation of the church to Christ ought to be that of a faithful spouse.
>
> By invitation I went to Plymouth to preach wherever people wished, whether in buildings or in private houses.[46]

Grayson Carter has concluded that: "One of the most significant developments in the early history of Brethrenism was its export from Ireland to England. Here, while the movement first took root at Oxford, it quickly branched out through the peripatetic activity of a handful of young adherents to two important West Country locations: Bristol and Plymouth."[47] This is a defensible judgment as long as one accepts (as does Carter) that there already were spontaneously generated proto-Brethren groups in southern and western England[48] and that,

44 Timothy C.F. Stunt, "Influences in the Early Development of J.N. Darby," in Gribben and Stunt (2004), 61.

45 Stunt (2000), 183–219, places the Oxford matters in detailed perspective.

46 Letter by J.N.D. to Prof Tholuck, *LJND*, vol. 3, no. 226. See chapter 4, note 4, for a discussion of the historicity of this item.

47 Carter, 231.

48 For example, John Gifford Bellett recalled meeting with Sir Edward Denny in Somersetshire "in 1831 or 1832" and discovering that Sir Edward and the daughter of the local Church of England cleric had come to the same beliefs as Bellett "for the last twelve months" and this independently of outside in-

while John Nelson Darby may have been a contributing principal to events, he was not the main cause.

More important in terms of Darby's growing powers of self-assertion, but harder to document, was his activity during his intermittent visits to Ireland. (Harder to document because the grey streets of the towns of western Ireland did not generate the self-celebrating memoirs of Oxford: merely memories of a transient holiness that became vague and disappeared in a generation or less.)[49] In Ireland, Darby engaged in what his critics later called poaching or raiding of the Church of Ireland henhouse. That is, he worked with small groups in the west and south that can be termed, with the benefit of hindsight, "proto-Brethren." Mostly these were Anglicans who met for prayer, intensive Bible study, and, in some groups, a weekly communion service without a clergyman in charge. At this stage, however, it is unfair to accuse Darby of poaching: as we have shown in chapter 7's discussion of ecclesiology, Darby was unclear if he would personally break definitively with the Church of Ireland until well into 1834 and perhaps not until his father's death in 1835.

Between the Powerscourt conferences of 1831 and of 1832, John Nelson Darby darted about – back to Ireland in 1831, on to Oxford again, and to Plymouth, and Bristol and several visits to western and far southern Ireland. Little of this restless motion is well-recorded as far as Ireland is concerned. In Ireland, unlike England, he was forming or nurturing infant assemblies rather than working with the theologically adept sorts of individuals he frequently dealt with in Oxford, London, and Plymouth. John Gifford Bellett remembered a very early proto-Brethren group founded in Ennis, Co. Clare, by "dear and

fluences ([Bellett], *Interesting Reminiscences,* 10). Sir Edward became a loyal adherent of the Brethren, an able hymn writer, and, because of his social position, something of an ornament to the movement.

49 As late as the mid-twentieth century, F. Roy Coad observed the memory-erase that made Brethren "shadowy figures to many even of their fellow-Christians. This fact arises partly from their quixotic (though well-intentioned) practice of anonymity" (*The History of the Brethren Movement*, 2nd ed. [Exeter 1968], 7). This held even more so in the generation of proto-Brethren, who kept no group records.

honoured J. Mahon,"[50] and this was the kind of group Darby would have visited. In May 1832, he wrote to his friends in Plymouth (who at this point clearly were a source of great personal support): "I probably, if the Lord will, shall get a week's rest of body on my way to the west."[51] He wrote from Limerick to a Miss Kingdom, that "I have yet Clare to visit and perhaps a day's run into Mayo," and then he would make a dash through to London, Oxford, Plymouth, and probably Bristol.[52] It was all slightly manic. His run to Clare and Mayo probably was to Ennis, Co. Clare, and in Mayo he was almost certainly visiting Westport, where the Church of Ireland rector and his curate were in a wobbly relationship with their bishop and were tending toward Irvingism. But the centre of Darby's early work was Limerick City: "We have set up weekly scripture reading meetings, two of them at the two most worldly houses in Limerick. Our only present difficulty is to keep people out."[53] Thus spoke growing confidence.

To return now to Lady Powerscourt's prophetic house parties: the arrangement of the scriptures to be discussed on the first day is a revealing map of how the exigetes mixed-and-matched items. The full devotional menu of her second big party, that of 1832, ran as follows:[54]

50 [Bellett], *Interesting Reminiscences,* 9–10. Bellett's dating of early events is often pointed out as being somewhat faulty. In this case, he anchored the foundation of the Ennis group (1828) in chronology by its being in existence before the proto-Brethren in Dublin moved to Francis Synge Hutchinson's residence.

51 J.N.D. to "Dearest Brethren and Sisters" [at Plymouth], from Dublin, May, 1832. *LJND,* vol. 1, no. 1.

52 J.N.D. to Miss __ Kingdom, ___ [1832]. The suppositional dating by the editors of *LJND,* vol. 1, no. 4, is not unlikely, but it possibly could be late autumn 1831.

53 Ibid.

54 As discussed in note 21 above, this part of a report in the *Christian Herald* was taken without acknowledgment from the Anglican periodical *The Christian Examiner and Church of Ireland Magazine* and was attached to an anonymous verbal report on the conference provided by John Nelson Darby. The program above was then included in *Questions for Eight Weeks' Consideration.*

MONDAY. Evening, Sept. 24. An examination into the quotations given in the New Testament from the Old Testament, with their connexion and explanation.

Matt.	1:23 —	Isa.	7:14	John	10:34 —	Ps. 82.6
	2:15 —	Hos.	11:1		19:37 —	Zech. 12:10
	2:18 —	Jer.	31:15	Acts.	2:17 —	{Isa. 44:3
	11:10 —	Mat.	3:1 & 4:5			{Joel 2:28
? Heb.	2:6}—	Ps.	8:2, 4		15:16 —	Amos 9:11,12
Mat.	21:16}			Rom.	9:25 —	{Hos. 2:23
	24:15 —	Dan.	9:27			{Deut. 32:43
	27:9 —	Zech.	11:12, 13	1 Cor.	9:9} —	Deut. 25:4
Eph	4:8 —	Ps.	68:18	1 Tim.	5:18}	
Heb.	2:13 —	Isa.	8:18	1 Cor.	15:15 —	Hos. 13:14
	8:8 —	Jer.	31:31, 34	Gal.	4:27 —	Isa. 54:1
	10:16 —		31:33	2 Pet.	3:13 —	{65:17
Luke	1:73, &c. —	Gen.	22:16			{66:22

TUESDAY. The prophetic character of each book in the Bible, including the three feasts of the Jews; the blessings of the Jews; the blessings pronounced on Jacob's sons; the Parables in the Gospels; and the Epistles to the seven churches in the Revelations?

WEDNESDAY. Should we expect a personal Antichrist; if so, to whom will he be revealed? Are there to be one or two great evil powers in the world at that time? Is there any uniform sense for the "*saints*" in the prophetic New Testament Scripture? By what covenant did the Jews, and shall the Jews, hold the land?

THURSDAY. An inquiry into, and a connexion between, Daniel and the Revelations.

FRIDAY. What light does Scripture throw on present events and their moral character? What is next to be looked for and expected? Is there a prospect of a revival of Apostolic Churches before the coming of Christ? What the duties arising

> out of present events? To what time and class of people do 2 Tim. iii; 1 Tim. iv; Jude; Matt. xxiv: 23, 24; and Peter iii refer?

Unlike the first prophetical house party at Powerscourt, we do not know how many persons attended (certainly it was a houseful but, then, it was a big house), but we do have a better measure of the heat that developed. In theory the house rules had not changed in that locals of reasonable social standing were permitted to attend (although not to speak), and the afternoon tea was as much a landlordly event as a religious exercise. A not-pleased Church of Ireland observer noted that one encountered "a miscellaneous assemblage, of which females and young persons form a large proportion."[55]

The stage, though, was monopolized by the clergy and male lay adepts. The Rev. Mr Daly was once again in the chair. In sharp contrast to the previous year's meeting, however, the congress was not limited to the reading of formal papers. Debate was permitted – or, at least, could not be prevented – and discussions became very heated. The Rev. Peter Roe, a leading evangelical but an opponent of apocalyptic millennialism, wrote the following in his diary:

> 1832. Sept 29th. – Spent from Tuesday morning to Friday evening at the Meeting at Powerscourt House, for the consideration of prophetical subjects and upon the whole it was unprofitable. Many of the subjects were evidently difficult to be understood. The most extravagant assertions were made, and dogmas quite opposed to each other maintained with the greatest pertinacity.[56]

While we must accept the lack of a transcript, or even an outline, of who said what, and on what subject, it is profitable to recognize that the second Powerscourt conference was following a tramline of thought that was made almost inevitable by the character of its theo-

55 "Domestic Religious Intelligence: Discussion on Prophecy," *Christian Examiner and Church of Ireland Magazine*, n.s., vol. 1 (October 1832), 790. This phrase and other descriptive items were excised from the plagiarized material used in the *Christian Herald*.

56 S. Madden (1842), 445.

logical tasting-menu: thus we know what the participants argued about. Hence, while fully acknowledging the new, rasping tone of the 1832 discussions, nevertheless they were a discursive continuation of 1831's more modulated and formal presentations.

The issue that had been on the menu, but quietly elided from full discussion at the first conference of 1831 – "the gifts of the Spirit to be considered" – was pressed forward in 1832. These were both a matter of the developing logic of the prophetic movement (what indeed was the ability to understand prophecy; was it not a gift from the Holy Spirit?) and a social imperative for John Nelson Darby: because Edward Irving and his followers were developing new spiritual gifts, and these had to be discredited if Darby were to shoulder aside Irving. The "gifts" in Edward Irving's ministry were, primarily, speaking, prophesying, and interpreting biblical prophecy in unknown languages (speaking-in-tongues – something known within the first two generations of Jesus-followers).[57] Faith-healing was a side matter and not central to the initial flap about spiritual gifts. The relevant course of events began in Row, Scotland, where in the late 1820s a Miss Margaret Macdonald, her two brothers, Port Glasgow shipwrights, and their Scots-Gaelic-speaking maid were seized by the Holy Spirit and started speaking-in-tongues. With reservations, Edward Irving was attracted by this phenomenon, although he did not experience it himself. In 1830, John Nelson Darby went to Scotland to investigate the matter and was not impressed.[58] The phenomenon might have faded out, but the tongues migrated to Irving's London congregation and, sometime

57 See, for example, the Pentecost events of Acts, ch. 2, where the tongues were existing languages that were miraculously acquired by the speakers, and 1 Cor. 14:1–4, where, in contrast, the tongues were unknown languages not understood by anyone.

58 Stunt (2004), "Influences in the Early Development of J.N. Darby," 65. Darby's own account, unusually direct and circumstantially detailed, is found in his *The Irrationalism of Infidelity, Being a Reply to "Phases of Faith"* (London: Groombridge and Son, 1853), 298ff. A more conveniently available version in CW, is 060002, 284ff. It is possible that George V. Wigram was involved in the 1830 investigation (Frederick R. Coad, *Prophetic Developments* [Pinner, Middlesex, 1966], 23).

Darby in 1844 recalled having met and had a discussion with Irving "at least fourteen years ago," which, if accurate, was in the late 1820s or in 1830.

between mid-October and mid-November 1831, Irving sanctioned the utterances as legitimate parts of worship inspired directly by the Holy Ghost. The occurrences were widely reported in the press, and Irving was called before the authorities of the General Assembly of the Church of Scotland and eventually lost his licence.[59] Though pushed aside at Lady Powerscourt's 1831 prophetic house party, "the gifts" inevitably came to the fore in 1832.

The "gifts of the spirit" were unsettling to several of the less radical Church of Ireland evangelicals as being unseemly. To study biblical prophecy was to decipher it and that was to declare it: students of prophecy were almost inevitably prophets themselves, so they had self-declared special spiritual gifts. Additionally, among the young Irish evangelicals, there was a belief in the possibility of receiving a special blessing from the Holy Spirit. To some, this was the equivalent of being "saved" a second time; to others it was the dispensing of some particular gift for teaching or learning or praying; the term "seal" or "sealing" by the Holy Spirit came into the vocabulary of some. None of this was focused at this time on any particular "gift," and there was, I would suggest, a strong sense of the borders that the special spiritual gifts must not violate, a consensus that stemmed from the shared social

---

Presumably it was before the tongues became closely associated with Irving. Darby says that the discussion was "before the system to which he gave his name was manifested" ("On the Presence and Action of the Holy Ghost in the Church in Answer to the Work of Mr P Wolff, Entitled, 'Ministry as Opposed to Hierarchism and Chiefly to Religious Radicalism'" (n.p.: Valence, 1844), CW 03007, 264). To be strict concerning Darby's observations, Irving did not "give his name" to any movement, either for spiritual gifts or for the creation of the Catholic Apostolic Church. "Irvingism" and its variations were slur-terms used by his critics and enemies. For useful background, see Tim Grass, "Edward Irving," in Gribben and Stunt (2004).

59 The torment caused Edward Irving by the tongues and the remarkable humility that made him accept their apparently spiritual validity and subsequently his own demotion into a mere acolyte of the Catholic Apostolic Church is well documented with large excerpts from his correspondence and diaries in Mrs Oliphant [Margaret Oliphant Wilson Oliphant], *The Life of Edward Irving* (New York 1862), 404–511. Irving died in autumn 1834. He was buried in the crypt of Glasgow cathedral in a grave that, in a lovely christological touch, was provided by a stranger.

class background of the Irish "prophets." They were willing to have the Holy Ghost lead them into the complexities of biblical Hebrew and New Testament Greek but not into gibberish; they were willing to permit the hallucinogenic visions of ancient Semites to provide them with clues to the future of all history, but were not going to waste their precious hours of devotional study trying to unwrap the misformed fricatives of ravening Scottish artisans, thank you. Thus, the battle that developed during Lady Powerscourt's 1832 house party was not about the idea that the Holy Ghost blessed special persons by providing special gifts – that was accepted by most. The argument centred on the narcissistic exercise of attempting to determine what were the special gifts that we, the special people, should expect?

This left the Rev. Peter Roe exasperated: "The duty of seeking for miraculous gifts was strongly insisted upon! Oh, what a fool is man!"[60] In contrast, when John Nelson Darby provided his anonymous report of the 1832 conference for the December issue of the *Christian Herald* he was well-pleased with the way the debate had gone on this front. The "most practically profitable" part of the conference was "the elucidation of the doctrine of the Holy Spirit casually drawn out; and the presiding presence of the Holy Spirit most marked, by a careful observer." He reported that "there was but one individual who introduced anything which could have given pain to any on these subjects and that was a reference to the reception of 'the gifts' and the principles connected with it." Most likely this troublesome individual was a so-called Irvingite: Jonathan Burnham is almost certainly correct that several of these "Irvingites" attended the conference.[61] Darby's assertion that "several defective and erroneous views prevalent (to the writer's knowledge) in England, [were] met by what appeared to be scriptural light"[62] was almost certainly a jab at the rival London prophets. As far as the Irish Anglicans were concerned, the "Irvingites" were routed.[63] That

60 S. Madden, 445. Roe did not attend subsequent Powerscourt conferences.

61 Burnham, 120n119.

62 The Darby quotations are from his report of the conference for the *Christian Herald*, attached by the editor to *LJND*, vol. 1, no. 2.

63 A few so-called Irvingites attended the 1833 conference according to a note by J.B. Stoney, 12 July 1871, in [Bellett], *Interesting Reminiscences*, 21. He added

"scriptural light" prevailed may have been the ultimate explanation for the victory, but one has to recognize as well John Nelson Darby's tactical sense in convening a phalanx of his supporters twice daily. In a private communication he noted that "We had (a few of us Brethren, more immediately known and together) prayer together, morning and afternoon, which helped us much, at least, ourselves; and doubtless, the Lord accepted us."[64]

Much closer in logical sequence to the "gifts" issue than it might at first appear were the discussion-menu's pairs of scriptural texts, a list of verses from the Hebrew scriptures yoked with verses from the Christian scriptures, that were to be discussed on the evening of the guests' arrival. This was a practical exercise in a form of hermeneutics not taught in orthodox institutions, such as Trinity College, Dublin. The implicit logic was that prophetic texts demanded readers with specific skills and insights and that among the special gifts given to the new young prophets was an ability to rightly divine at least some of the prophetic meaning of the deeply hermetic texts of both testaments. Thus, the second day, Tuesday, discussion revolved around the assertion that every single book of the Bible – Old and New Testament – was prophetical in character. Given that every single book was prophetic, licence was granted to take material from any one and fit it with any other – always of course within the guidance of the Holy Spirit. The attempted demonstration that every book of the Bible was saturated in prophetic meaning went even farther in its licensing of the chopping and rearranging of the scriptures than did the hunt-and-peck search for ecclesiological precedents from the era of the primitive Church that we observed in chapter 7. To demonstrate that on a verse-specific level the reader may wish to look at the twin sets of joined texts listed on the

---

in a gentle understatement that "those with Irvingite tendencies gradually drew away from us and their society was avoided." Less tactfully, he could have noted that the relationship between the Brethren, when they eventually emerged as a solidly definable group, and the Catholic Apostolic Church (which grew out of the Irvingites) was one of deep mutual loathing, eased only by the resolution of each group not to recognize the existence of the other.

64 J.N.D. to ___ [Plymouth], 15 October 1832, *LJND*, vol. 1, no. 2.

Monday agenda of the 1832 Powerscourt menu: examine each member of the set, not as an isolated verse of scripture, but in its full original documentary and historical context. Apparently, the interpretative principle involved is that a heavy enough hammer can get any foot into any boot. Alternately, the amount of torque required to shape every book of the Hebrew and Christian scriptures into a prophetical message can be metred in a simple exercise of looking at, say, Leviticus or, better, examining the worldly and jaded cynicism of the book of Ecclesiastes (also called Qoholeth), in which a "Preacher" flounces about as King Solomon and praises a form of religion that is close to hedonism – and somehow make that fit with the woe-betiding spiralings of John of Patmos. Thus, I suspect that one of the major points of tension in 1832 was between those who favoured this new mode of interpreting the scriptures and those who were committed to a more traditional, somewhat more reserved, treatment of the ancient texts.

Among the recondite items that the 1832 house party dealt with was the perennial issue of who, or what, was the Antichrist? This topic was left over from the 1831 meeting, when it had been indirectly raised in relation to the issue of the actors who would come to the fore before the final terrible conflict at Jesus's Second (or possibly his Third) Advent. The Antichrist is a rare beast in the scriptural sense, in that he only appears in the pseudonymous letters ascribed to "John": 1 John 2:18 and 22; 1 John 4:3; and 2 John 1:7, in each of which the reference is to a danger confronting believers that exists in the present. The reference is not prophetic, but the term – *Antichrist!* – has proved irresistible to generation after generation of Bible readers, particularly after the Reformation opened up the scriptures to vernacular audiences. Not surprisingly, among Protestants, the Antichrist frequently was identified as being the institution of the Roman Catholic Church and, most particularly, the papacy. The figure of the Antichrist was easily tied to one or more of the beasts of Revelation and, with a little ingenuity, shadows of the Antichrist (but not any direct reference) could be found in several other places in the scriptures (for example, 2 Thess. 2:3–10). Here we have a window into how far apocalyptic millennialism had advanced within the cohort of young radicals of the Church of Ireland. A less-than-enthusiastic participant at Lady Powerscourt's 1832 conference reported to the Anglican church magazine as follows:

> We subjoin the questions discussed. From these it will appear to our readers that the important questions connected with Millenarian topics are assumed, rather than proposed as debatable; and the discussions, of course, turned on the deductions from those *assumed* facts, and the doctrines supposed to be connected with them.[65]

Ignoring the censorious tone, the observation is salient: at least a significant proportion of Lady Powerscourt's guests were already wrapped into a belief system that took apocalyptic millennialism as a given. Therefore, they debated details rather than examined the validity of the whole idea. In such a situation, collective affirmation of the right interpretation of details became the goal. John Nelson Darby had embraced the idea that the Antichrist was not to be an institution but a literal figure who would appear as prophecy unwrapped itself. He was very pleased, therefore, to report that:

> The belief in the coming of a personal Antichrist was common, and that amongst many who, at a former meeting, had not received it at all; in this there was a very distinct and avowed change of opinion on the part of some. The discussion of the subject of Antichrist led to an extensive development of scripture, and to much very profitable detection of the spirit by which he might work in the nations.[66]

Darby's expanding self-confidence was well indicated in his summary that

> I think those in the church, [meaning the Church of Ireland], who are really in earnest, must most deeply feel, on the whole, that spread as that assembly will be over the country, the meeting was one of deep interest to the church of God at large.[67]

65 *Christian Examiner and Church of Ireland Magazine*, new ser., vol. 1 (October 1832), 790.

66 Darby quotation from his report of the 1832 conference for the *Christian Herald*, attached by the editor to *LJND*, vol. 1, no. 2.

67 Ibid.

The sense of the interaction of church and of prophecy, shown in Darby's report to the *Christian Herald,* leads to the inference that at some inevitable moment the relationship of ecclesiastical organization (ecclesiology) and end-time concepts (eschatology) would be explicitly joined.

That happened at the 1832 house party, and for some, notably Lady Powerscourt, the sky seemed to fall. As discussed in chapter 7, the proto-Brethren were studying scripture for guidance as to how the true Church should be organized, and their practice was to look at the primitive Church: the assembly closest in time to the ministry of Jesus of Nazareth and of Paul of Tarsus was taken as being the most desirable. (Not surprisingly, given the severe Protestantism of the proto-Brethren, little time was spent on the early ministry of Peter.) The tasting menu of the 1831 house party at Powerscourt had raised the question for the final day of that year's discussion, "What is to be the state of the world and state of the Church at the coming of Christ?" That was not necessarily an attack on the Church of Ireland. However, a cognate question posed for the last day of the 1832 conference unmistakeably bore a serrated edge: "Is there a prospect of a revival of Apostolic Churches before the coming of Christ?" The predicate of the question was the implication that the Christian Churches, including the Church of Ireland, had strayed from the original ("primitive") model and that it was unlikely that they could be put right before the Second Coming. That was precisely the sort of artery-severing attack that a faithful adherent of the Church of Ireland could not thole. Crucially, both the stand-firm Anglican evangelicals of Dalyland and the proto-Brethren were willing to build an elaborate apocalyptic edifice upon their own foundational beliefs about Church organization; but it turned out that these foundations were not the same. Those of the Church of Ireland followed the then-dominant Christian form of hierarchical authority and a belief in a genealogy-of-apostolic-succession; whereas the proto-Brethren were still working out what they believed, and it tended increasingly toward the rejection of all full-time clergy ("every man his own priest" was the crude expression of this view); with that would come a complete rejection of the formal arrangements of existing religious organizations. Things had not gone quite that far at the time of the 1832 Powerscourt conference, but the unity of Irish evangelicals, most particularly in their spiritual hub, Dalyland, was under great stress. Neither side in the discussion could accept an eschatology that denied the legitimacy of its own ecclesiology.

John Nelson Darby won. He saw off Robert Daly insofar as the continuing study of prophecy at Powerscourt was concerned. Fortunately, at least two of the Rev. Robert Daly's talks during the 1832 house party were transcribed by one of the audience; they are worth attention, not only because they show the emotional investment of a leading Anglican evangelical clergyman in prophetic interpretations of the scriptures but also his concerned, almost fatherly, fear that such exercises could be corrosive to the faith of everyday worshipers who needed constancy and stability in their lives:

> During these discussions two things have struck me forcibly – I see a cheering and comforting agreement upon the great features of promises and threatenings, and an equally great disagreement upon all the minor details of prophecy; which make me feel extremely anxious on this point to ask myself what is my duty, and the duty of any minister of God, with respect to introducing this subject, however interesting into ordinary pulpit instruction.[68]

This was the troubled voice of a deeply committed pastor worrying about his flock. Here we see one of the reasons that seasoned clergymen, even those themselves keen on prophetic study, were inclined to pull back from the ruthless radicalism of those who wanted simultaneously to break down the protective shield the Established Church provided for the average congregant and then to flood the everyday laypersons' minds with perceived truths that were as apt to be fright-

68 The excerpts from the transcriptions of Daly's talks that are quoted here are found in more extended form in Madden (1872), 19–22. Shorter excerpts of the same material are found in Mrs Hamilton Madden, *Memoir of the Late Right Rev. Robert Daly* (London 1875), 153–5.

eningly confusing as they were enlightening. Once again, social facts helped to determine theological dispositions: specifically, there was a marked age difference between the evangelical clergy of Daly's generation and the young men. Most in their late twenties or early thirties were willing to contemplate slash-and-burn apocalypticism and its attendant imitation of the primitive Church. Most of these young men, able and ambitious, at best were curates or were ordained but without benefice or were still contemplating ordination; not fully responsible for a congregation of worshippers. Robert Daly addressed them, "those ministers present who are younger than myself, and those who are likely at a future time to become ministers of the gospels." He tried to explain:

> I can state this to be the conviction of my mind, after much serious consideration, that whilst the great promises which we have considered are fit subjects for pulpit instruction, the minor points of detail, with regards to which we all admit there must be great inaccuracy in our views, it is our duty to withhold at such times … Our trumpet should not give an "uncertain sound"; we are not to say one day what we may have to contradict the next; we are not to preach this Sunday, that not one of the vials of God's wrath has been yet poured out, and to ask some of our beloved brethren here, to tell our congregation the following Sunday, that six of these vials have been poured out. This surely would not teach anyone their duty to God.

This explanation manifestly failed, as did Robert Daly's attempt to maintain the civility of the Powerscourt gathering and to moderate the aggression of John Nelson Darby and his followers.

Daly broke, and that says something about the power in closed-ring combat (such as occurred within the confines of the Powerscourt ballroom) of John Nelson Darby. Indeed, Daly was one of the strongest, most broad-shouldered of Irish evangelical leaders, with a long history of pressing the evangelical cause forward even when the Irish bishops were reluctant. He was experienced in the stand-up shouting matches with Catholic clergy that had marked the new-Reformation movement of the 1820s. He was not easily broken, but broken he was: "For myself,

I never felt so much inclined to say, 'Oh! That I had the wings of a dove, that I might flee away and be at rest.'"

This is the same Robert Daly who held the most perfect parish in the country, the nodal point for the conversion of ranking gentry and aristocrats, who as an animated evangelical was engaged in virtually every national evangelical society. His valedictory address closing the 1832 meeting had the heartbroken gravity of a burial service. He asked that those present on the final, divisive Friday evening should pray:

> that though there may have been error brought forward, the Lord may be pleased to lead us into all that is truth, all that is holiness; and if, in the various observations which have been made (this evening particularly) there have been great differences of opinion upon what appear to be fundamental points of doctrine, to pray that we may be enabled to exercise towards each other a spirit of love, and of interest for one another. For myself, I earnestly desire to ask that all should remember me as a Christian friend, and especially where they think I have erred, that they should ask the Lord to lead me into all truth.[69]

Robert Daly's leaving the Powerscourt prophecy circle was as dignified as it was consequential. Daly was still a major force in the Church of Ireland and continued to energetically administer the crown jewel of country parishes with evangelical fervour.

But the emergency brake was now removed from the carriage of proto-Brethren, which was beginning its run down the narrow gauge tracks from Powerscourt toward an undefined future. Revealingly, John Nelson Darby in reporting on the 1832 conference for the *Christian Herald,* noted only that "the Rev. Robert Daly, Rector of Powerscourt, as on a former occasion, unless casually absent, presided."[70]

69 In her 1872 memoir, Mrs Madden wrongly thought that Daly at the Powerscourt meeting was speaking against Irvingism – something he definitely opposed – but Irving was not in the frame at this point; Mrs Madden corrects that in her 1875 memoir and makes it clear that it was the emergent Brethren and their "peculiar views" he opposed.

70 Darby quotation from his report of the 1832 conference for the *Christian Herald,* attached by the editor to *LJND,* vol. 1, no. 2.

This, of course, is an example of an accurate report conveying a significant untruth. It implies that Robert Daly had held the same authority over the discussions in 1831 as he had in 1832. Much more misleadingly, Darby's report completely erased the most important point, that Daly had resigned from the assembly because of its fractiousness, excessive doctrinal variance, and its capacity for damage to the Church of Ireland – all of which had led to Daly's conclusion: "I certainly felt this evening a more awful sense of coming evil than I ever did before."

In contrast to Darby's dissimulation in his press reporting, Lady Powerscourt recognized and reacted at once to the reality of the split: she cried her eyes out. A personal friend of Lady Powerscourt (a parishioner of Robert Daly's parish) wrote to Daly in early October that "I did not hear your last address, but dear little Kate Wingfield came into my room after it quite melted in tears." She was referring to the Hon. Catherine Anne Wingfield, Lady Powerscourt's teenage stepdaughter, one of the many impressionable young people who were at the house party. The correspondent continued, "I slept in the bed-room next Lady Powerscourt's dressing-room and know from herself that most of that night was passed *in tears;* she was very much distressed for what you must have felt. Early in the morning I saw her, and she told me this; she felt as if all had gone wrong, but especially she felt for you."[71]

Lady Powerscourt took her worship to the Brethren room in the auction gallery at 11 Aungier Street in Dublin.[72] Despite this, she kept in close touch with her original spiritual mentor, the Rev. Robert Daly (as her letters clearly indicate), who did not turn against her.[73]

71 L___ M___ to Robert Daly, 5 October 1832, in Madden (1875), 155–7, quotation from 156. I do not wish to guess who "L.M." was: a possibility is someone from the Monck family, earls of Rathdown, who were centred at nearby Charleville. The writer was obviously an adult, a lady resident of the parish of Powerscourt, of sufficient social standing to be on terms of friendship with Lady Powerscourt, and she was a Church of Ireland evangelical who shared Lady Powerscourt's being attracted to the early Brethren. However, as she told Daly in a postscript, "I went to Aungier Street, but do not feel the least disposed to leave our own Church, from what I saw there" (ibid., 156–7).

72 Ibid., 158.

73 Daly preached her funeral sermon and was sincerely generous: "We feel assured that she was only actuated by a desire after more holiness, more perfect purity. She did it with much pain, much personal suffering and struggle,

Undoubtedly, her decision required a great deal of courage and soul-searching. She was moving to worship with what James Butler Stoney, when he adhered in 1834, referred to as "the unsightly few in Aungier Street."[74] John Gifford Bellett recalled that in Aungier Street what had once been a settled order of worship when the faithful few met in the Synge-Hutchinson residence in Fitzwilliam Square "gave place gradually; teaching and exhorting were first made common duties and services, while prayer was restricted under the care of two or three who were regarded as elders, but gradually all this yielded. In a little time no appointed or recognised eldership was understood to be in the midst of us, and all service was of a free character, the presence of God through the Spirit being more simply believed and used."[75]

In many ways, it was a long distance from Dalyland to Aungier Street. Lady Powerscourt possessed immense courage. Almost no one moved with her.[76]

---

and never in a spirit to lessen her love to those whom she valued as fellow-disciples of Jesus" (ibid., 157–8).

74 [Bellett], *Interesting Reminiscences*, note by J.B. Stoney, 20.

75 Ibid., 7–8.

76 Mrs Hamilton Madden, a thorough-going partisan, stated that "no one of the parish of Powerscourt followed her example" (Madden, 1875, 157). This well could have been true, but of course Powerscourt was only a single parish and Lady Powerscourt might have triggered an exodus from other parishes to Aungier Street. Possibly: but there is no direct evidence of this, or any circumstantial confirmation.Instead, we have a curious piece of undocumented assertion that needs to be expunged from our purview, not merely because it is misleading but because it is often quoted without any scrutiny of its probative base in histories of Brethrenism. This assertion usually is employed to suggest that Lady Powerscourt's declension led to a cascade of similar aristocratic and gentry departures from the Church of Ireland. The unfortunate text suggests that the Rev. Robert Daly "laboured so assiduously that only then Lady Powerscourt left his congregation. *In several parts of the country leading families joined the Brethren*" [emphasis added]. This is a statement by the Rev. N.D. Emerson, curate of Zion Church, Rathgar, in "Church Life in the 19th Century," in Walter Alison Phillips (ed.), *History of the Church of Ireland* (London 1933) vol. 3, 352. Emerson's assertion is made without either documentation or even instancing of individual families that left allegedly as a consequence of Lady Powerscourt's departure or, indeed, left the Church for

any other reason in the same time period. As we will discuss later, after John Nelson Darby fully withdrew from the Anglican communion, he continued his intermittent missionary work in Ireland into the mid- to later 1830s, but with minimal results. His converts, almost all of them disillusioned Anglicans, became usually known as "Darbyites." The sparseness of result in his work is probably largely ascribable to the strict sectarian divisions in Ireland, which made picking up loose Protestants much more difficult than in England or, later, in Canada and the United States.

That understood, the effect of Brethrenism ("Darbyites") *within* individual Church of Ireland families (such as the Synges) and *within* individual congregations is underestimated in every study of the Church of Ireland in the Victorian era that I have encountered (and here I include my own). That internal effect on the Anglican communion in Ireland is, I think, one key to understanding the strong evangelical emphasis and insistence on greatly increased lay control that followed upon disestablishment of the Church as a state institution in 1871.

CHAPTER TEN

Powerscourt 1833: Apogee or Syncline?

When trying to date the formation of the Brethren and of their distinctive form of evangelical Christianity, historians have usually sought precision in foundational datings. Brethren historians are hardly the only ones to work that way, but the habit of looking for first occurrences has become virtually an imperative for those who study "earlies," as the members of the founding generation sometimes are called. Further, within the evangelical form of Christianity that the Brethren embraced, decisive moments were central to the theology of each individual: the moment of conversion and especially the instant when the Holy Spirit came to animate a person's entire life. And that big-moment mentality transferred to collective histories.

An alternate way of thinking is that often big results occur by slow accumulation and that sometimes emphasising a single eureka moment becomes a dead weight, one that sinks the whole story into deep inaccuracy. Within Brethren memoirs and histories one can find a half-dozen or more occurrences between 1826 and 1838 denominated as the moment the Brethren as a group come into existence. My own view is that, while there are several occurrences of note, the story is more one of growth by accretion rather than foundation at a single transcendent moment and that the basic formation process was completed only in 1838, when a conference in Clifton, Gloucestershire, implicitly ratified a shift from Ireland to England as the metropole of the group. Simultaneously, a shift somewhat downward in the general social status of the assemblies became noticeable. Despite his own claims of having gotten things right in big epiphanous jumps, John Nelson Darby's views kept evolving all his life. However, his fecundity in ideas was greatest in his thirties; in the long run, the most important Brethren development as far as the history of evangelicalism as an international religious force is concerned was the emergence of John Nelson Darby as the primary vector for the creation and transmission of the innovative form of Christianity that eventually became known as "pre-millennial Dispensationalism."

After the power figure of Dalyland – the Rev. Robert Daly – walked away in despair from the 1832 Powerscourt house party, it would have been natural for an observer to predict that from then onward the keener evangelicals would break away from the social conventions of Dalyland and quickly convert themselves into a coven of free radicals. Not so: the social conventions of Dalyland were not dependent upon a single individual; "Dalyland" is our term-of-convenience for an interwoven set of religious and economic habits that reigned among a tranche of the Wicklow and south Dublin social élite and these still had influence even over the not-so-young persons (now mostly in their early thirties) who met again at Powerscourt in the autumn of 1833.

Crucially, an influential Anglo-Irish landlord, John "Pestalozzi" Synge of Glanmore Castle (1788–1845), stepped forward and not only chaired the 1833 meetings at Lady Powerscourt's big house but also hosted a pre-conference get-together at his own estate. John Synge came from one of the most distinguished clerical families in Ireland – its members being distinguished not just by their occasionally devoted Christianity but also by their ability, generation after generation, to fill plum clerical appointments and to obtain lands that once had belonged to the native Irish. John Synge was a layman, loyal to the Church of Ireland while being open-minded about its faults, and this made him more acceptable to the young radicals than if he had been an Anglican cleric: the proto-Brethren were moving steadily toward the notion that an ordained clerical caste was a mistake and incompatible with the precedents set by primitive Christianity. John Synge was also an especially useful bridge between the stay-in-church evangelicals and the potential separatists because one of his cousins, Francis Synge Hutchinson, had provided the early Brethren with their first assembly place in his residence on Fitzwilliam Square and had written short studies on prophecy. Further, John's younger brother, the Rev. Edward Synge, had become an evangelical clergyman in the far west of Ireland; and another cousin was a well-known proselytizing land agent in County Clare and a friend of John Nelson Darby. He also was named Edward Synge but was not an ordained cleric.[1]

John Synge resembled a large, loveable, slightly goofy English sheep dog, the sort whose amiable energy is compromised because it always has something slightly blocking its vision. John Synge kept bumping into things and losing money through a genuine but excessive humanitarianism. He was given management of his first Wicklow property, Roundwood, in 1818; when his father died in 1831 he inherited the wildly crenellated and turreted Glanmore Castle, and roughly 8,500 acres, overlooking the breathtaking Devil's Glen. John Synge from his twenties had been a disciple of the educationalist Johann Pestalozzi and he funded several schools. Also, he became an enthusiast of printing presses, of biblical Hebrew and Greek, of domestic industry for his tenants, and of large families (he had seven children from his first marriage, 1818–30, and another seven from his second, 1832ff) and generously supported poor relief during the late 1830s and early 1840s. Upon his death in 1845, his estate was found to be bankrupt.

As for the immediate context of his assuming chairmanship of the 1833 Powerscourt meeting, it is relevant that from mid-1827 to mid-1832, Synge was a frequent traveller back and forth between his Irish estate and another residence called Buckridge House near Teignmouth, Devonshire. The sea air was supposed to be good for the health of his ailing wife, but it seems also to have been chosen because it was within reasonable travelling distance of some of the leaders of proto-Brethren spirituality in England, notably Anthony Norris Groves, whom Synge greatly admired. In the actual event, Groves left for an epic missionary journey to Baghdad not long after Synge's arrival in Devon, but Synge engaged the former tutor of the Groves' children, Henry Craik, whose job now was not only to tutor Synge's boys but also to help John Synge get on top of biblical Hebrew and to oversee the printing of worthy material. In addition to minor anonymous works, Craik, with Synge acting as the silent publisher, produced *Principia Hebraica*, intended to

1 Documentation of the details of the background of the various Synges is provided in chapters 2, 7, and 9 of the present study and is not here repeated.

be an easy introduction to Hebrew based on twenty-four paradigmatic tables.[2] Bright as he was (Craik later wrote major scholarly works on Hebrew), he was more noteworthy for his deeply driven piety, strong even by early evangelical standards.[3] Craik self-converted to the Baptist faith and in April 1831, after almost three years living in John Synge's residence near Teignmouth, he moved away and became a preacher. At that point, John Synge could have lost a friend and ally, but instead he remained friendly with Craik and actually picked up two more confreres: in 1832 Craik formed a lifelong preaching-and-service alliance in Bristol with the remarkable George Müller (1805–1898), who was married to Mary Groves, sister of John Synge's hero, Anthony Norris Groves. Müller, a German immigrant, became famous in English philanthropic history as the founder of the Ashley Down Orphanage, and his general celebrity makes it easy to miss his early commitment to Brethren principles. Thus, William James, in *The Varieties of Religious Experience*, notes that Müller founded five large orphanages, educated 120,000 pupils and adults in schools he set up, and during his lifetime raised 1.5 million pounds sterling for social welfare causes, all without ever asking for money; he just prayed and demonstrated his work and prayed some more and help always flowed without his having to beg. William James viewed this as an extreme case of "the extraordinary narrowness of the man's intellectual horizon"[4] and missed completely that Müller was committed to the practice of what became standard Brethren procedure for fundraising and that this was a self-effacing form of devotional expression.[5]

2 I have not seen the 1831 original. The work was well-enough thought of to be reprinted in 1863 by Samuel Bagster of London, a standard Bible publisher: Henry Craik [revised, E.R. Hodges], *Principia Hebraica.*

3 See the excellent biography by W. Elfe Tayler, *Passages from the Diary and Letters of Henry Craik of Bristol*, 2nd ed. (London 1866. For basic career outline, see BDEB entry for Craik.

4 William James, *The Varieties of Religious Experience* (orig ed. 1902; New York 1958), 356.

5 In addition to the Müller entries in ODNB and BDEB, there are several biographies. The most useful is Frederick G. Warne, *George Müller: The Modern Apostle of Faith* (New York 1898). Also serviceable are Nancy Garton, *George Müller and His Orphans* (Worthington, Sussex, 1987), and Roger Steer, *George Müller: Delighted in God* (London, orig. ed. 1975, rev. ed. 1981). Müller wrote

John Synge's being in friendly contact with the Müller-Craik-Groves tranche of embryonic Brethrenism in England served as a double-purpose bridge. Synge helped to keep the Irish and English "earlys" in contact with each other (granted, he was scarcely the only sympathizer to have both the financial means and the inclination to go back and forth between southern Ireland and western England). Equally usefully, Synge served as a creditable conduit between the Church of Ireland and the young radical evangelicals in Ireland. It was natural that, when John Synge moved back to Ireland and took possession of Glanmore Castle, he would use it in part as a religious centre. Under his father, during the 1820s, the castle had been the site of some of the monthly clerical meetings that Robert Daly held for the clergy in the Dalyland region. This was a particularly prized venue because of the Synge family's generous hospitality, and on these occasions an average of forty Church of Ireland priests and deacons were present.[6] In the later 1820s, visits to the senior Synge's estate were part of the summer meetings that the Rev. Robert Daly ran for his own clergy and for promising divinity students from Trinity College.[7] John Synge had established his bona fides from the Irish Anglican point of view by a well-argued pamphlet published in 1831 that embraced the validity of earnest extra meetings such as the proto-Brethren were holding (so long as they did not clash with formal church hours) and at the same time put the case for remaining in the Church: after all, Jesus and his disciples continued to worship at the temple in Jerusalem, he said. As one scholar has shrewdly noted, John Synge's original vision was of "the Brethren as a sort of Evangelical Alliance before that organization had ever been thought of."[8]

---

six volumes of autobiographical narrative, overwhelmingly unrevealing in character; of which a version edited by G.F. Bergin was published, London: J. Nisbet and Co., 1905.

6 Mrs Hamilton Madden, *Memoir of the Late Right Rev. Robert Daly* (London 1875), 147–8.

7 Richard Sinclair Brooke, *Recollections of the Irish Church* (London 1877), 32–4.

8 John Synge, *Observations on "A Call to the Converted"* (Teignmouth 1831). This item is discussed in chapter 7 of the present study. For a fuller discussion as well an appreciation of Synge, see T.C.F. Stunt, "John Synge and the Early

Thus, when yet another Powerscourt conference was planned for the autumn of 1833, Synge arranged that, among others, Lady Powerscourt specifically invite Henry Craik and George Müller. Those two men were somewhat staggered by the invitation, but after long prayerful sessions they accepted. John Synge, who was to chair the 1833 sessions, was not being a social gadfly in intervening with the formal invitation list. He intended to influence events (at least make the discussions less heated) by convening an informal pre-conference meeting of his own at Glanmore Castle, before the main group assembled at Powerscourt for discussion on 23–27 September. Whatever John Synge's impracticalities as an improving resident landlord (like several of his class in Wicklow, he tried sinking mines in his hills, with more red ink than ore being the result), he was a sensitive host. When Craik and Müller arrived in Ireland on Wednesday, 18 September, he had them met by the Brethren-favourite publisher Richard Tims, who took them to his home in Dublin. There, *en famille,* they stayed overnight and in the morning, according to Craik, "had some important conversation with Mrs Tims; she is a true sister."[9] Then Synge came with his carriage and took them to Glanmore Castle. Without making a fuss, John Synge was helping the most alien of the conference participants to play themselves in: Craik and Müller were not part of the tight Plymouth group in England, for they both had moved to Bristol in spring 1832; in any case, they were not apt to be comfortable among the Anglo-Irish gentry. As a result of Synge's tactfulness, on Friday Craik felt confident enough to expound scripture to Synge's servants. Still, Craik was temporarily intimidated when several "brethren and sisters" arrived at the castle and he was scarcely able to speak: "The Lord humbled me in the presence of the brethren," he wrote in his diary.[10] (He was here using the term "brethren" in the sense of fellow-believers and not to refer to any organization.)

As the main conference approached, more guests arrived at Synge's estate. Naturally, the "moral agent" of the estate, William G. Rhind

Brethren," in *Christian Brethren Research Fellowship Journal* (1976); the quotation in the text is from 58.

9 Tayler, 167.

10 Ibid.

(1794–1863), a former Royal Navy officer, was present.[11] More central to later events, however, was the arrival at Synge's estate on Friday afternoon of several more "brethren and sisters" and most importantly Benjamin W. Newton, accompanied by Hannah, his wife.[12] He was seven years younger than John Nelson Darby (Newton's dates are 1807–1899) and for a time he had looked up to Darby with the sort of hero worship that a young freshman looks up to the senior captain of the starting fifteen. Newton had been greatly taken with the impression Darby made when he visited Oxford in 1830 and in late 1831 had preached with Darby to various small groups around Plymouth, where Newton had settled in. Though still in his mid-twenties, Newton already was a presence, the sort of person who is given command by his subordinates, rather than his having to assert it. His academic pedigree was better than Darby's – he was elected a fellow of Exeter College, Oxford, while still an undergraduate and then took a first in classics. He married in 1832, and thus vacated his fellowship; in

11 On Friday evening, "the brethren that united in prayer today were Synge, Hewit, Rhind, Müller and myself" (ibid., 167). Hewit is obscure. An appreciative short memoir of Rhind is found in Henry Pickering (ed.), *Chief Men among the Brethren* (1st ed. 1918; 2nd ed. London 1931), 23–6. See also Stunt (1976), 46–8. Rhind had spent two years as an American prisoner of war consequent upon being in a losing naval battle, had retired from the service to Plymouth, and then was employed by Synge in Ireland, 1832–38, to do everything from preaching to cottagers to running employment schemes and dispensing medicines. He can be thought of as a soft proselytizer, as distinct from, for example, those of the Farnham estates, who were hard proselytizers and who sometimes turfed out tenants who did not adopt the preferred religious line. The material in Pickering is convincing regarding Rhind's staying on mission until his death in 1863. Still, this has to be reconciled with Rhind's writing to a compiler of a dictionary of naval officers in 1844 and declaring that he been unemployed since being paid off by the navy in March 1816 (William G. Rhind to W.R. O'Byrne, 5 November 1844, British Library, add. ms 38,051, f.52, quoted in W.J. McCormack, *The Silence of Barbara Synge* [Manchester 2003], 178). I suspect that this is another, slightly maddening, instance of the posture of excessive modesty that characterized the founding generation of Brethren.

12 Stunt, (1976), 49, citing a letter by Newton to his mother, 23 September 1833, in the Fry Collection, now in CBA.

Plymouth, despite his youth, he became the presiding elder among the local early or proto-Brethren. (Newton's Oxford friend and later lieutenant of Darby, George V. Wigram, was in the fellowship, as was Capt. Percy Hall, to whom John Synge had directed his pamphlet against separation from the Established Church.) For the moment, Darby and Newton were friends, but they both were alpha-males: the relationship was not likely to be one of lasting cordiality.[13]

The high ambient temperature of the approaching main conference was well indicated by Henry Craik's recording in his diary for Saturday 21 September that, at Synge's residence, "from eleven to two, the brethren united in prayer for the success of the meeting. Surely these several hours crying unto our Father have not been in vain, though mixed with much imperfection."[14] There is no doubt of John Synge's sincerity in his participation in the fervid worship and animated discussions that the approaching conference promised; but as the designated chair of the proceedings he also wanted to control matters, at least to the extent of preventing an embarrassing public spectacle. Besides the houseguests at Glanmore Castle and at Powerscourt, clergy and evangelical laity from Dublin were expected – in the actual event, one late-century report was of nearly 400 attending.[15] This number may be a bit high, as such things grow in memory, but there is no question that over five days a lot of amped evangelicals filled the Powerscourt ballroom. Synge was trying to keep a core group together, bonded at least by the conventions of civility among those with whom one shared bed and board as guests. John Nelson Darby joined the castle group as did some of the cross-channel visitors who later became reference points

13 In addition to the entries on Newton in *ODNB* and *BDEB*, see F. Roy Coad, *A History of the Brethren Movement*, 2nd ed. (Exeter 1968), 59–63. A good deal of background and personal information on Newton is interspersed in Jonathan D. Burnham, *A Story of Conflict* (Carlisle 2004). Newton's remembrance late in life (1895) concerning early Plymouth was that "I was to sit at the head of the table and rule, and any one was allowed to speak who thought fit to do so; and if he did not speak to edification, I was to silence him" (CBA, Fry 7061, vol. 7, 50b).

14 Tayler, 168.

15 Burnham, 127, citing a Fry reference that I cannot verify.

in English Brethren history, such as James Lampden Harris, Miss Trelawney (later Mrs Christopher MacAdam), and Henry William Soltau. These individuals, along with Craik and Müller, formed a party that John Synge transported the thirty-eight miles from his estate to Powerscourt on the Monday morning of the conference.[16] It was reasonable for Synge to assume that he would receive support in maintaining order from others present, such as his cousin Edward Synge of Dysert and the gently influential John Gifford Bellett.[17]

In his attempt to bond together through social amity persons whom he did not wish to see become separate religiously from the Anglican Church, John Synge was on a very difficult mission. Alterations in orthopraxy were predictive of advances in orthodoxy – or, in less theological words, the behaviour of several of John Synge's core group told clearly that they were thinking as separatists already, even if they did not always articulate their ideas fully. Specifically, on Sunday, 22 September, the houseguests at Glanmore Castle met for prayer before breakfast and afterward read passages from the Epistle of Jude. Then "from ten till nearly twelve," according to Henry Craik's diary,[18] "meeting for breaking bread with the brethren." This was a practice that worried John Synge: holding a service at a time that clashed with the

16 Stunt (1976), 50, citing W.B. Newton to his mother, 23 September 1833.

17 I have not been able to find any Irish newspaper reporting of the conference. The available information on who the important attendees were leaves out locals and Church of Ireland clergy and focuses on British visitors and Irish evangelicals from outside the Dublin area. In late life, J.B. Stoney remembered the following, in addition to John G. Bellett: George Wigram, Captain Percy Hall, Sir Alexander Campbell, Thomas Mansell, __ Mahon, and Edward Synge. Also, "there were clergymen present and Irvingites" ([John Gifford Bellett], *Interesting Reminiscences* [London 1884], 20). Incidentally, that last phrase of Stoney's is important as it allows one to infer that the Edward Synge present was not the Rev. Edward Synge, but rather Edward Synge the Dysert evangelical land agent. The only purely Irish report of this conference is the secondhand twentieth-century report of Anna Stoney, daughter of J.B. Stoney, who recalled that in 1833 her maternal grandmother, Mrs Elwood, moved to the grounds of Powerscourt desmene for the conference and that Sir Edward Denny (1796–1889, of Tralee Castle, County Kerry), an early Irish stalwart, was in attendance (Anna M. Stoney, *An Account of Early Days of the So-Called Brethren Movement,* (London 1995; orig. pub. date unknown), 2).

18 Tayler, 168.

usual hours of Sunday morning Church of Ireland worship. (Indeed, as mentioned in chapter 7, John Nelson Darby was not yet ready to accept regular Sunday morning assembly.) On Monday, Synge's guests arrived at Powerscourt about one in the afternoon and immediately this select group, along with Lady Powerscourt, engaged once again in the breaking of bread. "Felt united to Lady Powerscourt, who seems a dear humble saint," Craik quickly decided.[19] This bread-breaking was not the equivalent of some pallid modern team-building exercise but an indication that a kernel of the larger group who would be at the conference already was behaving as if they were a small congregation of their own.

Crucially, at the end of the week's meetings, an incident whose importance was unmistakable took place. It occurred not in the main house but in a summer house on the grounds of the Powerscourt estate. "Before we broke up there was the Garden-house communion," Benjamin W. Newton recalled: "Seven of us, including [Capt.] Hall who was virtually an Irvingite, though he came out of that error afterwards."[20] Who the Select Seven were is uncertain. Messrs Craik and Newton were there according to their own testimony,[21] and by direct report so was Captain Hall. One infers with confidence, based on the wording in Craik's diary, that Müller was present. One can only guess concerning the identity of the remaining three. Lady Powerscourt and Hannah, Newtons' wife, probably were present. One wonders if the group included John Nelson Darby as, by the end of the 1833 conference, he and Newton were already circling each other preparing for a nasty fight sometime in the future. In any case, Darby was still uneasy about complete separation from the Anglican communion. Newton recalled that "we seven were all agreed as to the necessity of separation"[22] (which would exclude Darby). Still, the "Garden-house Communion" plausibly can be taken as one of the reasonable dates (among others) for the beginning of the Brethren as a formal entity[23] – this despite the

19 Ibid.

20 CBA, Fry 7061, vol. 7, 50a.

21 Ibid., and Tayler, 169.

22 CBA, Fry 7061, vol. 7, 50a.

23 The case is well put in Grayson Carter, *Anglican Evangelicals* (Oxford 2001), 206–7. Newton (CBA, Fry 7061, vol. 7, 126) immediately connects in his memory the Select Seven meeting to assembly in Plymouth. That said, his

first-generation Brethren's principle of not admitting that they were an organization. That suggestion is easiest to adopt if one sees the Brethren as a largely English group in their rank-and-file memberships,[24] which they certainly were by the 1840s, but is harder to accept for the early 1830s, when the hub still was Ireland, particularly south Dublin and Wicklow. If this was the true crystallization point of Brethrenism, then one must listen to Benjamin Wills Newton's full judgement: "Well, we seven were all agreed as to the necessity of separation, but as to doctrine – no two of us were agreed! And what folly it was to attempt to combine!"[25]

Behaviour clearly was ahead of belief on the part of some central participants at this, the last of Lady Powerscourt's grand house parties to be held on the Wicklow estate: thereafter the activities were moved to Dublin and became more modest. As was the case with her earlier house parties, the menu of topics in 1833 went in several directions at once:

memory may be faulty. Although I prefer leaving the matter indeterminate, see the alternative case by Peter L. Embley, "The Origins and Early Development of the Plymouth Brethren," (PhD, St Paul's College, Cheltenhan, 1967), 87–8, 243n152. He lists: Messrs Darby, Bellett, Newton, Craik, Müller, Capt. Hall, and Lady Powerscourt. He may not be wrong, but his citation to Craik's diary (ed. Tyler) as one source is inaccurate (Craik does not list the participants directly and certainly not Darby), and the Newton papers have been rearranged since he wrote, and thus his citation is no longer in order. Tim Grass, in *Gathering to His Name: The Story of Open Brethren in Britain and Ireland* (Milton Keynes 2006), 28n115, gives the same list as does Embley and also cites Craik's diary (ed. Tyler), although Craik does not provide that information. The problem is whether or not women counted. Among nineteenth-century Brethren, women were reckoned collectively as "sisters" but rarely accredited as individuals. From most Brethren memoirs one would never realize that assemblies were carried day-in, day-out by the constant background devotion of the sisters.

24 This probably was Newton's meaning in his late-life remembering (CBA, Fry, 7061, vol. 7, 126).

25 CBA, Fry 7061, vol. 7, 50a–50b.

MONDAY, Sept 3.	What the nature of the covenant of the land and what the everlasting covenant? Are they identical or diverse?
TUESDAY.	Is the visible Church founded on the basis of the Jewish? What the nature of the ministry and ordinances of the former? The promises to either or both conditional?
WEDNESDAY.	What analogy between the termination of the present and the last dispensation? Mystic Babylon what? The call out of her a divine call at a set period, or a continuous call?
THURSDAY.	The connexion of the present with the future dispensation? Do the same Scriptures admit of application to both?
FRIDAY.	What has been the different character of Satan's temptations in different ages? What now? What likely to be? Is our conduct to be regulated accordingly?[26]

To a present-day eye, this menu looks very peculiar. A large group of agitated evangelicals, mostly Irish Anglicans, were spending a week in parsing, interpreting, debating, and praying their way through an agenda of topics that gave priority to issues concerning Jewish matters, as they understood them. Seemingly, a very strange itinerary: but in fact it was a fundamental portion of a long arc of evangelical Protestant concerns with such matters, one that continues to have a strong influence on world geopolitics down to the present day. As with earlier conferences, there is no transcript of the 1833 debates, but later memoirs of this occasion strengthen the inferences one can draw from the fuzzy logic of the program. One can begin to see the emergence of the

26 [anon.], *Questions for Eight Weeks' Consideration: Addressed to the Church of God*, 2. The 1833 program has an independent attestation in the contemporary diary of Henry Craik (reproduced in Tayler, 168–9). The wording of some items is different from that of the Central Tract Depot publication, but not enough to change the meaning of the questions that were to be discussed. The 1838 published version is slightly fuller than is Craik's diary.

ideological spine that eventually undergird the Brethren rewriting of the scriptures and strongly influenced Protestant evangelicalism as it became an international force.

Recall the basic point that the Brethren's eschatology was based on the foundation of their ecclesiology – what they thought of themselves as a social entity was a prior determinant of what they, "the body of Christ," thought the future would bring. Their reading of the New Testament gave them the main outlines of the primitive Christian Church and indicated how they should comport themselves (the outlines only; there was still a lot to argue about). Thus, they were the true Church on Earth. One problem the Brethren faced was their own local version of one of the basic questions that all forms of Christianity have had to face: what was their relationship to the ancient Israelites and to the contemporary Jewish population?

At a high level of generalization, it is fair to say that the traditional answer of the Christian Church – Roman Catholic, Lutheran, Calvinist, for example – has been that there exists a strong strand of continuity between ancient Israel and the Christian tradition. Of course, one finds myriad explanations of what comprised that continuity. Equally obviously, the recognition of some form of continuous revelation between the Israelites and the Christians did not necessarily inhibit anti-Semitism; quite the opposite in some instances. But only rarely, as far as we know, were there attempts among the early Church fathers or among the several founders of Protestantism to amputate and cauterize the relationship with ancient Judaism. The most radical of these was engaged by Marcion, a "heretic" in Asia Minor during the first half of the second century ("heretic" means that he lost the battle with the "orthodox" winners). He is known only through his vilification by his opponents, but he was actually the first person of whom we have any record who thought systematically about the nature of the Christian canon. Among his heresies was the observation that Yahweh in the Hebrew scriptures was a nasty, vindictive, inconsistent, yet law-bound deity; in contrast, Jesus of Nazareth was the representative in some ethereal form of a god who was loving and forgiving. Thus, he proposed the exclusion from the Christian scriptures of the entire Old Testament, the gospels of Matthew, Mark, and John, and all of the epistles save the letters of Paul. Hence, Marcion's congregations had a sacred canon comprised of a cleaned up gospel of Luke and the Pauline letters, all bleached of ancient Israelite overtones, such as references to Abraham and his descendants.[27]

No one at the 1833 Powerscourt conference wanted to go that far, but John Nelson Darby in the late 1820s had begun to develop his own mode of patrolling the borders between the ancient Israelites, the true Christian Church, and the future Jewish nation. He discovered a way of preventing what he called "a confusion of the Jewish and Gentile dispensations."[28] Later in the nineteenth century, fully fledged "Dispensationalism" was to emerge, but at this early point for Darby only an incomplete system was involved and one should not here obsess about the word "dispensation." The focal word for Darby was that he had discovered a "hinge upon which the subject and the understanding of Scripture turns." In an early example of one of his frequent rhetorical tics, he used self-referentially a word – here "hinge," which joined in his own mind two difficult ideas – and projected it onto a statement which turns meaning on its head: his exposition reads as if he is joining "the Jewish and Gentile dispensations," when in fact he is dividing them from each other. Indeed, "dividing the word of truth" (a phrase from 2 Timothy 2:15) later becomes one of the code phrases by which Darby's spiritual descendants identify their mode of taking apart the scriptures and repackaging them.

Sometime before the beginning of 1830, Darby wrote to a friend in continuation of a previous conversation they had concerning the early Church. It was a hurried letter, and Darby had time only to assert, but

27 Robert M. Grant, "Marcion and the Critical Method," in Richardson and Hurd (1984); John Knox, *Marcion and the New Testament* (Chicago 1942).

28 "Reflections upon the Prophetic Inquiry and the Views Advanced in It" (CW, 02001, 17). The suggested date for this item, 1829, is probably correct. Although I admire much of the textual scholarship in Paul Richard Wilkinson, *For Zion's Sake: Christian Zionism and the Role of John Nelson Darby* (Milton Keynes 2007), I must here dissent from his assertion that "Darby's writings reveal a surprising degree of consistency in his thinking with very little evidence of any substantial change after 1829" (96). That, indeed, was Darby's own late-life view of himself, when he increasingly saw himself as something akin to an avatar of the Apostle Paul and therefore a product of his own Damoscene moment.

not explain, "how I distinguish Christianity from all that preceded it."[29] Unlike most Christian theologians, Darby did not accept the notion that Christianity in some way fulfilled the ancient Jewish faith and therefore that one should read the scriptures as in that sense continuous. Instead, he came to the view that, just as the Jewish and the Christian revelations were separate (in his opinion), so too were the parts of the scriptures that were directed, at the time of their composition, to the Jews and to the Christian Church. Few biblical interpreters would argue that the immediate audience for each document was insignificant, but Darby was asserting something much bigger. He was convinced that a deeply distinct eternal meaning was found in every word directed to the ancient Jews and in every word directed to the early Church and that these were not overlapping communications. Divided they had to be. Surprisingly, this principle applied even to writings *within* the New Testament. Indeed, much of the gospels and the book of Revelation was addressed to Jews and therefore under Darby's system had to be read as part of the inferior Jewish revelation. (This led to some amazingly strained readings, such as the idea that Matthew 24, where Jesus is said to predict a future Great Tribulation, only applied to Jews, specifically to a restored "Jewish remnant.")[30]

If one wishes to be generous to Darby, one could infer that the operational principle he was proposing as he approached Lady Powerscourt's 1833 conference was that the entire collection of Hebrew and Christian scriptures should be disassembled into Jewish and Christian portions and then should be read mostly literally when they dealt with the Jews (ancient and future) and mostly symbolically when they dealt with the Gentiles. (At this period of his life, Darby sometimes used "Gentile" to include Christians, or those who potentially could become Christians.) That almost epigrammatic summary of his way of dividing scripture is generous in its clarity (if dangling in logic) and is worth comparing to the closest statement we have by John Nelson Darby

29 J.N.D. to __Lovett, "before 1830," according to the copyist, *LJND*, vol. 3, appendix, no. 188.

30 Matthew 24:21. The "Jewish interpretation" of the passage is one of the things that in 1833 sent Benjamin Newton into near apoplexy (F. Roy Coad, *Prophetic Developments* (Pinner, Middlesex, 1966), 28–9; CBA, Fry 7061, vol. 7, 125b).

concerning biblical interpretation in the early 1830s. It comes from a review he wrote in 1831:

> There are two or three principles which I would lay down:
>
> First, in prophecy, when the Jewish church or nation, exclusive of the Gentile parenthesis in their history is concerned, ie., when the address is directly to the Jews, there we may look for a plain and direct testimony, because earthly things were the Jews proper portion. And, on the contrary, where the address is to be to the Gentiles, i.e., when the Gentiles are concerned in it, there we may look for symbol, because earthly things were not their portion, and the system of revelation must to them be symbolical …
>
> Secondly … wherever Scripture affords the history of a fact, there we may expect it to be distinctly and literally declared or predicated in prophecy … When the Scriptures do not extend to the giving [of] the history … then we must expect it to be declared only symbolically, i.e., propriately in its moral character …
>
> Thirdly, the Spirit loves to contemplate the desolation of the Jewish people – the prevalence of necessary wrath – and by consequence, mercy on the believing remnant of the seed of the Lord.[31]

That is John Nelson Darby at his clearest – he became more recondite and syntactically wondrous as he grew older – and even here it is impossible to ferret out exactly what he means and certainly not where the ideas came from. As T.C.F. Stunt wisely noted, "one of the challenges of historical inquiry is to try and get inside the mind of those with whom we are *not* instinctively in agreement and to discover how and why they came to their way of thinking. It is certainly quite possible that more than one person can come independently to the same conclusion. There are also good reasons for recognising that people

31 "On 'Days' Signifying 'Years' in Prophetic Language,' *CW*, 02002, 36. *CW* dates the original item as 1830, but it is 1831, being in part a reply to an item of December 1830 in the *Christian Herald*.

can absorb new ideas unconsciously and indeed that they may be unaware of the derivative nature of this thinking."[32]

A question that quickly comes to mind is: were not Darby and all who followed in his footsteps anti-Semites? No, I think not; and neither can he and his followers easily be labelled as philo-Semites. In fact, the query about anti-Semitism is in large part anachronistic, since the acid on the tip of the question's arrow was put there in the 1930s, a century after Darby's early ruminations. Still, assuming a licence to be slightly anachronistic, the body of work published by Darby in the 1830s and early 1840s shows the following patterns of biblical interpretation: Firstly, the Hebrew scriptures are accepted as being completely and literally accurate in historical terms. Secondly, the restoration of the Jews to the land of Israel is taken as being a literal future fact, a prophecy that is not metaphorical. In part this idea is taken from study of the Bible, and in part is a tactical employment of the literal future restoration of Israel as a concept that helps to wall off the Christian dispensation from Judaism.[33] This faith in the future literal existence

32 T.C.F. Stunt, "The Tribulation of Controversy: A Review Article," in *Brethren Archivists and Historians Network Review* (2003), 96. Stunt (97–8) makes it clear that Darby had by 1830 read various French and German theologians who advocated divisional thinking; they divided the various sorts of the saved into classes. I suspect that this mode of dividing spiritual categories easily could have been transposed into separating by classes the two sorts of chosen people, Jewish and Christians, and thence the portions of scripture addressed to each. Stunt's suggestion, essentially that Darby could have absorbed a new idea unconsciously, is not to be ignored. Darby himself rarely admitted the derivative nature of much of his own thinking and, indeed, probably did not recognize it. In his well-known (unsent) letter to Prof. F.A.G. Tholuck in the mid-1850s, he asserted that when on crutches because of his knee injury in 1827–28, he had meditated on Isaiah chapter 32 and come to reject the belief that the promises made to Israel were meant to be fulfilled in the Christian Church but rather they were distinct promises to Israel; see *Letter by J.N.D. to Prof Tholuck*, *LJND*, vol. 3, no.226, and J.N.D. to C. McAdam, 10 February 1863, *LJND*, vol. 1, no. 206.

33 The view of John Nelson Darby's influential sometime-disciple, the Rev. William Kelly, encapsulated this concept clearly: "Maintain simply and firmly the literal restoration of Israel as wholly distinct from Christianity, and you have a bulwark against pseudo-spiritualism, and a groundwork, if rightly used, for

of a reborn Israel led later followers of Darby's ideas (especially American evangelicals who had assimilated those ideas indirectly and who, indeed, did not even know Darby's name) to be strongly supportive of Zionism before 1948 and of the state of Israel thereafter. Mind you, a person can be pro-Zionist and anti-Semitic concerning diaspora Jews, but Christian Zionists have not usually been programmatically anti-Semitic.[34] Thirdly, the Christian Church, to which all the non-Jewish parts of the scriptures are said to apply, is not a human organization, but a heavenly one, some of whose members just happen to be on Earth for a time. Thus, the contrast of the heavenly Christian Church and earthly Judaism. Fourthly, although all the literal scriptural facts directed at the Jews are not applicable to the Christian "dispensation," each of them turns out to be relevant to true Christians when read in a certain manner. This manner is often called "typology," and when interpreting an historical event or narrative of ancient Israel there

---

seeing our special and heavenly privileges" (William Kelly, *Lectures Introductory to the Study of the Minor Prophets*, 26, quoted in Wilkinson, 115–16). To the uninitiated, this might have the ring of someone explaining how to keep Jews out of a country club or at least how to avoid admitting them to full membership.

34 Even limiting the matter to the nineteenth century, space precludes dealing with an extensive literature on the relationship of evangelical Christianity and ancient and modern Judaism. It is an immensely contradictory topic. For example, see Donald M. Lewis's splendid biography of Lord Shaftesbury, *The Origins of Christian Zionism* (Cambridge 2010). His lordship – effectively the godfather of the Balfour declaration and in a sense one of the patrons of modern Israel – nevertheless was opposed to Jewish Emancipation: he did not want the chosen of God sitting in the United Kingdom parliament. On the complexities of Christian philo-Semitism, Lewis's argument is that philo-Semitism on the part of many evangelicals was a portion of an identity reconstruction by Anglicans of Calvinist conviction that was precipitated by the French Revolution and by the confusions in the United Kingdom in the 1820s, including the rise in the political status of Roman Catholics. See also Gertrude Himmelfarb, *The People of the Book* (London 2013). Also relevant is John Wolffe, *The Protestant Crusade in Great Britain, 1829–1860* (Oxford 1991). A clear inverse correlation exists: in general, the keener emerging evangelicals were about the need for a Jewish restoration to their ancient homeland, the more anti-Catholic and anti-Anglocatholic they were. Whatever the explanation, the phenomenon itself is fully verifiable.

is almost nothing that some exegete cannot read as being a 'type" of something that is part of the later Christian dispensation. As practised by Darby and his followers, typology is really a way of reading texts metaphorically while maintaining that one is reading them literally.[35] Thus, finally, the entire set of writings accepted as being canonical by the Christian authorities in the fourth century is turned into a massive recursive and self-circling system. The literal ("Jewish") texts are read as literal, and the symbolic ("Christian") texts are read as symbolic, and then the literal portions are read as symbolic (through typology) and at the same time the sum total of the literal and the symbolic is taken as providing literal prophecies that both determine the future of Jews and Christians and also control the entire infinity of space and the eternity of time. There is no boundary to any of this; it is an ideational Mobius strip on which reality is located wherever one is not.

If the scriptures intended for the Jewish people and those intended for true Christians could be separated, then the two peoples of God

35 One should emphasize that typology was neither a creation of Darby and the Brethren nor practised solely by them. This hermeneutic method has a long history going back in the Christian tradition, some would say, to St Paul. It came energetically alive in the 1820s, with Henry Drummond's *Dialogues on Prophecy* (see chapter 7 in the present study), the writings and preaching of the Rev. Edward Irving, and, later, the Brethren as they coalesced in the 1830s and worked out their own way of reading the Bible. The typological method can be very productive, or can be turned into parody and cartoon. A good set of cartoon examples was instanced by a vexed Church of Ireland clergyman who read Drummond's *Dialogues* and came to the conclusion that he had just encountered "a most licentious mode of applying Scripture history … Thus … David's *life* during Saul's reign, sets forth the state of the Christian church … Michael, Saul's daughter, being given to David to wife, represents our Lord's disciples gathered from among the Israelites.—Saul among the prophets typifies the conversion of St Paul." The Irish Anglican critic gave several other examples and concluded regretfully that such extreme typologists were "giving way so obviously to the impulse of a heated imagination." "Sophron, letter to the editor," *Christian Examiner and Church of Ireland Magazine*, no. 50 (August 1829), 89–90.

could have separate futures, although they would ultimately be bound together as part of the intention and plan of the Almighty. The 1833 discussion on predictability would be exciting, and with John Nelson Darby to the fore, the 1833 conference seems to have been both exciting and ultimately divisive. Despite John Synge's formal chairmanship of the Powerscourt meetings, John Nelson Darby dominated. James Butler Stoney recalled: "I was at the meeting at Lady Powerscourt's in September 1833. Mr John Synge was in the chair. He called on each to speak on a given subject. Mr Darby spoke last, and for hours, touching on all that had been previously said."[36]

With Darby's having the last word (and, one speculates, with his having had his hand in setting the original program), there might well have been a good deal of supposedly open discussion, but the conclusions were predetermined. Benjamin W. Newton "complained bitterly that the conference had been organized in such a way as to 'control' private judgement."[37] Newton refused to attend any of the later Irish conferences and concentrated instead on becoming the parental figure in the Plymouth assembly. Newton displaced some of his frustration into a general faulting of the 1833 house party: "I went, and never was more disappointed. An amazing lack of both intelligent understanding and of devotedness," was his late-life judgment.[38] On the doctrinal level, he was appalled by the idea of splitting the scriptures into two parts according to their putative audience (as Darby was doing with Matthew, chapter 24) and was strongly hostile to a concept that Darby had only recently fully embraced: the "secret-Rapture."[39]

36 J.B. Stoney in [Bellett], *Interesting Reminiscences*, 11. Incidentally, Stoney's handwriting was interpreted as "183–" in transcription and this has led to errors in Brethren histories: until the early twenty-first century, the date was wrongly inferred to have been 1838. This is well explained by Burnham, 128–9n158. That the proper date was 1833 in made unambiguously clear in *Questions for Eight Weeks Consideration*, 2.

37 Carter, 206.

38 CBA, Fry 7061, vol. 7, 50a.

39 See ibid., 125a, 144b. Again one must note that these memories of Newton's were taken down in the mid-1890s and like Darby's own memories were retrospected not only through the normal haze of years but through the knowledge of the Darby-Newton warfare of the 1840s.

Rapture? Secret-Rapture? That set of terms opens a direct line of causality to a wide swatch of twentieth and twenty-first century evangelicalism: not all forms of later evangelicalism bought into it, but enough so that the concept of the rapture and its auxiliaries – Antichrist, the Great Tribulation, and Armageddon, among others – are known in the general culture, at least as stock figures in shocker films. Those demotic simplifications are in some ways a shame, for the ideational filigree is complex, highly creative, and at points elegant, albeit confusing.

That 1833 was a pivotal turning point for the evolution of the Brethren in Ireland is clear, but again with no transcripts of their prophetic house parties, we have to work down their probable decision tree. At each stage they became more precise in belief but narrower in their immediate constituency. Recall here the bare outline that brought the Dalyland evangelical radicals to 1833 as far as prophecy was concerned:

1. In, say, 1820, the dominant position within the Anglican communion was that there was indeed a single meaningful prediction of the millennium in the scriptures (Rev. 20:4–5), but that it was either metaphorical or would occur after the world had been made exponentially more righteous through Christian faith and action. Whether or not the Second Advent/Coming of Jesus was a literal or a metaphorical position was open to debate.

2. By the third of the Powercourt prophetic house parties, 1833, the dominant view among the guests almost certainly was that the Second Coming would be a literal event and that it would in some manner be apocalyptic.

3. Although it was possible to interpret prophecies of the Second Advent as bringing immediately the entire end of time (as argued by William Burgh in his 1821 monograph), the core participants at the conference of 1833 appear to have been committed to deciphering a linear program from biblical sources that would not be one big conclusive bang, but would run from Jesus's appearance – assumed to be soon, very soon – to the final judgment.

4. That left one central question and several peripheral ones. The main issue was whether or not the Second Coming could be predicted; if so, with what degree of precision? As late as 1831 John Nelson Darby had been willing to play with the day-year mode of decrypting the

books of Daniel and of Revelation.[40] Now, in 1833, he came out full force for unpredictability, as enhulled in the concept of the secret-Rapture.

5. Once Darby began to push for an unpredictable (but of course imminent) reappearance of Jesus, the cognitive map of the future became very plastic indeed: the more so because of the unpredictability of the just-declared concept of the secret-Rapture. If one went down the narrative line favoured by Darby, the Rapture would be followed by a further sequence of events, discernable in the present age through the right interpretation of scripture. This sequence of future events required dealing with several sub-questions. (a) Where did the Jews fit in? Given that Darby was simultaneously arguing his interpretation of all biblical history (past and future), which declared that the Christian Church would not be a straight-ahead fulfillment of God's covenant with Israel, and yet that there still were valid promises to Israel that were to be fulfilled, a lot of scripture-parsing was required. (b) Would the Rapture be so timed that true Christians would escape the messiness of the deteriorating world or would they have to wait painfully for the Second Coming while a "tribulation" occurred? (c) When would the one-thousand-year clock for the millennium start ticking? And (d) when would the final conquest of evil be complete and the last-judgment convened?

These were not small topics for a five-day conference to sort out, a task made no easier by the mode of reading scripture that pledged allegiance to the Bible as literal truth but interpreted much of it symbolically. Accepting that the 1833 conference was where John Nelson Darby first made a démarche with the concept of a secret-Rapture, it is wisdom not to become enmeshed in the question of where John Nelson Darby acquired the idea: the literature on that matter is mostly polemical and rancid, although there have been a few sensible, if inconclusive, interventions by disciplined historians.[41] For the purposes of our broad narrative, what counts is: that, wherever the secret-Rapture idea

40 Burnham, 116.

41 The contested literature on Darby's acquisition of the secret-Rapture is summarized in note 59, below.

came from, it served the needs of a relatively small group of disoriented and depressed members of the Irish elite; that it subsequently was woven into the core fabric of the Brethren movement in the wider British Isles (always remembering that some assembly somewhere always disagreed with all the others); and also that John Nelson Darby in the 1860s and '70s trucked the idea and its adjuvants to North America, where in the later nineteenth century it became a staple in the message of New World evangelists. One can see how it must have been at once appealing and appalling, unsettling for many, and a comforting concept for others.

In the term secret-Rapture the word "secret" had two meanings, and both meanings involved a wonderful heavenward ascension. Jesus would descend from Heaven; shattering noises would be heard, first the voice of the archangel and then the trumpet of God; and then the dead in Christ would ascend to meet the Lord and then all the faithful living on Earth would rise upward (1 Thess. 4:16–17). The early Darbyites believed that this noisy business would be secret in the sense of not being noticeable to unbelievers: the faithful would be missed, certainly, but the profane of this Earth would not have the vaguest idea of what had happened. Among Darby's spiritual heirs, this view of the secret-Rapture had pretty much been dropped by the last quarter of the nineteenth century, although strands of the idea remained.[42] However, the second meaning of "secret" was absolutely foundational to all the beliefs that followed upon John Nelson Darby's writing and preaching: the Rapture would come completely unannounced, and no human agency could know the secret time. The core group of believers gathered at Powerscourt came to accept that the Rapture would occur soon, although exactly when could not be known. There was indeed immense comfort to the Irish faithful who believed that they would escape heavenward from the slough of Ireland as it turned more and

42 J.S. Teulon, *The History and Teaching of the Plymouth Brethren*, 173–5. The full-bore Darbyite Andrew Miller in the late 1870s still maintained a version of the inaudibility concept, namely that all the saints would be gone – "not a particle of the redeemed dust of God's children left in the grave; and not a believer left on the face of the whole earth" – before a single trumpet was blown (*The Brethren: A Brief Sketch of Their Origin, Progress, and Testimony*, 151).

more septic. Comforting, certainly, emotionally intense, undeniably. Everyone had to worry whether or not they were among those who had been visited by the Holy Spirit and thus were not to be left on the darkling shore. Watch and pray without ceasing. Search the scriptures. Awake at midnight in terror, seek out one's fellow-believers, encourage each other, witness to the truth while avoiding contamination by the ungodly. So much worry, and what bliss at moments of confidence and peace.

At Powerscourt, in 1833, in pressing on an emotional nerve ending in the psyche of many of the Irish radical evangelicals, Darby also was exposing a massive ganglion that, it was later discovered, ran through the souls of many (actually millions) of Christians worldwide.[43]

Equally brilliantly, Darby was able to make this pressure point the fulcrum of a complete reorientation of the Jewish and Christian scriptures. The intellectual basis of that rewrite will, I hope, become clear, but it really should be intuitively obvious. For believers, the Rapture started the ultimate and eternal future. By situating ego – the swithering soul awaiting the any-moment, glorious heavenward escape from the distasteful Earth – at the edge of eternity, Darby had made the fulcrum point in history the just-about-to-happen Rapture. Thus the self-interest of ego and the divine control of eternity were approaching each other, racing toward a single point; even so, come quickly Lord Jesus.

The contrast between Darby's formulation and those of both ancient Jewish and of orthodox Christian thinking about where God placed

43 Charles B. Strozier, who worked with late twentieth-century evangelicals who adhered to the Rapture observed, "The escapism inherent in the end-time doctrine is also deeply personal. The rapture represents the great triumph of faith for those who consider themselves God's chosen people and in direct communion with him; the rapture justifies the wait and makes everything worthwhile. From the moment of the rapture eternal salvation is absolutely secure," *Apocalypse. On the Psychology of Fundamentalism in America* (Boston 1994), 120. This observation could equally be applied to the Powerscourt guests who followed Darby's formulations.

the fulcrum in history could scarcely be greater. The narrative of the Tanakh (the "Old Testament") rests on the fulcrum of the covenant between Yahweh and his Chosen People, beginning with Abraham. The Christian scriptures as read by most Christians in Darby's lifetime make the balance point of all time the life of Jesus of Nazareth, most precisely his resurrection. Darby moves the balance point to the present day, whenever that may be, and, yes, this very day might include the moment when God decides to end mere earthly time and start eternal time and you, my brethren and sisters, can be there.

In my view, John Nelson Darby's rewriting of the scriptures of Judaism and Christianity (worked out over several years; we are here dealing with only the front edge) was breathtakingly creative in its ambition and enormous in scope. It also was very messy in its details. A confusing amount of material was being considered at once, as the fractured agendas of the Powerscourt conferences indicate. For the sake of clarity, we should temporarily isolate from each other the concepts that relate to the far side of time's fulcrum – the Rapture and beyond – from everything on the near side, which is to say all real-time earthly events. Granting that in 1833 Darby literally had the last word at the end of each session, what did the Powerscourt guests actually hear and what did the main figures argue about in September 1833? Proceeding inferentially from related circumstantial material, we can reasonably speculate that the following was probably the way eternity was unrolled at Powerscourt.[44] Our main inference is that Darby was fairly far in advance of most of his audience at the 1833 meeting and that he had to work hard to get them to follow his line of thought. Even

44 Again, I must here emphasize the word "probably." There are no transcripts of the Powerscourt discussions. Most emphatically, I am not assuming that Darby's later writings and utterances as a larger-than-life prophetic figure were permanently crystallized in the late 1820s and early 1830s. However, one can make probability inferences from (a) the way that Darby acted in the early 1830s outside the Powerscourt demesne; (b) the evolution of the agenda that the early (or proto-) Brethren focused on in their Irish conferences 1831–36; and (c) how several of Darby's publication in the early 1840s (before the horrific split of the second half of that decade) show a predictable trajectory line of thought that is continuous from the line of evolution that characterized the conferences of 1831–36.

though the guests were individually predisposed to believe in biblical prophecy, Darby's scheme was (and still is) a long bridge to cross. Aside from Darby's assertion that there were no decipherable direct points of prediction of prophetic fulfillment in the Bible, he pushed another radical point: he rejected the dominant view of most evangelicals that Jesus would return and sort out the Earth in one big moment, and that would be his Second Coming.

Darby split Jesus's return into segments. First would come the Rapture to the heavens, of the true Church. Darby pushed for the secret-Rapture, but B.W. Newton and William Burgh disagreed and others must have. Most of Lady Powerscourt's guests would have equated Jesus's coming to gather his people in the Rapture with the Second Coming, and Darby had to move them away from that, while granting that there was room for debate about both terminology and timing. Second, after the Rapture a period of woe, the Tribulation would begin on Earth. Given the literalism concerning prophecy advocated by Darby and the insistence on using the seventy weeks of Daniel as a schematic, the natural reflex was to conclude that the Tribulation was to be a "week," that is seven years. That said, some of the guests, and probably Darby himself, would have entertained the idea that the Tribulation was a period divisible into two segments of three-and-a-half years (half-a-time, being one of the ways Daniel's prophecies were said to calibrate things), with the really terrible items reserved for the second period.[45] In any case, throughout the Tribulation members of the true Church, and the dead-in-Christ, would not be present (they

45 Burnham documents (122) that in 1845 Darby was proposing the notion of a three-and-half-year Tribulation, although exactly what he suggested in 1833 is unknown. I suspect that he was playing with the idea, sometimes floated by prophetic exigetes, that there would be a seven-year "Tribulation," in which the last three-and-half years would be the "Great Tribulation," for that would be when the Antichrist arrived. This certainly is what he believed in the 1870s: "That worldly minded Christian may go through the Tribulation (but not 'the Great Tribulation') to separate them from the world and make them expect Christ is very possible and very probable … The Great Tribulation is either Jewish as in Matthew 24, or over the whole world after the church is gone (Rev. 7)" (J.N.D. to ___Ulrich, n.d, but part of a letter sequence of 1870s. *LJND*, vol. 2, no. 139).

were with the Lord), but there would be action aplenty. The Antichrist would arise, a real person in the emerging Brethren scheme, not an institution: immense evil would wash over the Earth.[46] Third, Jesus and his people would "appear" on Earth, defeat the Antichrist at the battle of Armageddon, and reign with peace. This would be the second or third literal advent on Earth of Jesus, depending on whether or not the secret-Rapture was reckoned as an appearance on Earth. This slightly embarrassing numerical ambiguity was masked by a facile move, a distinction between the Rapture as Jesus's coming "for" his Church and the next arrival as his coming "with" his Church. A one-thousand year reign of peace, the millennium, would occur, during which Satan was bound and imprisoned in a bottomless pit. Fourth, near the end of the millennium the arch-devil was to be let out for a time. A final battle against Satan and his allies was to be engaged and the defeated arch-villains to be thrown into an eternal lake of fire and brimstone. The passage on which this end-of-all-time warfare is based (Rev. 20:7–10) is a stranger to the content of the rest of the Hebrew and Christian scriptures, but undeniably it is a strong and very effective piece of narrative. Fifth, a new Heaven and Earth and a New Jerusalem were to appear. Sixth, after that would come the second resurrection: the faithful dead had been raised with the Rapture, so it would be the multitudes of the unfaithful from world history and the relatively few persons who had lived and died in the millennium who would be resurrected at this end-time. And, seventh, those who were raised in the second resurrection would subsequently be judged. A proposition that most likely was attractive to the central group at Powerscourt in 1833 was that the rap-

46 B.W. Newton and (one suspects) his Plymouth followers were of the view that the Antichrist would arise before the Rapture and that the faithful therefore would have to go through at least part of the Tribulation and probably all of it (G.H. Lang, "Inquire of the Former Age," part 3, *The Disciple*, October 1953, 5). The prophetic distance in 1833 between the Plymouth (Newton) contingents at Powerscourt and the Darby-dominated Irish group probably was greater at this point than is usually reckoned; this suggests that the huge mid-1840s bust-up between the Darby and Newton factions was in part based on deep latent doctrinal fissure, not just matters of Church discipline and of strong competing personalities. The best discussion I have found of the long-standing fissure within the early Brethren is by the English independent brother G.H. Lang (see above, 51–66; CBA, no. 339).

tured faithful would not have to be judged: in the Lord's taking them up into the air, they already had been granted a heavenly passport.

Certainly every item there could be debated and probably was. If the direction toward which John Nelson Darby was pushing things was at times verbally ambiguous, that was not entirely a drawback. One of the great attractions of prophetic interpretation is the very human love of solving puzzles. Smart and well-educated people are especially attracted to this pursuit, and the young Irish evangelicals who came to the fore in Dalyland in the 1820s and 30s often were both clever and well schooled. Accepting the spiritual force of prophetic interpretation (after all, it does involve the eternal future of one's soul), there was also an entirely distinct intellectual joy (Augustine would have called it "carnal") in trying to unlock the cryptography of the Bible. Paradoxically, while insisting that the scriptures were to be read literally, they were transformed by the early Brethren and other enthusiasts of prophecy into code books that invited addictive and obsessive attention to their most peripheral details.

The questions that required the most nimbleness by Darby involved the items on the first day's conference menu, and these boiled down to: what about the Jews? Given that Darby had decided that some of the scriptures applied only to the true Church and some of them (including significant portions of the New Testament) applied only to the heirs of ancient Israel, he had a problem: at some point he had to integrate the Christian Church and the Jewish nation into the same picture. After all, there was only one God and only one eternity. Here, he had a compelling solution (within his interpretive framework) to half his problem. When the Great Tribulation was over, and Jesus and his faithful returned to rule during the millennium, the Jews would be restored to the land of Israel and there, under the Messiah, would be fulfilled the promises made to Abraham. Those were literal and unconditional promises and they would be fulfilled literally and unconditionally. Material such as Ezekiel ch. 36–48, which describes a restored land, the rebuilding of Jerusalem, and the rebuilding of the temple, could be slotted smoothly into Darby's dividing of scripture.[47]

47 The best evidence I can find concerning Darby's affirmation of this position is a decade later than the 1833 house party: "Substance of a Lecture on Prophecy," (delivered at Sidmouth, 1843, no publisher given), in *CW*, 05022, 107,

What about the Jewish people during the seven years of the Tribulation? They certainly would receive a thorough and well-deserved kicking according to Darby's reading of Jesus's "Olivet Discourse" (esp. Math. 24:15–31; Mark 13:14–27; Luke 21:20–28). That the Jews were to go through the Tribulation was because of Israel's "infidelity" to their covenant with Yahweh. The interesting point here is that Darby would have nothing to do with the medieval Catholic concept that the Jews deserved punishment because of the "deicide" of Jesus; and he would not limit himself to the common Protestant suggestion that they were to be punished for refusing to receive the true Messiah during his First Advent. Darby, in what was a very unusual explanation for the Jews deserved pain, ascribed it primarily to their not keeping their contract with Yahweh under the ancient law – this was their "infidelity." Within his method of reading and rewriting the Bible, his formulation worked: it walled off from each other the true Church and the ancient Jewish heritage, until the post-Tribulation restoration of Israel. As far as one can tell, Darby in the 1830s kept the story of two peoples – the Church and Israel – cleanly and clearly separate.[48]

117–18. The entire précis of the lecture is unusually clear concerning several items of Darby's thought. No indication is given of who took down the notes, but they received J.N.D.'s approval for inclusion in *CW*.

48 The closest I can find to a full statement on the Jews by Darby in his early period is "Divine Mercy in the Church and towards Israel," in *CW*, 02008, 122–63. This is a reprint of an undated tract, with publisher unstated. It was placed by Kelly and Darby in *CW*, just after an 1835 item and preceding "prophetic" items from the early 1840s. In the 1830s, Darby seems not to have speculated about matters that in the second half of the nineteenth century complicated this relatively clear early viewpoint: things such as the fate of the faithful Messiah-seeking Jewish remnant and whether or not the ten lost tribes of Israel would be included in the post-Tribulation restoration of the land of Israel. For his later view, apparently in the 1850s, see "The Rapture of the Saints and the Character of the Jewish Remnant," *CW*, 11007, 118–33, date and orig. publisher not given. A disappointing (but indirectly informative) item is Darby's "Notes on the Book of the Revelation; to Assist Enquirers in Searching into That Book," *CW* 02009, 165–265. It is a sequential commentary on Revelation that deals with the various beasts and horrors but does not reveal anything significant about Darby's early dispensational thought. Indirectly, though, it is useful. The item is dated "London: 1839" in *CW*. The

That, then, is a compressed set of inferences concerning the end-time issues that Lady Powerscourt's 1833 house party, like hounds tossing about a fox, were worrying to tatters. Those matters, though, were only the more sensational of the topics covered, and they were the far side of John Nelson Darby's new definition of God's time. In Darby's presentation, everything balanced on the moment when, at the Rapture, the course of earthly events was replaced by a calendar that ran directly to eternity. If his interpretation of the Almighty's mode of dealing with the future was to be pitched convincingly, Darby had to argue persuasively that God had ruled over every single day of time in the past – and that his rule would continue right up to the moment that Jesus came from the heavens to gather his faithful and, of course, thereafter.

On the face of things, this would be a hard sell: John Nelson Darby had separated the divine revelation concerning Israel from that concerning the true Church, and the scriptures were divided according to their direct applicability to the one audience or to the other. A different God, a different mountain? Actually, no: Darby was on his way to keeping everything – Israel, the true Church, Earth, and Heaven – on a single path. On Wednesday 25 September 1833, the day's opening topic at Powerscourt was "What analogy between the termination of the present and the last dispensation?" As a topic this was not exactly self-explanatory, but we should pay attention to the word "dispensation." It was mentioned in the 1831 program and then appeared with increasing centrality on the agendas for 1833, '34, '35, and '36.[49] The term is very important historically, but it has to be kept in context. To jump too quickly and say that in 1833 Darby was propounding all the tenets

publisher was the Central Tract Depot, London. What CW does not say is that the whole commentary was republished (London: W.H. Broom, 1876) with editorial notes by Darby added, and this is what is labelled 1839 in CW. Some of these change his interpretations markedly, but CW leaves that unnoted. This is not major misrepresentation, merely excessive license granted by William Kelly, the editor, to Darby. But it raises once again the constant worry about CW, namely the relationship of each reprint item to the original.

49 *Questions for Eight Weeks' Consideration*, 1–4.

of the theological school known as "Dispensationalism" would be a massive error. He was, however, starting the evolution of that school (or at least of his tranche of that school) and, if the immediate catalyst of his way of thinking was the darkening period of Irish history in which he and the Protestant elite of Dalyland lived, that does not vitiate our recognition that he was thinking very, very big thoughts.

For as long as we have written records of human belief systems, the evidence is undeniable that human beings have commonly controlled time by thinking of it as coming in lumps. This habit stems from several early mythologies that divide time according to the appearance and behaviour of their cultural gods, and it runs down to the present day, when academic historians think in terms of various periods of time, usually while we simultaneously deny that we are engaged in "simple periodization." In the grand ballroom of Powerscourt, "dispensation" was batted around, an ideational balloon that needed tethering, and this was John Nelson Darby's self-appointed task. It was easy enough to use "dispensation" to refer loosely, for example, to the Garden of Eden or to the era in Church history that occurred immediately after the apostles received the Holy Spirit at Pentecost. In more theologically sophisticated terms, the Old Testament dispensation of the divine covenant could be interpreted as leading naturally to the dispensation found in the New Covenant (that is, New Testament) scriptures. Indeed, that is the viewpoint of most Reformed Protestant theology; it has a long tradition of erudite explication. Darby would have none of that. Having split up the New Testament into "Jewish" and true-Church segments, he needed a way of dividing history into periods that (a) fit with this dividing of the Bible; (b) would meld with the various prophecies of ancient Israel that could be judged to be already fulfilled; (c) would fit with the seventy weeks of Daniel, the load-bearing lintel that prophetic evangelicals used to support the weight of most of their ideas; and (d) would lead to the secret-Rapture and all that was to follow.

Impressively inventive as Darby was in discerning the periods – dispensations – in the divine order, one has to recognize that he was a product of his own era in European intellectual life. Thus, when one observes Darby slicing up human time into segments that necessarily follow each other in an orderly pattern, one immediately thinks of his contemporaries, Karl Marx and Thomas Carlyle. As far from each other as they possible could be on the political spectrum, each thought the same way that Darby did about dividing time. Marx postulated successive canonical stages in the development of human society, running from primitive communism to slave society to feudalism to capitalism to socialism and finally to his own millennium, pure advanced communism. Each stage necessarily followed the previous one and led to its successor: call these stages "dispensations," and the point becomes clear. Similarly, although with less structural clarity, Thomas Carlyle (a longtime friend of the Rev. Edward Irving), put forward an evolutionary chart that ran from primitive mythology to major priests and prophets and would find its final fulfillment in a charismatic leader, the ultimate hero. Perhaps his *On Heroes, Hero-Worship, and the Heroic in History* (1841) was fascism before that ideology received a name; in any case, it certainly was a sequence of dispensations. Actually, Carlyle and Marx had a less demanding brief to meet than did John Nelson Darby: they did not have to work the angular awkwardness of the seventy weeks of Daniel into their dividing of time.

No one will be surprised to learn that Darby's succession of divinely ordered dispensations numbered seven – or would have if he had bothered to enumerate them.[50] (1) Noah and the total Earth-immersing Flood, for "here dispensations, properly speaking, begin."[51]

50 As is frequently the case, it is hard to obtain a tight bead on what Darby was formulating in the early 1830s – and certainly impossible to know with any precision what he argued at Powerscourt, 1833, in his long speeches that closed the several discussions. However, I think with some confidence one can take the following item, undated in CW, but reprinted from *Christian Witness* (October 1836), 359–66 (see Burnham, 133n192), as indicating what he was thinking when the question of dispensations became part of the debates: "The Apostasy of the Successive Dispensations," CW, 01009, 124–30. A seemingly promising essay, "The Dispensation of the Kingdom of Heaven," CW, 02004, 53–63, originally printed in *Christian Witness* (1834), 125–35, is a gnomic interpretation of the parables of Matthew chapter 13 and of little or no help on specifics.

51 Ibid., 125. The interesting point is that, unlike his mature works, here he is at pains to deny that the Garden of Eden and its subsequent history up to the Flood is a dispensation ("The Apostasy of Successive Dispensations," 125). One suspects this was necessary not for any theological reason but to keep the magic number seven in play.

(2) The revelation to Abraham. (3) Next, the period of Israel "under the law," beginning with Moses and the Aaronite priesthood. (4) Israel under the sequence of kings. (5) The period of the "Gentiles." (6) The "dispensation of the spirit," or "the present dispensation," which Darby, in the 1830s, finds a difficult beast to manage; he cannot even name it consistently, a tic that he evinced throughout his long life.[52] Finally (7) the divine sequence jumps over the fulcrum point in Darby's scheme and the Lord appears and all the things we have talked about in end-times prophecy are to occur.[53] Theologians had been doing periodization for centuries. The innovative point is the *mechanism* by which John Nelson Darby locks together successive dispensations: the divine order works through failure.

"I wish to draw the attention of those who have accompanied me in my researches," Darby wrote in the 1830s, pointing to the primary principle of dispensations, "that the promise and the prophecy as a witness of the promise, are always applicable to a state of failure."[54] Indeed, each dispensation was "no sooner fully established than it proved a failure."[55] Only the final one, after the Rapture, is not fated to end in deterioration and decay. Here Darby was proposing a rather unpleasant game being played by the Almighty, although he seems not to have found it rebarbative. In Darby's newly minted system, each dis-

52 Larry Crutchfield, who made an heroically unsuccessful attempt at providing a unified field theory of Darby's dispensational system, noted plaintively that "in reconstructing Darby's dispensational system, one is hard pressed to know exactly what to call this dispensation in which we now live – that which extends from the first to the second coming of Christ" (*The Origins of Dispensationalism* [Lanham, MD, 1991], 136n1). In various writings, besides "parenthesis," Darby uses "dispensation of the Spirit," "the present dispensation," and "Gentile dispensation."

53 The rapture-and-following events are not mentioned, but, unlike the Garden of Eden era, Darby does not deny that it is a dispensation, and the discussion menu of the 1833 house party specifically asserts that the "present" and "the last dispensation" are separate. That granted, it is fair to note that Darby's prose is very unclear; I probably have made him sound more ordered in mind than really he was.

54 "Divine Mercy in the Church and towards Israel," 147.

55 "The Apostasy of the Successive Dispensations," 129.

pensation was set up according to God's plan; so each was destined to be a failure. Even though humankind might try for a time to live up to divine requirements, humanity inevitably failed, and thus the relevant divine dispensation came to an end. Crucially, once failure had occurred no revival was possible.[56] Indeed, the compost of one failed dispensation was necessary for the creation of the next one – ill-destined though it too would be.

That earthly time was destined by God's plan to run through cycles of false progress and unavoidable failure had not previously been a significant feature of most Christian thought. Even more striking, though, was the emotional aspect of Darby's scheme: not merely pessimistic, but deeply dark. Darby was obsessed with failure; he seems to have longed for it. Only failure gave hope of a new beginning and, finally, of the secret-Rapture and the Second Advent of the Lord Jesus. The worse the world became, the more lost and bewildered its hordes were, the more randomly humanity's moral compass swung round, all godly guidance ignored, the sooner would be Christ's return. One is not being reductive in recalling at this point the basic human experience that John Nelson Darby and his closest Irish Anglican evangelical friends had been facing: a world they believed was being turned upside down and a Church that was hurtling toward its own peculiar ruin.

Still, Darby had one more needle to thread if he were to make his singular mode of reading the scriptures meld with his sequence of dispensations: he had to make everything fit with all prophecies in both the Hebrew and the Christian scriptures. Most importantly, his sequence of dispensations had to interlace with the seventy weeks of Daniel. The items on the Powerscourt discussion menu for Thursday, 26 September 1833, were an inquiry into "the connexion of the present with the future dispensation" and the subordinate question, "do the same Scriptures admit of application to both?" One does not need to know much about John Nelson Darby and his habit of dividing scripture to infer that the answer to the secondary question was, either, "not much" or "not at all." Within the vocabulary of the Powerscourt guests, the

56 "… neither does Scripture present the restoration of a dispensation" (ibid., 129).

one prophetic sequence that they undoubtedly shared was the seventy weeks of Daniel. One suspects (no more than that, given the lack of record) that this was the perfect moment for Darby to put forward his analysis of why the border between the sixty-ninth and the seventieth week of Daniel was coterminous with the wall he built between his sixth dispensation and the seventh, wherein the secret-Rapture suddenly began eternal time. As early as 1831, Darby had toyed with the concept of a "parenthesis" in the rolling out of dispensations.[57] One infers that at the 1833 conference (where the agenda was perfectly set up to lead to his presenting the secret-Rapture) he was trying out his most novel invention, the suspension – the "parenthesis" – between the sixty-ninth and seventieth week of Daniel. The parenthesis could be said to fit with Darby's definition of the sixth dispensation (which was of indeterminate length, as anyone who was sitting expectantly and waiting for Jesus to come again would have noticed) and his seventh, which would begin with the secret-Rapture. Quite amazing: no amount of what Darby's contemporary Benjamin Wills Newton called "grasshopper exegesis"[58] can make this into a reasonable reading of the compound entity that is the Tanakh and the Christian scriptures. Yet, it carried a certain logic within Darby's own system. The "parenthesis" in its still-fresh form in 1833 probably melded into Darby's evolving scheme like this: (1) the scriptures were divided between those that dealt with earthly Israel and the heavenly Christian Church; (2) prophecies that dealt with Israel were literal, while those that involved the true Church were symbolic and only were literalized if they concerned the period after the secret-Rapture; (3) the seventieth week of Daniel dealt with the post-Rapture world; (4) however, weeks one through sixty-nine dealt with the literal Earth and they had ended, by Darby's interpretation, with the crucifixion of Jesus, with Pentecost, or in some of Darby's musings, with the martyrdom of Stephen; (5) therefore there was a period of undefined length (remember, Darby by this time had rejected the idea that one could predict the Rapture

57 "On 'Days' Signifying 'Years' in Prophetic Language," 35.

58 Peter L. Embley, "The Early Development of the Plymouth Brethren," in Bryan R. Wilson (ed.), *Patterns of Sectariansim* (London 1967), 228.

and Second Coming) between the end of week sixty-nine and the start of week seventy and that period of undefined time was Darby's "parenthesis." Thus, the "parenthesis" – the "present dispensation" – was also his sixth of seven dispensations. The way that the secret-Rapture and the "parenthesis" interlocked becomes clear: neither concept was possible without the other. The only way the Second Advent of Jesus could be an event that was outside of prophetic calculation was if it followed a totally unpredictable announcement, which is what the secret-Rapture was; conversely, the only way that the secret-Rapture could be an unparalleled surprise to the world would be if it ended a period of time wherein predictive calculations of the Rapture taking place were impossible.

Darby's "parenthesis," though without much biblical warrant, was both creative and sharply clever. He introduced a startlingly new pair of linked ideas: God had declared the equivalent of a time-out in prophetic time (the "parenthesis," the "present dispensation"), and this particular dispensation would come to an end when the Almighty suddenly and unpredictably blew his referee's whistle so that the great whir of the secret-Rapture, the Tribulation, the millennium, and the final end-times could begin. The huge advantage Darby's new twin set of ideas possessed is that it encouraged the faithful to believe in the imminent return of the Lord and their own Rapture from the corrupt world, while at the same time precluding any attempt at precise calculations of the moment when the trumpet of the Lord would sound. Unlike schemes of interpretation of biblical prophecy that yielded specific predictions of the Second Advent, Darby's system was not vulnerable to calendral disproof. Further, it never became stale-dated. Members of each generation could be brought to palpitating anticipation of their Rapture to the heavens, and yet, when this did not happen, their beliefs were not obsolete: the Lord's "parenthesis" just was lasting a little longer than they wished. The only concession to the carnal need for worldly reference permitted in Darby's scheme was that non-specific but vaguely relevant "signs of the times" were said to precede the secret-Rapture. Such cloudy portents were certainly not predictions, but they helped to keep the emotional temperature high.

The entwined dogmas of the secret-Rapture and of the parenthesis in prophetic time were brand new. Either they spoke directly to the heart of devout evangelicals who were praying constantly for the any-moment return of Jesus, or the new ideas repelled them, utterly.

The Plymouth group, led by Benjamin Wills Newton, went back to their side of the Irish Sea and returned to less innovative ways of interpreting the Hebrew and Christian scriptures. They used methods that did not require the entire disassembly of the scriptures and their reassembly into a new and alien format.[59]

59 As indicated in the bibliography to the present study (and in several places in the text), John Nelson Darby's writings are insecurely dated for much of his life, and this is especially true of the 1830s, wherein the datings in the *Collected Writings* are often either missing or are guesswork by Darby and his editor William Kelly thirty or more years after their original publication. Some of these have been securely pinned down from external information, but not most. A degree of information on Darby's adopting ideas from others is found in a pamphlet published in French in 1850, in which Darby recalled that "twenty years ago," he had come to understand that the rapture of the saints would occur quite a time before the judgment of the living ("Short but Serious Examination of the Fundamental Principles Issued by Mr Gaussen in His Book Entitled 'Daniel the Prophet,'" Paris: Geneva and Montpellier, pub. not given, 1850, probably trans. by William Kelly, CW, 11005, 67). Darby here had embraced Rapture, by pondering 1 Thess. 2:1, but not a secret-Rapture. That fits with the point made in the text above: he was still juggling the predictive power of 1,260 days in his early 1831 review of Maitland, etc. (CW, 02002, 32–42). That being granted, then why was it necessary for Darby in 1850 to give a loose reference to having self-discovered the idea of "the Rapture of the saints before – perhaps a considerable time before – the day of the Lord (that is the judgment of the living)" in about 1830? Because the "Irvingite" paper *The Morning Watch* in September 1830 had published an article that talked abut the Rapture of believers into the sky (also called the "epiphany") and the later return of Jesus with his saints to rule Earth (the Second Advent/Coming or "parousia"). This material in the late 1840s and 1850s was used to suggest that Darby's ideas were of so-called Irvingite origin (see Rowdon, 16). Hence Darby's need to argue for his having created the idea on his own.

However, sometime before September 1833, Darby seemingly re-encountered the material in 1 Thess. ch. 2 and moved from a simple (and non-secret Rapture) to a secret (and therefore completely unpredictable) Rapture. Writing in 1903, William Kelly, Darby's sometime follower, editor, and bibliographer) believed that Darby had formed the idea for the secret-Rapture all by himself but that (in apparent contradiction) Darby had a bit of help, albeit certainly not from an Irvingite. Kelly reported that a sometime Church of Ireland layman and former Bible Society colporteur, later turned Brethren missionary in Demerara (British Guinea, now Guyana), Thomas Tweedy, recalled Darby's attention to the Thessalonians passage. In this new reflection on Thessalonians, Darby is said to have inferred the revelation of the secret-Rapture. In defending Darby's originating the concept of the secret-Rapture, Kelly cites a conversation of 1845 that Kelly himself had had with B.W. Newton; therein Newton told him of a (lost) letter from Darby to Newton crediting Tweedy with helping him to clear up the matter. Perhaps: but if that is the best statement of Darby's originality, the argument has not much probative force. See William Kelly, "The Rapture of the Saints: Who Suggested It, or Rather, on What Scripture?" (orig. pub. 1903), reprinted in William Kelly, *Christ's Coming Again: Chiefly on the Heavenly Side* (London: 1910), 114–135; see esp. 118–21.

None of that line of argument is polemical, merely attenuated and wobbly. Much more acidic is a swirl of modern polemic that argues either (a) that Darby picked up his Rapture viewpoint from Edward Irving, or at least from the so-called Irvingites and therefore this discredits Darby's theology, or [b] that Darby got nothing from the Irvingites, indeed was completely original in his thought, and that this automatically makes his theology valid. That this is a four-cell argument that leaves out two of the other possible cells – (c) that Darby acquired insight from the Irvingites and his theology is nevertheless valid and (d) that he was entirely original but his theology is rubbish – is not something that comes to the mind of the combatants. Their fight is a continuation on a slightly different battlefield of the nineteenth-century loathing of Darbyites and "Irvingites" (meaning those who formed the Catholic Apostolic Church and whose belief in spiritual gifts made them proto-Pentecostals) for each other. The present-day encapsulation of this fight is found in the work of Roy A. Huebner, *Precious Truths Revived*, 3 vols (Morganville, NJ, 1991), and his opposite, Dave MacPherson, *The Rapture Plot* (Simpsonville 1995), among other similar works.

For historians the matter would be easier if Edward Irving had been less prolix and unspecific in his preaching and writing, and if the Catholic Apostolic Church, which emerged among Irving's followers, had been less addicted to secrecy concerning its core beliefs. Fortunately, Fr Columba Flegg, of a longtime Catholic Apostolic family, had access to materials of the now nearly extinct denomination; his work makes it clear that both Irving and his successors in the Church believed in the Rapture, the glorious return of Jesus to Earth, and the millennium. The Irvingites, unlike most of the early Brethren, believed in the predictability of the Rapture and subsequent events. This skein was to begin in 1867 or 1868, although some plunked for the mid-1840s (Columba G. Flegg, "*Gathered under Apostles*" [Oxford 1991], 329; Tim Grass,

Edward Irving: The Lord's Watchman [Milton Keynes 2011], 172n112). The key point is that Darby's secret-Rapture was to happen at a future date that was humanly unknoweable: the "Irvingite" Rapture was predictable, albeit, in the actual event, not too accurately.

The grand sum is this: the verdict is open concerning what engendered John Nelson Darby's formulation of the secret-Rapture. That is not crippling. What counts is that Darby became the primary vector by which the idea was interjected into nineteenth- and twentieth-century transnational evangelicalism.

CHAPTER ELEVEN

The End of the Irish Evangelicals' Big-House Tradition, 1834–1837

September 1833 was not the last of Lady Powerscourt's prophetic house parties, but it was the end of the Grand Old Times. For both herself and John Nelson Darby a page seemed to have been turned, a new dispensation reached. On one scale, things ran almost entirely downhill: socially, as far as Lady Powerscourt's social position was concerned; organizationally, as far as there had been any hope of breaking a large band of Church of Ireland evangelicals away from their home Church; and, theologically, in that Darby developed his doctrine of the Christian Church "in ruins." Crucially, on quite another scale – that of Darby and Theodosia, Lady Powerscourt – these instances of apparent decline were anything but tragic. They, and related negative events, were good things, for decline-failure-ruin was the way that God moved time forward. Beyond the theological-apocalyptic implications of the increasingly ruinous condition of the Christian Church, there was an unusual pleasure, almost domestic in nature, shared by Lady Powerscourt and Darby in observing and participating in failure. They splashed about in failure as if it were summer rain. In their strange way, apparently they were happy.

Sometime after the 1833 house party, Lady Powerscourt began to move out of the Powerscourt estate. She and her stepson, Richard Wingfield, Sixth Viscount Powerscourt, who would come of age 18 January 1836, were not close. In 1833 he was eighteen years of age, his education completed, and he and his stepmother clearly would not be comfortable living in proximity to each other. This well may have had something to do with his disapproving of her leaving the Church of Ireland for the conventicle in Aungier Street, Dublin; and of a distaste for the well-publicized bust-up at the Powerscourt estate in 1832 when the Rev. Robert Daly, the totemic religious leader of Dalyland, had publicly broken with the developments at Lady Theodosia's prophetic house parties.[1] The young sixth viscount was on a North American grand tour with his cousin and neighbour John Henry Parnell from the autumn of 1834 into the late spring of 1835,[2] so friction was minimized for a time. Theodosia still had a right to reside until young Powerscourt gained his majority, but the calendar would defeat her.[3]

According to Benjamin Newton, even before the 1833 prophetic conference Lady Powerscourt was talking of moving to a humbler abode[4] – which, given the grandeur of Powerscourt house, necessarily would be the character of any new residence she took in Ireland. By late November 1833 she was living at a hunting-and-fishing lodge at the far back of the estate. She told a friend:

1 Peter L. Embley, "The Origins and Early Development of the Plymouth Brethren (PhD thesis, St Paul's College, Cheltenham, 1967), 88, states that "partly because of her family's disapproval of her religious activities" she moved out. His evidence is indirect, but his speculation is not unconvincing. The one qualification necessary is that, actually, "family disapproval" really meant the young sixth viscount's, as there were no other socially senior figures in the picture. It seems probable that the Wingfield family subsequently was embarrassed by the legacy of Lady Powerscourt's spiritual adventures. Thus, the history of the estate by Mervyn Wingfield, Seventh Viscount Powerscourt, allows her only one indirect mention in a reference to a memorial "to my grandfather, Richard, fifth Viscount, and his two wives" ([Mervyn Edward Wingfield], Viscount Powerscourt, *A Description and History of Powerscourt* [London 1903], 72).

2 Roy Foster, *Charles Stewart Parnell: The Man and His Family* (London 1976), 36.

3 Anna Stoney, whose dating of events is not always right but who is good on inside gossip, has the sixth viscount's coming into residence (albeit not necessarily being of age) and has Lady Powerscourt still living at the mansion, but "it no longer was her house" (Anna M. Stoney, *An Account of Early Days of the So-Called Brethren Movement* [London 1995; orig. pub. date unknown], 2).

4 Harold Rowdon, *The Origins of the Brethren* (London 1967), 107n104, citing a letter of Newton to his mother (n.d., but on the eve of the 1833 conference).

> I am writing, as you see, not from Powerscourt, but from Lough Bray, a little fishing cottage over a lake embraced in high mountains, of majestic, threatening appearance, seeming to defy the approach of any evil to the children of the Most High.[5]

A nineteenth-century ecclesiastical historian referred to the fishing lodge as a "mountain cloister" and as "a kind of Plymouth Brethren monastery." This was not unkind, as he shrewdly noted the strain of asceticism, almost medieval in nature, that ran through the first generation of Brethren.[6] With a Gothic shiver, Lady Powerscourt further described her new situation:

> It is a lone spot, three miles from Powerscourt, up the Glenchree mountains, where I used to visit the Roman Catholics; our nearest neighbour is the priest. People who judge only by sense, say we shall be shut up by snow and starved, not able to get help in illness – that we shall die of cold, inflammations, etc. – be murdered by the Roman Catholics, but I have an answer for all, "Let thy widows trust in me."[7]

Actually, Lough Bray was just off the Wicklow military road that was built after the 1798 Rising. The cottage was less than 1.5 kilometres from the Glenchree military barracks; and there was a second lodge just off the loughside.[8] This was the designer loneliness that was part of the Wicklow landlords' lust after the picturesque, accompanied of course by servants. Nevertheless, given the scale of Lady Powerscourt's usual accommodation, she was making a statement by roughing it:

> We know our *hearts* to be separated from these trifles; therefore we think the outward expression of it of little moment; but did

5 Lady Powerscourt to _____, 26 November 1833, reproduced in edited form in Robert Daly (ed.), *Letters and Papers by the Late Theodosia, Viscountess Powerscourt*, 3rd ed. (Dublin 1839), 192.

6 George T. Stokes, "John Nelson Darby," *Contemporary Review* 48 (1885), 544.

7 Lady Powerscourt letter, 26 November 1833, in Daly, 192.

8 See the Ordnance Survey for Wicklow.

> we declare plainly that our kingdom is not from hence, that we seek a city, so many whose hearts are not separated would at least count the cost. "They seek to carpet the way to heaven." It is therefore I have taken a cottage in the neighbourhood to make the principle more clear.[9]

How long she kept at it is unknown. If she wished, she continued to have access to Powerscourt demesne and house.[10] Also, Lady Powerscourt took additional lodgings in Dublin. It was not at all unusual for persons of her social class in Wicklow to split their living arrangements between Dublin and their residences in the county, and for men to have their sporting lodges as well. Three residences was minimum, and a London house was not uncommon. The unusual aspect of Lady Powerscourt's behaviour was that for a time she took to a hunting and fishing lodge (usually a male preserve) and she did so for religious reasons. Where she lodged in Dublin is unknown. In February 1835, she uses "5, Stephen's Green" on a letter.[11] This may have been a postal

9 Lady Powerscourt letter, 26 November 1833, in Daly, 193. The prose is a fair sample of her letters.

10 Anna Stoney, 2. One doubts if she took much advantage of the main Powerscourt estate, however. Dora Pennefather wrote in spring 1835 that "Lady Powerscourt is living at present in Dublin … Lady P. had not been living at Powerscourt for two or three years" (Dora Pennefather to Mrs C[rewdson], 14 March 1835, reproduced in Robert Braithwaite, *The Life and Letters of Rev. William Pennefather* [London 1878], 24).

11 Lady Powerscourt to unknown, February 1835 in Daly, 236. The address in 1834 was listed in the *Treble Almanac* as the location of Mary Mouton, confectioner. By 1840, the *Pettigrew and Oulton Dublin Almanac and General Register* listed it as the location of Booth and Talibart, watchmaker and jewellers. Alfred and Charles DeLessart, dentists, were also business tenants, and a James Boulton resided there, suggesting that living accommodations were found above the shops. (I am grateful to Fr James Quirk for this information.) Thus, Theodosia Lady Powerscourt could have been using the location as (a) her primary living quarters for a time, although it is hard to imagine the viscountess living in a claustral flat about a watchshop; (b) as a mail drop, if she was living at nearby Ely Place with Isabella, Lady Powerscourt, and she well might have wished to keep her mail away from the formidable Isabella or; (c) as a pied-à-terre for particularly private and intimate transactions.

accommodation address or a flat. In view of the frightening character of Isabella, relict of the Fourth Viscount Powerscourt (and since 1831 the Dowager Viscountess Powerscourt), it is noteworthy that the 1834 and 1835 prophecy meetings were held at no. 6 Ely Place in Dublin, which was effectively a Powerscourt dower house. If Theodosia, Lady Powerscourt, was allowed to reside there for a time, it must have been very unpleasant for her, and one can imagine with a shudder her having to live in the same cave as the creature that frightened even the confident young sixth viscount.[12]

Clearly, Lady Powerscourt was on a social decline, at least by the standards of the elite of Dalyland who set the metric by which she was viewed by "the world." Much the same conclusion concerning the drawing power of the mission that she and John Nelson Darby shared, the creation of an Irish equivalent of the primitive Church, arises from a simple set of observations: by charting the physical and social circumstances of the annual prophetic meetings, one has a nicely non-reactive (and blessedly non-doctrinal) measure of the declining prestige and impact of successive house parties. Note the following year-by-year changes:

1831. The first house party was chaired at Powerscourt by the godfather of Wicklow and south Dublin Anglican evangelicalism, the Rev. Robert Daly, with a socially elite attendance.

1832. Socially, the event still was exclusive and still held at the massive residence, and was chaired by Daly. However, the affair got out of hand and the Rev. Mr Daly publicly resigned and the event lost a goodly portion of its social cachet and its attraction to Church of Ireland evangelicals diminished.

1833. Nevertheless, the next conference, chaired by John Synge of Glanmore Castle, still maintained elite social weight. Synge used his estate to house special guests, and the actual conference, hosted by Lady Powerscourt, still was in the Big House. The discussions were dominated by John Nelson Darby.

1834. The era of the great Wicklow house parties was over. However, Lady Powerscourt was able to engage a smaller, but still impressive

12 See chapter 9 for information on Isabella Brownlow Wingfield, widow of the fourth viscount.

venue, the Wingfield family's Dublin house at Ely Place, Dublin.[13] Referring to the 1834 Ely Place meeting, the splendidly alert teenage gossip and apprentice in prophecy Dora Pennefather reported that "I hear many wild and unsatisfactory opinions were started – so much so that sober-minded people would not attend."[14]

1835. The last event to be held in a substantial private residence: again, hosted by Lady Powerscourt in the Ely Place mansion. The agenda was thoroughly basted in the *Christian Examiner and Church of Ireland Magazine* by an anonymous clergyman: "I confess that I think that even in this age of liberality, a clergyman of the Establishment may hesitate before he mixes himself up with such an assembly."[15] This sort of opinion had its effect.

1836. Only wisps of the original intention of pan-Protestant evangelical ecumenism remained. The meeting was held at a hotel in Sandymount Green, a decent-enough area of southeast Dublin (now "Dublin 4"). Nevertheless, to be forced to use commercial premises was a big social come-down. The character of the meeting can fairly be described as Darbyite.[16]

After that, no Irish meetings. By 1838 the centre of the now-distinct Brethren movement has migrated to England.

The downward trajectory here is obvious. Granted, one could assert that, as the original Irish evangelical-prophetic movement became smaller and smaller, it became purer and purer. But that seems like whistling past the graveyard. The believers who were allegiant to the study of prophecy as a key to both present behaviour and future hope became fewer, and they fought among themselves more and more. The diagnostic event in the Irish case was the decision of the Limerick

13 The venues and agendas of the 1834–36 meetings are found in [anon.], *Questions for Eight Weeks' Consideration: Addressed to the Church of God* (London 1838), 2–4. The same agenda as is given for 1835 is found in "Dionysius," "Prophetical Meetings," *Christian Examiner and Church of Ireland Magazine* (September 1835), 641–2.

14 Dora Pennefather to Mrs. C[rewdson], 14 March 1835 in Braithwaite, 24.

15 "Dionysius," 640.

16 The term is not an anachronism. Referring to the early 1830s, J.G. Bellett recalled that the assembly "in this country were called 'Darbyites'" ([John Gifford Bellett], *Interesting Reminsicences* [London 1884], 11).

Anglican clergyman the Rev. Edward Hoare, who had founded and edited an Irish periodical for advanced prophetic views. His paper, the *Christian Herald,* was where John Nelson Darby published some of his early material. As the mindset of writers on prophecy turned increasingly from investigation to dogmatic conviction, the paper became a free-fire zone for zealots, and the Rev. Mr Hoare found his public forum no longer tenable. In July 1835, he wound it all up. Hoare admitted that the *Christian Herald*'s circulation was dropping and that this caused a financial problem, but the real difficulty was the increasingly vitriolic and phantasmagorical ravenings of some of the prophetic adepts. When millennial doctrines first appeared, Hoare wrote, they were put forward by men "distinguished for orthodoxy in doctrine, and freedom from the spirit of dissent." No longer. Responsible people of faith were turning away from the topic. The whole subject was now being chewed to ribbons by persons who denounced each other as being heretics, schismatics and, one might infer, the spawn of the devil. Hoare closed down his paper by telling his readers not to let the devil "divert your minds from the subject of the Lord's second advent." In a voice of doom, he concluded, "Finally, brethren, farewell."[17]

The usual interpretation of this haemorrhage in the world of millenarian adherents is that it occurred because so-called Irvingites and Darbyites were gutting each other. Indeed, this was part of the problem, provided one does not directly blame the deeper nastiness on Edward Irving (he had died in 1834) or on John Nelson Darby, who in Hoare's periodical wrote edgy, but not hateful, pieces. However, each man had his wildly volatile outriders.[18] Further, there was a background torsion between Darby and Benjamin Wills Newton (and their respective followers) that begins in the early 1830s and eventually in the mid-1840s

17 Quotations from the *Christian Herald,* vol 5 (July 1835), in Le Roy Froom, *The Prophetic Faith of Our Fathers* (Washington 1946), vol. 3, 587. Large quotations are also found in Jonathan D. Burnham, *A Story of Conflict* (Carlisle 2004), 131–3.

18 The basic interpretation of the schismatics vs heretics being, respectively, Irvingites and Brethren is found in Rowdon (1967), 106n72. Burnham (132) sharpens "Brethren" to Darbyites, which is justified as the *Christian Herald* was an Irish publication and the Brethren were by 1835 known commonly, albeit not universally, as Darbyites.

splits the Brethren movement. The deepening latent fissure was as much about male power as anything else, but there was also an early doctrinal fault line. Newton and those who agreed with him could not abide Darby's discovery of the doctrine of the secret-Rapture, nor Darby's refusal to accept prophecy as applicable to the "present dispensation" other than through that great, surprising final heavenward elevation of the Rapture. Thus, Newton refused to attend Lady Powerscourt's 1834 Dublin meeting and instead set up a rival conference in England with the goal of pushing anti-Darby views.[19]

Whatever the fault lines between various prophecy adepts, if one takes a time frame running from autumn 1825 (when Darby was ordained deacon) through to autumn 1836 (the last Irish prophetic meeting), the long descent for the core group of young men and women who had been keen Anglican evangelicals is obvious. They had begun by believing that they could participate in a second or new-Reformation that would convert Ireland to a Protestant nation. This ambition was flattened by political and social reality, embodied in its most repellent (to them) form of Daniel O'Connell. The United Kingdom government in the 1830s suppressed several Church of Ireland bishoprics, removed the schools and other social welfare institution from Anglican control, and diminished tithe revenues of the clergy. The response of the keen among the young (now in their early thirties) was to study the earliest patterns of Church organization and, equally, to read furiously in the scriptures to see how the increasingly woeful world could be straightened out. They debated in the most economically secure and socially fashionable settings in rural Ireland. Inexorably, that all ended. John Nelson Darby, the dominant figure amongst the remnant, dealt with this decline, but hardly the way one would have expected.

The apparent slide toward ruin seems to have made Darby happy. We rarely catch a glimpse of him from the viewpoint of friendly outsiders – enemies, yes; and pious admirers, of course – so the view of Darby in this period by the young Dora Pennefather is valuable. She was the niece of Darby's sister, Susannah, and, irreproachably well and piously connected: her father, Richard Pennefather, was chief baron

19 Embley (1967), 93.

of the Irish court of exchequer; the family's Dublin residence was 5 Merrion Square South, and Darby felt comfortable dropping by when in town:

> Mr Darby is in Dublin and we have the enjoyment of seeing him sometimes. He calls here occasionally, and seems to communicate the joy in heavenly things which he feels. He presses *rejoicing* on believers very much, because he says, "Christ not only died but is risen and has purchased everything for us and believers are children and heirs." This joy in believing, he thinks, is the surest way of bringing about deadness to the world. I believe that you know his views about the Church of England: he wishes to draw believers out of it, although he admits there is salvation in it. On this subject he has not spoken to any of us.[20]

Aside from the anaesthetic joy that Darby feels in helping to bring about "deadness to the world," the striking point is that he was on mission. He is comfortable in targeting the people who were the primary audience – remember Anna Stoney's observation that "it often seems to be God's way to begin with the upper classes"[21] – but he is sensitive enough not to press. The Baron Pennefathers were Darby's sort, not merely because they were his relatives by marriage but because they were Anglican evangelicals who were willing to listen and to adopt some of his theology, although not his views on the Church of Ireland:

20 Dora Pennefather to Mrs C[rewdson] 14 March 1835, in Braithwaite, 23. Note: the Rev. Robert Braithwaite, vicar of Chipping Campden, England, removes entirely Darby's name from the letter but does not appear to otherwise censor it. The circumstantial details in the letter make me fully confident in filling in the name. Elsewhere in the book, religious luminaries, such as the Rev. Robert Daly, are clearly identified. The biography of William Pennefather was published in 1878. By then, for a churchman such as Braithwaite (editor of Pennefather's letters), and for a distinguished Church family such as the Pennefathers, Darby was the name that could not be written. (Of course he, like all Anglican clergy, was referred to socially as "Mr Darby" and not "Rev. Darby" by members of the Irish middle and upper classes.)

21 A. Stoney, 1.

> Many real Christians on this ground do not like to associate with Mr Darby; but this I cannot enter into, when there are so many delightful spots of common meeting. He appears to be engaged from morning till night preaching, expounding, visiting etc.: he now seems ready to go anywhere, either to dine or to call, always premising "If you will allow me to preach"; and he never goes anywhere unless about his Master's business. He says he feels his office principally lies in urging believers to walk worthy of their high and holy calling.[22]

Darby was right to be spending some of his seemingly manic energy on the young Pennefathers: William, slightly older than Dora, had already decided, following a childhood conversion, to become an Anglican clergyman and became something of a minor Victorian saint, and Dora married in 1839 the Hon Somerset Maxwell, younger brother of Lord Farnham of the fiercely proselytizing evangelical family of County Cavan. None of the young Pennefathers became Darby's disciples, but they were reasonable prospects. Dora and her older sister Susan attended a Brethren meeting; in Dora's report the social tone is as revealing as is the spiritual content:

> Lady Powerscourt is living at present in Dublin; through a mutual friend, S. and I were invited to attend a meeting for reading the Scriptures, which she has established once a week; we were there at one reading, and are going again to-day. I found it very profitable and, so did Susan; every one is allowed to give an opinion, or to ask questions. Mr Darby and two or three clergymen were present. The former read 1 John I, and spoke beautifully on the Christian's hopes and present comforts. Others said but little.[23]

This was a Darbyite assembly, convened by Lady Powerscourt, and controlled by Darby, about as pure an early Irish Brethren body as one could find:

22 Dora Pennefather in Braithwaite, 24.
23 Ibid.

> The ladies were silent, with the exception of two or three questions. Lady P. only asked one, which I could not hear. She is a lovely-looking creature, pale, elegant, dignified, and retiring; her face looks as if she were much in prayer and communication with God.[24]

Darby did not forget his primary market:

> Mr Darby and Lady Harberton kept up an interesting conversation, he urging rejoicing, she seeming to fear presumption.[25]

Dora Pennefather was a swift young mind with the eye of a social novelist. Her viewpoint is valuable because so much of John Nelson Darby's life was taken up with doctrinal and organizational warfare; most of his writings are terribly lumpy, dour, and often incomprehensible; and his presentation of his own family background is lifeless, cold, and emotionally autistic – so that one wonders, how in the world did he ever inspire such loyalty among his followers? Manifestly, there was something commanding and vivid in the man's character that is blanched away in the ocean of printed words and the hyper-pious memoirs that constitute most of the historical record.

Possibly this was one of the few times in his adult life that John Nelson Darby was comfortably at home both socially and religiously. The Holy Spirit dwelling in him would have been his explanation, but in the outer world it is worth noting that not long after the September 1834 Ely Place conference Darby's father died. A long and painful narrative ended, and the tendrils of that relationship were cauterized. Darby did not attend his father's funeral. With the bequest his father left him – £7,000 in stock – and with a previous £5,000 from his uncle, he now had an independent income of £300–400 a year. Alone among the males in his family, he was not given a gentleman's landed property, but if he was aggrieved he got over it quickly enough.[26] It appears

24 Ibid.

25 Ibid.

26 On testamentary matters relating to John Darby Sr, see chapter 7 of the present study.

that his life was good, as well as virtuous. He was treated as a figure of consequence by at least some of Dublin's quality: his being granted the right to preach at his hosts if he dined with them or called upon them was unusual. Along with his righteous calling, he clearly possessed a set of engraved calling cards and proper dinner clothes.[27] And Lady Powerscourt apparently did not spend most of her time sheltered away in the Wicklow hills.

The inference that John Nelson Darby and Lady Powerscourt spent a lot of time in each other's company after she had left the Powerscourt estate as her main residence leads to the distracting question of what, indeed, was their relationship? Distracting this is because it cannot be answered with any authority and because the query involves cutting our way through some unnecessarily tangled later Brethren folklore.

"Lady Powerscourt's secession may have been motivated, at least in part, by her having become romantically involved with Darby," writes the Rev. Dr Jonathan Burnham, an Oxford-trained historian and the pastor of a large Community Church in Florida.[28] He may be immediately wrong, but ultimately he is right that one cannot consider the spiritual turnings of either John Nelson Darby or Lady Powerscourt without being aware that in the 1830s they were the two foreground figures in the early days of Brethrenism in Ireland and that they certainly were far from being strangers to each other. Lady Powerscourt left for

27 One emphasizes Darby's having the clothes and manners to operate in upper-class Irish society because competitive austerity became a game among first- and second-generation Brethren of money and standing, somewhat distorting the historical record. Not surprisingly, memoirs emphasize Darby's own volitional poverty. William Kelly, Darby's longtime editor, in *John Nelson Darby as I Knew Him,* refers to an alleged incident in the 1830s: "His clothes were plain, and he wore them to shabbiness, though punctiliously clean in his person, which dressy people are not always. In Limerick once, kind friends took advantage of his sleep to replace the old with new, which he put on without a word, as the story went" (www.stempublishing.com/authors/kelly7 subjects/jnd__knew.html, accessed 23 September 2013).

28 Burnham, 121.

the Aungier Street assembly in late 1832, but Darby did not adhere to it until 1834 and, indeed, was not sure about leaving the Church of Ireland until late 1834 or soon thereafter.[29] Yet, if in the narrow sense Lady Powerscourt did not follow Darby to Aungier Street (she preceded him), she certainly was influenced by him: influenced, but not directed, for she had a very strong, if febrile, spiritual sense of her own. She was not Darby's glove puppet.

Like so much Brethren history, once one starts looking for an answer to the question of what actually was the social and emotional relationship between John Nelson Darby and Lady Powerscourt one enters a fairly barren land. The material that we have cited above makes it clear that in the mid-1830s Darby and the viscountess were often in each other's company, that they shared worship in small group settings, and that they had the residential accommodations and the social freedom for private intimacy of whatever sort they may have wished, physical or spiritual. These facts, though, do not take us very far.

Brethren folklore – still alive – holds that Darby and Lady Powerscourt became engaged to marry, but that their sense of spiritual duty drove them apart. The most extreme form of this story in print is Max Weremchuk's 1992 devotional biography of Darby:

> The story goes that when the Brethren in Dublin heard of Darby's engagement they prayed that the Lord might dissolve it and hinder a marriage; they felt that the Lord was using Darby mightily for His work and they feared that a wife would only hinder him in his service. When Darby heard of this reaction, he no longer felt at liberty to go on with the engagement. It is said that the engagement was mutually broken. Whether it is true that the letters they wrote one another in which they both spoke of breaking the engagement crossed in the mail is hard to say.[30]

29 See [Bellett], *Interesting Reminiscences*; both J.G. Bellett (8) and J.B. Stoney (20) indicate that Darby was indecisive well into 1834. Darby himself added a laconic note to *Interesting Reminiscences* that "I was not in Dublin when they went to Aungier Street, but I went there afterwards" (17).

30 Max S. Weremchuk, *John Nelson Darby* (Neptune, NJ, 1992; orginal German ed. 1988), 133–4.

Aside from the exogenous introduction of letters that cross in the mail (a standard device of Victorian romantic fiction), the events *could* have happened. But evidence? Timothy C.F. Stunt was justifiably vexed on this matter and, indeed, distrustful of Weremchuk's probative sense generally, as he indicated in reviewing Weremchuk's biography of Darby:

> These considerations are particularly important in the context of Weremchuk's conjectures about Darby's possible engagement to Lady Powerscourt. He is adamant that "we do know that they *did* meet each other and they fell in love and became engaged" (p. 133). In fact, it emerges on the following page that apart from an unreferenced "saying" of Darby and an unlocated letter of [William] Kelly (dated 1897), Weremchuk is *totally* dependent on oral tradition and conjecture for this episode. His suggestion is not necessarily wrong, but the source evaluation is inadequate. These questions, however, are only symptomatic of a wider historiographical issue.[31]

While Weremchuk clearly was relying on shaky oral tradition, he was unintentionally useful in telling us what later generations of Darby's followers wanted to believe about the emotional life and sense of duty of John Nelson Darby and his putative fiancée. This story appears to be an instance of a fairly common phenomenon: the way that folklore eventually gets into print and then is read and passed along as being pure oral folklore and subsequently generates a further reading of disparate printed sources as confirming and amplifying the reality of the original folklore.[32] I think the first writing-down of this Darby-Lady Powerscourt tradition in print was that of G.H. Lang in 1953 in *The Disciple*, a Brethren publication.[33] At least this was the first print version

31 Timothy C.F. Stunt, "Review of 'John Nelson Darby' by Max Weremchuk," *Brethren Archivists and Historians Network Review* (autumn 1997), 49.

32 Thus, as I explained in chapter 4, note 66, a letter to Robert Daly printed in Lady Powerscourt's correspondence gains a false identity as being to John Nelson Darby, which it certainly is not.

33 G.H. Lang, "Inquire of the Former Age," part 2, *The Disciple* (May 1953), 16.

that demonstrably affected subsequent memory. From that point, the story could be repeated and embroidered in Brethren assemblies and could also be spread in print form. Harold Rowdon in his pioneering study of Brethren origins cited the Lang article and gave it credentials: "Lang's father had been personally acquainted with Darby."[34] Almost precisely the same words are then repeated in later printed work.[35]

None of the few other bits of disjecta membra that can be brought to support the narrative of John Nelson Darby's breaking with Lady Powerscourt (or in some versions, vice versa) and Darby's then effectively taking a vow of lifelong celibacy has much probative force.[36] However, the story, accurate or not, clearly was useful to later generations of Brethren in creating a comforting history for themselves. Without the emollient of the Darby-Powerscourt folklore, Darby's lifelong behaviour was uncomfortably consistent with his practice of various medievalisms in the 1820s and especially his acting as a mendicant monk in the Calary uplands. In the second and subsequent generations of Brethrenism, Darby's failure to form a family must have appeared uncomfortably close to Roman Catholic priestly practice. Hence, one of the uses of the Darby-Powerscourt story is to legitimate Darby's rejection of sexuality: according to the story, it was a sacrifice he made at the request of his fellow Irish Brethren.

34 Rowdon, (1967), 104n1.

35 For example, Burnham, 122n124, without mention of Rowdon. Rather more gingerly, Tim Grass uses the Lang material to suggest that "Darby had thoughts of marrying her [Lady Powerscourt], although he was apparently advised that it would be better for his work if he remained single" (Grass, in Dickson and Grass, eds, 25).

36 Stunt, in his review of Weremchuk's biography, is right to ascerbically note the "unlocated letter" of William Kelly of 1897. And Weremchuk was shrewd not to include a reference. If Weremchuk was referring to William Kelly to ___ "P." [of Rotterham], 8 September 1897, the letter actually destroys a piece of the folklore, namely that the two now-distanced soulmates wrote hymns that showed their pain. "Lady Powerscourt wrote those lines ('too deep for human sympathy') but I am afraid it is legendary to connect them with Hargreaves etc getting J.N.D. to abandon the thought of marriage. And Mr D. composed his hymn 'Hark! Ten Thousand' … in the agony of gout in the eye (to which he was once subject) and wrote it down when recovering" (CBA, typescript of Kelly letters, box 33).

Of course it is possible to suggest a dozen or more scripts that cover the known facts of the Darby-Powerscourt relationship: such as that they never were affianced and eventually went their own ways after having shared some form of intimacy; or that they were so indiscreet that they caused gossip and their co-religionists in Wicklow and Dublin suggested to them that they break off their perceived impropriety. There are many more possibilities, but, until a trove of new material is uncovered, chasing this particular mirage is a waste of time.

What can profitably be affirmed is that Darby and Lady Powerscourt had the same real-world problem: not only were they part of the Anglo-Irish upper class that was losing purchase in several areas of Irish life, but in 1832–34 they both were in danger of becoming déclassé. Lady Powerscourt was moving inexorably toward the moment when her stepson would take over the estate, and she would be shifted; and until late 1834 Darby was not sure that his father would leave him with a penny. In many ways John Nelson Darby and Lady Powerscourt were a matched set: the same age, closely overlapping social-religious spheres, and similar social problems. Crucially, they practised together a form of worship that valued a high degree of intense small-group interaction; long, hand-wringing spontaneous prayers; petitions for inspiration to the Holy Spirit; and a belief that at any moment Jesus would literally appear again on the Earth and a new age would begin. They were dancing together on the edge of eternity. Both of them held the view that the present world had to fail. Thus, together they embraced the joy of failure.

John Nelson Darby's frenetic energy in the middle 1830s was not solely based in his *schadenfreude*, as he observed the tainted world around him lurch toward the abyss. I think we can see some of his joy, animation, and exhilaration in his successfully roughing out the final copestones that he placed atop his theological system. (This was not a final polished version of his theological architecture; Darby and his thoughts evolved until his last days.) In the 1834–35 meetings one catches a motif that becomes more and more prevalent in the discussions. Thus, the Ely Place, Dublin, conference in 1834, asked these questions:

> Can the Church account for her present state, *i.e.* that instead of unbelievers being mixed up with the children of God, these last are found as individuals among bodies of professing Christians, and joined in communion not as people of God, but upon other and different grounds?
>
> Was the dispensation of the Priesthood of Christ, in its graces, gifts, and hope of future glory, as proposed to the early Christian Church, at its foundation among the Jews, identical with that possessed by the Gentile Christian Church after the rejection of Israel?
>
> How far are ministers of the Word responsible for not proclaiming His speedy coming, or not warning of the Judgments to precede it?[37]

Aside from the syntactical tangle (which is pure John Nelson Darby in its messiness), these questions are difficult because of the plasticity with which Darby uses the word "church" – here and throughout his entire body of writing. The word has at least four usages and one has to guess what log Darby is birling at any particular moment: the Church as a purely heavenly body; the Church as the few real Christians on Earth who are the representatives of that heavenly body; the earthly, and corrupt, general Christian Church; or the wretched Church of Ireland. Whatever else was going on in the drawing room of Ely Place, Dublin, the Christian Church generally and the Church of Ireland were being held up – and not for praise.

Contemporaries in the Church of Ireland noted, quite correctly, that the annual meetings increasingly were loaded against the Anglican

37 The 1834–36 programs are found in *Questions for Eight Weeks' Consideration*, 2–4. They are a bit too full to reproduce here in their entirety. The presumptive case, unless evidence appears to the contrary, is that Darby drew up the agendas for these meetings. The 1834 meeting was held 15–19 September; that of 1835, 7–11 September; and that of 1836, 5–9 September.

Church: which explains why a circular that was attached to the invitation to the 1835 Ely Place conference tried to deflect attention to "the expectations of Mr Irving's followers" and more directly contained an assurance "that the meeting has no intention against the Established Church, as some seem to fear."[38] That assurance was markedly counterfactual, as the program indicates. The final full-day session in 1835 was focused on the following:

> Can we discover Satan's designs in the Church at large, from a study of our own hearts, or in our own hearts from his workings in the Church, or both from his attempts against Christ; the prophecies concerning the Antichrist, and the cries of the oppressed under him.
>
> What is the cause of the Church's sorrow? Can she be in a right state if not sorrowful? What will end her sorrowful days?[39]

These topics for discussion were not open-ended issues: the real agenda was for the guests to embroider in detail the theme of the failure of the formally organized Church in all its iterations. Given Darby's dominance in the Powerscourt meetings from 1833 onward, it is fair to conclude that by mid-1835 he finally was able to put definitively behind him the seesawing back-and-forth that had characterized him from late 1827 onward about whether or not he was in the Church of Ireland. My view is that only now, in the mid-1830s, did he complete the first iteration of a full theological system that permitted him to reject the

38 "Dionysius," 641. This circular is not included in the Brethren reprint of the successive conference programs in *Questions for Eight Weeks' Consideration*.

39 *Questions for Eight Weeks' Consideration*, 3. The Dublin hotel conference of 1836 had an agenda that was overwhelmingly about the sequence of the various dispensations. The Church issue was not directly on the table, save for glancing items, such as "Is there anything going on in the Church which calls for observation?" The agenda for that conference is valuable for indicating clearly that something very close to a full sequence of dispensations had been developed by Darby by that date. One of the big historical unknowns is how much colleagues such as G.V. Wigram and J.G. Bellett contributed to the development of the Irish paradigm that later evolved into the full-blown international belief system usually termed "Dispensationalism."

Church not just for reasons that were grounded in his own personality and social circumstances, but that were to him part of a full divinely ordered plan. This suggestion reflects awareness of the principle that we saw presented in "The Apostasy of the Successive Dispensations" (published in October 1836, but an outcome of his earlier thoughts on dispensations). The "Apostasy" essay articulated the fundamental belief that all dispensations, save the final one, end in failure. That is a covering principle that implied the doctrine Darby later articulated in print as "the ruin of the church": meaning that all extant ecclesiastical organizations of Christendom and, certainly, that of the Church of Ireland were not only very close to a state of ruin, but that their failures were irreparable.

One grants T.C.F. Stunt's observation that only in 1840 did Darby publish a full discussion of his concept of the "ruined condition of the church,"[40] and, indeed, it became a Brethren classic: as Clarence Bass noted, "this statement is one of the most often asserted in his volumes on ecclesiology and is one to which he repeatedly turns to answer any argument relative to the church as it exits in governmental form."[41]

40 Timothy C.F. Stunt, *Early Brethren and the Society of Friends* (n.p. 1970), 24–5. Darby's piece was written in French and published in Switzerland under the title "On the Formation of Churches." Significantly, when it was translated into English it was published as "Reflections on the Ruined Condition of the Church; and on the Efforts Making [*sic*] by Churchmen and Dissenters to Restore It to Its Primitive Order" (*CW*, 01011, 138–55). The essay's prime directive concerning Church organization was that "The children of God have nothing to do but to meet together in the name of the Lord" (149). As is the case with most items that Darby wrote in French and that were translated into English by someone else, the prose is uncharacteristically readable. For future reference relating to Darby's drive for dominance among the English Brethren in the mid-1840s, note the clear implication of a statement that follows a long argument for doing away with national Churches, hierarchies, and local choice of elders, presidents, and pastors: "I find the Holy Ghost directing submission to all who in devotedness of heart have given themselves to true labour of the Lord. So 1 Thessalonians 5:12 and Hebrews 13:17, teach the same godly submission to those who labour, and thus take the lead in the work of the Lord" (148). In other words, to labourer-leaders such as himself.

41 Clarence B. Bass, *Backgrounds to Dispensationalism* (Grand Rapids 1960), 100n2.

Although Darby only published the Church-in-ruin doctrine in 1840, he had been working on the idea for a long time previously. "As to the ruin of the church," he wrote to a French co-religionist in October 1840, "the theory came for me after the consciousness of it."[42] John Nelson Darby understood that the Church was ruined long before he turned the phrase Church-in-ruin into an ecclesiological drumbeat.

That this was the case is confirmed by the content of several of Darby's writings that had appeared earlier in the 1830s. Thus, in 1833 in a vigorous attack on the Church of Ireland bishops limiting the Irish Home Mission to persons of whom they approved, he rejected the validity of a system that was "episcopal and parochial." The parochial system – based on local geographic boundaries – was invalid. The exclusion of laymen was anti-biblical. "The Spirit of God is poured out on laymen and on clergy ... In fact, I can conceive of nothing more wicked than [the bishops] discrediting, as far as they can, the preaching of laymen."[43] He repeated his main contention in a short tract "On Lay Preaching": "The question is not whether all laymen are individually qualified; rather whether as laymen they are disqualified, unless they are what is commonly called ordained ... My assertion is, that they are entitled; that they did so in Scripture; were justified in doing so, God blessing them therein."[44]

By 1835, Darby was publishing an essay that attacked both the notion of apostolic succession, as found in Churches derived from the Catholic tradition, and the practice of Dissenting congregations calling their own ministers, as if they were hired labour. He refused, however,

42 J.N.D. to Mon. E. Maylon, 8 October 1840, orig. in French, probably trans. by W. Kelly in *LJND*, vol. 1, no. 19. Stunt (2000, 308) mentions the use of the term "ruined condition" in a Darby letter of October 1838.

43 "Thoughts on the Present Position of the Home Mission" [Dublin, 1833, pub. not given], in *CW*, 01004, 52, 55, 65.

44 "On Lay Preaching," *CW*, 01010, 131 (n.d., but part of 1833 home Mission debate). Significantly, in this tract, Darby is careful not to condemn conventional holy orders. "I do not despise pastoral care – I love it where it really exists as that savours in its place of the sweetest of God's service." His concluding sentence protects his own connection with the Church of Ireland: "Neither do I despise herein (God forbid that I do so) the holy setting apart, according to godliness, to any office."

to accept that he was rejecting the concept of the Christian ministry: "we reject nothing but *un*-Christian ministry. I do not believe that persons appointed by the king or chosen by the people, are therefore ministers." Yet, he continued, "I believe Christian ministry to be as essential to this dispensation, as the fact of Christ's coming. So far am I from setting it aside, I believe it to be essentially from God." Given that neither traditional Christian holy orders nor the Dissenting calling of pastors was valid spiritually, what was the alternative? "I read that when Christ ascended up on high, 'He gave some apostles, and some prophets; and some evangelists; and some, pastors and teachers.' This is the only source of ministry, not the appointment of a king, nor the choice of a people."[45] In practical terms, this meant that anyone who declared himself (it was a male prerogative for Darby) to be called by the Holy Spirit was a priest, subject only to criteria that Darby did not here spell out.

In the same essay, he essentially rejected the sacramental system of Catholic-derived Churches, such as the Church of Ireland. Darby forcefully articulated the implications of the "breaking of bread" – known as holy communion or the eucharist or the mass in sacramentally based churches – when it was practised within his system. "Further, I add, that while every office or gift is a blessing to the church and to be fully recognised, it is the clear privilege of any two or three Christians, where

45 "Letters to Addressed to ___, Parsonstown, in Reply to a Tract Entitled 'Three Considerations; Proving Unscriptural the Supposition of the Personal Reign of Christ on Earth during the Millennium" [Dublin: n.p., 1835], CW, 02006, 83. Two notes. First, again Darby is careful not to say that all persons called either to minister by the Established Church or by Dissenting congregations are unholy (see 84). The early Brethren embraced and recruited such persons if they were willing to worship on occasion in Brethren settings. Secondly, the Parsonstown reference is interesting in the context of Darby's own family background. Parsonstown was often known as Birr (its present name) in King's County. It was the nearest market town to the Darbys' Leap Castle and was also near where the Stoneys held their chief estate. The Rev. Edward Synge was the local Anglican priest. In the early 1840s, Parsonstown had one of the few well-organized Brethren assemblies in Ireland. See the printed notices of study meetings and printed topics of discussion posted by Thomas Mahon to Darby in England, with a personal note, April 1841 (CBA, J.N.D./1/1/20).

not done in the spirit of schism, to meet and break bread together, should they not have any ministry at all, nor any office whatever. It is their privilege as *Christians.*" The more timid of the early Brethren, most of them evangelical Anglicans, could go that far with him, but then he pounded a spike into any chance of compromise with the Church of Ireland. Concerning communion: "The necessity of a priest for this, for such it in fact comes to, is a mere remnant of the principle of apostasy in the church."[46] There we have it. If the most important sacrament of the apostolic-succession Churches was not a priest-actuated conduit of divine grace, then none of the lesser sacraments, whatever their number (the number varied among the various branches of the apostolic tradition), was subject to delivery by ordained clergy. Darby knew full well that he was telling those Christians who were within the tradition and theology of the Church of Ireland that either the Anglican concept of sacraments was invalid or that their Church structure was deeply flawed and that their priesthood could not validly deliver any sacrament whatsoever. Actually he meant both condemnations. He saw the formal priest-delivered sacraments as invalid – for the Holy Spirit gave grace directly to all God's people. To the extent that there were truly holy persons among the ordained clergy, when they presided over a true communion service it was a sacred collective experience not by virtue of their having any particular power as priests but by the power that they shared with every devout layman present.[47]

Hence: no priests, and no sacraments that were deliverable only through the conduit of an ordained priesthood. The Holy Spirit acted directly, without human mediation being necessary, as occurred at the breaking of bread among the Brethren.[48] By 1835 John Nelson Darby,

46 "A letter addressed to ___, Parsonstown," 86.

47 Later in life Darby got into a tangle on the question of whether breaking of bread was valid if only women were present. The specific argument is not here relevant, but one must point out that in the 1830s he was operating within a male-determined vocabulary concerning sacraments and collective devotional acts: this despite his efforts at recruitment of leading Irish society women.

48 At this point, the mid-1830s, Darby did not go into detail about the other traditional sacraments. Later in life he was something of an outlier among

like his American contemporary Joseph Smith Jr, had come to the conclusion that the Christian Church had taken the road to ruin when it put itself in the hands of paid professional clergy. The Brethren model as it developed in the Victorian era was for there to be no fulltime paid clergy, though of course there were to be stars, of which Darby would be in the first rank.

Thus, the process of roughing out John Nelson Darby's extraordinary ideological cathedral was complete. Roughing out only, the hard part done, but more details were to follow, year after year, as Darby laboured into the later Victorian era, and his followers continued adding details and ornamentation long after his death in 1882. As we observed in chapter 7, the framing process had begun at the base level. Hesitant and change-ridden as was the digging by the proto-Brethren into the architectural drawings of the primitive Church as found in the scriptures, that was the base level of all the superstructure that later was added. Although at no time did the Brethren practise the Imitation of Christ, they did practise to the best of their ability the imitation of the primitive Christian Church. This early, almost instinctive, primitive-Church ecclesiology determined the lines of possibility whereupon arose the hermeneutic involving the division of the scriptures, the eschatology of secret-Rapture and the subsequent rush into deep eternity, and, finally, the placement of polished capstones declaring the ruin of the Church, which, like any coping level of masonry both ultimately depended upon the building's foundations and protected the whole structure from external damage. The image of Antoni Gaudí's magnificent Basilica and Expiatory Church of the Holy Family returns to mind; Darby accomplished in theology, liturgy, Church organization, hermeneutics, and apocalyptic imaging an equivalent work of genius:

Brethren in his refusal to reject completely the baptism of infants and thus to privilege adult baptism by immersion. The topic did not agitate him; he saw useful meaning in infant baptism, albeit not the cleansing from original sin that many of the Christian Churches postulated.

less comfortable to the casual visitor than Guadi's Sagrada Familia but equally full of twisting columns, weird spires, and unexpected, soaring vaulted ceilings. The signal difference between Darby and Gaudí was that Gaudí was able to celebrate his own devotional originality, while Darby was by ideological necessity forced to pretend that he really had done nothing new, merely rediscovered truths that had always been there.

In one large segment of evangelical Christianity as it developed from the early nineteenth century into the twenty first, the work of John Nelson Darby was foundational. Although he would never admit to any originality, he was pyrotechnically creative. He took some old ideas, some new ones that his contemporaries provided, and added some original concepts of his own, and put them all together into a Gaudíesque edifice previously unknown. Like the creation of his Spanish comparator, Darby's new cathedral was a lifelong work that he never completely finished; it cast a long shadow over the minds and souls of his successors. By "foundational" in reference to John Nelson Darby's thought, one means two things. First, that his system annexed to it chronologically prior theological and devotional texts. Previous Christian theology was to be judged by Darby and his spiritual heirs according to whether or not any particular concept, belief, or devotional practice could be made to fit within Darby's massive, but angular and awkward, intellectual cathedral. Secondly, and even more revolutionarily, Darby's system produced a new arrangement of the Jewish and Christian scriptures, one that completely changed the meaning of any given word, paragraph, event, or image. A new Bible was created, one that was formalized in the early twentieth century when the Scofield Bible was published in 1909 by Oxford University Press.[49]

John Nelson Darby's development in the years 1827–35 had begun with a deep personal discomfort with the Church of Ireland, compounded by the failure of the Second Reformation movement in Ire-

49 In the present study, I have at various times foreshadowed the assimilation and adaptation of Darby's ideas into nineteenth- through twenty-first-century evangelicalism worldwide. The path of those developments was serpentine and unexpected indeed, and the methods of Darbyite influence were often covert. That story requires another book.

land and by his own problems with authority. Ireland as a nation was on its way to perdition. Darby had responded to his discovering himself to be a righteous man in a sea of shame by affirming a belief in ecclesiastical primitivism. He and his fellow proto-Brethren combined a literal reading of the New Testament as a guide to proper collective behaviour, with an animating experience they ascribed to the Holy Spirit's visiting them directly, most especially when they gathered in their small assemblies. Darby subsequently developed an ideology, and most especially an eschatology, that arose from his experience of proto-Brethren structures and practice in County Wicklow and south County Dublin. To a remarkable degree, orthopraxy preceded orthodoxy. The key to Darby's building upward was a complete rewriting of the Jewish and Christian scriptures, all within the context of a perfectly maintained claim to doing nothing new, just finding original truth. The rewriting was threefold: (1) the scriptural texts could be rearranged virtually at will to reveal God's original intent; (2) a novel dividing line was drawn between those scriptures that dealt with Israel and those that were directly applicable to the true Church, and, surprisingly, much of the New Testament was said to apply to "the Jews" rather than to the primitive Christian Church; and (3) a wonderfully plastic mode of interpreting the scriptures was propounded, where some portions were to be read "literally" and others "typologically," meaning as extended metaphors. This was prescribed, while simultaneously (and in apparent contradiction) the contemporary procedure of glossing many biblical texts as allegories was decried. In practice, these three principles constituted a license to chop-and-channel every word of the Bible. With these tools, Darby was able to create an hallucinogenic, immensely confusing, deeply encoded, highly addictive vision of the end-times, beginning with his employment of the then almost unknown concept of the secret-Rapture. Darby tied all his visions together with a prescriptive succession of divinely decreed steps – "dispensations" – that led from Creation to eternity. The flexible joint that linked each dispensation to the next was failure. As would be the case in a series of massive Darwinian extinctions, the end of one form of extant life was the predicate for the successive form, and there never was any going back. Finally, Darby had completed his amazing Gaudí-like structure by placing coping tiles at the very top. They were made from the same material as was his first foundational level – his disenchantment with the Church of Ireland. The last major doctrine that he annunciated was the "ruin of the church" – all Churches, and most particularly the one he had been ordained to serve.

While recognizing John Nelson Darby's immense creativity, one should note simultaneously the almost otiose fact that he was in fair degree manacled by the culture that produced his mindset. A pair of sharp modern observers has summarized the historical situation, by granting that John Nelson Darby took in the general European religious fashions of his era:

> but what is equally notable about the emergence of Darby's ideas is the degree to which his ideas were rooted in a particular social, national, and historical context. Darby's story and the story of Dispensationalism are closely imbricated with the contours of Irish history and the fortunes of ascendancy society. The Irishness of his theology has seldom been acknowledged, and the questions that this raises about the international, and especially the transatlantic success of Dispensationalism have seldom been addressed. The relationship between Ireland, Darby, and Dispensationalism is a complex and incomplete but fascinating picture.[50]

When considered as an entire edifice, John Nelson Darby's prodigious work in the late 1820s and 1830s was a cranky, brilliant, idiosyncratic, nearly impenetrably complicated solution to a uniquely Irish set of social and spiritual problems. That Darby's scheme would also serve a need in cultures others than the tight world of Dalyland's upper- and gentry-class evangelicals would, at the time, have seemed unlikely. Yet, fifty years later, Darby's construction was on its way to being the stealth ideology at the heart of transatlantic evangelicalism.

50 Mark Sweetman and Crawford Gribben, "J.N. Darby and the Irish Origins of Dispensationalism," *Journal of Evangelical Theological Studies*, vol. 52 (September 2009), 575.

In the short run, Darby's way of approaching the rewriting of the Bible and thus of all human time was a failure: in the sense that it did not immediately attract many adherents. As we noticed earlier, the 1836 Dublin conference was a marked come-down for the cause. The hotel at Sandymount Green was not the Powersourt estate and not even the family's central Dublin mansion. The menu for discussions almost entirely revolved about Darby's dispensational sequence. Thus, on the closing Friday the meeting opened with, "How do the faithful from an Apostasy differ in character and testimony from the opening of a Dispensation?"[51] There undoubtedly were several reasons for moving to a hotel, but in any case the agenda suggests strongly that the meeting was no longer intended to attract a broad base of Anglican evangelicals but was unabashedly Darbyite.

Lady Powerscourt died about Christmas day 1836. The exact date is unknown.[52] The cause of her passing goes unmentioned in reminiscences, which is not surprising, for mid-nineteenth century memoirs usually dwell obsessively on death and suffering without discussing directly the disease that caused an individual's demise. Max Weremchuk in his unreliable biography of Darby, reports that "it is said," in Brethren folklore, "she died of grief and a broken heart." As further explanation, he has recourse to mutually contradictory folk beliefs that she and John Nelson Darby mutually gave up plans to marry so that Darby could continue his work unhindered; that Lady Powerscourt took the leading part in breaking the alliance; and Weremchuk also reports that Darby (in plain words) dumped her. Weremchuk provides an uncited quotation, unknown to his fellow Brethren historians, that "years later, Darby said, 'I turned down a marriage and broke a heart by doing

51 *Questions for Eight Weeks' Consideration*, p.4.

52 Rowdon (1967), 86, has 30 December 1836. *CDIB*, entry for Theodosia Wingfield, reports 31 December 1836. These are probably a few days late. A letter of William Pennefather to ___, dated 28 December 1836, reports that he had received a letter telling him of the death of Lady Powerscourt (excerpt in Braithwaite, 47).

so.'"[53] Whatever the relationship of Lady Powerscourt and John Nelson Darby, her death most likely was caused by the Spanish flu, a variant of the virulent form of influenza that later caused the great 1918 death wave: it had hit Ireland in 1836–37.[54]

Lady Powerscourt's last year on Earth had more than its share of bitter gall. Her stepson, the sixth Viscount Powerscourt, came of age 18 January 1836 and almost immediately married in London Lady Elizabeth Jocelyn, eldest daughter of the third earl of Roden. The new Viscountess Powerscourt came from a more prestigious level of the intermarried Irish evangelical elite than did Theodosia and was not all that decorously evangelical. She was a famous London society beauty and active socially in her own way in Ireland: after the sixth viscount died in 1844, she married her lover, Viscount Castlereagh, who subsequently became the fourth marquis of Londonderry.[55] The relevant facts in 1836 were that Theodosia, Lady Powerscourt, faced a socially powerful young couple, a stepson now in full legal control of the several Wingfield properties, and she still had to deal with Isabella, Dowager Viscountess Powerscourt, who held the Ely Place, Dublin, house as a redoubt. One suspects that the new viscount expressed his disapproval of Theodosia's unusual spirituality and the associates it attracted by coming down hard against her further use of any of the family properties for meetings that might threaten the Established Church. Where John Nelson Darby was during Lady Powerscourt's difficult last year is uncertain. He held something of a watching brief over former Church of Ireland congregations in County Mayo. He spent time in Plymouth, where he was negotiating with a representative of the free assemblies in the French-speaking portion of Switzerland to facilitate his making an extended visit.[56]

53 Max S. Weremchuk, *John Nelson Darby*, 133–4.

54 Burnham (134) states that Lady Powerscourt died of "Spanish fever." Although his documentation is far from medically compelling, the influenza epidemic of those years indeed was severe and has a greater probability of being a cause of death than does her pining her way to demise.

55 Turtle Bunbury, *The Landed Gentry and Aristocracy of County Wicklow* (Dublin 2005), 73–6.

56 Stunt (2000), 304–5.

One of the few written memories of Lady Powescourt on the eve of her death comes from the local observer whom we know as "Mrs Hamilton Madden." In 1836, she was a fifteen-year-old middle-gentry daughter of Dalyland, keenly observant of the parish of Powerscourt's social and religious scene. She was fascinated by Lady Powerscourt and later in life recalled one of her ladyship's last visits to the parish where she had held spiritual court for so long:

> When paying a visit (which she did not very often do), she almost immediately introduced the subject which was nearest her heart. The last day I ever saw her, she talked a great deal about a favourite idea of hers, that our heaven was to be in a cloud, suspended over the new Jerusalem, which was to contain none but Jews; and when she got up to go away she said – "Well, I like the idea of my cloud." She died a short time afterwards.[57]

Lady Powerscourt was given a Church of Ireland funeral. There is no indication that John Nelson Darby attended, and I would be surprised if he had: Darby, after all, had not attended his father's funeral in 1834. Late in life he explained that he had refused to attend his father's memorial service on the principle that it was a corrupt ecclesiastical ceremony.[58] The final divine office for Lady Powerscourt was conducted by the Rev. Robert Daly, rector of the parish of Powerscourt.

Daly gave a sincere and deeply appreciative funeral sermon for Lady Powerscourt,[59] and in sermons and talks during the following year he referred generously to her search for holiness and purity.[60] Within two years of her death, Daly had collected, published, and considerably censored a volume of Lady Powerscourt's letters and devotional papers. The book went through several editions and translations into European languages.

57 [Mrs Hamilton Madden], *Personal Recollections of the Right Rev. Robert Daly* (Dublin 1872), 23. It seems likely that in her several personal recollections, Mrs Madden was working from her girlhood diary.

58 J.N.D. to _____, 1881, *LJND*, vol. 3, no. 353.

59 Madden (1872), 23, and (1875), 52n1, 157–8.

60 Madden (1872), 23.

Whatever she may have attempted in life, Lady Powerscourt did not in death leave her home parish. Dalyland ruled.

After Lady Powerscourt's death, John Nelson Darby again went walkabout. His movements have not left much trace in the historical record. In 1837 he was in London, Plymouth, Hereford, and Stafford and in Ireland in Westport, Co Mayo. At Westport he supported the work of the Rev. John M. Code, who was one of three former Church of Ireland clergymen who individually had fought with the evangelical archbishop of Tuam, the Rev. Hon Power Le Poer Trench, before leaving the Church. In 1837 only John Code, formerly curate of Westport, remained in the west of Ireland, He led a Brethren assembly, and Darby visited and encouraged him. Without ever admitting the parallel, Darby acted as a bishop on visitation: "watching over the saints I feel [is] a very primary thing," he told Code.[61] Aside from the Westport area, there were well-established assemblies in Limerick, Birr, Bandon, and smaller ones founded in the early 1830s probably still survived at places in the west of Ireland such as Ennis and Rathkeale.[62] That, how-

61 J.N.D., writing from Plymouth, to John Marsden Code 10 August 1837, *LJND*, vol. 3 (appendix), number 191. The other two clergy Westport area clerics were: the Rev. Charles Ferguson, rector of Westport, who with Code had seceded in 1835–36 and had become a full-time evangelist, and the Rev. Edward Hardman, son of one of the MPs for Drogheda, curate in Ballincholla, near Westport, who became an Irvingite in 1833 and subsequently became an angel in the Catholic Apostolic Church in Dublin. See Coad (1968), 83–5, and Rowdon, 100–4.

62 See Rowdon, 104. The meeting at Rathkeale, thirty kilometres southwest of Limerick City, is the assembly for which one most wishes there was more information. This is because, unlike virtually every place else in Ireland where small assemblies were created, the chief rival Protestant denomination in the locale was Methodist rather than Church of Ireland. The dispensational determinism increasingly assumed by the Brethren (which one might well view as an extreme variant of Calvinism) was the antipole to Methodism's acceptance of the efficacy of free will, which the Brethren denounced as "Perfectionism." Knowledge of the rivalry in Rathkeale would be fascinating for a second reason, namely intra-Protestant ethnic segmentation. Rathkeale's Methodists

ever, was the extent of the Brethren advance. It would not go much farther, a fact Darby assimilated quite quickly.

As early as 1835, Darby had visited French-speaking Switzerland and made contacts that would be useful if he decided to exit Ireland. In the summer of 1836, he had met with the Swiss dissenting clergyman Charles de Rodt, pastor of the Bourg-de-Four assembly in Geneva, and received an invitation to relocate to Geneva. In late August 1837, Darby moved his personal mission to the Continent. This connection with Switzerland "was significant as it opened up a new field of endeavour at a time when Darby's notoriety as a separatist had rendered him *persona non grata* in Ireland and when differences and tensions were beginning to emerge in Plymouth."[63]

On the eve of his leaving Ireland, Darby wrote an encouraging letter to John M. Code of Westport in the style of pastoral items early bishops had written to their clergy.[64] Thereafter, John Nelson Darby would be back in Ireland occasionally and would keep in written contact, but by the end of summer 1837 he was gone.

As the result of a surprising course of ideational transmission, Darby's central ideas became the ideological core of North American evangelicalism in the first half of the twentieth century. Of course there were a myriad other influences, and not all Darby's concepts were assimilated. But, quietly, almost silently, the theology of John Nelson Darby became the clenched fist within the America evangelical glove. His method of hyper-close Bible study; his insistence upon literalism in the reading of biblical texts, while permitting the rearrangement of the scriptures to show God's original intention; his assertion that humankind was inevitably a failure and, crucially, his making all

---

were mostly of German Palatine origin, a group for which John Wesley had a great affection; he visited Palatines on each of his missions to Ireland. For details, see Robert Haire, *Wesley's One-and-Twenty Visits to Ireland* (London 1947. The classic compressed statement is David Hempton, "Methodism in Irish Society, 1770–1830," *Transactions of the Royal Historical Society* (1986). Also indispensable is David Hempton, "The Methodist Crusade in Ireland, 1795–1845," *Irish Historical Studies* (1980).

63 Stunt (2000), 304.

64 That letter began "My Beloved Brother, I would not leave the country without a line in the Lord to you," J.N.D. to John M. Code, 10 August 1837.

FIGURE 11.1 JOHN NELSON DARBY IN MIDDLE AGE.

time balance on the any-moment return of Jesus in the secret-Rapture provided both an explanation of why the world was in such a mess and a formulation of sure promise for the future. The beliefs that had been developed to comfort the rich young rulers of County Wicklow worked even better when put forward by the waves of mass evangelists, beginning with the epochal Dwight L. Moody and proceeding like tumbling dominoes into the high years of Billy Graham's ministry. The path by which the theology of John Nelson Darby was Americanized swerved wildly. That gyring, in its complexity, its sinister and dextrous bends, is another story entirely.

BIBLIOGRAPHY

SYNOPSIS

BIBLIOGRAPHIC COMMENTS

General Comments on Basic John Nelson Darby Material

In the text, I noted that there has not as yet been a biography of John Nelson Darby that satisfactorily meets the demands of professional historians. The present book is not an attempt at his biography, but merely an effort to fit some of his beliefs and behaviours into their context: both their social context and the inevitably patchy knowledge available on the development of Darby's perspective on his own world and the next. I suspect that there never will be a full biography of John Nelson Darby, although I hope I am wrong. So far, the biographies of Darby have been by devotees of one of the branches of his faith – or its opponents. That said, any historian from outside the circle of Darby and his enemies will encounter technical difficulties that have nothing to do with whether or not the investigator enjoys the company of Darby as a subject. These are hinted at in the only successful scholarly discussion of Brethren literature, Arnold D. Ehlert's *Brethren Writers: A Checklist with an Introduction to Brethren Literature and Additional Lists* (Grand Rapids: Baker Book House, 1969). The following bibliographic and evidentiary comments are solely my own judgments, but I am very grateful for help and counsel to: Fr James Quirk, Queen's University, Kingston, Ontario; Dr Graham Johnson, the University Library, University of Manchester; Ms Joan Priest, Caven Library, Knox College, the University of Toronto; Professor Gerald Lincoln,

Lancaster Bible College; Dr Raymond Refaussé, the Representative Church Body of the Church of Ireland; Dr T.C.F. Stunt, notable independent scholar; and Professor Brian Walker, the Queen's University of Belfast.

Collected Letters

This is the most useful place to begin to approach the complexity of the Darby canon. There are few originals of letters written to John Nelson Darby still extant, though the Christian Brethren Archive, the University of Manchester, has some, and others are bound to show up over time. But the number inevitably will be limited, because Darby was truly an Irish peregrine, forever on the move, and he could not be expected to save much of his correspondence.

However, John Nelson Darby wrote thousands and thousands of letters and these often were prized keepsakes of the recipients. William Kelly, his longtime disciple and occasional adversary, compiled and published three volumes of Darby's letters (London: G. Morrish, undated, but 1886–99). The way that this collection was put together was for Kelly (and, apparently, the publisher George Morrish) to solicit from among their wide acquaintance of Darby's former associates as many original letters as possible. These were then redacted to remove the names of the recipients, to cut out sections that might be embarrassing, and to reduce individual name references within the body of the letters. This was done either by using only the person's initials or, more commonly, by employing a long dash. The practice went beyond the usual Victorian reticence in collections of printed correspondence. It was Brethren stealth at its purest: insiders would know who was involved, and outsiders would not. In *Letters of J.N.D.* answers to the obvious evidentiary questions – which of Darby's letters were chosen and which were not? – and how accurate were the transcriptions? – are largely indeterminate.

George Morrish published a second edition of the *Letters of J.N.D.* with some new material. This time the year of publication, 1914, was specified on the title page of volume 2. Whether or not these first two editions were identical with each other in terms of the content of the letters they had in common requires a complete digital comparison. I suspect they were, but a deep biographer of Darby would need to know if there were any differences and whether or not any differences followed a theological or ideological pattern.

The second edition was subsequently replaced as standard-issue among Brethren by a third edition published jointly in 1962–63 by H.L. Heijkoop, Windschoten, Netherlands, and by Stow Hill Bible and Tract Depot, Kingston-on-Thames. This is often called the "Heijkoop/Stow Hill edition." H.L. Heijkoop (1906–1995) was a venerable leader among the saints. This third edition was distributed in North America by Bible Truth Publishers of Oak Park, Illinois. Crucially the pagination of the third edition of the *Letters* is different from that of the preceding editions, although the content and details seem to be the same: as far as I can tell, but a biographer of Darby would have to do a precise line-by-line inventory. A related booklet was passed around among the initiated, giving the names of the previously anonymous recipients of Darby's communication. (More on that below.)

When the STEM Publishing electronic version was produced, it employed the third edition, the Heijkoop/Stow Hill edition, as its hardcopy base. Most helpfully, the editor of the electronic version, L.J.L. Hodgett, provided a key to all of the identifiable correspondents. This list is based on the booklet that had circulated among the select in England and Ireland and also contained some corrigenda. The information came originally from George Morrish's daughter, who confirmed that her father (the publisher and, clearly, at least a quasi-editor), had possessed the original letters. After the *Letters* were printed, he wrote the names of the correspondents on his own edition of the work and then sent the originals back to their owners. This information passed through various hands before the material and some additional corrective items were provided to the STEM publishers (see the statements of L.J.L. Hodgett, introducing the *Letters* and the *Corrigenda*, www.stempublishing.com/authors/darby/letters). Since the STEM electronic version is congruent with the Heijkoop/Stow Hill hardcopy edition, citations should be to the item number, this being the same in the STEM electronic version and in the hardcopy Heijkoop/Stow Hill edition. Such a citation system avoids the misleading specificity of page numbers (they vary through the various editions of Darby's letters, but the item numbers do not), and owners of older editions can easily identify the item being discussed.

Collected Writings

Here the problem facing any potential biographer becomes Herculean. By my own very rough count (it can only be that, given the technical problems), John Nelson Darby published (or had published for him by his followers) at least 850 separate items in his lifetime, and more items (some of questionable authenticity) keep turning up and being reprinted. Although some of Darby's material was written for periodicals, most of the work that he intended for publication (as distinct from notes on lectures and teaching sessions his followers put forward on their own) consisted of discrete individual items, ranging from tracts to exhaustive discussions of religious issues that ran to hundreds of pages.

The task of finding and then putting in an accurate chronological order the published writings of John Nelson Darby is daunting to consider; and unless some future scholar can precisely chronicle the development of his thought, a real biography will be impossible. Some of the difficulty arises from nineteenth-century Brethren of most schools (and certainly those of whatever section Darby was captaining at any given moment) having refused to recognize the power of the state as far as religious expression was concerned. In practical terms, this meant that they did not accept the deposit requirements of successive United Kingdom copyright acts. Thus, unlike the case of most writers, one cannot consult the British Library holdings for much help: the library's holdings comprise well under one hundred items from Darby's own lifetime, bolstered by a range of twentieth- and twenty-first-century reprints of untested authenticity.

The second problem is that, given the refusal to follow copyright requirements, the original printed version of most of Darby's works lack a date: not always, but in most cases. Granted, there was nothing preventing Darby from personally dating these works in some way (say, in a preface), but the Brethren emphasis on the fleeting and insignificant nature of worldly time meant that marking an earthly date was inconsistent with the appropriate focus on heavenly time.

Thirdly, a portentous modesty ran through most Brethren writing in the nineteenth century, and none more so than in Darby's own works. He often published (or allowed his followers to publish for him) items anonymously, and it is not at all clear what proportion of these have gone undetected. Less cryptically, he sometimes put "J.N.D." on the title page, or "J.N–." (Very usefully, Ehlert, 80–3, includes a list of all known initials and pseudonyms of Brethren writers and also, 22–3, provides a list of code words that usually indicate Brethren authorship.)

The library of the University of Manchester has received and splendidly curated a mass of material in its "Christian Brethren Archive." This collection is mostly from the private archives of the faithful and in fair degree makes up for the lacunae in the British Library and other deposit libraries. This is a much bigger achievement than it might at first appear: unlike most nineteenth-century literary items, this large body of work was mostly preserved privately and costively. As Arnold Ehlert noted in the late 1960s, "The fact of the matter is that the best of the older works never come onto the open market, but are passed along privately often to relatives or close friends for a small consideration or as a gift" (18). In addition to printed items, the Christian Brethren Archive has become the trusted repository for holographic items and for a few personal letters sent to John Nelson Darby. The main body of the archive's Darby material consists of several hundred individual printed Darby items, including duplicates and reprints. Even when dealing with original (meaning first edition) books and pamphlets, the basic problem remains: most items are undated.

Is this not all this merely huffing-and-puffing? – since almost every member of the faithful knows that John Nelson Darby's *Collected Writings* have been available for over 125 years, and several additional collections of miscellaneous material and Bible translations and a Bible synopsis have been printed as well. Granted, if one is a confessional follower of Darby, at whatever distance, the issue of dating and of authenticity of his *Collected Writings* and kindred compilation problems are irrelevant: for illumination is refulgent, whatever the bibliographic difficulties. However, for any future biographer, the *Collected Writings* will be simultaneously an irreplaceable source and a big headache. A migraine.

Before steeping any study of John Nelson Darby in the *Collected Writings,* one has to at least note and accept the fact that the writings are *not* an original source. The original source in the case of each reprinted item is the form that the piece of writing first took – the original of Darby's thought and expression at a given moment in time. The various editions of the *Collected Writings* (and there are several editions, not just one as is usually believed) are derivatives, not originals. Any deep biography of Darby will have to be based on the ur-edition of each item, that being the one in the form Darby framed his argument whether in pamphlet, hardcover, or periodical article. Here I must emphasize that the manner in which the derivative editions of Darby's works were assembled is highly problematic, and therefore the following inferences are made only tentatively and with full acceptance that they can be improved upon.

The first two derivatives of the mass of John Nelson Darby's publications were the *Collected Writings.* Two successive editions were compiled by Darby's sometime disciple William Kelly, who was the editor of the monthly *Bible Treasury* from 1856 onward. Kelly worked with Darby on the reprinting and compiling of the collected works (as is clearly indicated in the collected correspondence of J.N.D.). Without Kelly's persistence, Darby would chiefly be remembered as a bibliographic puzzle on the way to the litter bin.

Almost certainly, the first volume of the *Collected Writing* was published in 1866, the last volume of the first sequence (no. 32) in 1881. (The entire collection had been published in 192 fascicules between 1866 and 1881, so the bound edition was essentially a bookbinding rerun of the fascicules.) Darby died in

1882. Thirty-two volumes of *Collected Writings* were published by the London publisher George Morrish, a follower of Darby and at times his virtual stenographer. Two more volumes and a general index (London: G. Morrish) appeared, mostly likely in 1883, but this is by no means certain.

A second edition of the *Collected Writings* was also assembled by William Kelly but was not indicated as being a second edition. Kelly and Darby apparently had not got along concerning Darby's desire to censor or rewrite some of his own earlier words. (This is implied rather strongly in a thirteen-line footnote that stands at the front of volume twelve of both the first and second editions.) After Darby's death, Kelly revised volumes 12, 16, and 21, presumably to provide greater accuracy. This was not signalled with any clarity. The changes, however, are substantive, and the most important of these relate to material taken down in the late 1830s by one of Darby's followers, but not corrected by Darby at the time they were recorded. In an attenuated form they were printed with Darby's consent in the first edition of the *Collected Writings.* In the second edition some of these items are moved around as between volumes 12, 16, and 21, others are expanded, apparently to what their original length had been before Darby cut into them in a sunset rewrite of his beliefs.

A set of *Full Indexes to the Collected Writings of J.N. Darby, vols I–XXXIV* was published as a separate item by G. Morrish in 1902 (see BL and Rylands 4489). At that point the work of William Kelly as editor can be considered to have been closed. Kelly died in 1906.

The first two editions of Darby's *Writings* were very hard to come by. The bibliographer Arnold Ehlert, who was an avid collector from the 1940s through the 1960s , reported that "in all of my twenty-five years of theological librarianship I have heard of only two complete sets of Darby's *Collected Writings* coming on the market" (18). Given the scarcity of the complete sets, it is not surprising that there was little or no recognition among the faithful that there actually were two editions.

What may have been a third edition was advertised, its having been published just before the First World War by a London religious publisher, F.E. Race. I have been unable to find a Race edition, and it could have merely been a rebinding of one of the two previous editions with a new title page tipped in. (See the second edition, published posthumously by F.E. Race, probably 1913, of William Kelly's *Christ's Coming Again,* specifically the advertisements in the endpapers.)

Less obscurely, after the First World War, the firm of Morrish completely re-typeset the second edition of all thirty-four volumes. Thus: a fourth edition. This edition had a strange double titling. That is, each volume had a title page for the entire set of thirty-four volumes and also a separate title page for each individual volume. This is strange only in that (to take a specific example) the general title page said "Vol. XXI. [Second Edition.]." Yet that individual volume's inner title page gave no indication that this was a revised edition and simply said "Evangelic. Vol. II." Examination of contents of volumes 12, 16, and 21 makes it clear that this edition employed Kelly's second edition, not the first one that had been compiled when John Nelson Darby was still alive and able to meddle with the contents.

The bibliographic questions raised by subsequent editions are not entirely easy to answer. It is certain that in 1956 the Stow Hill Bible and Tract Depot, Kingston-on-Thames, in conjunction with H.L. Heijkoop in the Netherlands began to reissue the full thirty-four volume set of the *Collected Writings*. Thus: a fifth edition in the skein that is derivative from the original primary sources. Here things become somewhat messy. Although the Heijkoop/Stow Hill edition declared on its several titles pages that it was a "reprint edition," it was not a reprint in the sense that this word is used by historians, librarians, or bibliographers. Indeed, each volume presented an introductory tabulation of where each tract, sermon, or exposition was found in terms of the "original volume page" and in the "present volume page." I think what was intended here was to indicate to the faithful that this was a reprint in the sense of being an accurate rendering of Darby's words, albeit not a true reprinting of the first edition of his *Collected Writings*.

This situation raises a ticklish question: what were the editors of the Heijkoop/Stow Hill "reprint" of the *Collected Writings* working with as their sources? One would naturally assume that they used as their bedrock the 1866–83 first edition, but mostly they worked with the second edition. The Stow Hill title pages state that these are the collected writings of J.N. Darby "edited by William Kelly." But in fact these are not exactly either one of Kelly's editions. I do not think that anything misleading or mendacious was here intended. Rather, I suspect that the "reprint" editors just used what came to hand, mostly the second edition, and did not worry about bibliographic niceties or notice that they were dealing with broken sets.

What can be considered as a sixth edition was published electronically by STEM publishers. It follows the Heijkoop/Stow edition and adds, with clear citation, several new Darby items. This is a very stable electronic site, but for reasons of long-term durability, citation to the thirty-four original volumes should use the Heijkoop/Stow Hill pagination (except for volumes 12, 16, and 21, where one must obtain printed first and second editions on those items that have been amended between first and second editions. STEM references are necessary, however, for unique items that STEM has uncovered and published since the Heijkoop/Stem edition appeared; see below for comments on the best mode of STEM references).

With some regret, one must note that additional hardcopy versions of some of the volumes of the *Collected Writings*, or selected excerpts from the *Collected Writings*, have been appearing recently. These are made economically feasible by on-demand printing formats. My strong suggestion is that scholars stop with the STEM edition as the opportunities for deleterious changes are just too many and too hard to police in the various digital-print formats.

To summarize fundamental matters of historicity, consider the issues of *authenticity, chronology,* and *editorial responsibility.* Because of the intervention of Darby in the reprinting of his works, the authenticity of each separate item will have to be checked by any careful biographer against the original. My impression is that Darby was only minimally inclined to alter his earlier works, but that needs confirmation. A more pressing issue is the degree to which Darby's early editor – or editors – straightened out some of his messy and gnomic utterances. And one needs to address the "silence issue": the case of items that were extant but not reprinted. These are the elisions that could inform a biographer about issues of high sensitivity. Again, in Brethren fashion, the *Collected Writings* leave most items indeterminate as far as dating is concerned; nor is the originating publishing firm of the primary item credited on most items. Although William Kelly was loath to admit to having stamped his authority on the compilation, this could be the misleading result of Brethren modesty. He clearly overruled Darby in his second edition of volumes 12, 16, and 21, which include stenographic notes of early Darby sermons. Elsewhere, the editorial hand is virtually unseen, but that does not mean it was not present. One has to wonder not only about the extent of reshaping done by the interaction of Darby with Kelly, but also about how much the publisher George Morrish was involved.

In any case, if one is citing the *Collected Writings* rather than the original separate publication – and that will necessarily be the case with most items – it is well to remember that the collection was developed well before widespread photographic reprography, so that the pagination in the reprint (whatever the edition) does not jibe with that of the original independent publication of the specific item. Obviously, one has a chain-of-custody issue here. A Darby biographer would need to be very thorough.

Given the multiple editions of John Nelson Darby's *Collected Writings*, what is the most broadly useable way of citing items within the collections? Until bibliographers work out the stratigraphy of the material, or scholars find and reprint the true originals in their ur-form, I think the most ecumenical mode of approach is to use the Heijkoop/Stow Hill edition as a basis, as this is the most apt to be in libraries and personal collections. The STEM electronic form reproduces all the material in the Hiejkoop/Stow Hill edition, and this electronic form is most open to readers who do not have their own set. The only drawback is that the sequence of electronic presentation STEM employs scrambles the individual items in Heijkoop/Stow Hill. However this is not fatal, as STEM cites as part of the identification of each item, the information that one really wants: the volume number the article or reprinted book was put into in the 1866ff edition of the *Collected Writings;* its place within the sequential order within that volume (thus, "11007" in the STEM system refers to the seventh item in the eleventh volume of the 1866ff version of Darby's assembled writings); then, any subsequent page number is *not* that of the 1866ff edition (and, crucially, not even close to the pagination in the actual first-printed copy of each item when that item was a separate book or booklet) but that of the later Heijkoop/Stow Hill collected edition. Thus, to continue the example begun above, one would cite "The Rapture of the Saints and the Character of the Jewish Remnant," CW, 11007, and then give the page number [in this case between 118–67, inclusive] in the Heijkoop/Stow Hill edition. This system is not ideal, but it maximizes utility for users of the various editions, while at the same time permitting unambiguous citation.

In relation to the bibliographic and dating difficulties mentioned above, the reader may be tempted to seek refuge in the bibliographic handbook produced by the English group of Brethren often called the Taylorites (anon., *Dates of J.N. Darby's Collected Writings,* Chessington, Surrey: Bible and Gospel Trust, 2013). The handbook is very useful in its listing of Darby's publishers and of the periodicals in which his writing appeared. However, in its dating of the mass of items in the *Collected Writings*, it is both tantalizing and useless. The compilers of the bibliography accept (without being specific about substantive details) that there are multiple versions of CW and that "wording can vary between editions" (1). However, they deal directly with only the first two editions and mention only variations in the titles of individual items and where they are found. They report that they have carried out the admirable task of finding the first publication of 710 of the books, tracts, or articles that are among those in the CW. None of these original printings is cited in full and from the "Introduction" it appears that the compilers saw only some of the originals and relied on correspondence with librarians or on unspecified electronic forms for other items. What makes the final product potentially deeply misleading is that this handbook affixes a date to each item in the *Collected Writings* and this is done without any explanation of the source of the handbook's dating information or of why it has probative force. To state the obvious: the dates that were printed in the first edition of CW cannot be taken as proof that the date printed in CW was accurate. That being recognized, it is clear that the inaccuracies that John Nelson Darby, or his editor the Rev. William Kelly, affixed to some of the earliest writings are simply repeated.

Other Printed Books, Pamphlets, and Ephemera

In addition to the *Collected Writings* the Heijkoop/Stow Hill editors republished in the 1960s several substantial volumes of Darby's additional works: seven volumes of *Notes and Comments on Scripture*, one volume of *Notes and Jottings*, two volumes of *Miscellaneous Writings* (being volumes 4 and 5 of Darby's *Miscellaneous Writings*), and five volumes of the *Synopsis of the Books of the Bible*. Each of these additional series was allegedly written entirely by Darby and is part of the deutero-canon (if one can use a Catholic concept) of Darby's writings, as distinct from the primary canon: his writings and letters as edited by Kelly. The deutero-canon was completed and standardized after the *Collected Writings* and the *Letters* had been compiled: at indeterminate dates and by anonymous editors in the late Victorian or Edwardian eras.

In the mid-1990s STEM Publishing of Ramsgate, Kent, made the entire body of work available electronically, in CD-ROM form and on the web. In the deutero-canon, there are a few new editorial interpolations, but these are clearly marked. The credit for this probably goes to Les J.L. Hodgett of STEM. The awkward Oak Park index of 1971 is replaced by a search function.

The only complication here is that in 2005–06, a Brethren adherent [Roy Huebner] anonymously published *Additional Writings of J.N. Darby*, 2 vols (Jackson, NJ: Present Truth Publishers, 2005 and 2006). Some, but not all, of this material is found on the STEM site.

The Problematic Nature of the Synopsis of the Books of the Bible

This is a difficult historical matter. The Biblical Synopsis (as it usually is called) is a beloved item and a favourite of readers of J.N. Darby. It covers the entire Hebrew and Christian scriptures and does so with economy and even elegance. That is the problem. Its style is entirely different from any major item among Darby's writings. As is noted by a wide range of scholars, Darby was a terrible writer: involuted, solipsistic, tangential, and often downright incoherent in his arguments, albeit not always inapposite in his observations. None of those problems characterizes the Biblical Synopsis, which was originally written and published in French. It was published periodically in France beginning in 1849 and in book form in 1854 as *Études sur la parole destinées à aider le Chrétien dans la lecture du Saint-Livre* (Pau: E. Malan, 1854) and went through several editions. It was translated into English, by William Kelly, and edited by him and published serially in *The Present Testimony* under the editorship of George V. Wigram (see E.N. Cross, *The Irish Saint and Scholar: A Biography of William Kelly, 1821–1906*, London: Chapter Two, 2004, 63 and 82n79). In 1857, it began to be published in English in book form and in 1866 eventually reached five volumes. The *Synopsis* has been reprinted in whole or in part multiple times and often revised. The second English-language edition of the set has Darby's name on the title page and includes notice that the *Synopsis* was originally written and published in French. "It has been already translated into English and introduced Book by Book into a religious publication appearing from time to time." There is no doubt that the translation was by the Rev. William Kelly (on this Marion Field is good; see *John Nelson Darby: Prophetic Pioneer*, Godalming, Surrey: 2008, 192). One either has to infer that Darby wrote much better in French than in English or, more likely, that William Kelly has to be considered as a co-author of the *Synopsis of the Bible*. W.G. Turner, who was well connected with the Brethren of Kelly's generation, stated that Kelly "had himself revised Darby's *Synopsis of the Bible*" (*John Nelson Darby*, London: C.A. Hammond, 1944, 53). This means that studies of Darby's religious views cannot unreservedly use the *Synopsis* as a source. Thus, for example, Floyd S. Elmore's "A Critical Examination of the Doctrine of the Two Peoples of God in John Nelson Darby" (ThD, Dallas Theological Seminary, 1990) relies almost entirely on the *Synopsis*. One is walking on shaky tundra when the clearest and most loved of John Nelson Darby's putative writings is also the one item that most certainly was not produced by Darby's sole authorship; indeed, given that it first appeared in French and that he did not translate it himself, it most likely contains not even a single English-language sentence of his own composition.

Related Sources

In the Christian Brethren Archive in the University of Manchester Library, besides the core Darby collection (which was compiled privately by Henry Sibthorpe), there is the Fry Collection, named after Alfred Charles Fry. It contains material from first- and second-generation Brethren figures, most importantly Benjamin Wills Newton and Samuel P. Tregelles. The Christian Brethren Archive is becoming the natural magnet for material related to the group.

A particularly intriguing project is being engaged in through a partnership between the University of Manchester Library, Trinity College, Dublin, and the Panacea Society. It involves the digitilization of Darby's marginalia in a Greek New Testament that he had disassembled and rebound so that he could have plenty of space for handwritten comment. It is available online.

Conclusion

Despite the mountain of material by Darby that is available, the fundamental problem remains: we have a great deal of source material through which historians can come to know quite a bit about him, but as yet we do not yet have sufficient knowledge concerning the character and reliability of most of this material to be able to use it confidently and fully effectively.

UNITED KINGDOM PARLIAMENTARY PAPERS (IN CHRONOLOGICAL ORDER)

Reports from the Commissioners of the Board of Education in Ireland.
First, on Free Schools of Royal Foundation, H.C. 1809 (142), vii.
Second, on Schools of Private Foundation, H.C. 1809 (142), vii.
Third, on Protestant Charter Schools, H.C. 1809 (142), vii.
Fourth, on Diocesan Free Schools, H.C. 1810 (174), x.
Fifth, on Wilson's Hospital, H.C. 1810 (175), x.
Sixth, on the Blue Coat Hospital, H.C. 1810 (176), x.
Seventh, on the Hibernian School, H.C. 1810 (177), x.
Eighth, on the Foundling Hospital, H.C. 1810 (193), x.
Ninth, on Schools founded by Erasmus Smith, Esq., H.C. 1810 (194), x.
Tenth, on the Hibernian Marine School, H.C. 1810 (243), x.
Eleventh, on Parish Schools, 1810–11 (107), vi.
Twelfth, on Classical Schools of Private Foundation, H.C. 1812 (218), v.
Thirteenth, on English Schools of Private Foundation, H.C. 1812 (219), v.
Fourteenth, View of the Chief Foundations, with Some General Remarks, H.C. 1812–13 (21), vi. The fourteen reports reprinted, H.C. 1813–14 (47), v.

Papers Relating to the Foundling Hospital in Dublin, H.C. 1824 (281), xxi.

Minutes of Evidence Taken before the Select Committee of the House of Lords Appointed to Inquire into the State of Ireland … H.C. 1825 (521), ix.

First Report of the Commissioners of Irish Education Inquiry, H.C. 1825 (400), xii.

Second Report of the Commissioners of Irish Education Inquiry, H.C. 1826–27 (12), xii.

Third Report of the Commissioners of Irish Education Inquiry, H.C. 1826–27 (13), xiii.

Fourth Report of the Commissioners of Irish Education Inquiry, H.C. 1826–27 (89), xiii.
Fifth Report of the Commissioners of Irish Education Inquiry, H.C. 1826–27 (441), xiii.
Sixth Report of the Commissioners of Irish Education Inquiry, H.C. 1826–27 (442), xiii.
Seventh Report of the Commissioners of Irish Education Inquiry, H.C. 1826–27 (443), xiii.
Eighth Report of the Commissioners of Irish Education Inquiry, H.C. 1826–27 (509), xiii.
Ninth Report of the Commissioners of Irish Education Inquiry, H.C. 1826–27 (516), xiii.
Report from the Select Committee to Whom the Reports on the Subject of Education in Ireland Were Referred, H.C. 1828 (341), iv; reprinted H.C. 1829 (80), iv.
Report from the Select Committee Appointed to Take into Consideration the State of the Poorer Classes in Ireland, H.C. 1830 (667), vii.
Second Report of Evidence from the Select Committee on the State of the Poor in Ireland. Minutes of Evidence, 18 May – 5 June, H.C. 1830 (654), vii.
First Report of His Majesty's Commissioners on Ecclesiastical Revenue and Patronage, Ireland, H.C. 1833 (762), xxi.
Second Report of His Majesty's Commissioners on Ecclesiastical Revenue and Patronage, Ireland, H.C. 1834 (523), xxiii.
First Report of the Commissioners of Public Instruction, Ireland, (45 and 46), H.C. 1835, xxiii.
Second Report of the Commissioners of Public Instruction, Ireland, (47), H.C. 1835, xxxiv.
Third Report of His Majesty's Commissioners on Ecclesiastical Revenue and Patronage in Ireland, H.C. 1836 (246), xxv.
Fourth Report of His Majesty's Commissioners on Ecclesiastical Revenue and Patronage in Ireland, H.C. 1837 (500), xxi.
Irish Church Act (Commutation) Return, H.C. 1875 (52), lvii.
A Summary of the Returns of Owners of Land in Ireland, H.C. 1876 (422), lxxx.

INDIVIDUAL WORKS CITED IN THE TEXT

Aalen, F.H.A., and Kevin Whelan, eds. *Dublin City and County from Prehistory to Present*. Dublin: Geography Publications, 1992.
–, Kevin Whelan, and Matthew Stout. *Atlas of Irish Rural Landscape*. Toronto: University of Toronto Press, 1997.

Acheson, Alan. *A True and Lively Faith: Evangelical Revival in the Church of Ireland.* Dublin: Church of Ireland Evangelical Fellowship, 1992.

– *A History of the Church of Ireland, 1691–2001.* 2nd ed. Dublin: Columba Press and APCK, 2002.

– *Bishop John Jebb and the Nineteenth-Century Anglican Renaissance.* Toronto: Clements Academic, 2013.

Adams, J.R.R. "Swine-Tax and Eat-Him-All-Magee: The Hedge Schools and Popular Education in Ireland." In Donnelly and Miller, eds (Dublin: Irish Academic Press, 1998): 97–117.

Akenson, Donald H. *The Irish Education Experiment: The National System of Education in the Nineteenth Century.* London: Routledge and Kegan Paul, and Toronto: University of Toronto Press, 1970. Reprint, London and New York: Routledge, 2012.

– *The Church of Ireland: Ecclesiastical Reform and Revolution, 1800–1885.* New Haven: Yale University Press, 1971.

– *Education and Enmity: The Control of Schooling in Northern Ireland.* Newton Abbot: David and Charles Ltd, 1973. Reprint, London and New York: Routledge, 2012.

– *A Protestant in Purgatory: Richard Whately, Archbishop of Dublin.* Hamden, CT: Archon Books, for the Conference on British Studies, 1981.

– *The Orangeman: The Life and Times of Ogle Gowan.* Toronto: James Lorimer and Co., 1986.

– "Pre-university Education, 1782–1870." In W.E. Vaughan, ed., *A New History of Ireland, Vol. VI: Ireland under the Union, II, 1890–1921* (Oxford: Clarendon Press 1996): 523–37.

– *Surpassing Wonder: The Invention of the Bible and the Talmuds.* New York: Harcourt Brace and Co., and Montreal and Kingston: McGill-Queen's University Press, 1998.

– *Saint Saul: A Skeleton Key to the Historical Jesus.* New York: Oxford University Press, and Montreal and Kingston: McGill-Queen's University Press, 2000.

– *Some Family: The Mormons and How Humanity Keeps Track of Itself.* Montreal and Kingston: McGill-Queen's University Press, 2007.

– *Ireland, Sweden, and the Great European Migration, 1815–1914.* Liverpool: Liverpool University Press, and Montreal and Kingston: McGill-Queen's University Press, 2011.

Alborn, Timothy. "An Irish Eldorado: Recovering Gold in County Wicklow." *Journal of British Studies* 50 (2011): 359–80.

Alter, Robert. *The Art of Biblical Narrative.* New York: Basic Books, 1981.

Atkinson, Arthur. *The Irish Tourist: In a Series of Picturesque Views, Travelling Incidents and Statistical, Political and Moral Illustrations of the Character and Aspect of the Irish Nation*. Dublin: printed for the author, [1815].

Augustine of Hippo. *City of God against the Pagans*. Edited by William Chase Greene, vol. 6. Bilingual edition. London: William Heinemann, and Cambridge: Harvard University Press, 1960.

Bailey, Kenneth C. *A History of Trinity College Dublin, 1892–1945*. Dublin: Hodges, Figgis and Co., 1947.

Barker, G.F. Russell, and Alan H. Stenning. *The Record of Old Westminsters*. Vol. 1. London: Chiswick Press, 1928.

Barlow, H.B. "Intelligence: the Art of Good Guess-Work." In Richard L. Gregory, ed., *The Oxford Companion to the Mind* (Oxford: Oxford University Press, 1987).

Barnard, Toby. *A New History of Ireland: The Irish Protestants, 1649–1770*. New Haven: Yale University Press, 2003.

Bass, Clarence B. *Backgrounds to Dispensationalism: Its Historical Genesis and Ecclesiastical Implications*. Grand Rapids: William B. Eerdmans Publishing Co., 1960.

Bateman, John. *The Great Landowners of Great Britain and Ireland*. 4th ed. New York: Augustus M. Kelley Publishers, 1970. First published 1883.

Beatson, Robert. *A Political Index to the Histories of Great Britain and Ireland; or, a Complete Register of the Hereditary Honours, Public Offices, and Persons in Office from the Earliest Period to the Present Time*. 2nd ed., vol. 1. London: G.G.J. and J. Robinson, 1787.

Beaufort, Daniel. *Memoir of a Map of Ireland*. London: W. Faden and James Edwards, 1792.

Bebbington, David. *Evangelicalism in Modern Britain: A History from the 1730s to the 1980s*. London: Unwin Hyman, 1989.

– "Evangelical Conversion, c. 1740–1850." *Scottish Bulletin of Evangelical Theology* 18 (2000): 102–27.

Bebbington, Eileen. *A Patterned Life: Faith, History, and David Bebbington*. Eugene, OR: Wipf and Stock Publishers, 2014.

Beckett, James C. *Protestant Dissent in Ireland, 1687–1780*. London: Faber and Faber, 1948.

[Bellett, Dorothy]. *Memoirs of the Rev. George Bellett*. London: J. Masters and Co., 1889.

[Bellett, John Gifford]. *Interesting Reminiscences of the Early History of "Brethren": With a Letter from J.G. Bellett to J.N. Darby*. Weston-Super-Mare: Walter Scott and London: Alfred Holness, 1884.

[Bellett, Letty M.]. *Recollections of the Late J.G. Bellett by His Daughter.* London: A.S. Rouse, 1895.

Bence-Jones, Mark. *Burke's Guide to Country Houses: Vol. 1, Ireland.* London: Burke's Peerage Ltd, 1978.

Bergen, G. Fred, ed., *Autobiography of George Müller.* London: J. Nisbet, 1905.

The Blackwell Dictionary of Evangelical Biography. Oxford: Blackwell, 1995. 2 vols. Edited by Donald M. Lewis.

Bowen, Desmond. *Souperism: Myth or Reality?* Cork: Mercier Press, 1970.

– *The Protestant Crusade in Ireland, 1800–70: A Study of Protestant-Catholic Relations between the Act of Union and Disestablishment.* Dublin: Gill and Macmillan, and Montreal and Kingston: McGill-Queen's University Press, 1978.

– *History and the Shaping of Irish Protestantism.* New York: Peter Lang, 1995.

Brady, Ciaran. *James Anthony Froude: An Intellectual Biography of a Victorian Prophet.* Oxford: Oxford University Press, 2013.

Braithwaite, Robert. *The Life and Letters of Rev. William Pennefather, BA.* 2nd ed. London: John F. Shaw, 1878.

[anonymous]. *Brief Memorials of the Rev. B.W. Mathias, Late Chaplain of Bethesda Chapel.* Dublin: William Curry, 1842.

Brooke, Richard Sinclair. *Recollections of the Irish Church.* London: MacMillan and Co., 1877.

[Brookes, Joshua William]. *A Dictionary of Writers on the Prophecies with the Titles and Occasional Description of Their Works.* London: Simpkin, Marshall and Co., 1835.

Brown, Michael, Charles Ivar McGrath, and Thomas P. Power, eds. *Converts and Conversion in Ireland, 1650–1850.* Dublin: Four Courts Press, 2005.

Brown, Steward J. *The National Churches of England, Ireland, and Scotland, 1801–1846.* Oxford: Oxford University Press, 2001.

Brown, Terence. *Ireland's Literature: Selected Essays.* Mullingar: Lilliput Press, 1988.

Buchanan, Arthur W.P. *The Buchanan Book: The Life of Alexander Buchanan, QC, of Montreal, Followed by an Account of the Family of Buchanan.* Montreal, privately printed: 1911.

Buchanan, James. *The Religious Belief of James Buchanan.* London: privately printed, (n.p., 1834). Privately reprinted for George Whitlaw, 1896. Reprinted, Omagh: J. Quinn, 1956.

Buchwald, Jed, and Mordechai Feingold. *Newton and the Origin of Civilisation.* Princeton: Princeton University Press, 2012.

Bunbury, Turtle [and Art Kavanagh]. *The Landed Gentry and Aristocracy of County Wicklow.* Dublin: Irish Family Names, 2005.

[Burgh, William]. *The Coming of the Day of God, in Connexion with the First Resurrection – the Reign of Christ on Earth – the Restitution of All Things etc.: A Discourse on 2 Peter iii, 11, 12, 13, by an Humble Expectant of the Promise.* Dublin: Richard Moore Tims, 1821.

– *Lectures on the Second Advent of Our Lord Jesus Christ and Connected Events: With an Introduction on the Use of Unfulfilled Prophecy.* Dublin: Richard Moore Tims, 1832. 2nd expanded ed. Dublin: William Curry Jr, 1835.

– *The Apocalypse Unfulfilled.* Dublin: Richard M. Tims, 1832. 2nd ed., 1833.

– *An Exposition of the Book of Revelation.* 5th rev. ed. Dublin: Hodges, Smith and Co, 1857.

Burnham, Jonathan D. *A Story of Conflict: The Controversial Relationship between Benjamin Wills Newton and John Nelson Darby.* Carlisle: Paternoster Press, 2004.

Burtchaell, George Dames, and Thomas Ulick Sadleir. *Alumni Dublinensis.* London: Williams and Norgate, 1924.

Cambridge Dictionary of Irish Biography. Cambridge: Cambridge University Press, 2010.

Carlyle, Thomas. *On Heroes, Hero-Worship, and the Heroic in History.* James Fraser: London, 1841.

– *Reminescences.* 2 vols. Edited by James Anthony Froude. London: Longmans, Green, and Co. 1881.

Carter, Grayson. *Anglican Evangelicals: Protestant Secessions from the Via Media, c. 1800–1850.* Oxford: Oxford University Press, 2001.

[anonymous]. "The Catholic Question." *Blackwood's Edinburgh Magazine* 21 (May 1827): 575–96.

Cheney, C.R., ed. *Handbook of Dates for Students of English History.* London: Royal Historical Society, 1961.

Clark, Samuel, and James S. Donnelly, Jr. *Irish Peasants: Violence and Political Unrest, 1780–1914.* Madison: University of Wisconsin Press, 1983.

Clergy of Dublin and Glendalough: Biographical Succession Lists. Belfast: Ulster Historical Foundation, 2001. Compiled by James B. Leslie and corrected by W.J.R. Wallace.

Coad, F. Roy. *Prophetic Developments with Particular Reference to the Early Brethren Movement.* Pinner, Middlesex: Christian Brethren Research Fellowship, 1966.

– *A History of the Brethren Movement: Its Origins, Its Worldwide Development and Its Significance for the Present Day.* 2nd ed. Exeter: Paternoster Press, 1968.

Cohn, Norman. *The Pursuit of the Millennium: Revolutionary Millenarians and Mystical Anarchists of the Middle Ages.* London: Mercury Books, 1957. Rev. ed. New York: Oxford University Press, 1970.

Collins, John J., ed. *The Encyclopedia of Apocalypticism.* Vol. 1. New York: Continuum, 1998.

Comerford, Patrick. "An Innovative People: The Church of Ireland Laity, 1780–1830." In Gillespie and Neely, eds (Dublin, 2002): 170–95.

Comerford, R.V., Mary Cullen, Jacqueline R. Hill, and Colm Lennon. *Religion, Conflict and Coexistence in Ireland: Essays Presented to Monsignor Patrick Corish.* Dublin: Gill and MacMillan, 1990.

Connolly, Sean. *Priests and People in Pre-famine Ireland, 1780–1845.* Dublin: Gill and MacMillan, 1982.

– *Religion, Law and Power: The Making of Protestant Ireland, 1660–1760.* London: Oxford University Press, 1992.

– *Divided Kingdom: Ireland 1630–1800.* Oxford: Oxford University Press, 2008.

Cooke-Trench, Thomas R.C. *A Memoir of the Trench Family.* Privately printed: n.p., 1897.

Coolahan, John. "Primary Education as a Political Issue in O'Connell's Time." In O'Connell, ed. (1991): 87–100, 107–9.

Cornwall, E.E. "Thomas Kelly, 1769–1855," an excerpt from his "Songs of Pilgrimage and Glory," www.stempublishing.com/humns/biographies/kellyt.html. Accessed 5 July 2013.

Costecalde, Claude, and Brian Walker, eds. *The Church of Ireland: An Illustrated History.* Dublin: Booklin, 2013.

Craik, Henry. *Principia Hebraica; or, an Easy Introduction to the Hebrew Language, Exhibiting in Twenty-Four Tables the Interpretation of all the Hebrew and Chaldee Words, both Primitives and Derivatives, Contained in the Old Testament Scriptures.* Revised by E.R. Hodges. London: Samuel Bagster, [1863].

Croskerry, Thomas. *Plymouth-Brethrenism: A Refutation of Its Principles and Doctrines.* London and Belfast: William Mullan, 1879.

Crutchfield, Larry. *The Origins of Dispensationalism: The Darby Factor.* Lanham, MD: University Press of America, 1991.

Dallimore, Arnold A. *Forerunner of the Charismatic Movement: The Life of Edward Irving.* Chicago: Moody Press, 1983

D'Alton, John. *The Memoirs of the Archbishops of Dublin*. Dublin: Hodges and Smith, 1838.

Daly, Robert, ed. *Letters and Papers by the Late Theodosia A. Viscountess Powerscourt*. 3rd ed. Dublin: William Curry, 1839.

Darby, John Nelson. The multiple volumes of the *Letters of J.N.D.* and of his *Collected Writings* went through several editions. The details, as much as they can at present be known, are found in the Bibliographic Comments that precedes the present formal bibliography. Protocols for citation that bridge the various editions are indicated in those comments. Most of Darby's writings are included in those two sources, but for a few items that are in collected editions it nevertheless is useful to refer to the earlier printed editions:

[anonymous]. — *Considerations Addressed to the Archbishop of Dublin and the Clergy Who Signed the Petition to the House of Commons for Protection*. Dublin: privately printed: [1828]. Cf. CW 01001.

– *The Irrationalism of Infidelity, Being a Reply to "Phases of Faith."* London: Groombridge and Son: 1853. Cf. CW 06002.

– *Letter by J.N.D. to Prof Tholuck, "Translated from the French."* 2nd ed. Dublin: F.G. Burkitt: n.d. Cf. *LJND*, 3 (226).

– *Analysis of Dr Newman's Apologia Pro Vita Sua; With a Glance at the history of Popes, Councils, and the Church*. London: W.H. Broom, 1866. Cf. CW 18004.

[–, wrongly attributed]. *How the Lost Sheep Was Found: An Incident in the Life of the Late J.N. Darby*. n.p., 1930?

Darby, William H. *The Union of Believers*. Printed for the author, 1873.

[anonymous]. *Dates of J.N. Darby's Collected Writings*. Chessington, Surrey: Bible and Gospel Trust, 2013.

Delaney, Enda. *The Irish in Post-War Britain*. Oxford: Oxford University Press, 2007.

Dickson, David, ed. *The Gorgeous Mask: Dublin 1700–1750*. Dublin: Trinity History Workshop, 1987.

– *Dublin: The Making of a Capital City*. Cambridge: Harvard University Press, 2014.

– and Richard English. "The La Touche Dynasty." In Dickson (ed.). 1987: 17–29.

Dickson, J.N. Ian. *Beyond Religious Discourse: Sermons, Preaching and Evangelical Protestants in Nineteenth-Century Irish Society*. Milton Keynes: Paternoster, 2007.

Dickson, Neil. *Brethren in Scotland, 1838–2000: A Social Study in an Evangelical Movement*. Carlisle: Paternoster Press, 2002.

– and Tim Grass. *The Growth of the Brethren Movement: National and International Experiences. Essays in Honour of Harold H. Rowdon.* Carlisle: Paternoster, 2006.

[Digby, Kenelm Henry]. *The Broad Stone of Honour, or, Rules for the Gentlemen of England.* 1st ed. London: C. and J. Rivington, 1822. 2nd ed. (2 vols.) London: C. and J. Rivington, 1822 and 1823.

– *Broad Stone of Honour: The True Sense and Practice of Chivalry.* 4 vols. London: Bernard Quaritch, 1826–29.

"Dionysius." "Prophetical Meetings." *Christian Examiner and Church of Ireland Magazine*, new series, vol. 4 (September 1835): 639–42.

Dobbs, Francis. *Millennium, a Poem in Four Books, to Which Are Prefixed Reasons from Prophecy Why the Second Coming of Christ and the Commencement of His Personal Reign on Earth Are Immediately to Be Expected.* London: printed for the author by George Kearsley, 1787.

– *Mr Dobbs's Speech in the House of Commons of Ireland, on Tuesday the 5th of March, 1799, on Submitting Five Propositions for Tranquilizing the Country.* Dublin: J. Moore, 1799.

– *A Concise View from History and Prophecy of the Great Predictions in the Sacred Writings That Have Been Fulfilled; also of Those That Are Now Fulfilling and Remain to Be Accomplished: In Letters to His Eldest Son.* Dublin: printed for the author by John Jones, 1800.

– *First volume of Universal History.* 4 vols. London: printed for the author by G. Kearsley, 1787–1788; reprised and expanded in Dobbs, Francis. *A Summary of Universal History from the Creation to the Present Time: In Letters from a Father to His Son.* 9 vols. London: printed for the author by John Jones, 1800.

– *Memoirs of Francis Dobbs, Esq., also Genuine Reports of His Speeches in Parliament on the Subject on an Union and His Prediction of the Second Coming of the Messiah; with Extracts from His Poem on the Millennium.* Dublin: printed for the author by John Jones, 1800.

Dobbs, Richard. A *Remarkable Accomplishment of a Noted Scripture Prophecy as Applied to the History of England during the Last and Present Centuries, in a Thanksgiving Sermon … November 29th, 1759.* London: Thomas Wilcox, 1762.

Donnelly, James S. Jr. "Pastorini and Captain Rock: Millenarianism and Sectarianism in the Rockite Movement of 1821–4." In Clark and Donnelly, eds: 102–39.

– *Captain Rock: The Irish Agrarian Rebellion of 1821–1824.* Madison: University of Wisconsin Press, 2009.

Donnelly, James S., and Kerby A. Miller, eds. *Irish Popular Culture, 1650–1850.* Dublin: Irish Academic Press, 1998.

Dooley, Terence. *The Decline of the Big House in Ireland: A Study of Irish Landed Families, 1860–1960.* Dublin: Wolfhound Press, 2001.

W.H.D. [Dorman, William H]. *The Close of Twenty-Eight Years of Association with J.N.D.* London: Houlston and Wright, 1866.

[Doyle, James]. *A Reply by J.K.L. to the Late Charge of the Most Reverend Doctor Magee.* Dublin: Richard Coyne, 1827.

Drummond, Andrew L. *Edward Irving and His Circle, Including Some Consideration of the "Tongues" Movement in the Light of Modern Psychology.* London: J. Clarke, 1937.

[Drummond, Henry]. *Dialogues on Prophecy*, 3 vols. London: James Nisbet, vol. 1, 1828; vol. 2, 1828; vol. 3, 1829.

Dunlop, Robert, ed. *Evangelicals in Ireland: An Introduction.* Dublin: Columba Press, 2004.

Dunne, Waldo H. *James Anthony Froude: A Biography.* Vol. 1. Oxford: Oxford University Press, 1961.

[anonymous]. "Edward Irving." *North British Review* (August 1862): 94–131.

Ehlert, Arnold D. *Brethren Writers: A Checklist with an Introduction to Brethren Literature and Additional Lists.* Grand Rapids: Baker Book House, 1969.

Elmore, Floyd S. "A Critical Examination of the Doctrine of the Two Peoples of God in John Nelson Darby." ThD thesis, Dallas Theological Seminary, 1990.

Embley, Peter L. "The Early Development of the Plymouth Brethren." In Bryan R. Wilson, ed., *Patterns of Sectarianism* (London: Heinemann, 1967): 213–43.

– "The Origins and Early Development of the Plymouth Brethren." PhD thesis, St Paul's College, Cheltenham, 1967.

Emerson, N.D. "Church Life in the 19th Century." In Phillips, ed., vol. 3: 325–59.

Empey, C.A. "The Sacred and the Secular: The Augustinian Priory of Kells in Ossory, 1193–1541." *Irish Historical Studies* 24 (November 1984): 131–51.

Enright, Flan. "Edward Synge: The Dysert Proselytiser." *The Other Clare* 80 (1982): 8–11.

Field, Marion. *John Nelson Darby: Prophetic Pioneer.* Godalming, Surrey: Highland Books, 2008.

Fischer, David Hackett. *Historians' Fallacies: Toward a Logic of Historical Thought.* London: Routledge and Kegan Paul, 1971.

Fitzpatrick, David. *"Solitary and Wild": Frederick MacNeice and the Salvation of Ireland.* Dublin: Lilliput Press, 2012.

Fitzpatrick, William J. *The Life, Times and Correspondence of the Right Rev. Dr Doyle*. Dublin: James Duffy, 1861.

– *Memoirs of Richard Whately, Archbishop of Dublin, with a Glance at His Contemporaries and Times*, 2 vols. London: Richard Bentley, 1864.

Flegg, Columba Graham. "*Gathered under Apostles*": *A Study of the Catholic Apostolic Church*. Oxford: Clarendon Press, 1992.

Flynn, Arthur. *A History of County Wicklow*. Dublin: Gill and MacMillan, 2003.

Ford, Alan. *The Protestant Reformation in Ireland, 1540–1641*. Frankfurt am Main: P. Lang, 1985.

– James McGuire, and Kenneth Milne, eds. *As by Law Established: The Church of Ireland since the Reformation*. Dublin: Lilliput Press, 1995.

Foster, Roy F. *Charles Stewart Parnell: The Man and His Family*. London: Harvester Press Ltd, 1976.

– "Parnell and His Neighbours." In Hannigan and Nolan, eds: 895–910.

– "Good Behaviour: Yeats, Synge and Anglo-Irish Etiquette." In Grene, ed., *Interpreting Synge*, 41–55, 201–3.

Fox, Robin. *Kinship and Marriage: An Anthropological Perspective*. 2nd ed. Cambridge: Cambridge University Press, 1983.

Franklin, Benjamin. *Political, Miscellaneous, and Philosophical Pieces*. London: J. Johnson, 1779.

Fraser, George MacDonald. *Flashman: From the Flashman Papers, 1839–1842*. London: Herbert Jenkins, 1969.

Fraser, Robert. *General View of the Agriculture and Mineralogy, Present State and Circumstances of the County Wicklow*. Dublin: Dublin Society, 1801.

Freeman-Attwood, Marigold. *Leap Castle: A Place and Its People*. Norwich: Michael Russell, 2001.

Froom, Le Roy. *The Prophetic Faith of Our Fathers: The Historical Development of Prophetic Interpretation*. 3 vols. Washington: *Review and Herald*, 1946.

Garton, Nancy. *George Müller and His Orphans*. Worthington, Sussex: Churchman Publishing, 1987; First published London: Hodder and Stoughton, 1963.

Gillespie, Raymond, and W.G. Neely, eds. *The Laity and the Church of Ireland, 1000–2000*. Dublin: Four Courts Press, 2002.

Girouard, Mark. *The Return to Camelot: Chivalry and the English Gentleman*. New Haven and London: Yale University Press, 1981.

Gogarty, Oliver St John. "The Most Haunted House of Them All." In *A Weekend in the Middle of the Week, and Other Essays on the Bias* (New York: Doubleday, 1958): 202–9.

Grant, Robert M. "Marcion and the Critical Method." In Richardson and Hurd, eds (1984): 207–15.

Grass, Tim. *Gathering in His Name: The Story of the Open Brethren in Britain and Ireland.* Milton Keynes: Paternoster Press, 2006.

– "Edward Irving: Eschatology, Ecclesiology and Spiritual Gifts." In Gribben and Stunt, eds (2004): 95–121.

– *The Growth of the Brethren Movement, National and International Experiences: Essays in Honour of Harold H. Rowdon.* Carlisle: Paternoster, 2006.

– *Edward Irving: The Lord's Watchman.* Milton Keynes: Paternoster, 2011.

Grene, Nicholas. "Synge and County Wicklow." In Hannigan and Nolan, eds (1994): 693–721.

– ed. *Interpreting Synge: Essays from the Synge Summer School, 1991–2000.* Dublin: Lilliput Press, 2000.

Gribben, Crawford, "Evangelicalism, Historiography and the Possibility of Millennial Theory." In Searle and Newport, eds (2012): 1–19.

– and Andrew R. Holmes, eds. *Protestant Millennialism, Evangelicalism, and Irish Society, 1790–2005.* Basingstoke: Palgrave Macmillan, 2006.

– *Evangelical Millennialism in the Trans-Atlantic World, 1500–2000.* Basingstoke: Palgrave Macmillan, 2011.

– and Timothy C.F. Stunt, eds. *Prisoners of Hope? Aspects of Evangelical Millennialism in Britain and Ireland, 1800–1880.* Carlisle, Cumbria: Paternoster Press, 2004.

Guinness, Michele. *The Guinness Spirit: Brewers and Bankers, Ministers and Missionaries.* London: Hodder and Stoughton, 1999.

Gullen, David Pio. "Two Hundred Years from Lacunza: The Impact of His Eschatological Thought on Prophetic Studies and Modern Futurism," *Journal of the Adventist Theological Society* 9 (1998): 71–95.

Gurrin, Brian. *A Century of Struggle in Delgany and Kilcoole: An Exploration of the Social Implications of Population Change in North-East Wicklow, 1666–1779.* Dublin: Irish Academic Press, 2000.

Haigh, R.H., and P.W. Turner. *"Nickalsain": The Life and Times of John Nicholson, Brigadier-General in the Army of the Honourable East India Company, 1822–1857.* Manhattan, KS: Military Affairs/Aerospace Historian Publishing, 1980.

Haire, Robert. *Wesley's One-and-Twenty Visits to Ireland: A Short Survey.* London: Epworth Press, 1947.

Haldane, Alexander. *The Lives of Robert Haldane of Airthrey, and of His Brother James Alexander Haldane.* London: Hamilton, Adams and Co., 3rd ed., 1853; 1st ed., 1852.

Halévy, Élie. *A History of the English People in the Nineteenth Century, Vol. 2: The Liberal Awakening, 1815–30.* Trans. E.J. Watkin, London: Ernest Benn, 1961. Orig. ed., 1923.

Hall, Percy F. *Discipleship; or, Reasons for Resigning His Naval Rank and Pay.* London: J.K. Campbell, [1848].

Halpern, Baruch. *The First Historians: The Hebrew Bible and History.* San Francisco: Harper and Row. 1989.

Hannigan, Ken. "Wicklow before and after the Famine." In Hannigan and Nolan, eds: 709–822.

– and William Nolan, eds. *Wicklow History and Society: Interdisciplinary Essays on the History of an Irish County.* Dublin: Geography Publications, 1994.

Harden, R.W. *St John's Monkstown: The Story of an Irish Church.* Dublin: Hodges, Figgis, 1911.

Harrison, J.F.C. *The Second Coming: Popular Millenarianism 1780–1850.* New Brunswick, NJ: Rutgers University Press, 1979.

Hart, A.R. *A History of the King's Serjeants at Law in Ireland: Honour rather than Advantage.* Dublin: Four Courts Press for the Irish Legal History Society, 2000.

Hempton, David. "The Methodist Crusade in Ireland, 1795–1845." *Irish Historical Studies* 22 (1980): 33–48.

– "Evangelicalism and Eschatology." *Journal of Ecclesiastical History* 31 (April 1980): 179–94.

– *Methodism and Politics in British Society, 1750–1850.* Stanford: Stanford University Press, 1984.

– "Methodism in Irish Society, 1770–1830." Proxime accessit for the Alexander Prize, *Transactions of the Royal Historical Society*, 5 ser., 36 (1986): 117–42.

– (with Myrtle Hill). *Evangelical Protestantism in Ulster Society, 1740–1890.* London: Routledge, 1992.

– *Methodism: Empire of the Spirit.* New Haven: Yale University Press, 2005.

– *Evangelical Disenchantment: Nine Portraits of Faith and Doubt.* New Haven: Yale University Press, 2008.

Himmelfarb, Gertrude. *The People of the Book: Philosemitism in England from Cromwell to Churchill.* London: Encounter Books, 2013.

Hoffman, Ronald [with collaboration of Sally D. Mason]. *Princes of Ireland, Planters of Maryland: A Carroll Saga, 1500–1782.* Chapel Hill: University of North Carolina Press, 2000.

Holland, Bernard. *Memoir of Kenelm Henry Digby.* London: Longmans, Green, 1919.

Holmes, Andrew R. *The Shaping of Ulster Presbyterian Belief and Practice, 1770–1840*. Oxford: Oxford University Press, 2006.

[Hornby, James J., ed.]. *Remains of Alexander Knox, Esq.* 4 vols. London: James Duncan, 1834–1837.

Huebner, Roy A. *Precious Truths Revived and Defended through J.N. Darby.* Morganville, NJ: Present Truth Publishers, 3 vols., 1991.

[–, ed.] *Additional Writings of J.N. Darby.* 2 vols. Jackson, NJ: Present Truth Publishers, 2005 and 2006.

Hurley, Michael, ed. *Irish Anglicanism, 1869–1969*. Dublin: Allen Figgis, 1970.

Hutchinson, Francis Synge. *Letter to the "Christian Examiner," on the Opposition Manifested by Many in These Days, to the Study of the Prophetical Parts of the Word of God.* Dublin: Richard Moore Tims, 1830.

– *Remarks on Second Peter, Chap. 1, Ver. 19–21.* Dublin: Richard Moore Tims, 1830.

Irving, Edward. *The Last Days: A Discourse on the Evil Character of These Our Times.* London: Seeley and Burnside, 1829.

– "Preliminary Discourse" and additional comments, to Lacunza, vol. 1. 1827. Irregularly paginated, c. 194 pp.

Irwin, George O'Malley. *The Illustrated Handbook to the County of Wicklow.* London: Newman and Co., 1844.

James, William. *The Varieties of Religious Experience.* New York: North American Library ed., 1958 (orig. ed., 1902).

[Jones, William]. "Prefatory Matter." *The Millennial Harbinger; and Voluntary Church Advocate*, vol. 1 (1835): 1–130.

Jung, August. "Julius Anton von Poseck (1816–1898) and Brethren Origins in Germany." In Dickson and Grass, eds.

Keane, Edward, P. Beryl Phair, and Thomas U. Sadleir. *King's Inns Admission Papers, 1607–1867.* Dublin: Irish Manuscripts Commission, 1982.

Kelly, Thomas. "'Come, Lord Jesus, quickly come!' The Writing and Thought of Edward Nangle, 1828–1862." In Gribben and Holmes, eds: 99–118.

Kelly, William. *Lectures Introductory to the Study of the Minor Prophets.* London: W.H. Broom, 1871.

– "The Rapture of the Saints: who suggested it, or rather, on what Scripture?" Orig. pub. 1903. Reprinted in William Kelly, *Christ's Coming Again: Chiefly on the Heavenly Side* (London: F.E. Race, [1910]): 114–35.

Kenney, A.H. "Memoir of the Late Most Reverend William Magee, Archbishop of Dublin." In William Magee, *Collected Writings*, vol. 1 (1842).

Kenny, Colum. *King's Inns and the Kingdom of Ireland: The Irish "Inn of Court," 1541–1800.* Dublin: Irish Academic Press for the Irish Legal History Society, 1992.

– *Tristram Kennedy and the Revival of Irish Legal Training, 1835–1885*. Dublin: Irish Academic Press for the Irish Legal History Society, 1996.

Kirsch, Jonathan. *A History of the End of the World: How the Most Controversial Book in the Bible Changed the Course of Western Civilization*. New York: Harper San Francisco, 2006.

Knox, John. *Marcion and the New Testament: An Essay in the Early History of the Canon*. Chicago: University of Chicago Press, 1942.

Lacunza, Manuel. *The Coming of Messiah in Glory and Majesty by Juan Josafat Ben-Ezra, a Converted Jew*, 2 vols. Edited by Edward Irving. London: L.B. Seeley and Son, 1827.

Lambert, William George. *A Call to the Converted*. Oxford: 1831. Abridged reprint, Hereford: County Press Office, 1837.

Lang, G.H. "Inquire of the Former Age," part 2, *The Disciple*, vol. 1, no. 2 (1953): 13–22; "Inquire of the Former Age," part 3, *The Disciple*, vol. 1, no. 3 (1953): 51–66.

Larkin, Emmet. *The Pastoral Role of the Roman Catholic Church in Pre-famine Ireland, 1750–1850*. Dublin: Four Courts Press, 2006.

Laurence, Richard. *A Charge Delivered at the Triennial Visitation of the Province of Munster, in the Year 1826*. Dublin: Richard Milliken, 1826. (Google ebook, accessed 14 April 2013).

Law, James Thomas. *The Ecclesiastical Statutes at Large*. London: William Benning. 5 vols., 1847.

Lecky, William E.H. *A History of England in the Eighteenth Century*. London: Longmans, Green and Co, 2nd ed., vol. 2, 1879.

Leslie, James B. *Ossory Clergy and Parishes*. Enniskillen: "The Fermanagh Times" Office, 1933.

– *Ferns Clergy and Parishes*. Dublin: printed for the author, 1936.

– *Clergy of Connor, from Patrician Times to the Present Day*. Belfast: Ulster Historical Foundation, 1993.

[anonymous]. *Letters Concerning Their Principles and Order from Assemblies of Believers in 1818–20*. 1st ed., privately printed; reprint ed., London: Horner and Son, and Dublin: Robert Stewart, 1889.

Levenson, Jon. *Sinai and Zion: An Entry into the Jewish Bible*. San Francisco: Harper and Row, 1985.

Levi-Strauss, Claude. *The Elementary Structures of Kinship*. Trans. James H. Bell. John R. von Sturney and Rodney Needham (eds). London: Eyre and Spottiswoode, 1969, from the 2nd French ed. of 1967; orig. French ed., 1949.

– *Structural Anthropology*. London: Allen Lane, 1968 and 1973.

Lewis, Donald. *The Origins of Christian Zionism: Lord Shaftesbury and Evangelical Support for a Jewish Homeland.* Cambridge: Cambridge University Press, 2010.

Lewis, Samuel. *A Topographical Dictionary of Ireland.* London: S. Lewis and Co., 2 vols., 1837.

Liechty, Joseph. "Irish Evangelicalism, Trinity College, Dublin, and the Mission of the Church of Ireland at the End of the Eighteenth Century." PhD thesis, St Patrick's College: Maynooth, 1987.

– "The Popular Reformation Comes to Ireland: The Case of John Walker and the Foundation of the Church of God, 1804." In Comerford, Cullen, Hill, and Lennon, eds: 159–87, 324–31.

– "The Problem of Sectarianism and the Church of Ireland." In Ford, McGuire, and Milne, eds: 204–22, 278–9.

Little, J.I. "A.C. Buchanan and the Megantic Experiment: Promoting British Colonization in Lower Canada." *Histoire Social / Social History* 92 (November 2013): 298–9.

Lynch, Patrick, and John Vaizey. *Guinness's Brewery in the Irish Economy, 1759–1876.* Cambridge: Cambridge University Press, 1960.

MacPherson, Dave. *The Rapture Plot.* Simpsonville, SC: Millennium III Publishers, 1995.

[Madden, Mrs Hamilton]. *Personal Recollections of the Right Rev. Robert Daly, DD, Late Bishop of Cashel, at Powerscourt and Waterford, by an Old Parishioner.* Dublin: George Herbert, 1872.

– *Memoir of the Late Right Rev. Robert Daly, DD, Lord Bishop of Cashel.* London: James Nisbet, 1875.

Madden, Samuel. *Memoir of the Life of the Late Rev. Peter Roe, AM, Rector of Odogh, and Minister of St Mary's, Kilkenny, with Copious Extracts from His Correspondence, Diaries, and Other Remains.* Dublin: William Curry, 1842.

Magee, William. *The Collected Works of the Most Reverend William Magee, DD, Lord Archbishop of Dublin.* 2 vols. Edited by A.H. Kenney. London: T. Cadell, 1842.

– *A Sermon Preached before the Association for Discountenancing Vice, and Promoting the Practice of Religion and Virtue: In St Anne's Church, on Thursday 5th May 1796.* Dublin: W. Watson and Son, 1796.

– *A Charge Delivered at His Triennial and Metropolitan Visitation in St Patrick's Cathedral, Dublin in Oct. 1826.* London: T. Cadell and Dublin: K.P. Archer, 1827. (Google ebook accessed 2 August 2014). Reprinted in A.M. Kenney (ed.), vol. 2, 461–98, as "The Principle of the Union between Church and State in Christian Communities Explained; and Its Validity Defended against the Fictions of Warburton, and the Usurpations of Popery; in a Charge Delivered to His Clergy in St Patrick's Cathedral, Dublin in the Year 1827."

– *A Charge Delivered at His Primary Visitation* … In Kenney (ed.), vol. 2, *The Collected Works of the Most Reverend William Magee, DD, Lord Archbishop of Dublin* … (London: T. Cadell, 1842): 429–59.

Maguire, W.A. *The Downshire Estates in Ireland, 1801–1845: The Management of Irish Landed Estates in the Early Nineteenth Century.* Oxford: Clarendon Press, 1972.

Malcomson, A.P.W. *Archbishop Charles Agar: Churchmanship and Politics in Ireland, 1760–1810.* Dublin: Four Courts Press, 2002.

– *The Pursuit of the Heiress: Aristocratic Marriage in Ireland, 1740–1840.* 2nd ed. Belfast: Ulster Historical Foundation, 2006.

Marty, Martin E. *A Nation of Behavers.* Chicago: University of Chicago Press, 1976.

Maxwell, Constantia. *A History of Trinity College, Dublin, 1591–1892.* Dublin: The University Press of Trinity College, 1946.

McCormack, W.J. "The 'Plymouth' Brethren? Prolegomena to the Re-Writing of J.M. Synge's Biography." *Religion and Literature* 28 (summer–autumn 1996): 83–96.

– *Fool of the Family: A Life of J.M. Synge.* London: Weidenfeld and Nicolson, 2000.

– *The Silence of Barbara Synge.* Manchester: Manchester University Press, 2003.

– ed. *Memories of West Wicklow, 1813–1939: William Hanbridge and Mary Ann Hanbridge.* Dublin: University College Dublin Press, 2005.

McCullough, Niall. *Dublin: An Urban History.* Dublin: Anne St Press, 1989.

McDowell, R.B. *The Church of Ireland, 1869–1969.* London: Routledge and Kegan Paul, 1975.

– and D.A. Webb. *Trinity College Dublin, 1592–1951: An Academic History.* Cambridge: Cambridge University Press, 1982.

McGinn, Bernard, ed. *The Encyclopedia of Apocalypticism.* Vol. 2. New York: Continuum, 1998.

McGrath, Thomas. *Politics, Interdenominational Relations and Education in the Public Ministry of Bishop James Doyle of Kildare and Leighlin, 1786–1834.* Dublin: Four Courts Press, 1999.

– *Religious Renewal and Reform in the Pastoral Ministry of Bishop James Doyle of Kildare and Leighlin, 1786–1834.* Dublin: Four Courts Press, 1999.

McGregor, O.R. *Divorce in England.* Toronto: Heinemann, 1957.

McNally, Vincent. *Reform, Revolution and Reaction: Archbishop John Thomas Troy and the Catholic Church in Ireland, 1787–1817.* Lanham, MD: University Press of America, 1995.

Mede, Joseph. *Daniel's Weekes: An Interpretation of Part of the Prophecy of Daniel.* London: John Clarke, 1642. (Accessed via *Early English Books Online* on 12 November 2012 and qcat.library.queensu.ca/vweb/holdingsinfo?bibid=2164630 on 16 December 2013.)

– *The Key of the Revelation Searched and Demonstrated out of the Naturall and Proper Characters of the Visions …* London: Philip Stephens, 1650, qcat.library.queensu.ca/vwebv/holdingsinfor?bibld=2181337 (accessed 16 December 2013).

Melville, William R. *Crockford's Clerical Directory for 1868.* London: Horace Cox, 1868.

Miller, Andrew. *The Brethren: A Brief Sketch of Their Origin, Progress, and Testimony.* London: George Morrish, n.d. [1879?].

Miller, David. "Presbyterianism and 'Modernization' in Ulster." *Past and Present* 80 (1978): 66–90.

– "Varieties of Irish Evangelicalism." *Field Day Review* 3 (2007): 215–33.

Miller, Edward. *The History and Doctrine of Irvingism.* 2 vols. London: C. Kegan Paul and Co., 1878.

Milne, Kenneth. *The Irish Charter Schools, 1730–1830.* Dublin: Four Courts Press, 1997.

Moffitt, Miriam. *Soupers and Jumpers: The Protestant Missions in Connemara, 1848–1937.* Dublin: Nonsuch Publishing, 2008.

– *The Society for Irish Church Missions to the Roman Catholics, 1849–1950.* Manchester: Manchester University Press, 2010.

Mokyr, Joel. *Why Ireland Starved: A Quantitative and Analytical History of the Irish Economy, 1800–1850.* London: George Allen and Unwin, 1983.

Montgomery-Massingberd, Hugh, ed. *Burke's Irish Family Records.* London: UK Burke's Peerage Ltd, 1976.

Moore, H. Kingsmill. *An Unwritten Chapter in the History of Education, Being the History of the Society for the Education of the Poor in Ireland, Generally Known as the Kildare Place Society, 1811–1831.* London: Macmillan, 1904.

Mosely, Charles, ed. *Burke's Peerage, Baronetage and Knightage.* 107th ed. Wilmington: Genealogical Books, 2003.

Mullen, Jr., Thomas J. "Sayings by and about Irishmen at War." *Irish Sword* 11 (1973–74): 3–7.

Murdock, George Peter. *Ethnographic Atlas.* Pittsburgh: University of Pittsburgh Press, 1967.

Murphy, Ignatius. *The Diocese of Killaloe in the Eighteenth Century.* Dublin: Four Courts Press, 1991.

– *The Diocese of Killaloe, 1800–1850.* Dublin: Four Courts Press, 1992.

– *The Diocese of Killaloe, 1850–1904.* Dublin: Four Courts Press, 1995.

Murphy, James. *The Religious Problem in English Education: The Crucial Experiment.* Liverpool: Liverpool University Press, 1959.

Murray, James, Alan Ford, J.I. McGuire, S.J. Connolly, Fergus O'Ferrall, and Kenneth Milne. "The Church of Ireland: A Critical Bibliography, 1536–1992." *Irish Historical Studies* 28 (1993): 345–84.

Neatby, William Blair. *A History of the Plymouth Brethren.* 2nd ed. London: Hodder and Stoughton, 1902.

Nebeker, Gary L. "John Nelson Darby and Trinity College, Dublin: A Study in Eschatological Contrasts." *Fides et Historia* 34 (2002): 87–108.

Newman, Francis William. *Phases of Faith; or, Passages from the History of My Creed.* London: John Chapman, 1850. 9th ed., London: Trubner, 1874.

Newman, John Henry. *Apologia Pro Vita Sua.* Orig. ed., 1864; London: J.M. Dent edition, 1912.

Newton, Isaac. *Observations upon the Prophecies of Daniel and the Apocalypse of St John.* London: J. Darby and T. Browne, 1733. Available online at www.gutenberg.org/ebooks/16878. Accessed 20 December 2012.

Nockles, Peter B. *The Oxford Movement in Context: Anglican High Churchmanship, 1760–1857.* Cambridge: Cambridge University Press, 1994.

Noel, Napoleon. *The History of the Brethren.* 2 vols. Edited by William F. Knapp. Denver: privately pub. by William F. Knapp, 1936.

Nolan, William. "Land and Landscape in County Wicklow." In Hannigan and Nolan, eds: 649–92.

Noll, Mark A., David W. Bebbington, and George A. Rawlyk, eds. *Evangelicalism: Comparative Studies of Popular Protestantism in North America, the British Isles and Beyond, 1700–1990.* New York: Oxford University Press, 1994.

O'Brien, Conor Cruise. *The Great Melody: A Thematic Biography and Commented Anthology of Edmund Burke.* Chicago: University of Chicago Press, 1992.

O'Connell, Maurice R., ed. *The Correspondence of Daniel O'Connell.* 8 vols. Dublin: Irish Manuscripts Commission, 1972–1980.

– *O'Connell. Education, Church and State.* Dublin: Institute of Public Administration, 1991.

O'Donnell, Ruan, ed. *Insurgent Wicklow, 1798: The Story as Written by Luke Cullen, ODC.* Bray: Kestrel Books, 1998.

O'Faolain, Sean. *King of the Beggars: A Life of Daniel O'Connell.* London: Thomas Nelson and Sons, 1938.

O'Farrell, Patrick. "Millennialism, Messianism and Utopianism in Irish History." *Anglo-Irish Studies,* vol. 2, edited by P.J. Drudy (1976): 45–68.

Oliphant, Margaret Oliphant Wilson ["Mrs Oliphant"]. *The Life of Edward Irving, Minister of the National Scotch Church, London, Illustrated by His Journals and Correspondence.* 2 vols. London: Hurst and Blackett, 1862. 2nd ed. (1 vol.), New York: Harper and Brothers, 1862.

Oliver, William H. *Prophets and Millennialists: The Uses of Biblical Prophecy in England from the 1790s to the 1840s.* Auckland: Auckland University Press, and London: Oxford University Press, 1978.

O'Maitiu, Seamus. "Lacken, County Wicklow." In Paul Connell, Denis A. Cronin, and Brian O'Dalaigh, eds, *Irish Townlands: Studies in Local History* (Dublin: Four Courts Press, 1998): 203–19.

Oxford Dictionary of National Biography. Oxford: Oxford University Press, 2004.

Pagels, Elaine. *Revelations: Visions, Prophecy, and Politics in the Book of Revelation.* New York: Viking, 2012.

Palmer, Hurly Pring. *Joseph Wolff: His Romantic Life and Travels.* London: Heath Cranston, 1935.

Parkes, Susan M. *Kildare Place: The History of the Church of Ireland Teaching College, 1811–1969.* Dublin: Church of Ireland College of Education, 1984.

– *A Guide to Sources for the History of Irish Education, 1780–1922.* Dublin: Four Courts Press, 2010.

Parnell, John Howard. *C.S. Parnell: A Memoir.* New York: Henry Holt, 1914.

Parris, Matthew. *The Great Unfrocked: Two Thousand Years of Church Scandal.* London: Robson Books, 1998.

Pelikan, Jaroslav. *The Shape of Death: Life, Death, and Immortality in the Early Fathers.* New York: Abingdon Press, 1961.

Phillips, Walter A., ed. *History of the Church of Ireland from the Earliest Times to the Present Day.* 3 vols. London: Oxford University Press, 1933.

Pickering, Henry, ed. *Chief Men among the Brethren (Acts 15:22).* 1st ed. 1918. 2nd ed. London: Pickering and Inglis, 1931.

Porter, Stanley E. "Was Early Christianity a Millenarian Movement?" In Stanley E. Porter, Michael A. Hayes, and David Tombs, eds, *Faith in the Millennium* (Sheffield: Sheffield Academic Press, 2001): 234–59.

Powell, Fred. "Dean Swift and the Dublin Foundling Hospital." *Studies: An Irish Quarterly Review* 70 (summer/autumn 1981): 162–70.

Power, Thomas P. "'Of No Small Importance': Curricular Change in the School of Divinity, Trinity College Dublin, 1790–1850." In Power, ed., *Change and*

Transformation in Anglican History (Eugene, OR: Wipf and Stock Publishers, 2003): 140–83.

Powicke, F. Maurice, and E.B. Fryde, *Handbook of British Chronology*. London: Royal Historical Society, 2nd. ed., 1961.

[anonymous]. *Questions for Eight Weeks' Consideration. Addressed to the Church of God*. London: Central Tract Depot, 1838.

Rambo, Lewis W. *Understanding Religious Conversion*. New Haven: Yale University Press, 1993.

Richardson, Peter, and John C, Hurd, eds. *From Jesus to Paul: Studies in Honour of Francis Wright Beare*. Waterloo: Wilfrid Laurier University Press, 1994.

Robins, Joseph. *The Lost Children: A Study of Charity Children in Ireland, 1700–1900*. Dublin: Institute of Public Administration, 1980.

Roe, Peter, ed. *The Evil of Separation from the Church of England, Considered in a Series of Letters Addressed Chiefly to the Rev. Peter Roe, MA*. London: L.B. Seeley, 1st ed. 1815, 2nd ed. 1817.

Rowdon, Harold H. *The Origin of the Brethren, 1825–1850*. London: Pickering and Inglis Ltd, 1967.

– "Secession from the Established Church in the Early Nineteenth Century." *Vox Evangelica* 3 (1964): 76–88.

Rowell, George S. "Benjamin Vaughan – Patriot, Scholar, Diplomat." *The Magazine of History, with Notes and Queries* 22 (March 1916): 45–56.

Sandeen, Ernest R. *Roots of Fundamentalism: British and American Millenarianism, 1800–1930*. Chicago: University of Chicago Press, 1970.

Scott, John. *The Life of the Rev. Thomas Scott, Rector of Ashton Sandford, Bucks*. London: L.B. Seeley, 1822.

– *Letters and Papers of the Late Rev. Thomas Scott; with Occasional Observations*. London: L.B. Seeley and Son, 1826.

Scott, Thomas. *The Holy Bible, Containing the Old and New Testaments with Original Notes …* 2nd ed. London: Bellamy and Robarts, 1792.

Searle, Joshua, and Kenneth G.C. Newport. *Beyond the End: The Future of Millennial Studies*. Sheffield: Sheffield Phoenix Press, 2012.

Seymour, St John. *The Succession of Parochial Clergy in the United Diocese of Cashel and Emly*. Dublin: Church of Ireland Printing and Publishing Co., 1908.

Sheppard, John H. "Reminiscences and Genealogy of the Vaughan Family." *New England Historical and Genealogical Register* 19 (1865): 343–56.

Shiels, W.J., and Diana Wood, eds. *The Churches, Ireland and the Irish*. Oxford: Basil Blackwell, for the Ecclesiastical History Society, 1989.

Sirr, Joseph d'Arcy. *A Memoir of the Honorable and Most Reverend Power Le Poer Trench, Last Archbishop of Tuam*. Dublin: William Curry, 1845.

Staples, Hugh B., ed. *The Ireland of Sir Jonah Barrington: Selections from His Personal Sketches.* Seattle: University of Washington Press, 1967.

Steer, Roger. *George Müller: Delighted in God.* London: Hodder and Stoughton, orig. ed. 1975; rev. ed. 1981.

Stein, Stephen J., ed. *The Encyclopedia of Apocalypticism.* Vol. 3. New York: Continuum, 1998.

Stetson, Sarah P. "The Philadelphia Sojourn of Samuel Vaughan." *Pennsylvania Magazine of History and Biography* 73 (1949): 459–74.

Stewart, Kenneth J. *Restoring the Reformation: British Evangelicalism and the Francophone "Réveil," 1816–1849.* Milton Keynes: Paternoster, 2006.

Stokes, A.E. *The Parish of Powerscourt: A Centenary Lecture.* Bray: Old Bray Society, 1986.

Stokes, George T. "John Nelson Darby." *Contemporary Review* 48 (October 1885): 537–52.

Stoney, Anna M. *An Account of Early Days of the So-Called Brethren Movement.* London: Chapter Two, 1995; orig. pub. date unknown.

Strozier, Charles B. *Apocalypse: On the Psychology of Fundamentalism in America.* Boston: Beacon Press, 1994.

Stunt, Timothy C.F. *Early Brethren and the Society of Friends.* n.p.: Christian Brethren Research Fellowship, 1970.

– "John Synge and the Early Brethren." *Christian Brethren Research Fellowship Journal* 28 (1976): 39–62.

– "Evangelical Cross-Currents in the Church of Ireland, 1820–1833." In Shiels and Wood, eds (1989): 215–21.

– "Review of 'John Nelson Darby' by Max Weremchuk." *Brethren Archivists and Historians Network Review* (autumn 1997): 47–50.

– *From Awakening to Secession: Radical Evangelicals in Switzerland and Britain, 1815–35.* Edinburgh: T. and T. Clark, 2000.

– "The Tribulation of Controversy: A Review Article." *Brethren Archivists and Historians Network Review* 2 (2003): 91–8.

– "Influences in the Early Development of J.N. Darby." In Gribben and Stunt (2004): 44–68.

– "A Personal Odyssey." *Brethren Archivists' and Historians' Network Review* 3 (2006): 103–8.

– "John Nelson Darby: Contexts and Perceptions." In Gribben and Holmes, eds (2006): 83–98.

– "Trinity College, John Darby and the Powerscourt *Milieu.*" In Searle and Newport, eds (2012): 47–74.

– "An Early Account of the Brethren in 1838, with Some Explanation of Its Origin and Context." *Brethren Historical Review* 8 (2012): 1–9.

Sweetnam, Mark S., and Crawford Gribben, "J.N. Darby and the Irish Origins of Dispensationalism." *Journal of the Evangelical Theological Society* 52 (September 2009): 569–77.

Sykes, Norman. *Church and State in England in the XVIIIth Century.* Cambridge: Cambridge University Press, 1934.

[Synge, John]. *A Biographical Sketch of the Struggles of Pestalozzi to Establish His System of Education, by an Irish Traveller.* Dublin: Folds, 1815.

– *The Relations and Descriptions of Forms According to the Principles of Pestalozzi.* Roundwood: self-printed and sold, Dublin: Martine Klene, Thomas Bowes, and "at the Committee-House for Charitable Societies," 1817.

– *Observations on "A Call to the Converted," as It Relates to Members of the Church of England, Addressed to Captain P. Hall, RN.* Teignmouth: privately printed for Synge by Barnett Printer, 1831.

Synge, John Millington. "The Vagrants of Wicklow." In *The Complete Works of John M. Synge.* New York: Random House, 1935.

Tayler, W. Elfe, ed. *Passages from the Diary and Letters of Henry Craik, of Bristol.* 2nd ed. London: J.F. Shaw, 1866.

Teulon, J.S. *The History and Teaching of the Plymouth Brethren.* London: Society for Promoting Christian Knowledge, 1883.

Tierney, Andrew. "The Gothic and the Gaelic: Exploring the Place of Castles in Ireland's Celtic Revival." *International Journal of Historical Archaeology* 8 (September 2004): 185–98.

– "From Gothic to Gothic Revival: An Archaeology of Leap Castle, Co. Offaly." In Michael McCarthy and Karina O'Neill, eds, *Studies in the Gothic Revival* (Dublin: Four Courts Press, 2008).

– "Return of the Repressed? 'Haunted Castles' in Seventeenth-Century Munster." *Eire-Ireland* 45 (2010): 7–26.

Tregelles, Samuel P. *A Lecture on the Historic Evidence of the Authorship and Transmission of the Books of the New Testament.* London: Samuel Bagster and Son, 1857.

– *The Hope of Christ's Second Coming: How Is It Taught in Scripture? And Why?* London: Samuel Bagster and Sons, 1864.

Trimmer, Sarah. *An Abridgement of the New Testament, Consisting of Lessons Composed from the Writings of the Four Evangelists: For the Use of Schools and Families.* London: F. and C. Rivington, 1797.

Trotter, Lionel J. *The Life of John Nicholson, Soldier and Administrator.* London: John Murray, 1897.

Turner, W.G. *John Nelson Darby.* 2nd ed. London: C.A. Hammond, 1944.

Tuveson, Ernest Lee. *Redeemer Nation: The Idea of America's Millennial Role.* Chicago: University of Chicago Press, 1968.

Van Seters, John. *Abraham in History and Tradition.* New Haven: Yale University Press, 1975.

– *The Life of Moses: The Yahwist as Historian in Exodus-Numbers.* Louisville: Westminster John Knox Press, 1994.

Vaughan, W.E., ed. *A New History of Ireland, Vol. VI: Ireland under the Union, II, 1890–1921.* Oxford: Clarendon Press, 1996.

Vaughan, William. *The Golden-Grove, Moralized in Three Books: A Work Very Necessary for All Such as Would Know How to Governe Themselves, Their Houses, or Their Country.* [n.p.]: 1600. Available via *Early English Books Online.* Accessed 22 October 2013.

– *Tracts on Docks and Commerce, Printed between the Years 1793 and 1800, and Now First Collected with an Introduction, Memoir, and Miscellaneous Pieces.* London: Smith, Elder, and Co., 1839.

Wallace, W.J.R. *Clergy of Dublin and Glendalough: Biographical Succession Lists.* Belfast: Ulster Historical Foundation, 2001.

Walmsley, Charles ["Signor Pastorini"]. *The General History of the Christian Church: From Her Birth to Her Final Triumphant State in Heaven, Chiefly Deduced from the Apocalypse of St John the Apostle.* Dublin: privately printed, 1790 (archive.org, accessed 24 September 2013).

Walsh, Eamon. "Sackville Mall: The First One Hundred Years." In David Dickson, ed. (1987): 30–50.

Ward, John Percy. "The Eschatology of John Nelson Darby." PhD thesis. University of London, 1976.

Ward, W.R.. *The Protestant Evangelical Awakening.* Cambridge: Cambridge University Press, 1991.

– *Early Evangelicalism: A Global Intellectual History, 1670–1789.* Cambridge: Cambridge University Press, 2006.

Ware, George M. *A Review of Certain Contentions for the Faith.* London: L.M. Haverly, [1937].

Warne, Frederick G., *George Müller: The Modern Apostle of Faith.* New York: Fleming H. Revell Co., 1898.

Waugh, Evelyn. *Put out More Flags.* New York: Dell Publishing, 1961.

Weremchuk, Max S. *John Nelson Darby.* Neptune, NJ: Loizeaux Brothers, English ed., 1992; orig. German ed., 1988.

– "Darby of the Leap." Research Papers nos 3, 4, 5, and 13. Available at www.mybrethren.org. Accessed 20 October 2011.

Whately, Elizabeth Jane [with Herman Merrivale]. *Life and Correspondence of Richard Whately, DD, Late Archbishop of Dublin.* 2 vols. London: Longmans, Green and Co., 1866.

– *Plymouth Brethrenism.* London: Hatchard, 1877.

Whelan, Irene. "The Stigma of Souperism." In Cathal Poirteir, ed., *The Great Irish Famine* (Cork: Mercier Press, 1995): 133–54.

– *The Bible War in Ireland: The "Second Reformation" and the Polarization of Protestant-Catholic Relations, 1800–1840.* Dublin: Lilliput Press and Madison: University of Wisconsin Press, 2005.

Wilkinson, Paul Richard. *For Zion's Sake: Christian Zionism and the Role of John Nelson Darby.* Milton Keynes: Paternoster, 2007.

[Wingfield, Mervyn Edward], 7th Viscount Powerscourt. *A Description and History of Powerscourt.* London: Mitchell and Hughes, 1903.

Wolffe, John. *The Protestant Crusade in Great Britain, 1829–1860.* Oxford: Clarendon Press, 1991.

Wright, G.N. *A Guide to the County of Wicklow.* London: Baldwin, Cradock and Joy, and Dublin, W. Wakeman, 1827: 171–3.

Wyse, Thomas. *The Political Catechism Explanatory of the Constitutional Rights and Civil Disabilities of the Catholics of Ireland.* London: 1829.

Yarde, D.M. *The Life and Works of Sarah Trimmer: A Lady of Brentford.* Hounslow: Hounslow and District History Society, 1972.

INDEX